Student Solutions Manual

Laurel Technical Services

Beginning Algebra

THIRD EDITION

K. Elayn Martin-Gay

Upper Saddle River, NJ 07458

Executive Editor: Karin E. Wagner
Project Manager: Mary Beckwith
Special Projects Manager: Barbara A. Murray
Production Editor: Maat Van Uitert
Supplement Cover Manager: Paul Gourhan
Supplement Cover Designer: PM Workshop Inc.
Manufacturing Manager: Trudy Pisciotti

Printed in the United States of America

10 9 8 7

ISBN 0-13-087209-1

Prentice-Hall International (UK) Limited, London
Prentice-Hall of Australia Pty. Limited, Sydney
Prentice-Hall Canada, Inc., Toronto
Prentice-Hall Hispanoamericana, S.A., Mexico
Prentice-Hall of India Private Limited, New Delhi
Pearson Education Asia Pte. Ltd., Singapore
Prentice-Hall of Japan, Inc., Tokyo
Editora Prentice-Hall do Brazil, Ltda., Rio de Janeiro

Table of Contents

Chapter 1	1
Chapter 2	23
Chapter 3	71
Chapter 4	111
Chapter 5	142
Chapter 6	169
Chapter 7	225
Chapter 8	247
Chapter 9	292
Chapter 10	318
Appendix A	365
Appendix B	367
Appendix D	368
Appendix F	370

Chapter 1

Exercise Set 1.2

1. $4 < 10$

3. $7 > 3$

5. $6.26 = 6.26$

7. $0 < 7$

9. $32 < 212$

11. $44{,}300 > 34{,}611$

13 True

15. False

17. $3 + 8 \geq 3(8)$
$11 \geq 24$ False

19. True

21. $30 \leq 45$

23. $8 < 12$

25. $5 \geq 4$

27. $15 \neq -2$

29. The integer 535 represents 535 feet.
The integer –8 represents 8 feet below sea level.

31. The integer –433,853 represents a decrease in attendance of 433,853.

33. The integer 350 represents a deposit of $350.
The integer –126 represents a withdrawal of $126.

35. 1988

37. 1988, 1989, 1990, 1991

39. $6068 \geq 2649$

41. whole, integers, rational, real

43. integers, rational, real

45. natural, whole, integers, rational, real

47. rational, real

49. irrational, real

51. False

53. True

55. True

57. True

59. False

61. $-10 > -100$

63. $32 > 5.2$

65. $\frac{18}{3} < \frac{24}{3}$

67. $-51 < -50$

69. $|-5| > -4$

71. $|-1| = |1|$

73. $|-2| < |-3|$

75. $|0| < |-8|$

77. $-0.04 > -26.7$

79. The sun is brighter, since $-26.7 < -0.04$.

81. The sun, since on the number line –26.7 is to the left of all other numbers listed, and therefore, –26.7 is smaller than all other numbers listed.

83. $20 \leq 25$

85. $6 > 0$

87. $-12 < -10$

89. Answers may vary.

Section 1.3

Mental Math

1. $\frac{3}{8}$

2. $\frac{1}{4}$

3. $\frac{5}{7}$

4. $\frac{2}{5}$

5. numerator, denominator

6. $\frac{11}{7}$

Exercise Set 1.3

1. $33 = 3 \cdot 11$

3. $98 = 2 \cdot 49 = 2 \cdot 7 \cdot 7$

5. $20 = 2 \cdot 2 \cdot 5$

7. $75 = 3 \cdot 5 \cdot 5$

9. $45 = 3 \cdot 3 \cdot 5$

11. $\frac{2}{4} = \frac{2}{2 \cdot 2} = \frac{1}{2}$

13. $\frac{10}{15} = \frac{2 \cdot 5}{3 \cdot 5} = \frac{2}{3}$

15. $\frac{3}{7}$ is in lowest terms.

17. $\frac{18}{30} = \frac{2 \cdot 3 \cdot 3}{2 \cdot 3 \cdot 5} = \frac{3}{5}$

19. $\frac{1}{2} \cdot \frac{3}{4} = \frac{3}{8}$

21. $\frac{2}{3} \cdot \frac{3}{4} = \frac{2 \cdot 3}{3 \cdot 2 \cdot 2} = \frac{1}{2}$

23. $\frac{1}{2} \div \frac{7}{12} = \frac{1}{2} \cdot \frac{12}{7} = \frac{1 \cdot 2 \cdot 2 \cdot 3}{2 \cdot 7} = \frac{6}{7}$

25. $\frac{3}{4} \div \frac{1}{20} = \frac{3}{4} \cdot \frac{20}{1} = \frac{3 \cdot 2 \cdot 2 \cdot 5}{2 \cdot 2} = 15$

27. $\frac{7}{10} \cdot \frac{5}{21} = \frac{7 \cdot 5}{2 \cdot 5 \cdot 3 \cdot 7} = \frac{1}{6}$

29. $2\frac{7}{9} \cdot \frac{1}{3} = \frac{25}{9} \cdot \frac{1}{3} = \frac{5 \cdot 5 \cdot 1}{3 \cdot 3 \cdot 3} = \frac{25}{27}$

31. $l \cdot w = \frac{11}{12} \cdot \frac{3}{5} = \frac{11 \cdot 3}{2 \cdot 2 \cdot 3 \cdot 5} = \frac{11}{20}$ sq. miles

33. $\frac{4}{5} - \frac{1}{5} = \frac{4-1}{5} = \frac{3}{5}$

35. $\frac{4}{5} + \frac{1}{5} = \frac{4+1}{5} = \frac{5}{5} = 1$

37. $\frac{17}{21} - \frac{10}{21} = \frac{17-10}{21} = \frac{7}{21} = \frac{7}{7 \cdot 3} = \frac{1}{3}$

39. $\frac{23}{105} + \frac{4}{105} = \frac{23+4}{105} = \frac{27}{105} = \frac{3 \cdot 3 \cdot 3}{3 \cdot 5 \cdot 7} = \frac{9}{35}$

41. $\frac{7}{10} \cdot \frac{3}{3} = \frac{21}{30}$

43. $\frac{2}{9} \cdot \frac{2}{2} = \frac{4}{18}$

45. $\frac{4}{5} \cdot \frac{4}{4} = \frac{16}{20}$

47. $\frac{2}{3}+\frac{3}{7}$ LCD = 21
$\frac{2}{3}\cdot\frac{7}{7}=\frac{14}{21}$
$\frac{3}{7}\cdot\frac{3}{3}=\frac{9}{21}$
$\frac{14}{21}+\frac{9}{21}=\frac{14+9}{21}=\frac{23}{21}$

49. $2\frac{13}{15}-1\frac{1}{5}=\frac{43}{15}-\frac{6}{5}$ LCD = 15
$\frac{6}{5}\cdot\frac{3}{3}=\frac{18}{15}$
$\frac{43}{15}-\frac{18}{15}=\frac{43-18}{15}=\frac{25}{15}=1\frac{2}{3}$

51. $\frac{5}{22}-\frac{5}{33}$ LCD = 66
$\frac{5}{22}\cdot\frac{3}{3}=\frac{15}{66}$
$\frac{5}{33}\cdot\frac{2}{2}=\frac{10}{66}$
$\frac{15}{66}-\frac{10}{66}=\frac{5}{66}$

53. $\frac{12}{5}-1$ LCD = 5
$1\cdot\frac{5}{5}=\frac{5}{5}$
$\frac{12}{5}-\frac{5}{5}=\frac{7}{5}$

55. $1-\frac{3}{10}-\frac{5}{10}=\frac{10}{10}-\frac{3}{10}-\frac{5}{10}$
$=\frac{10-3-5}{10}$
$=\frac{2}{10}$
$=\frac{1}{5}$

57. $1-\frac{1}{4}-\frac{3}{8}=\frac{8}{8}-\frac{2}{8}-\frac{3}{8}=\frac{8-2-3}{8}=\frac{3}{8}$

59. $1-\frac{1}{2}-\frac{1}{6}-\frac{2}{9}=\frac{18}{18}-\frac{9}{18}-\frac{3}{18}-\frac{4}{18}$
$=\frac{2}{18}$
$=\frac{1}{9}$

61. $\frac{10}{21}+\frac{5}{21}=\frac{10+5}{21}=\frac{15}{21}$
$\frac{15}{21}=\frac{3\cdot 5}{3\cdot 7}=\frac{5}{7}$

63. $\frac{10}{3}-\frac{5}{21}$ LCD = 21
$\frac{10}{3}\cdot\frac{7}{7}=\frac{70}{21}$
$\frac{70}{21}-\frac{5}{21}=\frac{65}{21}$

65. $\frac{2}{3}\cdot\frac{3}{5}=\frac{2\cdot 3}{3\cdot 5}=\frac{2}{5}$

67. $\frac{3}{4}\div\frac{7}{12}=\frac{3}{4}\cdot\frac{12}{7}=\frac{3\cdot 2\cdot 2\cdot 3}{2\cdot 2\cdot 7}=\frac{9}{7}$

69. $\frac{5}{12}+\frac{4}{12}=\frac{4+5}{12}=\frac{9}{12}=\frac{3\cdot 3}{2\cdot 2\cdot 3}=\frac{3}{4}$

71. $5+\frac{2}{3}$ LCD = 3
$\frac{5}{1}\cdot\frac{3}{3}=\frac{15}{3}$
$\frac{15}{3}+\frac{2}{3}=\frac{17}{3}$

73. $\frac{7}{8}\div 3\frac{1}{4}=\frac{7}{8}\div\frac{13}{4}=\frac{7}{8}\cdot\frac{4}{13}=\frac{7\cdot 2\cdot 2}{2\cdot 2\cdot 2\cdot 13}=\frac{7}{26}$

75. $\frac{7}{18}\div\frac{14}{36}=\frac{7}{18}\cdot\frac{36}{14}=\frac{7\cdot 2\cdot 2\cdot 3\cdot 3}{2\cdot 3\cdot 3\cdot 2\cdot 7}=1$

77. $\frac{23}{105}-\frac{2}{105}=\frac{23-2}{105}=\frac{21}{105}$
$\frac{21}{105}=\frac{3\cdot 7}{3\cdot 5\cdot 7}=\frac{1}{5}$

79. $1\frac{1}{2}+3\frac{2}{3}=\frac{3}{2}+\frac{11}{3}$ LCD = 6
$\frac{3}{2}\cdot\frac{3}{3}=\frac{9}{6}$
$\frac{11}{3}\cdot\frac{2}{2}=\frac{22}{6}$
$\frac{9}{6}+\frac{22}{6}=\frac{31}{6}=5\frac{1}{6}$

81. $\frac{2}{3}-\frac{5}{9}+\frac{5}{6}$ LCD = 18
$\frac{2}{3}\cdot\frac{6}{6}=\frac{12}{18}$
$\frac{5}{9}\cdot\frac{2}{2}=\frac{10}{18}$
$\frac{5}{6}\cdot\frac{3}{3}=\frac{15}{18}$
$\frac{12}{18}-\frac{10}{18}+\frac{15}{18}=\frac{12-10+15}{18}=\frac{17}{18}$

83. $5+4\frac{1}{8}+15\frac{3}{4}+10\frac{1}{2}+15\frac{3}{4}+4\frac{1}{8}$
$=5+\frac{33}{8}+\frac{63}{4}+\frac{21}{2}+\frac{63}{4}+\frac{33}{8}$
$=\frac{40}{8}+\frac{33}{8}+\frac{126}{8}+\frac{84}{8}+\frac{126}{8}+\frac{33}{8}$
$=\frac{40+33+126+84+126+33}{8}$
$=\frac{442}{8}$
$=55\frac{1}{4}$ feet

85. $80-74\frac{17}{25}=\frac{2000}{25}-\frac{1867}{25}$
$=\frac{133}{25}$
$=5\frac{8}{25}$ meters

87. Answers may vary.

89. $5\frac{1}{2}-2\frac{1}{8}=\frac{11}{2}-\frac{17}{8}$
$=\frac{44}{8}-\frac{17}{8}$
$=\frac{44-17}{8}$
$=\frac{27}{8}$
$=3\frac{3}{8}$ miles

91. $\frac{3}{4}$

93. $1-\frac{3}{4}-\frac{1}{200}=\frac{200}{200}-\frac{150}{200}-\frac{1}{200}$
$=\frac{200-150-1}{200}$
$=\frac{49}{200}$

Section 1.4

Calculator Explorations

1. 125

3. 59,049

5. 30

7. 9857

9. 2376

Mental Math

1. multiply

2. add

3. subtract

4. divide

Exercise Set 1.4

1. $3^5 = 3 \cdot 3 \cdot 3 \cdot 3 \cdot 3 = 243$

3. $3^3 = 3 \cdot 3 \cdot 3 = 27$

5. $1^5 = 1 \cdot 1 \cdot 1 \cdot 1 \cdot 1 = 1$

7. $5^1 = 5$

9. $\left(\frac{1}{5}\right)^3 = \frac{1}{5} \cdot \frac{1}{5} \cdot \frac{1}{5} = \frac{1}{125}$

11. $\left(\frac{2}{3}\right)^4 = \frac{2}{3} \cdot \frac{2}{3} \cdot \frac{2}{3} \cdot \frac{2}{3} = \frac{16}{81}$

13. $7^2 = 7 \cdot 7 = 49$

15. $4^2 = 4 \cdot 4 = 16$

17. $(1.2)^2 = 1.2 \cdot 1.2 = 1.44$

19. $5 + 6 \cdot 2 = 5 + 12 = 17$

21. $4 \cdot 8 - 6 \cdot 2 = 32 - 12 = 20$

23. $2(8 - 3) = 2(5) = 10$

25.
$$\begin{aligned} 2 + (5 - 2) + 4^2 &= 2 + 3 + 4^2 \\ &= 2 + 3 + 16 \\ &= 5 + 16 \\ &= 21 \end{aligned}$$

27. $5 \cdot 3^2 = 5 \cdot 9 = 45$

29. $\frac{1}{4} \cdot \frac{2}{3} - \frac{1}{6} = \frac{2}{12} - \frac{1}{6} = \frac{1}{6} - \frac{1}{6} = 0$

31. $\frac{6-4}{9-2} = \frac{2}{7}$

33.
$$\begin{aligned} 2[5 + 2(8 - 3)] &= 2[5 + 2(5)] \\ &= 2[5 + 10] \\ &= 2[15] \\ &= 30 \end{aligned}$$

35. $\frac{19 - 3 \cdot 5}{6 - 4} = \frac{19 - 15}{2} = \frac{4}{2} = 2$

37. $\frac{|6-2|+3}{8+2 \cdot 5} = \frac{4+3}{8+10} = \frac{7}{18}$

39. $\frac{3+3(5+3)}{3^2+1} = \frac{3+3(8)}{9+1} = \frac{3+24}{10} = \frac{27}{10}$

41.
$$\begin{aligned} \frac{6+|8-2|+3^2}{18-3} &= \frac{6+|6|+3^2}{15} \\ &= \frac{6+6+9}{15} \\ &= \frac{21}{15} \\ &= \frac{3 \cdot 7}{3 \cdot 5} \\ &= \frac{7}{5} \end{aligned}$$

43. No, since in the absence of grouping symbols we always perform multiplications or divisions before additions or subtractions in any expression. Thus, in the expression $2 + 3 \cdot 5$, we should first find the product $3 \cdot 5$ and then add 2.
$2 + 3 \cdot 5 = 2 + 15 = 17$

45. **a.** $(6 + 2) \cdot (5 + 3) = 8 \cdot 8 = 64$

b.
$$\begin{aligned} (6 + 2) \cdot 5 + 3 &= 8 \cdot 5 + 3 \\ &= 40 + 3 \\ &= 43 \end{aligned}$$

c. $6 + 2 \cdot 5 + 3 = 6 + 10 + 3 = 19$

d. $6 + 2 \cdot (5 + 3) = 6 + 2 \cdot 8 = 6 + 16 = 22$

47. Replace y with 3.
$3y = 3(3) = 9$

49. Replace x with 1 and z with 5.
$\frac{z}{5x} = \frac{5}{5(1)} = \frac{5}{5} = 1$

51. Replace x with 1.
$3x - 2 = 3(1) - 2 = 3 - 2 = 1$

53. Replace x with 1 and y with 3.
$|2x + 3y| = |2(1) + 3(3)| = |2 + 9| = |11| = 11$

55. Replace y with 3.
$5y^2 = 5 \cdot 3^2 = 5 \cdot 9 = 45$

57. If $x = 12$, $y = 8$, and $z = 4$, then
$\frac{x}{z} + 3y = \frac{12}{4} + 3(8) = 3 + 24 = 27.$

59. If $x = 12$ and $y = 8$, then
$$\begin{aligned} x^2 - 3y + x &= (12)^2 - 3(8) + 1\text{:} \\ &= 144 - 24 + 12 \\ &= 132 \end{aligned}$$

61. If $x = 12$, $y = 8$, and $z = 4$, then
$$\frac{x^2 + z}{y^2 + 2z} = \frac{(12)^2 + 4}{(8)^2 + 2(4)} = \frac{144 + 4}{64 + 8} = \frac{148}{72} = \frac{37}{18}.$$

63. We evaluate the expression $16t^2$ for each value of t.
When $t = 1$, we have
$16t^2 = 16 \cdot 1^2 = 16 \cdot 1 = 16.$
When $t = 2$ we have
$16t^2 = 16 \cdot 2^2 = 16 \cdot 4 = 64.$
When $t = 3$ we have
$16t^2 = 16 \cdot 3^2 = 16 \cdot 9 = 144.$
When $t = 4$, we have
$16t^2 = 16 \cdot 4^2 = 16 \cdot 16 = 256.$

Time t (in seconds)	Distance $16t^2$ (in feet)
1	16
2	64
3	144
4	256

65.
$$\begin{aligned} 3x - 6 &= 9 \\ 3(5) - 6 &\stackrel{?}{=} 9 \\ 15 - 6 &\stackrel{?}{=} 9 \\ 9 &= 9 \end{aligned}$$
Solution

67.
$$\begin{aligned} 2x + 6 &= 5x - 1 \\ 2 \cdot 0 + 6 &\stackrel{?}{=} 5 \cdot 0 - 1 \\ 0 + 6 &\stackrel{?}{=} 0 - 1 \\ 6 &\neq -1 \end{aligned}$$
Not a solution

69.
$$\begin{aligned} 2x - 5 &= 5 \\ 2 \cdot 8 - 5 &\stackrel{?}{=} 5 \\ 16 - 5 &\stackrel{?}{=} 5 \\ 11 &\neq 5 \end{aligned}$$
Not a solution

71. $x + 6 = x + 6$
$2 + 6 \stackrel{?}{=} 2 + 6$
$8 = 8$
Solution

73. $x = 5x + 15$
$0 \stackrel{?}{=} 5 \cdot 0 + 15$
$0 \stackrel{?}{=} 0 + 15$
$0 \neq 15$
Not a solution

75. $x + 15$

77. $x - 5$

79. $3x + 22$

81. $1 + 2 = 9 \div 3$

83. $3 \neq 4 \div 2$

85. $5 + x = 20$

87. $13 - 3x = 13$

89. $\frac{12}{x} = \frac{1}{2}$

91. Answers may vary.

93. $P = 2l + 2w$
$P = 2(8) + 2(6)$
$P = 16 + 12$
$P = 28$ meters

95. $A = lw$
$A = (120)(100)$
$A = 12{,}000$ sq. ft

97. $R = \dfrac{I}{PT}$
$R = \dfrac{126.75}{(650)(3)}$
$R = \dfrac{126.75}{1950} = .065 = 6.5\%$

99. If $m = 228$ min, then
$4.95 + 0.10m = 4.95 + 0.10(228)$
$= 4.95 + 22.8$
$= \$27.75$

Section 1.5

Mental Math

1. negative
2. positive
3. 0
4. negative
5. negative
6. 0

Exercise Set 1.5

1. $6 + 3 = 9$

3. $-6 + (-8) = -14$

5. $8 + (-7) = 1$

7. $-14 + 2 = -12$

9. $-2 + (-3) = -5$

11. $-9 + (-3) = -12$

13. $-7 + 3 = -4$

15. $10 + (-3) = 7$

17. $5 + (-7) = -2$

19. $-16 + 16 = 0$

21. $27 + (-46) = -19$

23. $-18 + 49 = 31$

25. $-33 + (-14) = -47$

27. $6.3 + (-8.4) = -2.1$

29. $|-8| + (-16) = 8 + (-16) = -8$

31. $117 + (-79) = 38$

33. $-9.6 + (-3.5) = -13.1$

35. $-\frac{3}{8} + \frac{5}{8} = \frac{2}{8} = \frac{1}{4}$

37. $-\frac{7}{16} + \frac{1}{4} = -\frac{7}{16} + \frac{4 \cdot 1}{4 \cdot 4} = -\frac{7}{16} + \frac{4}{16} = -\frac{3}{16}$

39. $-\dfrac{7}{10} + \left(-\dfrac{3}{5}\right) = -\dfrac{7}{10} + \left(-\dfrac{2 \cdot 3}{2 \cdot 5}\right)$
$= -\dfrac{7}{10} + \left(-\dfrac{6}{10}\right)$
$= -\dfrac{3}{10}$

41. $-15 + 9 + (-2) = -6 + (-2) = -8$

43. $-21 + (-16) + (-22) = -37 + (-22) = -59$

45. $-23 + 16 + (-2) = -7 + (-2) = -9$

47. $|5 + (-10)| = |-5| = 5$

49. $6 + (-4) + 9 = 2 + 9 = 11$

51. $[-17 + (-4)] + [-12 + 15] = [-21] + [3]$
$= -18$

53. $|9 + (-12)| + |-16| = |-3| + |-16| = 3 + 16 = 19$

55. $-1.3 + [0.5 + (-0.3) + 0.4]$
$= -1.3 + (0.2 + 0.4)$
$= -1.3 + 0.6$
$= -0.7$

57. Tuesday

59. 7°

61. $\frac{-4°+3°+7°-2°+1°}{5} = \frac{5°}{5} = 1°$

63. $-15°+9° = -6°$

65. $-1312+658 = -654$ feet

67. $-41.1+(-126.7)+(-51.0)$
$= -167.8+(-51.0)$
$= -218.8$ million dollars

69. $-6+(-7)+(-4) = -13+(-4) = -17$

71. The opposite of 6 is −6.

73. The opposite of −2 is 2.

75. The opposite of 0 is 0.

77. Since $|-6| = 6$, the opposite of $|-6|$ is −6.

79. Answers may vary.

81. Since $|-2| = 2$, $-|-2| = -2$.

83. $-|0| = -0 = 0$

85. Since $\left|-\frac{2}{3}\right| = \frac{2}{3}$, $-\left|-\frac{2}{3}\right| = -\frac{2}{3}$.

87. Answers may vary.

89. $-a$ is a negative number.

91. $a + a$ is a positive number.

93. $x+9 = 5$
$-4+9 \stackrel{?}{=} 5$
$5 = 5$
Solution

95. $2y+(-3) = -7$
$2(-1)+(-3) \stackrel{?}{=} -7$
$-2+(-3) \stackrel{?}{=} -7$
$-5 \neq -7$
Not a solution

Section 1.6

Exercise Set 1.6

1. $-6-4 = -6+(-4) = -10$

3. $4-9 = 4+(-9) = -5$

5. $16-(-3) = 16+(3) = 19$

7. $\frac{1}{2}-\frac{1}{3} = \frac{1}{2}+\left(-\frac{1}{3}\right)$
$= \frac{3\cdot 1}{3\cdot 2}+\left(-\frac{2\cdot 1}{2\cdot 3}\right)$
$= \frac{3}{6}+\left(-\frac{2}{6}\right)$
$= \frac{1}{6}$

9. $-16-(-18) = -16+(18) = 2$

11. $-6-5 = -6+(-5) = -11$

13. $7-(-4) = 7+(4) = 11$

15. $-6-(-11) = -6+(11) = 5$

17. $16-(-21) = 16+(21) = 37$

19. $9.7-16.1 = 9.7+(-16.1) = -6.4$

21. $-44-27 = -44+(-27) = -71$

23. $-21-(-21) = -21+(21) = 0$

25. $-2.6-(-6.7) = -2.6+(6.7) = 4.1$

27. $-\frac{3}{11}-\left(-\frac{5}{11}\right) = -\frac{3}{11}+\left(\frac{5}{11}\right) = \frac{2}{11}$

29. $-\frac{1}{6}-\frac{3}{4}=-\frac{1}{6}+\left(-\frac{3}{4}\right)$
$=\frac{4\cdot 1}{4\cdot 6}+\left(-\frac{6\cdot 3}{6\cdot 4}\right)$
$=-\frac{4}{24}+\left(-\frac{18}{24}\right)$
$=-\frac{22}{24}$
$=-\frac{2\cdot 11}{2\cdot 12}$
$=-\frac{11}{12}$

31. $8.3-(-0.62)=8.3+(0.62)=8.92$

33. $8-(-5)=8+5=13$

35. $-6-(-1)=-6+1=-5$

37. $7-8=-1$

39. $-8-15=-23$

41. Answers may vary.

43. $-10-(-8)+(-4)-20$
$=-10+8+(-4)+(-20)$
$=-2+(-4)+(-20)$
$=-6+(-20)$
$=-26$

45. $5-9+(-4)-8-8$
$=5+(-9)+(-4)+(-8)+(-8)$
$=-4+(-4)+(-8)+(-8)$
$=-8+(-8)+(-8)$
$=-16+(-8)$
$=-24$

47. $-6-(2-11)=-6-(-9)=-6+9=3$

49. $3^3-8\cdot 9=27-8\cdot 9$
$=27-72$
$=27+(-72)$
$=-45$

51. $2-3(8-6)=2-3(8+(-6))$
$=2-3(2)$
$=2-6$
$=2+(-6)$
$=-4$

53. $(3-6)+4^2=(3+(-6))+4^2$
$=(-3)+4^2$
$=-3+16$
$=13$

55. $-2+[(8-11)-(-2-9)]$
$=-2+[(8+(-11))-(-2+(-9)]$
$=-2+[(-3)-(-11)]$
$=-2+[-3+11]$
$=-2+[8]$
$=6$

57. $|-3|+2^2+[-4-(-6)]=3+2^2+[-4+6]$
$=3+2^2+[2]$
$=3+4+2$
$=7+2$
$=9$

59. Replace x with -5 and y with 4.
$x-y=-5-4=-5+(-4)=-9$

61. Replace x with -5, y with 4, and t with 10.
$|x|+2t-8y=|-5|+2(10)-8(4)$
$=5+20-32$
$=5+20+(-32)$
$=25+(-32)$
$=-7$

63. Replace x with -5 and y with 4.
$\frac{9-x}{y+6}=\frac{9-(-5)}{4+6}=\frac{9+5}{4+6}=\frac{14}{10}=\frac{2\cdot 7}{2\cdot 5}=\frac{7}{5}$

65. Replace x with -5 and y with 4.
$y^2-x=4^2-(-5)$
$=16-(-5)$
$=16+5$
$=21$

67. Replace x with –5 and t with 10.

$$\frac{|x-(-10)|}{2t}=\frac{|-5-(-10)|}{2(10)}$$
$$=\frac{|-5+10|}{20}$$
$$=\frac{|5|}{20}$$
$$=\frac{5}{20}$$
$$=\frac{5}{4\cdot 5}$$
$$=\frac{1}{4}$$

69. January, –22°

71. $6-18°=-12°$

73. $30-(-19)=30+19=49°$

75. $-56°-(44°)=-56°+(-44°)=-100°$
The negative sign indicates a drop in temperature.
Therefore the temperature fell 100°.

77. $+2-5-20=+2+(-5)+(-20)$
$=-3+(-20)$
$=-23$ yd or 23 yard loss

79. $-322-62=-384$ or 384 B.C.

81. $-1\frac{5}{8}+\left(-\frac{3}{4}\right)=-\frac{13}{8}+\left(-\frac{3}{4}\right)$
$=-\frac{13}{8}+\left(-\frac{6}{8}\right)$
$=-\frac{19}{8}$
$=-2\frac{3}{8}$ points

83. $22{,}834-(-131)=22{,}834+131$
$=22{,}965$ feet

85. These angles are supplementary, so their sum is 180°.
$y=180°-50°=130°$

87. These angles are complementary, so their sum is 90°.
$x=90°-60°=30°$

89. $x-9=5$
$-4-9\overset{?}{=}5$
$-13\neq 5$
Not a solution

91. $-x+6=-x-1$
$-(-2)+6\overset{?}{=}-(-2)-1$
$2+6\overset{?}{=}2-1$
$8\neq 1$
Not a solution

93. $-x-13=-15$
$-2-13\overset{?}{=}-15$
$-15=-15$
Solution

95. True

97. False

99. $56{,}875+(-87{,}262)$
Negative since $87{,}262>56{,}875$
$56{,}875-87{,}262=-30{,}387$

Section 1.7

Calculator Explorations

1. $-38(26-27)=38$

3. $134+25(68-91)=-441$

5. $\frac{-50(294)}{175-265}=\frac{-14{,}700}{-90}=\frac{490}{3}=163.\overline{3}$

7. $9^5-4550=54{,}499$

9. $(-125)^2=15{,}625$

Mental Math

1. positive

2. positive

3. negative

4. negative

5. positive

6. negative

Exercise Set 1.7

1. $-6(4) = -24$

3. $2(-1) = -2$

5. $-5(-10) = 50$

7. $-3 \cdot 4 = -12$

9. $-6(-7) = 42$

11. $2(-9) = -18$

13. $-\frac{1}{2}\left(-\frac{3}{5}\right) = -\left(-\frac{1 \cdot 3}{2 \cdot 5}\right) = -\left(-\frac{3}{10}\right) = \frac{3}{10}$

15.
$$\begin{aligned} -\frac{3}{4}\left(-\frac{8}{9}\right) &= -\left(-\frac{3 \cdot 8}{4 \cdot 9}\right) \\ &= -\left(-\frac{24}{36}\right) \\ &= \frac{24}{36} \\ &= \frac{2 \cdot 12}{3 \cdot 12} \\ &= \frac{2}{3} \end{aligned}$$

17. $5(-1.4) = -7$

19. $-0.2(-0.7) = 0.14$

21. $-10(80) = -800$

23. $4(-7) = -28$

25. $(-5)(-5) = 25$

27. $\frac{2}{3}\left(-\frac{4}{9}\right) = -\frac{2 \cdot 4}{3 \cdot 9} = -\frac{8}{27}$

29. $-11(11) = -121$

31.
$$\begin{aligned} -\frac{20}{25}\left(\frac{5}{16}\right) &= -\frac{20 \cdot 5}{25 \cdot 16} \\ &= -\frac{100}{400} \\ &= -\frac{4 \cdot 5 \cdot 5}{5 \cdot 5 \cdot 4 \cdot 4} \\ &= -\frac{1}{4} \end{aligned}$$

33. $-2.1(-0.4) = 0.84$

35.
$$\begin{aligned} (-1)(2)(-3)(-5) &= (-2)(-3)(-5) \\ &= (6)(-5) \\ &= -30 \end{aligned}$$

37.
$$\begin{aligned} (2)(-1)(-3)(5)(3) &= (-2)(-3)(5)(3) \\ &= (+6)(5)(3) \\ &= (30)(3) \\ &= 90 \end{aligned}$$

39. True

41. False

43. $(-2)^4 = (-2)(-2)(-2)(-2) = 16$

45. $-1^5 = -(1 \cdot 1 \cdot 1 \cdot 1 \cdot 1) = -1$

47. $(-5)^2 = (-5)(-5) = 25$

49. $-7^2 = -(7 \cdot 7) = -49$

51. The reciprocal of 9 is $\frac{1}{9}$ since $9 \cdot \frac{1}{9} = 1$.

53. The reciprocal of $\frac{2}{3}$ is $\frac{3}{2}$ since $\frac{2}{3} \cdot \frac{3}{2} = 1$.

55. The reciprocal of -14 is $-\frac{1}{14}$ since $(-14)\left(-\frac{1}{14}\right) = 1$.

57. The reciprocal of $-\frac{3}{11}$ is $-\frac{11}{3}$ since $\left(-\frac{3}{11}\right)\left(-\frac{11}{3}\right) = 1$.

59. The reciprocal of 0.2 is $\frac{1}{0.2}$ since $0.2 \cdot \frac{1}{0.2} = 1$.

61. The reciprocal of $\frac{1}{-6.3}$ is –6.3 since $\left(\frac{1}{-6.3}\right)(-6.3) = 1$.

63. $\frac{18}{-2} = 18 \cdot -\frac{1}{2} = -9$

65. $\frac{-16}{-4} = -16 \cdot -\frac{1}{4} = 4$

67. $\frac{-48}{12} = -48 \cdot \frac{1}{12} = -4$

69. $\frac{0}{-4} = 0 \cdot -\frac{1}{4} = 0$

71. $-\frac{15}{3} = -15 \cdot \frac{1}{3} = -5$

73. $\frac{5}{0}$ is undefined

75. $\frac{-12}{-4} = -12 \cdot -\frac{1}{4} = 3$

77. $\frac{30}{-2} = 30 \cdot -\frac{1}{2} = -15$

79. $\frac{6}{7} \div \left(-\frac{1}{3}\right) = \frac{6}{7} \cdot \left(-\frac{3}{1}\right) = -\frac{18}{7}$

81. $-\frac{5}{9} \div \left(-\frac{3}{4}\right) = -\frac{5}{9} \cdot \left(-\frac{4}{3}\right) = \frac{20}{27}$

83. $-\frac{4}{9} \div \frac{4}{9} = -\frac{4}{9} \cdot \frac{9}{4} = -1$

85. $\frac{-9(-3)}{-6} = \frac{27}{-6} = -\frac{9}{2}$

87. $\frac{12}{9-12} = \frac{12}{-3} = -4$

89. $\frac{-6^2+4}{-2} = \frac{-36+4}{-2} = \frac{-32}{-2} = 16$

91. $\frac{8+(-4)^2}{4-12} = \frac{8+16}{4-12} = \frac{24}{-8} = -3$

93. $\frac{22+(3)(-2)}{-5-2} = \frac{22-6}{-5-2} = \frac{16}{-7} = -\frac{16}{7}$

95. $\frac{-3-5^2}{2(-7)} = \frac{-3-25}{-14} = \frac{-28}{-14} = 2$

97. $\frac{6-2(-3)}{4-3(-2)} = \frac{6+6}{4+6} = \frac{12}{10} = \frac{6}{5}$

99. $\frac{-3-2(-9)}{-15-3(-4)} = \frac{-3+18}{-15+12} = \frac{15}{-3} = -5$

101.
$$\begin{aligned}\frac{|5-9|+|10-15|}{|2(-3)|} &= \frac{|-4|+|-5|}{|-6|}\\ &= \frac{4+5}{6}\\ &= \frac{9}{6}\\ &= \frac{3}{2}\end{aligned}$$

103.
$$\begin{aligned}3x+2y &= 3(-5)+2(-3)\\ &= -15+(-6)\\ &= -21\end{aligned}$$

105.
$$\begin{aligned}2x^2-y^2 &= 2(-5)^2-(-3)^2\\ &= 2(25)-(9)\\ &= 50+(-9)\\ &= 41\end{aligned}$$

107.
$$\begin{aligned}x^3+3y &= (-5)^3+3(-3)\\ &= -125+(-9)\\ &= -134\end{aligned}$$

109.
$$\begin{aligned}\frac{2x-5}{y-2} &= \frac{2(-5)-5}{-3-2}\\ &= \frac{-10+(-5)}{-3-2}\\ &= \frac{-15}{-5}\\ &= 3\end{aligned}$$

111. $\frac{6-y}{x-4} = \frac{6-(-3)}{-5-4} = \frac{6+(+3)}{-5+(-4)} = \frac{9}{-9} = -1$

113. 4(–\$124.5 million) = –\$498 million

115. Answers may vary.

117. 1, −1

119. Positive

121. Not possible to determine

123. Negative

125. $-2+\frac{-15}{3}=-2-5=-7$

127. $2[-5+(-3)]=2[-8]=-16$

129. $-5x=-35$
$-5(7) \stackrel{?}{=} -35$
$-35=-35$
Solution

131. $\frac{x}{-10}=2$
$\frac{-20}{-10} \stackrel{?}{=} 2$
$2=2$
Solution

133. $-3x-5=-20$
$-3(5)-5 \stackrel{?}{=} -20$
$-15-5 \stackrel{?}{=} -20$
$-20=-20$
Solution

Section 1.8

Exercise Set 1.8

1. $x+16=16+x$

3. $-4\cdot y=y\cdot(-4)$

5. $xy=yx$

7. $2x+13=13+2x$

9. $(xy)\cdot z=x\cdot(yz)$

11. $2+(a+b)=(2+a)+b$

13. $4\cdot(ab)=4ab=(4a)\cdot b$

15. $(a+b)+c=a+(b+c)$

17. $8+(9+b)=(8+9)+b=17+b$

19. $4(6y)=(4\cdot 6)\cdot y=24\cdot y=24y$

21. $\frac{1}{5}(5y)=\left(\frac{1}{5}\cdot 5\right)\cdot y=1\cdot y=y$

23. $(13+a)+13=13+(a+13)$
$=13+(13+a)$
$=(13+13)+a$
$=26+a$

25. $-9(8x)=(-9\cdot 8)\cdot x=-72\cdot x=-72x$

27. $\frac{3}{4}\left(\frac{4}{3}s\right)=\left(\frac{3}{4}\cdot\frac{4}{3}\right)\cdot s=1\cdot s=s$

29. Answers may vary.

31. $4(x+y)=4(x)+4(y)=4x+4y$

33. $9(x-6)=9(x)-9(6)=9x-54$

35. $2(3x+5)=2(3x)+2(5)=6x+10$

37. $7(4x-3)=7(4x)-7(3)=28x-21$

39. $3(6+x)=3(6)+3(x)=18+3x$

41. $-2(y-z)=-2(y)-(-2)(z)=-2y+2z$

43. $-7(3y+5)=-7(3y)+(-7)(5)=-21y-35$

45. $5(x+4m+2)=5(x)+5(4m)+5(2)$
$=5x+20m+10$

47. $-4(1-2m+n)=-4(1)-(-4)(2m)+(-4)(n)$
$=-4+8m-4n$

49. $-(5x+2)=-1(5x+2)$
$=(-1)(5x)+(-1)(2)$
$=-5x-2$

51. $-(r-3-7p)=-1(r-3-7p)$
$=(-1)(r)-(-1)(3)-(-1)(7p)$
$=-r+3+7p$

53. $\frac{1}{2}(6x+8) = \frac{1}{2}(6x) + \frac{1}{2}(8)$
$= \left(\frac{1}{2}\cdot 6\right)x + \left(\frac{1}{2}\cdot 8\right)$
$= 3x + 4$

55. $-\frac{1}{3}(3x-9y) = -\frac{1}{3}(3x) - \left(-\frac{1}{3}\right)(9y)$
$= \left(-\frac{1}{3}\cdot 3\right)x - \left(-\frac{1}{3}\cdot 9\right)y$
$= (-1)x - (-3)y$
$= -x + 3y$

57. $3(2r+5) - 7 = 3(2r) + 3(5) - 7$
$= 6r + 15 - 7$
$= 6r + 8$

59. $-9(4x+8) + 2 = -9(4x) + (-9)(8) + 2$
$= -36x - 72 + 2$
$= -36x - 70$

61. $-4(4x+5) - 5 = -4(4x) + (-4)(5) - 5$
$= -16x - 20 - 5$
$= -16x - 25$

63. $4 \cdot 1 + 4 \cdot y = 4(1 + y)$

65. $11x + 11y = 11(x + y)$

67. $(-1) \cdot 5 + (-1) \cdot x = -1(5 + x)$

69. $30a + 30b = 30(a + b)$

71. The commutative property of multiplication

73. The associative property of addition

75. The distributive property

77. The associative property of multiplication

79. The identity property of addition

81. The distributive property

83. The associative and commutative properties of multiplication

85.

Expression	Opposite	Reciprocal
8	−8	$\frac{1}{8}$

87.

Expression	Opposite	Reciprocal
x	$-x$	$\frac{1}{x}$

89.

Expression	Opposite	Reciprocal
$2x$	$-2x$	$\frac{1}{2x}$

91. not commutative

93. commutative

95. Answers may vary.

Exercise Set 1.9

1. The number of teenagers expected to use the Internet in 1999 is about 7.8 million.

3. From the graph, the greatest increase in the heights of successive bars is from 1999 to 2002. The greatest increase is in 2002.

5. Look for the shortest bar, which is the bar representing the PGA/LPGA tours. The PGA/LPGA tours spent the least amount of money on advertising.

7. Major League Baseball and the NBA each spent over $10,000,000 on advertising.

9. The NBA spent about $15 million on advertising.

11. France

13. France, U.S., Spain, Italy

15. 34 million

17. *Pocahontas* generated approximately 142 million dollars, or $142,000,000.

19. *Snow White and the Seven Dwarfs*

21. Answers may vary.

23. Find the highest point of the line graph. The highest percent of arson fires started by juveniles occurred in 1994.

25. 1989 and 1990

27. approximately 54%

29. The greatest increase in the percent of arson fires started by juveniles occurred in 1994. Notice that the line graph is steepest between the years 1993 and 1994.

31. The pulse rate was approximately 59 beats per minute 5 minutes before lighting a cigarette.

33. 5 minutes before lighting a cigarette, the pulse rate was approximately 59 beats per minute. 10 minutes after lighting a cigarette, the pulse rate had increased to about 85 beats per minute.
$85 - 59 = 26$
The pulse rate increased by 26 beats per minute between 5 minutes before and 10 minutes after lighting a cigarette.

35. 20 students

37. 1985

39. Answers may vary.

41. 4 million

43. 69 million

45. 1960

47. $69 - 57 = 12$; 12 million

49. New Orleans, Louisiana is located at latitude 30° north and longitude 90° west.

51. Answers may vary.

Chapter 1 Review Exercises

1. $8 < 10$

2. $7 > 2$

3. $-4 > -5$

4. $\frac{12}{2} > -8$

5. $|-7| < |-8|$

6. $|-9| > -9$

7. $-|-1| = -1$

8. $|-14| = -(-14)$

9. $1.2 > 1.02$

10. $-\frac{3}{2} < -\frac{3}{4}$

11. $4 \geq -3$

12. $6 \neq 5$

13. $0.03 < 0.3$

14. $50 > 40$

15. **a.** $\{1, 3\}$

b. $\{0, 1, 3\}$

c. $\{-6, 0, 1, 3\}$

d. $\{-6, 0, 1, 1\frac{1}{2}, 3, 9.62\}$

e. $\{\pi\}$

f. $\{-6, 0, 1, 1\frac{1}{2}, 3, \pi, 9.62\}$

16. **a.** $\{2, 5\}$

b. $\{2, 5\}$

c. $\{-3, 2, 5\}$

d. $\{-3, -1.6, 2, 5, \frac{11}{2}, 15.1\}$

e. $\{\sqrt{5}, 2\pi\}$

f. $\{-3, -1.6, 2, 5, \frac{11}{2}, 15.1, \sqrt{5}, 2\pi\}$

17. Friday

18. Wednesday

19. $36 = 2 \cdot 2 \cdot 3 \cdot 3$

20. $120 = 2 \cdot 2 \cdot 2 \cdot 3 \cdot 5$

21. $\frac{8}{15} \cdot \frac{27}{30} = \frac{2 \cdot 2 \cdot 2}{3 \cdot 5} \cdot \frac{3 \cdot 3 \cdot 3}{2 \cdot 3 \cdot 5} = \frac{12}{25}$

22. $\frac{7}{8} \div \frac{21}{32} = \frac{7}{8} \cdot \frac{32}{21} = \frac{1}{1} \cdot \frac{4}{3} = \frac{4}{3}$

23.
$$\begin{aligned} \frac{7}{15} + \frac{5}{6} &= \frac{7}{15} \cdot \frac{2}{2} + \frac{5}{6} \cdot \frac{5}{5} \\ &= \frac{14}{30} + \frac{25}{30} \\ &= \frac{39}{30} \\ &= \frac{3 \cdot 13}{2 \cdot 3 \cdot 5} \\ &= \frac{13}{10} \end{aligned}$$

24. $\frac{3}{4} - \frac{3}{20} = \frac{15}{20} - \frac{3}{20} = \frac{12}{20} = \frac{3}{5}$

25.
$$\begin{aligned} 2\frac{3}{4} + 6\frac{5}{8} &= \frac{11}{4} \cdot \frac{2}{2} + \frac{53}{8} \\ &= \frac{22}{8} + \frac{53}{8} \\ &= \frac{75}{8} \\ &= 9\frac{3}{8} \end{aligned}$$

26.
$$\begin{aligned} 7\frac{1}{6} - 2\frac{2}{3} &= \frac{43}{6} - \frac{8}{3} \\ &= \frac{43}{6} - \frac{16}{6} \\ &= \frac{27}{6} \\ &= \frac{9}{2} \\ &= 4\frac{1}{2} \end{aligned}$$

27. $5 \div \frac{1}{3} = 5 \cdot \frac{3}{1} = 15$

28. $2 \cdot 8\frac{3}{4} = 2 \cdot \frac{35}{4} = \frac{35}{2} = 17\frac{1}{2}$

29.
$$\begin{aligned} 1 - \frac{1}{6} - \frac{1}{4} &= 1 \cdot \frac{12}{12} - \frac{1}{6} \cdot \frac{2}{2} - \frac{1}{4} \cdot \frac{3}{3} \\ &= \frac{12}{12} - \frac{2}{12} - \frac{3}{12} \\ &= \frac{12 - 2 - 3}{12} \\ &= \frac{7}{12} \end{aligned}$$

30. Area $= 1\frac{1}{3} \cdot \frac{7}{8} = \frac{4}{3} \cdot \frac{7}{8} = \frac{7}{6} = 1\frac{1}{6}$ sq. m

$$\begin{aligned} \text{Perimeter} &= \frac{7}{8} + \frac{7}{8} + 1\frac{1}{3} + 1\frac{1}{3} \\ &= \frac{7}{8} + \frac{7}{8} + \frac{4}{3} + \frac{4}{3} \\ &= \frac{7}{8} \cdot \frac{3}{3} + \frac{7}{8} \cdot \frac{3}{3} + \frac{4}{3} \cdot \frac{8}{8} + \frac{4}{3} \cdot \frac{8}{8} \\ &= \frac{21}{24} + \frac{21}{24} + \frac{32}{24} + \frac{32}{24} \\ &= \frac{106}{24} \\ &= 4\frac{5}{12} \text{ meters} \end{aligned}$$

31. Area $= \frac{3}{11} \cdot \frac{3}{11} + \frac{5}{11} \cdot \frac{5}{11}$
$= \frac{9}{121} + \frac{25}{121}$
$= \frac{34}{121}$ sq. in.

Perimeter
$= \frac{5}{11} + \frac{5}{11} + \frac{3}{11} + \frac{2}{11} + \frac{3}{11} + \frac{3}{11} + \frac{5}{11}$
$= \frac{26}{11}$
$= 2\frac{4}{11}$ in.

32. $7\frac{1}{2} - 6\frac{1}{8} = \frac{15}{2} - \frac{49}{8}$
$= \frac{15}{2} \cdot \frac{4}{4} - \frac{49}{8}$
$= \frac{60}{8} - \frac{49}{8}$
$= \frac{11}{8}$
$= 1\frac{3}{8}$ ft

33. $1\frac{1}{8} + 1\frac{13}{16} = \frac{9}{8} + \frac{29}{16}$
$= \frac{18}{16} + \frac{29}{16}$
$= \frac{47}{16}$
$= 2\frac{15}{16}$ pounds

34. $1\frac{1}{2} + 1\frac{11}{16} + 1\frac{3}{4} + 1\frac{5}{8} + \frac{11}{16} + 1\frac{1}{8}$
$= \frac{3}{2} + \frac{27}{16} + \frac{7}{4} + \frac{13}{8} + \frac{11}{16} + \frac{9}{8}$
$= \frac{24}{16} + \frac{27}{16} + \frac{28}{16} + \frac{26}{16} + \frac{11}{16} + \frac{18}{16}$
$= \frac{134}{16}$
$= \frac{67}{8}$
$= 8\frac{3}{8}$ pounds

35. $2\frac{15}{16} + 8\frac{3}{8} = \frac{47}{16} + \frac{67}{8}$
$= \frac{47}{16} + \frac{134}{16}$
$= \frac{181}{16}$
$= 11\frac{5}{16}$ pounds

36. Jioke

37. Odera

38. $1\frac{13}{16} - \frac{11}{16} = \frac{29}{16} - \frac{11}{16} = \frac{18}{16} = \frac{9}{8} = 1\frac{1}{8}$ pounds

39. $5\frac{1}{2} - 1\frac{5}{8} = \frac{11}{2} - \frac{13}{8}$
$= \frac{44}{8} - \frac{13}{8}$
$= \frac{31}{8}$
$= 3\frac{7}{8}$ pounds

40. $4\frac{5}{32} - 1\frac{1}{8} = \frac{133}{32} - \frac{9}{8}$
$= \frac{133}{32} - \frac{36}{32}$
$= \frac{97}{32}$
$= 3\frac{1}{32}$ pounds

41. $2^4 = 2 \cdot 2 \cdot 2 \cdot 2 = 16$

42. $5^2 = 5 \cdot 5 = 25$

43. $\left(\frac{2}{7}\right)^2 = \frac{2}{7} \cdot \frac{2}{7} = \frac{4}{49}$

44. $\left(\frac{3}{4}\right)^3 = \frac{3}{4} \cdot \frac{3}{4} \cdot \frac{3}{4} = \frac{27}{64}$

45. $6 \cdot 3^2 + 2 \cdot 8 = 6 \cdot 9 + 2 \cdot 8 = 54 + 16 = 70$

46. $68-5\cdot 2^3=68-5\cdot 8=68-40=28$

47. $3(1+2\cdot 5)+4=3(1+10)+4$
$=3(11)+4$
$=33+4$
$=37$

48. $8+3(2\cdot 6-1)=8+3(12-1)$
$=8+3(11)$
$=8+33$
$=41$

49. $\dfrac{4+|6-2|+8^2}{4+6\cdot 4}=\dfrac{4+4+64}{4+24}$
$=\dfrac{72}{28}$
$=\dfrac{2\cdot 2\cdot 2\cdot 3\cdot 3}{2\cdot 2\cdot 7}$
$=\dfrac{18}{7}$

50. $5[3(2+5)-5]=5[3(7)-5]$
$=5[21-5]$
$=5[16]$
$=80$

51. $20-12=2\cdot 4$

52. $\dfrac{9}{2}>-5$

53. $2x+3y=2(6)+3(2)=12+6=18$

54. If $x=6$, $y=2$ and $z=8$, then
$x(y+2z)=6[2+2(8)]$
$=6[2+16]$
$=6[18]$
$=108$

55. $\dfrac{x}{y}+\dfrac{z}{2y}=\dfrac{6}{2}+\dfrac{8}{2(2)}=3+\dfrac{8}{4}=3+2=5$

56. If $x=6$ and $y=2$, then
$x^2-3y^2=6^2-3(2)^2$
$=36-3(4)$
$=36-12$
$=24$

57. $180-37-80=63°$

58. $7x-3=18$
$7\cdot 3-3\stackrel{?}{=}18$
$21-3\stackrel{?}{=}18$
$18=18$
Solution

59. $3x^2+4=x-1$
$3\cdot 1^2+4\stackrel{?}{=}1-1$
$3\cdot 1+4\stackrel{?}{=}0$
$3+4\stackrel{?}{=}0$
$7\neq 0$
Not a solution

60. $-9\Rightarrow 9$

61. $\dfrac{2}{3}\Rightarrow -\dfrac{2}{3}$

62. $|-2|=2\Rightarrow -2$

63. $-|-7|=-7\Rightarrow 7$

64. $-15+4=-11$

65. $-6+(-11)=-17$

66. $\dfrac{1}{16}+\left(-\dfrac{1}{4}\right)=\dfrac{1}{16}-\dfrac{1}{4}\cdot\dfrac{4}{4}=\dfrac{1}{16}-\dfrac{4}{16}=-\dfrac{3}{16}$

67. $-8+|-3|=-8+3=-5$

68. $-4.6+(-9.3)=-13.9$

69. $-2.8+6.7=3.9$

70. $-282+728=446$ ft

71. $6-20=-14$

72. $-3.1-8.4=-11.5$

73. $-6-(-11)=-6+(+11)=5$

74. $4-15=-11$

75. $-21-16+3(8-2)=-21-16+3(6)$
$=-21-16+18$
$=-19$

76. $\frac{11-(-9)+6(8-2)}{2+3\cdot 4}=\frac{11+9+6(6)}{2+12}$
$=\frac{11+9+36}{14}$
$=\frac{56}{14}$
$=4$

77. $2x^2-y+z=2(3)^2-(-6)+(-9)$
$=2(9)-(-6)+(-9)$
$=18-(-6)+(-9)$
$=18+(+6)+(-9)$
$=24+(-9)$
$=15$

78. If $x=3$ and $y=-6$, then
$\frac{y-x+5x}{2x}=\frac{-6-3+5(3)}{2(3)}$
$=\frac{-6-3+15}{6}$
$=\frac{6}{6}$
$=1$

79. $50+1-2+5+1-4=\$51$

80. If E is 412 and I is 536, then
$E-I=412-536=-124$.
-$124 billion

81. $-6\Rightarrow-\frac{1}{6}$

82. $\frac{3}{5}\Rightarrow\frac{5}{3}$

83. $6(-8)=-48$

84. $(-2)(-14)=28$

85. $\frac{-18}{-6}=3$

86. $\frac{42}{-3}=-14$

87. $-3(-6)(-2)=+18(-2)=-36$

88. $(-4)(-3)(0)(-6)=(12)(0)(-6)=(0)(-6)=0$

89. $\frac{4\cdot(-3)+(-8)}{2+(-2)}=\frac{-12+(-8)}{2+(-2)}$
$=\frac{-20}{0}$
undefined—division by zero is not defined

90. $\frac{3(-2)^2-5}{-14}=\frac{3(4)-5}{-14}$
$=\frac{12-5}{-14}$
$=\frac{7}{-14}$
$=-\frac{1}{2}$

91. $-\frac{6}{0}$ is undefined.

92. $\frac{0}{-2}=0$

93. $\frac{-9-7+1}{3}=\frac{-16+1}{3}=\frac{-15}{3}=-5$

94. $\frac{-1+0-3+0}{4}=\frac{-1-3}{4}=\frac{-4}{4}=-1$

95. $-6+5=5+(-6)$
commutative property of addition

96. $6\cdot 1=6$
multiplicative identity property

97. $3(8-5)=3(8)+3(-5)$
distributive property

98. $4+(-4)=0$
additive inverse property

99. $2+(3+9)=(2+3)+9$
associative property of addition

100. $2 \cdot 8 = 8 \cdot 2$
commutative property of multiplication

101. $6(8 + 5) = 6(8) + 6(5)$
distributive property

102. $(3 \cdot 8) \cdot 4 = 3 \cdot (8 \cdot 4)$
associative property of multiplication

103. $4 \cdot \frac{1}{4} = 1$
multiplicative inverse

104. $8 + 0 = 8$
additive identity property

105. $4(8 + 3) = 4(3 + 8)$
commutative property of addition

106. 76 million

107. $76 - 69 = 7$; 7 million

108. 1999

109. number of subscribers is increasing

110. San Francisco, 8.3%

111. Miami, 1.8%

112. Detroit, Los Angeles/Orange County, Washington/Baltimore, Philadelphia, Miami

113. New York, Cleveland, Houston, Chicago, Boston, Dallas/Ft. Worth, San Francisco

Chapter 1 Test

1. $|-7| > 5$

2. $(9 + 5) \geq 4$

3. $-13 + 8 = -5$

4. $-13 - (-2) = -13 + (+2) = -11$

5. $6 \cdot 3 - 8 \cdot 4 = 18 - 32 = 18 + (-32) = -14$

6. $(13)(-3) = -39$

7. $(-6)(-2) = 12$

8. $\frac{|-16|}{-8} = \frac{16}{-8} = -2$

9. $\frac{-8}{0}$
undefined—division by zero is not defined

10. $\frac{|-6|+2}{5-6} = \frac{6+2}{5-6} = \frac{8}{5+(-6)} = \frac{8}{-1} = -8$

11. $$\begin{aligned}\frac{1}{2} - \frac{5}{6} &= \frac{1}{2} + \left(-\frac{5}{6}\right) \\ &= \frac{1}{2} \cdot \frac{3}{3} + \left(-\frac{5}{6}\right) \\ &= \frac{3}{6} + \left(-\frac{5}{6}\right) \\ &= -\frac{2}{6} \\ &= \frac{2}{2 \cdot 3} \\ &= -\frac{1}{3}\end{aligned}$$

12. $$\begin{aligned}-1\frac{1}{8} + 5\frac{3}{4} &= -\frac{9}{8} + \frac{23}{4} \\ &= -\frac{9}{8} + \frac{23}{4} \cdot \frac{2}{2} \\ &= -\frac{9}{8} + \frac{46}{8} \\ &= \frac{37}{8} \\ &= 4\frac{5}{8}\end{aligned}$$

13. $$\begin{aligned}-\frac{3}{5} + \frac{15}{8} &= \frac{3}{5} \cdot \frac{8}{8} + \frac{15}{8} \cdot \frac{5}{5} \\ &= -\frac{24}{40} + \frac{75}{40} \\ &= \frac{51}{40}\end{aligned}$$

14. $3(-4)^2 - 80 = 3(16) - 80$
$= 48 - 80$
$= 48 + (-80)$
$= -32$

15. $6[5 + 2(3 - 8) - 3] = 6[5 + 2(3 + (-8)) - 3]$
$= 6[5 + 2(-5) - 3]$
$= 6[5 + (-10) - 3]$
$= 6[5 + (-10) + (-3)]$
$= 6[-5 + (-3)]$
$= 6[-8]$
$= -48$

16. $\frac{-12 + 3 \cdot 8}{4} = \frac{-12 + 24}{4} = \frac{12}{4} = 3$

17. $\frac{(-2)(0)(-3)}{-6} = \frac{0}{-6} = 0$

18. $-3 > -7$

19. $4 > -8$

20. $|-3| \ ? \ 2$
$3 \ ? \ 2$
$3 > 2$
$|-3| > 2$

21. $|-2| \ ? -1 - (-3)$
$2 \ ? -1 + (+3)$
$2 \ ? \ 2$
$2 = 2$
$|-2| = -1 - (-3)$

22. $2221 < 10{,}993$

23. **a.** $\{1, 7\}$

b. $\{0, 1, 7\}$

c. $\{-5, -1, 0, 1, 7\}$

d. $\left\{-5, -1, 0, \frac{1}{4}, 1, 7, 11.6\right\}$

e. $\{\sqrt{7}, 3\pi\}$

f. $\left\{-5, -1, 0, \frac{1}{4}, 1, 7, 11.6, \sqrt{7}, 3\pi\right\}$

24. $x^2 + y^2 = (6)^2 + (-2)^2 = 36 + 4 = 40$

25. $x + yz = 6 + (-2)(-3) = 6 + 6 = 12$

26. $2 + 3x - y = 2 + 3(6) - (-2)$
$= 2 + 18 + (+2)$
$= 22$

27. $\frac{y + z - 1}{x} = \frac{-2 + (-3) - 1}{6}$
$= \frac{-2 + (-3) + (-1)}{6}$
$= \frac{-6}{6}$
$= -1$

28. $8 + (9 + 3) = (8 + 9) + 3$
associative property of addition

29. $6 \cdot 8 = 8 \cdot 6$
commutative property of multiplication

30. $-6(2 + 4) = -6(2) + (-6)(4)$
distributive property

31. $\frac{1}{6}(6) = 1$
multiplicative inverse

32. 9
The opposite of –9 is 9.

33. –3
The reciprocal of $-\frac{1}{3}$ is –3.

34. Second down

35. Yes

36. $-14 + 31 = 17°$

37. $356 + 460 - 166 = 816 - 166 = 650$
$650 million

38. $280 \cdot 1.5 = 420$
loss of $420

39. $8 billion

40. $25 billion

41. $13.5 - 8 = 5.5$
$5.5 billion

42. 1996, since the increase from 1995 to 1996 is greater than any other year.

43. Indiana, 25.2 million tons

44. Texas, 5 million tons

45. 16 million tons

46. $8 - 5 = 3$; 3 million tons

Chapter 2

Section 2.1

Mental Math

1. The numerical coefficient of $-7y$ is -7.
2. The numerical coefficient of $3x$ is 3.
3. The numerical coefficient of x is 1 since x is $1x$.
4. The numerical coefficient of $-y$ is -1 since $-y$ is $-1y$.
5. The numerical coefficient of $17x^2y$ is 17.
6. The numerical coefficient of $1.2xyz$ is 1.2.
7. Like terms, since the variable and its exponent match.
8. Unlike terms, since the exponents on x are not the same.
9. Unlike terms, since the exponents on z are not the same.
10. Like terms, since each variable and its exponent match.
11. Like terms, since $wz = zw$ by the commutative property.
12. Unlike terms, since the variables do not match.

Exercise Set 2.1

1. $7y + 8y = (7 + 8)y = 15y$

3. $8w - w + 6w = (8 - 1 + 6)w = 13w$

5. $$\begin{aligned} 3b - 5 - 10b - 4 &= 3b - 10b - 5 - 4 \\ &= (3 - 10)b + (-5 - 4) \\ &= -7b - 9 \end{aligned}$$

7. $$\begin{aligned} m - 4m + 2m - 6 &= (1 - 4 + 2)m - 6 \\ &= -m - 6 \end{aligned}$$

9. $5(y - 4) = 5y - 20$

11. $7(d - 3) + 10 = 7d - 21 + 10 = 7d - 11$

13. $-(3x - 2y + 1) = -3x + 2y - 1$

15. $$\begin{aligned} 5(x + 2) - (3x - 4) &= 5x + 10 - 3x + 4 \\ &= 5x - 3x + 10 + 4 \\ &= 2x + 14 \end{aligned}$$

17. Answers may vary.

19. $$\begin{aligned} (6x + 7) + (4x - 10) &= 6x + 7 + 4x - 10 \\ &= 6x + 4x + 7 - 10 \\ &= 10x - 3 \end{aligned}$$

21. $$\begin{aligned} (3x - 8) - (7x + 1) &= 3x - 8 - 7x - 1 \\ &= 3x - 7x - 8 - 1 \\ &= -4x - 9 \end{aligned}$$

23. $7x^2 + 8x^2 - 10x^2 = 5x^2$

25. $$\begin{aligned} 6x - 5x + x - 3 + 2x &= 6x - 5x + x + 2x - 3 \\ &= 4x - 3 \end{aligned}$$

27. $$\begin{aligned} -5 + 8(x - 6) &= -5 + 8x - 48 \\ &= 8x - 5 - 48 \\ &= 8x - 53 \end{aligned}$$

29. $$\begin{aligned} 5g - 3 - 5 - 5g &= 5g - 5g - 3 - 5 \\ &= -8 \end{aligned}$$

31. $$\begin{aligned} 6.2x - 4 + x - 1.2 &= 6.2x + x - 4 - 1.2 \\ &= 7.2x - 5.2 \end{aligned}$$

33. $2k - k - 6 = k - 6$

35. $$\begin{aligned} 0.5(m + 2) + 0.4m &= 0.5m + 1.0 + 0.4m \\ &= 0.5m + 0.4m + 1.0 \\ &= 0.9m + 1.0 \end{aligned}$$

37. $-4(3y - 4) = -12y + 16$

39. $$\begin{aligned} 3(2x - 5) - 5(x - 4) &= 6x - 15 - 5x + 20 \\ &= 6x - 5x - 15 + 20 \\ &= x + 5 \end{aligned}$$

41. $3.4m-4-3.4m-7=3.4m-3.4m-4-7$
$=-11$

43. $6x+0.5-4.3x-0.4x+3$
$=6x-4.3x-0.4x+0.5+3$
$=6.0x-4.3x-0.4x+0.5+3.0$
$=1.3x+3.5$

45. $-2(3x-4)+7x-6=-6x+8+7x-6$
$=-6x+7x+8-6$
$=x+2$

47. $-9x+4x+18-10x=-9x+4x-10x+18$
$=-15x+18$

49. $5k-(3k-10)=5k-3k+10=2k+10$

51. $(3x+4)-(6x-1)=3x+4-6x+1$
$=3x-6x+4+1$
$=-3x+5$

53.

twice a number	decreased by	4
$2x$	$-$	4

$2x-4$

55.

three-fourths of a number	increased by	12
$\frac{3}{4}x$	+	12

$\frac{3}{4}x+12$

57.

the sum of 5 times a number and –2	added to	7 times a number
$5x+(-2)$	+	$7x$

$5x+(-2)+7x=-2+12x$

59. Subtract $5m-6$ from $m-9$
$(m-9)-(5m-6)=m-9-5m+6$
$=-4m-3$

61.

eight	times	the sum of a number and 6
8	$\cdot$	$(x+6)$

$8(x+6)$

63.

double a number	minus	the sum of a number and 10
$2x$	$-$	$(x+10)$

$2x-(x+10)=2x-x-10=x-10$

65.

seven	multiplied by	the quotient of a number and 6
7	$\cdot$	$\frac{x}{6}$

$7\cdot\frac{x}{6}=\frac{7x}{6}$

67.

the sum of			
2	3 times a number	–9	4 times a number
2 +	$3x$	+ (–9) +	$4x$

$2+3x-9+4x=7x-7$

69. $2(5x)+2(4x-1)=10x+8x-2=18x-2$
$(18x-2)$ft

71. Balanced

73. Balanced

75. $12\cdot(x+2)+(3x-1)=12x+24+3x-1$
$=12x+3x+24-1$
$=15x+23$

$(15x+23)$ inches

77. $y-x^2$ when $x=-1$ and $y=3$
$3-(-1)^2=3-(+1)$
$=3-1$
$=2$

79. If $a = 2$ and $b = -5$, then
$a - b^2 = 2 - (-5)^2 = 2 - 25 = -23$

81. $yz - y^2$ when $y = -5$ and $z = 0$
$(-5)(0) - (-5)^2 = 0 - (+25) = 0 - 25 = -25$

83. $5b^2c^3 + 8b^3c^2 - 7b^3c^2 = 5b^2c^3 + b^3c^2$

85.
$$\begin{aligned} &3x - (2x^2 - 6x) + 7x^2 \\ &= 3x - 2x^2 + 6x + 7x^2 \\ &= -2x^2 + 7x^2 + 3x + 6x \\ &= 5x^2 + 9x \end{aligned}$$

87.
$$\begin{aligned} &-(2x^2y + 3z) + 3z - 5x^2y \\ &= -2x^2y - 3z + 3z - 5x^2y \\ &= -2x^2y - 5x^2y - 3z + 3z \\ &= -7x^2y \end{aligned}$$

Section 2.2

Mental Math

1. $x + 4 = 6$
$x = 2$

2. $x + 7 = 10$
$x = 3$

3. $n + 18 = 30$
$n = 12$

4. $z + 22 = 40$
$z = 18$

5. $b - 11 = 6$
$b = 17$

6. $d - 16 = 5$
$d = 21$

Exercise Set 2.2

1.
$$\begin{aligned} x + 7 &= 10 \\ x + 7 - 7 &= 10 - 7 \\ x &= 3 \end{aligned}$$

Check:
$$\begin{aligned} x + 7 &= 10 \\ 3 + 7 &\stackrel{?}{=} 10 \\ 10 &= 10 \end{aligned}$$

The solution is 3.

3.
$$\begin{aligned} x - 2 &= -4 \\ x - 2 + 2 &= -4 + 2 \\ x &= -2 \end{aligned}$$

Check:
$$\begin{aligned} x - 2 &= -4 \\ -2 - 2 &\stackrel{?}{=} -4 \\ -4 &= -4 \end{aligned}$$

The solution is -2.

5.
$$\begin{aligned} 3 + x &= -11 \\ 3 + x - 3 &= -11 - 3 \\ x &= -14 \end{aligned}$$

Check:
$$\begin{aligned} 3 + x &= -11 \\ 3 + (-14) &\stackrel{?}{=} -11 \\ -11 &= -11 \end{aligned}$$

The solution is -14.

7.
$$\begin{aligned} r - 8.6 &= -8.1 \\ r - 8.6 + 8.6 &= -8.1 + 8.6 \\ r &= 0.5 \end{aligned}$$

Check:
$$\begin{aligned} r - 8.6 &= -8.1 \\ 0.5 - 8.6 &\stackrel{?}{=} -8.1 \\ -8.1 &= -8.1 \end{aligned}$$

The solution is 0.5.

9.
$$\frac{1}{3}+f=\frac{3}{4}$$
$$\frac{1}{3}+f-\frac{1}{3}=\frac{3}{4}-\frac{1}{3}$$
$$f=\frac{9}{12}-\frac{4}{12}$$
$$f=\frac{5}{12}$$

Check:
$$\frac{1}{3}+f=\frac{3}{4}$$
$$\frac{1}{3}+\frac{5}{12}\stackrel{?}{=}\frac{3}{4}$$
$$\frac{4}{12}+\frac{5}{12}\stackrel{?}{=}\frac{3}{4}$$
$$\frac{9}{12}\stackrel{?}{=}\frac{3}{4}$$
$$\frac{3}{4}=\frac{3}{4}$$

The solution is $\frac{5}{12}$.

11.
$$5b-0.7=6b$$
$$5b-0.7-5b=6b-5b$$
$$-0.7=b$$

Check:
$$5b-0.7=6b$$
$$5(-0.7)-0.7\stackrel{?}{=}6(-0.7)$$
$$-3.5-0.7\stackrel{?}{=}-4.2$$
$$-4.2=-4.2$$

The solution is –0.7.

13.
$$7x-3=6x$$
$$7x-3-6x=6x-6x$$
$$x-3=0$$
$$x-3+3=0+3$$
$$x=3$$

Check:
$$7x-3=6x$$
$$7(3)-3\stackrel{?}{=}6(3)$$
$$21-3\stackrel{?}{=}18$$
$$18=18$$

The solution is 3.

15. Answers may vary.

17.
$$7x+2x=8x-3$$
$$9x=8x-3$$
$$9x-8x=8x-3-8x$$
$$x=-3$$

Check:
$$7x+2x=8x-3$$
$$7(-3)+2(-3)\stackrel{?}{=}8(-3)-3$$
$$-21-6\stackrel{?}{=}-24-3$$
$$-27=-27$$

The solution is –3.

19.
$$2y+10=5y-4y$$
$$2y+10=y$$
$$2y+10-y=y-y$$
$$y+10=0$$
$$y+10-10=0-10$$
$$y=-10$$

Check:
$$2y+10=5y-4y$$
$$2(-10)+10\stackrel{?}{=}5(-10)-4(-10)$$
$$-20+10\stackrel{?}{=}-50+40$$
$$-10=-10$$

The solution is –10.

21.
$$3x-6=2x+5$$
$$3x-6-2x=2x+5-2x$$
$$x-6=5$$
$$x-6+6=5+6$$
$$x=11$$

Check:
$$3x-6=2x+5$$
$$3(11)-6\stackrel{?}{=}2(11)+5$$
$$33-6\stackrel{?}{=}22+5$$
$$27=27$$

The solution is 11.

23.
$$5x - \frac{1}{6} = 6x - \frac{5}{6}$$
$$5x - \frac{1}{6} + \frac{5}{6} = 6x - \frac{5}{6} + \frac{5}{6}$$
$$5x + \frac{4}{6} = 6x$$
$$5x - 5x + \frac{4}{6} = 6x - 5x$$
$$\frac{4}{6} = x$$
$$x = \frac{2}{3}$$

Check:
$$5x - \frac{1}{6} = 6x - \frac{5}{6}$$
$$5\left(\frac{2}{3}\right) - \frac{1}{6} \stackrel{?}{=} 6\left(\frac{2}{3}\right) - \frac{5}{6}$$
$$\frac{10}{3} - \frac{1}{6} \stackrel{?}{=} \frac{12}{3} - \frac{5}{6}$$
$$\frac{20}{6} - \frac{1}{6} \stackrel{?}{=} \frac{24}{6} - \frac{5}{6}$$
$$\frac{19}{6} = \frac{19}{6}$$

The solution is $\frac{2}{3}$.

25.
$$8y + 2 - 6y = 3 + y - 10$$
$$2y + 2 = y - 7$$
$$2y + 2 - y = y - 7 - y$$
$$y + 2 = -7$$
$$y + 2 - 2 = -7 - 2$$
$$y = -9$$

Check:
$$8y + 2 - 6y = 3 + y - 10$$
$$8(-9) + 2 - 6(-9) \stackrel{?}{=} 3 + (-9) - 10$$
$$-72 + 2 + 54 \stackrel{?}{=} 3 - 9 - 10$$
$$-16 = -16$$

The solution is –9.

27.
$$13x - 9 + 2x - 5 = 12x - 1 + 2x$$
$$15x - 14 = 14x - 1$$
$$15x - 14 - 14x = 14x - 1 - 14x$$
$$x - 14 = -1$$
$$x - 14 + 14 = -1 + 14$$
$$x = 13$$

Check:
$$13x - 9 + 2x - 5 = 12x - 1 + 2x$$
$$13(13) - 9 + 2(13) - 5 \stackrel{?}{=} 12(13) - 1 + 2(13)$$
$$169 - 9 + 26 - 5 \stackrel{?}{=} 156 - 1 + 26$$
$$181 = 181$$

The solution is 13.

29.
$$-6.5 - 4x - 1.6 - 3x = -6x + 9.8$$
$$-8.1 - 7x = -6x + 9.8$$
$$-8.1 - 7x + 7x = -6x + 9.8 + 7x$$
$$-8.1 = x + 9.8$$
$$-9.8 - 8.1 = x + 9.8 - 9.8$$
$$-17.9 = x$$

Check:
$$-6.5 - 4x - 1.6 - 3x = -6x + 9.8$$
$$-6.5 - 4(-17.9) - 1.6 - 3(-17.9) \stackrel{?}{=} -6(-17.9) + 9.8$$
$$-6.5 + 71.6 - 1.6 + 53.7 \stackrel{?}{=} 107.4 + 9.8$$
$$117.2 = 117.2$$

The solution is –17.9.

31.
$$\frac{3}{8}x - \frac{1}{6} = -\frac{5}{8}x - \frac{2}{3}$$
$$\frac{3}{8}x - \frac{1}{6} - \frac{3}{8}x = -\frac{5}{8}x - \frac{2}{3} - \frac{3}{8}x$$
$$-\frac{1}{6} = -\frac{8}{8}x - \frac{2}{3}$$
$$-\frac{1}{6} + \frac{2}{3} = -x - \frac{2}{3} + \frac{2}{3}$$
$$-\frac{1}{6} + \frac{4}{6} = -x$$
$$\frac{3}{6} = -x$$
$$\frac{1}{2} = -x$$

If $\frac{1}{2} = -x$, then $-\frac{1}{2} = x$.

Check:
$$\frac{3}{8}x-\frac{1}{6}=-\frac{5}{8}x-\frac{2}{3}$$
$$\frac{3}{8}\left(-\frac{1}{2}\right)-\frac{1}{6}\stackrel{?}{=}-\frac{5}{8}\left(-\frac{1}{2}\right)-\frac{2}{3}$$
$$-\frac{3}{16}-\frac{1}{6}\stackrel{?}{=}\frac{5}{16}-\frac{2}{3}$$
$$-\frac{9}{48}-\frac{8}{48}\stackrel{?}{=}\frac{15}{48}-\frac{32}{48}$$
$$-\frac{17}{48}=-\frac{17}{48}$$

The solution is $-\frac{1}{2}$.

33.
$$2(x-4)=x+3$$
$$2(x)+2(-4)=x+3$$
$$2x-8=x+3$$
$$2x-8-x=x+3-x$$
$$x-8=3$$
$$x-8+8=3+8$$
$$x=11$$

Check:
$$2(x-4)=x+3$$
$$2(11-4)\stackrel{?}{=}11+3$$
$$2(7)\stackrel{?}{=}14$$
$$14=14$$

The solution is 11.

35.
$$7(6+w)=6(2+w)$$
$$7(6)+7(w)=6(2)+6(w)$$
$$42+7w=12+6w$$
$$42+7w-6w=12+6w-6w$$
$$42+w=12$$
$$42+w-42=12-42$$
$$w=-30$$

Check:
$$7(6+w)=6(2+w)$$
$$7(6+(-30))\stackrel{?}{=}6(2+(-30))$$
$$7(-24)\stackrel{?}{=}6(-28)$$
$$-168=-168$$

The solution is –30.

37.
$$10-(2x-4)=7-3x$$
$$10-1(2x-4)=7-3x$$
$$10-1(2x)-1(-4)=7-3x$$
$$10-2x+4=7-3x$$
$$14-2x=7-3x$$
$$14-2x+3x=7-3x+3x$$
$$x+14=7$$
$$x+14-14=7-14$$
$$x=-7$$

Check:
$$10-(2x-4)=7-3x$$
$$10-(2(-7)-4)\stackrel{?}{=}7-3(-7)$$
$$10-(-14-4)\stackrel{?}{=}7+21$$
$$10-(-18)\stackrel{?}{=}28$$
$$10+18\stackrel{?}{=}28$$
$$28=28$$

The solution is –7.

39.
$$-5(n-2)=8-4n$$
$$-5(n)-5(-2)=8-4n$$
$$-5n+10=8-4n$$
$$-5n+10+5n=8-4n+5n$$
$$10=8+n$$
$$10-8=8+n-8$$
$$2=n$$

Check:
$$-5(n-2)=8-4n$$
$$-5(2-2)\stackrel{?}{=}8-4(2)$$
$$-5(0)\stackrel{?}{=}8-8$$
$$0=0$$

The solution is 2.

41.
$$-3\left(x-\frac{1}{4}\right)=-4x$$
$$-3x+\frac{3}{4}=-4x$$
$$4x-3x+\frac{3}{4}=4x-4x$$
$$x+\frac{3}{4}=0$$
$$x+\frac{3}{4}-\frac{3}{4}=0-\frac{3}{4}$$
$$x=-\frac{3}{4}$$

Check:

$$-3\left(x-\frac{1}{4}\right)=-4x$$
$$-3\left(-\frac{3}{4}-\frac{1}{4}\right)\stackrel{?}{=}-4\left(-\frac{3}{4}\right)$$
$$-3(-1)\stackrel{?}{=}3$$
$$3=3$$

The solution is $-\frac{3}{4}$.

43.
$$3(n-5)-(6-2n)=4n$$
$$3(n-5)-1(6-2n)=4n$$
$$3(n)+3(-5)-1(6)-1(-2n)=4n$$
$$3n-15-6+2n=4n$$
$$5n-21=4n$$
$$5n-21-4n=4n-4n$$
$$n-21=0$$
$$n-21+21=0+21$$
$$n=21$$

Check:
$$3(n-5)-(6-2n)=4n$$
$$3(21-5)-(6-2(21))\stackrel{?}{=}4(21)$$
$$3(16)-(6-42)\stackrel{?}{=}84$$
$$48-(-36)\stackrel{?}{=}84$$
$$48+36\stackrel{?}{=}84$$
$$84=84$$

The solution is 21.

45.
$$-2(x+6)+3(2x-5)=3(x-4)+10$$
$$-2(x)-2(6)+3(2x)+3(-5)=3(x)+3(-4)+10$$
$$-2x-12+6x-15=3x-12+10$$
$$4x-27=3x-2$$
$$4x-27-3x=3x-2-3x$$
$$x-27=-2$$
$$x-27+27=-2+27$$
$$x=25$$

Check:
$$-2(x+6)+3(2x-5)=3(x-4)+10$$
$$-2(25+6)+3(2(25)-5)\stackrel{?}{=}3(25-4)+10$$
$$-2(31)+3(50-5)\stackrel{?}{=}3(21)+10$$
$$-62+3(45)\stackrel{?}{=}63+10$$
$$-62+135\stackrel{?}{=}73$$
$$73=73$$

The solution is 25.

47.
$$7(m-2)-6(m+1)=-20$$
$$7m-14-6m-6=-27$$
$$m-20=-20$$
$$m-20+20=-20+20$$
$$m=0$$

Check:
$$7(m-2)-6(m+1)=-20$$
$$7(0-2)-6(0+1)\stackrel{?}{=}-20$$
$$7(-2)-6(1)\stackrel{?}{=}-20$$
$$-14-6\stackrel{?}{=}-20$$
$$-20=-20$$

The solution is 0.

49.
$$0.8t+0.2(t-0.4)=1.75$$
$$0.8t+0.2t-0.08=1.75$$
$$1.0t-0.08=1.75$$
$$t-0.08+0.08=1.75+0.08$$
$$t=1.83$$

Check:
$$0.8t+0.2(t-0.4)=1.75$$
$$0.8(1.83)+0.2(1.83-0.4)\stackrel{?}{=}1.75$$
$$1.464+0.2(1.43)\stackrel{?}{=}1.75$$
$$1.464+0.286\stackrel{?}{=}1.75$$
$$1.75=1.75$$

The solution is 1.83.

51. $20-p$

53. $(10-x)$ feet

55. $(180-x)°$

57. $(n+284)$ votes

59. If the length of the Verrazano-Narrows Bridge is m feet and the Golden Gate Bridge is 60 feet shorter than the Verrazano-Narrows Bridge, we find the length of the Golden Gate Bridge by subtracting 60 from m. Thus, the length of the Golden Gate Bridge is $(m-60)$ feet.

61.
$$180-x-(2x+7)=180-x-2x-7$$
$$=(173-3x)°$$

63. $0.06 - 0.01(x + 1) = -0.02(2 - x)$
$$200 + 150 + 400 + x = 1000$$
$$750 + x = 1000$$
$$750 - 750 + x = 1000 - 750$$
$$x = 250 \text{ ml}$$

65. Answers may vary.

67.
$$8.13 + 5.85y = 20.05y - 8.91$$
$$8.13 + 5.85 \cdot 1.2 \stackrel{?}{=} 20.05 \cdot 1.2 - 8.91$$
$$8.13 + 7.02 \stackrel{?}{=} 24.06 - 8.91$$
$$15.15 = 15.15$$
Solution

69.
$$7(z - 1.7) + 9.5 = 5(z + 3.2) - 9.2$$
$$7(4.8 - 1.7) + 9.5 \stackrel{?}{=} 5(4.8 + 3.2) - 9.2$$
$$7(3.1) + 9.5 \stackrel{?}{=} 5(8) - 9.2$$
$$21.7 + 9.5 \stackrel{?}{=} 40 - 9.2$$
$$31.2 \neq 30.8$$
Not a solution

71. $\frac{7}{6} \Rightarrow \frac{6}{7}$

73. $5 \Rightarrow \frac{1}{5}$

75. $-\frac{3}{5} \Rightarrow -\frac{5}{3}$

77. $\frac{-2y}{-2} = \left(\frac{-2}{-2}\right)y = (1)y = y$

79. $7\left(\frac{1}{7}r\right) = \left(7 \cdot \frac{1}{7}\right)r = (1)r = r$

81. $\frac{9}{2}\left(\frac{2}{9}x\right) = \left(\frac{9}{2} \cdot \frac{2}{9}\right)x = (1)x = x$

Section 2.3

Mental Math

1. $3a = 27$
$a = 9$

2. $9c = 54$
$c = 6$

3. $5b = 10$
$b = 2$

4. $7t = 14$
$t = 2$

5. $6x = -30$
$x = -5$

6. $8r = -64$
$r = -8$

Exercise Set 2.3

1.
$$-5x = 20$$
$$\frac{-5x}{-5} = \frac{20}{-5}$$
$$x = -4$$
Check:
$$-5x = 20$$
$$-5(-4) \stackrel{?}{=} 20$$
$$20 = 20$$
The solution is -4.

3.
$$3x = 0$$
$$\frac{3x}{3} = \frac{0}{3}$$
$$x = 0$$
Check:
$$3x = 0$$
$$3(0) \stackrel{?}{=} 0$$
$$0 = 0$$
The solution is 0.

5.
$$-x = -12$$
$$\frac{-x}{-1} = \frac{-12}{-1}$$
$$x = 12$$
Check:
$$-x = -12$$
$$-(12) \stackrel{?}{=} -12$$
$$-12 = -12$$
The solution is 12.

7.
$$\frac{2}{3}x = -8$$
$$\frac{3}{2}\left(\frac{2}{3}x\right) = \frac{3}{2}(-8)$$
$$x = -12$$

Check: $\frac{2}{3}x = -8$

$\frac{2}{3}(-12) \stackrel{?}{=} -8$

$-8 = -8$

The solution is –12.

9. $\frac{1}{6}d = \frac{1}{2}$

$6\left(\frac{1}{6}d\right) = 6\left(\frac{1}{2}\right)$

$d = 3$

Check: $\frac{1}{6}d = \frac{1}{2}$

$\frac{1}{6}(3) \stackrel{?}{=} \frac{1}{2}$

$\frac{1}{2} = \frac{1}{2}$

The solution is 3.

11. $\frac{a}{2} = 1$

$2\left(\frac{a}{2}\right) = 2(1)$

$a = 2$

Check: $\frac{a}{2} = 1$

$\frac{2}{2} \stackrel{?}{=} 1$

$1 = 1$

The solution is 2.

13. $\frac{k}{-7} = 0$

$-7\left(\frac{k}{-7}\right) = -7(0)$

$k = 0$

Check: $\frac{k}{-7} = 0$

$\frac{0}{-7} \stackrel{?}{=} 0$

$0 = 0$

The solution is 0.

15. $1.7x = 10.71$

$\frac{1.7x}{1.7} = \frac{10.71}{1.7}$

$x = 6.3$

Check: $1.7x = 10.71$

$1.7(6.3) \stackrel{?}{=} 10.71$

$10.71 = 10.71$

The solution is 6.3.

17. $42 = 7x$

$\frac{42}{7} = \frac{7x}{7}$

$6 = x$

Check: $42 = 7x$

$42 \stackrel{?}{=} 7(6)$

$42 = 42$

The solution is 6.

19. $4.4 = -0.8x$

$\frac{4.4}{-0.8} = \frac{-0.8x}{-0.8}$

$-5.5 = x$

Check: $4.4 = -0.8x$

$4.4 \stackrel{?}{=} -0.8(-5.5)$

$4.4 = 4.4$

The solution is –5.5.

21. $-\frac{3}{7}p = -2$

$-\frac{7}{3}\left(-\frac{3}{7}p\right) = -\frac{7}{3}(-2)$

$p = \frac{14}{3}$

Check: $-\frac{3}{7}p = -2$

$-\frac{3}{7}\left(\frac{14}{3}\right) \stackrel{?}{=} -2$

$-2 = -2$

The solution is $\frac{14}{3}$.

23. $-\frac{4}{3}x = 12$

$-\frac{3}{4}\left(-\frac{4}{3}x\right) = -\frac{3}{4}(12)$

$x = -9$

Check: $-\frac{4}{3}x = 12$

$-\frac{4}{3}(-9) \stackrel{?}{=} 12$

$12 = 12$

The solution is –9.

25. $2x - 4 = 16$

$2x - 4 + 4 = 16 + 4$

$2x = 20$

$\frac{2x}{2} = \frac{20}{2}$

$x = 10$

Check: $2x - 4 = 16$

$2(10) - 4 \stackrel{?}{=} 16$

$20 - 4 \stackrel{?}{=} 16$

$16 = 16$

The solution is 10.

27. $-x + 2 = 22$

$-x + 2 - 2 = 22 - 2$

$-x = 20$

$\frac{-x}{-1} = \frac{20}{-1}$

$x = -20$

Check: $-x + 2 = 22$

$-(-20) + 2 \stackrel{?}{=} 22$

$20 + 2 \stackrel{?}{=} 22$

$22 = 22$

The solution is –20.

29. $6a + 3 = 3$

$6a + 3 - 3 = 3 - 3$

$6a = 0$

$\frac{6a}{6} = \frac{0}{6}$

$a = 0$

Check: $6a + 3 = 3$

$6(0) + 3 \stackrel{?}{=} 3$

$0 + 3 \stackrel{?}{=} 3$

$3 = 3$

The solution is 0.

31. $6x + 10 = -20$

$6x + 10 - 10 = -20 - 10$

$6x = -30$

$\frac{6x}{6} = \frac{-30}{6}$

$x = -5$

Check: $6x + 10 = -20$

$6(-5) + 10 \stackrel{?}{=} -20$

$-30 + 10 \stackrel{?}{=} -20$

$-20 = -20$

The solution is –5.

33. $5 - 0.3k = 5$

$5 - 0.3k - 5 = 5 - 5$

$-0.3k = 0$

$\frac{-0.3k}{-0.3} = \frac{0}{-0.3}$

$k = 0$

Check: $5 - 0.3k = 5$

$5 - 0.3(0) \stackrel{?}{=} 5$

$5 - 0 \stackrel{?}{=} 5$

$5 = 5$

The solution is 0.

35. $-2x + \frac{1}{2} = \frac{7}{2}$

$-2x + \frac{1}{2} - \frac{1}{2} = \frac{7}{2} - \frac{1}{2}$

$-2x = \frac{6}{2}$

$-2x = 3$

$\frac{-2x}{-2} = \frac{3}{-2}$

$x = -\frac{3}{2}$

Check:

$$-2x+\frac{1}{2}=\frac{7}{2}$$
$$-2\left(-\frac{3}{2}\right)+\frac{1}{2}\stackrel{?}{=}\frac{7}{2}$$
$$3+\frac{1}{2}\stackrel{?}{=}\frac{7}{2}$$
$$\frac{6}{2}+\frac{1}{2}\stackrel{?}{=}\frac{7}{2}$$
$$\frac{7}{2}=\frac{7}{2}$$

The solution is $-\frac{3}{2}$.

37.
$$\frac{x}{3}+2=-5$$
$$\frac{x}{3}+2-2=-5-2$$
$$\frac{x}{3}=-7$$
$$3\left(\frac{x}{3}\right)=3(-7)$$
$$x=-21$$

Check:
$$\frac{x}{3}+2=-5$$
$$\frac{-21}{3}+2\stackrel{?}{=}-5$$
$$-7+2\stackrel{?}{=}-5$$
$$-5=-5$$

The solution is –21.

39.
$$10=2x-1$$
$$10+1=2x-1+1$$
$$11=2x$$
$$\frac{11}{2}=\frac{2x}{2}$$
$$\frac{11}{2}=x$$

Check:
$$10=2x-1$$
$$10\stackrel{?}{=}2\left(\frac{11}{2}\right)-1$$
$$10\stackrel{?}{=}11-1$$
$$10=10$$

The solution is $\frac{11}{2}$.

41.
$$6z-8-z+3=0$$
$$5z-5=0$$
$$5z-5+5=0+5$$
$$5z=5$$
$$\frac{5z}{5}=\frac{5}{5}$$
$$z=1$$

Check:
$$6z-8-z+3=0$$
$$6(1)-8-1+3\stackrel{?}{=}0$$
$$6-8-1+\stackrel{?}{=}0$$
$$0=0$$

The solution is 1.

43.
$$10-3x-6-9x=7$$
$$4-12x=7$$
$$4-12x-4=7-4$$
$$-12x=3$$
$$\frac{-12x}{-12}=\frac{3}{-12}$$
$$x=-\frac{1}{4}$$

Check:
$$10-3x-6-9x=7$$
$$10-3\left(-\frac{1}{4}\right)-6-9\left(-\frac{1}{4}\right)\stackrel{?}{=}7$$
$$10+\frac{3}{4}-6+\frac{9}{4}\stackrel{?}{=}7$$
$$10-6+\frac{3}{4}+\frac{9}{4}\stackrel{?}{=}7$$
$$4+\frac{12}{4}\stackrel{?}{=}7$$
$$4+3\stackrel{?}{=}7$$
$$7=7$$

The solution is $-\frac{1}{4}$.

45.
$$1=0.4x-0.6x-5$$
$$1=-0.2x-5$$
$$1+5=-0.2x-5+5$$
$$6=-0.2x$$
$$\frac{6}{-0.2}=\frac{-0.2x}{-0.2}$$
$$-30=x$$

Check: $1 = 0.4x - 0.6x - 5$
$1 \stackrel{?}{=} 0.4(-30) - 0.6(-30) - 5$
$1 \stackrel{?}{=} -12 + 18 - 5$
$1 = 1$

The solution is –30.

47. $z - 5z = 7z - 9 - z$
$-4z = 6z - 9$
$-4z - 6z = 6z - 9 - 6z$
$-10z = -9$
$\frac{-10z}{-10} = \frac{-9}{-10}$
$z = \frac{9}{10}$

Check: $z - 5z = 7z - 9 - z$
$\frac{9}{10} - 5\left(\frac{9}{10}\right) \stackrel{?}{=} 7\left(\frac{9}{10}\right) - 9 - \frac{9}{10}$
$\frac{9}{10} - \frac{45}{10} \stackrel{?}{=} \frac{63}{10} - 9 - \frac{9}{10}$
$-\frac{36}{10} \stackrel{?}{=} \frac{54}{10} - 9$
$-\frac{36}{10} \stackrel{?}{=} \frac{54}{10} - \frac{90}{10}$
$-\frac{36}{10} = -\frac{36}{10}$

The solution is $\frac{9}{10}$.

49. $0.4x - 0.6x - 5 = 1$
$-0.2x - 5 = 1$
$-0.2x - 5 + 5 = 1 + 5$
$-0.2x = 6$
$\frac{-0.2x}{-0.2} = \frac{6}{-0.2}$
$x = -30$

Check: $0.4x - 0.6x - 5 = 1$
$0.4(-30) - 0.6(-30) - 5 \stackrel{?}{=} 1$
$-12 + 18 - 5 \stackrel{?}{=} 1$
$1 = 1$

The solution is –30.

51. $6 - 2x + 8 = 10$
$14 - 2x = 10$
$14 - 14 - 2x = 10 - 14$
$-2x = -4$
$\frac{-2x}{-2} = \frac{-4}{-2}$
$x = 2$

Check: $6 - 2x + 8 = 10$
$6 - 2(2) + 8 \stackrel{?}{=} 10$
$6 - 4 + 8 \stackrel{?}{=} 10$
$10 = 10$

The solution is 2.

53. $-3a + 6 + 5a = 7a - 8a$
$2a + 6 = -a$
$2a - 2a + 6 = -a - 2a$
$6 = -3a$
$\frac{6}{-3} = \frac{-3a}{-3}$
$-2 = a$

Check: $-3a + 6 + 5a = 7a - 8a$
$-3(-2) + 6 + 5(-2) \stackrel{?}{=} 7(-2) - 8(-2)$
$6 + 6 - 10 \stackrel{?}{=} -14 + 16$
$2 = 2$

The solution is –2.

55. Answers may vary.

57. Answers may vary.

59. If x = the first odd integer, then $x + 2$ = the next odd integer. Their sum is $x + (x + 2) = x + x + 2 = 2x + 2$.

61. If x = the first integer, then $x + 1$ = the second consecutive integer, and $x + 2$ = the third consecutive integer. The sum of the first and third integers is $x + (x + 2) = x + x + 2 = 2x + 2$.

63. $9x = 2100$

$\frac{9x}{9} = \frac{2100}{9}$

$x = \frac{700}{3}$

The dose is $\frac{700}{3}$ mg.

65. $4.95y = -31.185$

$\frac{4.95y}{4.95} = \frac{-31.185}{4.95}$

$y = -6.3$

67. $0.06y + 2.63 = 2.5562$

$0.06y + 2.63 - 2.63 = 2.5562 - 2.63$

$0.06y = -0.0738$

$\frac{0.06y}{0.06} = \frac{-0.0738}{0.06}$

$y = -1.23$

69. $-7y + 2y - 3(y+1) = -7y + 2y - 3y - 3$

$= -8y - 3$

71. $-(3a-3) + 2a - 6 = -3a + 3 + 2a - 6$

$= -a - 3$

73. $8(z-6) + 7z - 1 = 8z - 48 + 7z - 1$

$= 15z - 49$

75. $(-2)^4 > -2^4$

$16 > -16$

77. $(-4)^3 = -4^3$

$-64 = -64$

79. $-|-0.7| = -0.7$

$-0.7 = -0.7$

Section 2.4

Calculator Explorations

1. $2x = 48 + 6x;\ x = -12$

$2(-12) = -24$

$48 + 6(-12) = -24$

Solution, since the left side equals the right side.

3. $5x - 2.6 = 2(x + 0.8);\ x = 4.4$

$5(4.4) - 2.6 = 19.4$

$2(4.4 + 0.8) = 10.4$

Not a solution, since the left side does not equal the right side.

5. $\frac{564x}{4} = 200x - 11(649);\ x = 121$

$\frac{564(121)}{4} = 17,061$

$200(121) - 11(649) = 17,061$

Solution, since the left side equals the right side.

Exercise Set 2.4

1. $-2(3x-4) = 2x$

$-6x + 8 = 2x$

$-6x - 2x + 8 = 2x - 2x$

$-8x + 8 = 0$

$-8x + 8 - 8 = 0 - 8$

$-8x = -8$

$\frac{-8x}{-8} = \frac{-8}{-8}$

$x = 1$

3. $4(2n-1) = (6n+4) + 1$

$8n - 4 = 6n + 4 + 1$

$8n - 4 = 6n + 5$

$8n - 6n - 4 = 6n - 6n + 5$

$2n - 4 = 5$

$2n - 4 + 4 = 5 + 4$

$2n = 9$

$\frac{2n}{2} = \frac{9}{2}$

$n = \frac{9}{2}$

5. $$\begin{aligned} 5(2x-1)-2(3x)&=1\\ 10x-5-6x&=1\\ 4x-5&=1\\ 4x-5+5&=1+5\\ 4x&=6\\ \frac{4x}{4}&=\frac{6}{4}\\ x&=\frac{3}{2} \end{aligned}$$

7. $$\begin{aligned} 6(x-3)+10&=-8\\ 6x-18+10&=-8\\ 6x-8&=-8\\ 6x-8+8&=-8+8\\ 6x&=0\\ \frac{6x}{6}&=\frac{0}{6}\\ x&=0 \end{aligned}$$

9. $$\begin{aligned} \frac{3}{4}x-\frac{1}{2}&=1\\ 4\left(\frac{3}{4}x-\frac{1}{2}\right)&=4\cdot 1\\ 4\left(\frac{3}{4}x\right)-4\left(\frac{1}{2}\right)&=4\\ 3x-2&=4\\ 3x-2+2&=4+2\\ 3x&=6\\ \frac{3x}{3}&=\frac{6}{3}\\ x&=2 \end{aligned}$$

11. $$\begin{aligned} x+\frac{5}{4}&=\frac{3}{4}x\\ 4\left(x+\frac{5}{4}\right)&=4\left(\frac{3}{4}x\right)\\ 4(x)+4\left(\frac{5}{4}\right)&=4\left(\frac{3}{4}x\right)\\ 4x+5&=3x\\ 4x-3x+5&=3x-3x\\ x+5&=0\\ x+5-5&=0-5\\ x&=-5 \end{aligned}$$

13. $$\begin{aligned} \frac{x}{2}-1&=\frac{x}{5}+2\\ 10\left(\frac{x}{2}-1\right)&=10\left(\frac{x}{5}+2\right)\\ 10\left(\frac{x}{2}\right)-10\cdot 1&=10\left(\frac{x}{5}\right)+10\cdot 2\\ 5x-10&=2x+20\\ 5x-2x-10&=2x-2x+20\\ 3x-10&=20\\ 3x-10+10&=20+10\\ 3x&=30\\ \frac{3x}{3}&=\frac{30}{3}\\ x&=10 \end{aligned}$$

15. $$\begin{aligned} \frac{6(3-z)}{5}&=-z\\ 5\cdot\frac{6(3-z)}{5}&=5(-z)\\ 6(3-z)&=-5z\\ 18-6z&=-5z\\ 18-6z+6z&=-5z+6z\\ 18&=z \end{aligned}$$

17. $$\begin{aligned} \frac{2(x+1)}{4}&=3x-2\\ 4\cdot\frac{2(x+1)}{4}&=4(3x-2)\\ 2(x+1)&=12x-8\\ 2x+2&=12x-8\\ 2x-2x+2&=12x-2x-8\\ 2&=10x-8\\ 2+8&=10x-8+8\\ 10&=10x\\ \frac{10}{10}&=\frac{10x}{10}\\ 1&=x \end{aligned}$$

19. $$\begin{aligned} 0.50x+0.15(70)&=0.25(142)\\ 50x+15(70)&=25(142)\\ 50x+1050&=3550\\ 50x+1050-1050&=3550-1050\\ 50x&=2500\\ x&=50 \end{aligned}$$

21.
$$\begin{aligned} 0.12(y-6)+0.06y &= 0.08y-0.07(10) \\ 12(y-6)+6y &= 8y-7(10) \\ 12y-72+6y &= 8y-70 \\ 18y-72 &= 8y-70 \\ 18y-72-8y &= 8y-70-8y \\ 10y-72 &= -70 \\ 10y-72+72 &= -70+72 \\ 10y &= 2 \\ \frac{10y}{10} &= \frac{2}{10} \\ y &= 0.2 \end{aligned}$$

23.
$$\begin{aligned} 5x-5 &= 2(x+1)+3x-7 \\ 5x-5 &= 2x+2+3x-7 \\ 5x-5 &= 5x-5 \\ 5x-5x-5 &= 5x-5x-5 \\ -5 &= -5 \\ -5+5 &= -5+5 \\ 0 &= 0 \end{aligned}$$
All real numbers

25.
$$\begin{aligned} \frac{x}{4}+1 &= \frac{x}{4} \\ 4\left(\frac{x}{4}+1\right) &= 4\left(\frac{x}{4}\right) \\ 4\left(\frac{x}{4}\right)+4(1) &= 4\left(\frac{x}{4}\right) \\ x+4 &= x \\ x-x+4 &= x-x \\ 4 &= 0 \end{aligned}$$
No solution

27.
$$\begin{aligned} 3x-7 &= 3(x+1) \\ 3x-7 &= 3x+3 \\ 3x-3x-7 &= 3x-3x+3 \\ -7 &= 3 \end{aligned}$$
No solution

29. Answers may vary.

31. Answers may vary.

33.
$$\begin{aligned} 4x+3 &= 2x+11 \\ 4x-2x+3 &= 2x-2x+11 \\ 2x+3 &= 11 \\ 2x+3-3 &= 11-3 \\ 2x &= 8 \\ \frac{2x}{2} &= \frac{8}{2} \\ x &= 4 \end{aligned}$$

35.
$$\begin{aligned} -2y-10 &= 5y+18 \\ -2y+2y-10 &= 5y+2y+18 \\ -10 &= 7y+18 \\ -10-18 &= 7y+18-18 \\ -28 &= 7y \\ \frac{-28}{7} &= \frac{7y}{7} \\ -4 &= y \end{aligned}$$

37.
$$\begin{aligned} 0.6x-0.1 &= 0.5x+0.2 \\ 6x-1 &= 5x+2 \\ 6x-5x-1 &= 5x-5x+2 \\ x-1 &= 2 \\ x-1+1 &= 2+1 \\ x &= 3 \end{aligned}$$

39.
$$\begin{aligned} 2y+2 &= y \\ 2y-2y+2 &= y-2y \\ 2 &= -y \\ \frac{2}{-1} &= \frac{-y}{-1} \\ -2 &= y \end{aligned}$$

41.
$$\begin{aligned} 3(5c-1)-2 &= 13c+3 \\ 15c-3-2 &= 13c+3 \\ 15c-5 &= 13c+3 \\ 15c-13c-5 &= 13c-13c+3 \\ 2c-5 &= 3 \\ 2c-5+5 &= 3+5 \\ 2c &= 8 \\ \frac{2c}{2} &= \frac{8}{2} \\ c &= 4 \end{aligned}$$

43.
$$x+\frac{7}{6}=2x-\frac{7}{6}$$
$$6\left(x+\frac{7}{6}\right)=6\left(2x-\frac{7}{6}\right)$$
$$6(x)+6\left(\frac{7}{6}\right)=6(2x)+6\left(-\frac{7}{6}\right)$$
$$6x+7=12x-7$$
$$6x-12x+7=12x-12x-7$$
$$-6x+7=-7$$
$$-6x+7-7=-7-7$$
$$-6x=-14$$
$$\frac{-6x}{-6}=\frac{-14}{-6}$$
$$x=\frac{14}{6}$$
$$x=\frac{7}{3}$$

45.
$$2(x-5)=7+2x$$
$$2x-10=7+2x$$
$$2x-2x-10=7+2x-2x$$
$$-10=7$$
No solution

47.
$$\frac{2(z+3)}{3}=5-z$$
$$3\cdot\frac{2(z+3)}{3}=3(5-z)$$
$$2(z+3)=3(5-z)$$
$$2z+6=15-3z$$
$$2z+3z+6=15-3z+3z$$
$$5z+6=15$$
$$5z+6-6=15-6$$
$$5z=9$$
$$\frac{5z}{5}=\frac{9}{5}$$
$$z=\frac{9}{5}$$

49.
$$\frac{4(y-1)}{5}=-3y$$
$$5\cdot\frac{4(y-1)}{5}=5(-3y)$$
$$4(y-1)=5(-3y)$$
$$4y-4=-15y$$
$$4y-4y-4=-15y-4y$$
$$-4=-19y$$
$$\frac{-4}{-19}=\frac{-19y}{-19}$$
$$\frac{4}{19}=y$$

51.
$$8-2(a-1)=7+a$$
$$8-2a+2=7+a$$
$$-2a+10=7+a$$
$$-2a-a+10=7+a-a$$
$$-3a+10=7$$
$$-3a+10-10=7-10$$
$$-3a=-3$$
$$\frac{-3a}{-3}=\frac{-3}{-3}$$
$$a=1$$

53.
$$2(x+3)-5=5x-3(1+x)$$
$$2x+6-5=5x-3-3x$$
$$2x+1=2x-3$$
$$2x-2x+1=2x-2x-3$$
$$1=-3$$
No solution

55.
$$\frac{5x-7}{3}=x$$
$$3\cdot\frac{5x-7}{3}=3(x)$$
$$5x-7=3x$$
$$5x-5x-7=3x-5x$$
$$-7=-2x$$
$$\frac{-7}{-2}=\frac{-2x}{-2}$$
$$\frac{7}{2}=x$$

57.
$$\frac{9+5v}{2} = 2v-4$$
$$2\cdot\frac{9+5v}{22} = 2(2v-4)$$
$$9+5v = 4v-8$$
$$9+5v-4v = 4v-4v-8$$
$$9+v = -8$$
$$9-9+v = -8-9$$
$$v = -17$$

59.
$$-3(t-5)+2t = 5t-4$$
$$-3t+15+2t = 5t-4$$
$$-t+15 = 5t-4$$
$$-t+t+15 = 5t+t-4$$
$$15 = 6t-4$$
$$15+4 = 6t-4+4$$
$$19 = 6t$$
$$\frac{19}{6} = \frac{6t}{6}$$
$$\frac{19}{6} = t$$

61.
$$0.02(6t-3) = 0.12(t-2)+0.18$$
$$2(6t-3) = 12(t-2)+18$$
$$12t-6 = 12t-24+18$$
$$12t-6 = 12t-6$$
$$12t-6-12t = 12t-6-12t$$
$$6 = 6$$
All real numbers

63.
$$0.06-0.01(x+1) = -0.02(2-x)$$
$$6-1(x+1) = -2(2-x)$$
$$6-x-1 = -4+2x$$
$$5-x = -4+2x$$
$$5-x+x = -4+2x+x$$
$$5 = -4+3x$$
$$5+4 = -4+4+3x$$
$$9 = 3x$$
$$\frac{9}{3} = \frac{3x}{3}$$
$$3 = x$$

65.
$$\frac{3(x-5)}{2} = \frac{2(x+5)}{3}$$
$$6\cdot\frac{3(x-5)}{2} = 6\cdot\frac{2(x+5)}{3}$$
$$3\cdot\frac{3(x-5)}{1} = 2\cdot\frac{2(x+5)}{1}$$
$$9(x-5) = 4(x+5)$$
$$9x-45 = 4x+20$$
$$9x-4x-45 = 4x-4x+20$$
$$5x-45 = 20$$
$$5x-45+45 = 20+45$$
$$5x = 65$$
$$\frac{5x}{5} = \frac{65}{5}$$
$$x = 13$$

67.
$$\begin{aligned}
1000(7x-10) &= 50(412+100x)\\
7000x-10{,}000 &= 20{,}600+5000x\\
7000x-5000x-10{,}000 &= 20{,}600+5000x-5000x\\
2000x-10{,}000 &= 20{,}600\\
2000x-10{,}000+10{,}000 &= 20{,}600+10{,}000\\
2000x &= 30{,}600\\
\frac{2000x}{2000} &= \frac{30{,}600}{2000}\\
x &= 15.3
\end{aligned}$$

69.
$$\begin{aligned}
0.035x+5.112 &= 0.010x+5.107\\
35x+5112 &= 10x+5107\\
35x-10x+5112 &= 10x-10x+5107\\
25x+5112 &= 5107\\
25x+5112-5112 &= 5107-5112\\
25x &= -5\\
\frac{25x}{25} &= \frac{-5}{25}\\
x &= -0.2
\end{aligned}$$

71. Let x represent the number.
$$\begin{aligned}
2x+\frac{1}{5} &= 3x-\frac{4}{5}\\
5\left(2x+\frac{1}{5}\right) &= 5\left(3x-\frac{4}{5}\right)\\
5(2x)+5\left(\frac{1}{5}\right) &= 5(3x)+5\left(-\frac{4}{5}\right)\\
10x+1 &= 15x-4\\
10x-15x+1 &= 15x-15x-4\\
-5x+1 &= -4\\
-5x+1-1 &= -4-1\\
-5x &= -5\\
\frac{-5x}{-5} &= \frac{-5}{-5}\\
x &= 1
\end{aligned}$$

73.
$$\begin{aligned}
2x+7 &= x+6\\
2x-x+7 &= x-x+6\\
x+7 &= 6\\
x+7-7 &= 6-7\\
x &= -1
\end{aligned}$$

75.
$$\begin{aligned} 3x-6&=2x+8\\ 3x-2x-6&=2x-2x+8\\ x-6&=8\\ x-6+6&=8+6\\ x&=14 \end{aligned}$$

77.
$$\begin{aligned} \frac{1}{3}x&=\frac{5}{6}\\ \frac{3}{1}\cdot\frac{1}{3}x&=\frac{5}{6}\cdot\frac{3}{1}\\ x&=\frac{5}{2}=2\frac{1}{2} \end{aligned}$$

79.
$$\begin{aligned} x-4&=2x\\ x-x-4&=2x-x\\ -4&=x \end{aligned}$$

81.
$$\begin{aligned} \frac{x}{4}+\frac{1}{2}&=\frac{3}{4}\\ \frac{x}{4}+\frac{1}{2}-\frac{1}{2}&=\frac{3}{4}-\frac{1}{2}\\ \frac{x}{4}&=\frac{3}{4}-\frac{1}{2}\cdot\frac{2}{2}\\ \frac{x}{4}&=\frac{3}{4}-\frac{2}{4}\\ \frac{x}{4}&=\frac{1}{4}\\ 4\cdot\frac{x}{4}&=\frac{1}{4}\cdot 4\\ x&=1 \end{aligned}$$

83.
$$\begin{aligned} x+x+x+2x+2x&=28\\ 7x&=28\\ \frac{7x}{7}&=\frac{28}{7}\\ x&=4\text{ cm}\\ 2x&=8\text{ cm} \end{aligned}$$

85.
$$\begin{aligned} 10-5x&=3x\\ 10-5x+5x&=3x+5x\\ 10&=8x\\ \frac{10}{8}&=\frac{8x}{8}\\ \frac{5}{4}&=x \end{aligned}$$

87. Midway; since it has the tallest graph.

89.
$$\begin{aligned} x+55&=2x-90\\ x-x+55&=2x-x-90\\ 55&=x-90\\ 55+90&=x-90+90\\ 145&=x \end{aligned}$$
145 cities, towns, or villages

91.
$$\begin{aligned} \left|2^3-3^2\right|-|5-7|&=|8-9|-|5-7|\\ &=|-1|-|-2|\\ &=1-2\\ &=-1 \end{aligned}$$

93. $\frac{5}{4+3\cdot 7}=\frac{5}{4+21}=\frac{5}{25}=\frac{1}{5}$

95. $x+(2x-3)+(3x-5)=6x-8$
$(6x-8)$ meters

97.
$$\begin{aligned} x(x-3)&=x^2+5x+7\\ x^2-3x&=x^2+5x+7\\ x^2-x^2-3x&=x^2-x^2+5x+7\\ -3x&=5x+7\\ -3x-5x&=5x-5x+7\\ -8x&=7\\ \frac{-8x}{-8}&=\frac{7}{-8}\\ x&=-\frac{7}{8} \end{aligned}$$

99.
$$\begin{aligned} 2z(z+6)&=2z^2+12z-8\\ 2z^2+12z&=2z^2+12z-8\\ 2z^2-2z^2+12z&=2z^2-2z^2+12z-8\\ 12z&=12z-8\\ 12z-12z&=12z-12z-8\\ 0&=-8 \end{aligned}$$
No solution

101.
$$\begin{aligned} n(3+n)&=n^2+4n\\ 3n+n^2&=n^2+4n\\ 3n+n^2-n^2&=n^2-n^2+4n\\ 3n&=4n\\ 3n-3n&=4n-3n\\ 0&=n \end{aligned}$$

Exercise Set 2.5

1. Let x represent the number.

$$2x+\frac{1}{5}=3x-\frac{4}{5}$$
$$5\left(2x+\frac{1}{5}\right)=5\left(3x-\frac{4}{5}\right)$$
$$10x+1=15x-4$$
$$10x+1-10x=15x-4-10x$$
$$1=5x-4$$
$$1+4=5x-4+4$$
$$5=5x$$
$$\frac{5}{5}=\frac{5x}{5}$$
$$1=x$$

The number is 1.

3. Let x represent the number.

$$2(x-8)=3(x+3)$$
$$2x-16=3x+9$$
$$2x-16-2x=3x+9-2x$$
$$-16=x+9$$
$$-16-9=x+9-9$$
$$-25=x$$

The number is –25.

5. Let x represent the number.

$$2x\cdot 3=5x-\frac{3}{4}$$
$$6x=5x-\frac{3}{4}$$
$$6x-5x=5x-\frac{3}{4}-5x$$
$$x=-\frac{3}{4}$$

The number is $-\frac{3}{4}$.

7. Let x represent the number.

$$3(x+5)=2x-1$$
$$3x+15=2x-1$$
$$3x+15-2x=2x-1-2x$$
$$x+15=-1$$
$$x+15-15=-1-15$$
$$x=-16$$

The number is –16.

9. Let x = salary of the governor of Nebraska, then $2x$ = salary of the governor of Washington.

$$x+2x=195{,}000$$
$$3x=195{,}000$$
$$\frac{3x}{3}=\frac{195{,}000}{3}$$
$$x=65{,}000$$

The salary of the governor of Nebraska is $65,000. The salary of the governor of Washington is 2 · 65,000 = $130,000.

11. If x = length of the first piece, then $2x$ = length of the second piece, and $5x$ = length of the third piece.

$$x+2x+5x=40$$
$$8x=40$$
$$\frac{8x}{8}=\frac{40}{8}$$
$$x=5$$

The first piece is 5 inches long, the second piece is 2 · 5 = 10 inches long, and the third piece is 5 · 5 = 25 inches long.

13. The cost of renting the car is equal to the daily rental charge plus $0.29 per mile. Let x = number of miles.

$$2\cdot 24.95+0.29x=100$$
$$49.90+0.29x=100$$
$$49.90+0.29x-49.90=100-49.90$$
$$0.29x=50.10$$
$$\frac{0.29x}{0.29}=\frac{50.10}{0.29}$$
$$x=172$$

You can drive 172 whole miles on a budget of $100.

15. Let x = measure of each of the two equal angles, then $2x + 30$ = measure of the third angle.

$$x+x+2x+30=180$$
$$4x+30=180$$
$$4x+30-30=180-30$$
$$4x=150$$
$$\frac{4x}{4}=\frac{150}{4}$$
$$x=37.5$$

The angles measure 37.5°, 37.5°, and 105°.

17. Let x = number of votes for Randall, then $x + 13{,}288$ = number of votes for Brown.

$$x + x + 13{,}288 = 119{,}436$$
$$2x + 13{,}288 = 119{,}436$$
$$2x + 13{,}288 - 13{,}288 = 119{,}436 - 13{,}288$$
$$2x = 106{,}148$$
$$\frac{2x}{2} = 106{,}148$$
$$x = 53{,}074$$

$x + 13{,}288 = 66{,}362$
Brown: 66,362 votes
Randall: 53,074 votes

19.
$$x + 3x = 180$$
$$4x = 180$$
$$\frac{4x}{4} = \frac{180}{4}$$
$$x = 45$$

$3x = 135$
45° and 135°

21. Let x = code for Belgium, then $x + 1$ = code for France, and $x + 2$ = code for Spain.

$$x + (x + 1) + (x + 2) = 99$$
$$3x + 3 = 99$$
$$3x + 3 = 99 - 3$$
$$3x = 96$$
$$\frac{3x}{3} = \frac{96}{3}$$
$$x = 32$$

$x + 1 = 33$
$x + 2 = 34$
Belgium: 32
France: 33
Spain: 34

23. Let x = growth rate of human toenails.

$$4x = 0.8$$
$$\frac{4x}{4} = \frac{0.8}{4}$$
$$x = 0.2$$

Human toenails grow at a rate of 0.2 inch per year.

25. Let x = height of the probe, then $2x - 19$ = diameter of the probe.

$$x + (2x - 19) = 83$$
$$x + 2x - 19 = 83$$
$$3x - 19 = 83$$
$$3x - 19 + 19 = 83 + 19$$
$$3x = 102$$
$$\frac{3x}{3} = \frac{102}{3}$$
$$x = 34$$

The probe is 34 inches tall and has a diameter of $2(34) - 19 = 49$ inches.

27. Let x = Knicks' score, then $x + 1$ = Spurs' score.

$$x + x + 1 = 155$$
$$2x + 1 = 155$$
$$2x + 1 - 1 = 155 - 1$$
$$2x = 154$$
$$\frac{2x}{2} = \frac{154}{2}$$
$$x = 77$$

$x + 1 = 78$
Spurs: 78
Knicks: 77

29. Let x = number of rotations.

$$360x = 900$$
$$\frac{360x}{360} = \frac{900}{360}$$
$$x = 2\frac{1}{2}$$

There were $2\frac{1}{2}$ rotations.

31. Let x = number of Democratic governors, then $x + 14$ = number of Republican governors.

$$x + x + 14 = 50 - 2$$
$$2x + 14 = 48$$
$$2x + 14 - 14 = 48 - 14$$
$$2x = 34$$
$$\frac{2x}{2} = \frac{34}{2}$$
$$x = 17$$

$x + 14 = 31$
17 Democratic governors
31 Republican governors

33. If x = length of the shorter piece, then $2x + 2$ = length of the longer piece.

$$x+(2x+2)=17$$
$$x+2x+2=17$$
$$3x+2=17$$
$$3x+2-2=17-2$$
$$3x=15$$
$$\frac{3x}{3}=\frac{15}{3}$$
$$x=5$$

The shorter piece is 5 feet long. The longer piece is 12 feet long.

35. Let x = smallest angle.

$$x+(x+2)+(x+4)=180$$
$$3x+6=180$$
$$3x+6-6=180-6$$
$$3x=174$$
$$\frac{3x}{3}=\frac{174}{3}$$
$$x=58$$

$x+2=60$
$x+4=62$
The angles are 58°, 60°, and 62°.

37. Let x = number of miles.

$$34+0.20x=104$$
$$-34+34+0.20x=-34+104$$
$$0.20x=70$$
$$\frac{0.20x}{0.20}=\frac{70}{0.20}$$
$$x=350$$

You drove 350 miles.

39. Answers may vary.

41. Texas and Florida

43. Let x = amount spent by Pennsylvania, then $2x - 8.1$ = amount spent by Hawaii.

$$x+2x-8.1=60.9$$
$$3x-8.1=60.9$$
$$3x-8.1+8.1=60.9+8.1$$
$$3x=69.0$$
$$\frac{3x}{3}=\frac{69.0}{3}$$
$$x=23.0$$

$2x-8.1=37.9$
Hawaii: $37.9 million
Pennsylvania: $23 million

45. Let x = width, then $1.6x$ = length.

$$2x+2(1.6x)=78$$
$$2x+3.2x=78$$
$$5.2x=78$$
$$x=15$$

$1.6x=24$
The dimensions are 15 ft by 24 ft.

47. Answers may vary.

49. Answers may vary.

51. c

53. $-2+(-8)=-2-8=-10$

55. $-11+2=-9$

57. $-12-3=-15$

59. $5(-x)=x+60$

61. $50-(x+9)=0$

Exercise Set 2.6

1.

$$A=bh$$
$$45=15\cdot h$$
$$\frac{45}{15}=\frac{15\cdot h}{15}$$
$$3=h$$

3.
$$S = 4lw + 2wh$$
$$102 = 4(7)(3) + 2(3)h$$
$$102 = 84 + 6h$$
$$102 - 84 = 84 + 6h - 84$$
$$18 = 6h$$
$$\frac{18}{6} = \frac{6h}{6}$$
$$3 = h$$

5.
$$A = \frac{1}{2}h(B + b)$$
$$180 = \frac{1}{2}h(11 + 7)$$
$$180 = \frac{1}{2}h(18)$$
$$180 = 9h$$
$$\frac{180}{9} = \frac{9h}{9}$$
$$20 = h$$

7.
$$P = a + b + c$$
$$30 = 8 + 10 + c$$
$$30 = 18 + c$$
$$30 - 18 = 18 + c - 18$$
$$12 = c$$

9.
$$C = 2\pi r$$
$$15.7 = 2\pi r$$
$$\frac{15.7}{2\pi} = \frac{2\pi r}{2\pi}$$
$$\frac{15.7}{2(3.14)} = r$$
$$2.5 = r$$

11.
$$I = PRT$$
$$3750 = (25,000)(0.05)T$$
$$3750 = 1250T$$
$$\frac{3750}{1250} = \frac{1250T}{1250}$$
$$3 = T$$

13.
$$V = \frac{1}{3}\pi r^2 h$$
$$565.2 = \frac{1}{3}\pi(6^2)h$$
$$565.2 = \frac{1}{3}\pi(36)h$$
$$565.2 = 12\pi h$$
$$\frac{565.2}{12\pi} = \frac{12\pi h}{12\pi}$$
$$\frac{565.2}{12(3.14)} = h$$
$$15 = h$$

15.
$$f = 5gh$$
$$\frac{f}{5g} = \frac{5gh}{5g}$$
$$\frac{f}{5g} = h$$

17.
$$V = LWH$$
$$\frac{V}{LH} = \frac{LWH}{LH}$$
$$\frac{V}{LH} = W$$

19.
$$3x + y = 7$$
$$3x - 3x + y = 7 - 3x$$
$$y = 7 - 3x$$

21.
$$A = P + PRT$$
$$A - P = P - P + PRT$$
$$A - P = PRT$$
$$\frac{A - P}{PT} = \frac{PRT}{PT}$$
$$\frac{A - P}{PT} = R$$

23.
$$V = \frac{1}{3}Ah$$
$$3(V) = 3\left(\frac{1}{3}Ah\right)$$
$$3V = Ah$$
$$\frac{3V}{h} = \frac{Ah}{h}$$
$$\frac{3V}{h} = A$$

25.
$$P = a + b + c$$
$$P - b = a + b - b + c$$
$$P - b = a + c$$
$$P - b - c = a + c - c$$
$$P - b - c = a$$

27.
$$S = 2\pi rh + 2\pi r^2$$
$$S - 2\pi r^2 = 2\pi rh + 2\pi r^2 - 2\pi r^2$$
$$S - 2\pi r^2 = 2\pi rh$$
$$\frac{S - 2\pi r^2}{2\pi r} = \frac{2\pi rh}{2\pi r}$$
$$\frac{S - 2\pi r^2}{2\pi r} = h$$

29.
$$A = bh$$
$$52,400 = 400 \cdot h$$
$$\frac{52,400}{400} = \frac{400 \cdot h}{400}$$
$$131 = h$$
The width of the sign is 131 feet.

31.
$$d = rt$$
$$375 = 50 \cdot t$$
$$\frac{375}{50} = \frac{50 \cdot t}{50}$$
$$7.5 = t$$
It would take 7.5 hours.

33. Use the formula $C = \frac{5}{9}(F - 32)$ with $F = 14$.
$$C = \left(\frac{5}{9}\right)(14 - 32) = \left(\frac{5}{9}\right)(-18) = -10$$
14°F is the same as –10°C.

35. $V = lwh$
$V = (8)(3)(6)$
$V = 144$
Since the tank has a volume of 144 cubic feet, and each piranha requires 1.5 cubic feet, the tank can hold $\frac{144}{1.5} = 96$ piranhas.

37. $d = rt$
$d = 55(2.5)$
$d = 137.5$
The cities are 137.5 miles apart.

39. $A = \frac{1}{2}h(B + b)$
$$A = \frac{1}{2}(60)(130 + 70) = \frac{1}{2}(60)(200) = 6000$$
Since the area of the lawn is 6000 square feet and since each bag covers 4000 square feet, two bags must be purchased.

41.
$$d = rt$$
$$25,000 = 4000 \cdot t$$
$$\frac{25,000}{4000} = \frac{4000 \cdot t}{4000}$$
$$6.25 = t$$
It will take 6.25 hours.

43. $V = lwh$
$V = (10)(8)(10)$
$V = 800$
The minimum volume of the box must be 800 cubic feet.

45. Use the formula for the area of a circle, $A = \pi r^2$, to solve for the number of square inches of pizza purchased in each case. For one 16-inch pizza use $r = 8$.
$A = \pi r^2 = \pi\left(8^2\right) = 64\pi$ square inches. For two 10-inch pizzas use $r = 5$ and multiply the result by 2.
$A = 2(\pi r^2) = 2\pi(5^2) = 2\pi(25) = 50\pi$ square inches
One 16-inch pizza gives more pizza for the price.

47.
$$d = rt$$
$$42.8 = 552t$$
$$\frac{42.8}{552} = \frac{552t}{552}$$
$$0.077536 = t$$
$$(0.077536 \text{ hours})\left(\frac{60 \text{ minutes}}{\text{hour}}\right)$$
$$= 4.65 \text{ minutes}$$
The test run would last 4.65 minutes.

49. $d = rt$
$135 = 60 \cdot t$
$\frac{135}{60} = \frac{60 \cdot t}{60}$
$2.25 = t$
It will take 2.25 hours.

51. Use $F = \left(\frac{9}{5}\right)C + 32$ with $C = -78.5$.
$F = \left(\frac{9}{5}\right)C + 32$
$F = \left(\frac{9}{5}\right)(-78.5) + 32$
$= -141.3 + 32$
$= -109.3$
-78.5°C is the same as -109.3°F.

53. Use $d = rt$ with $d = 93{,}000{,}000$ and $r = 186{,}000$.
$d = rt$
$93{,}000{,}000 = 186{,}000 \cdot t$
$\frac{93{,}000{,}000}{186{,}000} = \frac{186{,}000 \cdot t}{186{,}000}$
$500 = t$
It takes 500 seconds or $8\frac{1}{3}$ minutes.

55. Use the formula for the volume of a sphere, $V = \frac{4}{3}\pi r^3$, with $r = 2000$.
$V = \frac{4}{3}\pi(2000)^3$
$= \frac{4}{3}\pi(8{,}000{,}000{,}000)$
$= 33{,}493{,}333{,}333$
The volume of the fireball was 33,493,333,333 cubic miles.

57. Use the formula $d = rt$ with $d = 25{,}120$ and $r = 270{,}000$.
$d = rt$
$25{,}120 = 270{,}000 \cdot t$
$\frac{25{,}120}{270{,}000} = \frac{270{,}000 \cdot t}{270{,}000}$
$0.093 = t$
Thus, it takes 0.093 second for a bolt of lightning to travel around the world once. In one second it can travel around the world $\frac{1}{0.093} = 10.7$ times.

59. $\frac{20 \text{ miles}}{1 \text{ hour}} = \frac{20 \text{ miles}}{1 \text{ hour}} \cdot \frac{5280 \text{ feet}}{1 \text{ mile}} \cdot \frac{1 \text{ hour}}{3600 \text{ sec}}$
$= \frac{88}{3}$ feet per second
Use $d = rt$ with $d = 1300$ feet and $r = \frac{88}{3}$ feet per second.
$1300 = \frac{88}{3}t$
$\frac{3}{88}(1300) = \left(\frac{3}{88}\right)\left(\frac{88}{3}t\right)$
$44.3 = t$
It took about 44.3 seconds.

61. Use the formula $C = \left(\frac{5}{9}\right)(F - 32)$ to find when $C = F$.
$C = \left(\frac{5}{9}\right)(F - 32)$
$F = \left(\frac{5}{9}\right)(F - 32)$
$9(F) = 9\left[\left(\frac{5}{9}\right)(F - 32)\right]$
$9F = 5(F - 32)$
$9F = 5F - 160$
$9F - 5F = 5F - 160 - 5F$
$4F = -160$
$\frac{4F}{4} = \frac{-160}{4}$
$F = -40$
-40°F is the same as -40°C.

63. $V = (2 \cdot L)(2 \cdot W)(2 \cdot H) = 8LWH$
The volume is multiplied by 8.

65. Let x = number
$\frac{9}{x + 5}$

67. $3(x + 4)$

69. Let x = number
$2(10 + 4x)$

71. $3(x - 12)$

Section 2.7

Mental Math

1. not correct

2. not correct

3. correct

4. correct

Exercise Set 2.7

1. $120\% = 1.20$

3. $22.5\% = 0.225$

5. $0.12\% = 0.0012$

7. $0.75 = 75\%$

9. $2 = 200\%$

11. $\frac{1}{8} = 0.125 = 12.5\%$

13. 38%

15. $38\% + 16\% = 54\%$

17. 38% of 360°
$0.38(360°) = 136.8°$

19. Answers may vary.

21. 4%

23. 4% of 360° = $0.04(360°) = 14.4°$

25. 37% of 135,000 = $0.37(135,000) = 49,950$

27. Let x = unknown number
$x = 0.16(70)$
$x = 11.2$

29. Let x = unknown percent
$28.6 = x(52)$
$0.55 = x$
55%

31. Let x = unknown number
$45 = 0.25x$
$180 = x$

33. $0.23(20) = 4.6$

35. Let x = unknown number
$40 = 0.80x$
$50 = x$

37. Let x = unknown percent
$144 = x(480)$
$0.3 = x$
30%

39. Decrease = 156(0.25) = \$39
Sale price = 156 – 39 = \$117

41. To find how much shorter the men's record throw is than the women's, we find 3.7% of 252 feet.
3.7% of 252 = $0.037(252)$
$= 9.324$
The men's record throw is 9.324 feet less than the women's.
$252 - 9.324 = 243$
The men's record is 243 feet.

43. 55.40% of those surveyed have used over-the-counter drugs to combat the common cold.

45. Since 23.70% of those surveyed have used over-the-counter drugs for allergies, we find 23.70% of 230.
23.70% of 230 = $0.237(230) = 54.51$
54 people used over-the-counter drugs for allergies.

47. No, because many people have used over-the-counter drugs for more than one of the categories listed.

49. Since 26% of men doze off, we find 26% of 121.
26% of 121 = $0.26(121) = 31.46$
We would expect 31 of the men to have dozed off.

51. The percent of total number of women from each service is the ratio of the number of women of the service to the total.

Navy: $\frac{50,287}{186,697} \approx 27\%$

Marines: $\frac{9696}{186,697} \approx 5\%$

Air Force: $\frac{64,427}{186,697} \approx 35\%$

Coast Guard: $\frac{3879}{186,697} \approx 2\%$

Total:
$31\% + 27\% + 5\% + 35\% + 2\% = 100\%$

53. $\frac{1800}{1,200,000} = 0.0015 = 0.15\%$

55. $0.44x = 10.4$
$\frac{0.44x}{0.44} = \frac{10.4}{0.44}$
$x = 23.6$
23.6 million

57. Increase $= 70 - 40 = 30$
$30 = x(40)$
$0.75 = x$
75% increase

59. Increase $= 15.65 - 12.62 = 3.03$
$3.03 = x(12.62)$
$0.24 = x$
24% increase; No

61. Increase $= 5000 - 3 = 4997$
$4997 = x(3)$
$1665.67 = x$
166,567% increase

63. 16%

65. 24% of $50 = 0.24(50) = 12$

67. Answers may vary.

69. $\frac{34,611 - 38,831}{38,831} = \frac{-4220}{38,831} = -0.109$
There was an 11% decrease.

71. $\frac{23}{300} \approx 0.077 = 7.7\%$
About 7.7% of the daily recommended carbohydrate intake is contained in one serving.

73. Find the ratio of the calories from fat to the total calories. Each serving contains 6 g of fat.
$6 \cdot 9 = 54$ calories
$\frac{54}{280} \approx 0.193 = 19.3\%$
About 19.3% of the calories in each serving comes from fat.

75. Answers may vary.

77. $2a + b - c = 2(5) + (-1) - 3 = 10 - 1 - 3 = 6$

79. $4ab - 3bc = 4(-5)(-8) - 3(-8)(2)$
$= 160 + 48 = 208$

81. $n^2 - m^2 = (-3)^2 - (-8)^2 = 9 - 64 = -55$

Exercise Set 2.8

1. Let $x =$ length
then $\frac{2}{3}x =$ width

$$P = 2L + 2W$$
$$260 = 2(x) + 2\left(\frac{2}{3}x\right)$$
$$260 = 2x + \frac{4}{3}x$$
$$260 = \frac{6}{3}x + \frac{4}{3}x$$
$$260 = \frac{10}{3}x$$
$$\frac{3}{10}(260) = \frac{3}{10} \cdot \frac{10}{3}x$$
$$78 \text{ ft} = x$$

length = 78 ft
width $= \frac{2}{3}(78 \text{ ft}) = 52$ ft

3.

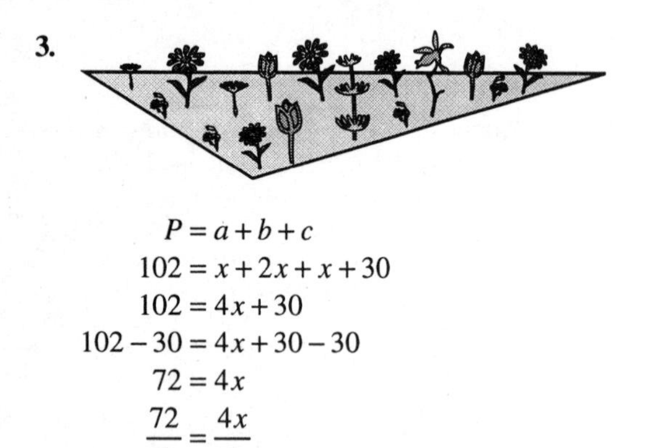

$$P = a + b + c$$
$$102 = x + 2x + x + 30$$
$$102 = 4x + 30$$
$$102 - 30 = 4x + 30 - 30$$
$$72 = 4x$$
$$\frac{72}{4} = \frac{4x}{4}$$
$$18 \text{ ft} = x$$

The sides are 18 ft, 36 ft, and 48 ft.

5.

rate · time = distance			
Jet	500	x	$500x$
Propeller	200	$x+2$	$200(x+2)$

$$500x = 200(x+2)$$
$$500x = 200x + 400$$
$$500x - 200x = 200x - 200x + 400$$
$$300x = 400$$
$$\frac{300x}{300} = \frac{400}{300}$$
$$x = \frac{4}{3}$$
$$\text{Distance} = 500\left(\frac{4}{3}\right) = \frac{2000}{3} = 666\frac{2}{3} \text{ miles}$$

7.

rate · time = distance			
To Disneyland	50	x	$50x$
From Disneyland	40	$7.2 - x$	$40(7.2 - x)$

$$50x = 40(7.2 - x)$$
$$50x = 288 - 40x$$
$$50x + 40x = 388 - 40x + 40x$$
$$\frac{90x}{90} = \frac{288}{90}$$
$$90x = 288$$
$$x = 3.2 \text{ hours}$$
$$\text{Distance} = 50(3.2) = 160 \text{ miles}$$

9.

Strength of solution	Liters of Solution	Gallons of Acid
100%	x	$1.00x$
40%	2	0.40(2)
70%	$x+2$	$0.70(x+2)$

$$1.00x + 0.40(2) = 0.70(x+2)$$
$$1.00x + 0.80 = 0.70x + 1.40$$
$$1.00x - 0.70x + 0.80 = 0.70x - 0.70x + 1.40$$
$$0.30x + 0.80 = 1.40$$
$$0.30x + 0.80 - 0.80 = 1.40 - 0.80$$
$$0.30x = 0.60$$
$$\frac{0.30x}{0.30} = \frac{0.60}{0.30}$$
$$x = 2 \text{ gallons}$$

11.

Pounds of Nuts	Cost of One Pound	Total Cost
20	3	60
x	5	$5x$
$20 + x$	3.50	$3.50(20 + x)$

$$60 + 5x = 3.50(20 + x)$$
$$60 + 5x = 70 + 3.50x$$
$$60 + 5x - 3.50x = 70 + 3.50x - 3.50x$$
$$60 + 1.50x = 70$$
$$60 - 60 + 1.50x = 70 - 60$$
$$1.50x = 10$$
$$\frac{1.50x}{1.50} = \frac{10}{1.5}$$
$$x = 6.\overline{6} \text{ or } 6\frac{2}{3} \text{ lb}$$

13. No; the mixture will have a percent antifreeze content between 30% and 50%.

15.

	Principal · Rate · Time = Interest			
8%	x	0.08	1	$0.08x$
9%	$25{,}000-x$	0.09	1	$0.09(25{,}000-x)$
Total	25,000			2135

$$0.08x+0.09(25,000-x)=2135$$
$$0.08x+2250-0.09x=2135$$
$$-0.01x+2250=2135$$
$$-0.01x+2250-2250=2135-2250$$
$$-0.01x=-115$$
$$\frac{-0.01x}{-0.01}=\frac{-115}{-0.01}$$
$$x=\$11,500$$

\$11,500 at 8% and \$13,500 at 9%.

17. 1st investment at $11\% = x$
2nd investment at 4% loss $= 10,000 - x$

$$0.11(x)-0.04(10,000-x)=650$$
$$11x-4(10,000-x)=65,000$$
$$11x-40,000+4x=65,000$$
$$15x-40,000=65,000$$
$$\frac{15x}{15}=\frac{105,000}{15}$$
$$x=7000$$

$10,000 - x = 3000$
\$7,000 @ 11% profit
\$3,000 @ 4% loss

19. Let x = side of square
$x + 5$ = side of triangle

$$3(x+5)=7+4x$$
$$3x+15=7+4x$$
$$8=x$$

$x+5=13$
Square's side length: 8 in.
Triangle's side length: 13 in.

21.

Principal · Rate · Time = Interest			
x	0.08	1	$0.08x$
$54{,}000-x$	0.10	1	$0.10(54{,}000-x)$

$$0.08x=0.10(54,000-x)$$
$$0.08x=5400-0.10x$$
$$0.08x+0.10x=5400-0.10x+0.10x$$
$$0.18x=5400$$
$$\frac{0.18x}{0.18}=\frac{5400}{0.18}$$
$$x=30,000$$

\$30,000 at 8% and \$24,000 at 10%

23. 1st investment $= x$
2nd investment $= 20,000 - x$

$$0.12(x)-0.04(20,000-x)=0$$
$$12x-80,000+4x=0$$
$$\frac{16x}{16}=\frac{80,000}{16}$$
$$x=5,000$$

$20,000 - x = 15,000$
\$5,000 at 12%
\$15,000 at 4%

25.

Principal · Rate · Time = Interest			
3000	0.06	1	180
x	0.09	1	$0.09x$

$$180+0.09x=585$$
$$180-180+0.09x=585-180$$
$$0.09x=405$$
$$\frac{0.09x}{0.09}=\frac{405}{0.09}$$
$$x=\$4500$$

27. amount invested at 9% = x
amount invested at 10% = $2x$
amount invested at 11% = $3x$

$$\$2790 = 0.09(x) + 0.10(2x) + 0.11(3x)$$
$$279,000 = 9x + 20x + 33x$$
$$\frac{279,000}{62} = \frac{62x}{62}$$
$$x = 4,500$$

$2x = 9,000$
$3x = 13,500$
\$4,500 at 9%
\$9,000 at 10%
\$13,500 at 11%

29.

	Number of Tickets	Cost of One Ticket	Total Cost
Adults	x	5.75	$5.75x$
Children	$8 - x$	3.00	$3.00(8 - x)$

$$5.75x + 3.00(8 - x) = 32.25$$
$$5.75x + 24.00 - 3.00x = 32.25$$
$$2.75x + 24.00 = 32.25$$
$$2.75x + 24.00 - 24.00 = 32.25 - 24.00$$
$$2.75x = 8.25$$
$$\frac{2.75x}{2.75} = \frac{8.25}{2.75}$$
$$x = 3$$

3 adult tickets

31. Rate of 1st hiker = x
Rate of 2nd hiker = $1.1 + x$

$$2x + 2(1.1 + x) = 11$$
$$2x + 2.2 + 2x = 11$$
$$4x + 2.2 = 11$$
$$4x = 8.8$$
$$\frac{4x}{4} = \frac{8.8}{4}$$
$$x = 2.2 \text{ mph}$$

$1.1 + x = 3.3$ mph

33.

	Rate	Time
Upstream	5	x
Downstream	11	$4 - x$

$$5x = 11(4 - x)$$
$$5x = 44 - 11x$$
$$\frac{16x}{16} = \frac{44}{16}$$
$$x = 2.75$$

Distance:

$$5x + 11(4 - x) = 5(2.75) + 11(4 - 2.75)$$
$$= 13.75 + 11(1.25)$$
$$= 13.75 + 13.75$$
$$= 27.5 \text{ miles}$$

35. $R = 60x$
$C = 50x + 5000$

$$60x = 50x + 5000$$
$$10x = 5000$$
$$x = 500$$

$C = 50(500) + 5000 = \$30,000$

37. $C = 870 + 70x$
$R = 105x$

$$870 + 70x = 105x$$
$$870 = 35x$$
$$24.9 = x$$

25 monitors

39. $3 + (-7) = -4$

41. $\frac{3}{4} - \frac{3}{16} = \frac{12}{16} - \frac{3}{16} = \frac{9}{16}$

43. $-5 - (-1) = -5 + 1 = -4$

45. $-5 > -7$

47.
$$|-5| = 5$$
$$-(-5) = 5$$
$$|-5| = -(-5)$$

Section 2.9

Mental Math

1. $5x > 10$
   $x > 2$

2. $4x < 20$
   $x < 5$

3. $2x \geq 16$
   $x \geq 8$

4. $9x \leq 63$
   $x \leq 7$

Exercise Set 2.9

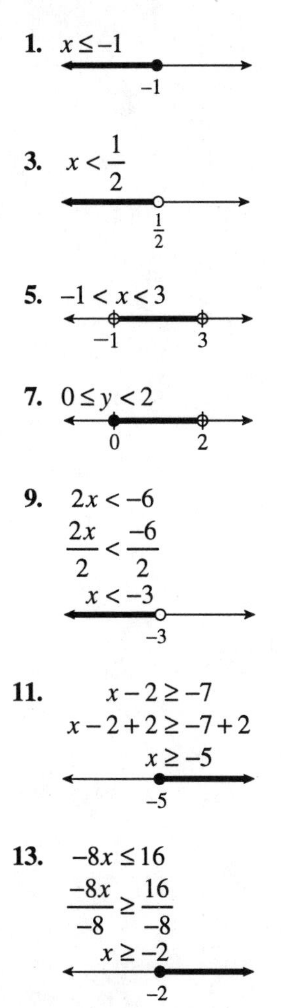

1. $x \leq -1$

3. $x < \frac{1}{2}$

5. $-1 < x < 3$

7. $0 \leq y < 2$

9. $2x < -6$
   $\frac{2x}{2} < \frac{-6}{2}$
   $x < -3$

11. $x - 2 \geq -7$
    $x - 2 + 2 \geq -7 + 2$
    $x \geq -5$

13. $-8x \leq 16$
    $\frac{-8x}{-8} \geq \frac{16}{-8}$
    $x \geq -2$

15. $3x - 5 > 2x - 8$
    $3x - 5 + 5 > 2x - 8 + 5$
    $3x > 2x - 3$
    $3x - 2x > 2x - 3 - 2x$
    $x > -3$

17. $4x - 1 \leq 5x - 2x$
    $4x - 1 \leq 3x$
    $4x - 1 - 3x \leq 3x - 3x$
    $x - 1 \leq 0$
    $x - 1 + 1 \leq 0 + 1$
    $x \leq 1$

19. $x - 7 < 3(x + 1)$
    $x - 7 < 3x + 3$
    $x - x - 7 < 3x - x + 3$
    $-7 < 2x + 3$
    $-7 - 3 < 2x + 3 - 3$
    $-10 < 2x$
    $\frac{-10}{2} < \frac{2x}{2}$
    $-5 < x$

21. $-6x + 2 \geq 2(5 - x)$
    $-6x + 2 \geq 10 - 2x$
    $-6x + 2x + 2 \geq 10 - 2x + 2x$
    $-4x + 2 \geq 10$
    $-4x + 2 - 2 \geq 10 - 2$
    $-4x \geq 8$
    $\frac{-4x}{-4} \leq \frac{8}{-4}$
    $x \leq -2$

23.
$$4(3x-1) \le 5(2x-4)$$
$$12x-4 \le 10x-20$$
$$12x-10x-4 \le 10x-10x-20$$
$$2x-4 \le -20$$
$$2x-4+4 \le -20+4$$
$$2x \le -16$$
$$\frac{2x}{2} \le \frac{-16}{2}$$
$$x \le -8$$

−8

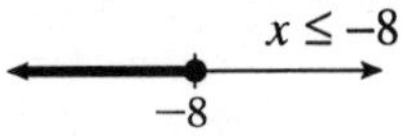

25.
$$3(x+2)-6 > -2(x-3)+14$$
$$3x+6-6 > -2x+6+14$$
$$3x > -2x+20$$
$$3x+2x > -2x+2x+20$$
$$5x > 20$$
$$\frac{5x}{5} > \frac{20}{5}$$
$$x > 4$$

4

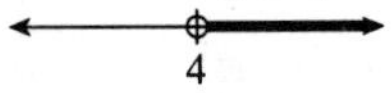

27.
$$-3 < 3x < 6$$
$$\frac{-3}{3} < \frac{3x}{3} < \frac{6}{3}$$
$$-1 < x < 2$$

−1 2

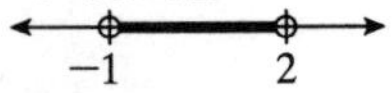

29.
$$2 \le 3x - 10 \le 5$$
$$2 + 10 \le 3x - 10 + 10 \le 5 + 10$$
$$12 \le 3x \le 15$$
$$\frac{12}{3} \le \frac{3x}{3} \le \frac{15}{3}$$
$$4 \le x \le 5$$

4 5

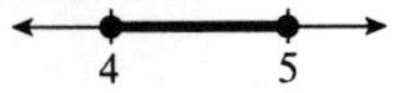

31.
$$-4 < 2(x-3) < 4$$
$$-4 < 2x-6 < 4$$
$$-4+6 < 2x-6+6 < 4+6$$
$$2 < 2x < 10$$
$$\frac{2}{2} < \frac{2x}{2} < \frac{10}{2}$$
$$1 < x < 5$$

1 5

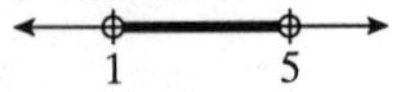

33. Answers may vary.

35.
$$-2x \le -40$$
$$\frac{-2x}{-2} \ge \frac{-40}{-2}$$
$$x \ge 20$$

20

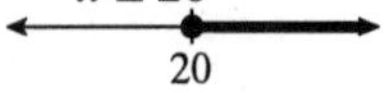

37.
$$-9+x > 7$$
$$-9+9+x > 7+9$$
$$x > 16$$

16

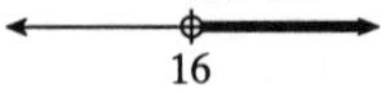

39.
$$3x-7 < 6x+2$$
$$3x-3x-7 < 6x-3x+2$$
$$-7 < 3x+2$$
$$-7-2 < 3x+2-2$$
$$-9 < 3x$$
$$\frac{-9}{3} < \frac{3x}{3}$$
$$-3 < x$$

−3

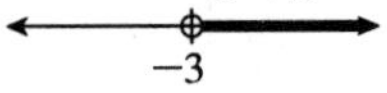

41.
$$5x-7x \le x+2$$
$$-2x \le x+2$$
$$-2x-x \le x-x+2$$
$$-3x \le 2$$
$$\frac{-3x}{-3} \ge \frac{2}{-3}$$
$$x \ge -\frac{2}{3}$$

$-\frac{2}{3}$

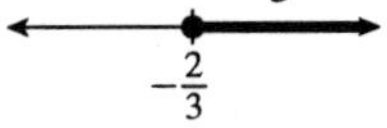

43.
$$\frac{3}{4}x > 2$$
$$\frac{4}{3}\left(\frac{3}{4}x\right) > \frac{4}{3}(2)$$
$$x > \frac{8}{3}$$
$$x > 2\frac{2}{3}$$

$\frac{8}{3}$

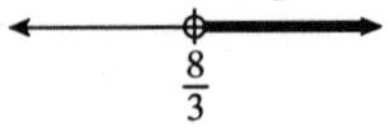

45.
$$\begin{aligned} 3(x-5) &< 2(2x-1) \\ 3x-15 &< 4x-2 \\ 3x-3x-15 &< 4x-3x-2 \\ -15 &< x-2 \\ -15+2 &< x-2+2 \\ -13 &< x \end{aligned}$$

Number line: open circle at −13, shaded to the right.

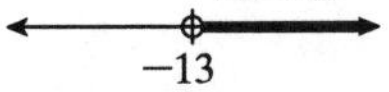

47.
$$\begin{aligned} 4(2x+1) &> 4 \\ 8x+4 &> 4 \\ 8x+4-4 &> 4-4 \\ 8x &> 0 \\ \frac{8x}{8} &> \frac{0}{8} \\ x &> 0 \end{aligned}$$

Number line: open circle at 0, shaded to the right.

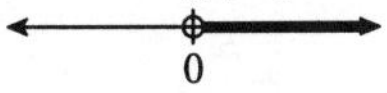

49.
$$\begin{aligned} -5x+4 &\le -4(x-1) \\ -5x+4 &\le -4x+4 \\ -5x+5x+4 &\le -4x+5x+4 \\ 4 &\le x+4 \\ 4-4 &\le x+4-4 \\ 0 &\le x \end{aligned}$$

Number line: closed circle at 0, shaded to the right.

51.
$$\begin{aligned} &-2 < 3x-5 < 7 \\ &-2+5 < 3x-5+5 < 7+5 \\ &3 < 3x < 12 \\ &\frac{3}{3} < \frac{3x}{3} < \frac{12}{3} \\ &1 < x < 4 \end{aligned}$$

Number line: open circles at 1 and 4, shaded between.

53.
$$\begin{aligned} -2(x-4)-3x &< -(4x+1)+2x \\ -2x+8-3x &< -4x-1+2x \\ -5x+8 &< -2x-1 \\ -5x+2x+8 &< -2x+2x-1 \\ -3x+8 &< -1 \\ -3x+8-8 &< -1-8 \\ -3x &< -9 \\ \frac{-3x}{-3} &> \frac{-9}{-3} \\ x &> 3 \end{aligned}$$

Number line: open circle at 3, shaded to the right.

55.
$$\begin{aligned} -3x+6 &\ge 2x+6 \\ -3x+3x+6 &\ge 2x+3x+6 \\ 6 &\ge 5x+6 \\ 6-6 &\ge 5x+6-6 \\ 0 &\ge 5x \\ \frac{0}{5} &\ge \frac{5x}{5} \\ 0 &\ge x \end{aligned}$$

Number line: closed circle at 0, shaded to the left.

57.
$$\begin{aligned} &-6 < 3(x-2) < 8 \\ &-6 < 3x-6 < 8 \\ &-6+6 < 3x-6+6 < 8+6 \\ &0 < 3x < 14 \\ &\frac{0}{3} < \frac{3x}{3} < \frac{14}{3} \\ &0 < x < 4\frac{2}{3} \end{aligned}$$

Number line: open circles at 0 and $\frac{14}{3}$, shaded between.

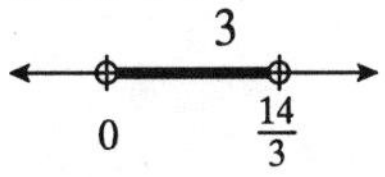

59. $x < 200$ recommended
$200 \le x \le 240$ borderline
$x > 240$ high

61. Let $x =$ number.
$$\begin{aligned} 2x+6 &> -14 \\ 2x+6-6 &> -14-6 \\ 2x &> -20 \\ \frac{2x}{2} &> \frac{-20}{2} \\ x &> -10 \end{aligned}$$

63. Let $x =$ number of people.
$$\begin{aligned} 50+34x &\le 3000 \\ 50+34x-50 &\le 3000-50 \\ 34x &\le 2950 \\ \frac{34x}{34} &\le \frac{2950}{34} \\ x &\le 86.7 \end{aligned}$$

They can invite a maximum of 86 people.

65. $P = 2L + 2W$
$$2x + 2(15) \le 100$$
$$2x + 30 \ge 100$$
$$2x + 30 - 30 \le 100 - 30$$
$$2x \le 70$$
$$\frac{2x}{2} \le \frac{70}{2}$$
$$x \le 35 \text{ cm}$$

67. $-39 \le \frac{5}{9}(F - 32) \le 45$
$$-70.2 \le F - 32 \le 81$$
$$-38.2° \le F \le 113°$$

69. $2.9 \le 3.14d \le 3.1$
$$\frac{2.9}{3.14} \le \frac{3.14d}{3.14} \le \frac{3.1}{3.14}$$
$$0.924 \le d \le 0.987$$

71. Let x = number.
$$-5 < 2x + 1 < 7$$
$$-5 - 1 < 2x + 1 - 1 < 7 - 1$$
$$-6 < 2x < 6$$
$$\frac{-6}{2} < \frac{2x}{2} < \frac{6}{2}$$
$$-3 < x < 3$$

73.

Principal · Rate · Time = Interest			
10,000	0.11	1	1100
5,000	x	1	$5000x$

$$1100 + 5000x \ge 1600$$
$$1100 - 1100 + 5000x \ge 1600 - 1100$$
$$5000x \ge 500$$
$$\frac{5000x}{5000} \ge \frac{500}{5000}$$
$$x \ge 0.10$$
$$x \ge 10\%$$

75. Let x = score of 3rd game.
$$\frac{146 + 201 + x}{3} \ge 180$$
$$3\left(\frac{146 + 201 + x}{3}\right) \ge (3)180$$
$$146 + 201 + x \ge 540$$
$$347 + x \ge 540$$
$$347 - 347 + x \ge 540 - 347$$
$$x \ge 193$$

77. $(2)^3 = 8$

79. $(1)^{12} = 1$

81. $\left(\frac{4}{7}\right)^2 = \frac{4^2}{7^2} = \frac{16}{49}$

83. 32 million; point on graph is (1995, 51)

85. 1996; the increase from 1995 to 1996 is the greatest

87.
$$x(x + 4) > x^2 - 2x + 6$$
$$x^2 + 4x > x^2 - 2x + 6$$
$$x^2 - x^2 + 4x > x^2 - x^2 - 2x + 6$$
$$4x > -2x + 6$$
$$4x + 2x > -2x + 2x + 6$$
$$6x > 6$$
$$\frac{6x}{6} > \frac{6}{6}$$
$$x > 1$$

1

89.
$$\begin{aligned} x^2+6x-10 &< x(x-10) \\ x^2+6x-10 &< x^2-10x \\ x^2-x^2+6x-10 &< x^2-x^2-10x \\ 6x-10 &< -10x \\ 6x-6x-10 &< -10x-6x \\ -10 &< -16x \\ \frac{-10}{-16} &> \frac{-16x}{-16} \\ \frac{10}{16} &> x \\ \frac{5}{8} &> x \end{aligned}$$

$\frac{5}{8}$

91.
$$\begin{aligned} x(2x-3) &\le 2x^2-5x \\ 2x^2-3x &\le 2x^2-5x \\ 2x^2-2x^2-3x &\le 2x^2-2x^2-5x \\ -3x &\le -5x \\ -3x+5x &\le -5x+5x \\ 2x &\le 0 \\ \frac{2x}{2} &\le \frac{0}{2} \\ x &\le 0 \end{aligned}$$

0

Chapter 2 Review Exercises

1. $5x-x+2x=4x+2x=6x$

2. $0.2z-4.6x-7.4z=-4.6x-7.2z$

3. $\frac{1}{2}x+3+\frac{7}{2}x-5=\frac{8}{2}x-2=4x-2$

4. $\frac{4}{5}y+1+\frac{6}{5}y+2=\frac{10}{5}y+3=2y+3$

5. $2(n-4)+n-10=2n-8+n-10=3n-18$

6. $3(w+2)-(12-w)=3w+6-12+w$
$=4w-6$

7. $x+5-(7x-2)=x+5-7x+2=-6x+7$

8. $y-0.7-(1.4y-3)=y-0.7-1.4y+3$
$=-0.4y+2.3$

9. Let x = number
$3x-7$

10. Let x = number
$2(x+2.8)+3x$

11.
$$\begin{aligned} 8x+4 &= 9x \\ 8x-8x+4 &= 9x-8x \\ 4 &= x \end{aligned}$$

12.
$$\begin{aligned} 5y-3 &= 6y \\ -3 &= y \end{aligned}$$

13.
$$\begin{aligned} 3x-5 &= 4x+1 \\ 3x-3x-5 &= 4x-3x+1 \\ -5 &= x+1 \\ -5-1 &= x+1-1 \\ -6 &= x \end{aligned}$$

14.
$$\begin{aligned} 2x-6 &= x-6 \\ 2x-6+6 &= x-6+6 \\ 2x &= x \\ 2x-x &= x-x \\ x &= 0 \end{aligned}$$

15.
$$\begin{aligned} 4(x+3) &= 3(1+x) \\ 4x+12 &= 3+3x \\ 4x-3x+12 &= 3+3x-3x \\ x+12 &= 3 \\ x+12-12 &= 3-12 \\ x &= -9 \end{aligned}$$

16.
$$\begin{aligned} 6(3+n) &= 5(n-1) \\ 18+6n &= 5n-5 \\ 18+6n-5n &= 5n-5n-5 \\ 18+n &= -5 \\ 18-18+n &= -5-18 \\ n &= -23 \end{aligned}$$

17. 5

18. 9

19. Let x = number
$10-x$ = other number

20. $(x - 5)$ inches

21. $180 - (x + 5) = 180 - x - 5 = 175 - x$ or $(175 - x)°$

22.
$$\frac{3}{4}x = -9$$
$$\frac{4}{3}\left(\frac{3}{4}x\right) = \frac{4}{3}(-9)$$
$$x = -12$$

23.
$$\frac{x}{6} = \frac{2}{3}$$
$$6 \cdot \frac{x}{6} = 6 \cdot \frac{2}{3}$$
$$x = 4$$

24.
$$-3x + 1 = 19$$
$$-3x + 1 - 1 = 19 - 1$$
$$-3x = 18$$
$$\frac{-3x}{-3} = \frac{18}{-3}$$
$$x = -6$$

25.
$$5x + 25 = 20$$
$$5x + 25 - 25 = 20 - 25$$
$$5x = -5$$
$$\frac{5x}{5} = \frac{-5}{5}$$
$$x = -1$$

26.
$$5x + x = 9 + 4x - 1 + 6$$
$$6x = 4x + 14$$
$$-4x + 6x = -4x + 4x + 14$$
$$2x = 14$$
$$\frac{2x}{2} = \frac{14}{2}$$
$$x = 7$$

27.
$$-y + 4y = 7 - y - 3 - 8$$
$$3y = -y - 4$$
$$y + 3y = y - y - 4$$
$$4y = -4$$
$$\frac{4y}{4} = -\frac{4}{4}$$
$$y = -1$$

28. $x + (x + 2) + (x + 4) = 3x + 6$

29.
$$\frac{2}{7}x - \frac{5}{7} = 1$$
$$2x - 5 = 7$$
$$2x = 12$$
$$\frac{2x}{2} = \frac{12}{2}$$
$$x = 6$$

30.
$$\frac{5}{3}x + 4 = \frac{2}{3}x$$
$$\frac{5}{3}x - \frac{5}{3}x + 4 = \frac{2}{3}x - \frac{5}{3}x$$
$$4 = -\frac{3}{3}x$$
$$4 = -x$$
$$\frac{4}{-1} = \frac{-x}{-1}$$
$$-4 = x$$

31.
$$-(5x + 1) = -7x + 3$$
$$-5x - 1 = -7x + 3$$
$$-5x + 7x - 1 = -7x + 7x + 3$$
$$2x - 1 = 3$$
$$2x - 1 + 1 = 3 + 1$$
$$2x = 4$$
$$\frac{2x}{2} = \frac{4}{2}$$
$$x = 2$$

32.
$$-4(2x + 1) = -5x + 5$$
$$-8x - 4 = -5x + 5$$
$$-8x + 5x - 4 = -5x + 5x + 5$$
$$-3x - 4 = 5$$
$$-3x - 4 + 4 = 5 + 4$$
$$-3x = 9$$
$$\frac{-3x}{-3} = \frac{9}{-3}$$
$$x = -3$$

33.
$$-6(2x - 5) = -3(9 + 4x)$$
$$-12x + 30 = -27 - 12x$$
$$-12x + 12x + 30 = -27 - 12x + 12x$$
$$30 = -27$$

No solution

34.
$$3(8y-1)=6(5+4y)$$
$$24y-3=30+24y$$
$$24y-24y-3=30+24y-24y$$
$$-3=30$$
No solution

35.
$$\frac{3(2-z)}{5}=z$$
$$5\cdot\frac{3(2-z)}{5}=5\cdot z$$
$$3(2-z)=5z$$
$$6-3z=5z$$
$$6-3z+3z=5z+3z$$
$$6=8z$$
$$\frac{6}{8}=\frac{8z}{8}$$
$$\frac{6}{8}=z$$
$$z=\frac{3}{4}$$

36.
$$\frac{4(n+2)}{5}=-n$$
$$5\left[\frac{4(n+2)}{5}\right]=5(-n)$$
$$4(n+2)=-5n$$
$$4n+8=-5n$$
$$4n-4n+8=-5n-4n$$
$$8=-9n$$
$$\frac{8}{-9}=\frac{-9n}{-9}$$
$$-\frac{8}{9}=n$$

37.
$$5(2n-3)-1=4(6+2n)$$
$$10n-15-1=24+8n$$
$$10n-16=24+8n$$
$$10n-16+16=24+16+8n$$
$$10n=40+8n$$
$$10n-8n=40+8n-8n$$
$$2n=40$$
$$\frac{2n}{2}=\frac{40}{2}$$
$$n=20$$

38.
$$-2(4y-3)+4=3(5-y)$$
$$-8y+6+4=15-3y$$
$$-8y+10=15-3y$$
$$-8y+3y+10=15-3y+3y$$
$$-5y+10=15$$
$$-5y+10-10=15-10$$
$$-5y=5$$
$$\frac{-5y}{-5}=\frac{5}{-5}$$
$$y=-1$$

39.
$$9z-z+1=6(z-1)+7$$
$$8z+1=6z-6+7$$
$$8z+1=6z+1$$
$$8z-6z+1=6z-6z+1$$
$$2z+1=1$$
$$2z+1-1=1-1$$
$$2z=0$$
$$\frac{2z}{2}=\frac{0}{2}$$
$$z=0$$

40.
$$5t-3-t=3(t+4)-15$$
$$4t-3=3t+12-15$$
$$4t-3=3t-3$$
$$4t-3t-3=3t-3t-3$$
$$t-3=-3$$
$$t-3+3=-3+3$$
$$t=0$$

41.
$$-n+10=2(3n-5)$$
$$-n+10=6n-10$$
$$-n+n+10=6n+n-10$$
$$10=7n-10$$
$$10+10=7n-10+10$$
$$20=7n$$
$$\frac{20}{7}=\frac{7n}{7}$$
$$\frac{20}{7}=n$$

42.

$$\begin{aligned} -9-5a &= 3(6a-1) \\ -9-5a &= 18a-3 \\ -9-5a+5a &= 18a+5a-3 \\ -9 &= 23a-3 \\ -9+3 &= 23a-3+3 \\ -6 &= 23a \\ \frac{-6}{23} &= \frac{23a}{23} \\ -\frac{6}{23} &= a \end{aligned}$$

43.

$$\begin{aligned} \frac{5(c+1)}{6} &= 2c-3 \\ 5(c+1) &= 6(2c-3) \\ 5c+5 &= 12c-18 \\ 5c-5c+5 &= 12c-5c-18 \\ 5 &= 7c-18 \\ 5+18 &= 7c-18+18 \\ 23 &= 7c \\ \frac{23}{7} &= \frac{7c}{7} \\ \frac{23}{7} &= c \end{aligned}$$

44.

$$\begin{aligned} \frac{2(8-a)}{3} &= 4-4a \\ 3\left[\frac{2(8-a)}{3}\right] &= 3(4-4a) \\ 2(8-a) &= 12-12a \\ 16-2a &= 12-12a \\ 16-2a+12a &= 12-12a+12a \\ 16+10a &= 12 \\ 16-16+10a &= 12-16 \\ 10a &= -4 \\ \frac{10a}{10} &= \frac{-4}{10} \\ a &= -\frac{4}{10} = -\frac{2}{5} \end{aligned}$$

45.
$$\begin{aligned}
200(70x-3560) &= -179(150x-19{,}300)\\
14{,}000x-712{,}000 &= -26{,}850x+3{,}454{,}700\\
14{,}000x+26{,}850x-712{,}000 &= -26{,}850x+26{,}850x+3{,}454{,}700\\
40{,}850x-712{,}000 &= 3{,}454{,}700\\
40{,}850x-712{,}000+712{,}000 &= 3{,}454{,}700+712{,}000\\
40{,}850x &= 4{,}166{,}700\\
\frac{40{,}850x}{40{,}850} &= \frac{4{,}166{,}700}{40{,}850}\\
x &= 102
\end{aligned}$$

46.
$$\begin{aligned}
1.72y-0.04y &= 0.42\\
1.68y &= 0.42\\
\frac{1.68y}{1.68} &= \frac{0.42}{1.68}\\
y &= 0.25
\end{aligned}$$

47.
$$\begin{aligned}
\frac{x}{3} &= x-2\\
x &= 3(x-2)\\
x &= 3x-6\\
x-x &= 3x-x-6\\
0 &= 2x-6\\
0+6 &= 2x-6+6\\
6 &= 2x\\
\frac{6}{2} &= \frac{2x}{2}\\
3 &= x
\end{aligned}$$

48. Let x = number
$$\begin{aligned}
2(x+6) &= -x\\
2x+12 &= -x\\
2x-2x+12 &= -x-2x\\
12 &= -3x\\
\frac{12}{-3} &= \frac{-3x}{-3}\\
-4 &= x
\end{aligned}$$

49. Let x = side of base
$$\begin{aligned}
68+3x+x &= 1380\\
68+4x &= 1380\\
68-68+4x &= 1380-68\\
4x &= 1312\\
\frac{4x}{4} &= \frac{1312}{4}\\
x &= 328
\end{aligned}$$
height = 68 + 3(328) = 1052 ft

50. $x+2x=12$
$3x=12$
$\frac{3x}{3}=\frac{12}{3}$
$x=4$
$2x=8$
4 ft and 8 ft

51. Let x = smaller area code
$34+3x+x=1262$
$34+4x=1262$
$34-34+4x=1262-34$
$4x=1228$
$\frac{4x}{4}=\frac{1228}{4}$
$x=307$
$34+3x=955$
The codes are 307 and 955.

52. Let x = smallest integer
$x+(x+2)+(x+4)=-114$
$3x+6=-114$
$3x=-120$
$x=-40$
$x+2=-38$
$x+4=-36$
The integers are –40, –38, and –36.

53. $P=2l+2w$
$46=2(14)+2w$
$46=28+2w$
$18=2w$
$9=w$

54. $V=lwh$
$192=8(6)h$
$192=48h$
$4=h$

55. $y=mx+b$
$y-b=mx+b-b$
$y-b=mx$
$\frac{y-b}{x}=\frac{mx}{x}$
$\frac{y-b}{x}=m$

56. $r=vst-9$
$r+9=vst-9+9$
$r+9=vst$
$\frac{r+9}{vt}=\frac{vst}{vt}$
$\frac{r+9}{vt}=s$

57. $2y-5x=7$
$2y-5x+5x=7+5x$
$2y=7+5x$
$2y-7=7-7+5x$
$2y-7=5x$
$\frac{2y-7}{5}=\frac{5x}{5}$
$\frac{2y-7}{5}=x$

58. $3x-6y=-2$
$3x-3x-6y=-2-3x$
$-6y=-2-3x$
$\frac{-6y}{-6}=\frac{-2-3x}{-6}$
$y=\frac{-2-3x}{-6}$
$y=\frac{-1(-2-3x)}{-1(-6)}$
$y=\frac{2+3x}{6}$

59. $C=\pi D$
$\frac{C}{D}=\frac{\pi D}{D}$
$\frac{C}{D}=\pi$

60. $C=2\pi r$
$\frac{C}{2r}=\frac{2\pi r}{2r}$
$\frac{C}{2r}=\pi$

61.
$$V = lwh$$
$$900 = (20)(w)(3)$$
$$900 = 60w$$
$$\frac{900}{60} = \frac{60w}{60}$$
$$15 = w$$
$w = 15$ meters

62.
$$C = \frac{5}{9}(F - 32)$$
$$C = \frac{5}{9}(104 - 32)$$
$$C = \frac{5}{9}(72)$$
$$C = 40°$$

63.
$$D = RT$$
$$10,000 = 125T$$
$$\frac{10,000}{125} = \frac{125T}{125}$$
80 minutes $= T$
1 hour 20 minutes $= T$

64. $0.12(250) = 30$

65. $1.10(85) = 93.5$

66. Let x = percent
$$9 = x(45)$$
$$\frac{9}{45} = \frac{45x}{45}$$
$$0.2 = x$$
20%

67. Let x = percent
$$59.5 = x(85)$$
$$\frac{59.5}{85} = \frac{85x}{85}$$
$$0.7 = x$$
70%

68. Let x = unknown number
$$137.5 = 1.25x$$
$$\frac{137.5}{1.25} = \frac{1.25x}{1.25}$$
$$110 = x$$

69. Let x = unknown number

$$768 = 0.6x$$
$$\frac{768}{0.6} = \frac{0.6x}{0.6}$$
$$1280 = x$$

70. $0.126(50{,}000) = 6300$

71. 6%; the height of the 'Nap' bar is at 6%.

72. Eat from the Minibar; because this is the tallest bar.

73. $0.40(300) = 120$ travelers

74. No; some business travelers may have chosen more than one category.

75. $\frac{210-180}{210} = \frac{30}{210} = 0.143$

14.3%

76.

Principal · rate · time = interest				
Money Market	x	0.085	1	$0.085x$
C.D.	$50{,}000-x$	0.105	1	$0.105(50{,}000-x)$

$$0.085x + 0.105(50{,}000 - x) = 4550$$
$$0.085x + 5250 - 0.105x = 4550$$
$$-0.02x + 5250 = 4550$$
$$-0.02x + 5250 - 5250 = 4550 - 5250$$
$$-0.02x = -700$$
$$\frac{-0.02x}{-0.02} = \frac{-700}{-0.02}$$
$$x = 35{,}000$$

\$35,000 in the money market and \$15,000 in the C.D.

77. dimes = x

quarters = $2x$

nickels = $500 - 3x$

$$0.10(x) + 0.25(2x) + 0.05(500 - 3x) = 88$$
$$10x + 25(2x) + 5(500 - 3x) = 8800$$
$$10x + 50x + 2500 - 15x = 8800$$
$$45x + 2500 = 8800$$
$$45x = 6300$$
$$\frac{45x}{45} = \frac{6300}{45}$$
$$x = 140, \text{ so}$$

$500 - 3x = 500 - 3(140) = 80$

80 nickels

78.

	Rate	Time	Distance
Passenger Train	60 mph	x	$60x$
Freight Train	45 mph	$x+\frac{3}{2}$	$45\left(x+\frac{3}{2}\right)$

$$60x = 45\left(x+\frac{3}{2}\right)$$
$$60x = 45x+\frac{135}{2}$$
$$120x = 90x+135$$
$$30x = 135$$
$$\frac{30x}{30} = \frac{135}{30}$$
$$x = 4.5 \text{ hrs}$$

79.

	Rate	Time	Distance
Up	8	x	$8x$
Down	12	$5-x$	$12(5-x)$

$$8x = 12(5-x)$$
$$8x = 60-12x$$
$$8x+12x = 60-12x+12x$$
$$20x = 60$$
$$\frac{20x}{20} = \frac{60}{20}$$
$$x = 3$$
$$8(3) = 24$$
$$12(5-3) = 24$$

Round trip distance: 48 miles

80. $x \le -2$

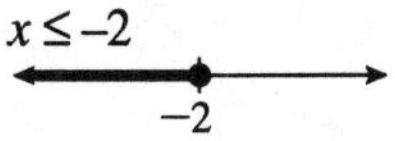

−2

81. $x > 0$

0

82. $-1 < x < 1$

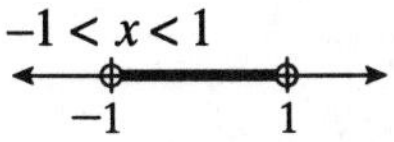

−1 1

83. $0.5 \le y < 1.5$

0.5 1.5

84. $-2x \ge -20$

$\frac{-2x}{-2} \le \frac{-20}{-2}$

$x \le 10$

10

85. $-3x > 12$

$\frac{-3x}{-3} < \frac{12}{-3}$

$x < -4$

−4

86. $5x - 7 > 8x + 5$

$5x - 7 - 5x > 8x - 5x + 5$

$-7 > 3x + 5$

$-7 - 5 > 3x + 5 - 5$

$-12 > 3x$

$\frac{-12}{3} > \frac{3x}{3}$

$-4 > x$

−4

87. $x + 4 \ge 6x - 16$

$x - x + 4 \ge 6x - x - 16$

$4 \ge 5x - 16$

$4 + 16 \ge 5x - 16 + 16$

$20 \ge 5x$

$\frac{20}{5} \ge \frac{5x}{5}$

$4 \ge x$

4

88. $2 \le 3x - 4 < 6$

$2 + 4 \le 3x - 4 + 4 < 6 + 4$

$6 \le 3x < 10$

$\frac{6}{3} \le \frac{3x}{3} < \frac{10}{3}$

$2 \le x < \frac{10}{3}$

2 $\frac{10}{3}$

89. $-3 < 4x - 1 < 2$

$-3 + 1 < 4x - 1 + 1 < 2 + 1$

$-2 < 4x < 3$

$\frac{-2}{4} < \frac{4x}{4} < \frac{3}{4}$

$-\frac{1}{2} < x < \frac{3}{4}$

$-\frac{1}{2}$ $\frac{3}{4}$

90. $-2(x - 5) > 2(3x - 2)$

$-2x + 10 > 6x - 4$

$-2x + 2x + 10 > 6x + 2x - 4$

$10 > 8x - 4$

$10 + 4 > 8x - 4 + 4$

$14 > 8x$

$\frac{14}{8} > \frac{8x}{8}$

$\frac{7}{4} > x$

$\frac{7}{4}$

91. $4(2x - 5) \le 5x - 1$

$8x - 20 \le 5x - 1$

$8x - 5x - 20 \le 5x - 5x - 1$

$3x - 20 \le -1$

$3x - 20 + 20 \le -1 + 20$

$3x \le 19$

$\frac{3x}{3} \le \frac{19}{3}$

$x \le \frac{19}{3}$

$x \le 6\frac{1}{3}$

$\frac{19}{3}$

92. $175 + 0.05(x) \ge 300$

$17{,}500 + 5x \ge 30{,}000$

$5x \ge 12{,}500$

$\frac{5x}{5} \ge \frac{12{,}500}{5}$

$x \ge 2500$

Her minimum sales must be \$2500.

93. Let x = score on next round

$$\frac{76+82+79+x}{4} < 80$$
$$4\left[\frac{76+82+79+x}{4}\right] < 4(80)$$
$$76+82+79+x < 320$$
$$237+x < 320$$
$$237-237+x < 320-237$$
$$x < 83$$

Her next score must be less than 83.

Chapter 2 Test

1. $2y-6-y-4 = y-10$

2. $2.7x + 6.1 + 3.2x - 4.9 = 5.9x + 1.2$

3. $4(x-2)-3(2x-6) = 4x-8-6x+18 = -2x + 10$

4.
$$-5(y+1)+2(3-5y) = -5y-5+6-10y$$
$$= -15y+1$$

5.
$$-\frac{4}{5}x = 4$$
$$-\frac{5}{4}\left(-\frac{4}{5}x\right) = -\frac{5}{4}(4)$$
$$x = -5$$

6.
$$4(n-5) = -(4-2n)$$
$$4n-20 = -4+2n$$
$$4n-2n-20 = -4+2n-2n$$
$$2n-20 = -4$$
$$2n-20+20 = -4+20$$
$$2n = 16$$
$$\frac{2n}{2} = \frac{16}{2}$$
$$n = 8$$

7.
$$5y-7+y = -(y+3y)$$
$$5y-7+y = -y-3y$$
$$6y-7 = -4y$$
$$6y-6y-7 = -4y-6y$$
$$-7 = -10y$$
$$\frac{-7}{-10} = \frac{-10y}{-10}$$
$$\frac{-7}{-10} = y$$
$$\frac{7}{10} = y$$

8.
$$4z+1-z = 1+z$$
$$3z+1 = 1+z$$
$$3z-z+1 = 1+z-z$$
$$2z+1 = 1$$
$$2z+1-1 = 1-1$$
$$2z = 0$$
$$\frac{2z}{2} = \frac{0}{2}$$
$$z = 0$$

9.
$$\frac{2(x+6)}{3} = x-5$$
$$3\left[\frac{2(x+6)}{3}\right] = 3(x-5)$$
$$2(x+6) = 3(x-5)$$
$$2x+12 = 3x-15$$
$$2x-2x+12 = 3x-2x-15$$
$$12 = x-15$$
$$12+15 = x-15+15$$
$$27 = x$$

10.
$$\frac{4(y-1)}{5}=2y+3$$
$$5\left[\frac{4(y-1)}{5}\right]=5(2y+3)$$
$$4(y-1)=5(2y+3)$$
$$4y-4=10y+15$$
$$4y-10y-4=10y-10y+15$$
$$-6y-4=15$$
$$-6y-4+4=15+4$$
$$-6y=19$$
$$\frac{-6y}{-6}=\frac{19}{-6}$$
$$y=-\frac{19}{6}$$

11.
$$\frac{1}{2}-x+\frac{3}{2}=x-4$$
$$-x+\frac{4}{2}=x-4$$
$$-x+2=x-4$$
$$-x+x+2=x+x-4$$
$$2=2x-4$$
$$2+4=2x-4+4$$
$$6=2x$$
$$\frac{6}{2}=\frac{2x}{2}$$
$$3=x$$

12.
$$\frac{1}{3}(y+3)=4y$$
$$3\left[\frac{1}{3}(y+3)\right]=3(4y)$$
$$y+3=12y$$
$$y-y+3=12y-y$$
$$3=11y$$
$$\frac{3}{11}=\frac{11y}{11}$$
$$\frac{3}{11}=y$$

13.
$$-0.3(x-4)+x=0.5(3-x)$$
$$-3(x-4)+10x=5(3-x)$$
$$-3x+12+10x=15-5x$$
$$12+7x=15-5x$$
$$12+7x+5x=15-5x+5x$$
$$12+12x=15$$
$$12-12+12x=15-12$$
$$12x=3$$
$$\frac{12x}{12}=\frac{3}{12}$$
$$x=0.25$$

14.
$$-4(a+1)-3a=-7(2a-3)$$
$$-4a-4-3a=-14a+21$$
$$-7a-4=-14a+21$$
$$-7a+14a-4=-14a+14a+21$$
$$7a-4=21$$
$$7a-4+4=21+4$$
$$7a=25$$
$$\frac{7a}{7}=\frac{25}{7}$$
$$a=\frac{25}{7}$$

15. Let x = number
$$x+\frac{2}{3}x=35$$
$$\frac{3}{3}x+\frac{2}{3}x=35$$
$$\frac{5}{3}x=35$$
$$\frac{3}{5}\left(\frac{5}{3}x\right)=\frac{3}{5}(35)$$
$$x=21$$

16. Area of deck

$A = lw$

$A = (20\text{ ft})(35\text{ ft})$

$A = 700$ sq ft

Two coats are needed.

Twice the Area = 2(700 sq ft)

Twice the Area = 1400 sq ft

$$\frac{1400\text{ sq ft}}{200\text{ sq ft / gal}}$$

7 gallons

17.

Principal · rate · time = interest				
Amoxil	x	0.10	1	$0.10x$
IBM	$2x$	0.12	1	$0.24x$

$$0.10x + 0.24x = 2890$$
$$0.34x = 2890$$
$$x = 8500$$
$2x = 17{,}000$
Amoxil: $8500
IBM: $17,000

18.

rate · time = distance			
1st train	50	x	$50x$
2nd train	64	x	$64x$

$$50x + 64x = 285$$
$$114x = 285$$
$$\frac{114x}{114} = \frac{285}{114}$$
$x = 2.5$ hours

19.
$$y = mx + b$$
$$-14 = -2x - 2$$
$$-12 = -2x$$
$$6 = x$$

20.
$$V = \pi r^2 h$$
$$\frac{V}{\pi r^2} = \frac{\pi r^2 h}{\pi r^2}$$
$$\frac{V}{\pi r^2} = h$$

21.
$$3x - 4y = 10$$
$$3x - 3x - 4y = 10 - 3x$$
$$-4y = 10 - 3x$$
$$\frac{-4y}{-4} = \frac{10 - 3x}{-4}$$
$$y = \frac{10 - 3x}{-4}$$
$$y = \frac{-1(10 - 3x)}{-1(-4)}$$
$$y = \frac{-10 + 3x}{4}$$
$$y = \frac{3x - 10}{4}$$

22.
$$3x - 5 > 7x + 3$$
$$3x - 7x - 5 > 7x - 7x + 3$$
$$-4x - 5 > 3$$
$$-4x - 5 + 5 > 3 + 5$$
$$-4x > 8$$
$$\frac{-4x}{-4} < \frac{8}{-4}$$
$$x < -2$$

−2

23.
$$x + 6 > 4x - 6$$
$$x - 4x + 6 > 4x - 4x - 6$$
$$-3x + 6 > -6$$
$$-3x + 6 - 6 > -6 - 6$$
$$-3x > -12$$
$$\frac{-3x}{-3} < \frac{-12}{-3}$$
$$x < 4$$

4

24.
$$-2 < 3x + 1 < 8$$
$$-2 - 1 < 3x + 1 - 1 < 8 - 1$$
$$-3 < 3x < 7$$
$$-\frac{3}{3} < \frac{3x}{3} < \frac{7}{3}$$
$$-1 < x < \frac{7}{3}$$
$$-1 < x < 2\frac{1}{3}$$

−1　　$\frac{7}{3}$

25. $0 < 4x - 7 < 9$
$0 + 7 < 4x - 7 + 7 < 9 + 7$
$7 < 4x < 16$
$\frac{7}{4} < \frac{4x}{4} < \frac{16}{4}$
$\frac{7}{4} < x < 4$
$1\frac{3}{4} < x < 4$

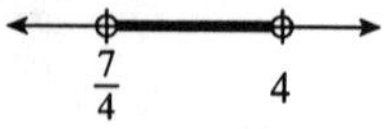

26.
$$\frac{2(5x+1)}{3} > 2$$
$$3\left[\frac{2(5x+1)}{3}\right] > 3(2)$$
$$2(5x+1) > 3(2)$$
$$10x + 2 > 6$$
$$10x + 2 - 2 > 6 - 2$$
$$10x > 4$$
$$\frac{10x}{10} > \frac{4}{10}$$
$$x > \frac{4}{10}$$
$$x > \frac{2}{5}$$

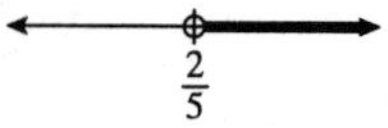

27. 81.3%

28. $0.047(126.2) = \$5.9314$ billion

29. $0.067(360) = 24.12°$

30. 17%; the bar for 1997, e-mail extends to 17%.

31. $37\% - 24\% = 13\%$; the lengths of the bars for computers for 1997 and 1994 are 37% and 24% respectively.

32. 26% of $23,000 = 0.26(23,000)$
$= 5980$

Chapter 3

Section 3.1

Mental Math

1. Answers may vary; Ex. (5, 5), (7, 3)
2. Answers may vary; Ex. (0, 6), (6, 0)
3. Answers may vary; Ex. (3, 5), (3, 0)
4. Answers may vary; Ex. (0, –2), (1, –2)

Exercise Set 3.1

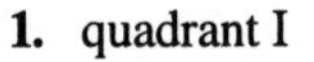

1. quadrant I

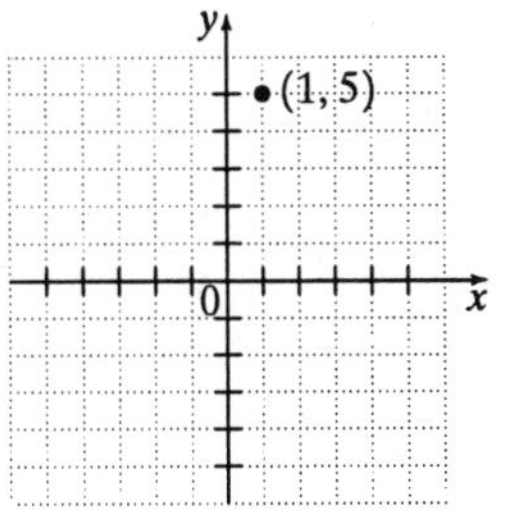

3. no quadrant, x-axis

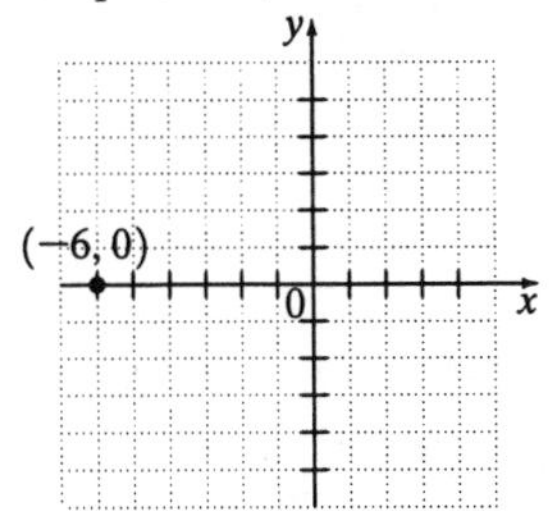

5. quadrant IV

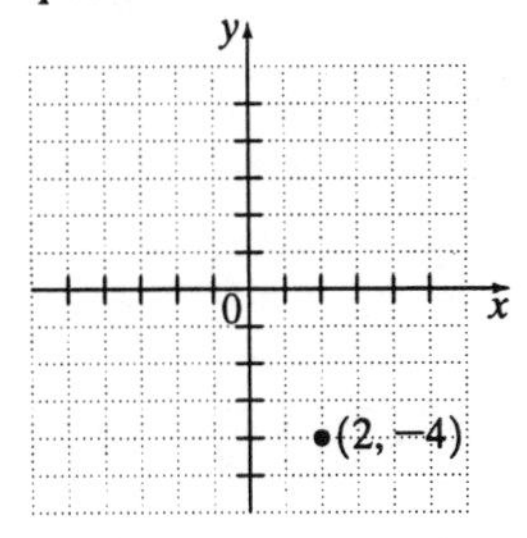

7. no quadrant, x-axis

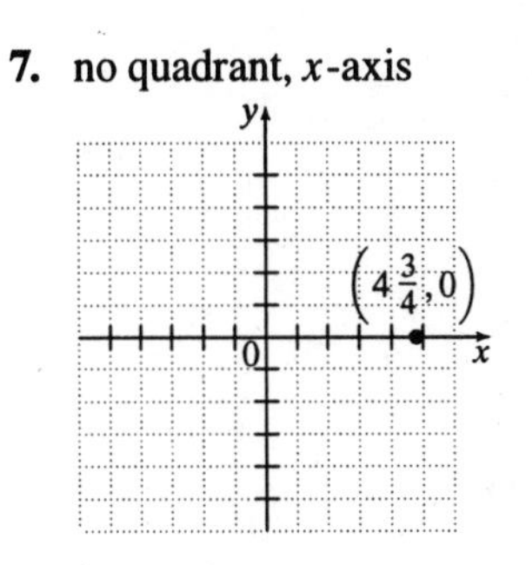

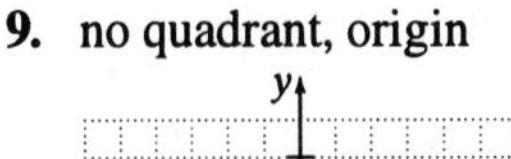

9. no quadrant, origin

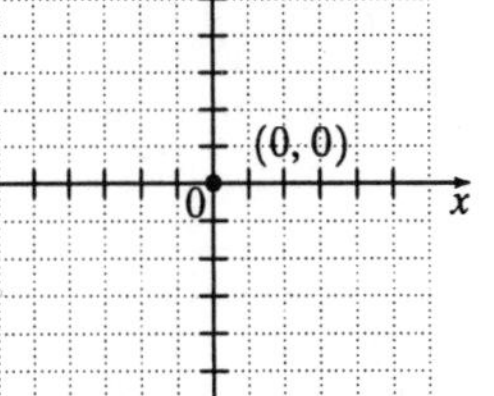

11. no quadrant, y-axis

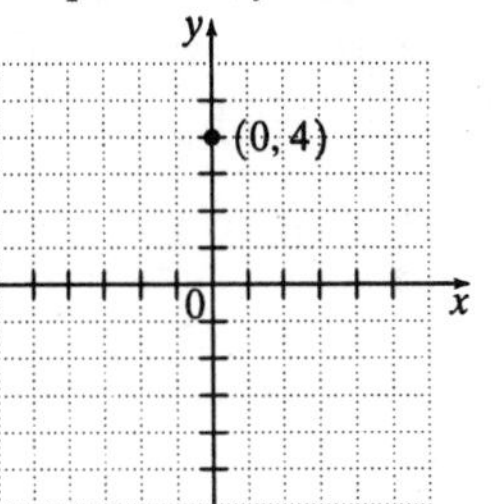

13. A: (0, 0); B: $\left(3\frac{1}{2}, 0\right)$; C: (3, 2); D: (–1, 3); E: (–2, –2); F: (0, –1); G: (2, –1)

15. 2(4) + 2(9) = 26 units

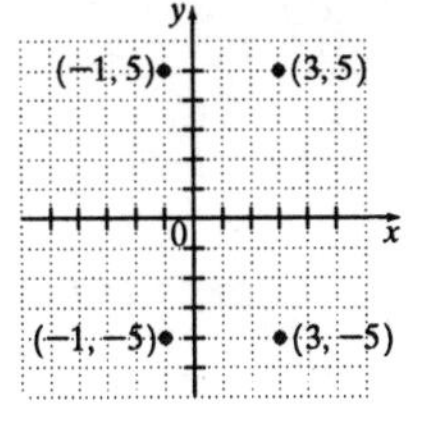

17. a. (1991, 1.14), (1992, 1.13), (1993, 1.11), (1994, 1.11), (1995, 1.15), (1996, 1.23), (1997, 1.23), (1998, 1.06), (1999, 1.17)

b.

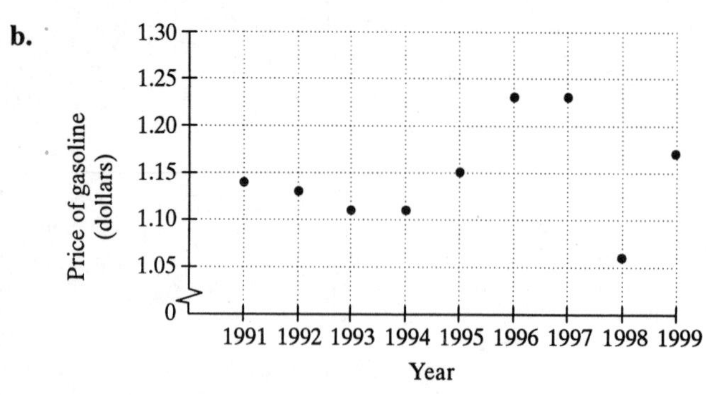

19. a. (1994, 578), (1995, 613), (1996, 654), (1997, 675), (1998, 717)

b.

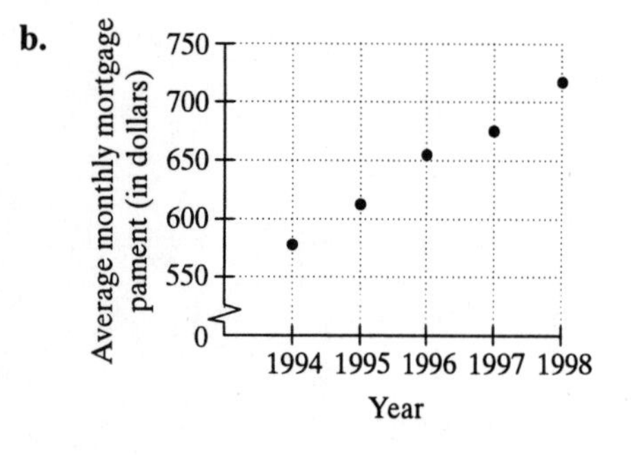

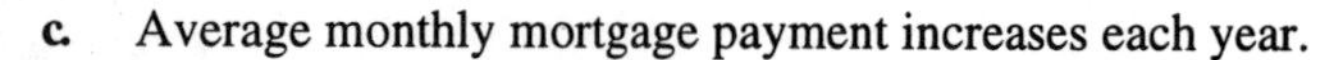
c. Average monthly mortgage payment increases each year.

21.

(3, 1)

$$2x + y = 7$$
$$2(3) + 1 \; ? \; 7$$
$$6 + 1 \; ? \; 7$$
$$7 = 7$$

yes

(7, 0)

$$2x + y = 7$$
$$2(7) + 0 \; ? \; 7$$
$$14 + 0 \; ? \; 7$$
$$14 \neq 7$$

no

(0, 7)

$$2x + y = 7$$
$$2(0) + 7 \; ? \; 7$$
$$0 + 7 \; ? \; 7$$
$$7 = 7$$

yes

23.

$(-1, -5)$ no
$$y = -5x$$
$$-5 \ ? -5(-1)$$
$$-5 \neq +5$$

$(0, 0)$ yes
$$y = -5x$$
$$0 \ ? -5(0)$$
$$0 = 0$$

$(2, -10)$ yes
$$y = -5x$$
$$-10 \ ? -5(2)$$
$$-10 = -10$$

25.
$$x = 5$$
$(4, 5)$ $4 \neq 5$ no
$(5, 4)$ $5 = 5$ yes
$(5, 0)$ $5 = 5$ yes

27.

$(5, 2)$ yes
$$x + 2y = 9;$$
$$5 + 2(2) \ ? \ 9$$
$$5 + 4 \ ? \ 9$$
$$9 = 9$$

$(0, 9)$ no
$$x + 2y = 9$$
$$0 + 2(9) \ ? \ 9$$
$$18 \neq 9$$

29.

$(3, -4)$ no
$$2x - y = 11$$
$$2(3) - (-4) \ ? \ 11$$
$$6 + 4 \ ? \ 11$$
$$10 \neq 11$$

$(9, 8)$ no
$$2x - y = 11$$
$$2(9) - 8 \ ? \ 11$$
$$18 - 8 \ ? \ 11$$
$$10 \neq 11$$

31.

$(0, 0)$ yes
$$x = \frac{1}{3}y$$
$$0 \ ? \ \frac{1}{3}(0)$$
$$0 = 0$$

$(3, 9)$ yes
$$x = \frac{1}{3}y$$
$$3 \ ? \ \frac{1}{3}(9)$$
$$3 = 3$$

33.

$(-2, -2)$ yes
$$y = -2$$
$$-2 = -2$$

$(5, -2)$ yes
$$y = -2$$
$$-2 = -2$$

35.
$$x - 4y = 4$$
$$x - 4(-2) = 4$$
$$x + 8 = 4$$
$$x = -4$$
$(-4, -2)$
$$x - 4y = 4$$
$$4 - 4y = 4$$
$$-4y = 0$$
$$y = 0$$
$(4, 0)$

37.
$$3x + y = 9$$
$$3(0) + y = 9$$
$$0 + y = 9$$
$$y = 9$$
$(0, 9)$

$$3x + y = 9$$
$$3x + 0 = 9$$
$$3x = 9$$
$$x = 3$$
$(3, 0)$

39.
$$y = -7$$
$$y = -7$$
$(11, -7)$

$$y = -7$$
$$-7 = -7$$
identity, true for all x.
Example $(2, -7)$

41.
$$x + 3y = 6$$
Complete (0,):
$$x = 0$$
$$0 + 3y = 6$$
$$y = 2$$
$(0, 2)$
Complete (, 0):
$$y = 0$$
$$x + 3(0) = 6$$
$$x = 6$$
$(6, 0)$

Complete (, 1):

$y = 1$

$x + 3(1) = 6$

$x + 3 = 6$

$x = 3$

(3, 1)

x	y
0	2
6	0
3	1

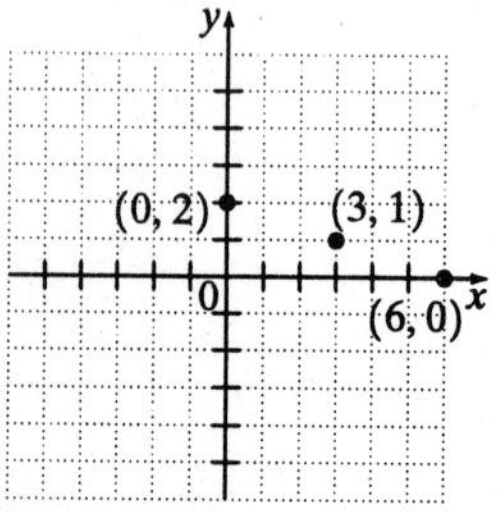

43. $2x - y = 12$

Complete (0,):

$x = 0$

$2(0) - y = 12$

$-y = 12$

$y = -12$

(0, –12)

Complete (, –2):

$y = -2$

$2x - (-2) = 12$

$2x + 2 = 12$

$2x = 10$

$x = 5$

(5, –2)

Complete (–3,):

$x = -3$

$2(-3) - y = 12$

$-6 - y = 12$

$-y = 18$

$y = -18$

(3, –18)

x	y
0	–12
5	–2
–3	–18

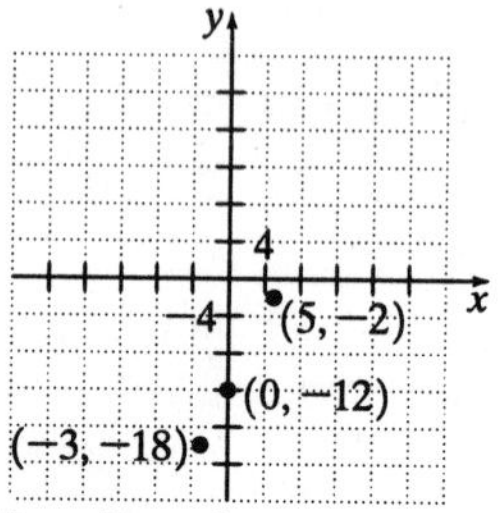

45. $2x + 7y = 5$

Complete (0,):

$x = 0$

$2(0) + 7y = 5$

$7y = 5$

$y = \frac{5}{7}$

$\left(0, \frac{5}{7}\right)$

Complete (, 0):

$y = 0$

$2x + 7(0) = 5$

$2x = 5$

$x = \frac{5}{2}$

$\left(\frac{5}{2}, 0\right)$

Complete (, 1):

$y = 1$

$2x + 7(1) = 5$

$2x + 7 = 5$

$2x = -2$

$x = -1$

(–1, 1)

x	y
0	$\frac{5}{7}$
$\frac{5}{2}$	0
–1	1

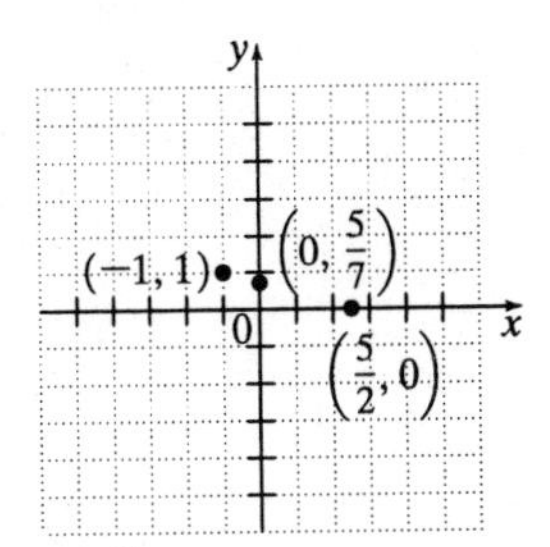

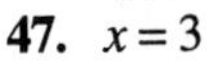

47. $x = 3$
All x table values are 3.

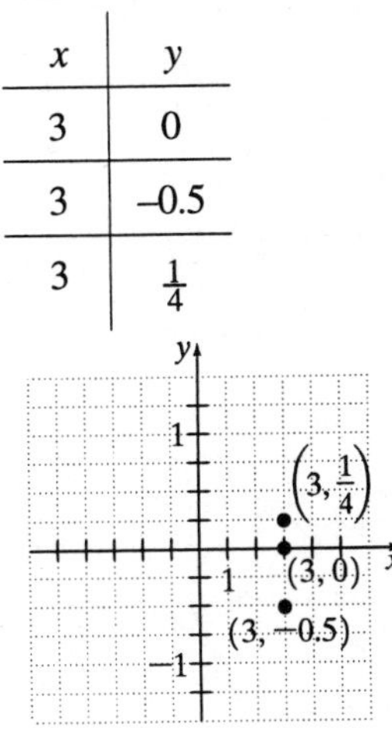

x	y
3	0
3	–0.5
3	$\frac{1}{4}$

49. $x = -5y$
Complete (, 0):
$y = 0$
$x = 5(0)$
$x = 0$
(0, 0)
Complete (, 1):
$y = 1$
$x = -5(1)$
$x = -5$
(–5, 1)
Complete (10,):
$x = 10$
$10 = -5y$
$y = -2$
(10, –2)

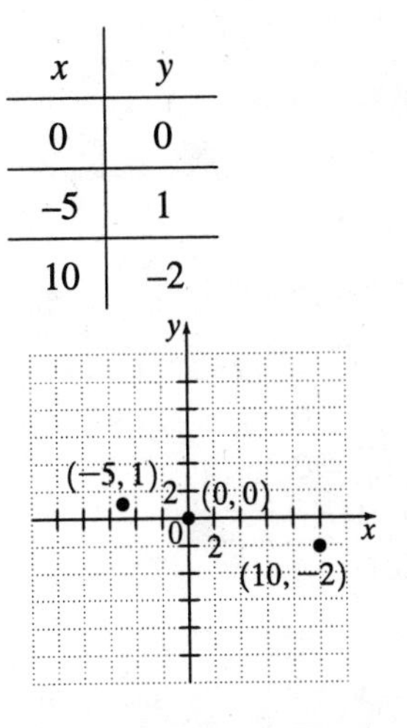

x	y
0	0
–5	1
10	–2

51. Answers may vary.

53. $y = 80(100) + 5000 = 13,000$
$y = 80(200) + 5000 = 21,000$
$y = 80(300) + 5000 = 29,000$

a.

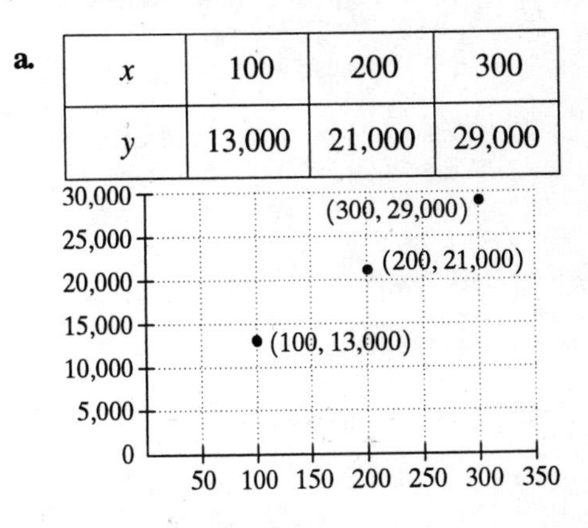

x	100	200	300
y	13,000	21,000	29,000

b.
$$y = 80x + 5000$$
$$8600 = 80x + 5000$$
$$3600 = 80x$$
$$45 = x$$
45 desks can be produced for \$8600.

55. $y = 0.364(20) + 21.939 = 29.219$
$y = 0.364(65) + 21.939 = 45.599$
$y = 0.364(90) + 21.939 = 54.699$

a.

x	20	65	90
y	29.219	45.599	54.699

b.
$$50 = 0.364x + 21.939$$
$$50 - 21.939 = 0.364x + 21.939 - 21.939$$
$$28.061 = 0.364x$$
$$\frac{28.061}{0.364} = \frac{0.364x}{0.364}$$
$$77 = x$$
$1900 + 77 = 1977$
In 1977 the population density was approximately 50 people per square mile.

57. $(5, 670)$
5 corresponds to the year 1995.
670 corresponds to the number of Target stores.
In 1995, these were 670 Target stores.

59. Year 6: $736 - 670 = 66$ stores
Year 7: $796 - 736 = 60$ stores
Year 8: $851 - 796 = 55$ stores

61. when $a = b$

63. $(+, -)$; quadrant IV

65. $(-, y)$; quadrant II or III

67.
$$x + y = 5$$
$$x - x + y = 5 - x$$
$$y = 5 - x$$

69.
$$2x + 4y = 5$$
$$2x - 2x + 4y = 5 - 2x$$
$$4y = 5 - 2x$$
$$\frac{4y}{4} = \frac{5 - 2x}{4}$$
$$y = \frac{5}{4} - \frac{1}{2}x$$

71.
$$10x = -5y$$
$$\frac{10x}{-5} = \frac{-5y}{-5}$$
$$-2x = y$$
or
$$y = -2x$$

73.
$$x - 3y = 6$$
$$x - 3y - x = 6 - x$$
$$-3y = 6 - x$$
$$\frac{-3y}{-3} = \frac{6 - x}{-3}$$
$$y = -2 + \frac{1}{3}x$$

Section 3.2

Graphing Calculator Explorations

1. $y = -3x + 7$

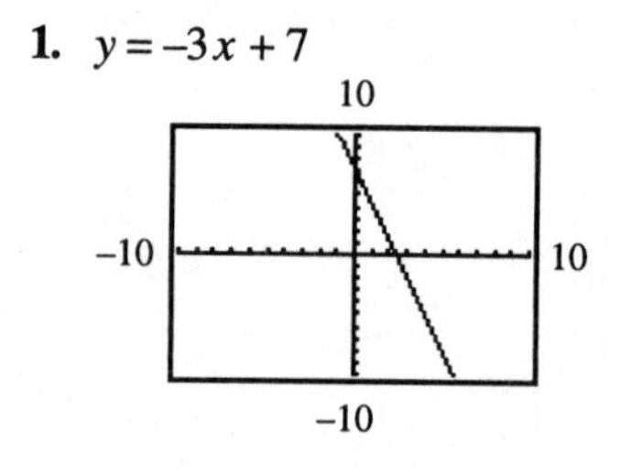

3. $y = 2.5x - 7.9$

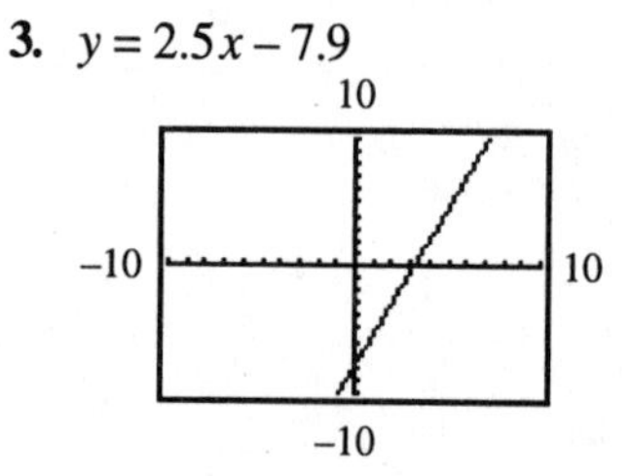

5. $y = -\frac{3}{10}x + \frac{32}{5}$

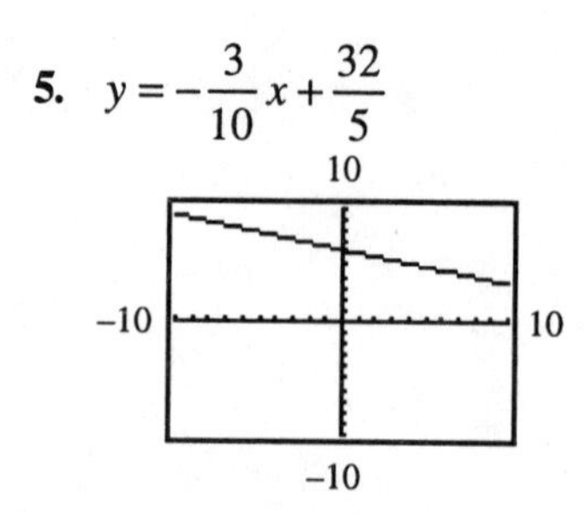

Exercise Set 3.2

1. Yes; it can be written in the form $Ax + By = C$.

3. Yes; it can be written in the form $Ax + By = C$.

5. No; x is squared.

7. Yes; it can be written in the form $Ax + By = C$.

9. $x + y = 4$
   Find three points:

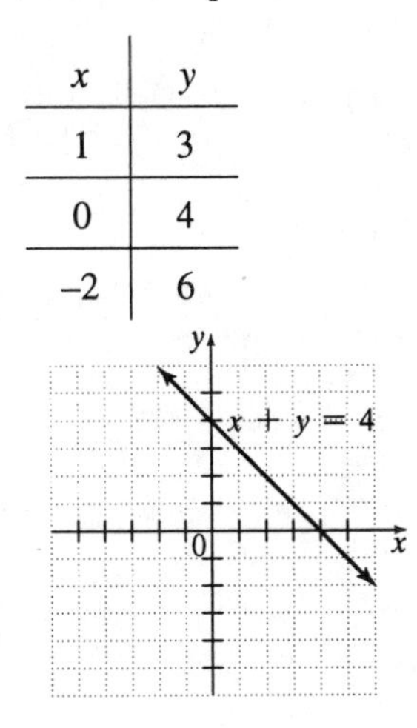

x	y
1	3
0	4
–2	6

11. 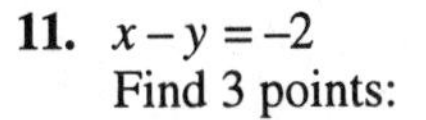
    $x - y = -2$
    Find 3 points:

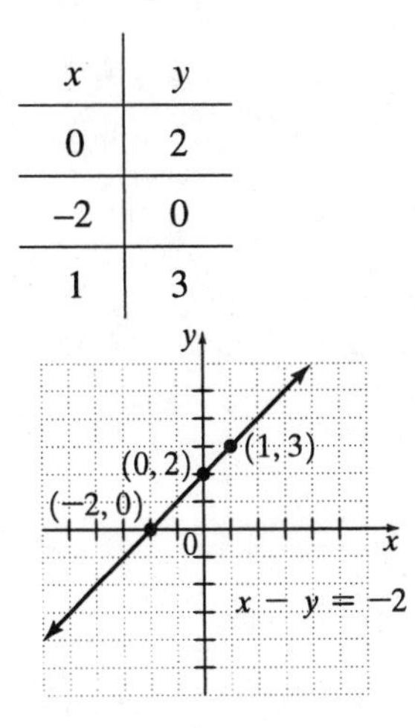

x	y
0	2
–2	0
1	3

13. 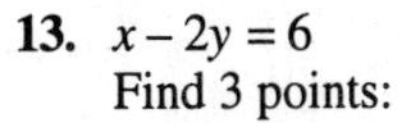
    $x - 2y = 6$
    Find 3 points:

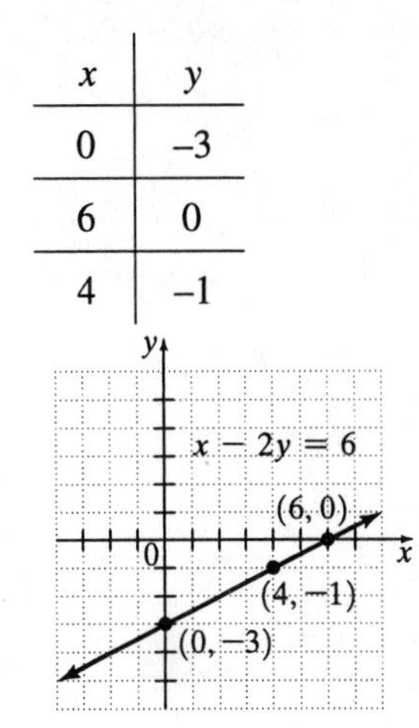

x	y
0	–3
6	0
4	–1

15. $y = 6x + 3$
    Find 3 points:

x	y
0	3
–1	–3
1	9

17. $x - 2y = -6$
Find 3 points:

x	y
0	3
–6	0
–4	1

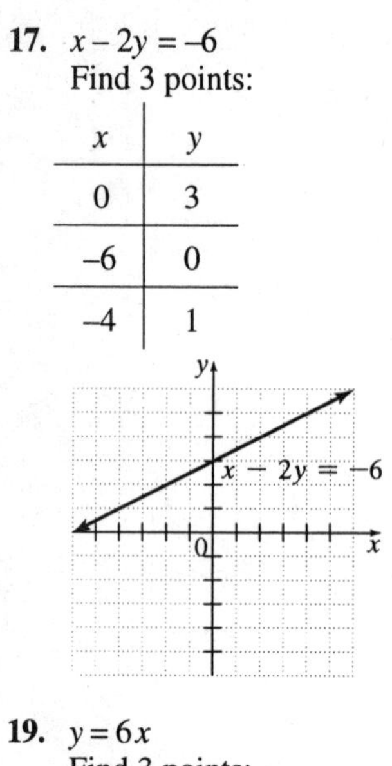

19. $y = 6x$
Find 3 points:

x	y
0	0
1	6
–1	–6

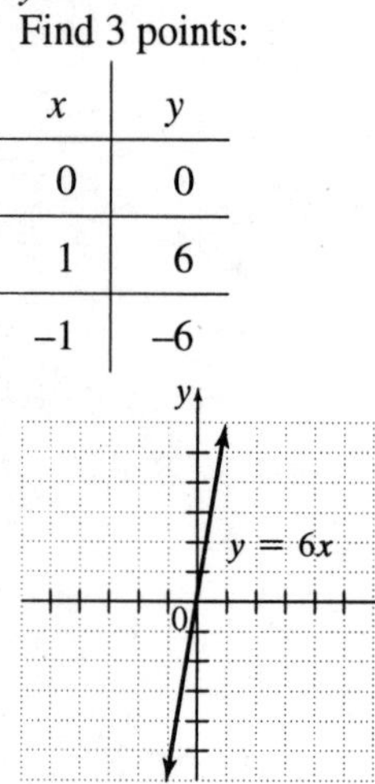

21. $3y - 10 = 5x$
Find 3 points:

x	y
0	$\frac{10}{3}$
–2	0
1	5

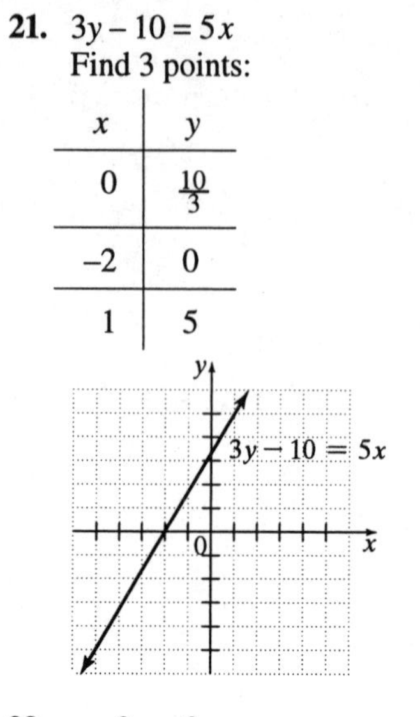

23. $x + 3y = 9$
Find 3 points:

x	y
0	3
3	2
–3	4

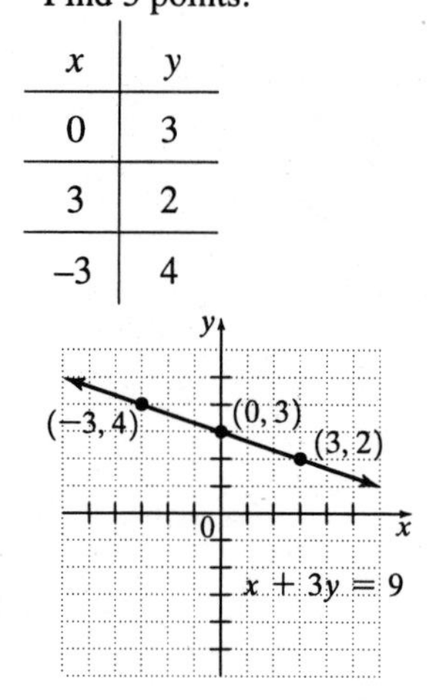

25. $y - x = -1$
Find 3 points:

x	y
0	–1
1	0
2	1

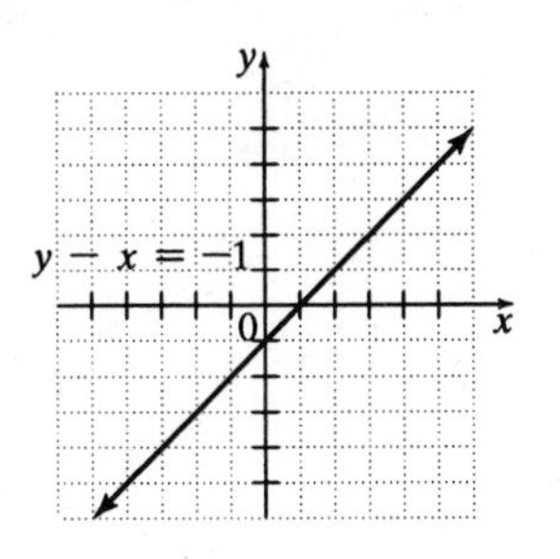

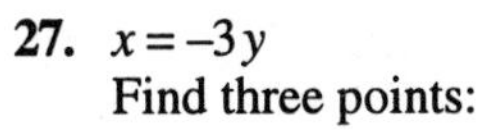

27. $x = -3y$
Find three points:

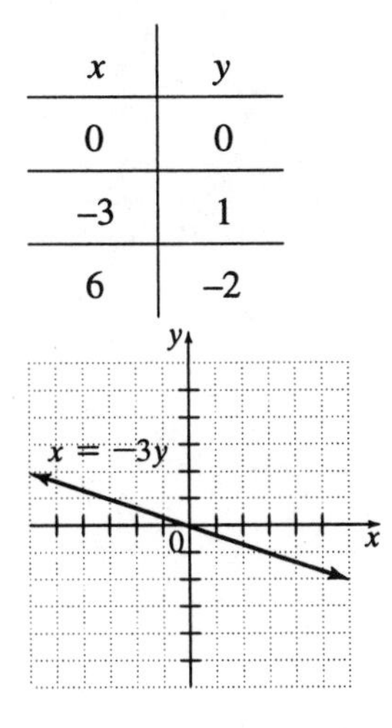

x	y
0	0
–3	1
6	–2

29. $5x - y = 10$
Find three points:

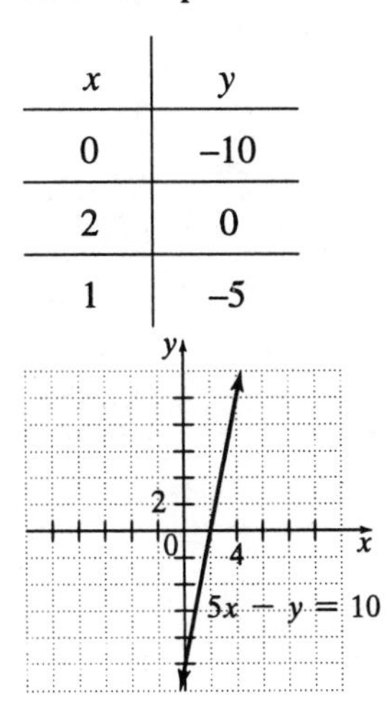

x	y
0	–10
2	0
1	–5

31. $y = \frac{1}{2}x + 2$
Find three points:

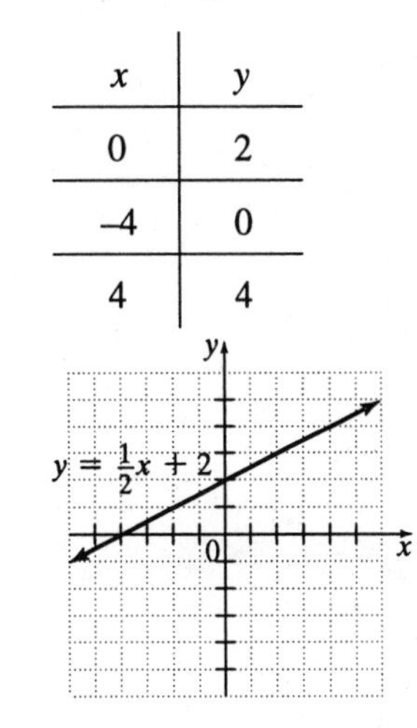

x	y
0	2
–4	0
4	4

33. Find 3 points for each line:

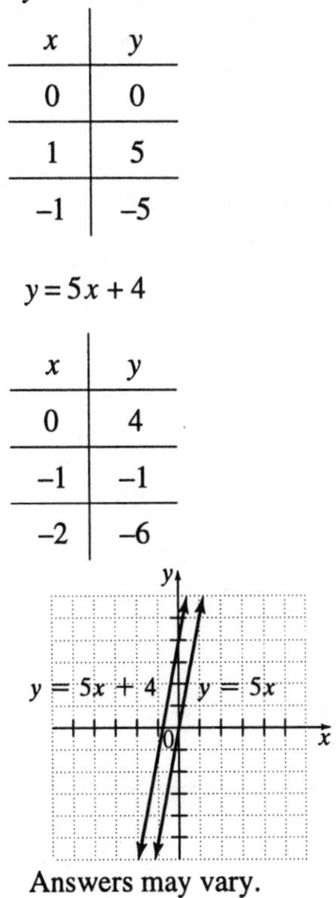

$y = 5x$

x	y
0	0
1	5
–1	–5

$y = 5x + 4$

x	y
0	4
–1	–1
–2	–6

Answers may vary.

35. Find 3 points for each line:

$y = -2x$

x	y
2	–4
0	0
–2	4

$y = -2x - 3$

x	y
–2	1
–1	–1
0	–3

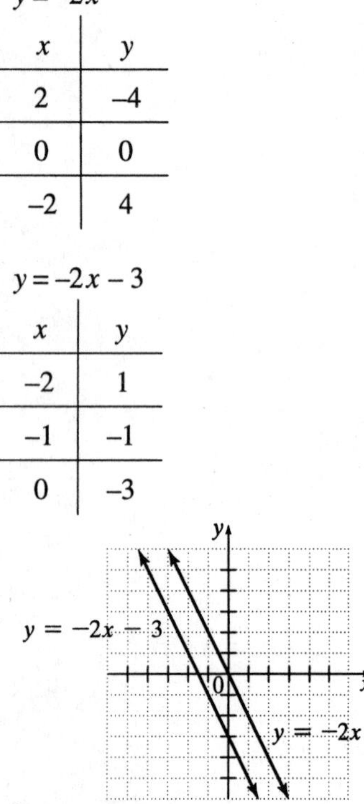

Answers may vary.

37. Find three points for each line.

$y = \frac{1}{2}x + 2$

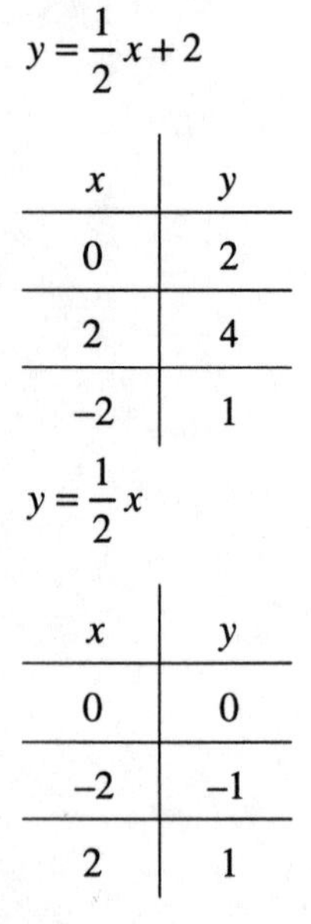

x	y
0	2
2	4
–2	1

$y = \frac{1}{2}x$

x	y
0	0
–2	–1
2	1

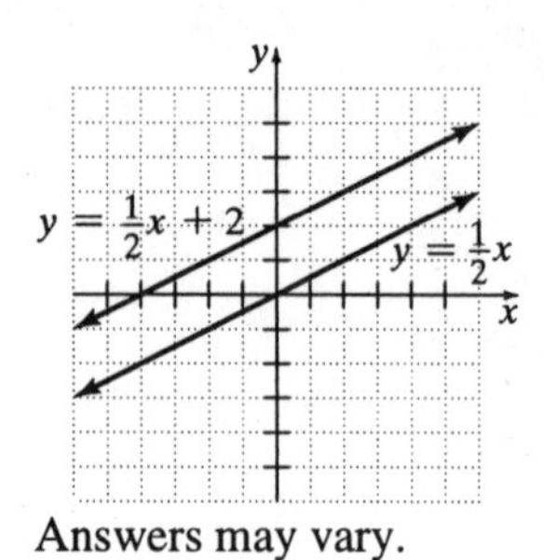

Answers may vary.

39. c

41. d

43. $y = 5x + 15$

x	y
0	15
4	35
10	65

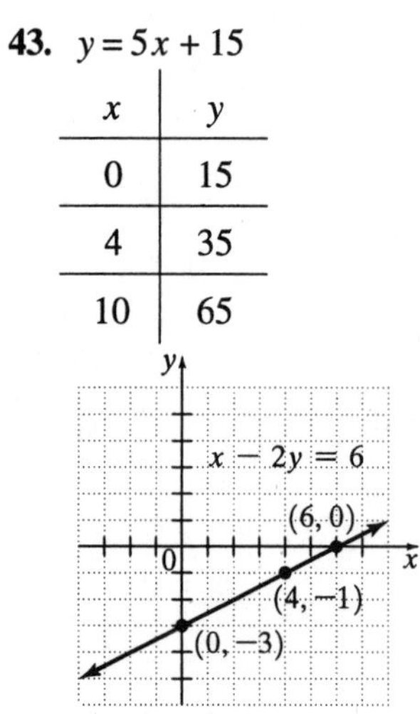

In 2006 ($x = 10$), the revenue will be 65 billion dollars.

45. $y = 20x + 1539$

x	y
0	1539
5	1639
10	1739

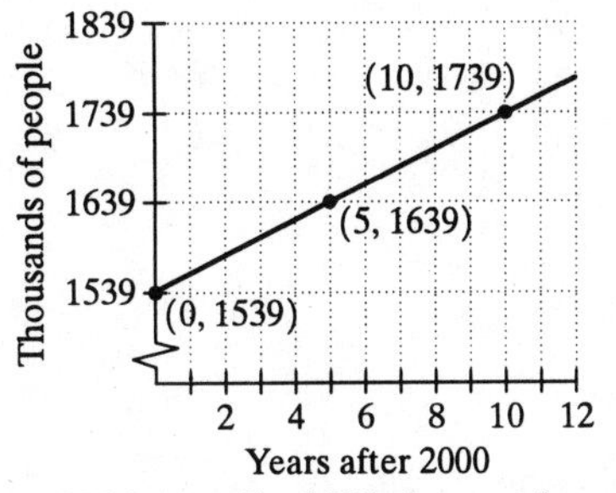

In 2008 ($x = 8$), 1699 thousand people will be employed as elementary teachers.

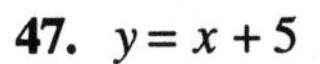

47. $y = x + 5$

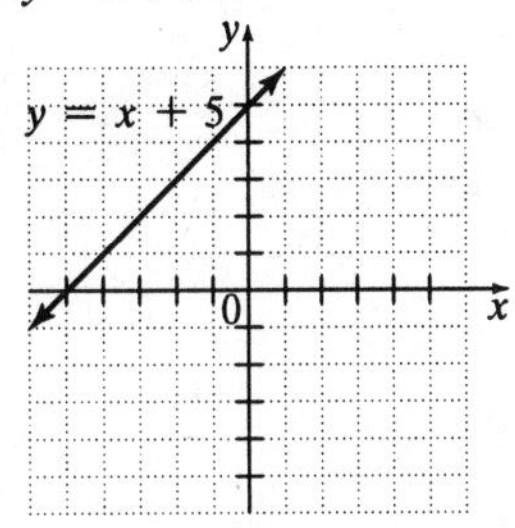

49. $2x + 3y = 6$

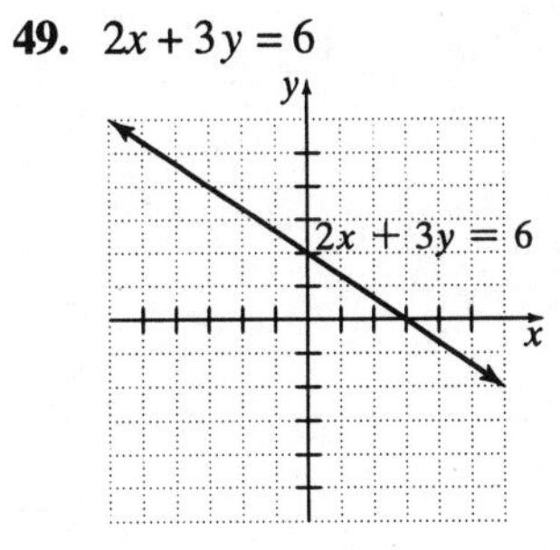

51. Answers may vary.

53. Yes; answers may vary.

55. $y = x^2$

x	y
0	0
1	1
–1	1
2	4
–2	4

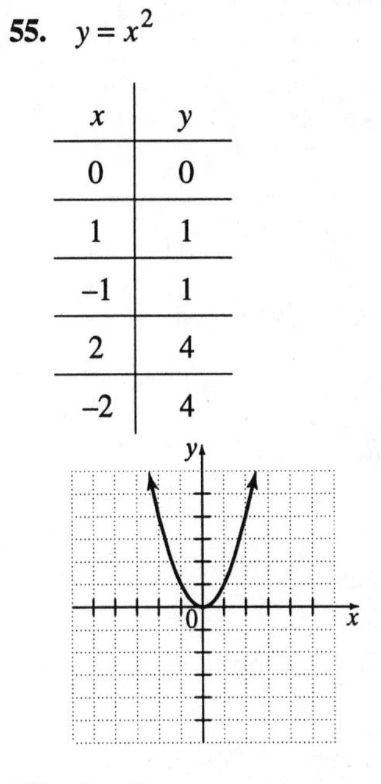

57. $(4, -1)$

59.
$$\begin{aligned} 3(x-2)+5x &= 6x-16 \\ 3x-6+5x &= 6x-16 \\ 8x-6 &= 6x-16 \\ 2x-6 &= -16 \\ 2x &= -10 \\ x &= -5 \end{aligned}$$

61.
$$\begin{aligned} 3x+\frac{2}{5} &= \frac{1}{10} \\ 3x &= \frac{1}{10}-\frac{2}{5} \\ 3x &= \frac{1}{10}-\frac{4}{10} \\ 3x &= -\frac{3}{10} \\ x &= -\frac{1}{10} \end{aligned}$$

63. $x - y = -3$

x	y
0	3
–3	0

65. $y = 2x$

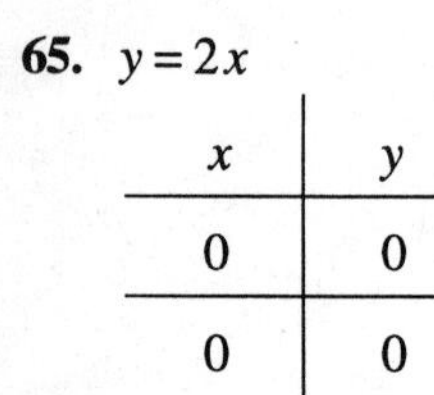

x	y
0	0
0	0

Section 3.3

Graphing Calculator Explorations

1.
$$x = 3.78y$$
$$\frac{x}{3.78} = \frac{3.78y}{3.78}$$
$$\frac{1}{3.78}x = y$$

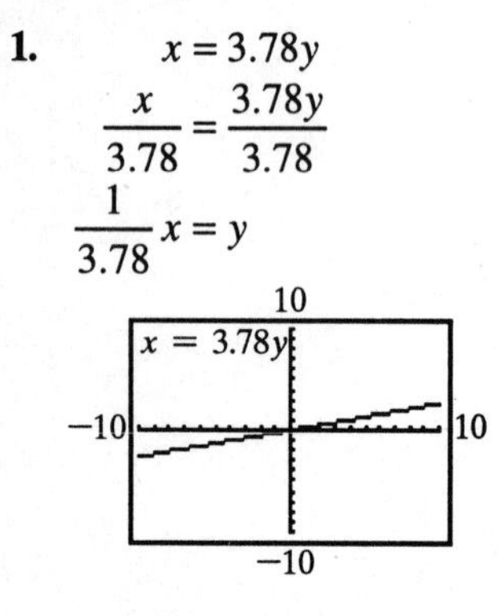

3. $3x + 7y = 21$
$$7y = 21 - 3x$$
$$\frac{7y}{7} = \frac{21}{7} - \frac{3x}{7}$$
$$y = 3 - \frac{3}{7}x$$

5. $-2.2x + 6.8y = 15.5$
$$6.8y = 2.2x + 15.5$$
$$\frac{6.8y}{6.8} = \frac{2.2x}{6.8} + \frac{15.5}{6.8}$$
$$y = 0.32x + 2.3$$

Mental Math

1. False
2. False
3. True
4. True

Exercise Set 3.3

1. (–1, 0); (0, 1)

3. (–2, 0)

5. (–1, 0); (1, 0); (0, 1); (0, –2)

7. infinite

9. zero

11. $x - y = 3$
If $x = 0$, then $y = -3$
If $y = 0$, then $x = 3$
Plot using (0, –3) and (3, 0):

13. $x = 5y$
If $x = 0$, then $y = 0$
Need another point:
If $y = 1$, then $x = 5$
Plot using (0, 0) and (5, 1):

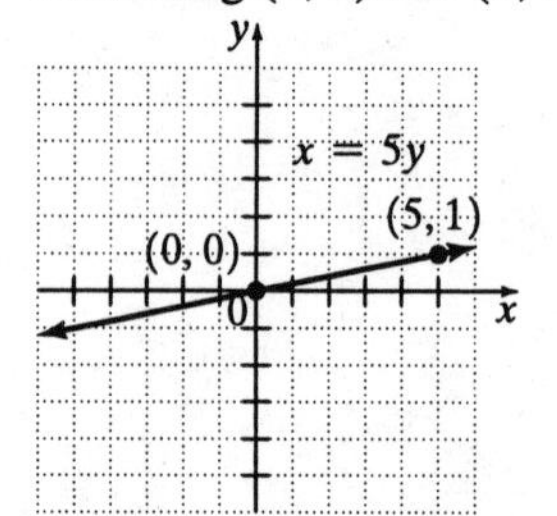

15. $-x+2y=6$
If $x=0$, then $y=3$
If $y=0$, then $x=-6$
Plot using (0, 3) and (– 6, 0):

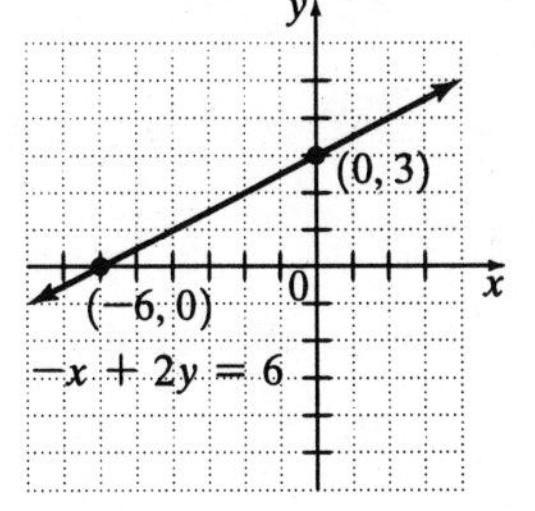

17. $2x-4y=8$
If $x=0$, then $y=-2$
If $y=0$, then $x=4$
Plot using (0, –2) and (4, 0):

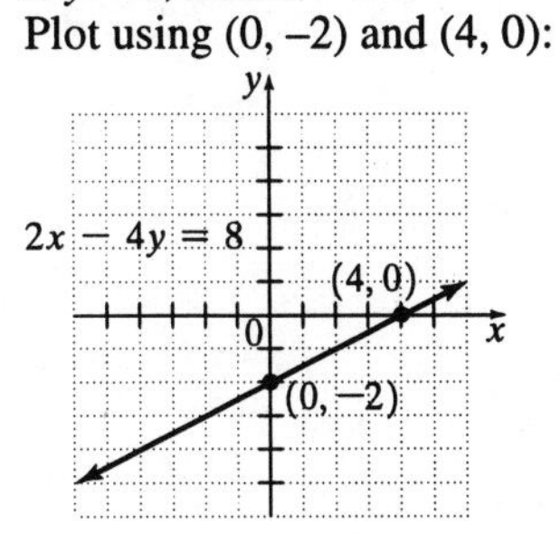

19. $x=-1$
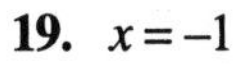
For any y-value, x is –1.

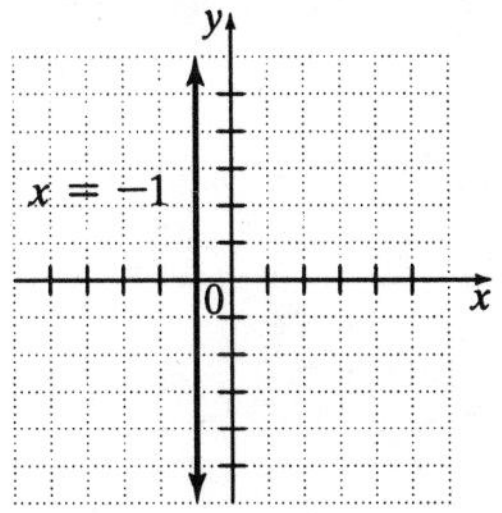

21. $y=0$
For any x-value, y is 0.

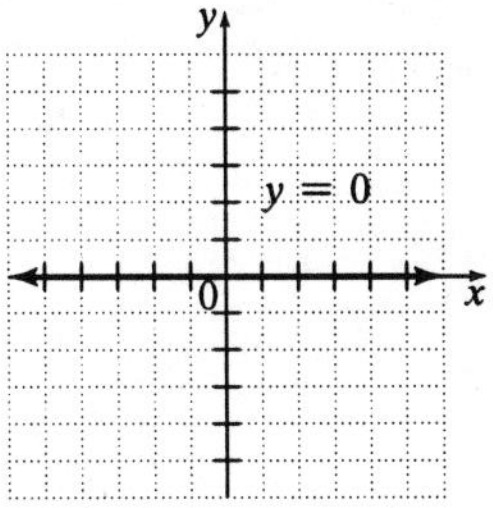

23. $y+7=0$
$y=-7$
For any x-value, y is –7.

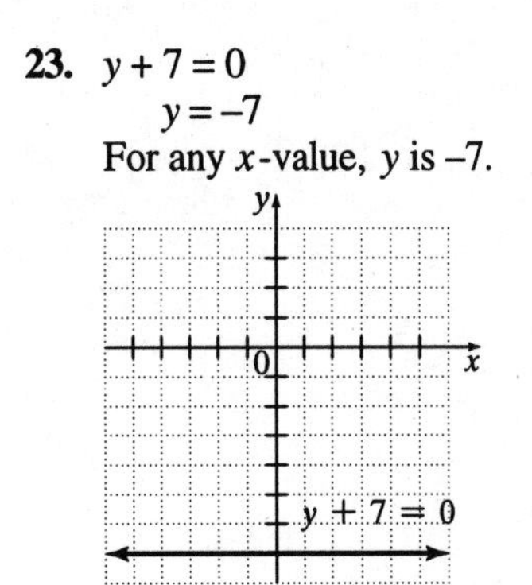

25. $x + 2y = 8$

Let $x = 0$,	$y = 0$,	$y = 1$
$0 + 2y = 8$	$x + 2(0) = 8$	$x + 2(1) = 8$
$2y = 8$	$x + 0 = 8$	$x + 2 = 8$
$y = 4$	$x = 8$	$x = 6$
$(0, 4)$	$(8, 0)$	$(6, 1)$

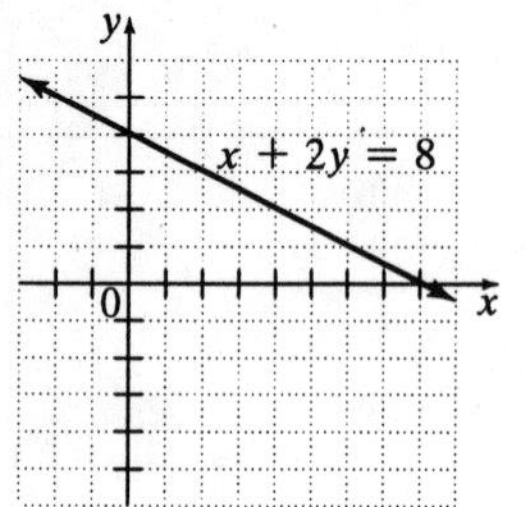

27. $x - 7 = 3y$

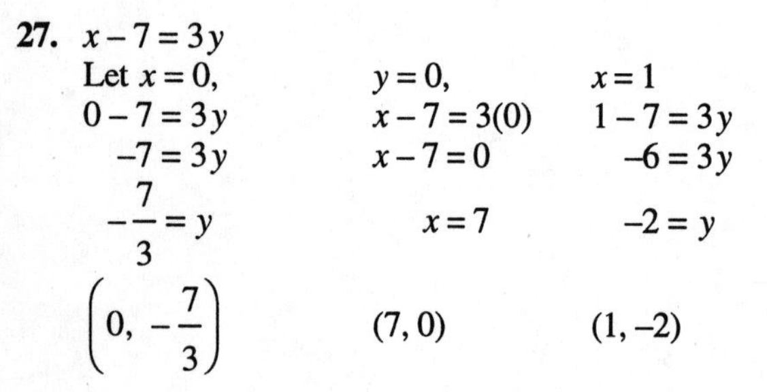

Let $x = 0$,	$y = 0$,	$x = 1$
$0 - 7 = 3y$	$x - 7 = 3(0)$	$1 - 7 = 3y$
$-7 = 3y$	$x - 7 = 0$	$-6 = 3y$
$-\frac{7}{3} = y$	$x = 7$	$-2 = y$
$\left(0, -\frac{7}{3}\right)$	$(7, 0)$	$(1, -2)$

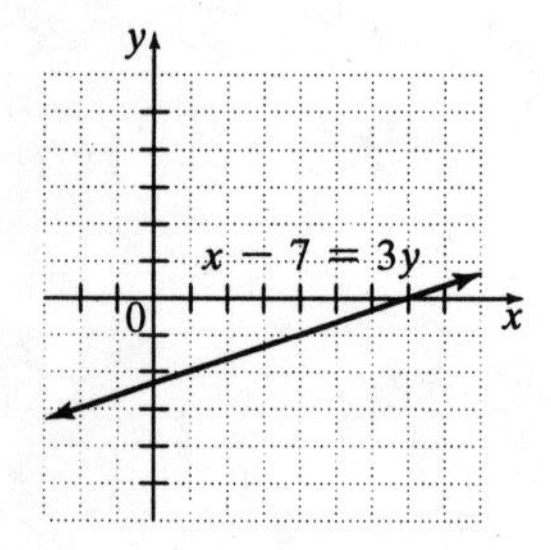

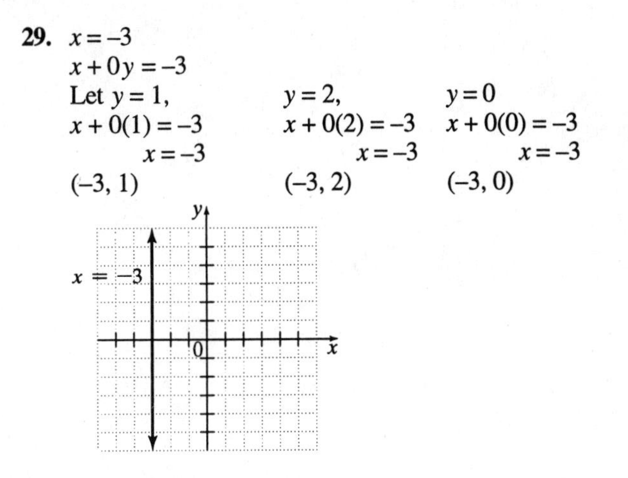

29. $x = -3$

$x + 0y = -3$

Let $y = 1$,	$y = 2$,	$y = 0$
$x + 0(1) = -3$	$x + 0(2) = -3$	$x + 0(0) = -3$
$x = -3$	$x = -3$	$x = -3$
$(-3, 1)$	$(-3, 2)$	$(-3, 0)$

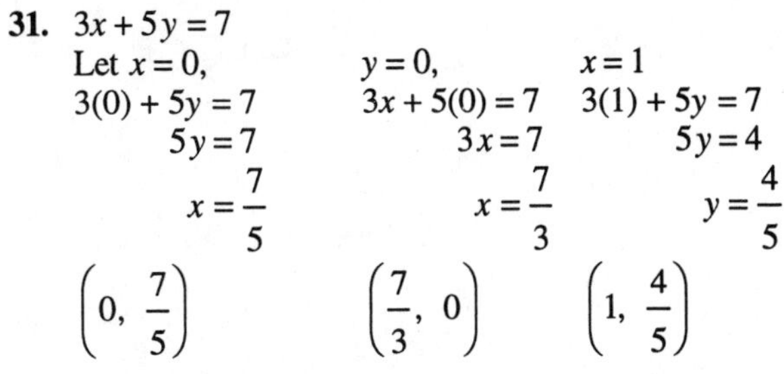

31. $3x + 5y = 7$

Let $x = 0$,	$y = 0$,	$x = 1$
$3(0) + 5y = 7$	$3x + 5(0) = 7$	$3(1) + 5y = 7$
$5y = 7$	$3x = 7$	$5y = 4$
$x = \frac{7}{5}$	$x = \frac{7}{3}$	$y = \frac{4}{5}$
$\left(0, \frac{7}{5}\right)$	$\left(\frac{7}{3}, 0\right)$	$\left(1, \frac{4}{5}\right)$

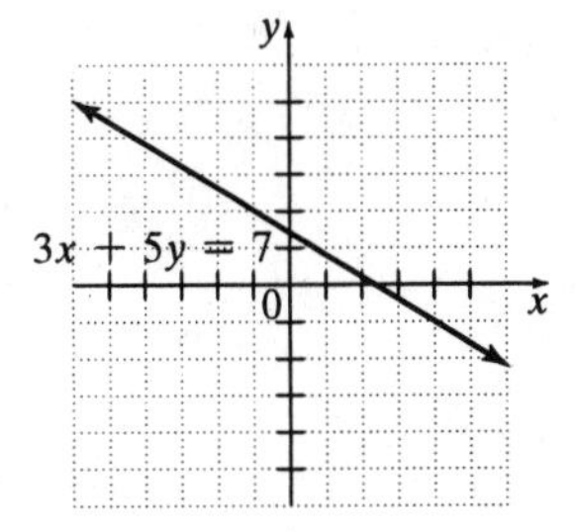

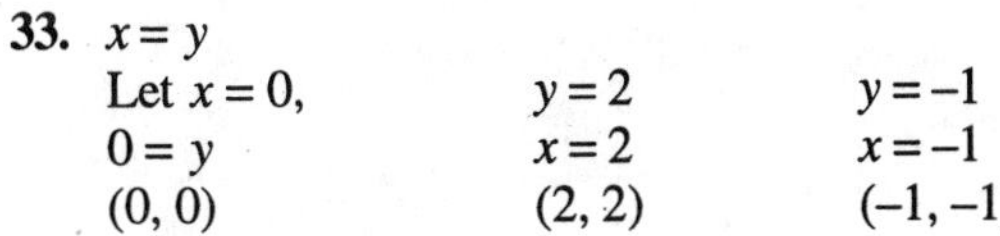

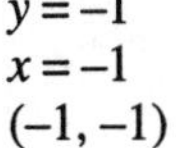

33. $x = y$

Let $x = 0$,	$y = 2$	$y = -1$
$0 = y$	$x = 2$	$x = -1$
$(0, 0)$	$(2, 2)$	$(-1, -1)$

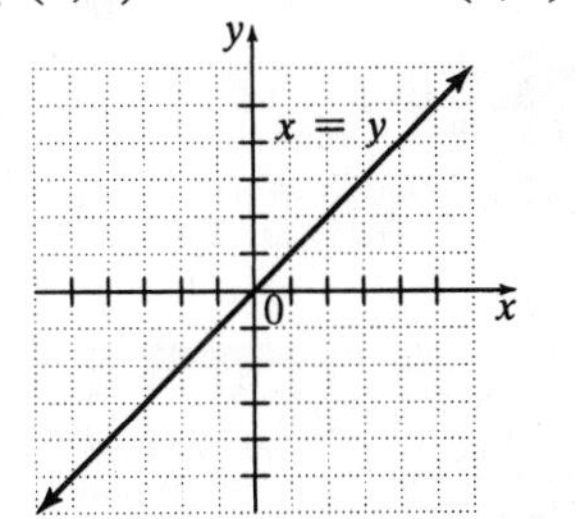

35. $x + 8y = 8$

Let $x = 0$,	$y = 0$,	$x = 3$
$0 + 8y = 8$	$x + 8(0) = 8$	$3 + 8y = 8$
$8y = 8$	$x = 8$	$8y = 5$
$y = 1$	$(8, 0)$	$y = \frac{5}{8}$
$(0, 1)$		$\left(3, \frac{5}{8}\right)$

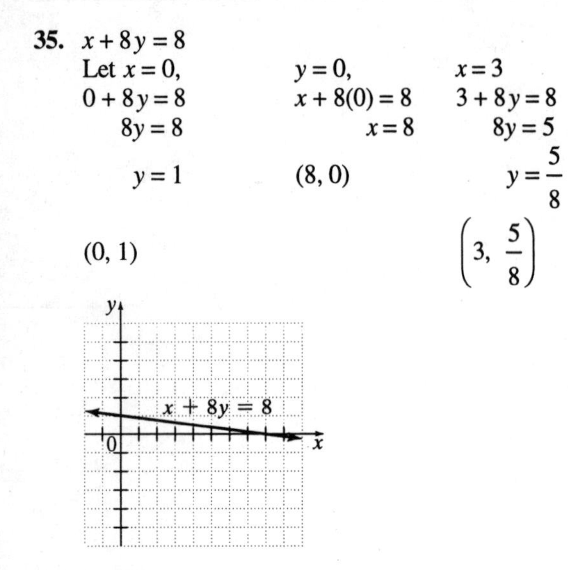

37. $5 = 6x - y$

Let $x = 0$,	$y = 0$,	$y = 1$
$5 = 6(0) - y$	$5 = 6x - 0$	$5 = 6x - 1$
$5 = -y$	$5 = 6x$	$6 = 6x$
$-5 = y$	$\frac{5}{6} = x$	$1 = x$
$(0, -5)$	$\left(\frac{5}{6}, 0\right)$	$(1, 1)$

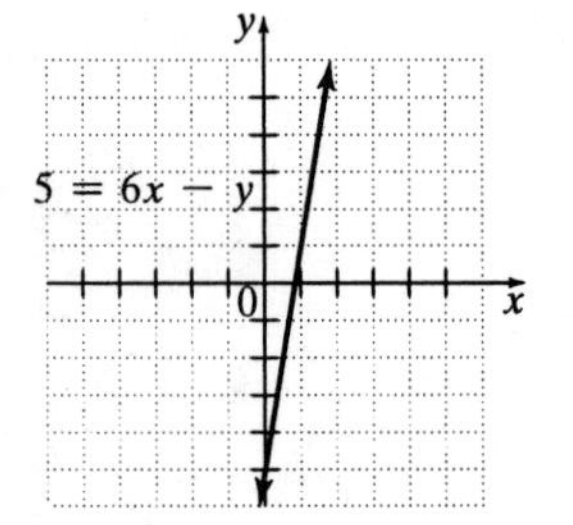

39. $-x + 10y = 11$

Let $x = 0$,	$y = 0$,	$x = -1$
$-0 + 10y = 11$	$-x + 10(0) = 11$	$-1(-1) + 10y = 11$
$10y = 11$	$-x = 11$	$1 + 10y = 11$
$y = \frac{11}{10}$	$x = -11$	$10y = 10$
$\left(0, \frac{11}{10}\right)$	$(-11, 0)$	$y = 1$
		$(-1, 1)$

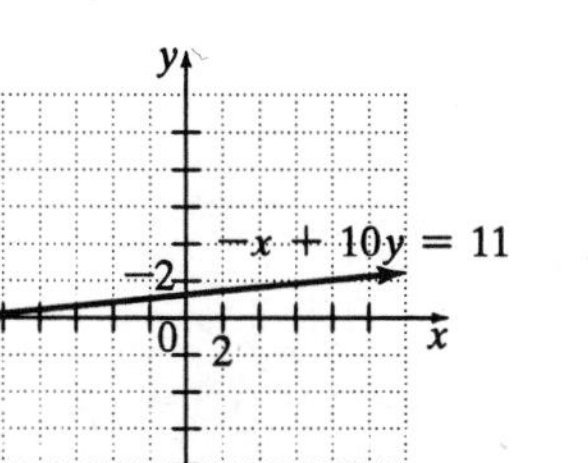

41. $y = 1$

$0x + y = 1$

Let $x = 1$,	$x = 2$,	$x = 0$
$0(1) + y = 1$	$0(2) + y = 1$	$0(0) + y = 1$
$y = 1$	$y = 1$	$y = 1$
$(1, 1)$	$(2, 1)$	$(0, 1)$

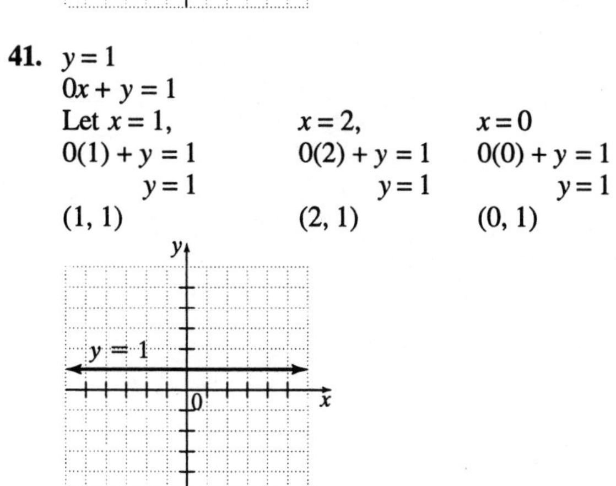

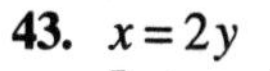

43. $x = 2y$

Let $y = 0$,	$y = 1$,	$y = -2$
$x = 2(0)$	$x = 2(1)$	$x = 2(-2)$
$x = 0$	$x = 2$	$x = -4$
$(0, 0)$	$(2, 1)$	$(-4, -2)$

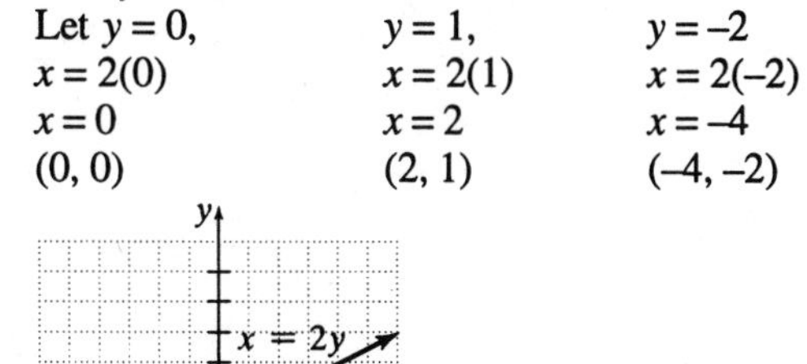

45. $x + 3 = 0$

$x = -3$

$x + 0y = -3$

Let $y = 1$,	$y = 2$,	$y = 0$
$x + 0(1) = -3$	$x + 0(2) = -3$	$x + 0(0) = -3$
$x = -3$	$x = -3$	$x = -3$
$(-3, 1)$	$(-3, 2)$	$(-3, 0)$

47. $x = 4y - \frac{1}{3}$

Let $y = 0$,	$y = \frac{1}{3}$,	$y = -\frac{2}{3}$
$x = 4(0) - \frac{1}{3}$	$x = 4\left(\frac{1}{3}\right) - \frac{1}{3}$	$x = 4\left(-\frac{2}{3}\right) - \frac{1}{3}$
$x = -\frac{1}{3}$	$x = \frac{4}{3} - \frac{1}{3}$	$x = -\frac{8}{3} - \frac{1}{3}$
$\left(-\frac{1}{3}, 0\right)$	$x = \frac{3}{3} = 1$	$x = -\frac{9}{3} = -3$
	$\left(1, \frac{1}{3}\right)$	$\left(-3, -\frac{2}{3}\right)$

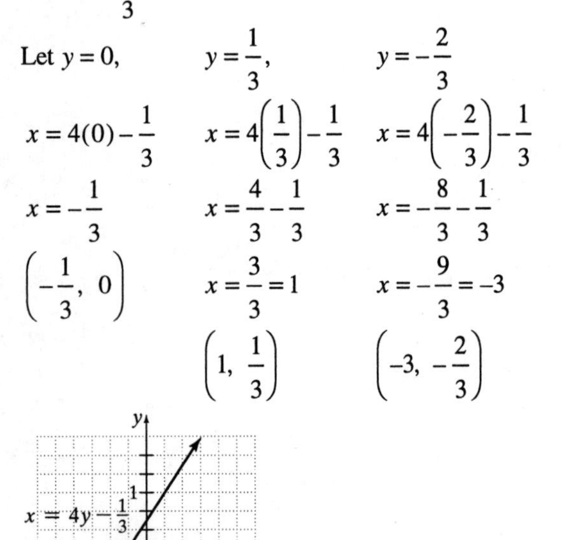

49. $2x+3y=6$

Let $x=0$,	$y=0$,	$x=1$
$2(0)+3y=6$	$2x+3(0)=6$	$2(1)+3y=6$
$3y=6$	$2x=6$	$2+3y=6$
$y=2$	$x=3$	$3y=4$
$(0, 2)$	$(3, 0)$	$y=\frac{4}{3}$
		$\left(1, \frac{4}{3}\right)$

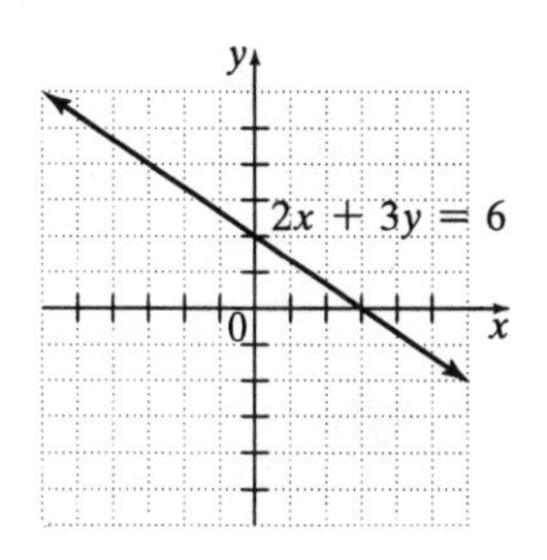

51. C

53. E

55. B

57. **a.**
$$3x+6y=1200$$
$$3(0)+6y=1200$$
$$0+6y=1200$$
$$6y=1200$$
$$y=200$$
(0, 200); Answers may vary.

b.
$$3x+6y=1200$$
$$3x+6(0)=1200$$
$$3x+0=1200$$
$$3x=1200$$
$$x=400$$
(400, 0); Answers may vary.

c.

d. $3x+6(50)=1200$
$3x+300=1200$
$3x=900$
$x=300$
300 chairs can be made.

59. a. $0=-22.5x+467.0$
$22.5x=467.0$
$\frac{22.5x}{22.5}=\frac{467.0}{22.5}$
$x=20.8$
(20.8, 0)

b. About 20.8 years after 1987, 0 music cassettes will be shipped.

61. Answers may vary.

63. Answers may vary.

65. $y=-4$

67. $\frac{4-5}{-1-0}=\frac{-1}{-1}=1$

69. $\frac{12-3}{10-9}=\frac{9}{1}=9$

71. $\frac{2-2}{3-5}=\frac{0}{-2}=0$

Section 3.4

Graphing Calculator Explorations

1. $y_1=3.8x$
$y_2=3.8x-3$
$y_3=3.8x+9$

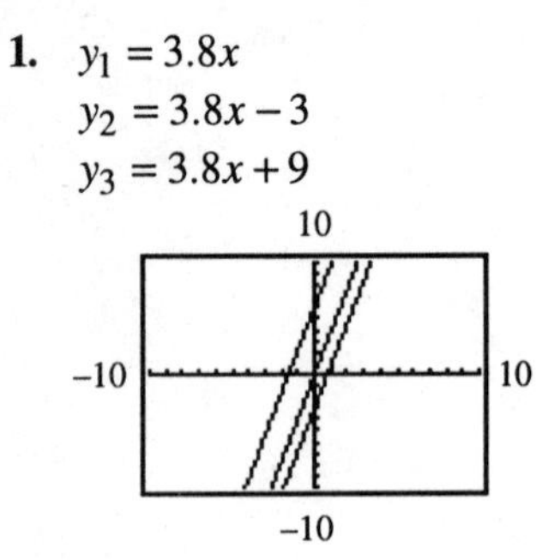

3. $y_1=\frac{1}{4}x$
$y_2=\frac{1}{4}x+5$
$y_3=\frac{1}{4}x-8$

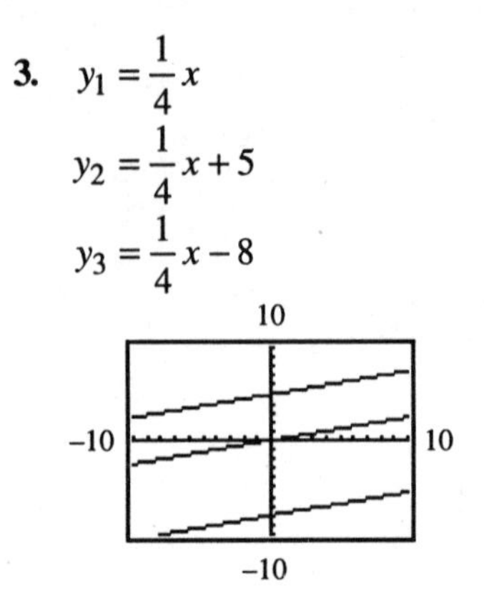

Mental Math

1. upward
2. downward
3. horizontal
4. vertical

Exercise Set 3.4

1. (–1, 2) and (2, –2)
$m=\frac{-2-2}{2-(-1)}=\frac{-4}{2+1}=-\frac{4}{3}$

3. (2, 3) and (2, –1)
$m=\frac{-1-3}{2-2}=\frac{-4}{0}$
undefined slope

5. (–3, –2) and (–1, 3)
$m=\frac{3-(-2)}{-1-(-3)}=\frac{3+2}{-1+3}=\frac{5}{2}$

7. (0, 0) and (7, 8)
$m=\frac{8-0}{7-0}=\frac{8}{7}$

9. (–1, 5) and (6, –2)
$m=\frac{-2-5}{6-(-1)}=\frac{-7}{6+1}=\frac{-7}{7}=-1$

11. (1, 4) and (5, 3)
$m = \frac{3-4}{5-1} = \frac{-1}{4} = -\frac{1}{4}$

13. (– 4, 3) and (– 4, 5)
$m = \frac{5-3}{4-(-4)} = \frac{2}{0}$
undefined

15. (–2, 8) and (1, 6)
$m = \frac{6-8}{1-(-2)} = \frac{-2}{1+2} = -\frac{2}{3}$

17. (1, 0) and (1, 1)
$m = \frac{1-0}{1-1} = \frac{1}{0}$
undefined

19. (5, 1) and (–2, 1)
$m = \frac{1-1}{-2-5} = \frac{0}{-7} = 0$

21. line 1

23. line 2

25. D

27. B

29. E

31. no slope

33. $m = 0$

35. no slope

37. $m = 0$

39. **a.** $m = \frac{0-(-3)}{0-(-3)} = \frac{3}{3} = 1$

b. –1

41. **a.** $m = \frac{5-(-4)}{3-(-8)} = \frac{5+4}{3+8} = \frac{9}{11}$

b. $-\frac{11}{9}$

43. $m = \frac{0-6}{-2-0} = \frac{-6}{-2} = 3$
$m = \frac{8-5}{1-0} = \frac{3}{1} = 3$
parallel

45. $m = \frac{8-6}{-2-2} = \frac{2}{-4} = -\frac{1}{2}$
$m = \frac{5-3}{1-0} = \frac{2}{1} = 2$
perpendicular

47. $m = \frac{8-6}{7-3} = \frac{2}{4} = \frac{1}{2}$
$m = \frac{7-6}{2-0} = \frac{1}{2}$
parallel

49. $m = \frac{-5-(-3)}{6-2} = \frac{-5+3}{4} = \frac{-2}{4} = -\frac{1}{2}$
$m = \frac{-4-(-2)}{-3-5} = \frac{-4+2}{-8} = \frac{-2}{-8} = \frac{1}{4}$
neither

51. $m = \frac{0-(-3)}{-1-(-4)} = \frac{3}{-1+4} = \frac{3}{3} = 1$
$m = \frac{0-(-4)}{0-4} = \frac{4}{-4} = -1$
perpendicular

53. $m = \frac{-6-(-5)}{-2-(-7)} = \frac{-6+5}{-2+7} = -\frac{1}{5}$

55. $m = \frac{-3-0}{1-0} = \frac{-3}{1} = -3$
$m = \frac{1}{3}$

57. $m = \frac{-3-3}{-3-3} = \frac{-6}{-6} = 1$
$m = 1$

59. $\frac{\text{rise}}{\text{run}} = \frac{6}{10} = \frac{3}{5}$

61. $\frac{\text{rise}}{\text{run}} = \frac{2}{16} = 0.125$
12.5%

63. $\frac{\text{rise}}{\text{run}} = \frac{2580}{6450} = 0.40$
40%

65. $\frac{\text{rise}}{\text{run}} = \frac{0.25}{12} = 0.02$
$m = 0.02$

67. (1999, 99), (2002, 144)
$m = \frac{144-99}{2002-1999} = \frac{45}{3} = 15$
Every one year there are/should be 15 million more internet users.

69. (5000, 1800), (20,000, 7200)
$m = \frac{7200-1800}{20{,}000-5000} = \frac{5400}{15{,}000} = 0.36$
It costs \$0.36 per 1 mile to own and operate a compact car.

71. (1988, 18.7)
18.7 mpg

73. 21.3 – 17.5 = 3.8 mpg

75. from 1989 to 1990

77. 1990

79. $\frac{x}{18} = \frac{1}{3}$
$18 \cdot \frac{x}{18} = \frac{1}{3} \cdot 18$
$x = 6$

81. Answers may vary.

83. $m = \frac{9.3-6.7}{-8.3-2.1} = \frac{2.6}{-10.4} = -0.25$

85. $m = \frac{5.1-0.2}{7.9-2.3} = \frac{4.9}{5.6} = 0.875$

87. The line becomes steeper.

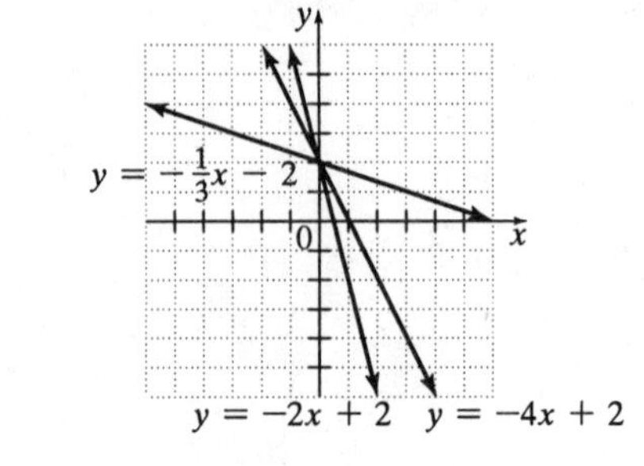

89. $-x > -16$
$\frac{-x}{-1} < \frac{-16}{-1}$
$x < 16$

91. $\frac{2x+1}{3} \geq -1$
$3\left(\frac{2x+1}{3}\right) \geq -1 \cdot 3$
$2x+1 \geq -3$
$2x+1-1 \geq -3-1$
$2x \geq -4$
$x \geq -2$

93. $x = -2y$
If $y = 0$ then $x = -2 \cdot 0 = 0$
If $y = 1$ then $x = -2 \cdot 1 = -2$
If $y = 2$ then $x = -2 \cdot 2 = -4$

x	y
0	0
–2	1
–4	2

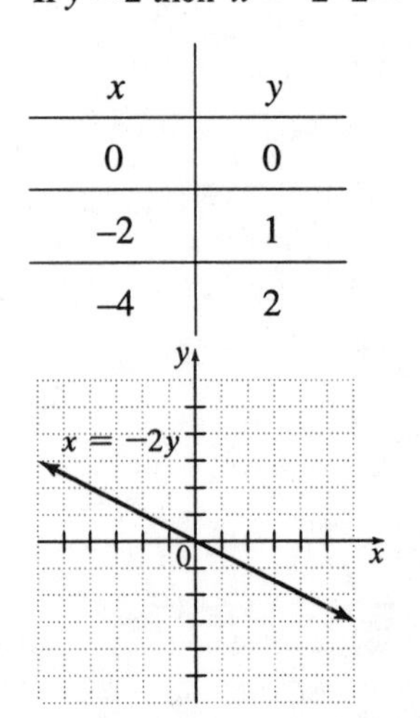

95. $5x + 3y = 15$ or $y = -\frac{5}{3}x + 5$

If $x = 3$, then $y = -\frac{5}{3} \cdot 3 + 5 = 0$

If $x = 0$, then $y = -\frac{5}{3} \cdot 0 + 5 = 5$

If $x = -\frac{3}{5}$, then $y = -\frac{5}{3} \cdot \left(-\frac{3}{5}\right) + 5 = 6$

x	y
3	0
0	5
$-\frac{3}{5}$	6

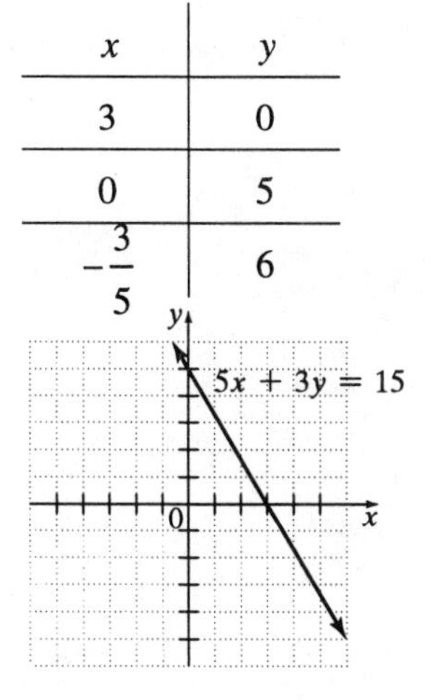

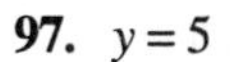

97. $y = 5$

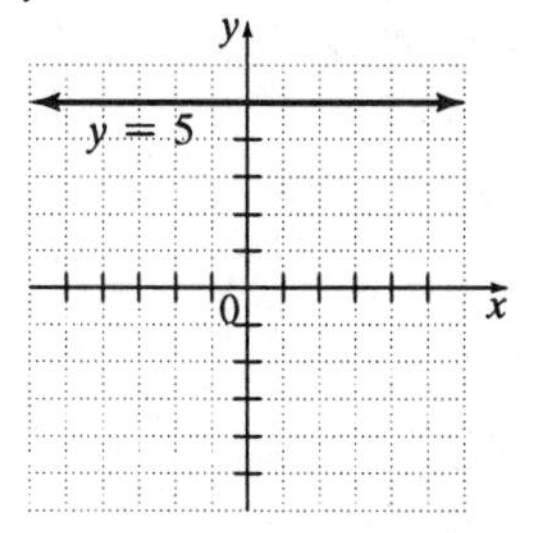

Section 3.5

Mental Math

1. yes
2. no
3. yes
4. no

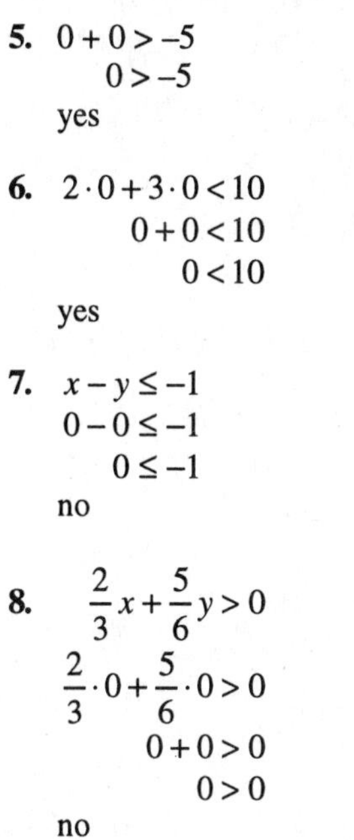

5. $0 + 0 > -5$
$0 > -5$
yes

6. $2 \cdot 0 + 3 \cdot 0 < 10$
$0 + 0 < 10$
$0 < 10$
yes

7. $x - y \le -1$
$0 - 0 \le -1$
$0 \le -1$
no

8. $\frac{2}{3}x + \frac{5}{6}y > 0$
$\frac{2}{3} \cdot 0 + \frac{5}{6} \cdot 0 > 0$
$0 + 0 > 0$
$0 > 0$
no

Exercise Set 3.5

1. $x - y > 3$

$(2, -1)$
$2 - (-1) > 3$
$2 + 1 > 3$
$3 > 3$ no

$(5, 1)$
$5 - 1 > 3$
$4 > 3$ yes

3. $3x - 5y \le -4$

$(-1, -1)$
$3(-1) - 5(-1) \le -4$
$-3 + 5 \le -4$
$2 \le -4$ no

$(4, 0)$
$3(4) - 5(0) \le -4$
$12 - 0 \le -4$
$12 \le -4$ no

5. $x < -y$

$(0, 2)$
$0 < -2$ no

$(-5, 1)$
$-5 < -1$ yes

7. $x + y \le 1$
Find the intercepts.
Let $x = 0$, $0 + y = 1$, $y = 1$, $(0, 1)$
Let $y = 0$, $x + 0 = 1$, $x = 1$, $(1, 0)$
The boundary line is solid.
Choose $(0, 0)$ as a test point.
$x + y \le 1$
$0 + 0 \, ? \, 1$
Since $0 < 1$, the side containing $(0, 0)$ is shaded.

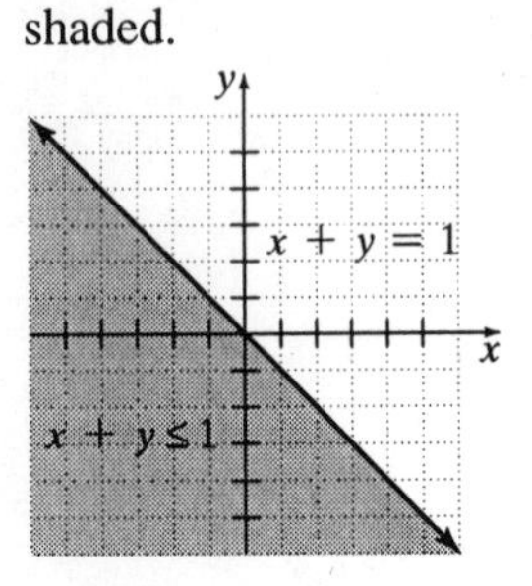

9. $2x + y > -4$
Find the intercepts.
Let $x = 0$, $2(0) + y = -4$, $y = -4$, $(0, -4)$
Let $y = 0$, $2x + 0 = -4$, $2x = -4$, $x = -2$, $(-2, 0)$
The boundary line is dashed.
Choose $(0, 0)$ as a test point.
$2x + y > -4$
$2(0) + 0 \, ? -4$
$0 \, ? -4$
Since $0 > -4$, the side of the line containing $(0, 0)$ is shaded.

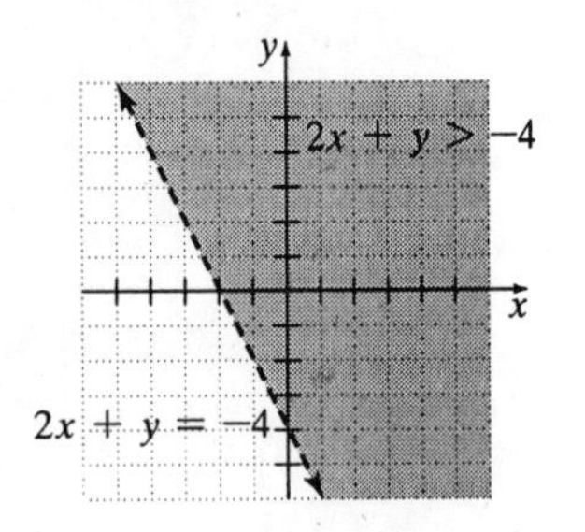

11. $x + 6y \le -6$
Find the intercepts.
Let $x = 0$, $0 + 6y = -6$, $6y = -6$, $y = -1$, $(0, -1)$
Let $y = 0$, $x + 6(0) = -6$, $x = -6$, $(-6, 0)$
The boundary line is solid.
Choose $(0, 0)$ as a test point.
$x + 6y \le -6$
$0 + 6(0) \, ? -6$
$0 \, ? -6$
Since $0 \not< -6$, the side *not* containing $(0, 0)$ is shaded.

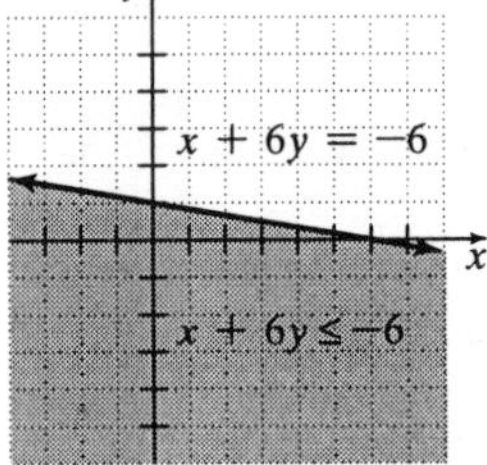

13. $2x + 5y > -10$
Find the intercepts.
Let $x = 0$, $2(0) + 5y = -10$, $5y = -10$, $y = -2$, $(0, -2)$
Let $y = 0$, $2x + 5(0) = -10$, $2x = -10$, $x = -5$, $(-5, 0)$
The boundary line is dashed.
Choose $(0, 0)$ as a test point.
$2x + 5y > -10$
$2(0) + 5(0) \, ? -10$
$0 \, ? -10$
Since $0 > -10$, the side containing $(0, 0)$ is shaded.

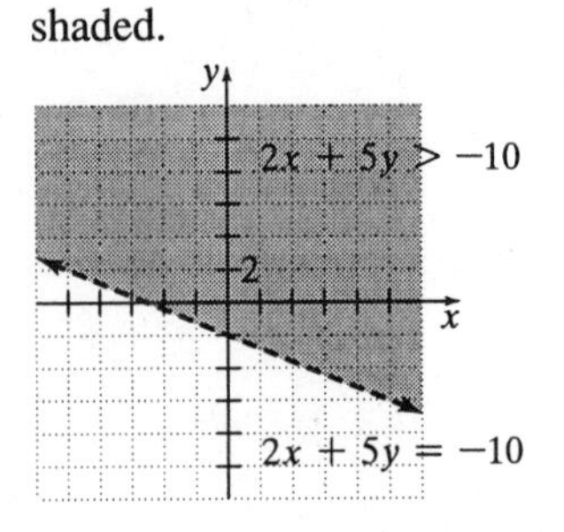

15. $x + 2y \le 3$
Find the intercepts.
Let $x = 0$, $0 + 2y = 3$, $2y = 3$,
$y = \frac{3}{2}$, $\left(0, \frac{3}{2}\right)$
Let $y = 0$, $x + 2(0) = 3$, $x = 3$, $(3, 0)$
The boundary line is solid.
Choose (0, 0) as a test point.
$x + 2y \le 3$
$0 + 2(0) \ ? \ 3$
$0 \ ? \ 3$
Since $0 \le 3$, the side containing (0, 0) is shaded.

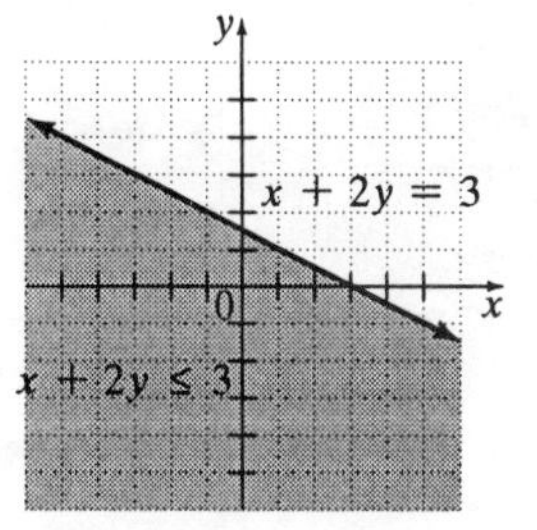

17. $2x + 7y > 5$
Find the intercepts.
Let $x = 0$, $2(0) + 7y = 5$, $7y = 5$,
$y = \frac{5}{7}$, $\left(0, \frac{5}{7}\right)$
Let $y = 0$, $2x + 7(0) = 5$, $2x = 5$,
$x = \frac{5}{2}$, $\left(\frac{5}{2}, 0\right)$
The boundary line is dashed.
Choose (0, 0) as a test point.
$2x + 7y > 5$
$2(0) + 7(0) \ ? \ 5$
$0 \ ? \ 5$
Since $0 \not> 5$, the side *not* containing (0, 0) is shaded.

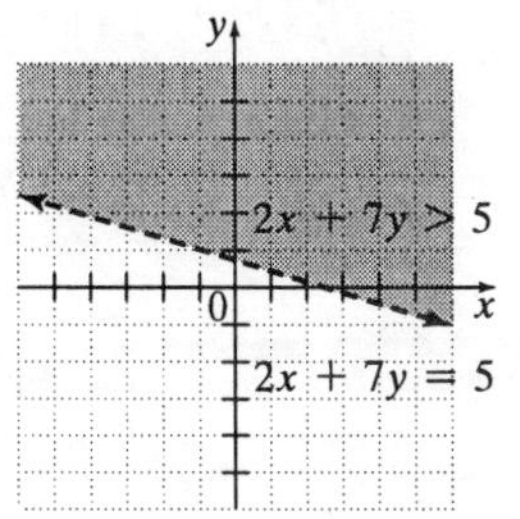

19. $x - 2y \ge 3$
Find the intercepts.
Let $x = 0$, $0 - 2y = 3$, $-2y = 3$,
$y = -\frac{3}{2}$, $\left(0, -\frac{3}{2}\right)$
Let $y = 0$, $x - 2(0) = 3$, $x = 3$, $(3, 0)$
The boundary line is solid.
Choose (0, 0) as a test point.
$x - 2y \ge 3$
$0 - 2(0) \ ? \ 3$
$0 \ ? \ 3$
Since $0 \not\ge 3$, the side *not* containing (0, 0) is shaded.

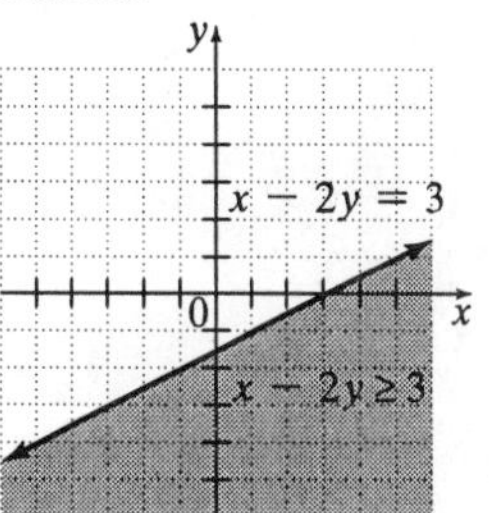

21. $5x + y < 3$
Find the intercepts.
Let $x = 0$, $5(0) + y = 3$, $y = 3$, $(0, 3)$
Let $y = 0$, $5x + 0 = 3$, $5x = 3$,
$x = \frac{3}{5}$, $\left(\frac{3}{5}, 0\right)$
The boundary line is dashed.
Choose (0, 0) as a test point.
$5x + y < 3$
$5(0) + 0 \ ? \ 3$
$0 \ ? \ 3$
Since $0 < 3$, the side containing (0, 0) is shaded.

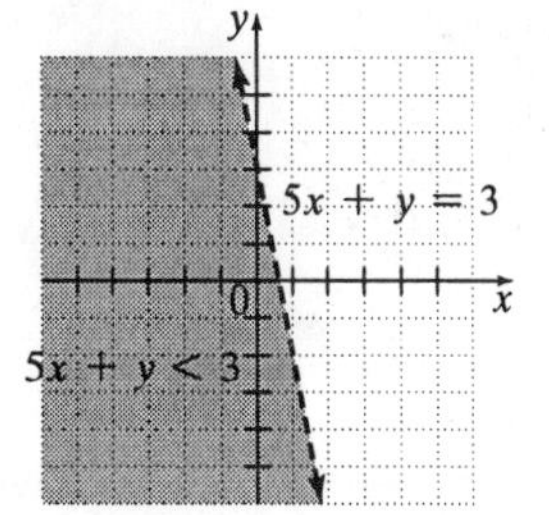

23. $4x + y < 8$
Find the intercepts.
Let $x = 0$, $4(0) + y = 8$, $y = 8$, $(0, 8)$
Let $y = 0$, $4x + 0 = 8$, $4x = 8$, $x = 2$, $(2, 0)$
The boundary line is dashed.
Choose (0, 0) as a test point.
$4x + y < 8$
$4(0) + 0 \ ?\ 8$
$0 \ ?\ 8$
Since $0 < 8$, the side containing (0, 0) is shaded.

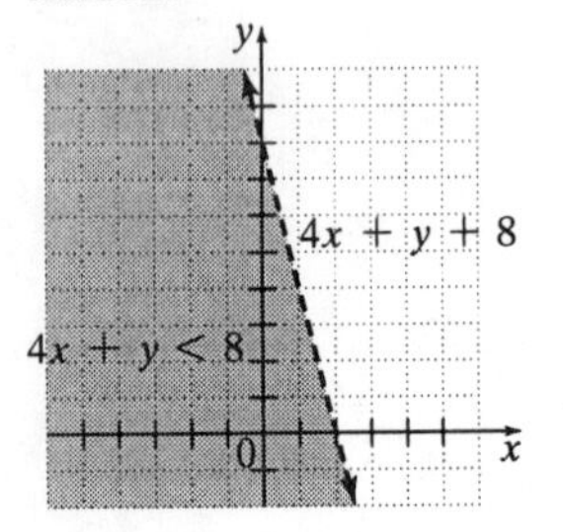

25. $y \geq 2x$
Find the two points.
Let $x = 0$, $y = 2(0)$, $y = 0$, $(0, 0)$
Let $x = 3$, $y = 2(3)$, $y = 6$, $(3, 6)$
The boundary line is solid.
Choose (5, 0) as a test point.
$y \geq 2x$
$0 \ ?\ 2(5)$
$0 \ ?\ 10$
Since $0 \not\geq 10$, the side *not* containing (5, 0) is shaded.

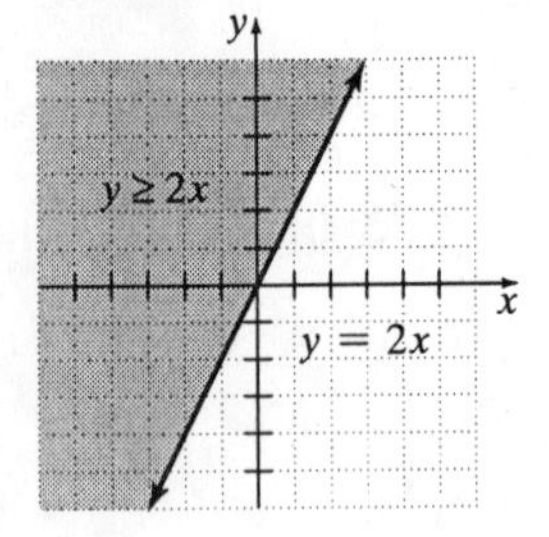

27. $x \geq 0$
$x = 0$ is a vertical line passing through (0, 0).
The boundary line is solid.
Choose (4, 1) as a test point.
$x \geq 0$
$4 \ ?\ 0$
Since $4 \geq 0$, the side containing (4, 1) is shaded.

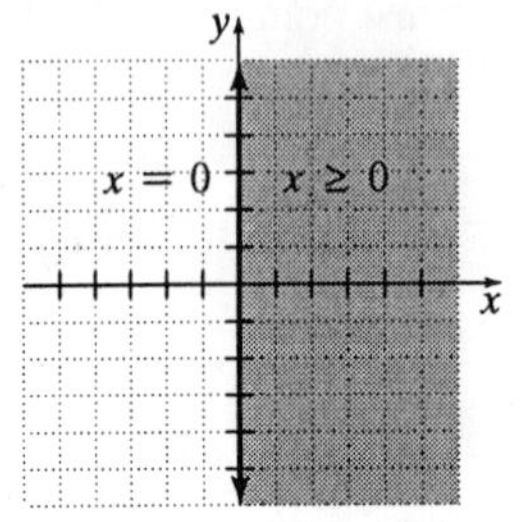

29. $y \leq -3$
$y = -3$ is a horizontal line passing through (0, –3).
The boundary line is solid.
Choose (1, 0) as a test point.
$y \leq -3$
$0 \ ?\ -3$
Since $0 \not\leq -3$, the side *not* containing (1, 0) is shaded.

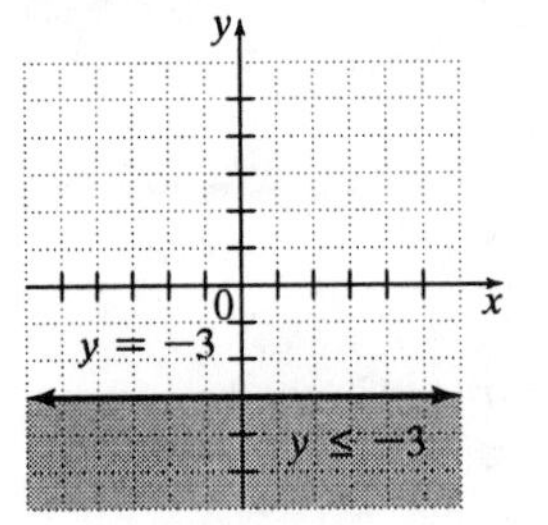

31. $2x - 7y > 0$
Find two points.
Let $x = 0$, $2(0) - 7y = 0$, $-7y = 0$, $y = 0$, $(0, 0)$
Let $x = 2$, $2(2) - 7y = 0$, $4 - 7y = 0$, $-7y = -4$,
$y = \frac{4}{7}$, $\left(2, \frac{4}{7}\right)$
The boundary line is dashed.
Choose (0, 4) as a test point.
$2x - 7y > 0$
$2(0) - 7(4) \ ?\ 0$
$-28 \ ?\ 0$
Since $-28 \not> 0$, the side *not* containing (0, 4) is shaded.

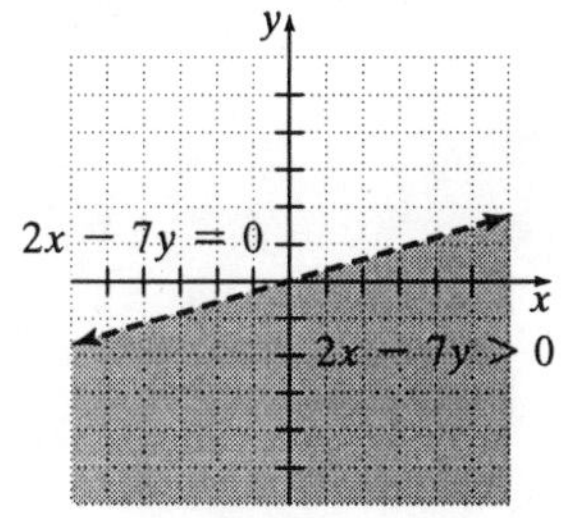

33. $3x - 7y \geq 0$
Find two points.
Let $x = 0$, $3(0) - 7y = 0$, $-7y = 0$, $y = 0$, $(0, 0)$
Let $x = 1$, $3(1) - 7y = 0$, $3 - 7y = 0$, $-7y =$
-3, $y = \frac{3}{7}$, $\left(1, \frac{3}{7}\right)$
The boundary line is solid.
Choose (0, 4) as a test point.
$3x - 7y \geq 0$
$3(0) - 7(4) \ ?\ 0$
$-28 \ ?\ 0$
Since $-28 \not\geq 0$, the side *not* containing (0, 4) is shaded.

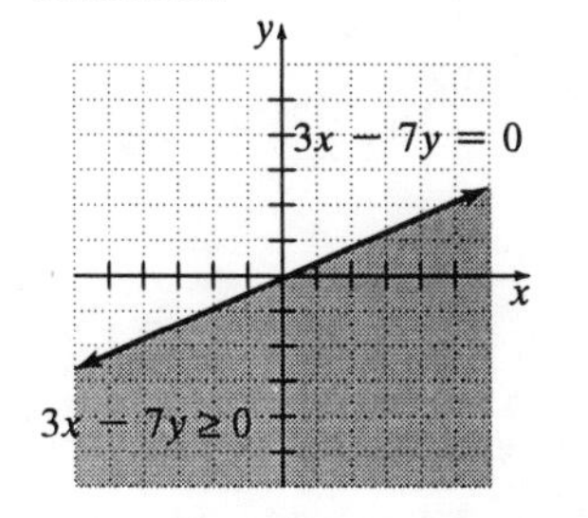

35. $x > y$
Find two points.
Let $x = 0$, $0 = y$, $(0, 0)$
Let $x = 4$, $4 = y$, $(4, 4)$
The boundary line is dashed.
Choose (5, 0) as a test point.
$x > y$
$5 \ ?\ 0$
Since $5 > 0$, the side containing (5, 0) is shaded.

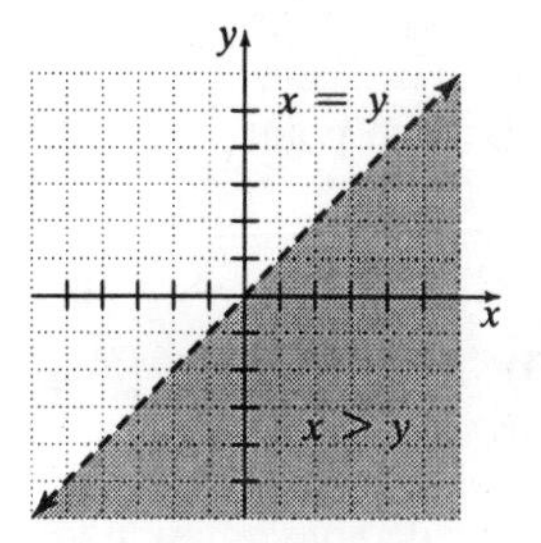

37. $x - y \leq 6$
Find the intercepts.
Let $x = 0$, $0 - y = 6$, $-y = 6$, $y = -6$, $(0, -6)$
Let $y = 0$, $x - 0 = 6$, $x = 6$, $(6, 0)$
The boundary line is solid.
Choose (0, 0) as a test point.
$x - y \leq 6$
$0 - 0 \ ?\ 6$
$0 \ ?\ 6$
Since $0 \leq 6$, the side containing (0, 0) is shaded.

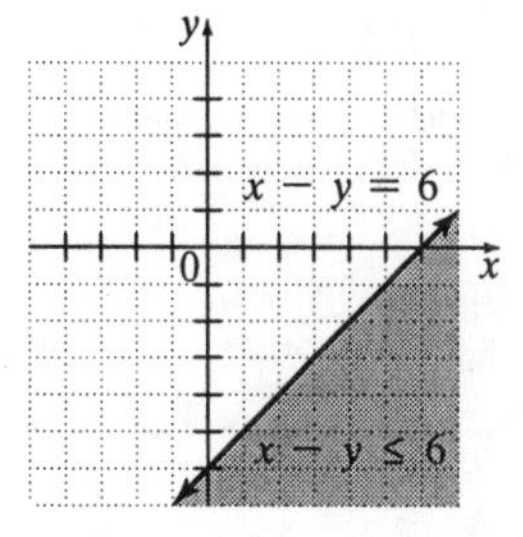

39. $-\frac{1}{4}y+\frac{1}{3}x>1$
Find the intercepts.
Let $x=0$, $-\frac{1}{4}y+\frac{1}{3}(0)=1$, $-\frac{1}{4}y=1$,
$y=-4$,
$(0,-4)$
Let $y=0$, $-\frac{1}{4}(0)+\frac{1}{3}x=1$, $\frac{1}{3}x=1$, $x=3$,
$(3, 0)$
The boundary line is dashed.
Choose (0, 0) as a test point.
$$-\frac{1}{4}y+\frac{1}{3}x>1$$
$$-\frac{1}{4}(0)+\frac{1}{3}(0)\ ?\ 1$$
$$0\ ?\ 1$$
Since $0 \not> 1$, the side *not* containing (0, 0) is shaded.

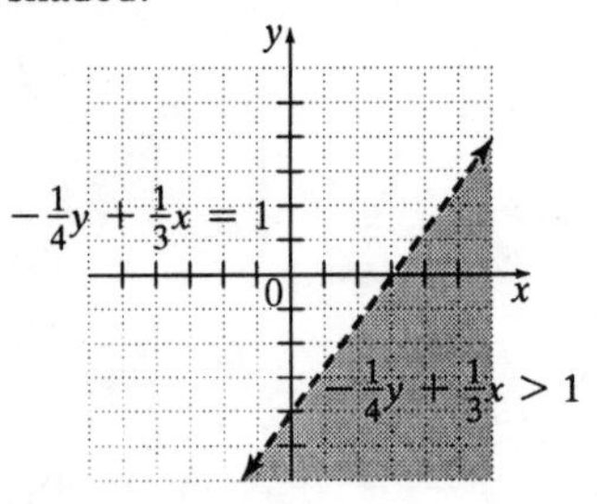

41. $-x<0.4y$
Find two points.
Let $y=0$, $-x=0.4(0)$, $-x=0$, $x=0$, (0, 0)
Let $y=10$, $-x=0.4(10)$, $-x=4$, $x=-4$, (–4, 10)
The boundary line is dashed.
Choose (5, 0) as a test point.
$-x<0.4y$
$-5\ ?\ 0.4(0)$
$-5\ ?\ 0$
Since $-5<0$, the side containing (5, 0) is shaded.

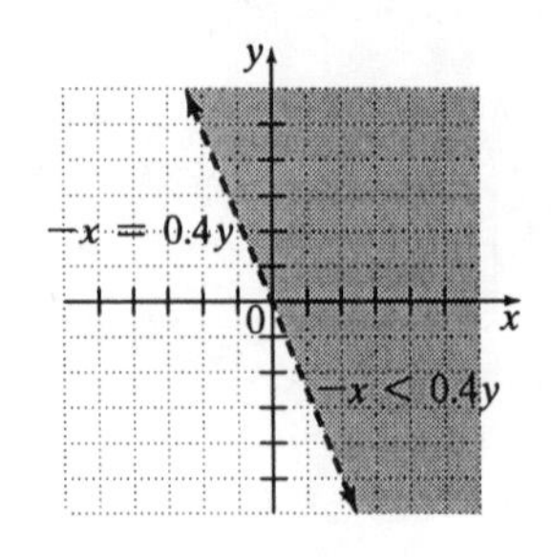

43. e

45. c

47. f

49. $x+y\geq 13$
Find the intercepts.
Let $x=0$, $0+y=13$, $y=13$, (0, 13)
Let $y=0$, $x+0=13$, $x=13$, (13, 0)
The boundary line is solid.
Choose (0, 0) as a test point.
$x+y\geq 13$
$0+0\ ?\ 13$
$0\ ?\ 13$
Since $0 \not\geq 13$ the side *not* containing (0, 0) is shaded.

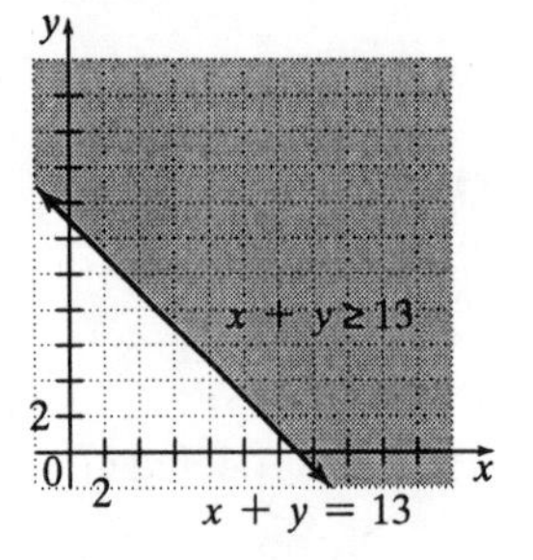

51. Answers may vary.

53. $2^3=2\cdot 2\cdot 2=8$

55. $(-2)^5=(-2)(-2)(-2)(-2)(-2)=-32$

57. $3\cdot 4^2=3\cdot 4\cdot 4=48$

59. $x^2=(-5)^2=(-5)(-5)=25$

61. $2x^3=2(-1)^3=2(-1)(-1)(-1)=-2$

Chapter 3 Review Exercises

1.

2.

3.

4.

5.

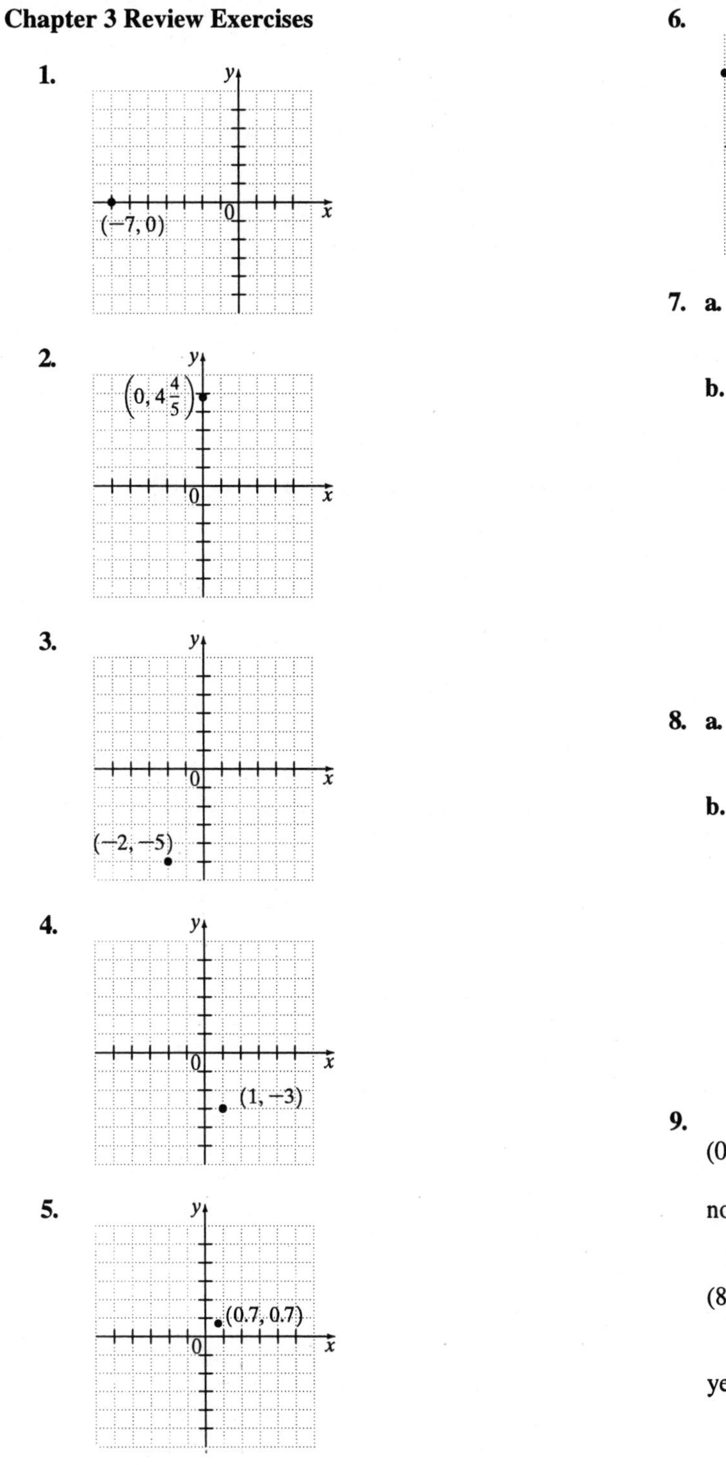

6.

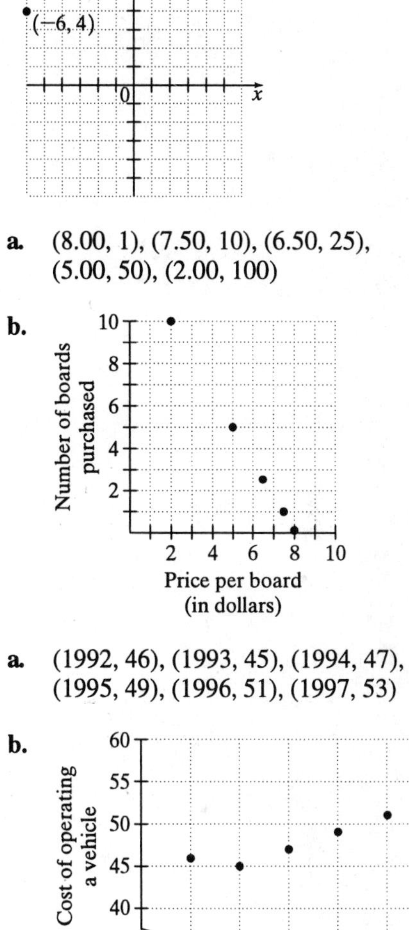

7. a. (8.00, 1), (7.50, 10), (6.50, 25), (5.00, 50), (2.00, 100)

b.

8. a. (1992, 46), (1993, 45), (1994, 47), (1995, 49), (1996, 51), (1997, 53)

b.

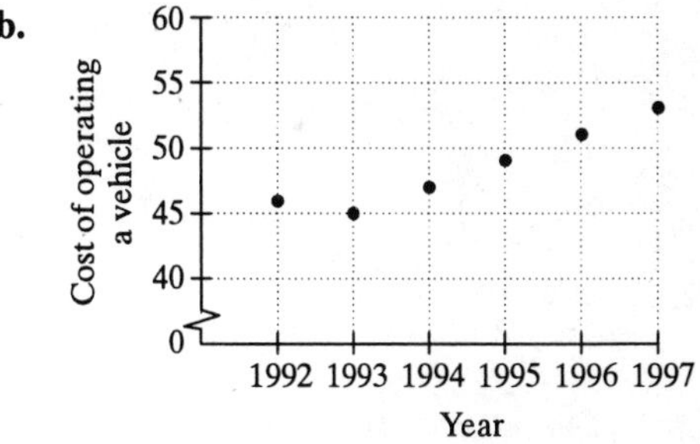

9.

$7x - 8y = 56$

(0, 56) $7(0) - 8(56) \stackrel{?}{=} 56$

$-448 \stackrel{?}{=} 56$

no $-448 \neq 56$

$7x - 8y = 56$

(8, 0) $7(8) - 8(0) \stackrel{?}{=} 56$

$56 - 0 \stackrel{?}{=} 56$

$56 \stackrel{?}{=} 56$

yes $56 = 56$

10. $-2x + 5y = 10$

(–5, 0) $-2(-5) + 5(0) = 10$

$10 + 0 = 10$

Yes $10 = 10$

(1, 1) $-2(1) + 5(1) = 10$

$-2 + 5 = 10$

No $3 \neq 10$

11. $x = 13$

(13, 5) $13 \;?\; 13$

yes $13 = 13$

$x = 13$

(13, 13) $13 \;?\; 13$

yes $13 = 13$

12. $y = 2$

(7, 2): $2 \;?\; 2$

Yes $2 = 2$

$y = 2$

(2, 7) $7 \;?\; 2$

No $7 \neq 2$

13.
$$\begin{aligned} -2 + y &= 6x \\ -2 + y &= 6(7) \\ -2 + y &= 42 \\ y &= 42 + 2 \\ y &= 44 \end{aligned}$$
(7, 44)

14.
$$\begin{aligned} y - 3x &= 5 \\ -8 - 3x &= 5 \\ \frac{-3x}{-3} &= \frac{13}{3} \\ x &= -\frac{13}{3} \end{aligned}$$
$$\left(-\frac{13}{3}, -8\right)$$

15.
$$\begin{aligned} 9 &= -3x + 4y \\ 9 &= -3x + 4(0) \\ 9 &= -3x + 0 \\ 9 &= -3x \\ -3 &= x \end{aligned}$$
(–3, 0)

$$\begin{aligned} 9 &= -3x + 4y \\ 9 &= -3x + 4(3) \\ 9 &= -3x + 12 \\ 9 - 12 &= -3x \\ -3 &= -3x \\ 1 &= x \end{aligned}$$
(1, 3)

$$\begin{aligned} 9 &= -3x + 4y \\ 9 &= -3(9) + 4y \\ 9 &= -27 + 4y \\ 9 + 27 &= 4y \\ 36 &= 4y \\ 9 &= y \end{aligned}$$
(9, 9)

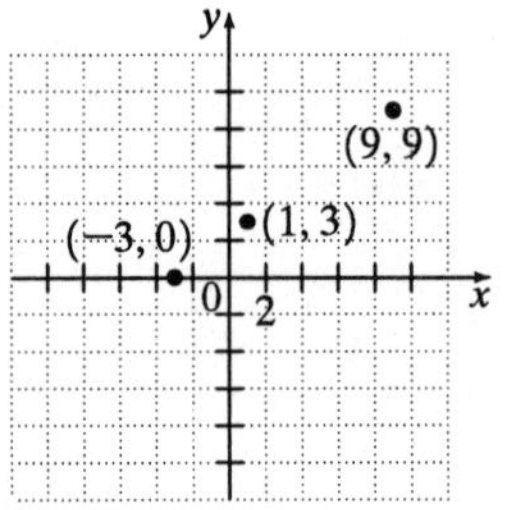

16. $y = 5$

(7, 5)

(–7, 5)

(0, 5)

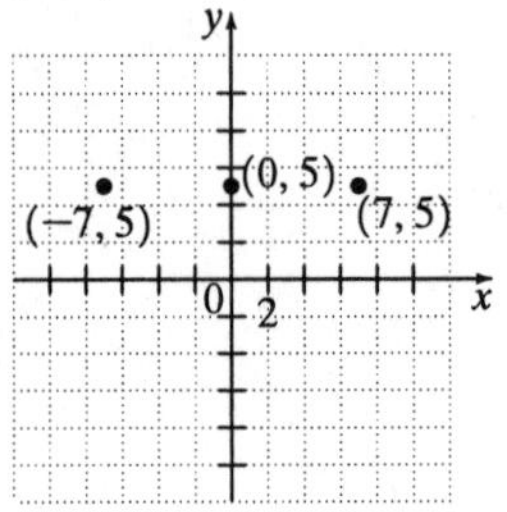

17. $x = 2$
$x = 2(0)$
$x = 0$
$(0, 0)$

$x = 2y$
$x = 2(5)$
$x = 10$
$(10, 5)$

$x = 2y$
$x = 2(-5)$
$x = -10$
$(-10, -5)$

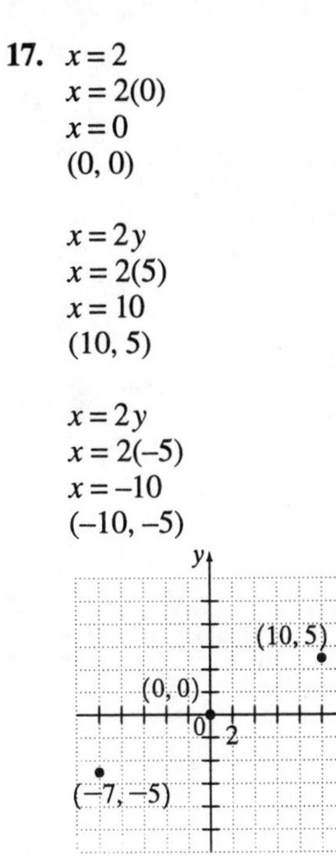

18. a. $y = 5x + 2000$
$y = 5(1) + 2000 = 2005$
$y = 5(100) + 2000 = 2500$
$y = 5(1000) + 2000 = 7000$

x	1	100	1000
y	2005	2500	7000

b. $6430 = 5x + 2000$
$4430 = 5x$
$886 = x$
886 compact disks can be produced for $6430.

19. $x - y = 1$
Find 3 points.

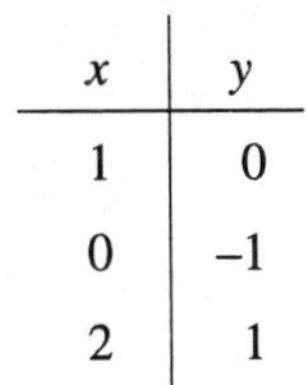

x	y
1	0
0	−1
2	1

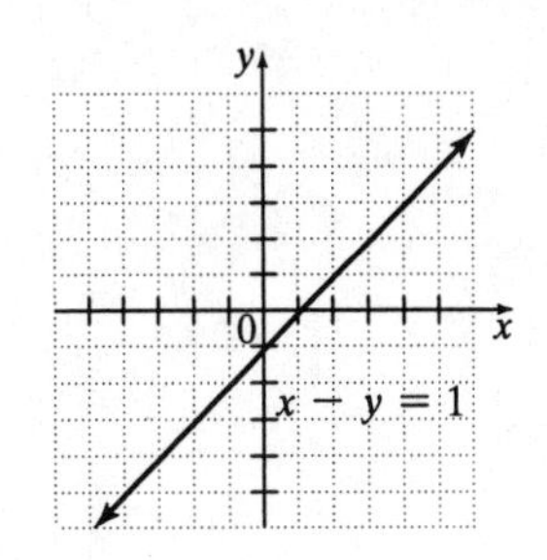

20. $x + y = 6$
Find 3 points.

x	y
0	6
6	0
1	5

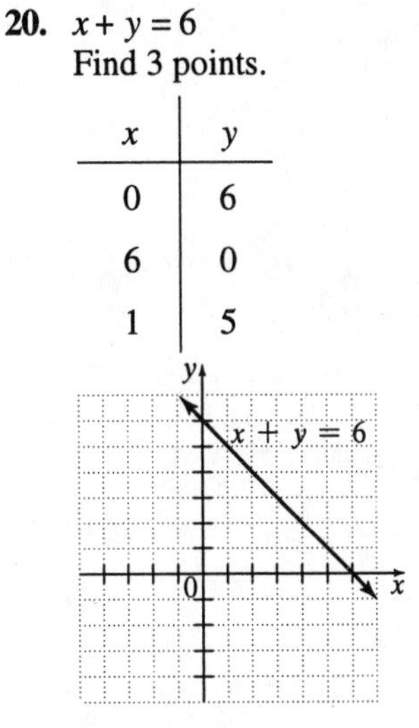

21. $x - 3y = 12$
Find 3 points.

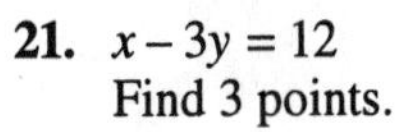

x	y
12	0
0	−4
9	−1

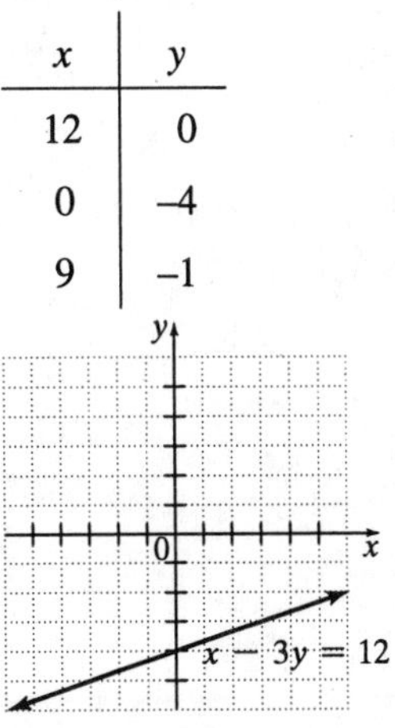

22. $5x - y = -8$
Find 3 points.

x	y
0	8
$-\frac{8}{5}$	0
-1	3

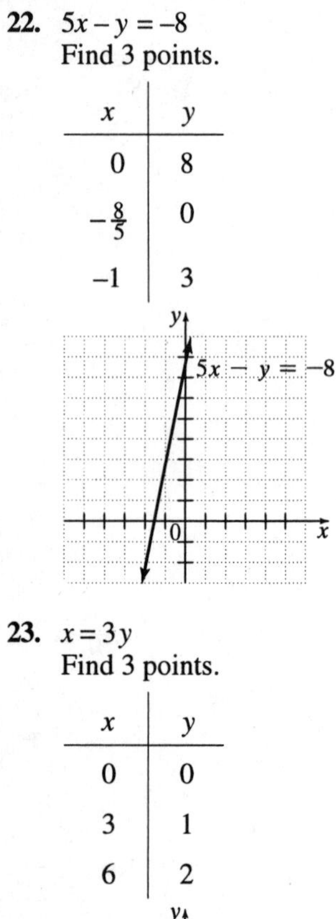

23. $x = 3y$
Find 3 points.

x	y
0	0
3	1
6	2

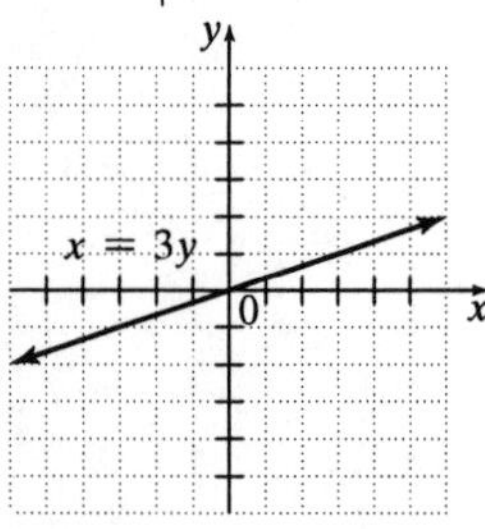

24. $y = -2x$
Find 3 points.

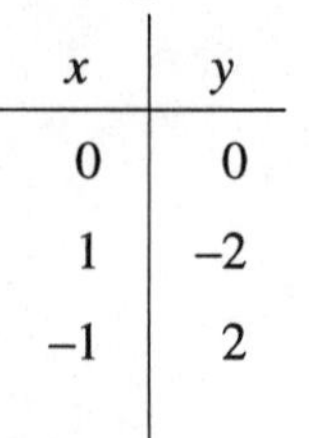

x	y
0	0
1	-2
-1	2

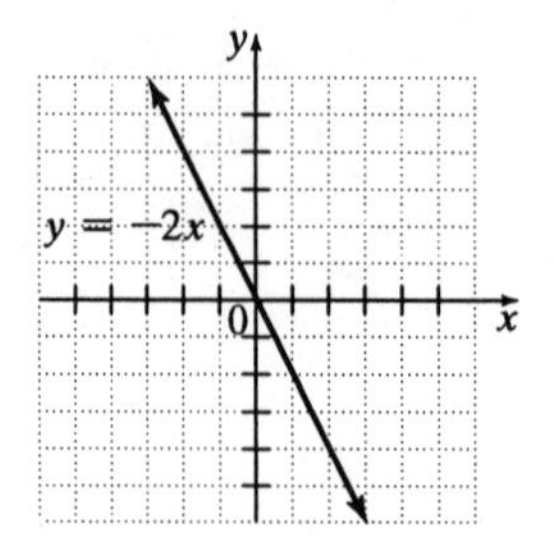

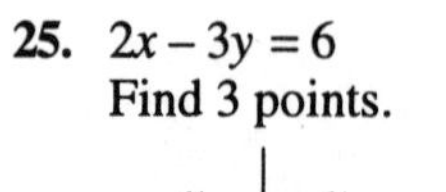

25. $2x - 3y = 6$
Find 3 points.

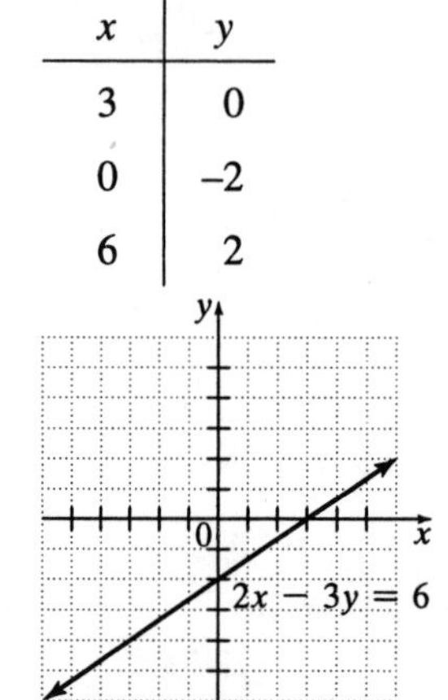

x	y
3	0
0	-2
6	2

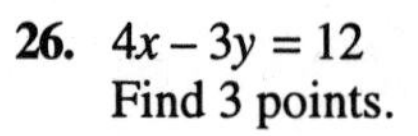

26. $4x - 3y = 12$
Find 3 points.

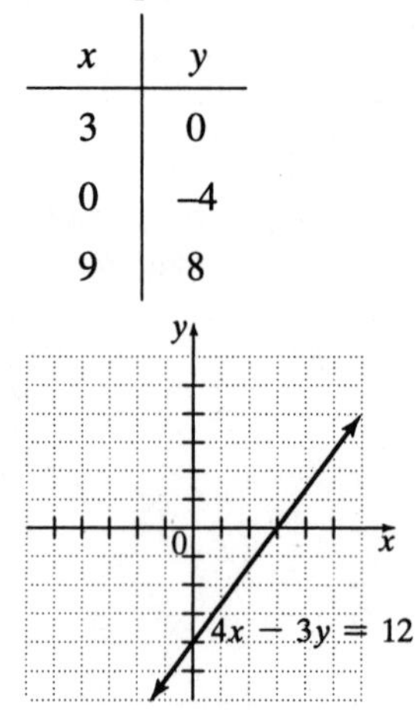

x	y
3	0
0	-4
9	8

27. $y = 16x + 250$

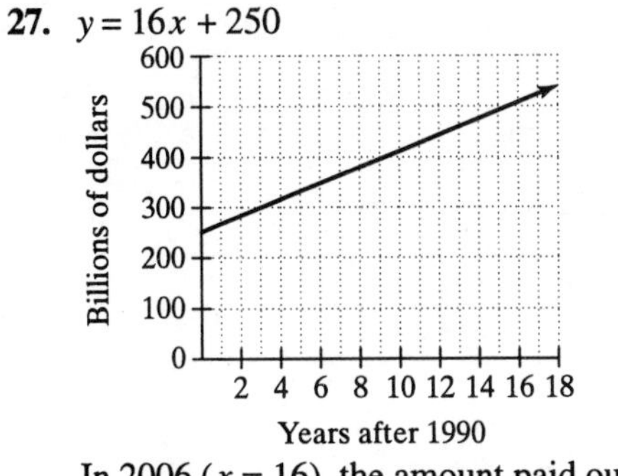

In 2006 ($x = 16$), the amount paid out for social security payments will be \$506 billion.

28. $x = 4$; $y = -2$; (4, 0); (0, −2)

29. $y = -3$; (0, −3)

30. $x = -2$; $x = 2$; $y = 2$; $y = -2$; (−2, 0); (2, 0); (0, 2); (0, −2)

31. $x = -1$; $x = 2$; $x = 3$; $y = -2$; (−1, 0); (2, 0); (3, 0); (0, −2)

32. $x - 3y = 12$

If $x = 0$, then
$0 - 3y = 12$
$-3y = 12$
$y = -4$
(0, −4)

If $y = 0$, then
$x - 3(0) = 12$
$x - 0 = 12$
$x = 12$
(12, 0)

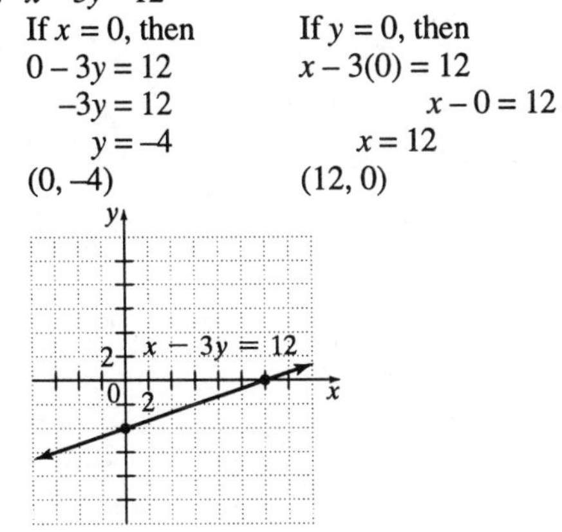

33. $-4x + y = 8$

If $x = 0$, then
$-4(0) + y = 8$
$0 + y = 8$
$y = 8$
(0, 8)

If $y = 0$, then
$-4x + 0 = 8$
$-4x = 8$
$x = -2$
(−2, 0)

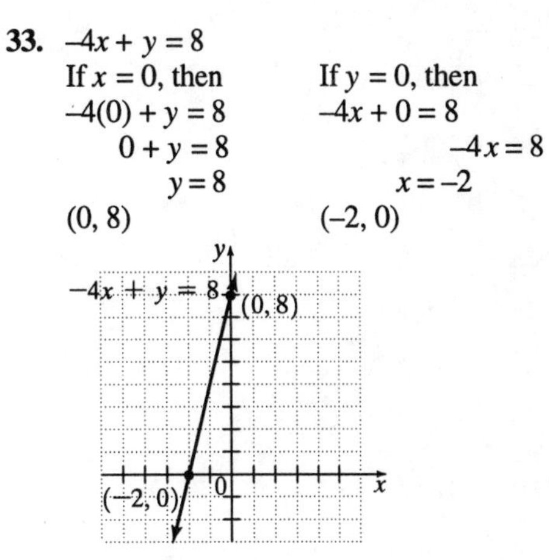

34. $y = -3$

If $x = 0$, then $y = -3$; (0, −3)

Since y cannot equal 0 there is no x-intercept.

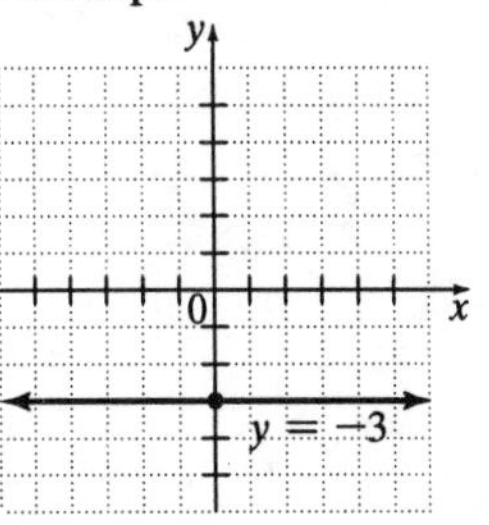

35. $x = 5$

Since x cannot equal 0 there is no y-intercept.

If $y = 0$, then $x = 5$; (5, 0)

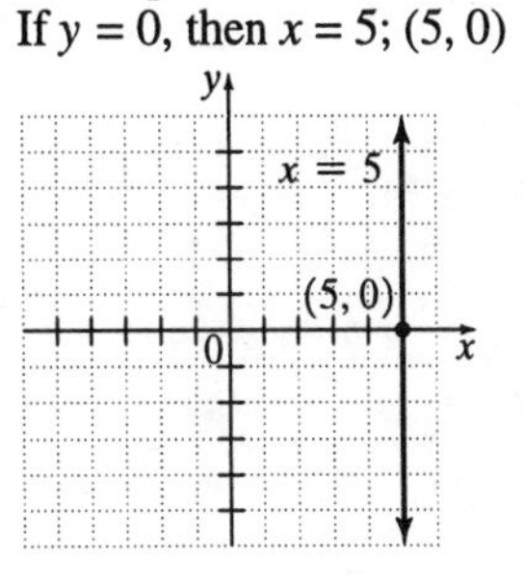

36. $y = -3x$
If $x = 0$, then $y = -3(0) = 0$; (0, 0)

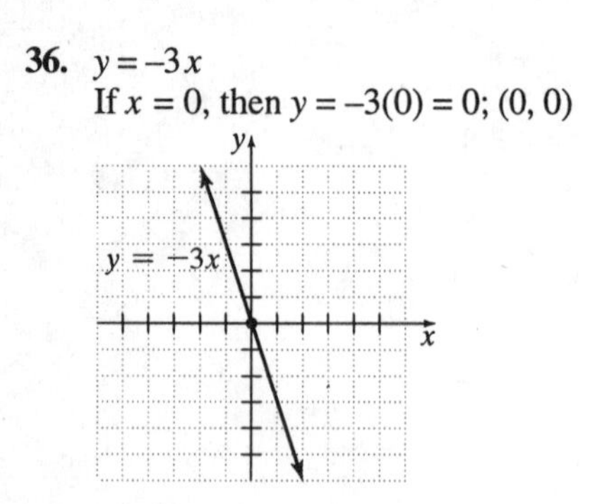

37. $x = 5y$
If $x = 0$, then $0 = 5y$ or $y = 0$; (0, 0)

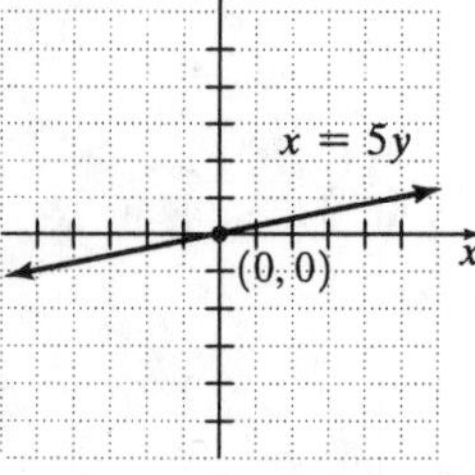

38. $x - 2 = 0$ or $x = 2$
Since x cannot equal 0, there is no y-intercept.
If $y = 0$, then $x = 2$; (2, 0)

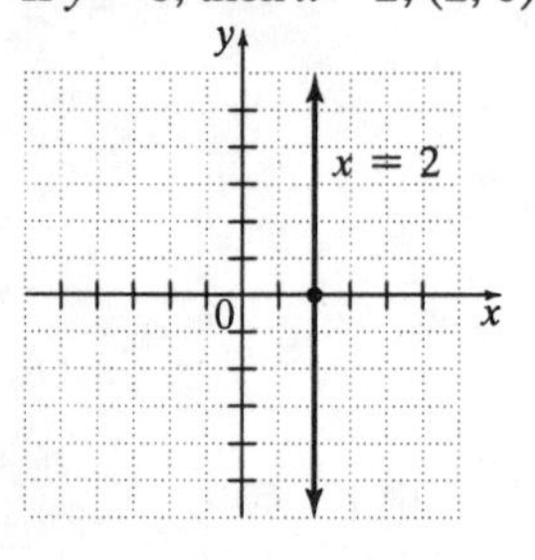

39. $y + 6 = 0$ or $y = -6$
If $x = 0$, then $y = -6$; (0, −6)
Since y cannot equal zero there is no x-intercept.

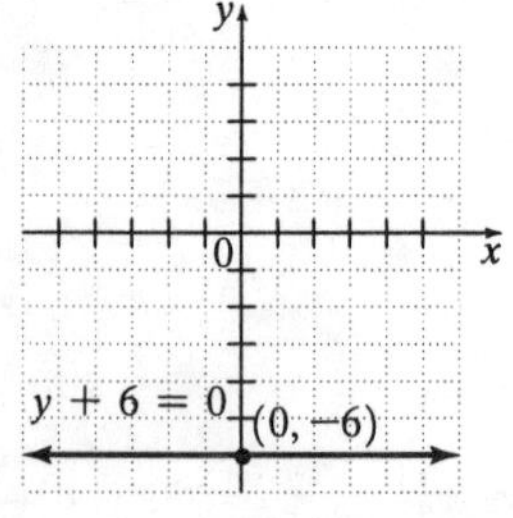

40. (−1, 2) and (3, −1)
$$m = \frac{-1-2}{3-(-1)} = \frac{-3}{3+1} = -\frac{3}{4}$$

41. (−2, −2) and (3, −1)
$$m = \frac{-1-(-2)}{3-(-2)} = \frac{-1+2}{3+2} = \frac{1}{5}$$

42. d

43. b

44. c

45. a

46. e

47. (2, 5) and (6, 8)
$$m = \frac{8-5}{6-2} = \frac{3}{4}$$

48. (4, 7) and (1, 2)
$$m = \frac{2-7}{1-4} = \frac{-5}{-3} = \frac{5}{3}$$

49. (1, 3) and (−2, −9)
$$m = \frac{-9-3}{-2-1} = \frac{-12}{-3} = 4$$

50. (−4, 1) and (3, −6)
$$m = \frac{-6-1}{3-(-4)} = \frac{-7}{3+4} = \frac{-7}{7} = -1$$

51. $x = 5$, undefined slope

52. $y = -1$, $m = 0$

53. $y = -2$, $m = 0$

54. $x = 0$, undefined slope

55. $m = \frac{-2-1}{1-(-3)} = \frac{-3}{1+3} = -\frac{3}{4}$
$$m = \frac{1-4}{6-2} = -\frac{3}{4}$$
parallel

56. $m = \dfrac{4-6}{0-(-7)} = \dfrac{-2}{0+7} = -\dfrac{2}{7}$

$m = \dfrac{5-(-3)}{1-(-9)} = \dfrac{5+3}{1+9} = \dfrac{8}{10} = \dfrac{4}{5}$

neither

57. $m = \dfrac{-7-10}{8-9} = \dfrac{-17}{-1} = 17$

$m = \dfrac{-8-(-3)}{2-(-1)} = \dfrac{-8+3}{2+1} = -\dfrac{5}{3}$

neither

58. $m = \dfrac{-2-3}{3-(-1)} = \dfrac{-5}{3+1} = -\dfrac{5}{4}$

$m = \dfrac{2-(-2)}{3-(-2)} = \dfrac{2+2}{3+2} = \dfrac{4}{5}$

perpendicular

59. (1995, 39.2), (1998, 42.92).

$m = \dfrac{42.92-39.2}{1998-1995} = \dfrac{37.2}{3} = 1.24$

Every 1 year, 1.24 million more persons have a bachelors degree or higher.

60. (1995, 805), (1997, 859)

$m = \dfrac{859-805}{1997-1995} = \dfrac{54}{2} = 27$

Every 1 year, 27 million more people go on vacations.

61. $3x - 4y \le 0$

Graph $3x - 4y = 0$. The boundary line is solid.

Test: (0, 1):

$3(0) - 4(1) \le 0$

$0 - 4 \le 0$

$-4 \le 0$ True

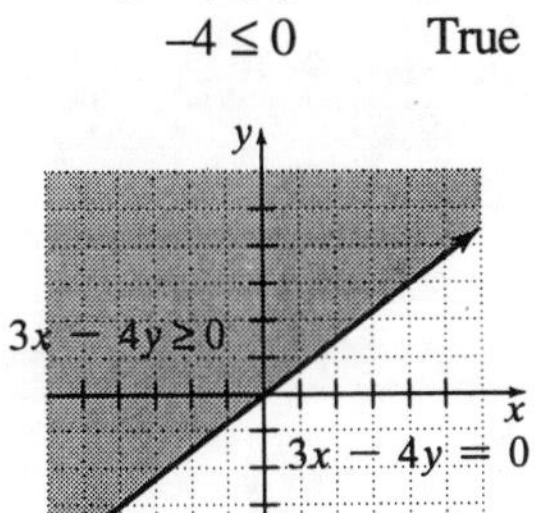

62. $3x - 4y \ge 0$

Find two points.

Let $x = 0$, $3(0) - 4y = 0$, $-4y = 0$, $y = 0$, (0, 0)

Let $x = 4$, $3(4) - 4y = 0$, $12 - 4y = 0$,

$-4y = -12$,

$y = 3$, (4, 3)

The boundary line is solid.

Choose (5, 0) for a test point.

$3x - 4y \ge 0$

$3(5) - 4(0) \ge 0$

$15 - 0 \ge 0$

$15 \ge 0$

Since $15 \ge 0$, the side containing (5, 0) is shaded.

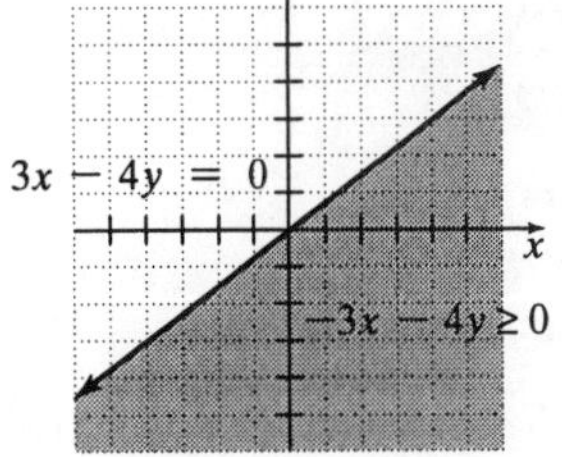

63. $x + 6y < 0$

Graph $x + 6y = 0$. The boundary line is dashed.

Test (0, −1):

$0 + 6(-1) < 0$

$0 - 6 < 0$

$-6 < 0$ True

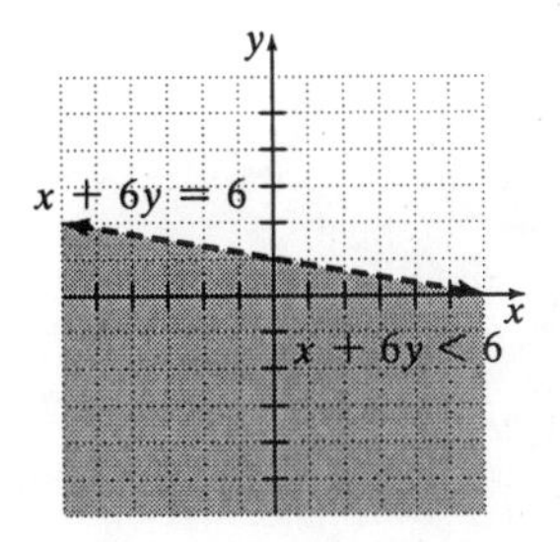

64. $x + y > -2$
Find the intercepts.
Let $x = 0$, $0 + y = -2$, $y = -2$, $(0, -2)$
Let $y = 0$, $x + 0 = -2$, $x = -2$, $(-2, 0)$
The boundary line is dashed.
Choose $(0, 0)$ as a test point.
$x + y > -2$
$0 + 0 > -2$
$0 > -2$
Since $0 > -2$, the side containing $(0, 0)$ is shaded.

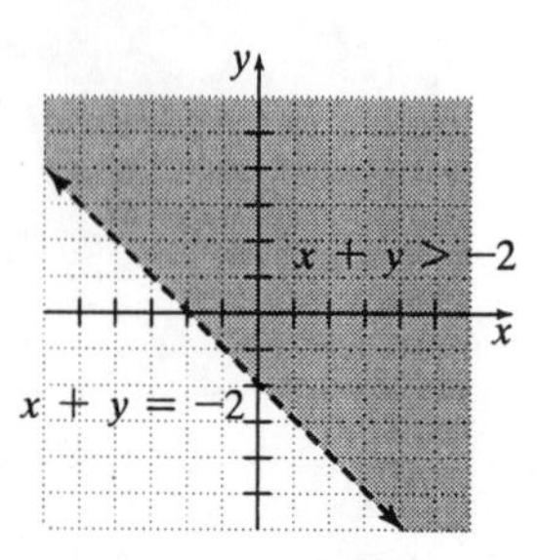

65. $y \geq -7$
Graph $y = -7$. The boundary line is solid.

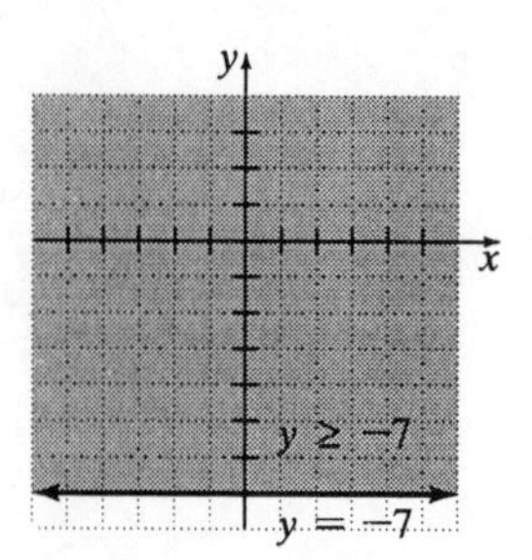

66. $y \leq -4$
Find two points.
Let $x = 1$, $y = -4$, $(1, -4)$
Let $x = 3$, $y = -4$, $(3, -4)$
The boundary line is solid.
Choose $(0, 0)$ as a test point.
$y \leq -4$
$0 \; ? -4$
Since $0 \not\leq -4$, the side *not* containing $(0, 0)$ is shaded.

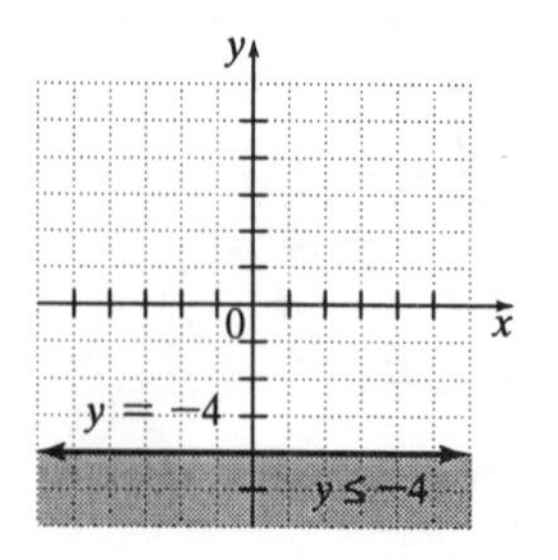

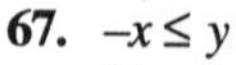
67. $-x \leq y$
Graph $-x = y$. The boundary line is solid.
Test $(0, 1)$: $-(0) \leq 1$
$0 \leq 1$ True

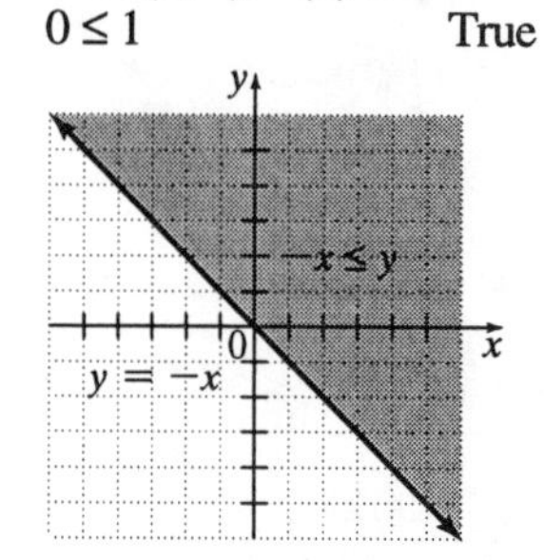

68. $x \geq -y$
Find two points.
Let $y = 0$, $x = -0$, $x = 0$, $(0, 0)$
Let $y = 3$, $x = -3$, $(-3, 3)$
The boundary line is solid.
Choose $(4, 0)$ as a test point.
$x \geq -y$
$4 \geq -0$
$4 \geq 0$
Since $4 \geq 0$ the side containing $(4, 0)$ is shaded.

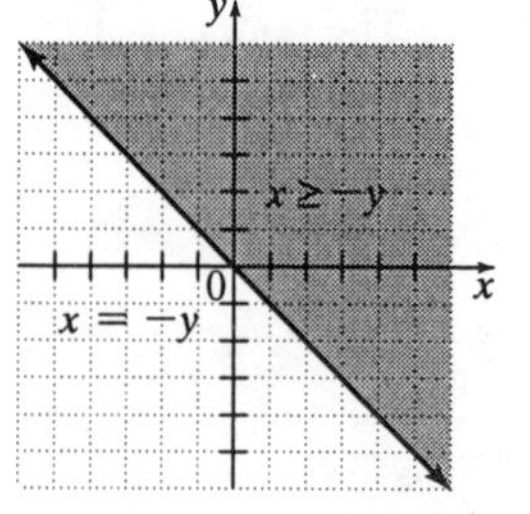

Chapter 3 Test

1. $x - 2y = 3 \qquad (1, 1)$

$1 - 2(1) \; ? \; 3$

$1 - 2 \; ? \; 3$

$-1 \; ? \; 3$

$-1 \neq 3 \qquad$ No

2. $2x + 3y = 6 \qquad (0, -2)$

$2(0) + 3(-2) \; ? \; 6$

$0 - 6 \; ? \; 6$

$-6 \; ? \; 6$

$-6 \neq 6 \qquad$ No

3. $12y - 7x = 5$

$12y - 7(1) = 5$

$12y - 7 = 5$

$12y = 5 + 7$

$12y = 12$

$y = 1$

$(1, 1)$

4. $y = 17$

$(-4, 17)$

5. $(-1, -1)$ and $(4, 1)$

$$m = \frac{1-(-1)}{4-(-1)} = \frac{1+1}{4+1} = \frac{2}{5}$$

6. $m = 0$ for horizontal line

7. $$m = \frac{2-(-5)}{-1-6} = \frac{2+5}{-7} = \frac{7}{-7} = -1$$

8. $$m = \frac{-1-(-8)}{-1-0} = \frac{-1+8}{-1} = \frac{7}{-1} = -7$$

9. $-3x + y = 5$

$y = 3x + 5$

$m = 3$

10. $x = 6$

Undefined slope

11. $$m = \frac{-3-3}{1-(-1)} = \frac{-6}{1+1} = \frac{-6}{2} = -3$$

$$m = \frac{-7-(-1)}{4-2} = \frac{-7+1}{2} = \frac{-6}{2} = -3$$

parallel

12. $$m = \frac{-2-(-6)}{-1-(-6)} = \frac{-2+6}{-1+6} = \frac{4}{5}$$

$$m = \frac{-3-3}{3-(-4)} = \frac{-6}{3+4} = -\frac{6}{7}$$

neither

13. $2x + y = 8$

Find the intercepts.

Let $x = 0$, $2(0) + y = 8$, $y = 8$, $(0, 8)$

Let $y = 0$, $2x + 0 = 8$, $2x = 8$, $x = 4$ $(4, 0)$

14. $-x + 4y = 5$

Find the intercepts.

Let $x = 0$, $-0 + 4y = 5$, $4y = 5$, $y = \frac{5}{4}$

$\left(0, \frac{5}{4}\right)$

Let $y = 0$, $-x + 4(0) = 5$, $-x = 5$, $x = -5$, $(-5, 0)$

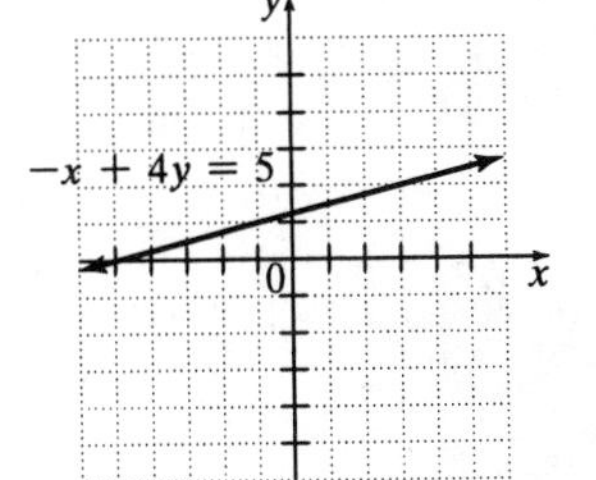

15. $x - y \geq -2$
Find the intercepts.
Let $x = 0$, $0 - y = -2$, $-y = -2$,
$y = \dfrac{-2}{-1} = 2$, $(0, 2)$
let $y = 0$, $x - 0 = -2$, $x = -2$, $(-2, 0)$
The boundary line is solid.
Choose $(0, 0)$ as a test point.
$x - y \geq -2$
$0 - 0 \ ? -2$
$0 \ ? -2$
Since $0 \geq -2$, the side containing $(0, 0)$ is shaded.

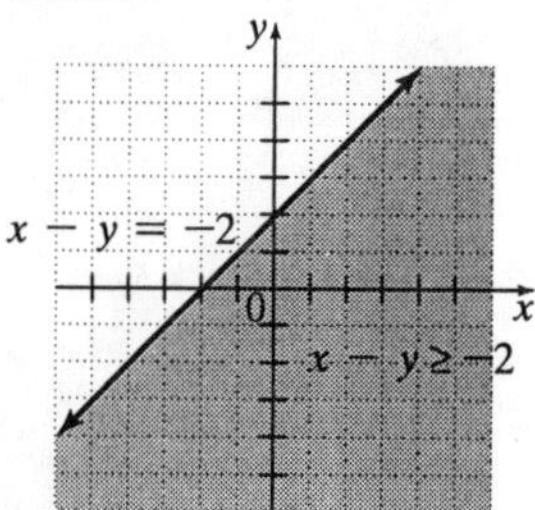

16. $y \geq -4x$
Find two points.
Let $x = 0$, $y = -4(0)$, $y = 0$, $(0, 0)$
Let $x = 1$, $y = -4(1)$, $y = -4$ $(1, -4)$
The boundary line is solid.
Choose $(5, 0)$ as a test point.
$y \geq -4x$
$0 \ ? -4(5)$
$0 \ ? -20$
Since $0 \geq -20$, the side containing $(5, 0)$ is shaded.

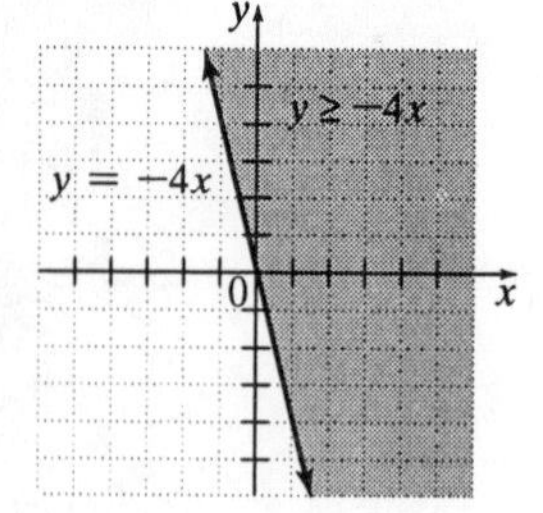

17. $5x - 7y = 10$
Find the intercepts.
Let $x = 0$, $5(0) - 7y = 10$, $-7y = 10$,
$y = -\dfrac{10}{7}$, $\left(0, -\dfrac{10}{7}\right)$
Let $y = 0$, $5x - 7(0) = 10$, $5x = 10$, $x = 2$, $(2, 0)$

18. $2x - 3y > -6$
Find the intercepts. Let $x = 0$, $2(0) - 3y = -6$,
$-3y = -6$, $y = \dfrac{-6}{-3} = 2$, $(0, 2)$
Let $y = 0$, $2x - 3(0) = -6$, $2x = -6$, $x = -3$, $(-3, 0)$
The boundary line is dashed.
Choose $(0, 0)$ for a test point.
$2x - 3y > -6$
$2(0) - 3(0) \ ? -6$
$0 + 0 \ ? -6$
$0 \ ? -6$
Since $0 > -6$, the side containing $(0, 0)$ is shaded.

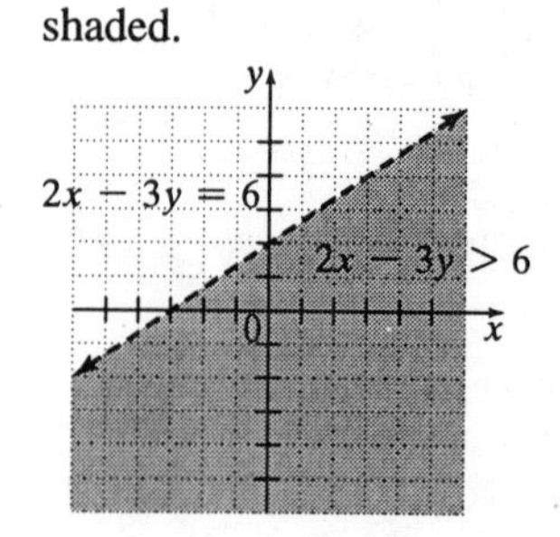

19. $6x + y > -1$

Find the intercepts.

Let $x = 0$, $6(0) + y = -1$, $y = -1$, $(0, -1)$

Let $y = 0$, $6x + 0 = -1$, $6x = -1$, $x = -\frac{1}{6}$

$\left(-\frac{1}{6}, 0\right)$

The boundary line is dashed.

Choose (0, 0) as a test point.

$$6x + y > -1$$
$$6(0) + 0 \ ? -1$$
$$0 + 0 \ ? -1$$
$$0 \ ? -1$$

Since $0 > -1$ the side containing (0, 0) is shaded.

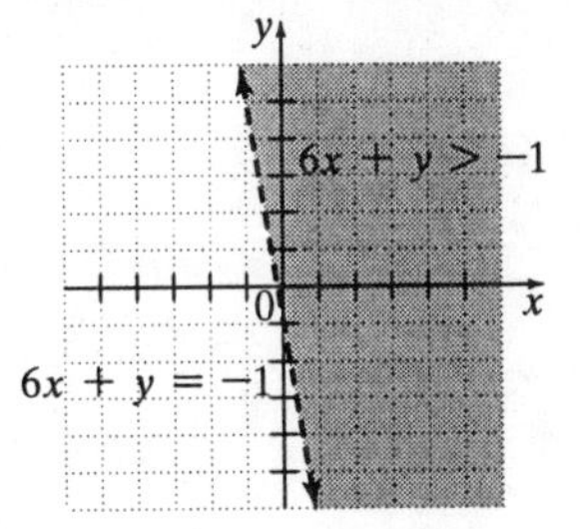

20. $y = -1$

Find two points.

Let $x = 0$, $y = -1$, $(0, -1)$

Let $x = 3$, $y = -1$, $(3, -1)$

21. $x - 3 = 0$

$x = 3$

Find two points.

Let $y = 0$, $x = 3$ (3, 0)

Let $y = 2$, $x = 3$ (3, 2)

22. $5x - 3y = 15$

Find the intercepts.

Let $x = 0$, $5(0) - 3y = 15$, $-3y = 15$, $y = -5$, $(0, -5)$

Let $y = 0$, $5x - 3(0) = 15$, $5x = 15$, $x = 3$, $(3, 0)$

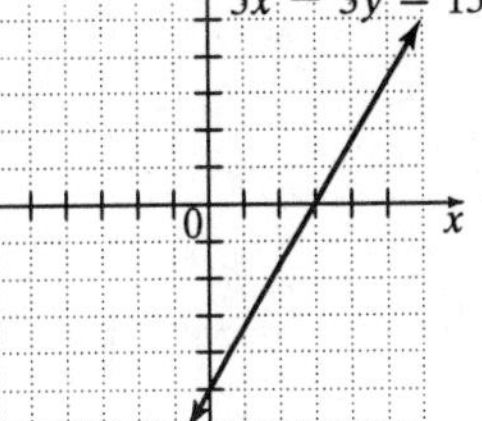

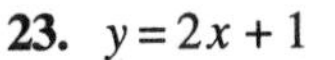

23. $y = 2x + 1$

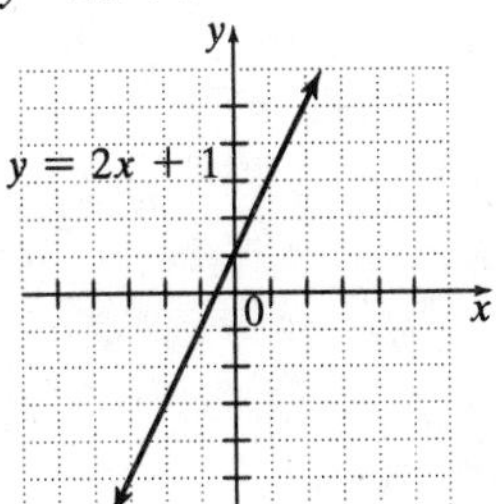

24. $x+4y<-4$

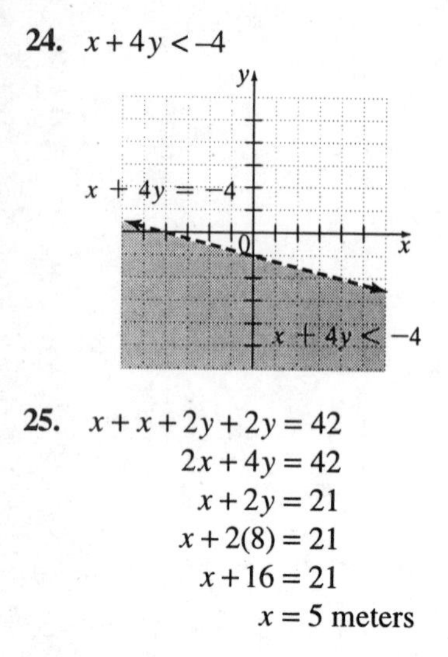

25. $x+x+2y+2y=42$

$$2x+4y=42$$
$$x+2y=21$$
$$x+2(8)=21$$
$$x+16=21$$
$$x=5 \text{ meters}$$

26. a. (1986, 38), (1988, 44), (1990, 50), (1992, 53), (1994, 57), (1996, 62), (1997, 64)

b.

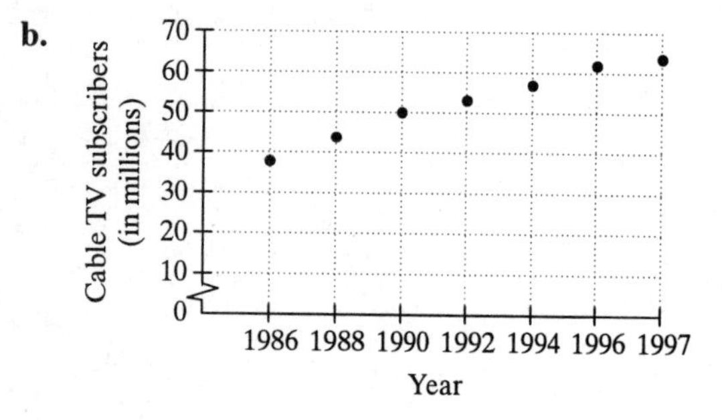

27. (1996, 1332), (1998, 1474)

$$m=\frac{1474-1332}{1998-1996}=\frac{142}{2}=71$$

Every 1 year, 71 million more movie tickets are sold.

Chapter 4

Section 4.1

Mental Math

1. 3^2
   base: 3; exponent: 2

2. 5^4
   base: 5; exponent: 4

3. $(-3)^6$
   base: –3; exponent: 6

4. -3^7
   base: 3; exponent: 7

5. -4^2
   base: 4; exponent: 2

6. $(-4)^3$
   base: –4; exponent: 3

7. $5 \cdot 3^4$
   base: 5; exponent: 1
   base: 3; exponent: 4

8. $9 \cdot 7^6$
   base: 9; exponent: 1
   base 7; exponent: 6

9. $5x^2$
   base: 5; exponent: 1
   base: x, exponent: 2

10. $(5x)^2$
    base: $5x$; exponent: 2

Exercise Set 4.1

1. $7^2 = 7 \cdot 7 = 49$

3. $(-5)^1 = -5$

5. $-2^4 = -2 \cdot 2 \cdot 2 \cdot 2 = -16$

7. $(-2)^4 = (-2)(-2)(-2)(-2) = 16$

9. $\left(\frac{1}{3}\right)^3 = \left(\frac{1}{3}\right)\left(\frac{1}{3}\right)\left(\frac{1}{3}\right) = \frac{1}{27}$

11. $7 \cdot 2^4 = 7 \cdot 2 \cdot 2 \cdot 2 \cdot 2 = 112$

13. Answers may vary.

15. $x^2 = (-2)^2 = (-2)(-2) = 4$

17. $5x^3 = 5(3)^3 = 5 \cdot 3 \cdot 3 \cdot 3 = 135$

19. $2xy^2 = 2(3)(5)^2 = 2(3)(5)(5) = 150$

21. $\frac{2z^4}{5} = \frac{2(-2)^4}{5} = \frac{2(-2)(-2)(-2)(-2)}{5} = \frac{32}{5}$

23. $V = x^3 = 7^3 = 7 \cdot 7 \cdot 7 = 343$
    The volume is 343 cubic meters.

25. We use the volume formula.

27. $x^2 \cdot x^5 = x^{2+5} = x^7$

29. $(-3)^3 \cdot (-3)^9 = (-3)^{3+9} = (-3)^{12}$

31. $(5y^4)(3y) = 5(3)y^{4+1} = 15y^5$

33. $(4z^{10})(-6z^7)(z^3) = 4(-6)z^{10+7+3} = -24z^{20}$

35. $(pq)^7 = p^7q^7$

37. $\left(\frac{m}{n}\right)^9 = \frac{m^9}{n^9}$

39. $(x^2y^3)^5 = x^{2\cdot5}y^{3\cdot5} = x^{10}y^{15}$

41. $\left(\frac{-2xz}{y^5}\right)^2 = \frac{(-2)^2x^2z^2}{y^{5\cdot2}} = \frac{4x^2z^2}{y^{10}}$

43. $\frac{x^3}{x} = x^{3-1} = x^2$

45. $\frac{(-2)^5}{(-2)^3} = (-2)^{5-3} = (-2)^2 = 4$

47. $\frac{p^7 q^{20}}{pq^{15}} = p^{7-1} q^{20-15} = p^6 q^5$

49. $\frac{7x^2y^6}{14x^2y^3} = \frac{7}{14} x^{2-2} y^{6-3}$
$= \frac{1}{2} x^0 y^3$
$= \frac{1}{2}(1)y^3$
$= \frac{y^3}{2}$

51. $(2x)^0 = 1$

53. $-2x^0 = -2(1) = -2$

55. $5^0 + y^0 = 1 + 1 = 2$

57. $\left(\frac{-3a^2}{b^3}\right)^3 = \frac{(-3)^3 a^{2\cdot 3}}{b^{3\cdot 3}} = -\frac{27a^6}{b^9}$

59. $\frac{(x^5)^7 \cdot x^8}{x^4} = \frac{x^{5\cdot 7} x^8}{x^4}$
$= \frac{x^{35} x^8}{x^4}$
$= x^{35+8-4}$
$= x^{39}$

61. $\frac{(z^3)^6}{(5z)^4} = \frac{z^{3\cdot 6}}{5^4 \cdot z^4} = \frac{z^{18}}{625z^4} = \frac{z^{18-4}}{625} = \frac{z^{14}}{625}$

63. $\frac{(6mn)^5}{mn^2} = \frac{6^5 \cdot m^5 \cdot n^5}{mn^2}$
$= 7776m^{5-1}n^{5-2}$
$= 7776m^4n^3$

65. $-5^2 = -1 \cdot 5^2 = -(5)(5) = -25$

67. $\left(\frac{1}{4}\right)^3 = \left(\frac{1}{4}\right)\left(\frac{1}{4}\right)\left(\frac{1}{4}\right) = \frac{1}{64}$

69. $(9xy)^2 = 9^2 x^2 y^2 = 81x^2y^2$

71. $(6b)^0 = 1$

73. $2^3 + 2^5 = 2\cdot 2\cdot 2 + 2\cdot 2\cdot 2\cdot 2\cdot 2$
$= 8 + 32$
$= 40$

75. $b^4 b^2 = b^{4+2} = b^6$

77. $a^2 a^3 a^4 = a^{2+3+4} = a^9$

79. $(2x^3)(-8x^4) = (2)(-8)x^{3+4} = -16x^7$

81. $(4a)^3 = 4^3 a^3 = 64a^3$

83. $(-6xyz^3)^2 = (-6)^2 x^2 y^2 z^{3\cdot 2} = 36x^2y^2z^6$

85.

$\left(\frac{3y^5}{6x^4}\right)^3 = \left(\frac{y^5}{2x^4}\right)^3$ Reduce fraction
$= \frac{y^{5\cdot 3}}{2^3 x^{4\cdot 3}}$
$= \frac{y^{15}}{8x^{12}}$

87. $\frac{x^5}{x^4} = x^{5-4} = x$

89. $\frac{2x^3y^2z}{xyz} = 2x^{3-1}y^{2-1}z^{1-1}$
$= 2x^2y^1z^0$
$= 2x^2y(1)$
$= 2x^2y$

91. $\frac{(3x^2y^5)^5}{x^3y} = \frac{3^5 \cdot x^{2\cdot 5} \cdot y^{5\cdot 5}}{x^3y}$
$= \frac{243x^{10}y^{25}}{x^3y}$
$= 243x^{10-3}y^{25-1}$
$= 243x^7y^{24}$

93. Answers may vary.

95. $A = l \cdot w$
$A = (5x^3 \text{ ft})(4x^2 \text{ ft})$
$A = 5 \cdot 4 \cdot x^{3+2}\text{sq. ft} = 20x^5 \text{ sq. ft}$

97. $A = \pi r^2$
$A = \pi(5y \text{ cm})^2$
$= \pi(5)^2y^2 \text{ sq. cm}$
$= 25y^2\pi \text{ sq. cm}$

99. $V = s^3$
$V = (3y^4 \text{ ft})^3$
$= 3^3y^{4\cdot 3} \text{ cu. ft}$
$= 27y^{12} \text{ cu ft}$

101. $3x - 5x + 7 = -2x + 7$

103. $y - 10 + y = 2y - 10$

105. $7x + 2 - 8x - 6 = -x - 4$

107. $2(x-5) + 3(5-x) = 2x - 10 + 15 - 3x$
$= -x + 5$

109. $x^{5a}x^{4a} = x^{5a+4a} = x^{9a}$

111. $(a^b)^5 = a^{b\cdot 5} = a^{5b}$

113. $\frac{x^{9a}}{x^{4a}} = x^{9a-4a} = x^{5a}$

115. $(x^ay^bz^c)^{5a} = x^{a\cdot 5a}y^{b\cdot 5a}z^{c\cdot 5a}$
$= x^{5a^2}y^{5ab}z^{5ac}$

Section 4.2

Mental Math

1. $-9y - 5y = -14y$
2. $6m^5 + 7m^5 = 13m^5$
3. $4y^3 + 3y^3 = 7y^3$
4. $21y^5 - 19y^5 = 2y^5$
5. $x + 6x = 7x$
6. $7z - z = 6z$

Exercise Set 4.2

1. $x + 2$
degree is 1; binomial

3. $9m^3 - 5m^2 + 4m - 8$
degree is 3; none of these

5. $12x^4y - x^2y^2 - 12x^2y^4$
degree is 6; trinomial

7. $3zx - 5x^2$
degree is 2; binomial

9. $3xy^2 - 4$
degree 3

11. $5a^2 - 2a + 1$
degree 2

13. Answers may vary.

15. Answers may vary.

17. $x+6$

a. $x=0$
$0+6=6$

b. $x=-1$
$-1+6=5$

19. x^2-5x-2

a. $x=0$
$0^2-5(0)-2=0+0-2=-2$

b. $x=-1$
$(-1)^2-5(-1)-2=1+5-2=4$

21. x^3-15

a. $x=0$
$0^3-15=-15$

b. $x=-1$
$(-1)^3-15=-1-15=-16$

23. $-16t^2+1821=-16(10.8)^2+1821$
$=-45.24$ ft
The object has reached the ground.

25. $14x^2+9x^2=23x^2$

27. $15x^2-3x^2-y=12x^2-y$

29. $8s-5s+4s=3s+4s=7s$

31. $0.1y^2-1.2y^2+6.7-1.9=-1.1y^2+4.8$

33. $\frac{2}{5}x^2-\frac{1}{3}x^3+x^2-\frac{1}{4}x^3+6$
$=-\frac{7}{12}x^3+\frac{7}{5}x^2+6$

35. $6a^2-4ab+7b^2-a^2-5ab+9b^2$
$=5a^2-9ab+16b^2$

37. $(3x+7)+(9x+5)=3x+7+9x+5$
$=12x+12$

39. $(-7x+5)+(-3x^2+7x+5)$
$=-7x+5-3x^2+7x+5$
$=-3x^2+0x+10$
$=-3x^2+10$

41. $(2x^2+5)-(3x^2-9)=2x^2+5-3x^2+9$
$=-x^2+14$

43. $3x-(5x-9)=3x-5x+9=-2x+9$

45. $(2x^2+3x-9)-(-4x+7)$
$=2x^2+3x-9+4x-7$
$=2x^2+7x-16$

47. $P=a+b+c$
$P=(-x^2+3x)\text{ ft}+(2x^2+5)\text{ ft}+(4x-1)\text{ ft}$
$P=(-x^2+3x+2x^2+5+4x-1)\text{ ft}$
$P=(x^2+7x+4)\text{ ft}$

49. $(4y^2+4y+1)\text{ m}-(y^2-10)\text{ m}$
$=(4y^2+4y+1-y^2+10)\text{ m}$
$=(3y^2+4y+11)\text{ m}$

51.
$$\begin{array}{r} 3t^2+4 \\ +\ 5t^2-8 \\ \hline 8t^2-4 \end{array}$$

53.
$$\begin{array}{r} 4z^2-8z+3 \\ -(6z^2+8z-3) \\ \hline \end{array}$$

$$\begin{array}{r} 4z^2-8z+3 \\ -6z^2-8z+3 \\ \hline -2z^2-16z+6 \end{array}$$

55.
$$\begin{array}{r} 5x^3-4x^2+6x-2 \\ -(3x^3-2x^2-\ x-4) \\ \hline \end{array}$$

$$\begin{array}{r} 5x^3-4x^2+6x-2 \\ -3x^3+2x^2+\ x+4 \\ \hline 2x^3-2x^2+7x+2 \end{array}$$

57. $81x^2+10-(19x^2+5)=81x^2+10-19x^2-5$
$=62x^2+5$

59. $[(8x+1)+(6x+3)]-(2x+2)=8x+1+6x+3-2x-2$
$=8x+6x-2x+1+3-2$
$=12x+2$

61. $-15x-(-4x)=-15x+4x=-11x$

63. $2x-5+5x-8=7x-13$

65. $(-3y^2-4y)+(2y^2+y-1)=-3y^2-4y+2y^2+y-1$
$=-y^2-3y-1$

67. $(5x+8)-(-2x^2-6x+8)=5x+8+2x^2+6x-8$
$=2x^2+11x$

69. $(-8x^4+7x)+(-8x^4+x+9)=-8x^4+7x-8x^4+x+9$
$=-16x^4+8x+9$

71. $(3x^2+5x-8)+(5x^2+9x+12)-(x^2-14)$
$=3x^2+5x-8+5x^2+9x+12-x^2+14$
$=7x^2+14x+18$

73. $7x-3-(4x)=7x-3-4x=3x-3$

75. $(7x^2+3x+9)-(5x+7)=7x^2+3x+9-5x-7$
$=7x^2-2x+2$

77. $[(8y^2+7)+(6y+9)]-(4y^2-6y-3)$
$=8y^2+7+6y+9-4y^2+6y+3$
$=8y^2-4y^2+6y+6y+7+9+3$
$=4y^2+12y+19$

79. $[(-x^2-2x)+(5x^2+x+9)]-(-2x^2+4x-12)$
$=-x^2-2x+5x^2+x+9+2x^2-4x+12$
$=-x^2+5x^2+2x^2-2x+x-4x+9+12$
$=6x^2-5x+21$

81. $[(1.2x^2-3x+9.1)-(7.8x^2-3.1+8)]+(1.2x-6)$
$=1.2x^2-3x+9.1-7.8x^2+3.1-8+1.2x-6$
$=-6.6x^2-1.8x-1.8$

83. $(2x)(2x)+7x+(x)(x)+5x=4x^2+7x+x^2+5x;$
$4x^2+7x+x^2+5x=5x^2+12x$

85. $-16t^2+200t$

a. $t=1$ second
$-16(1)^2+200(1)=184$ ft

b. $t=5$ seconds
$-16(5)^2+200(5)=600$ ft

c. $t=7.6$ seconds
$-16(7.6)^2+200(7.6)=595.84$ ft

d. $t=10.3$ seconds
$-16(10.3)^2+200(10.3)=362.56$ ft

87. $-16t^2+200t=0$
$t(-16t+200)=0$
$-16t+200=0$
$t=\dfrac{-200}{-16}=12.5$ seconds

89. $(9a+6b-5)+(-11a-7b+6)$
$=9a+6b-5-11a-7b+6$
$=-2a-b+1$

91. $(4x^2+y^2+3)-(x^2+y^2-2)$
$=4x^2+y^2+3-x^2-y^2+2$
$=3x^2+5$

93. $(x^2+2xy-y^2)+(5x^2-4xy+20y^2)$
$=x^2+2xy-y^2+5x^2-4xy+20y^2$
$=6x^2-2xy+19y^2$

95. $(11r^2s+16rs-3-2r^2s^2)-(3sr^2+5-9r^2s^2)$
$=11r^2s+16rs-3-2r^2s^2-3sr^2-5+9r^2s^2$
$=11r^2s-3r^2s+16rs-3-5-2r^2s^2+9r^2s^2$
$=8r^2s+16rs-8+7r^2s^2$

97. $0.15x^2 + 0.15x + 7.2$
When $x = 5$, we have
$$0.15(5)^2 + 0.15(5) + 7.2 = 3.75 + 0.75 + 7.2 = 11.7$$
The model predicts that there were 11.7 million departures in 1998.

99. $(152.5x^2 - 187.5x + 25,525) + (775.5x^2 - 670.5x + 17,763)$
$= 152.5x^2 - 187.5x + 25,525 + 775.5x^2 - 670.5x + 17,763$
$= 152.5x^2 + 775.5x^2 - 187.5x - 670.5x + 25,525 + 17,763$
$= 928x^2 - 858x + 43,288$

101. $3x(2x) = 3 \cdot 2 \cdot x^{1+1} = 6x^2$

103. $(12x^3)(-x^5) = (12)(-1)x^{3+5} = -12x^8$

105. $10x^2(20xy^2) = 10 \cdot 20 \cdot x^{2+1}y^2 = 200x^3y^2$

Section 4.3

Mental Math

1. $5x(2y) = 5 \cdot 2xy = 10xy$

2. $7a(4b) = 7 \cdot 4ab = 28ab$

3. $x^2x^5 = x^{2+5} = x^7$

4. $z \cdot z^4 = z^{1+4} = z^5$

5. $6x(3x^2) = 6 \cdot 3 \cdot x^{1+2} = 18x^3$

6. $5a^2(3a^2) = 5 \cdot 3 \cdot a^{2+2} = 15a^4$

Exercise Set 4.3

1. $2a(2a - 4) = 2a(2a) + 2a(-4) = 4a^2 - 8a$

3. $7x(x^2 + 2x - 1) = 7x(x^2) + 7x(2x) + 7x(-1)$
$= 7x^3 + 14x^2 - 7x$

5. $3x^2(2x^2 - x) = 3x^2(2x^2) + 3x^2(-x)$
$= 6x^4 - 3x^3$

7. $x^2 + 3x$

9. $(a+7)(a-2) = a(a) + a(-2) + 7(a) + 7(-2)$
$= a^2 - 2a + 7a - 14$
$= a^2 + 5a - 14$

11. $(2y-4)^2 = (2y-4)(2y-4)$
$= 2y(2y) + 2y(-4) - 4(2y) - 4(-4)$
$= 4y^2 - 8y - 8y + 16$
$= 4y^2 - 16y + 16$

13. $(5x-9y)(6x-5y) = 5x(6x) + 5x(-5y) - 9y(6x) - 9y(-5y)$
$= 30x^2 - 25xy - 54xy + 45y^2$
$= 30x^2 - 79xy + 45y^2$

15. $(2x^2-5)^2 = (2x^2-5)(2x^2-5)$
$= 2x^2(2x^2) + 2x^2(-5) - 5(2x^2) - 5(-5)$
$= 4x^4 - 10x^2 - 10x^2 + 25$
$= 4x^4 - 20x^2 + 25$

17. $x^2 + 3x + 2x + 2 \cdot 3 = x^2 + 5x + 6$

19. $(x-2)(x^2-3x+7) = x(x^2) + x(-3x) + x(7) - 2(x^2) - 2(-3x) - 2(7)$
$= x^3 - 3x^2 + 7x - 2x^2 + 6x - 14$
$= x^3 - 5x^2 + 13x - 14$

21. $(x+5)(x^3-3x+4) = x(x^3) + x(-3x) + x(4) + 5(x^3) + 5(-2x) + 5(4)$
$= x^4 - 3x^2 + 4x + 5x^3 - 15x + 20$
$= x^4 + 5x^3 - 3x^2 - 11x + 20$

23. $(2a-3)(5a^2-6a+4) = 2a(5a^2) + 2a(-6a) + 2a(4) - 3(5a^2) - 3(-6a) - 3(4)$
$= 10a^3 - 12a^2 + 8a - 15a^2 + 18a - 12$
$= 10a^3 - 27a^2 + 26a - 12$

25. $(x+2)^3 = (x+2)(x+2)(x+2)$
$= (x^2 + 2x + 2x + 4)(x+2)$
$= (x^2 + 4x + 4)(x+2)$
$= (x^2 + 4x + 4)x + (x^2 + 4x + 4)2$
$= x^3 + 4x^2 + 4x + 2x^2 + 8x + 8$
$= x^3 + 6x^2 + 12x + 8$

27. $$\begin{aligned}(2y-3)^3 &= (2y-3)(2y-3)(2y-3)\\ &= (4y^2-6y-6y+9)(2y-3)\\ &= (4y^2-12y+9)(2y-3)\\ &= (4y^2-12y+9)2y+(4y^2-12y+9)(-3)\\ &= 8y^3-24y^2+18y-12y^2+36y-27\\ &= 8y^3-36y^2+54y-27\end{aligned}$$

29. $$\begin{array}{r} 2x^2+4x-1 \\ \times \qquad x+3 \\ \hline 6x^2+12x-3 \\ 2x^3+4x^2-x \quad \\ \hline 2x^3+10x^2+11x-3 \end{array}$$

31. $$\begin{array}{r} x^3 \qquad +5x-7 \\ \times \qquad x^2 \qquad -9 \\ \hline -9x^3 \qquad -45x+63 \\ x^5+5x^3-7x^2 \qquad\qquad \\ \hline x^5-4x^3-7x^2+45x+63 \end{array}$$

33. **a.** $(2+3)^2 = 5^2 = 25$
$2^2+3^2 = 4+9 = 13$

b. $(8+10)^2 = (18)^2 = 324$
$8^2+10^2 = 64+100 = 164$

c. No; answers may vary.

35. $2a(a+4) = 2a(a)+2a(4) = 2a^2+8a$

37. $$\begin{aligned}3x(2x^2-3x+4) &= 3x(2x^2)+3x(-3x)+3x(4)\\ &= 6x^3-9x^2+12x\end{aligned}$$

39. $$\begin{aligned}(5x+9y)(3x+2y) &= 5x(3x)+5x(2y)+9y(3x)+9y(2y)\\ &= 15x^2+10xy+27xy+18y^2\\ &= 15x^2+37xy+18y^2\end{aligned}$$

41. $$\begin{aligned}(x+2)(x^2+5x+6) &= x(x^2)+x(5x)+x(6)+2(x^2)+2(5x)+2(6)\\ &= x^3+5x^2+6x+2x^2+10x+12\\ &= x^3+7x^2+16x+12\end{aligned}$$

43. $(7x+4)^2 = (7x+4)(7x+4)$
$= 7x(7x) + 7x(4) + 4(7x) + 4(4)$
$= 49x^2 + 28x + 28x + 16$
$= 49x^2 + 56x + 16$

45. $-2a^2(3a^2 - 2a + 3) = -2a^2(3a^2) - 2a^2(-2a) - 2a^2(3)$
$= -6a^4 + 4a^3 - 6a^2$

47. $(x+3)(x^2 + 7x + 12) = x(x^2) + x(7x) + x(12) + 3(x^2) + 3(7x) + 3(12)$
$= x^3 + 7x^2 + 12x + 3x^2 + 21x + 36$
$= x^3 + 10x^2 + 33x + 36$

49. $(a+1)^3 = (a+1)(a+1)(a+1)$
$= (a^2 + a + a + 1)(a+1)$
$= (a^2 + 2a + 1)(a+1)$
$= (a^2 + 2a + 1)a + (a^2 + 2a + 1)1$
$= a^3 + 2a^2 + a + a^2 + 2a + 1$
$= a^3 + 3a^2 + 3a + 1$

51. $(x+y)(x+y) = x(x) + x(y) + y(x) + y(y)$
$= x^2 + xy + xy + y^2$
$= x^2 + 2xy + y^2$

53. $(x-7)(x-6) = x(x) + x(-6) - 7(x) - 7(-6)$
$= x^2 - 6x - 7x + 42$
$= x^2 - 13x + 42$

55. $3a(a^2 + 2) = 3a(a^2) + 3a(2) = 3a^3 + 6a$

57. $-4y(y^2 + 3y - 11) = -4y(y^2) - 4y(3y) - 4y(-11)$
$= -4y^3 - 12y^2 + 44y$

59. $(5x+1)(5x-1) = 5x(5x) + 5x(-1) + 1(5x) + 1(-1)$
$= 25x^2 - 5x + 5x - 1$
$= 25x^2 - 1$

61. $(5x+4)(x^2 - x + 4) = 5x(x^2) + 5x(-x) + 5x(4) + 4(x^2) + 4(-x) + 4(4)$
$= 5x^3 - 5x^2 + 20x + 4x^2 - 4x + 16$
$= 5x^3 - x^2 + 16x + 16$

63. $(2x-5)^3 = (2x-5)(2x-5)(2x-5)$
$= (4x^2 - 10x + 25)(2x-5)$
$= (4x^2 - 20x + 25)(2x-5)$
$= (4x^2 - 20x + 25)2x + (4x^2 - 20x + 25)(-5)$
$= 8x^3 - 40x^2 + 50x - 20x^2 + 100x - 125$
$= 8x^3 - 60x^2 + 150x - 125$

65. $(4x+5)(8x^2 + 2x - 4)$
$= 4x(8x^2) + 4x(2x) + 4x(-4) + 5(8x^2) + 5(2x) + 5(-4)$
$= 32x^3 + 8x^2 - 16x + 40x^2 + 10x - 20$
$= 32x^3 + 48x^2 - 6x - 20$

67. $(7xy - y)^2 = (7xy - y)(7xy - y)$
$= 7xy(7xy) + 7xy(-y) - y(7xy) - y(-y)$
$= 49x^2y^2 - 7xy^2 - 7xy^2 + y^2$
$= 49x^2y^2 - 14xy^2 + y^2$

69.
$$\begin{array}{r} 5y^2 - y + 3 \\ \times \qquad y^2 - 3y - 2 \\ \hline -10y^2 + 2y - 6 \\ -15y^3 + 3y^2 - 9y \qquad \\ 5y^4 - y^3 + 3y^2 \qquad\qquad \\ \hline 5y^4 - 16y^3 - 4y^2 - 7y - 6 \end{array}$$

71.
$$\begin{array}{r} 3x^2 + 2x - 4 \\ \times \qquad 2x^2 - 4x + 3 \\ \hline 9x^2 + 6x - 12 \\ -12x^3 - 8x^2 + 16x \qquad \\ 6x^4 + 4x^3 - 8x^2 \qquad\qquad \\ \hline 6x^4 - 8x^3 - 7x^2 + 22x - 12 \end{array}$$

73. $A = l \cdot w$
$A = (2x+5)(2x-5)$
$A = 2x(2x) + 2x(-5) + 5(2x) + 5(-5)$
$A = 4x^2 - 10x + 10x - 25$
$A = (4x^2 - 25)$ square yards

75. $A = \frac{1}{2}b \cdot h$

$A = \frac{1}{2}(4x)(3x-2)$

$A = (2x)(3x-2)$

$A = (6x^2 - 4x)$ square inches

77. $(x+3)(x+3) - 2.2$

$= (x^2 + 3x + 3x + 9) - 4$

$= x^2 + 6x + 9 - 4$

$= (x^2 + 6x + 5)$ square units

79. a. $(a+b)(a-b) = a \cdot a - ab + ab - b \cdot b$

$= a^2 - b^2$

b. $(2x+3y)(2x-3y)$

$= 2x(2x) - 2x(3y) + 2x(3y) - 3y(3y)$

$= 4x^2 - 9y^2$

c. $(4x+7)(4x-7)$

$= 4x(4x) - 4x(7) + 4x(7) - 7(7)$

$= 16x^2 - 49$

d. Answers may vary.

81. $(4p)^2 = 4p(4p) = 4 \cdot 4p^{1+1} = 16p^2$

83. $(-7m^2)^2 = (-7m^2)(-7m^2)$

$= (-7)(-7)m^{2+2}$

$= 49m^4$

85. $3500

87. $6500 – $6000 = $500

89. There is a loss in value each year.

Section 4.4

Mental Math

1. False

$(x+4)^2 = x^2 + 8x + 16$

2. True

3. False

$(x+4)(x-4) = x^2 - 16$

4. False

The product of $(x-1)(x^3 + 3x - 1)$ is a polynomial of degree 4.

Exercise Set 4.4

1. $(x+3)(x+4)$

F O I L

$= x(x) + x(4) + 3(x) + 3(4)$

$= x^2 + 4x + 3x + 12$

$= x^2 + 7x + 12$

3. $(x-5)(x+10)$

F O I L

$= x(x) + x(10) - 5(x) - 5(10)$

$= x^2 + 10x - 5x - 50$

$= x^2 + 5x - 50$

5. $(5x-6)(x+2)$

F O I L

$= 5x(x) + 5x(2) - 6(x) - 6(2)$

$= 5x^2 + 10x - 6x - 12$

$= 5x^2 + 4x - 12$

7. $(y-6)(4y-1)$

F O I L

$= y(4y) + y(-1) - 6(4y) - 6(-1)$

$= 4y^2 - y - 24y + 6$

$= 4y^2 - 25y + 6$

9. $(2x+5)(3x-1)$

F O I L

$= 2x(3x) + 2x(-1) + 5(3x) + 5(-1)$

$= 6x^2 - 2x + 15x - 5$

$= 6x^2 + 13x - 5$

11. $(x-2)^2 = x^2 - 2(x)(2) + (2)^2 = x^2 - 4x + 4$

13. $(2x-1)^2 = (2x)^2 - 2(2x)(1) + (1)^2$

$= 4x^2 - 4x + 1$

15. $(3a-5)^2 = (3a)^2 - 2(3a)(5) + (5)^2$
$= 9a^2 - 30a + 25$

17. $(5x+9)^2 = (5x)^2 + 2(5x)(9) + (9)^2$
$= 25x^2 + 90x + 81$

19. Answers may vary.

21. $(a-7)(a+7) = (a)^2 - (7)^2 = a^2 - 49$

23. $(3x-1)(3x+1) = (3x)^2 - (1)^2 = 9x^2 - 1$

25. $\left(3x - \frac{1}{2}\right)\left(3x + \frac{1}{2}\right) = (3x)^2 - \left(\frac{1}{2}\right)^2$
$= 9x^2 - \frac{1}{4}$

27. $(9x+y)(9x-y) = (9x)^2 - (y)^2 = 81x^2 - y^2$

29. $A = l \cdot w$
$A = (2x+1)(2x+1)$
$A = 2x(2x) + 2x(1) + 1(2x) + 1(1)$
$A = 4x^2 + 2x + 2x + 1$
$A = (4x^2 + 4x + 1)$ square feet

31. $(a+5)(a+4) = a^2 + 4a + 5a + 20$
$= a^2 + 9a + 20$

33. $(a+7)^2 = (a)^2 + 2(a)(7) + (7)^2$
$= a^2 + 14a + 49$

35. $(4a+1)(3a-1)$
$= 12a^2 - 4a + 3a - 1$
$= 12a^2 - a - 1$

37. $(x+2)(x-2) = (x)^2 - (2)^2$
$= x^2 - 4$

39. $(3a+1)^2 = (3a)^2 + 2(3a)(1) + (1)^2$
$= 9a^2 + 6a + 1$

41. $(x+y)(4x-y) = 4x^2 - xy + 4xy - y^2$
$= 4x^2 + 3xy - y^2$

43. $(x+3)(x^2 - 6x + 1)$
$= x(x^2) + x(-6x) + x(1) + 3(x^2) + 3(-6x) + 3(1)$
$= x^3 - 6x^2 + x + 3x^2 - 18x + 3$
$= x^3 - 3x^2 - 17x + 3$

45. $(2a-3)^2 = (2a)^2 - 2(2a)(3) + (3)^2$
$= 4a^2 - 12a + 9$

47. $(5x-6z)(5x+6z) = (5x)^2 - (6z)^2$
$= 25x^2 - 36z^2$

49. $(x-3)(x-5) = x^2 - 5x - 3x + 15$
$= x^2 - 8x + 15$

51. $\left(x - \frac{1}{3}\right)\left(x + \frac{1}{3}\right) = (x)^2 - \left(\frac{1}{3}\right)^2 = x^2 - \frac{1}{9}$

53. $(a+11)(a-3) = a^2 - 3a + 11a - 33$
$= a^2 + 8a - 33$

55. $(x-2)^2 = (x)^2 - 2(x)(2) + (2)^2$
$= x^2 - 4x + 4$

57. $(3b+7)(2b-5) = 6b^2 - 15b + 14b - 35$
$= 6b^2 - b - 35$

59. $(7p-8)(7p+8) = (7p)^2 - (8)^2$
$= 49p^2 - 64$

61. $\left(\frac{1}{3}a^2 - 7\right)\left(\frac{1}{3}a^2 + 7\right) = \left(\frac{1}{3}a^2\right)^2 - (7)^2$
$= \frac{1}{9}a^4 - 49$

63. $5x^2(3x^2 - x + 2)$
$= 5x^2(3x^2) + 5x^2(-x) + 5x^2(2)$
$= 15x^4 - 5x^3 + 10x^2$

65. $(2r-3s)(2r+3s) = (2r)^2 - (3s)^2$
$= 4r^2 - 9s^2$

67. $(3x-7y)^2 = (3x)^2 - 2(3x)(7y) + (7y)^2$
$= 9x^2 - 42xy + 49y^2$

69. $(4x+5)(4x-5) = (4x)^2 - (5)^2$
$= 16x^2 - 25$

71. $(x+4)(x+4) = x^2 + 4x + 4x + 16$
$= x^2 + 8x + 16$

73. $\left(a - \frac{1}{2}y\right)\left(a + \frac{1}{2}y\right) = (a)^2 - \left(\frac{1}{2}y\right)^2$
$= a^2 - \frac{1}{4}y^2$

75. $\left(\frac{1}{5}x - y\right)\left(\frac{1}{5}x + y\right) = \left(\frac{1}{5}x\right)^2 - (y)^2$
$= \frac{1}{25}x^2 - y^2$

77. $(a+1)(3a^2 - a + 1)$
$= a(3a^2) + a(-a) + a(1) + 1(3a^2) + 1(-a) + 1(1)$
$= 3a^3 - a^2 + a + 3a^2 - a + 1$
$= 3a^3 + 2a^2 + 1$

79. $(2x-3)(2x+3) - x^2$
$= 4x^2 - 9 - x^2$
$= (3x^2 - 9)$ square units

81. $(5x-3)^2 - (x+1)^2$
$= 25x^2 - 30x + 9 - (x^2 + 2x + 1)$
$= 25x^2 - 30x + 9 - x^2 - 2x - 1$
$= (24x^2 - 32x + 8)$ square meters

83. Answers may vary.

85. $\frac{x^3y^6}{xy^2} = x^{3-1}y^{6-2} = x^2y^4$

87. $\frac{-6a^8y}{3a^4y} = -2a^{8-4}y^{1-1}$
$= -2a^4y^0$
$= -2a^4 \cdot 1$
$= -2a^4$

89. $\frac{-48ab^6}{32ab^3} = -\frac{3}{2}a^{1-1}b^{6-3}$
$= -\frac{3}{2}a^0b^3$
$= -\frac{3}{2} \cdot 1 \cdot b^3$
$= -\frac{3b^3}{2}$

91. (−1, 2) and (1, 1)
$m = \frac{1-2}{1-(-1)} = \frac{-1}{1+1} = -\frac{1}{2}$

93. (0, 3) and (2, 0)
$m = \frac{0-3}{2-0} = \frac{-3}{2} = -\frac{3}{2}$

95. $[(a+c)-5][(a+c)+5]$
$= (a+c)^2 + 5(a+c) - 5(a+c) - 25$
$= a^2 + 2ac + c^2 - 25$

97. $[(x-2)+y][(x-2)-y]$
$= (x-2)^2 - y(x-2) + y(x-2) - y^2$
$= x^2 - 4x + 4 - y^2$

Section 4.5

Calculator Explorations

1. 5.31×10^3 is entered as 5.31 EE 3.

3. 6.6×10^{-9} is entered as 6.6 EE −9.

5. $3{,}000{,}000 \times 5{,}000{,}000 = 1.5 \times 10^{13}$

7. $(3.26 \times 10^6)(2.5 \times 10^{13}) = 8.15 \times 10^{19}$

Mental Math

1. $5x^{-2} = \frac{5}{x^2}$

2. $3x^{-3} = \frac{3}{x^3}$

3. $\frac{1}{y^{-6}} = y^6$

4. $\frac{1}{x^{-3}} = x^3$

5. $\frac{4}{y^{-3}} = 4y^3$

6. $\frac{16}{y^{-7}} = 16y^7$

Exercise Set 4.5

1. $4^{-3} = \frac{1}{4^3} = \frac{1}{64}$

3. $7x^{-3} = 7 \cdot \frac{1}{x^3} = \frac{7}{x^3}$

5. $\left(-\frac{1}{4}\right)^{-3} = \frac{(-1)^{-3}}{(4)^{-3}} = \frac{4^3}{(-1)^3} = \frac{64}{-1} = -64$

7. $3^{-1} + 2^{-1} = \frac{1}{3} + \frac{1}{2} = \frac{2}{6} + \frac{3}{6} = \frac{5}{6}$

9. $\frac{1}{p^{-3}} = p^3$

11. $\frac{p^{-5}}{q^{-4}} = \frac{q^4}{p^5}$

13. $\frac{x^{-2}}{x} = x^{-2-1} = x^{-3} = \frac{1}{x^3}$

15. $\frac{z^{-4}}{z^{-7}} = z^{-4-(-7)} = z^3$

17. $2^0 + 3^{-1} = 1 + \frac{1}{3} = \frac{3}{3} + \frac{1}{3} = \frac{4}{3}$

19. $(-3)^{-2} = \frac{1}{(-3)^2} = \frac{1}{9}$

21. $\frac{-1}{p^{-4}} = -1\left(p^4\right) = -p^4$

23. $-2^0 - 3^0 = -1(1) - 1 = -2$

25. $\frac{x^2x^5}{x^3} = x^{2+5-3} = x^4$

27. $\frac{p^2p}{p^{-1}} = p^{2+1-(-1)} = p^{2+1+1} = p^4$

29. $\frac{\left(m^5\right)^4 m}{m^{10}} = m^{5(4)+1-10} = m^{20+1-10} = m^{11}$

31. $\frac{r}{r^{-3}r^{-2}} = r^{1-(-3)-(-2)} = r^{1+3+2} = r^6$

33. $\left(x^5y^3\right)^{-3} = x^{5(-3)}y^{3(-3)} = x^{-15}y^{-9} = \frac{1}{x^{15}y^9}$

35. $\frac{\left(x^2\right)^3}{x^{10}} = \frac{x^6}{x^{10}} = x^{6-10} = x^{-4} = \frac{1}{x^4}$

37. $\frac{\left(a^5\right)^2}{\left(a^3\right)^4} = \frac{a^{10}}{a^{12}} = a^{10-12} = a^{-2} = \frac{1}{a^2}$

39. $\frac{8k^4}{2k} = \frac{8}{2} \cdot k^{4-1} = 4k^3$

41. $\frac{-6m^4}{-2m^3} = \frac{-6}{-2} \cdot m^{4-3} = 3m$

43. $\frac{-24a^6b}{6ab^2} = \frac{-24}{6} \cdot a^{6-1}b^{1-2}$
$= -4a^5b^{-1}$
$= -\frac{4a^5}{b}$

45. $\dfrac{6x^2y^3}{-7xy^5} = -\dfrac{6}{7}x^{2-1}y^{3-5}$
$= -\dfrac{6}{7}x^1y^{-2}$
$= -\dfrac{6x}{7y^2}$

47. $\left(a^{-5}b^2\right)^{-6} = a^{-5(-6)}b^{2(-6)} = a^{30}b^{-12} = \dfrac{a^{30}}{b^{12}}$

49. $\left(\dfrac{x^{-2}y^4}{x^3y^7}\right)^2 = \dfrac{x^{-2(2)}y^{4(2)}}{x^{3(2)}y^{7(2)}}$
$= \dfrac{x^{-4}y^8}{x^6y^{14}}$
$= x^{-4-6}y^{8-14}$
$= x^{-10}y^{-6}$
$= \dfrac{1}{x^{10}y^6}$

51. $\dfrac{4^2z^{-3}}{4^3z^{-5}} = 4^{2-3}z^{-3-(-5)} = 4^{-1}z^2 = \dfrac{z^2}{4}$

53. $\dfrac{2^{-3}x^{-4}}{2^2x} = 2^{-3-2}x^{-4-1}$
$= 2^{-5}x^{-5}$
$= \dfrac{1}{2^5x^5}$
$= \dfrac{1}{32x^5}$

55. $\dfrac{7ab^{-4}}{7^{-1}a^{-3}b^2} = 7^{1-(-1)}a^{1-(-3)}b^{-4-2}$
$= 7^2a^4b^{-6}$
$= \dfrac{49a^4}{b^6}$

57. $\left(\dfrac{a^{-5}b}{ab^3}\right)^{-4} = \dfrac{a^{-5(-4)}b^{-4}}{a^{-4}b^{3(-4)}}$
$= \dfrac{a^{20}b^{-4}}{a^{-4}b^{-12}}$
$= a^{20-(-4)}b^{-4-(-12)}$
$= a^{24}b^8$

59. $\dfrac{\left(xy^3\right)^5}{(xy)^{-4}} = \dfrac{x^5y^{3(5)}}{x^{-4}y^{-4}}$
$= \dfrac{x^5y^{15}}{x^{-4}y^{-4}}$
$= x^{5-(-4)}y^{15-(-4)}$
$= x^9y^{19}$

61. $\dfrac{\left(-2xy^{-3}\right)^{-3}}{\left(xy^{-1}\right)^{-1}} = \dfrac{(-2)^{-3}x^{-3}y^{-3(-3)}}{x^{-1}y^{-1(-1)}}$
$= \dfrac{(-2)^{-3}x^{-3}y^9}{x^{-1}y^1}$
$= (-2)^{-3}x^{-3-(-1)}y^{9-1}$
$= (-2)^{-3}x^{-2}y^8$
$= \dfrac{y^2}{(-2)^3x^2}$
$= \dfrac{y^2}{-8x^2}$
$= -\dfrac{y^8}{8x^2}$

63. $\left(\dfrac{3x^{-2}}{z}\right)^3 = \dfrac{3^3x^{-6}}{z^3} = \dfrac{27}{x^6z^3}$

The volume is $\dfrac{27}{x^6z^3}$ cubic inches.

65. $78,000 = 7.8 \times 10^4$

67. $0.00000167 = 1.67 \times 10^{-6}$

69. $0.00635 = 6.35 \times 10^{-3}$

71. $1,160,000 = 1.16 \times 10^6$

73. $20,000,000 = 2.0 \times 10^7$

75. $93,000,000 = 9.3 \times 10^7$

77. $120,000,000 = 1.2 \times 10^8$

79. $8.673 \times 10^{-10} = 0.0000000008673$

81. $3.3 \times 10^{-2} = 0.033$

83. $2.032 \times 10^4 = 20,320$

85. $6.25 \times 10^{18} = 6,250,000,000,000,000,000$

87. $9.460 \times 10^{12} = 9,460,000,000,000$

89. $$\begin{aligned}(1.2 \times 10^{-3})(3 \times 10^{-2}) &= 1.2 \cdot 3 \cdot 10^{-3} \cdot 10^{-2}\\ &= 3.6 \times 10^{-5}\\ &= 0.000036\end{aligned}$$

91. $$\begin{aligned}&(4 \times 10^{-10})(7 \times 10^{-9})\\ &= 4 \cdot 7 \cdot 10^{-10} \cdot 10^{-9}\\ &= 28 \times 10^{-19}\\ &= 0.0000000000000000028\end{aligned}$$

93. $$\begin{aligned}\frac{8 \times 10^{-1}}{16 \times 10^5} &= \frac{8}{16} \times 10^{-1-5}\\ &= 0.5 \times 10^{-6}\\ &= 0.0000005\end{aligned}$$

95. $$\begin{aligned}\frac{1.4 \times 10^{-2}}{7 \times 10^{-8}} &= \frac{1.4}{7} \times 10^{-2-(-8)}\\ &= 0.2 \times 10^6\\ &= 200,000\end{aligned}$$

97. $$\begin{aligned}3600 \times 4.2 \times 10^6 &= 3.6 \times 10^3 \times 4.2 \times 10^6\\ &= 3.6 \times 4.2 \times 10^3 \times 10^6\\ &= 15.12 \times 10^9\\ &= 1.512 \times 10^{10} \text{ cubic feet}\end{aligned}$$

99. Answers may vary.

101. $$\begin{aligned}a^{-2} &= \left(\frac{1}{10}\right)^{-2}\\ &= \frac{1^{-2}}{10^{-2}}\\ &= \frac{10^2}{1^2}\\ &= \frac{100}{1}\\ &= 100\end{aligned}$$

103. $$\begin{aligned}&(2.63 \times 10^{12})(-1.5 \times 10^{-10})\\ &= 2.63 \cdot (-1.5) \cdot 10^{12} \cdot 10^{-10}\\ &= -3.945 \times 10^2\\ &= -394.5\end{aligned}$$

105. $$\begin{aligned}&d = r \cdot t\\ &238,857 = (1.86 \times 10^5)t\\ &t = \frac{238,857}{1.86 \times 10^5}\\ &t = \frac{2.38857}{1.86} \times 10^{5-5}\\ &t \approx 1.3 \text{ seconds}\end{aligned}$$

107. $$\frac{5x^7}{3x^4} = \frac{5x^{7-4}}{3} = \frac{5x^3}{3}$$

109. $$\frac{15z^4y^3}{21zy} = \frac{5z^{4-1}y^{3-1}}{7} = \frac{5z^3y^2}{7}$$

111. $$\begin{aligned}\frac{1}{y}(5y^2 - 6y + 5) &= \frac{5y^2}{y} - \frac{6y}{y} + \frac{5}{y}\\ &= 5y - 6 + \frac{5}{y}\end{aligned}$$

113. $$\begin{aligned}&2x^2\left(10x - 6 + \frac{1}{x}\right)\\ &= 2 \cdot 10x^{2+1} - 6 \cdot 2x^2 + \frac{2x^2}{x}\\ &= 20x^3 - 12x^2 + 2x\end{aligned}$$

115. $a^{-4m} \cdot a^{5m} = a^{-4m+5m} = a^m$

117. $\left(3y^{2z}\right)^3 = 3^3 y^{2\cdot 3z} = 27y^{6z}$

119. $\dfrac{y^{4a}}{y^{-a}} = y^{4a-(-a)} = y^{4a+a} = y^{5a}$

121. $\left(z^{3a+2}\right)^{-2} = \dfrac{1}{\left(z^{3a+2}\right)^2} = \dfrac{1}{z^{(3a+2)(2)}} = \dfrac{1}{z^{6a+4}}$

Section 4.6

Mental Math

1. $\dfrac{a^6}{a^4} = a^{6-4} = a^2$

2. $\dfrac{y^2}{y} = y^{2-1} = y$

3. $\dfrac{a^3}{a} = a^{3-1} = a^2$

4. $\dfrac{p^8}{p^3} = p^{8-3} = p^5$

5. $\dfrac{k^5}{k^2} = k^{5-2} = k^3$

6. $\dfrac{k^7}{k^5} = k^{7-5} = k^2$

7. $\dfrac{p^8}{p^3} = p^{8-3} = p^5$

8. $\dfrac{k^5}{k^2} = k^{5-2} = k^3$

9. $\dfrac{k^7}{k^5} = k^{7-5} = k^2$

Exercise Set 4.6

1. $\dfrac{15p^3+18p^2}{3p} = \dfrac{15p^3}{3p} + \dfrac{18p^2}{3p} = 5p^2+6p$

3. $\dfrac{-9x^4+18x^5}{6x^5} = \dfrac{-9x^4}{6x^5} + \dfrac{18x^5}{6x^5} = -\dfrac{3}{2x}+3$

5. $\dfrac{-9x^5+3x^4-12}{3x^3} = \dfrac{-9x^5}{3x^3} + \dfrac{3x^4}{3x^3} - \dfrac{12}{3x^3}$
$= -3x^2 + x - \dfrac{4}{x^3}$

7. $\dfrac{4x^4-6x^3+7}{-4x^4} = \dfrac{4x^4}{-4x^4} + \dfrac{-6x^3}{-4x^4} + \dfrac{7}{-4x^4}$
$= -1 + \dfrac{3}{2x} - \dfrac{7}{4x^4}$

9. $\dfrac{25x^5-15x^3+5}{5x^2} = \dfrac{25x^5}{5x^2} - \dfrac{15x^3}{5x^2} + \dfrac{5}{5x^2}$
$= 5x^3 - 3x + \dfrac{1}{x^2}$

11. Perimeter = 4 times a side
Let s = length of a side.
$4s = 12x^3+4x-16$
$s = \dfrac{12x^3+4x-16}{4}$
$s = \dfrac{12x^3}{4} + \dfrac{4x}{4} - \dfrac{16}{4}$
$s = (3x^3+x-4)$ feet

13.
$$\begin{array}{r|l} & x+1 \\ \hline x+3 & x^2+4x+3 \\ & \underline{x^2+3x} \\ & \quad\;\; x+3 \\ & \quad\;\; \underline{x+3} \\ & \qquad\;\; 0 \end{array}$$
$x+1$

15.
$$\begin{array}{r} 2x+3 \\ x+5\overline{)2x^2+13x+15} \\ \underline{2x^2+10x} \\ 3x+15 \\ \underline{3x+15} \\ 0 \end{array}$$

$2x+3$

17.
$$\begin{array}{r} 2x+1 \\ x-4\overline{)2x^2-7x+3} \\ \underline{2x^2-8x} \\ x+3 \\ \underline{x-4} \\ 7 \end{array}$$

$2x+1+\frac{7}{x-4}$

19.
$$\begin{array}{r} 4x+9 \\ 2x-3\overline{)8x^2+6x-27} \\ \underline{8x^2-12x} \\ 18x-27 \\ \underline{18x-27} \\ 0 \end{array}$$

$4x+9$

21.
$$\begin{array}{r} 3a^2-3a+1 \\ 3a+2\overline{)9a^3-3a^2-3a+4} \\ \underline{9a^3+6a^2} \\ -9a^2-3a \\ \underline{-9a^2-6a} \\ 3a+4 \\ \underline{3a+2} \\ 2 \end{array}$$

$3a^2-3a+1+\frac{2}{3a+2}$

23.
$$\begin{array}{r} 2b^2+b+2 \\ b+4\overline{)2b^3+9b^2+6b-4} \\ \underline{2b^3+8b^2} \\ b^2+6b \\ \underline{b^2+4b} \\ 2b-4 \\ \underline{2b+8} \\ -12 \end{array}$$

$2b^2+b+2-\frac{12}{b+4}$

25. Answers may vary.

27.
$$\begin{array}{r} 2x+5 \\ 5x+3\overline{)10x^2+31x+15} \\ \underline{10x^2+6x} \\ 25x+15 \\ \underline{25x+15} \\ 0 \end{array}$$

Its height is $(2x + 5)$ meters.

29.
$$\frac{20x^2+5x+9}{5x^3}=\frac{20x^2}{5x^3}+\frac{5x}{5x^3}+\frac{9}{5x^3}=\frac{4}{x}+\frac{1}{x^2}+\frac{9}{5x^3}$$

31.
$$\begin{array}{r} 5x-2 \\ x+6\overline{)5x^2+28x-10} \\ \underline{5x^2+30x} \\ -2x-10 \\ \underline{-2x-12} \\ 2 \end{array}$$

$5x-2+\frac{2}{x+6}$

33.
$$\frac{10x^3-24x^2-10x}{10x}=\frac{10x^3}{10x}-\frac{24x^2}{10x}-\frac{10x}{10x}=x^2-\frac{12x}{5}-1$$

35.
$$\begin{array}{r} 6x-1 \\ x+3\overline{)6x^2+17x-4} \\ \underline{6x^2+18x} \\ -x-4 \\ \underline{-x-3} \\ -1 \end{array}$$

$$6x-1-\frac{1}{x+3}$$

37. $$\frac{12x^4+3x^2}{3x^2}=\frac{12x^4}{3x^2}+\frac{3x^2}{3x^2}=4x^2+1$$

39.
$$\begin{array}{r} 2x^2+6x-5 \\ x-2\overline{)2x^3+2x^2-17x+8} \\ \underline{2x^3-4x^2} \\ 6x^2-17x \\ \underline{6x^2-12x} \\ -5x+8 \\ \underline{-5x+10} \\ -2 \end{array}$$

$$2x^2+6x-5-\frac{2}{x-2}$$

41.
$$\begin{array}{r} 6x-1 \\ 5x-2\overline{)30x^2-17x+2} \\ \underline{30x^2-12x} \\ -5x+2 \\ \underline{-5x+2} \\ 0 \end{array}$$

$6x-1$

43. $$\frac{3x^4-9x^3+12}{-3x}=\frac{3x^4}{-3x}+\frac{-9x^3}{-3x}+\frac{12}{-3x}$$
$$=-x^3+3x^2-\frac{4}{x}$$

45.
$$\begin{array}{r} 4x+3 \\ 2x+1\overline{)8x^2+10x+1} \\ \underline{8x^2+4x} \\ 6x+1 \\ \underline{6x+3} \\ -2 \end{array}$$

$$4x+3-\frac{2}{2x+1}$$

47.
$$\begin{array}{r} 2x+9 \\ 2x-9\overline{)4x^2+0x-81} \\ \underline{4x^2-18x} \\ 18x-81 \\ \underline{18x-81} \\ 0 \end{array}$$

$2x+9$

49.
$$\begin{array}{r} 2x^2+3x-4 \\ 2x+3\overline{)4x^3+12x^2+x-12} \\ \underline{4x^3+6x^2} \\ 6x^2+x \\ \underline{6x^2+9x} \\ -8x-12 \\ \underline{-8x-12} \\ 0 \end{array}$$

$2x^2+3x-4$

51.
$$\begin{array}{r} x^2+3x+9 \\ x-3\overline{)x^3+0x^2+0x-27} \\ \underline{x^3-3x^2} \\ 3x^2+0x \\ \underline{3x^2-9x} \\ 9x-27 \\ \underline{9x-27} \\ 0 \end{array}$$

x^2+3x+9

53.
$$\begin{array}{r} x^2 - x + 1 \\ x+1 \overline{)\, x^3 + 0x^2 + 0x + 1} \\ \underline{x^3 + x^2} \qquad\qquad \\ -x^2 + 0x \qquad \\ \underline{-x^2 - \ \ x} \qquad \\ x + 1 \\ \underline{x + 1} \\ 0 \end{array}$$

$x^2 - x + 1$

55.
$$\begin{array}{r} -3x + 6 \\ x+2 \overline{)\, -3x^2 + 0x + 1} \\ \underline{-3x^2 - 6x} \qquad \\ 6x + \ \ 1 \\ \underline{6x + 12} \\ -11 \end{array}$$

$-3x + 6 - \dfrac{11}{x+2}$

57.
$$\begin{array}{r} 2b - 1 \\ 2b-1 \overline{)\, 4b^2 - 4b - 5} \\ \underline{4b^2 - 2b} \qquad \\ -2b - 5 \\ \underline{-2b + 1} \\ -6 \end{array}$$

$2b - 1 - \dfrac{6}{2b-1}$

59. $2a(a^2 + 1) = 2a^3 + 2a$

61. $2x(x^2 + 7x - 5) = 2x^3 + 14x^2 - 10x$

63. $-3xy(xy^2 + 7x^2y + 8)$
$= -3x^2y^3 - 21x^3y^2 - 24xy$

65. $9ab(ab^2c + 4bc - 8)$
$= 9a^2b^3c + 36ab^2c - 72ab$

67. The Rolling Stones (1994)

69. $80 million

Chapter 4 Review Exercises

1. 3^2
base = 3; exponent = 2

2. $(-5)^4$
base = –5; exponent = 4

3. -5^4
base = 5; exponent = 4

4. $8^3 = 8 \cdot 8 \cdot 8 = 512$

5. $(-6)^2 = (-6)(-6) = 36$

6. $-6^2 = -36$

7. $-4^3 - 4^0 = -(64) - (1) = -64 - 1 = -65$

8. $(3b)^0 = 1$

9. $\dfrac{8b}{8b} = 1$

10. $5b^3b^5a^6 = 5a^6b^8$

11. $2^3 \cdot x^0 = 8 \cdot 1 = 8$

12. $\left[(-3)^2\right]^3 = (9)^3 = 9 \cdot 9 \cdot 9 = 729$

13. $(2x^3)(-5x^2) = (2)(-5)(x^3)(x^2) = -10x^5$

14. $\left(\dfrac{mn}{q}\right)^2 \cdot \left(\dfrac{mn}{q}\right) = \dfrac{m^2n^2}{q^2} \cdot \dfrac{mn}{q} = \dfrac{m^3n^3}{q^3}$

15. $\left(\dfrac{3ab^2}{6ab}\right)^4 = \left(\dfrac{b}{2}\right)^4 = \dfrac{b^4}{2^4} = \dfrac{b^4}{16}$

16. $\dfrac{x^9}{x^4} = x^{9-4} = x^5$

17. $\frac{2x^7y^8}{8xy^2} = \frac{x^6y^6}{4}$

18. $\frac{12xy^6}{3x^4y^{10}} = \frac{4}{x^3y^4}$

19. $5a^7(2a^4)^3 = 5a^7(2^3a^{12})$
$= 5a^7(8a^{12})$
$= 40a^{19}$

20. $(2x)^2(9x) = (4x^2)(9x) = 36x^3$

21. $\frac{(-4)^2(3^3)}{(4^5)(3^2)} = \frac{(-1\cdot 4)^2(3^3)}{(4^5)(3^2)}$
$= \frac{(-1)^2(4^2)(3^3)}{(4^5)(3^2)}$
$= \frac{(-1)^2(3)}{4^3}$
$= \frac{3}{64}$

22. $\frac{(-7)^2(3^5)}{(-7)^3(3^4)} = \frac{3}{-7} = -\frac{3}{7}$

23. $\frac{(2x)^0(-4)^2}{16x} = \frac{1\cdot 16}{16x} = \frac{1}{x}$

24. $\frac{(8xy)(3xy)}{18x^2y^2} = \frac{24x^2y^2}{18x^2y^2} = \frac{4}{3}$

25. $m^0 + p^0 + 3q^0 = 1 + 1 + 3(1)$
$= 1 + 1 + 3$
$= 5$

26. $(-5a)^0 + 7^0 + 8^0 = 1+1+1 = 3$

27. $(3xy^2 + 8x + 9)^0 = 1$

28. $8x^0 + 9^0 = 8(1) + 1 = 9$

29. $6(a^2b^3)^3 = 6(a^6b^9) = 6a^6b^9$

30. $\frac{(x^3z)^a}{x^2z^2} = \frac{x^{3a}z^a}{x^2z^2} = x^{3a-2}z^{a-2}$

31. $-5x^4y^3$
The degree is 4 + 3 = 7.

32. $10x^3y^2z$
The degree is 3 + 2 + 1 = 6.

33. $35a^5bc^2$
The degree is 5 + 1 + 2 = 8.

34. $95xyz$
The degree is 1 + 1 + 1 = 3.

35. $y^5 + 7x - 8x^4$
The degree is 5.

36. $9y^2 + 30y + 25$
The degree is 2.

37. $-14x^2y - 28x^2y^3 - 42x^2y^2$
The degree of $-14x^2y$ is 3.
The degree of $-28x^2y^3$ is 5.
The degree of $-42x^2y^2$ is 4.
Therefore, the degree of the polynomial is 5.

38. $6x^2y^2z^2 + 5x^2y^3 - 12xyz$
The degree of $6x^2y^2z^2$ is 6.
The degree of $5x^2y^3$ is 5.
The degree of $-12xyz$ is 3.
Therefore, the degree of the polynomial is 6.

39. a. $3a^2b-2a^2+ab-b^2-6$

Term	Numerical Coefficient	Degree of Term
$3a^2b$	3	3
$-2a^2$	−2	2
ab	1	2
$-b^2$	−1	2
−6	−6	0

b. 3

40. a. $x^2y^2+5x^2-7y^2+11xy-1$

Term	Numerical Coefficient	Degree of Term
x^2y^2	1	4
$5x^2$	5	2
$-7y^2$	−7	2
$11xy$	11	2
−1	−1	0

b. 4

41.

x	1	3	5.1	10
$2x^2+20x$	22	78	154.02	400

42. $6a^2b^2+4ab+9a^2b^2=15a^2b^2+4ab$

43. $21x^2y^3+3xy+x^2y^3+6$
$=22x^2y^3+3xy+6$

44. $4a^2b-3b^2-8q^2-10a^2b+7q^2$
$=-6a^2b-3b^2-q^2$

45. $2s^{14}+3s^{13}+12s^{12}-s^{10}$
Since there are no like terms, no terms can be combined.

46. $(3k^2+2k+6)+(5k^2+k)$
$=3k^2+2k+6+5k^2+k$
$=8k^2+3k+6$

47. $(2s^5+3s^4+4s^3+5s^2)-(4s^2+7s+6)$
$=2s^5+3s^4+4s^3+5s^2-4s^2-7s-6$
$=2s^5+3s^4+4s^3+s^2-7s-6$

48. $(2m^7+3x^4+7m^6)-(8m^7+4m^2+6x^4)$
$=2m^7+3x^4+7m^6-8m^7-4m^2-6x^4$
$=-6m^7-3x^4+7m^6-4m^2$

49. $(11r^2+16rs-2s^2)-(3r^2+5rs-9s^2)$
$=11r^2+16rs-2s^2-3r^2-5rs+9s^2$
$=8r^2+11r^2+7s^2$

50. $(3x^2-6xy+y^2)-(11x^2-xy+5y^2)$
$=3x^2-6xy+y^2-11x^2+xy-5y^2$
$=-8x^2-5xy-4y^2$

51. $(7x-14y)-(3x-y)=7x-14y-3x+y$
$=4x-13y$

52. $[(x^2+7x+9)+(x^2+4)]-(4x^2+8x-7)$
$=x^2+7x+9+x^2+4-4x^2-8x+7$
$=-2x^2-x+20$

53. $0.365x^2-0.244x+57.958$
When $x=11$, we have
$0.365(11)^2-0.244(11)+57.958$
$=44.165-2.684+57.958$
$=99.439$
This model predicts that the room rate in 2001 will be \$99.44.

54. $9x(x^2y)=9x^3y$

55. $-7(8xz^2)=-56xz^2$

56. $(6xa^2)(xya^3)=6x^2a^5y$

57. $(4xy)(-3xa^2y^3) = -12x^2a^2y^4$

58. $6(x+5) = 6x + 6(5) = 6x + 30$

59. $9(x-7) = 9x - 63$

60. $4(2a+7) = 4(2a) + 4(7) = 8a + 28$

61. $9(6a-3) = 54a - 27$

62. $-7x(x^2+5) = -7x(x^2) - 7x(5)$
$= -7x^3 - 35x$

63. $-8y(4y^2-6) = -32y^3 + 48y$

64. $-2(x^3 - 9x^2 + x) = -2(x^3) - 2(-9x^2) - 2(x)$
$= -2x^3 + 18x^2 - 2x$

65. $-3a(a^2b + ab + b^2) = -3a^3b - 3a^2b - 3ab^2$

66. $(3a^3 - 4a + 1)(-2a)$
$= (3a^3)(-2a) + (-4a)(-2a) + (1)(-2a)$
$= -6a^4 + 8a^2 - 2a$

67. $(6b^3 - 4b + 2)(7b) = 42b^4 - 28b^2 + 14b$

68. $(2x+2)(x-7) = 2x^2 - 14x + 2x - 14$
$= 2x^2 - 12x - 14$

69. $(2x-5)(3x+2) = 6x^2 + 4x - 15x - 10$
$= 6x^2 - 11x - 10$

70. $(4a-1)(a+7) = 4a^2 + 28a - a - 7$
$= 4a^2 + 27a - 7$

71. $(6a-1)(7a+3) = 42a^2 + 18a - 7a - 3$
$= 42a^2 + 11a - 3$

72. $(x+7)(x^3+4x-5)$
$= x^4 + 4x^2 - 5x + 7x^3 + 28x - 35$
$= x^4 + 7x^3 + 4x^2 + 23x - 35$

73. $(x+2)(x^5+x+1)$
$= x^6 + x^2 + x + 2x^5 + 2x + 2$
$= x^6 + 2x^5 + x^2 + 3x + 2$

74.
$$\begin{array}{rrrrr} & & x^2 & +2x & +4 \\ \times & & x^2 & +2x & -4 \\ \hline & & -4x^2 & -8x & -16 \\ & 2x^3 & +4x^2 & +8x & \\ x^4 & +2x^3 & +4x^2 & & \\ \hline x^4 & +4x^3 & +4x^2 & & -16 \end{array}$$

75. $(x^3+4x+4)(x^3+4x-4) = x^6+4x^4-4x^3+4x^4+16x^2-16x+4x^3+16x-16$
$= x^6+8x^4+16x^2-16$

76. $(x+7)^3 = (x+7)(x+7)(x+7)$
$= (x^2+7x+7x+49)(x+7)$
$= (x^2+14x+49)(x+7)$
$= x^3+14x^2+49x+7x^2+98x+343$
$= x^3+21x^2+147x+343$

77. $(2x-5)^3 = (2x-5)(2x-5)(2x-5)$
$= (4x^2-10x-10x+25)(2x-5)$
$= (4x^2-20x+25)(2x-5)$
$= 8x^3-40x^2+50x-20x^2+100x-125$
$= 8x^3-60x^2+150x-125$

78. $2x(3x^2-7x+1) = 2x(3x^2)+2x(-7x)+2x(1)$
$= 6x^3-14x^2+2x$

79. $3y(5y^2-y+2) = 3y(5y^2)+3y(-y)+3y(2)$
$= 15y^3-3y^2+6y$

80. $(6x-1)(4x+3) = 24x^2+18x-4x-3$
F O I L
$= (6x)(4x)+6x(3)+(-1)(4x)+(-1)(3)$
$= 24x^2+14x-3$

81. $(4a-1)(3a+7)$
F O I L
$= 4a(3a)+4a(7)+(-1)(3a)+(-1)(7)$
$= 12a^2+28a-3a-7$
$= 12a^2+25a-7$

82. $(x+7)^2 = x^2+2(x)(7)+7^2$
$= x^2+14x+49$

83. $(x-5)^2 = x^2-2(x)(5)+5^2$
$= x^2-10x+25$

84. $(3x-7)^2 = (3x)^2-2(3x)(7)+(7)^2$
$= 9x^2-42x+49$

85. $(4x+2)^2 = (4x)^2 + 2(4x)(2) + 2^2$
$= 16x^2 + 16x + 4$

86. $(y+1)(y^2 - 6y - 5) = y(y^2) + y(-6y) + y(-5) + 1(y^2) + 1(-6y) + 1(-5)$
$= y^3 - 6y^2 - 5y + y^2 - 6y - 5$
$= y^3 - 5y^2 - 11y - 5$

87. $(x-2)(x^2 - x - 2) = x(x^2) + x(-x) + x(-2) + (-2)(x^2) + (-2)(-x) + (-2)(-2)$
$= x^3 - x^2 - 2x - 2x^2 + 2x + 4$
$= x^3 - 3x^2 + 4$

88. $(5x-9)^2 = (5x)^2 - 2(5x)(9) + (9)^2$
$= 25x^2 - 90x + 81$

89. $(5x+1)(5x-1) = (5x)^2 - (1)^2 = 25x^2 - 1$

90. $(7x+4)(7x-4) = (7x)^2 - (4)^2 = 49x^2 - 16$

91. $(a+2b)(a-2b) = a^2 - (2b)^2 = a^2 - 4b^2$

92. $(2x-6)(2x+6) = (2x)^2 - (6)^2 = 4x^2 - 36$

93. $(4a^2 - 2b)(4a^2 + 2b) = (4a)^2 - (2b)^2$
$= 16a^4 - 4b^2$

94. $7^{-2} = \frac{1}{7^2} = \frac{1}{49}$

95. $-7^{-2} = -\frac{1}{7^2} = -\frac{1}{49}$

96. $2x^{-4} = 2\left(\frac{1}{x^4}\right) = \frac{2}{x^4}$

97. $(2x)^{-4} = \frac{1}{(2x)^4} = \frac{1}{16x^4}$

98. $\left(\frac{1}{5}\right)^{-3} = \frac{1^{-3}}{5^{-3}} = \frac{5^3}{1^3} = \frac{125}{1} = 125$

99. $\left(\frac{-2}{3}\right)^{-2} = \frac{(-2)^{-2}}{3^{-2}} = \frac{3^2}{(-2)^2} = \frac{9}{4}$

100. $2^0 + 2^{-4} = 1 + \frac{1}{2^4} = 1 + \frac{1}{16} = \frac{16}{16} + \frac{1}{16} = \frac{17}{16}$

101. $6^{-1} - 7^{-1} = \frac{1}{6} - \frac{1}{7} = \frac{7}{42} - \frac{6}{42} = \frac{1}{42}$

102. $\frac{1}{(2q)^{-3}} = 1 \cdot (2q)^3$

$= 1 \cdot 2^3 \cdot q^3$

$= 1 \cdot 8 \cdot q^3$

$= 8q^3$

103. $\frac{-1}{(qr)^{-3}} = -1 \cdot (qr)^3 = -1 \cdot q^3 \cdot r^3 = -q^3 r^3$

104. $\frac{r^{-3}}{s^{-4}} = \frac{s^4}{r^3}$

105. $\frac{rs^{-3}}{r^{-4}} = r^{1-(-4)} s^{-3} = \frac{r^5}{s^3}$

106. $\frac{-6}{8x^{-3}r^4} = \frac{-6x^3}{8r^4} = -\frac{3x^3}{4r^4}$

107. $\frac{-4s}{16s^{-3}} = -\frac{s^{1-(-3)}}{4} = -\frac{s^4}{4}$

108. $\left(2x^{-5}\right)^{-3} = 2^{-3} x^{15} = \frac{x^{15}}{2^3} = \frac{x^{15}}{8}$

109. $\left(3y^{-6}\right)^{-1} = 3^{-1} y^6 = \frac{y^6}{3}$

110. $\left(3a^{-1}b^{-1}c^{-2}\right)^{-2} = 3^{-2} a^2 b^2 c^4$

$= \frac{a^2 b^2 c^4}{3^2}$

$= \frac{a^2 b^2 c^4}{9}$

111. $\left(4x^{-2}y^{-3}z\right)^{-3} = 4^{-3} x^6 y^9 z^{-3}$

$= \frac{x^6 y^9}{4^3 z^3}$

$= \frac{x^6 y^9}{64 z^3}$

112. $\frac{5^{-2} x^8}{5^{-3} x^{11}} = 5^{-2-(-3)} x^{8-11}$

$= 5^{-2+3} x^{8-11}$

$= 5^1 x^{-3}$

$= \frac{5}{x^3}$

113. $\frac{7^5 y^{-2}}{7^7 y^{-10}} = 7^{5-7} \cdot y^{-2-(-10)}$

$= 7^{-2} \cdot y^8$

$= \frac{y^8}{7^2}$

$= \frac{y^8}{49}$

114. $\left(\frac{bc^{-2}}{bc^{-3}}\right)^4 = \left(b^{1-1} c^{-2-(-3)}\right)^4$

$= (b^0 c^{-2+3})^4$

$= (1 \cdot c^1)^4$

$= 1^4 c^4$

$= c^4$

115. $\left(\frac{x^{-3}y^{-4}}{x^{-2}y^{-5}}\right)^{-3} = \frac{x^9 y^{12}}{x^6 y^{15}}$

$= x^{9-6} \cdot y^{12-15}$

$= x^3 y^{-3}$

$= \frac{x^3}{y^3}$

116. $\frac{x^{-4} y^{-6}}{x^2 y^7} = x^{-4-2} y^{-6-7} = x^{-6} y^{-13} = \frac{1}{x^6 y^{13}}$

117. $\dfrac{a^5b^{-5}}{a^{-5}b^5} = a^{5-(-5)}b^{-5-5} = a^{10}b^{-10} = \dfrac{a^{10}}{b^{10}}$

118. $-2^0 + 2^{-4} = -1\cdot 2^0 + \dfrac{1}{2^4}$
$= -1\cdot 1 + \dfrac{1}{16}$
$= -1 + \dfrac{1}{16}$
$= -\dfrac{16}{16} + \dfrac{1}{16}$
$= -\dfrac{15}{16}$

119. $-3^{-2} - 3^{-3} = -\dfrac{1}{3^2} - \dfrac{1}{3^3}$
$= -\dfrac{1}{9} - \dfrac{1}{27}$
$= -\dfrac{3}{27} - \dfrac{1}{27}$
$= -\dfrac{4}{27}$

120. $a^{6m}a^{5m} = a^{6m+5m} = a^{11m}$

121. $\dfrac{\left(x^{5+h}\right)^3}{x^5} = \dfrac{x^{3(5+h)}}{x^5}$
$= \dfrac{x^{15+3h}}{x^5}$
$= x^{15+3h-5}$
$= x^{10+3h}$

122. $(3xy^{2z})^3 = 3^3x^3y^{2z(3)} = 27x^3y^{6z}$

123. $a^{m+2}\cdot a^{m+3} = a^{m+2+m+3} = a^{2m+5}$

124. $0.00027 = 2.7\times 10^{-4}$

125. $0.8868 = 8.868\times 10^{-1}$

126. $80,800,000 = 8.08\times 10^7$

127. $-868,000 = -8.68\times 10^5$

128. $32,667,000 = 3.2667\times 10^7$

129. $4000 = 4.0\times 10^3$

130. $8.67\times 10^5 = 867,000$

131. $3.86\times 10^{-3} = 0.00386$

132. $8.6\times 10^{-4} = 0.00086$

133. $8.936\times 10^5 = 893,600$

134. $1\times 10^{20} = 100,000,000,000,000,000,000$

135. 3×10^{-25}
$= 0.0000000000000000000000003$

136. $(8\times 10^4)(2\times 10^{-7}) = 8\times 2\times 10^{4+(-7)}$
$= 16\times 10^{-3}$
$= 0.016$

137. $\dfrac{8\times 10^4}{2\times 10^{-7}} = 4\times 10^{4-(-7)}$
$= 4\times 10^{11}$
$= 4(100,000,000,000)$
$= 400,000,000,000$

138. $\dfrac{x^2+21x+49}{7x^2} = \dfrac{x^2}{7x^2} + \dfrac{21x}{7x^2} + \dfrac{49}{7x^2}$
$= \dfrac{1}{7} + \dfrac{3}{x} + \dfrac{7}{x^2}$

139. $\dfrac{5a^3b - 15ab^2 + 20ab}{-5ab}$
$= \dfrac{5a^3b}{-5ab} + \dfrac{-15ab^2}{-5ab} + \dfrac{20ab}{-5ab}$
$= -a^2 + 3b - 4$

140.
$$\begin{array}{r} a+1 \\ a-2\overline{)a^2-a+4} \\ \underline{a^2-2a} \\ a+4 \\ \underline{a-2} \\ 6 \end{array}$$

$$a+1+\frac{6}{a-2}$$

141.
$$\begin{array}{r} 4x+0 \\ x+5\overline{)4x^2+20x+7} \\ \underline{4x^2+20x} \\ 0x+7 \\ \underline{0x+0} \\ 7 \end{array}$$

$$4x+\frac{7}{x+5}$$

142.
$$\begin{array}{r} a^2+3a+8 \\ a-2\overline{)a^3+a^2+2a+6} \\ \underline{a^3-2a^2} \\ 3a^2+2a \\ \underline{3a^2-6a} \\ 8a+6 \\ \underline{8a-16} \\ 22 \end{array}$$

$$a^2+3a+8+\frac{22}{a-2}$$

143.
$$\begin{array}{r} 3b^2-4b+0 \\ 3b-2\overline{)9b^3-18b^2+8b-1} \\ \underline{9b^3-6b^2} \\ -12b^2+8b \\ \underline{-12b^2+8b} \\ 0b-1 \\ \underline{0b+0} \\ -1 \end{array}$$

$$3b^2-4b-\frac{1}{3b-2}$$

144.
$$\begin{array}{r} 2x^3-x^2+2 \\ 2x-1\overline{)4x^4-4x^3+x^2+4x-3} \\ \underline{4x^4-2x^3} \\ -2x^3+x^2 \\ \underline{-2x^3+x^2} \\ 0+4x-3 \\ \underline{4x-2} \\ -1 \end{array}$$

$$2x^3-x^2+2-\frac{1}{2x-1}$$

145.
$$\begin{array}{r} -x^2-16x-117 \\ x-6\overline{)-x^3-10x^2-21x+18} \\ \underline{-x^3+6x^2} \\ -16x^2-21x \\ \underline{-16x^2+96x} \\ -117x+18 \\ \underline{-117x+702} \\ -684 \end{array}$$

$$-x^2-16x-117-\frac{684}{x-6}$$

Chapter 4 Test

1. $2^5=2\cdot2\cdot2\cdot2\cdot2=32$

2. $(-3)^4=(-3)(-3)(-3)(-3)=81$

3. $-3^4=-(3\cdot3\cdot3\cdot3)=-81$

4. $4^{-3}=\frac{1}{4^3}=\frac{1}{64}$

5. $\left(3x^2\right)\left(-5x^9\right)=(3)(-5)\left(x^2\cdot x^9\right)=-15x^{11}$

6. $\frac{y^7}{y^2}=y^{7-2}=y^5$

7. $\frac{r^{-8}}{r^{-3}}=r^{-8-(-3)}=r^{-5}=\frac{1}{r^5}$

8. $\left(\frac{x^2y^3}{x^3y^{-4}}\right)^2 = \frac{x^4y^6}{x^6y^{-8}}$
$= x^{4-6}y^{6-(-8)}$
$= x^{-2}y^{14}$
$= \frac{y^{14}}{x^2}$

9. $\frac{6^2x^{-4}y^{-1}}{6^3x^{-3}y^7} = 6^{2-3}x^{-4-(-3)}y^{-1-7}$
$= 6^{-1}x^{-1}y^{-8}$
$= \frac{1}{6xy^8}$

10. $563,000 = 5.63 \times 10^5$

11. $0.0000863 = 8.63 \times 10^{-5}$

12. $1.5 \times 10^{-3} = 0.0015$

13. $6.23 \times 10^4 = 62,300$

14. $(1.2 \times 10^5)(3 \times 10^{-7}) = (1.2)(3) \times 10^{5-7}$
$= 3.6 \times 10^{-2}$
$= 0.036$

15. a. $4xy^2 + 7xyz + x^3y - 2$

Term	Numerical Coefficient	Degree of Term
$4xy^2$	4	3
$7xyz$	7	3
x^3y	1	4
−2	−2	0

b. 4

16. $5x^2 + 4xy - 7x^2 + 11 + 8xy$
$= -2x^2 + 12xy + 11$

17. $(8x^3 + 7x^2 + 4x - 7) + (8x^3 - 7x - 6)$
$= 8x^3 + 7x^2 + 4x - 7 + 8x^3 - 7x - 6$
$= 16x^3 + 7x^2 - 3x - 13$

18.
$$\begin{array}{r} 5x^3 + x^2 + 5x - 2 \\ -(8x^3 - 4x^2 + x - 7) \\ \hline 5x^3 + x^2 + 5x - 2 \\ -8x^3 + 4x^2 - x + 7 \\ \hline -3x^3 + 5x^2 + 4x + 5 \end{array}$$

19. $[(8x^2 + 7x + 5) + (x^3 - 8)] - (4x + 2)$
$= 8x^2 + 7x + 5 + x^3 - 8 - 4x - 2$
$= x^3 + 8x^2 + 3x - 5$

20. $(3x + 7)(x^2 + 5x + 2)$
$= 3x^3 + 15x^2 + 6x + 7x^2 + 35x + 14$
$= 3x^3 + 22x^2 + 41x + 14$

21. $3x^2(2x^2 - 3x + 7)$
$= 3x^2(2x^2) + 3x^2(-3x) + 3x^2(7)$
$= 6x^4 - 9x^3 + 21x^2$

22. $(x + 7)(3x - 5)$
F O I L
$= x(3x) + x(-5) + 7(3x) + 7(-5)$
$= 3x^2 - 5x + 21x - 35$
$= 3x^2 + 16x - 35$

23. $(3x - 7)(3x + 7) = (3x)^2 - (7)^2 = 9x^2 - 49$

24. $(4x - 2)^2 = (4x)^2 - 2(4x)(2) + (2)^2$
$= 16x^2 - 16x + 4$

25. $(8x + 3)^2 = (8x)^2 + 2(8x)(3) + (3)^2$
$= 64x^2 + 48x + 9$

26. $(x^2 - 9b)(x^2 + 9b) = (x^2)^2 - (9b)^2$
$= x^4 - 81b^2$

27.

t	0 sec	1 sec	3 sec	5 sec
$-16t^2+1001$	1001 ft	985 ft	857 ft	601 ft

28. $\frac{8xy^2}{4x^3y^3z}=\frac{8x^{1-3}y^{2-3}}{4z}=\frac{2x^{-2}y^{-1}}{z}=\frac{2}{x^2yz}$

29. $\frac{4x^2+2xy-7x}{8xy}=\frac{4x^2}{8xy}+\frac{2xy}{8xy}-\frac{7x}{8xy}$

$=\frac{x}{2y}+\frac{1}{4}-\frac{7}{8y}$

30.

$$
\begin{array}{r}
x+\ \ 2 \\
x+5\overline{\smash{\big)}\,x^2+7x+10} \\
\underline{x^2+5x} \\
2x+10 \\
\underline{2x+10} \\
0
\end{array}
$$

$x+2$

31.

$$
\begin{array}{r}
9x^2-\ 6x+\ 4 \\
3x+2\overline{\smash{\big)}\,27x^3+\ 0x^2+\ 0x-\ 8} \\
\underline{27x^3+18x^2} \\
-18x^2+\ 0x \\
\underline{-18x^2-12x} \\
12x-\ 8 \\
\underline{12x+\ 8} \\
-16
\end{array}
$$

$9x^2-6x+4-\frac{16}{3x+2}$

32. $62x^2-149x+922$

When $x=7$, we have

$62(7)^2-149(7)+922=3038-1043+922$

$=2917$

The model predicts that there were 2917 thousand cases in 2000 ($x=7$).

Chapter 5

Section 5.1

Mental Math

1. $14 = 2 \cdot 7$

2. $15 = 3 \cdot 5$

3. $10 = 2 \cdot 5$

4. $70 = 2 \cdot 5 \cdot 7$

5. $6 = 2 \cdot 3$
   $15 = 3 \cdot 5$
   $\text{GCF} = 3$

6. $20 = 2 \cdot 2 \cdot 5$
   $15 = 3 \cdot 5$
   $\text{GCF} = 5$

7. 3
   $18 = 2 \cdot 3 \cdot 3$
   $\text{GCF} = 3$

8. $14 = 2 \cdot 7$
   $35 = 5 \cdot 7$
   $\text{GCF} = 7$

Exercise Set 5.1

1. $32 = 2 \cdot 2 \cdot 2 \cdot 2 \cdot 2$
   $36 = 2 \cdot 2 \cdot 3 \cdot 3$
   $\text{GCF} = 2 \cdot 2 = 4$

3. $12 = 2 \cdot 2 \cdot 3 = 2^2 \cdot 3$
   $18 = 2 \cdot 3 \cdot 3 = 2 \cdot 3^2$
   $36 = 2 \cdot 2 \cdot 3 \cdot 3 = 2^2 \cdot 3^2$
   $\text{GCF} = 2 \cdot 3 = 6$

5. $y^2,\ y^4,\ y^7$
   $\text{GCF} = y^2$

7. $x^{10}y^2,\ xy^2,\ x^3y^3$
   $\text{GCF} = xy^2$

9. $8x = 2 \cdot 2 \cdot 2 \cdot x$
   $4 = 2 \cdot 2$
   $\text{GCF} = 2 \cdot 2 = 4$

11. $12y^4 = 2 \cdot 2 \cdot 3y^4$
    $20y^3 = 2 \cdot 2 \cdot 5y^3$
    $\text{GCF} = 2 \cdot 2 \cdot y^3 = 4y^3$

13. $12x^3 = 2 \cdot 2 \cdot 3x^3$
    $6x^4 = 2 \cdot 3x^4$
    $3x^5 = 3x^5$
    $\text{GCF} = 3x^3$

15. $18x^2y = 2 \cdot 3 \cdot 3 \cdot x^2y$
    $9x^3y^3 = 3 \cdot 3 \cdot x^3y^3$
    $36x^3y = 2 \cdot 2 \cdot 3 \cdot 3 \cdot x^3y$
    $\text{GCF} = 3 \cdot 3x^2y = 9x^2y$

17. $30x - 15$; $\text{GCF} = 15$
    $15 \cdot 2x - 15 \cdot 1 = 15(2x - 1)$

19. $24cd^3 - 18c^2d$; $\text{GCF} = 6cd$
    $6cd \cdot 4d^2 - 6cd \cdot 3c = 6cd(4d^2 - 3c)$

21. $-24a^4x + 18a^3x$; $\text{GCF} = -6a^3x$
    $-6a^3x(4a) - 6a^3x(-3) = -6a^3x(4a - 3)$

23. $12x^3 + 16x^2 - 8x$; $\text{GCF} = 4x$
    $4x(3x^2) + 4x(4x) + 4x(-2)$
    $= 4x(3x^2 + 4x - 2)$

25. $5x^3y - 15x^2y + 10xy$; $\text{GCF} = 5xy$
    $5xy(x^2) + 5xy(-3x) + 5xy(2)$
    $= 5xy(x^2 - 3x + 2)$

27. Answers may vary.

29. $y(x + 2) + 3(x + 2)$; $\text{GCF} = (x + 2)$
    $(x + 2)(y + 3)$

31. $x(y-3)-4(y-3)$; GCF = $(y-3)$
$(y-3)(x-4)$

33. $2x(x+y)-(x+y)$; GCF = $(x+y)$
$2x(x+y)+(x+y)(-1)=(x+y)(2x-1)$

35. $5x+15+xy+3y=5(x)+5(3)+x(y)+3(y)$
$=5(x+3)+y(x+3)$
$=(x+3)(5+y)$

37. $2y-8+xy-4x=2(y-4)+x(y-4)$
$=(y-4)(2+x)$

39. $3xy-6x+8y-16=3x(y-2)+8(y-2)$
$=(y-2)(3x+8)$

41. $y^3+3y^2+y+3=y^2(y+3)+1(y+3)$
$=(y+3)(y^2+1)$

43. $12x(x^2)-2x=12x^3-2x=2x(6x^2-1)$

45. $20x(10)+\pi\cdot 5^2=200x+25\pi=25(8x+\pi)$

47. $3x-6$; GCF = 3
$3\cdot x-3\cdot 2=3(x-2)$

49. $32xy-18x^2$; GCF = $2x$
$2x(16y)-2x(9x)=2x(16y-9x)$

51. $4x-8y+4$; GCF = 4
$4\cdot x-4\cdot 2y+4\cdot 1=4(x-2y+1)$

53. $8(x+2)-y(x+2)$; GCF = $(x+2)$
$(x+2)(8-y)$

55. $-40x^8y^6-16x^9y^5$; GCF = $-8x^8y^5$
$-8x^8y^5\cdot 5y-8x^8y^5\cdot 2x=-8x^8y^5(5y+2x)$

57. $-3x+12$; GCF = -3
$-3\cdot x-3(-4)=-3(x-4)$

59. $18x^3y^3-12x^3y^2+6x^5y^2$; GCF = $6x^3y^2$
$6x^3y^2\cdot 3y+6x^3y^2(-2)+6x^3y^2\cdot x^2$
$=6x^3y^2(3y-2+x^2)$

61. $y^2(x-2)+(x-2)$; GCF = $(x-2)$
$y^2(x-2)+1(x-2)=(x-2)(y^2+1)$

63. $5xy+15x+6y+18=5x(y+3)+6(y+3)$
$=(y+3)(5x+6)$

65. $4x^2-8xy-3x+6y=4x(x-2y)-3(x-2y)$
$=(x-2y)(4x-3)$

67. $126x^3yz+210y^4z^3$; GCF = $42yz$
$42yz\cdot 3x^3+42yz\cdot 5y^3z^2$
$=42yz(3x^3+5y^3z^2)$

69. $3y-5x+15-xy$
$=3y+15-5x-xy$
$=3(y+5)-x(5+y)$
$=3(y+5)-x(y+5)$
$=(y+5)(3-x)$ or $(3-x)(y+5)$

71. $12x^2y-42x^2-4y+14$; GCF = 2
$2[6x^2y-21x^2-2y+7]$
$=2[3x^2(2y-7)-1(2y-7)]$
$=2[(2y-7)(3x^2-1)]$
$=2(2y-7)(3x^2-1)$

73. Answers may vary.

75. $(a+6)(b-2)$ is factored.

77. $5(2y+z)-b(2y+z)$ is not factored.

79. $\dfrac{4n^4-24n}{4n}=\dfrac{4n^4}{4n}-\dfrac{24n}{4n}=(n^3-6)$ units

81. **a.** $60x^2-85x+780$
$=60(2)^2-85(2)+780$
$=240-170+780$
$=850$
850 million CDs were sold in 1998.

b. $x = 2001 - 1996 = 5$
$60x^2 - 85x + 780$
$= 60(5)^2 - 85(5) + 780$
$= 1500 - 425 + 780$
$= 1855$
1855 million CDs will be sold in 2001.

c. $60x^2 - 85x + 780$
$= 5 \cdot 12x^2 + 5(-17x) + 5(156)$
$= 5(12x^2 - 17x + 156)$

83. $(x+2)(x+5) = x^2 + 5x + 2x + 10$
$= x^2 + 7x + 10$

85. $(a-7)(a-8) = a^2 - 8a - 7a + 56$
$= a^2 - 15a + 56$

87. The two numbers are 2 and 6.
$2 \cdot 6 = 12; 2 + 6 = 8$

89. The two numbers are -1 and -8.
$-1 \cdot (-8) = 8; -1 + (-8) = -9$

91. The two numbers are -2 and 5.
$-2 \cdot 5 = -10; -2 + 5 = 3$

93. The two numbers are -8 and 3.
$-8 \cdot 3 = -24; -8 + 3 = -5$

Section 5.2

Mental Math

1. $x^2 + 9x + 20 = (x+4)(x+5)$
2. $x^2 + 12x + 35 = (x+5)(x+7)$
3. $x^2 - 7x + 12 = (x-4)(x-3)$
4. $x^2 - 13x + 22 = (x-2)(x-11)$
5. $x^2 + 4x + 4 = (x+2)(x+2)$
6. $x^2 + 10x + 24 = (x+6)(x+4)$

Exercise Set 5.2

1. $x^2 + 7x + 6 = (x+6)(x+1)$

3. $x^2 + 9x + 20 = (x+5)(x+4)$

5. $x^2 - 8x + 15 = (x-5)(x-3)$

7. $x^2 - 10x + 9 = (x-9)(x-1)$

9. $x^2 - 15x + 5$
not factorable, prime

11. $x^2 - 3x - 18 = (x-6)(x+3)$

13. $x^2 + 5x + 2$
not factorable, prime

15. $x^2 + 8xy + 15y^2 = (x+3y)(x+5y)$

17. $x^2 - 2xy + y^2 = (x-y)(x-y)$

19. $x^2 - 3xy - 4y^2 = (x-4y)(x+y)$

21. $2z^2 + 20z + 32$; GCF = 2
$2(z^2 + 10z + 16) = 2(z+8)(z+2)$

23. $2x^3 - 18x^2 + 40x$; GCF = $2x$
$2x(x^2 - 9x + 20) = 2x(x-5)(x-4)$

25. $7x^2 + 14xy - 21y^2$; GCF = 7
$7(x^2 + 2xy - 3y^2) = 7(x+3y)(x-y)$

27. product, sum

29. $x^2 + 15x + 36 = (x+12)(x+3)$

31. $x^2 - x - 2 = (x-2)(x+1)$

33. $r^2 - 16r + 48 = (r-12)(r-4)$

35. $x^2 - 4x - 21 = (x-7)(x+3)$

37. $x^2 + 7xy + 10y^2 = (x + 2y)(x + 5y)$

39. $r^2 - 3r + 6$
not factorable, prime

41. $2t^2 + 24t + 64$; GCF = 2
$2(t^2 + 12t + 32) = 2(t + 4)(t + 8)$

43. $x^3 - 2x^2 - 24x$; GCF = x
$x(x^2 - 2x - 24) = x(x - 6)(x + 4)$

45. $x^2 - 16x + 63 = (x - 9)(x - 7)$

47. $x^2 + xy - 2y^2 = (x + 2y)(x - y)$

49. $3x^2 - 60x + 108$; GCF = 3
$3(x^2 - 20x + 36) = 3(x - 18)(x - 2)$

51. $x^2 - 18x - 144 = (x - 24)(x + 6)$

53. $6x^3 + 54x^2 + 120x$; GCF = $6x$
$6x(x^2 + 9x + 20) = 6x(x + 5)(x + 4)$

55. $2t^5 - 14t^4 + 24t^3$; GCF = $2t^3$
$2t^3(t^2 - 7t + 12) = 2t^3(t - 4)(t - 3)$

57. $5x^3y - 25x^2y^2 - 120xy^3$; GCF = $5xy$
$5xy(x^2 - 5xy - 24y^2)$
$= 5xy(x - 8y)(x + 3y)$

59. $4x^2y + 4xy - 12y$; GCF = $4y$
$4y(x^2 + x - 3)$

61. $2a^2b - 20ab^2 + 42b^3$; GCF = $2b$
$2b(a^2 - 10ab + 21b^2) = 2b(a - 7b)(a - 3b)$

63. $b = 8$;
$x^2 + 8x + 15 = (x + 3)(x + 5)$
$b = 16$;
$x^2 + 16x + 15 = (x + 15)(x + 1)$

65. $b = 6$;
$m^2 + 6m - 27 = (m + 9)(m - 3)$
$b = 26$;
$m^2 + 26m - 27 = (m + 27)(m - 1)$

67. $c = 5$;
$x^2 + 6x + 5 = (x + 5)(x + 1)$
$c = 8$;
$x^2 + 6x + 8 = (x + 4)(x + 2)$
$c = 9$;
$x^2 + 6x + 9 = (x + 3)(x + 3)$

69. $c = 3$;
$y^2 - 4y + 3 = (y - 3)(y - 1)$
$c = 4$;
$y^2 - 4y + 4 = (y - 2)(y - 2)$

71. Answers may vary.

73. $(2x + 1)(x + 5) = 2x^2 + 10x + x + 5$
$= 2x^2 + 11x + 5$

75. $(5y - 4)(3y - 1) = 15y^2 - 5y - 12y + 4$
$= 15y^2 - 17y + 4$

77. $(a + 3)(9a - 4) = 9a^2 - 4a + 27a - 12$
$= 9a^2 + 23a - 12$

79.

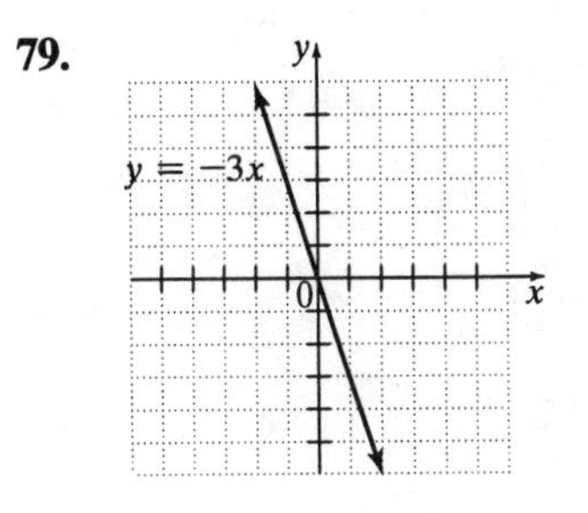

81.

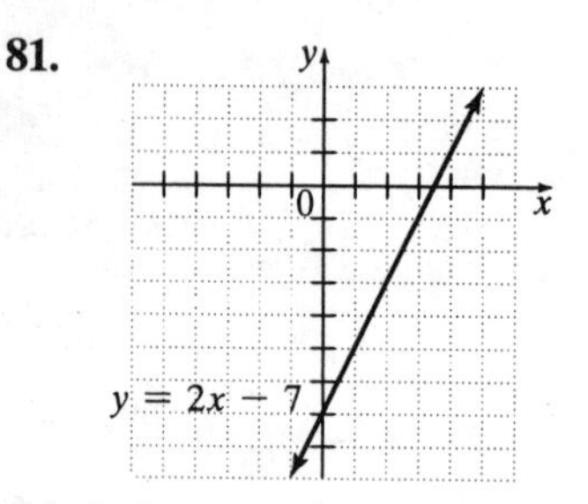

83. $2x^2y + 30xy + 100y$; GCF = $2y$
$2y(x^2 + 15x + 50) = 2y(x+5)(x+10)$

85. $-12x^2y^3 - 24xy^3 - 36y^3$; GCF = $-12y^3$
$-12y^3(x^2 + 2x + 3)$

87. $y^2(x+1) - 2y(x+1) - 15(x+1)$;
GCF = $(x + 1)$
$(x+1)(y^2 - 2y - 15) = (x+1)(y-5)(y+3)$

Section 5.3

Mental Math

1. $x^2 + 14x + 49 = x^2 + 2 \cdot x \cdot 7 + 7^2 = (x+7)^2$;
Yes

2. $9x^2 - 12x + 4 = (3x)^2 - 2 \cdot 3x \cdot 2 + 2^2$
$= (3x-2)^2$;
Yes

3. No

4. No

5. $9y^2 + 6y + 1 = (3y)^2 + 2 \cdot 3y \cdot 1 + 1^2$
$= (3y+1)^2$;
Yes

6. $y^2 - 16y + 64 = y^2 - 2 \cdot y \cdot 8 + 8 = (y-8)^2$;
Yes

Exercise Set 5.3

1. $2x^2 + 13x + 15 = (2x+3)(x+5)$

3. $2x^2 - 9x - 5 = (2x+1)(x-5)$

5. $2y^2 - y - 6 = (2y+3)(y-2)$

7. $16a^2 - 24a + 9 = (4a-3)(4a-3)$
$= (4a-3)^2$

9. $36r^2 - 5r - 24 = (9r-8)(4r+3)$

11. $10x^2 + 17x + 3 = (5x+1)(2x+3)$

13. $21x^2 - 48x - 45$; GCF = 3
$3(7x^2 - 16x - 15) = 3(7x+5)(x-3)$

15. $12x^2 - 14x - 6$; GCF = 2
$2(6x^2 - 7x - 3) = 2(2x-3)(3x+1)$

17. $4x^3 - 9x^2 - 9x$; GCF = x
$x(4x^2 - 9x - 9) = x(4x+3)(x-3)$

19. $x^2 + 22x + 121 = (x+11)(x+11)$
$= (x+11)^2$

21. $x^2 - 16x + 64 = (x-8)(x-8) = (x-8)^2$

23. $16y^2 - 40y + 25 = (4y-5)(4y-5)$
$= (4y-5)^2$

25. $x^2y^2 - 10xy + 25 = (xy-5)(xy-5)$
$= (xy-5)^2$

27. Answers may vary.

29. $2x^2 - 7x - 99 = (2x+11)(x-9)$

31. $4x^2 - 8x - 21 = (2x-7)(2x+3)$

33. $30x^2 - 53x + 21 = (6x-7)(5x-3)$

35. $24x^2 - 58x + 9 = (4x-9)(6x-1)$

37. $9x^2 - 24xy + 16y^2 = (3x - 4y)(3x - 4y)$
$= (3x - 4y)^2$

39. $x^2 - 14xy + 49y^2 = (x - 7y)(x - 7y)$
$= (x - 7y)^2$

41. $2x^2 + 7x + 5 = (2x + 5)(x + 1)$

43. $3x^2 - 5x + 1$
not factorable, prime

45. $-2y^2 + y + 10 = 10 + y - 2y^2$
$= (5 - 2y)(2 + y)$

47. $16x^2 + 24xy + 9y^2 = (4x + 3y)(4x + 3y)$
$= (4x + 3y)^2$

49. $8x^2y + 34xy - 84y$; GCF $= 2y$
$2y(4x^2 + 17x - 42) = 2y(4x - 7)(x + 6)$

51. $3x^2 + x - 2 = (3x - 2)(x + 1)$

53. $x^2y^2 + 4xy + 4 = (xy + 2)(xy + 2)$
$= (xy + 2)^2$

55. $49y^2 + 42xy + 9x^2 = (7y + 3x)(7y + 3x)$
$= (7y + 3x)^2$

57. $3x^2 - 42x + 63$; GCF $= 3$
$3(x^2 - 14x + 21)$

59. $42a^2 - 43a + 6 = (7a - 6)(6a - 1)$

61. $18x^2 - 9x - 14 = (6x - 7)(3x + 2)$

63. $25p^2 - 70pq + 49q^2 = (5p - 7q)(5p - 7q)$
$= (5p - 7q)^2$

65. $15x^2 - 16x - 15 = (5x + 3)(3x - 5)$

67. $-27t + 7t^2 - 4 = 7t^2 - 27t - 4$
$= (7t + 1)(t - 4)$

69. $a^2 + ab + ab + b^2 = a^2 + 2ab + b^2$

71. $b = 2$; $3x^2 + 2x - 5 = (3x + 5)(x - 1)$
$b = 14$; $3x^2 + 14x - 5 = (3x - 1)(x + 5)$

73. $b = 5$; $2z^2 + 5z - 7 = (2z + 7)(z - 1)$
$b = 13$; $2z^2 + 13z - 7 = (2z - 1)(z + 7)$

75. $c = 2$; $5x^2 + 7x + 2 = (5x + 2)(x + 1)$

77. $c = 4$; $3x^2 - 8x + 4 = (3x - 2)(x - 2)$
$c = 5$; $3x^2 - 8x + 5 = (3x - 5)(x - 1)$

79. $(x - 2)(x + 2) = x^2 - 2x + 2x - 4 = x^2 - 4$

81. $(a + 3)(a^2 - 3a + 9)$
$= a^3 - 3a^2 + 9a + 3a^2 - 9a + 27$
$= a^3 + 27$

83. $(y - 5)(y^2 + 5y + 25)$
$= y^3 + 5y^2 + 25y - 5y^2 - 25y - 125$
$= y^3 - 125$

85. \$75,000 and above because the graph for this income is the tallest.

87. Answers may vary.

89. $-12x^3y^2 + 3x^2y^2 + 15xy^2$; GCF $= -3xy^2$
$-3xy^2(4x^2 - x - 5) = -3xy^2(4x - 5)(x + 1)$

91. $-30p^3q + 88p^2q^2 + 6pq^3$; GCF $= -2pq$
$-2pq(15p^2 - 44pq - 3q^2)$
$= -2pq(15p + q)(p - 3q)$

93. $4x^2(y-1)^2+10x(y-1)^2+25(y-1)^2$
GCF = $(y-1)^2$
$(y-1)^2(4x^2+10x+25)$

Section 5.4

Calculator Explorations

	x^2-2x+1	x^2-2x-1	$(x-1)^2$
$x=5$	16	14	16
$x=-3$	16	14	16
$x=2.7$	2.89	0.89	2.89
$x=-12.1$	171.61	169.61	171.61
$x=0$	1	–1	1

Mental Math

1. $1=1^2$

2. $25=5^2$

3. $81=9^2$

4. $64=8^2$

5. $9=3^2$

6. $100=10^2$

7. $1=1^3$

8. $64=4^3$

9. $8=2^3$

10. $27=3^3$

Exercise Set 5.4

1. $x^2-4=x^2-2^2=(x+2)(x-2)$

3. $y^2-49=y^2-7^2=(y+7)(y-7)$

5. $25y^2 - 9 = (5y)^2 - 3^2 = (5y+3)(5y-3)$

7. $121 - 100x^2 = 11^2 - (10x)^2$
$= (11-10x)(11+10x)$

9. $12x^2 - 27$; GCF = 3
$3(4x^2 - 9) = 3[(2x)^2 - 3^2]$
$= (13a+7b)(13a-7b)$

11. $169a^2 - 49b^2 = (13a)^2 - (7b)^2$
$= (13a+7b)(13a-7b)$

13. $x^2y^2 - 1 = (xy)^2 - 1^2$
$= (xy+1)(xy-1)$

15. $x^4 - 9 = (x^2)^2 - 3^2 = (x^2+3)(x^2-3)$

17. $49a^4 - 16 = (7a^2)^2 - 4^2$
$= (7a^2+4)(7a^2-4)$

19. $x^4 - y^{10} = (x^2)^2 - (y^5)^2$
$= (x^2+y^5)(x^2-y^5)$

21. $x+6$ because $(x-6)(x+6) = x^2$.

23. $a^3 + 27 = a^3 + 3^3 = (a+3)(a^2-3a+9)$

25. $8a^3 + 1 = (2a)^3 + 1^3$
$= (3a+1)(4a^2-2a+1)$

27. $5k^3 + 40$; GCF = 5
$5(k^3+8) = 5(k^3+2^3)$
$= 5(k+2)(k^2-2k+4)$

29. $x^3y^3 - 64 = (xy)^3 - 4^3$
$= (xy-4)(x^2y^2+4xy+16)$

31. $x^3 + 125 = x^3 + 5^3 = (x+5)(x^2-5x+25)$

33. $24x^4 - 81xy^3$; GCF $= 3x$
$3x(8x^3 - 27y^3)$
$= 3x[(2x)^3 - (3y)^3]$
$= 3x(2x-3y)(4x^2+6xy+9y^2)$

35. $(2x+y)$ because
$(2x+y)(4x^2-2xy+y^2)$
$= (2x)^3 + y^3$
$= 8x^3 + y^3$.

37. $x^2 - 4 = x^2 - 2^2 = (x-2)(x+2)$

39. $81 - p^2 = 9^2 - p^2 = (9-p)(9+p)$

41. $4r^2 - 1 = (2r)^2 - 1^2 = (2r-1)(2r+1)$

43. $9x^2 - 16^2 = (3x)^2 - 4^2 = (3x-4)(3x+4)$

45. $16r^2 + 1$
not factorable, prime

47. $27 - t^3 = 3^3 - t^3 = (3-t)(9+3t+t^2)$

49. $8r^3 - 64$; GCF = 8
$8(r^3-8) = 8(r^3-2^3)$
$= 8(r-2)(r^2+2r+4)$

51. $t^3 - 343 = t^3 - 7^3 = (t-7)(t^2+7t+49)$

53. $x^2 - 169y^2 = x^2 - (13y)^2$
$= (x-13y)(x+13y)$

55. $x^2y^2 - z^2 = (xy)^2 - z^2 = (xy-z)(xy+z)$

57. $x^3y^3 + 1 = (xy)^3 + 1^3$
$= (xy+1)(x^2y^2-xy+1)$

59. $s^3 - 64t^3 = s^3 - (4t)^3$
$= (s-4t)(s^2+4st+16t^2)$

61. $18r^2 - 8$; GCF = 26

$$2(9r^2 - 4) = 2[(3r)^2 - 2^2]$$
$$= 2(3r - 2)(3r + 2)$$

63. $9xy^2 - 4x$; GCF = x

$$x(9y^2 - 4) = x[(3y)^2 - 2^2]$$
$$= x(3y + 2)(3y - 2)$$

65. $25y^4 - 100y^2$; GCF = $25y^2$

$$25y^2(y^2 - 4) = 25y^2(y^2 - 2^2)$$
$$= 25y^2(y + 2)(y - 2)$$

67. $x^3y - 4xy^3$; GCF = xy

$$xy(x^2 - 4y^2) = xy[x^2 - (2y)^2]$$
$$= xy(x - 2y)(x + 2y)$$

69. $8s^6t^3 + 100s^3t^6$; GCF = $4s^3t^3$

$$4s^3t^3(2s^3 + 25t^3)$$

71. $27x^2y^3 - xy^2$; GCF = xy^2

$$xy^2(27xy - 1)$$

73. a. Let $t = 2$.

$$841 - 16t^2 = 841 - 16(2^2)$$
$$= 841 - 16(4)$$
$$= 841 - 64$$
$$= 777$$

After 2 seconds, the height of the object is 777 feet.

b. Let $t = 5$.

$$841 - 16t^2 = 841 - 16(5^2)$$
$$= 841 - 16(25)$$
$$= 841 - 400$$
$$= 441$$

After 5 seconds, the height of the object is 441 feet.

c. When the object hits the ground, its height is zero feet. Thus, to find the time, t, when the object's height is zero feet above the ground, we set the expression $841 - 16t^2$ equal to 0 and solve for t.

$$841 - 16t^2 = 0$$
$$841 - 16t^2 + 16t^2 = 0 + 16t^2$$
$$841 = 16t^2$$
$$\frac{841}{16} = \frac{16t^2}{16}$$
$$52.5625 = t^2$$
$$\sqrt{52.5625} = \sqrt{t^2}$$
$$7.25 = t$$

Thus, the object will hit the ground after approximately 7 seconds.

d. $841 - 16t^2 = 29^2 - (4t)^2$

$$= (29 + 4t)(29 - 4t)$$

75. Answers may vary.

77. $\dfrac{8x^4 + 4x^3 - 2x + 6}{2x} = \dfrac{8x^4}{2x} + \dfrac{4x^3}{2x} - \dfrac{2x}{2x} + \dfrac{6}{2x}$

$$= 4x^3 + 2x^2 - 1 + \frac{3}{x}$$

79.

$$\begin{array}{r} 2x+1 \\ x-2\overline{\big)\,2x^2-3x-2} \\ \underline{2x^2-4x} \\ x-2 \\ \underline{x-2} \\ 0 \end{array}$$

$2x + 1$

81.

$$\begin{array}{r} 3x+4 \\ x+3\overline{\big)\,3x^2+13x+10} \\ \underline{3x^2+\ \ 9x} \\ 4x+10 \\ \underline{4x+12} \\ -2 \end{array}$$

83. $a^2 - (2 + b)^2 = [a + (2 + b)][a - (2 + b)]$

$$= (a + 2 + b)(a - 2 - b)$$

85. $(x^2-4)^2-(x-2)^2$
$=[(x^2-4)+(x-2)][(x^2-4)-(x-2)]$
$=(x^2-4+x-2)(x^2-4-x+2)$
$=(x^2+x-6)(x^2-x-2)$
$=(x+3)(x-2)(x-2)(x+1)$
$=(x-2)^2(x+1)(x+3)$

Exercise Set 5.5

1. $a^2+2ab+b^2=(a+b)(a+b)=(a+b)^2$

3. $a^2+a-12=(a-3)(a+4)$

5. $a^2-a-6=(a-3)(a+2)$

7. $x^2+2x+1=(x+1)(x+1)=(x+1)^2$

9. $x^2+4x+3=(x+3)(x+1)$

11. $x^2+7x+12=(x+3)(x+4)$

13. $x^2+3x-4=(x+4)(x-1)$

15. $x^2+2x-15=(x+5)(x-3)$

17. $x^2-x-30=(x-6)(x+5)$

19. $2x^2-98$; GCF $=2$
$2(x^2-49)=2(x^2-7^2)=2(x+7)(x-7)$

21. $x^2+3x+xy+3y=x(x+3)+y(x+3)$
$=(x+3)(x+y)$

23. $x^2+6x-16=(x+8)(x-2)$

25. $4x^3+20x^2-56x$; GCF $=4x$
$4x(x^2+5x-14)=4x(x+7)(x-2)$

27. $12x^2+34x+24$; GCF $=2$
$2(6x^2+17x+12)=2(3x+4)(2x+3)$

29. $4a^2-b^2=(2a)^2-b^2=(2a+b)(2a-b)$

31. $20-3x-2x^2=(5-2x)(4+x)$

33. a^2+a-3
not factorable, prime

35. $4x^2-x-5=(4x-5)(x+1)$

37. $4t^2+36$; GCF $=4$
$4(t^2+9)$

39. $ax+2x+a+2=x(a+2)+1(a+2)$
$=(a+2)(x+1)$

41. $12a^3-24a^2+4a$; GCF $=4a$
$4a(3a^2-6a+1)$

43. $x^2-14x-48$
not factorable, prime

45. $25p^2-70pq+49q^2=(5p-7q)(5p-7q)$
$=(5p-7q)^2$

47. $125-8y^3=5^3-(2y)^3$
$=(5-2y)(25+10y+4y^2)$

49. $-x^2-x+30=30-x-x^2=(6+x)(5-x)$

51. $14+5x-x^2=(7-x)(2+x)$

53. $3x^4y+6x^3y-72x^2y$; GCF $=3x^2y$
$3x^2y(x^2+2x-24)=3x^2y(x+6)(x-4)$

55. $5x^3y^2-40x^2y^3+35xy^4$; GCF $=5xy^2$
$5xy^2(x^2-8xy+7y^2)$
$=5xy^2(x-7y)(x-y)$

57. $12x^3y+243xy$; GCF $=3xy$
$3xy(4x^2+81)$

59. $(x-y)^2-z^2=[(x-y)+z][(x-y)-z]$
$=(x-y+z)(x-y-z)$

61. $3rs - s + 12r - 4 = s(3r-1) + 4(3r-1)$
$= (3r-1)(s+4)$

63. $4x^2 - 8xy - 3x + 6y = 4x(x-2y) - 3(x-2y)$
$= (x-2y)(4x-3)$

65. $6x^2 + 18xy + 12y^2$; GCF = 6
$6(x^2 + 3xy + 2y^2) = 6(x+2y)(x+y)$

67. $xy^2 - 4x + 3y^2 - 12 = x(y^2-4) + 3(y^2-4)$
$= (y^2-4)(x+3)$
$= (y^2-2^2)(x+3)$
$= (y+2)(y-2)(x+3)$

69. $5(x+y) + x(x+y) = (x+y)(5+x)$

71. $14t^2 - 9t + 1 = (7t-1)(2t-1)$

73. $3x^2 + 2x - 5 = (3x+5)(x-1)$

75. $x^2 + 9xy - 36y^2 = (x+12y)(x-3y)$

77. $1 - 8ab - 20a^2b^2 = (1-10ab)(1+2ab)$

79. $x^4 - 10x^2 + 9 = (x^2-1)(x^2-9)$
$= (x^2-1^2)(x^2-3^2)$
$= (x+1)(x-1)(x+3)(x-3)$

81. $x^4 - 14x^2 - 32 = (x^2-16)(x^2+2)$
$= (x^2-4^2)(x^2+2)$
$= (x+4)(x-4)(x^2+2)$

83. $x^2 - 23x + 120 = (x-15)(x-8)$

85. $6x^3 - 28x^2 + 16x$; GCF = $2x$
$2x(3x^2 - 14x + 8) = 2x(3x-2)(x-4)$

87. $27x^3 - 125y^3$
$= (3x)^3 - (5y)^3$
$= (3x-5y)(9x^2 + 15xy + 25y^2)$

89. $x^3y^3 + 8z^3 = (xy)^3 + (2z)^3$
$= (xy+2z)(x^2y^2 - 2xyz + 4z^2)$

91. $2xy - 72x^3y$; GCF = $2xy$
$2xy(1-36x^2) = 2xy(1-6x)(1+6x)$

93. $x^3 + 6x^2 - 4x - 24 = x^2(x+6) - 4(x+6)$
$= (x+6)(x^2-4)$
$= (x+6)(x+2)(x-2)$

95. $6a^3 + 10a^2$; GCF = $2a^2$
$2a^2(3a+5)$

97. $a^2(a+2) + 2(a+2) = (a+2)(a^2+2)$

99. $x^3 - 28 + 7x^2 - 4x = x^3 + 7x^2 - 28 - 4x$
$= x^2(x+7) - 4(7+x)$
$= x^2(x+7) - 4(x+7)$
$= (x+7)(x^2-4)$
$= (x+7)(x+2)(x-2)$

101. Answers may vary.

103.
$$x - 6 = 0$$
$$x - 6 + 6 = 0 + 6$$
$$x = 6$$

105.
$$2m + 4 = 0$$
$$2m + 4 - 4 = 0 - 4$$
$$2m = -4$$
$$\frac{2m}{2} = \frac{-4}{2}$$
$$m = -2$$

107.
$$5z - 1 = 0$$
$$5z - 1 + 1 = 0 + 1$$
$$5z = 1$$
$$\frac{5z}{5} = \frac{1}{5}$$
$$z = \frac{1}{5}$$

109. $V = lwh$
$960 = (12)(x)(10)$
$960 = 120x$
$\frac{960}{120} = \frac{120x}{120}$
$8 = x$
8 inches

111. (−2, 0), (4, 0), (0, 2), (0, −2)

113. (2, 0), (4, 0), (0, 4)

Section 5.6

Calculator Explorations

1. $3x^2 - 4x - 6 = 0$

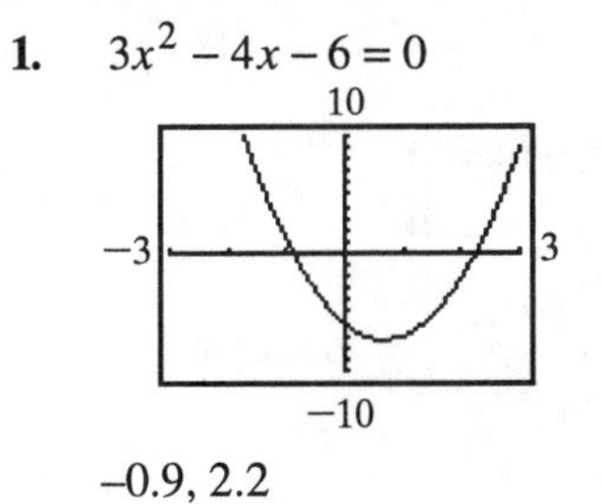

−0.9, 2.2

3. $2x^2 + x + 2 = 0$

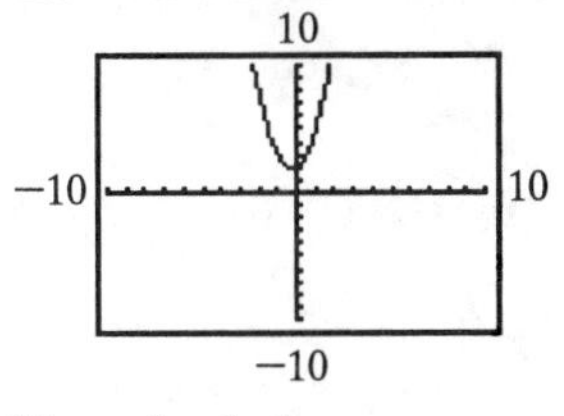

No real solution

5. $-x^2 + x + 5 = 0$

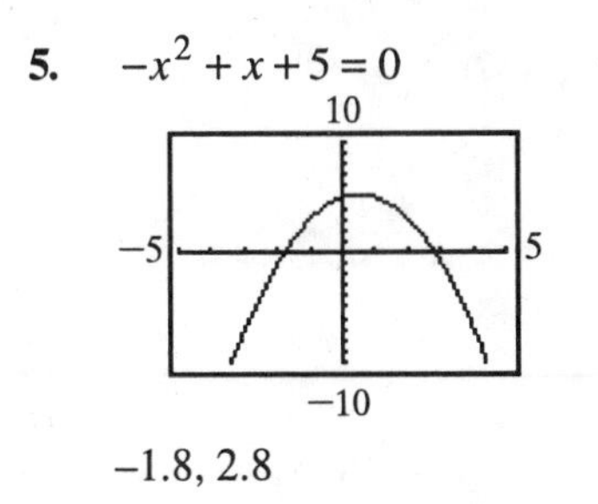

−1.8, 2.8

Mental Math

1. $(a-3)(a-7) = 0$
$a - 3 = 0$ or $a - 7 = 0$
$a = 3$ or $a = 7$

2. $(a-5)(a-2) = 0$
$a - 5 = 0$ or $a - 2 = 0$
$a = 5$ or $a = 2$

3. $(x+8)(x+6) = 0$
$x + 8 = 0$ or $x + 6 = 0$
$x = -8$ or $x = -6$

4. $(x+2)(x+3) = 0$
$x + 2 = 0$ or $x + 3 = 0$
$x = -2$ or $x = -3$

5. $(x+1)(x-3) = 0$
$x + 1 = 0$ or $x - 3 = 0$
$x = -1$ or $x = 3$

6. $(x-1)(x+2) = 0$
$x - 1 = 0$ or $x + 2 = 0$
$x = 1$ or $x = -2$

Exercise Set 5.6

1. $(x-2)(x+1) = 0$
$x - 2 = 0$ or $x + 1 = 0$
$x = 2$ or $x = -1$

3. $x(x+6) = 0$
$x = 0$ or $x + 6 = 0$
$x = 0$ or $x = -6$

5. $(2x+3)(4x-5) = 0$
$2x + 3 = 0$ or $4x - 5 = 0$
$2x = -3$ or $4x = 5$
$x = -\frac{3}{2}$ or $x = \frac{5}{4}$

7. $(2x-7)(7x+2) = 0$
$2x - 7 = 0$ or $7x + 2 = 0$
$2x = 7$ or $7x = -2$
$x = \frac{7}{2}$ or $x = -\frac{2}{7}$

9. $(x-6)(x+1) = 0$

11. $x^2 - 13x + 36 = 0$
$(x-4)(x-9) = 0$
$x - 4 = 0$ or $x - 9 = 0$
$x = 4$ or $x = 9$

13. $x^2 + 2x - 8 = 0$
$(x+4)(x-2) = 0$
$x + 4 = 0$ or $x - 2 = 0$
$x = -4$ or $x = 2$

15. $x^2 - 4x = 32$
$x^2 - 4x - 32 = 0$
$(x-8)(x+4) = 0$
$x - 8 = 0$ or $x + 4 = 0$
$x = 8$ or $x = -4$

17. $x(3x-1) = 14$
$3x^2 - x = 14$
$3x^2 - x - 14 = 0$
$(3x-7)(x+2) = 0$
$3x - 7 = 0$ or $x + 2 = 0$
$3x = 7$ or $x = -2$
$x = \frac{7}{3}$ or $x = -2$

19. $3x^2 + 19x - 72 = 0$
$(3x-8)(x+9) = 0$
$3x - 8 = 0$ or $x + 9 = 0$
$3x = 8$ or $x = -9$
$x = \frac{8}{3}$ or $x = -9$

21. Two solutions, 5 and 7.
$x = 5$ or $x = 7$
$x - 5 = 0$ or $x - 7 = 0$
$(x-5)(x-7) = 0$
$x^2 - 7x - 5x + 35 = 0$
$x^2 - 12x + 35 = 0$

23. $x^3 - 12x^2 + 32x = 0$
$x(x^2 - 12x + 32) = 0$
$x(x-8)(x-4) = 0$
$x = 0$ or $x - 8 = 0$ or $x - 4 = 0$
$x = 0$ or $x = 8$ or $x = 4$

25. $(4x-3)(16x^2 - 24x + 9) = 0$
$(4x-3)(4x-3)(4x-3) = 0$
Since all factors are the same:
$4x - 3 = 0$
$4x = 3$
$x = \frac{3}{4}$

27. $4x^3 - x = 0$
$x(4x^2 - 1) = 0$
$x(2x+1)(2x-1) = 0$
$x = 0$ or $2x + 1 = 0$ or $2x - 1 = 0$
$x = 0$ or $2x = -1$ or $2x = 1$
$x = 0$ or $x = -\frac{1}{2}$ or $x = \frac{1}{2}$

29. $32x^3 - 4x^2 - 6x = 0$
$2x(16x^2 - 2x - 3) = 0$
$2x(2x-1)(8x+3) = 0$
$2x = 0$ or $2x - 1 = 0$ or $8x + 3 = 0$
$x = \frac{0}{2}$ or $2x = 1$ or $8x = -3$
$x = 0$ or $x = \frac{1}{2}$ or $x = -\frac{3}{8}$

31. $x(x+7) = 0$
$x = 0$ or $x + 7 = 0$
$x = 0$ or $x = -7$

33. $(x+5)(x-4) = 0$
$x + 5 = 0$ or $x - 4 = 0$
$x = -5$ or $x = 4$

35. $x^2 - x = 30$
$x^2 - x - 30 = 0$
$(x-6)(x+5) = 0$
$x - 6 = 0$ or $x + 5 = 0$
$x = 6$ or $x = -5$

37. $6y^2 - 22y - 40 = 0$
$2(3y^2 - 11y - 20) = 0$
$2(3y+4)(y-5) = 0$
$3y + 4 = 0$ or $y - 5 = 0$
$3y = -4$ or $y = 5$
$y = -\frac{4}{3}$ or $y = 5$

39. $(2x+3)(2x^2 - 5x - 3) = 0$
$(2x+3)(2x+1)(x-3) = 0$
$2x + 3 = 0$ or $2x + 1 = 0$ or $x - 3 = 0$
$2x = -3$ or $2x = -1$ or $x = 3$
$x = -\frac{3}{2}$ or $x = -\frac{1}{2}$ or $x = 3$

41. $x^2 - 15 = -2x$
$x^2 + 2x - 15 = 0$
$(x+5)(x-3) = 0$
$x + 5 = 0$ or $x - 3 = 0$
$x = -5$ or $x = 3$

43. $x^2 - 16x = 0$
$x(x-16) = 0$
$x = 0$ or $x - 16 = 0$
$x = 0$ or $x = 16$

45. $-18y^2 - 33y + 216 = 0$
$-3(6y^2 + 11y - 72) = 0$
$-3(3y-8)(2y+9) = 0$
$3y - 8 = 0$ or $2y + 9 = 0$
$3y = 8$ or $2y = -9$
$y = \frac{8}{3}$ or $y = -\frac{9}{2}$

47. $12x^2 - 59x + 55 = 0$
$(4x-5)(3x-11) = 0$
$4x - 5 = 0$ or $3x - 11 = 0$
$4x = 5$ or $3x = 11$
$x = \frac{5}{4}$ or $x = \frac{11}{3}$

49. $18x^2 + 9x - 2 = 0$
$(3x+2)(6x-1) = 0$
$3x + 2 = 0$ or $6x - 1 = 0$
$3x = -2$ or $6x = 1$
$x = -\frac{2}{3}$ or $x = \frac{1}{6}$

51. $x(6x+7) = 5$
$6x^2 + 7x = 5$
$6x^2 + 7x - 5 = 0$
$(3x+5)(2x-1) = 0$
$3x + 5 = 0$ or $2x - 1 = 0$
$3x = -5$ or $2x = 1$
$x = -\frac{5}{3}$ or $x = \frac{1}{2}$

53. $4(x-7) = 6$
$4x - 28 = 6$
$4x = 6 + 28$
$4x = 34$
$x = \frac{34}{4} = \frac{17}{2}$

55. $5x^2 - 6x - 8 = 0$
$(5x+4)(x-2) = 0$
$5x + 4 = 0$ or $x - 2 = 0$
$5x = -4$ or $x = 2$
$x = -\frac{4}{5}$ or $x = 2$

57. $(y-2)(y+3) = 6$
$y^2 + 3y - 2y - 6 = 6$
$y^2 + y - 6 = 6$
$y^2 + y - 6 - 6 = 0$
$y^2 + y - 12 = 0$
$(y+4)(y-3) = 0$
$y + 4 = 0$ or $y - 3 = 0$
$y = -4$ or $y = 3$

59. $4y^2 - 1 = 0$
$(2y+1)(2y-1) = 0$
$2y + 1 = 0$ or $2y - 1 = 0$
$2y = -1$ or $2y = 1$
$y = -\frac{1}{2}$ or $y = \frac{1}{2}$

61. $t^2 + 13t + 22 = 0$
$(t+11)(t+2) = 0$
$t + 11 = 0$ or $t + 2 = 0$
$t = -11$ or $t = -2$

63. $5t - 3 = 12$
$5t = 12 + 3$
$5t = 15$
$t = \frac{15}{5}$
$t = 3$

65. $x^2 + 6x - 17 = -26$
$x^2 + 6x - 17 + 26 = 0$
$x^2 + 6x + 9 = 0$
$(x+3)(x+3) = 0$
$x + 3 = 0$
$x = -3$

67. $12x^2 + 7x - 12 = 0$
$(3x+4)(4x-3) = 0$
$3x + 4 = 0$ or $4x - 3 = 0$
$3x = -4$ or $4x = 3$
$x = -\frac{4}{3}$ or $x = \frac{3}{4}$

69. $10t^3 - 25t - 15t^2 = 0$
$10t^3 - 15t^2 - 25t = 0$
$5t(2t^2 - 3t - 5) = 0$
$5t(2t-5)(t+1) = 0$
$5t = 0$ or $2t - 5 = 0$ or $t + 1 = 0$
$t = \frac{0}{5}$ or $2t = 5$ or $t = -1$
$t = 0$ or $t = \frac{5}{2}$ or $t = -1$

71. Let $y = 0$ and solve for x.
$y = (3x+4)(x-1)$
$0 = (3x+4)(x-1)$
$3x + 4 = 0$ or $x - 1 = 0$
$3x = -4$ or $x = 1$
$x = -\frac{4}{3}$

The x-intercepts are $\left(-\frac{4}{3}, 0\right)$ and (1, 0).

73. Let $y = 0$ and solve for x.
$y = x^2 - 3x - 10$
$0 = x^2 - 3x - 10$
$0 = (x-5)(x+2)$
$x - 5 = 0$ or $x + 2 = 0$
$x = 5$ or $x = -2$
The x-intercepts are (5, 0) and (–2, 0).

75. Let $y = 0$ and solve for x.
$y = 2x^2 + 11x - 6$
$0 = 2x^2 + 11x - 6$
$0 = (2x-1)(x+6)$
$2x - 1 = 0$ or $x + 6 = 0$
$2x = 1$ or $x = -6$
$x = \frac{1}{2}$

The x-intercepts are $\left(\frac{1}{2}, 0\right)$ and (–6, 0).

77. E; x-intercepts are (–2, 0), (1, 0)

79. B; x-intercepts are (0, 0), (–3, 0)

81. C; $y = 2x^2 - 8 = 2(x-2)(x+2)$
x-intercepts are (2, 0) and (–2, 0)

83. **a.** $y = -16x^2 + 20x + 300$

x	0	1	2	3	4	5	6
y	300	304	276	216	124	0	–156

b. 5 seconds

c. 304 feet

d.

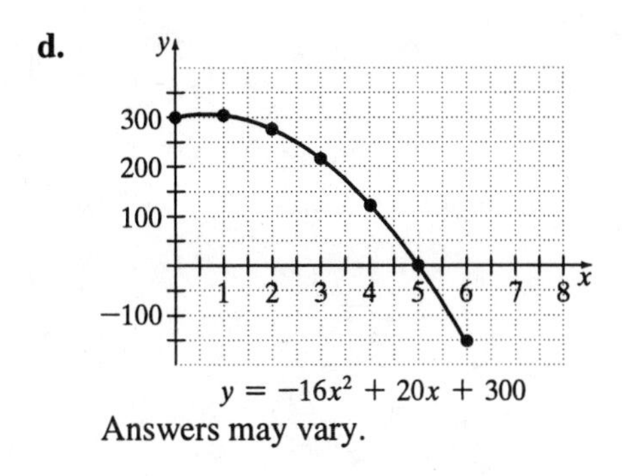

Answers may vary.

85. $\frac{3}{5}+\frac{4}{9}=\frac{3}{5}\cdot\frac{9}{9}+\frac{4}{9}\cdot\frac{5}{5}=\frac{27}{45}+\frac{20}{45}=\frac{47}{45}$

87. $\frac{7}{10}-\frac{5}{12}=\frac{7}{10}\cdot\frac{6}{6}-\frac{5}{12}\cdot\frac{5}{5}=\frac{42}{60}-\frac{25}{60}=\frac{17}{60}$

89. $\frac{7}{8}\div\frac{7}{15}=\frac{7}{8}\cdot\frac{15}{7}=\frac{15}{8}$

91. $\frac{4}{5}\cdot\frac{7}{8}=\frac{4\cdot 7}{5\cdot 8}=\frac{28}{40}=\frac{7}{10}$

93.

$$(x-3)(3x+4) = (x+2)(x-6)$$
$$3x^2+4x-9x-12 = x^2-6x+2x-12$$
$$3x^2-5x-12 = x^2-4x-12$$
$$3x^2-x^2-5x+4x-12+12 = 0$$
$$2x^2-x = 0$$
$$x(2x-1) = 0$$

$x = 0$ or $2x-1=0$

$x = 0$ or $2x = 1$

$x = 0$ or $x = \frac{1}{2}$

95.

$$(2x-3)(x+8)=(x-6)(x+4)$$
$$2x^2+16x-3x-24=x^2+4x-6x-24$$
$$2x^2+13x-24=x^2-2x-24$$
$$2x^2-x+13x+2x-24+24=0$$
$$x^2+15x=0$$
$$x(x+15)=0$$
$$x=0 \quad \text{or} \quad x+15=0$$
$$x=0 \quad \text{or} \quad x=-15$$

97.

$$(4x-1)(x-8)=(x+2)(x+4)$$
$$4x^2-32x-x+8=x^2+4x+2x+8$$
$$4x^2-33x+8=x^2+6x+8$$
$$4x^2-x^2-33x-6x+8-8=0$$
$$3x^2-39x=0$$
$$3x(x-13)=0$$
$$3x=0 \quad \text{or} \quad x-13=0$$
$$\frac{3x}{3}=\frac{0}{3} \quad \text{or} \quad x=13$$
$$x=0 \quad \text{or} \quad x=13$$

Exercise Set 5.7

1. Let x = the width, then $x + 4$ = the length.

3. Let x = the first odd integer, then
   $x + 2$ = the next consecutive odd integer.

5. Let x = the base, then $4x + 1$ = the height.

7. Let x = the length of one side.
   $$A=x^2$$
   $$121=x^2$$
   $$0=x^2-121$$
   $$0=x^2-11^2$$
   $$0=(x+11)(x-11)$$
   $$x+11=0 \quad \text{or} \quad x-11=0$$
   $$x=-11 \qquad x=11$$
   Since the length cannot be negative, the sides are 11 units long.

9. The perimeter is the sum of the lengths of the sides.

$$120 = (x+5)+(x^2-3x)+(3x-8)+(x+3)$$
$$120 = x+5+x^2-3x+3x-8+x+3$$
$$120 = x^2+2x$$
$$0 = x^2+2x-120$$

$x^2+2x-120=0$

$(x+12)(x-10)=0$

$x+12=0$ or $x-10=0$

$x=-12$ $\quad$ $x=10$

Since the dimensions cannot be negative, the lengths of the sides are: $10+5=15$ cm, $10^2-3(10)=70$ cm, $3(10)-8=22$ cm, and $10+3=13$ cm.

11. $x+5$ = the base and $x-5$ = the height.

$$A = bh$$
$$96 = (x+5)(x-5)$$
$$96 = x^2+5x-5x-25$$
$$96 = x^2-25$$
$$0 = x^2-121$$

$x^2-121=0$

$(x+11)(x-11)=0$

$x+11=0$ or $x-11=0$

$x=-11$ $\quad$ $x=11$

Since the dimensions cannot be negative, $x=11$. The base is $11+5=16$ miles, and the height is $11-5=6$ miles.

13. Find t when $h=0$.

$h=-16t^2+64t+80$

$0=-16t^2+64t+80$

$0=-16(t^2-4t-5)$

$0=-16(t-5)(t+1)$

$t-5=0$ or $t+1=0$

$t=5$ $\quad$ $t=-1$

Since the time t cannot be negative, the object hits the ground after 5 seconds.

15. Let x = the width, then $2x-7$ = the length.

$A=lw$

$30=(2x-7)(x)$

$30=2x^2-7x$

$0=2x^2-7x-30$

$0=(2x+5)(x-6)$

$2x+5=0$ or $x-6=0$

$2x=-5$ $\quad$ $x=6$

$x=-\frac{5}{2}$

Since the dimensions cannot be negative, the width is 6 cm and the length is $2(6)-7=5$ cm.

17. Let $n = 12$.

$$D = \frac{1}{2}n(n-3)$$

$$D = \frac{1}{2} \cdot 12(12-3) = 6(9) = 54$$

A polygon with 12 sides has 54 diagonals.

19. Let $D = 35$ and solve for n.

$$D = \frac{1}{2}n(n-3)$$

$$35 = \frac{1}{2}n(n-3)$$

$$35 = \frac{1}{2}n^2 - \frac{3}{2}n$$

$$0 = \frac{1}{2}n^2 - \frac{3}{2}n - 35$$

$$0 = \frac{1}{2}(n^2 - 3n - 70)$$

$$0 = \frac{1}{2}(n-10)(n+7)$$

$n - 10 = 0$ or $n + 7 = 0$

$n = 10$ $\quad$ $n = -7$

The polygon has 10 sides.

21. Let x = the unknown number.

$$x + x^2 = 132$$

$$x^2 + x - 132 = 0$$

$$(x+12)(x-11) = 0$$

$x + 12 = 0$ or $x - 11 = 0$

$x = -12$ $\quad$ $x = 11$

There are two numbers. They are -12 and 11.

23. Let x = the rate (in mph) of the slower boat, then
$x + 7$ = the rate (in mph) of the faster boat.
After one hour, the slower boat has traveled x miles and the faster boat has traveled $x + 7$ miles. By the Pythagorean theorem,

$$x^2 + (x+7)^2 = 17^2$$

$$x^2 + x^2 + 14x + 49 = 289$$

$$2x^2 + 14x + 49 = 289$$

$$2x^2 + 14x - 240 = 0$$

$$2(x^2 + 7x - 120) = 0$$

$$2(x+15)(x-8) = 0$$

$x + 15 = 0$ or $x - 8 = 0$

$x = -15$ $\quad$ $x = 8$

Since the rate cannot be negative, the slower boat travels at 8 mph. The faster boat travels at $8 + 7 = 15$ mph.

25. Let x = the first number, then
$20 - x$ = the other number.

$$x^2 + (20-x)^2 = 218$$

$$x^2 + 400 - 40x + x^2 = 218$$

$$2x^2 - 40x + 400 = 218$$

$$2x^2 - 40x + 182 = 0$$

$$2(x^2 - 20x + 91) = 0$$

$$2(x-13)(x-7) = 0$$

$x - 13 = 0$ or $x - 7 = 0$

$x = 13$ $\quad$ $x = 7$

The numbers are 13 and 7.

27. Let x = the length of a side of the original square. Then $x + 3$ = the length of a side of the larger square.

$$64 = (x+3)^2$$

$$64 = x^2 + 6x + 9$$

$$0 = x^2 + 6x - 55$$

$$0 = (x+11)(x-5)$$

$x + 11 = 0$ or $x - 5 = 0$

$x = -11$ $\quad$ $x = 5$

Since the length cannot be negative, the sides of the original square are 5 inches long.

29. Let x = the length of the shorter leg. Then $x + 4$ = the length of the longer leg and $x + 8$ = the length of the hypotenuse.
By the Pythagorean theorem

$$x^2 + (x+4)^2 = (x+8)^2$$
$$x^2 + x^2 + 8x + 16 = x^2 + 16x + 64$$
$$2x^2 + 8x + 16 = x^2 + 16x + 64$$
$$x^2 - 8x - 48 = 0$$
$$(x-12)(x+4) = 0$$
$$x - 12 = 0 \quad \text{or} \quad x + 4 = 0$$
$$x = 12 \qquad\qquad x = -4$$

Since the length cannot be negative, the sides of the triangle are 12 mm, 12 + 4 = 16 mm, and 12 + 8 = 20 mm.

31. Let x = the height of the triangle, then $2x$ = the base.

$$A = \frac{1}{2}bh$$
$$100 = \frac{1}{2}(2x)(x)$$
$$100 = x^2$$
$$0 = x^2 - 100$$
$$0 = (x+10)(x-10)$$
$$x + 10 = 0 \quad \text{or} \quad x - 10 = 0$$
$$x = -10 \qquad\qquad x = 10$$

Since the altitude cannot be negative, the height of the triangle is 10 km.

33. Let x = the length of the shorter leg, then $x + 12$ = the length of the longer leg and $2x - 12$ = the length of the hypotenuse.
By the Pythagorean theorem

$$x^2 + (x+12)^2 = (2x-12)^2$$
$$x^2 + x^2 + 24x + 144 = 4x^2 - 48x + 144$$
$$2x^2 + 24x + 144 = 4x^2 - 48x + 144$$
$$0 = 2x^2 - 72x$$
$$0 = 2x(x-36)$$
$$2x = 0 \quad \text{or} \quad x - 36 = 0$$
$$x = 0 \qquad\qquad x = 36$$

Since the length cannot be zero feet, the shorter leg is 36 feet long.

35. Find t when $h = 0$.

$$h = -16t^2 + 625$$
$$0 = -16t^2 + 625$$
$$0 = -(16t^2 - 625)$$
$$0 = -(4t+25)(4t-25)$$
$$4t + 25 = 0 \quad \text{or} \quad 4t - 25 = 0$$
$$4t = -25 \qquad\qquad 4t = 25$$
$$t = -\frac{25}{4} \qquad\qquad t = \frac{25}{4}$$
$$t = -6.25 \qquad\qquad t = 6.25$$

Since the time cannot be negative, the object will reach the ground after 6.25 seconds.

37.

$$A = P(1+r)^2$$
$$144 = 100(1+r)^2$$
$$144 = 100(1+2r+r^2)$$
$$144 = 100 + 200r + 100r^2$$
$$0 = 100r^2 + 200r - 44$$
$$0 = 4(25r^2 + 50r - 11)$$
$$0 = 4(5r-1)(5r+11)$$
$$5r - 1 = 0 \quad \text{or} \quad 5r + 11 = 0$$
$$5r = 1 \quad \text{or} \quad 5r = -11$$
$$r = \frac{1}{5} \quad \text{or} \quad r = -\frac{11}{5}$$
$$r = \frac{1}{5} = 0.20 = 20\%$$

39. length = x
width = $x - 7$

$$x(x-7) = 120$$
$$x^2 - 7x - 120 = 0$$
$$(x-15)(x+8) = 0$$
$$x - 15 = 0 \quad \text{or} \quad x + 8 = 0$$
$$x = 15 \quad \text{or} \quad x = -8$$

length = 15 miles
width = 8 miles

41.

$$C = x^2 - 15x + 50$$
$$9500 = x^2 - 15x + 50$$
$$0 = x^2 - 15x - 9450$$
$$0 = (x-105)(x+90)$$
$$x - 105 = 0 \quad \text{or} \quad x + 90 = 0$$
$$x = 105 \quad \text{or} \quad x = -90$$

105 units were manufactured.

43. x = length of boom
$2x + 28$ = height of mainsail

$$\frac{1}{2}bh = A$$
$$\frac{1}{2}x(2x+28) = 0.60(3000)$$
$$\frac{1}{2}x(2x) + \frac{1}{2}x(28) = 1800$$
$$x^2 + 14x = 1800$$
$$x^2 + 14x - 1800 = 1800 - 1800$$
$$x^2 + 14x - 1800 = 0$$
$$(x+50)(x-36) = 0$$
$$x + 50 = 0 \quad \text{or} \quad x - 36 = 0$$
$$x = -50 \quad \text{or} \quad x = 36$$

$x = 36$
$2x + 28 = 100$
boom length: 36 ft
height of mainsail: 100 ft

45. 435 acres; the graph at 1998 is about 435.

47. 2 million; the graph at 1998 is about 2.

49. Answers may vary.

51. $\frac{20}{35} = \frac{2\cdot 2\cdot 5}{5\cdot 7} = \frac{4}{7}$

53. $\frac{27}{18} = \frac{3\cdot 3\cdot 3}{2\cdot 3\cdot 3} = \frac{3}{2}$

55. $\frac{14}{42} = \frac{2\cdot 7}{2\cdot 3\cdot 7} = \frac{1}{3}$

Chapter 5 Review Exercises

1. $6x^2 - 15x = 3x(2x-5)$

2. $2x^3y - 6x^2y^2 - 8xy^3 = 2xy(x^2 - 3xy - 4y^2)$
$= 2xy(x-4y)(x+y)$

3. $20x^2 + 12x$; GCF $= 4x$
$4x(5x+3)$

4. $6x^2y^2 - 3xy^3 = 3xy^2(2x-y)$

5. $-8x^3y + 6x^2y^2$; GCF $= -2x^2y$
$-2x^2y(4x-3y)$

6. $3x(2x+3) - 5(2x+3) = (2x+3)(3x-5)$

7. $5x(x+1) - (x+1)$; GCF
$5x(x+1) - 1(x+1) = (x+1)(5x-1)$

8. $3x^2 - 3x + 2x - 2 = 3x(x-1) + 2(x-1)$
$= (x-1)(3x+2)$

9. $6x^2 + 10x - 3x - 5 = 2x(3x+5) - 1(3x+5)$
$= (3x+5)(2x-1)$

10. $3a^2 + 9ab + 3b^2 + ab$
$= 3a(a+3b) + b(a+3b)$
$= (a+3b)(3a+b)$

11. $x^2 + 6x + 8 = (x+4)(x+2)$

12. $x^2 - 11x + 24 = (x-8)(x-3)$

13. $x^2 + x + 2$
not factorable, prime

14. $x^2 - 5x - 6 = (x-6)(x+1)$

15. $x^2 + 2x - 8 = (x+4)(x-2)$

16. $x^2 + 4xy - 12y^2 = (x+6y)(x-2y)$

17. $x^2 + 8xy + 15y^2 = (x+3y)(x+5y)$

18. $3x^2y + 6xy^2 + 3y^3 = 3y(x^2 + 2xy + y^2)$
$= 3y(x+y)(x+y)$
$= 3y(x+y)^2$

19. $72 - 18x - 2x^2$; GCF $= 2$
$2(36 - 9x - x^2) = 2(12+x)(3-x)$

20. $32 + 12x - 4x^2 = 4(8 + 3x - x^2)$

21. $2x^2 + 11x - 6 = (2x-1)(x+6)$

22. $4x^2 - 7x + 4$
not factorable, prime

23. $4x^2 + 4x - 3 = (2x+3)(2x-1)$

24. $6x^2 + 5xy - 4y^2 = 6x^2 + 8xy - 3xy - 4y^2$
$= 2x(3x+4y) - y(3x+4y)$
$= (3x+4y)(2x-y)$

25. $6x^2 - 25xy + 4y^2 = (6x-y)(x-4y)$

26. $18x^2 - 60x + 50 = 2(9x^2 - 30x + 25)$
$= 2(3x-5)(3x-5)$
$= 2(3x-5)^2$

27. $2x^2 - 23xy - 39y^2 = (2x+3y)(x-13y)$

28. $4x^2 - 28xy + 49y^2 = (2x-7y)(2x-7y)$
$= (2x-7y)^2$

29. $18x^2 - 9xy - 20y^2 = (6x+5y)(3x-4y)$

30. $36x^3y + 24x^2y^2 - 45xy^3$
$= 3xy(12x^2 + 8xy - 15y^2)$
$= 3xy(12x^2 + 18xy - 10y^2 - 15y^2)$
$= 3xy[6x(2x+3y) - 5y(2x+3y)]$
$= 3xy(2x+3y)(6x-5y)$

31. $4x^2 - 9 = (2x)^2 - 3^2 = (2x+3)(2x-3)$

32. $9t^2 - 25s^2 = (3t-5s)(3t+5s)$

33. $16x^2 + y^2$
not factorable, prime

34. $x^3 - 8y^3 = x^3 - (2y)^3$
$= (x-2y)(x^2 + 2xy + 4y^2)$

35. $8x^3 + 27 = (2x)^3 + 3^3$
$= (2x+3)(4x^2 - 6x + 9)$

36. $2x^3 + 8x = 2x(x^2 + 4)$

37. $54 - 2x^3y^3$; GCF = 2
$2(27 - x^3y^3) = 2[3^3 - (xy)^3]$
$= 2(3-xy)(9 + 3xy + x^2y^2)$

38. $9x^2 - 4y^2$
$= (3x)^2 - (2y)^2$
$= (3x-2y)(3x+2y)$

39. $16x^4 - 1 = (4x^2)^2 - 1^2$
$= (4x^2+1)(4x^2-1)$
$= (4x^2+1)[(2x)^2 - 1^2]$
$= (4x^2+1)(2x+1)(2x-1)$

40. $x^4 + 16$
not factorable, prime

41. $2x^2 + 5x - 12 = (2x-3)(x+4)$

42. $3x^2 - 12 = 3(x^2 - 4) = 3(x-2)(x+2)$

43. $x(x-1) + 3(x-1)$; GCF = $(x-1)$
$(x-1)(x+3)$

44. $x^2 + xy - 3x - 3y = x(x+y) - 3(x+y)$
$= (x+y)(x-3)$

45. $4x^2y - 6xy^2$; GCF = $2xy$
$2xy(2x-3y)$

46. $8x^2 - 15x - x^3 = -x(-8x + 15 + x^2)$
$= -x(x^2 - 8x + 15)$
$= -x(x-5)(x-3)$

47. $125x^3 + 27 = (5x)^3 + 3^3$
$= (5x+3)(25x^2 - 15x + 9)$

48. $24x^2 - 3x - 18 = 3(8x^2 - x - 6)$

49. $(x+7)^2 - y^2 = [(x+7)+y][(x+7)-y]$
$= (x+7+y)(x+7-y)$

50. $x^2(x+3)-4(x+3)=(x+3)(x^2-4)$
$=(x+3)(x-2)(x+2)$

51. $(x+6)(x-2)=0$
$x+6=0$ or $x-2=0$
$x=-6$ or $x=2$

52. $3x(x+1)(7x-2)=0$
$3x=0$ or $x+1=0$ or $7x-2=0$
$x=0$ or $x=-1$ or $7x=2$

$x=\frac{2}{7}$

53. $4(5x+1)(x+3)=0$
$5x+1=0$ or $x+3=0$
$5x=-1$ or $x=-3$
$x=-\frac{1}{5}$ or $x=-3$

54. $x^2+8x+7=0$
$(x+7)(x+1)=0$
$x+7=0$ or $x+1=0$
$x=-7$ or $x=-1$

55. $x^2-2x-24=0$
$(x-6)(x+4)=0$
$x-6=0$ or $x+4=0$
$x=6$ or $x=-4$

56. $x^2+10x=-25$
$x^2+10x+25=0$
$(x+5)(x+5)=0$
$x+5=0$
$x=-5$

57. $x(x-10)=-16$
$x^2-10x=-16$
$x^2-10x+16=0$
$(x-8)(x-2)=0$
$x-8=0$ or $x-2=0$
$x=8$ or $x=2$

58. $(3x-1)(9x^2+3x+1)=0$
$3x-1=0$
$3x=1$
$x=\frac{1}{3}$

59. $56x^2-5x-6=0$
$(7x+2)(8x-3)=0$
$7x+2=0$ or $8x-3=0$
$7x=-2$ or $8x=3$
$x=-\frac{2}{7}$ or $x=\frac{3}{8}$

60. $20x^2-7x-6=0$
$(4x-3)(5x+2)=0$
$4x-3=0$ or $5x+2=0$
$4x=3$ or $5x=-2$
$x=\frac{3}{4}$ or $x=-\frac{2}{5}$

61. $5(3x+2)=4$
$15x+10=4$
$15x=4-10$
$15x=-6$
$x=-\frac{6}{15}=-\frac{2}{5}$

62. $6x^2-3x+8=0$
no real solution

63. $12-5t=-3$
$-5t=-3-12$
$-5t=-15$
$t=\frac{-15}{-5}$
$t=3$

64. $5x^3+20x^2+20x=0$
$5x(x^2+4x+4)=0$
$5x(x+2)(x+2)=0$
$x+2=0$ or $5x=0$
$x=-2$ or $x=0$

65. $4t^3 - 5t^2 - 21t = 0$

$t(4t^2 - 5t - 21) = 0$

$t(4t + 7)(t - 3) = 0$

$t = 0$ or $4t + 7 = 0$ or $t - 3 = 0$

$t = 0$ or $4t = -7$ or $t = 3$

$t = 0$ or $t = -\frac{7}{4}$ or $t = 3$

66. Let x = width

Then $2x - 15$ = length

$A = lw$

$500 = (2x - 15)(x)$

$500 = 2x^2 - 15x$

$0 = 2x^2 - 15x - 500$

$0 = (2x + 25)(x - 20)$

$2x + 25 = 0$ or $x - 20 = 0$

$x = -\frac{25}{2}$ or $x = 20$

Since the width cannot be negative, the width = 20 inches and the length = 25 inches.

67. base = $4x$

height = x

$A = \frac{1}{2}bh$

$162 = \frac{1}{2}(4x)(x)$

$162 = 2x^2$

$81 = x^2$

$x^2 - 81 = 0$

$(x + 9)(x - 9) = 0$

$x - 9 = 0$ or $x + 9 = 0$

$x = 9$ or $x = -9$

Since the length cannot be negative, then the base is 4(9) = 36 yards.

68. 1st positive integer = x

2nd positive integer = $x + 1$

$x(x + 1) = 380$

$x^2 + x - 380 = 0$

$(x + 20)(x - 19) = 0$

$x + 20 = 0$ or $x - 19 = 0$

$x = -20$ or $x = 19$

Since -20 is not positive, the 1st integer = 19 and the 2nd integer = 20.

69. a. $h = -16t^2 + 440t$

$2800 = -16t^2 + 440t$

$0 = -16t^2 + 440t - 2800$

$0 = -8(2t^2 - 55t + 350)$

$0 = -8(2t - 35)(t - 10)$

$2t - 35 = 0$ or $t - 10 = 0$

$t = \frac{35}{2} = 17\frac{1}{2}$ or $t = 10$

17.5 seconds and 10 seconds

The rocket reaches a height of 2800 ft on its way up and on its way back down.

b. $h = -16t^2 + 440t$

$0 = -16t^2 + 440t$

$0 = -16t(t - 27.5)$

$t - 27.5 = 0$

$t = 27.5$ seconds

70. short leg = $x - 8$
long leg = x
hypotenuse = $x + 8$
By the Pythagorean theorem,

$$(x-8)^2 + x^2 = (x+8)^2$$
$$x^2 + 2(x)(-8) + 8^2 + x^2 = x^2 + 2(x)(8) + 8^2$$
$$x^2 - 16x + 64 + x^2 = x^2 + 16x + 64$$
$$2x^2 - 16x + 64 = x^2 + 16x + 64$$
$$2x^2 - x^2 - 16x - 16x + 64 - 64 = 0$$
$$x^2 - 32x = 0$$
$$x(x-32) = 0$$

$x = 0$ or $x - 32 = 0$
$x = 0$ or $x = 32$
The long leg is 32 cm.

Chapter 5 Test

1. $9x^3 + 39x^2 + 12x$; GCF = $3x$
$3x(3x^2 + 13x + 4) = 3x(3x+1)(x+4)$

2. $x^2 + x - 10$
not factorable, prime

3. $x^2 + 4$
not factorable, prime

4. $y^2 - 8y - 48 = (y-12)(y+4)$

5. $3a^2 + 3ab - 7a - 7b = 3a(a+b) - 7(a+b)$
$= (a+b)(3a-7)$

6. $3x^2 - 5x + 2 = (3x-2)(x-1)$

7. $x^2 + 20x + 90$
not factorable, prime

8. $x^2 + 14xy + 24y^2 = (x+12y)(x+2y)$

9. $26x^6 - x^4$; GCF = x^4
$x^4(26x^2 - 1)$

10. $50x^3 + 10x^2 - 35x$; GCF = $5x$
$5x(10x^2 + 2x - 7)$

11. $180-5x^2$; GCF = 5

$5(36-x^2)=5(6-x)(6+x)$

12. $64x^3-1=(4x)^3-1^3$

$=(4x-1)(16x^2+4x+1)$

13. $6t^2-t-5=(6t+5)(t-1)$

14. $xy^2-7y^2-4x+28=y^2(x-7)-4(x-7)$

$=(x-7)(y^2-4)$

$=(x-7)(y+2)(y-2)$

15. $x-x^5$; GCF = x

$x(1-x^4)=x[(1^2)^2-(x^2)^2]$

$=x(1^2-x^2)(1^2+x^2)$

$=x(1-x)(1+x)(1+x^2)$

16. $-xy^3-x^3y$; GCF = $-xy$

$-xy(y^2+x^2)$

17. $x^2+5x=14$

$x^2+5x-14=0$

$(x+7)(x-2)=0$

$x+7=0$ or $x-2=0$

$x=-7$ or $x=2$

18. $(x+3)^2=16$

$x^2+2(x)(3)+3^2=16$

$x^2+6x+9=16$

$x^2+6x+9-16=0$

$x^2+6x-7=0$

$(x+7)(x-1)=0$

$x+7=0$ or $x-1=0$

$x=-7$ or $x=1$

19. $3x(2x-3)(3x+4)=0$

$3x=0$ or $2x-3=0$ or $3x+4=0$

$x=\frac{0}{3}$ or $2x=3$ or $3x=-4$

$x=0$ or $x=\frac{3}{2}$ or $x=-\frac{4}{3}$

20. $5t^3-45t=0$

$5t(t^2-9)=0$

$5t(t+3)(t-3)=0$

$5t=0$ or $t+3=0$ or $t-3=0$

$t=0$ or $t=-3$ or $t=3$

21. $3x^2=-12x$

$3x^2+12x=0$

$3x(x+4)=0$

$3x=0$ or $x+4=0$

$x=0$ or $x=-4$

22. $t^2-2t-15=0$

$(t-5)(t+3)=0$

$t-5=0$ or $t+3=0$

$t=5$ or $t=-3$

23. $7x^2=168+35x$

$7x^2-35x-168=0$

$7(x^2-5x-24)=0$

$7(x-8)(x+3)=0$

$x-8=0$ or $x+3=0$

$x=8$ or $x=-3$

24. $6x^2=15x$

$6x^2-15x=0$

$3x(2x-5)=0$

$3x=0$ or $2x-5=0$

$x=0$ or $2x=5$

$x=\frac{5}{2}$

25. width = x
length = $x + 5$

$$A = lw$$
$$66 = (x+5)(x)$$
$$66 = x^2 + 5x$$
$$0 = x^2 + 5x - 66$$
$$0 = (x+11)(x-6)$$
$$x + 11 = 0 \quad \text{or} \quad x - 6 = 0$$
$$x = -11 \quad \text{or} \quad x = 6$$

The dimensions are 6 ft. by 11 ft.

26. altitude = x
base = $x + 9$

$$A = \frac{1}{2}bh$$
$$68 = \frac{1}{2}(x+9)(x)$$
$$2(68) = 2\left[\frac{1}{2}(x+9)(x)\right]$$
$$136 = (x+9)(x)$$
$$136 = x^2 + 9x$$
$$0 = x^2 + 9x - 136$$
$$0 = (x+17)(x-8)$$
$$x + 17 = 0 \quad \text{or} \quad x - 8 = 0$$
$$x = -17 \quad \text{or} \quad x = 8$$

The base is 17 feet.

27. one number = x
other number = $17 - x$

$$x^2 + (17-x)^2 = 145$$
$$x^2 + 289 + 2(17)(-x) + x^2 = 145$$
$$x^2 + 289 - 34x + x^2 = 145$$
$$2x^2 - 34x + 289 = 145$$
$$2x^2 - 34x + 289 - 145 = 0$$
$$2x^2 - 34x + 144 = 0$$
$$2(x^2 - 17x + 72) = 0$$
$$2(x-8)(x-9) = 0$$
$$x - 8 = 0 \quad \text{or} \quad x - 9 = 0$$
$$x = 8 \quad \text{or} \quad x = 9$$

The numbers are 8 and 9.

28.

$$h = -16t^2 + 784$$
$$0 = -16t^2 + 784$$
$$0 = -16(t^2 - 49)$$
$$0 = -16(t-7)(t+7)$$
$$t - 7 = 0 \quad \text{or} \quad t + 7 = 0$$
$$t = 7 \quad \text{or} \quad t = -7$$

Since time cannot be negative, the object reaches the ground after 7 seconds.

Chapter 6

Section 6.1

Mental Math

1. $\frac{x+5}{x}$; $x=0$

2. $\frac{x^2-5x}{x-3}$; $x=3$

3. $\frac{x^2+4x-2}{x(x-1)}$; $x=0$, $x=1$

4. $\frac{x+2}{(x-5)(x-6)}$; $x=5$, $x=6$

Exercise Set 6.1

1. $x=2$
$$\frac{x+5}{x+2}=\frac{2+5}{2+2}=\frac{7}{4}$$

3. $z=-5$
$$\frac{z-8}{z+2}=\frac{-5-8}{-5+2}=\frac{-13}{-3}=\frac{13}{3}$$

5. $x=2$
$$\frac{x^2+8x+2}{x^2-x-6}=\frac{2^2+8(2)+2}{2^2-2-6}=\frac{4+16+2}{4-2-6}=\frac{22}{-4}=-\frac{11}{2}$$

7. $x=2$
$$\frac{x+5}{x^2+4x-8}=\frac{2+5}{2^2+4(2)-8}=\frac{7}{4+8-8}=\frac{7}{4}$$

9. $y=-2$
$$\frac{y^3}{y^2-1}=\frac{(-2)^3}{(-2)^2-1}=\frac{-8}{4-1}=\frac{-8}{3}=-\frac{8}{3}$$

11. $\frac{x+3}{x+2}$ undefined if
$$x+2=0$$
$$x=-2$$

13. $\frac{4x^2+9}{2x-8}$ undefined if
$$2x-8=0$$
$$2x=8$$
$$x=\frac{8}{2}=4$$

15. $\frac{9x^3+4}{15x+30}$ undefined if
$$15x+30=0$$
$$15x=-30$$
$$x=\frac{-30}{15}=-2$$

17. $\frac{x^2-5x-2}{x^2+4}$ undefined if
$$x^2+4=0$$
$$x^2=-4$$
$$x=\pm\sqrt{-4}$$
Since $\pm\sqrt{-4}$ is not a real number, there is no real number for which it is not defined.

19. Answers may vary.

21. $\frac{8x^5}{4x^9}=\frac{2\cdot 4\cdot x^5}{4\cdot x^5\cdot x^4}=\frac{2}{x^4}$

23. $\frac{5(x-2)}{(x-2)(x+1)}=\frac{5}{x+1}$

25. $\frac{-5a-5b}{a+b}=\frac{-5(a+b)}{a+b}=-5$

27. $\frac{x+5}{x^2-4x-45}=\frac{x+5}{(x-9)(x+5)}=\frac{1}{(x-9)}$

29. $\frac{5x^2+11x+2}{x+2}=\frac{(5x+1)(x+2)}{x+2}=5x+1$

31. $\frac{x^2+x-12}{2x^2-5x-3}=\frac{(x+4)(x-3)}{(2x+1)(x-3)}=\frac{x+4}{2x+1}$

33. Answers may vary.

35. $\frac{x-7}{7-x}=\frac{x-7}{-1(x-7)}=-1$

37. $\frac{y^2-2y}{4-2y}=\frac{y(y-2)}{-2(y-2)}=-\frac{y}{2}$

39. $\frac{x^2-4x+4}{4-x^2}=\frac{(x-2)(x-2)}{-1(x^2-4)}$

$=\frac{(x-2)(x-2)}{-1(x+2)(x-2)}$

$=-\frac{x-2}{x+2}$

$=\frac{2-x}{x+2}$

41. $\frac{15x^4y^8}{-5x^8y^3}=\frac{-3\cdot -5\cdot x^4\cdot y^3\cdot y^5}{-5\cdot x^4\cdot x^4\cdot y^3}$

$=\frac{-3y^5}{x^4}$

$=-\frac{3y^5}{x^4}$

43. $\frac{(x-2)(x+3)}{5(x+3)}=\frac{x-2}{5}$

45. $\frac{-6a-6b}{a+b}=\frac{-6(a+b)}{a+b}=-6$

47. $\frac{2x^2-8}{4x-8}=\frac{2(x^2-4)}{4(x-2)}$

$=\frac{2(x+2)(x-2)}{2\cdot 2(x-2)}$

$=\frac{x+2}{2}$

49. $\frac{11x^2-22x^3}{6x-12x^2}=\frac{11x^2(1-2x)}{6x(1-2x)}=\frac{11x\cdot x}{6x}=\frac{11x}{6}$

51. $\frac{x+7}{x^2+5x-14}=\frac{x+7}{(x+7)(x-2)}=\frac{1}{x-2}$

53. $\frac{2x^2+3x-2}{2x-1}=\frac{(2x-1)(x+2)}{2x-1}=x+2$

55. $\frac{x^2-1}{x^2-2x+1}=\frac{(x+1)(x-1)}{(x-1)(x-1)}=\frac{x+1}{x-1}$

57. $\frac{m^2-6m+9}{m^2-9}=\frac{(m-3)(m-3)}{(m+3)(m-3)}=\frac{m-3}{m+3}$

59. $\frac{-2a^2+12a-18}{9-a^2}=\frac{-2(a^2-6a+9)}{-1(a^2-9)}$

$=\frac{-2(a-3)(a-3)}{-1(a+3)(a-3)}$

$=\frac{2(a-3)}{a+3}$ or $\frac{2a-6}{a+3}$

61. $\frac{2-x}{x-2}=\frac{-1(x-2)}{x-2}=-1$

63. $\frac{x^2-1}{1-x}=\frac{(x+1)(x-1)}{-1(x-1)}=-(x+1)=-x-1$

65. $\frac{x^2+7x+10}{x^2-3x-10}=\frac{(x+5)(x+2)}{(x-5)(x+2)}=\frac{x+5}{x-5}$

67. $\frac{3x^2+7x+2}{3x^2+13x+4}=\frac{(3x+1)(x+2)}{(3x+1)(x+4)}=\frac{x+2}{x+4}$

69. $C=\frac{DA}{A+12}$; $A=8, D=1000$

$C=\frac{1000\cdot 8}{8+12}=\frac{8000}{20}=400$ mg

71. $B=\frac{705w}{h^2}$; $w=148,\ h=66$

$B=\frac{705\cdot 148}{(66)^2}=\frac{104,340}{4356}\approx 24.0$

No

73. a. $R=\frac{150x^2}{x^2+3}$

$=\frac{150(1)^2}{1^2+3}$

$=\frac{150}{4}$

$=\$37.5$ million

b. $R=\frac{150x^2}{x^2+3}$

$=\frac{150(2)^2}{2^2+3}$

$=\frac{600}{7}$

$\approx \$85.7$ million

c. $85.7-37.5=\$48.2$ million

75. a, c

Answers may vary.

77. $\frac{ab+ac+b^2+bc}{b+c}=\frac{a(b+c)+b(b+c)}{b+c}$

$=\frac{(b+c)(a+b)}{(b+c)}$

$=a+b$

79. $\frac{xy-6x+2y-12}{y^2-6y}=\frac{x(y-6)+2(y-6)}{y(y-6)}$

$=\frac{(y-6)(x+2)}{y(y-6)}$

$=\frac{x+2}{y}$

81. $\frac{x^3+64}{x+4}=\frac{(x+4)(x^2-4x+16)}{x+4}$

$=x^2-4x+16$

83. $\frac{3-x}{x^3-27}=\frac{-(x-3)}{(x-3)(x^2+3x+9)}$

$=-\frac{1}{x^2+3x+9}$

85. $y=\frac{x^2-16}{x-4}=\frac{(x+4)(x-4)}{(x-4)}=x+4,\ x\neq 4$

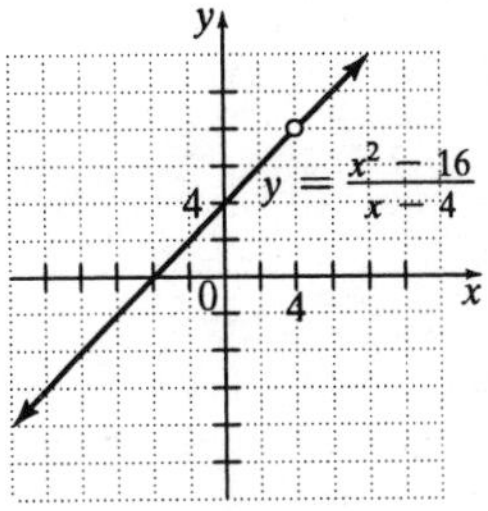

87. $y=\frac{x^2-6x+8}{x-2}$

$=\frac{(x-2)(x-4)}{(x-2)}$

$=x-4,\ x\neq 2$

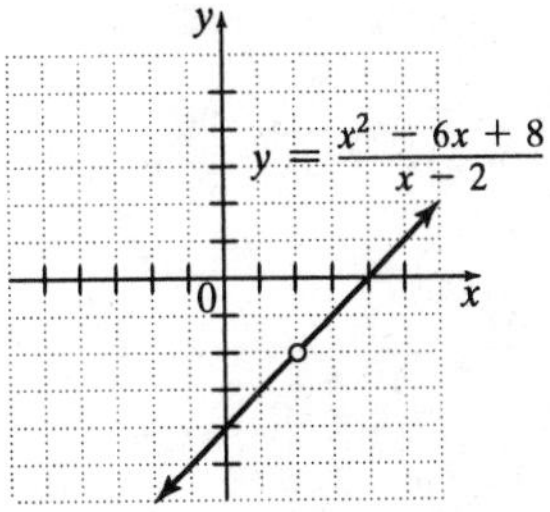

89. $\frac{5}{27}\cdot\frac{2}{5}=\frac{5\cdot 2}{3\cdot 3\cdot 3\cdot 5}=\frac{2}{27}$

91. $\frac{7}{8}\div\frac{1}{2}=\frac{7}{8}\cdot\frac{2}{1}=\frac{7\cdot 2}{2\cdot 2\cdot 2}=\frac{7}{4}$

93. $\frac{4}{3}\cdot\frac{1}{7}\cdot\frac{10}{13}=\frac{2\cdot 2\cdot 1\cdot 2\cdot 5}{3\cdot 7\cdot 13}=\frac{40}{273}$

95. $\frac{8}{15} \div \frac{5}{8} = \frac{8}{15} \cdot \frac{8}{5} = \frac{2 \cdot 2 \cdot 2 \cdot 2 \cdot 2 \cdot 2}{3 \cdot 5 \cdot 5} = \frac{64}{75}$

Section 6.2

Mental Math

1. $\frac{2}{y} \cdot \frac{x}{3} = \frac{2 \cdot x}{y \cdot 3} = \frac{2x}{3y}$

2. $\frac{3x}{4} \cdot \frac{1}{y} = \frac{3x \cdot 1}{4 \cdot y} = \frac{3x}{4y}$

3. $\frac{5}{7} \cdot \frac{y^2}{x^2} = \frac{5 \cdot y^2}{7 \cdot x^2} = \frac{5y^2}{7x^2}$

4. $\frac{x^5}{11} \cdot \frac{4}{z^3} = \frac{x^5 \cdot 4}{11 \cdot z^3} = \frac{4x^5}{11z^3}$

5. $\frac{9}{x} \cdot \frac{x}{5} = \frac{9 \cdot x}{x \cdot 5} = \frac{9}{5}$

6. $\frac{y}{7} \cdot \frac{3}{y} = \frac{y \cdot 3}{7 \cdot y} = \frac{3}{7}$

Exercise Set 6.2

1. $\frac{3x}{y^2} \cdot \frac{7y}{4x} = \frac{21xy}{4x \cdot y \cdot y} = \frac{21}{4y}$

3. $\frac{8x}{2} \cdot \frac{x^5}{4x^2} = \frac{8x^6}{8x^2} = \frac{8 \cdot x^2 \cdot x^4}{8 \cdot x^2} = x^4$

5. $$-\frac{5a^2b}{30a^2b^2} \cdot b^3 = -\frac{5a^2b^4}{30a^2b^2} = -\frac{5 \cdot a^2 \cdot b^2 \cdot b^2}{5 \cdot 6 \cdot a^2 \cdot b^2} = -\frac{b^2}{6}$$

7. $$\frac{x}{2x-14} \cdot \frac{x^2-7x}{5} = \frac{x}{2(x-7)} \cdot \frac{x(x-7)}{5} = \frac{x \cdot x \cdot (x-7)}{2 \cdot 5 \cdot (x-7)} = \frac{x^2}{10}$$

9. $$\frac{6x+6}{5} \cdot \frac{10}{36x+36} = \frac{6(x+1)}{5} \cdot \frac{10}{36(x+1)} = \frac{6 \cdot 2 \cdot 5 \cdot (x+1)}{5 \cdot 6 \cdot 2 \cdot 3 \cdot (x+1)} = \frac{1}{3}$$

11. $$\frac{m^2-n^2}{m+n} \cdot \frac{m}{m^2-mn} = \frac{(m+n)(m-n)}{m+n} \cdot \frac{m}{m(m-n)} = \frac{m \cdot (m+n) \cdot (m-n)}{m \cdot (m+n) \cdot (m-n)} = 1$$

13. $$\frac{x^2-25}{x^2-3x-10} \cdot \frac{x+2}{x} = \frac{(x+5)(x-5)}{(x+2)(x-5)} \cdot \frac{x+2}{x} = \frac{(x+5) \cdot (x-5) \cdot (x+2)}{(x+2) \cdot (x-5) \cdot x} = \frac{x+5}{x}$$

15. $A = l \cdot w$

$$A = \frac{2x}{x^2-25} \cdot \frac{x+5}{9x^3}$$

$$A = \frac{2x}{(x+5)(x-5)} \cdot \frac{x+5}{9x^3}$$

$$A = \frac{2x \cdot (x+5)}{9 \cdot x \cdot x^2 \cdot (x+5)(x-5)}$$

$$A = \frac{2}{9x^2(x-5)} \text{ square feet}$$

17. $\frac{5x^7}{2x^5} \div \frac{10x}{4x^3} = \frac{5x^7}{2x^5} \cdot \frac{4x^3}{10x}$
$= \frac{20x^{10}}{20x^6}$
$= \frac{20x^6 \cdot x^4}{20x^6}$
$= x^4$

19. $\frac{8x^2}{y^3} \div \frac{4x^2y^3}{6} = \frac{8x^2}{y^3} \cdot \frac{6}{4x^2y^3}$
$= \frac{48x^2}{4x^2y^6}$
$= \frac{12 \cdot 4x^2}{4x^2 \cdot y^6}$
$= \frac{12}{y^6}$

21. $\frac{(x-6)(x+4)}{4x} \div \frac{2x-12}{8x^2}$
$= \frac{(x-6)(x+4)}{4x} \cdot \frac{8x^2}{2x-12}$
$= \frac{(x-6)(x+4)}{4x} \cdot \frac{8x^2}{2(x-6)}$
$= \frac{8x \cdot x(x-6)(x+4)}{8x \cdot (x-6)}$
$= x(x+4)$

23. $\frac{3x^2}{x^2-1} \div \frac{x^5}{(x+1)^2}$
$= \frac{3x^2}{(x+1)(x-1)} \cdot \frac{(x+1)(x+1)}{x^5}$
$= \frac{3x^2 \cdot (x+1) \cdot (x+1)}{x^2 \cdot x^3 \cdot (x+1)(x-1)}$
$= \frac{3(x+1)}{x^3(x-1)}$

25. $\frac{m^2-n^2}{m+n} \div \frac{m}{m^2+nm}$
$= \frac{m^2-n^2}{m+n} \cdot \frac{m^2+nm}{m}$
$= \frac{(m+n)(m-n)}{m+n} \cdot \frac{m(m+n)}{m}$
$= \frac{m \cdot (m+n) \cdot (m-n) \cdot (m+n)}{m(m+n)}$
$= m^2 - n^2$

27. $\frac{x+2}{7-x} \div \frac{x^2-5x+6}{x^2-9x+14}$
$= \frac{x+2}{7-x} \cdot \frac{x^2-9x+14}{x^2-5x+6}$
$= \frac{x+2}{-1(x-7)} \cdot \frac{(x-7)(x-2)}{(x-3)(x-2)}$
$= \frac{(x+2) \cdot (x-7) \cdot (x-2)}{-1 \cdot (x-7) \cdot (x-3) \cdot (x-2)}$
$= -\frac{x+2}{x-3}$

29. $\frac{x^2+7x+10}{1-x} \div \frac{x^2+2x-15}{x-1}$
$= \frac{x^2+7x+10}{1-x} \cdot \frac{x-1}{x^2+2x-15}$
$= \frac{(x+5)(x+2)}{-1(x-1)} \cdot \frac{x-1}{(x+5)(x-3)}$
$= \frac{(x+5) \cdot (x+2) \cdot (x-1)}{-1 \cdot (x-1) \cdot (x+5)(x-3)}$
$= -\frac{x+2}{x-3}$

31. Answers may vary.

33. $\frac{5a^2b}{30a^2b^2} \cdot \frac{1}{b^3} = \frac{5a^2b}{30a^2b^5} = \frac{1}{6b^4}$

35. $\frac{12x^3y}{8xy^7} \div \frac{7x^5y}{6x} = \frac{12x^3y}{8xy^7} \cdot \frac{6x}{7x^5y}$
$= \frac{72x^4y}{56x^6y^8}$
$= \frac{9}{7x^2y^7}$

37. $\frac{5x-10}{12} \div \frac{4x-8}{8} = \frac{5x-10}{12} \cdot \frac{8}{4x-8}$
$= \frac{5(x-2)}{12} \cdot \frac{8}{4(x-2)}$
$= \frac{5 \cdot 4 \cdot 2 \cdot (x-2)}{2 \cdot 6 \cdot 4 \cdot (x-2)}$
$= \frac{5}{6}$

39. $\frac{x^2+5x}{8} \cdot \frac{9}{3x+15} = \frac{x(x+5)}{8} \cdot \frac{9}{3(x+5)}$
$= \frac{3 \cdot 3 \cdot x \cdot (x+5)}{3 \cdot 8 \cdot (x+5)}$
$= \frac{3x}{8}$

41. $\frac{7}{6p^2+q} \div \frac{14}{18p^2+3q}$
$= \frac{7}{6p^2+q} \cdot \frac{18p^2+3q}{14}$
$= \frac{7}{6p^2+q} \cdot \frac{3(6p^2+q)}{14}$
$= \frac{7 \cdot 3 \cdot (6p^2+q)}{2 \cdot 7 \cdot (6p^2-q)}$
$= \frac{3}{2}$

43. $\frac{3x+4y}{x^2+4xy+4y^2} \cdot \frac{x+2y}{2}$
$= \frac{3x+4y}{(x+2y)(x+2y)} \cdot \frac{x+2y}{2}$
$= \frac{(3x+4y) \cdot (x+2y)}{2 \cdot (x+2y) \cdot (x+2y)}$
$= \frac{3x+4y}{2(x+2y)}$

45. $\frac{x^2-9}{x^2+8} \div \frac{3-x}{2x^2+16}$
$= \frac{x^2-9}{x^2+8} \cdot \frac{2x^2+16}{3-x}$
$= \frac{(x+3)(x-3)}{x^2+8} \cdot \frac{2(x^2+8)}{-1(x-3)}$
$= \frac{2 \cdot (x+3) \cdot (x-3) \cdot (x^2+8)}{-1 \cdot (x^2+8) \cdot (x-3)}$
$= -2(x+3)$

47. $\frac{(x+2)^2}{x-2} \div \frac{x^2-4}{2x-4}$
$= \frac{(x+2)^2}{(x-2)} \cdot \frac{2x-4}{x^2-4}$
$= \frac{(x+2)(x+2)}{(x-2)} \cdot \frac{2(x-2)}{(x+2)(x-2)}$
$= \frac{2 \cdot (x+2)(x+2) \cdot (x-2)}{(x-2) \cdot (x+2)(x-2)}$
$= \frac{2(x+2)}{x-2}$

49. $\frac{a^2+7a+12}{a^2+5a+6} \cdot \frac{a^2+8a+15}{a^2+5a+4}$
$= \frac{(a+3)(a+4)}{(a+3)(a+2)} \cdot \frac{(a+3)(a+5)}{(a+1)(a+4)}$
$= \frac{(a+3) \cdot (a+4) \cdot (a+3) \cdot (a+5)}{(a+3) \cdot (a+2) \cdot (a+1) \cdot (a+4)}$
$= \frac{(a+3)(a+5)}{(a+2)(a+1)}$

51. $\frac{1}{-x-4} \div \frac{x^2-7x}{x^2-3x-28}$
$= \frac{1}{-x-4} \cdot \frac{x^2-3x-28}{x^2-7x}$
$= \frac{1}{-1(x+4)} \cdot \frac{(x-7)(x+4)}{x(x-7)}$
$= \frac{(x-7) \cdot (x+4)}{-1 \cdot x \cdot (x+4) \cdot (x-7)}$
$= -\frac{1}{x}$

53. $\frac{x^2-5x-24}{2x^2-2x-24}\cdot\frac{4x^2+4x-24}{x^2-10x+16}$
$=\frac{(x-8)(x+3)}{2(x^2-x-12)}\cdot\frac{4(x^2+x-6)}{(x-8)(x-2)}$
$=\frac{(x-8)(x+3)}{2(x-4)(x+3)}\cdot\frac{4(x+3)(x-2)}{(x-8)(x-2)}$
$=\frac{2\cdot2\cdot(x-8)\cdot(x+3)\cdot(x+3)\cdot(x-2)}{2\cdot(x-4)\cdot(x+3)\cdot(x-8)\cdot(x-2)}$
$=\frac{2(x+3)}{x-4}$

55. $(x-5)\div\frac{5-x}{x^2+2}=(x-5)\cdot\frac{x^2+2}{5-x}$
$=(x-5)\cdot\frac{x^2+2}{-1(x-5)}$
$=\frac{(x-5)\cdot(x^2+2)}{-1\cdot(x-5)}$
$=-(x^2+2)$

57. $\frac{x^2-y^2}{x^2-2xy+y^2}\cdot\frac{y-x}{x+y}$
$=\frac{(x+y)(x-y)}{(x-y)(x-y)}\cdot\frac{-1(x-y)}{x+y}$
$=\frac{-1\cdot(x+y)\cdot(x-y)\cdot(x-y)}{(x-y)\cdot(x-y)\cdot(x+y)}$
$=-1$

59. $\frac{x^2-9}{2x}\div\frac{x+3}{8x^4}=\frac{x^2-9}{2x}\cdot\frac{8x^4}{x+3}$
$=\frac{(x+3)(x-3)}{2x}\cdot\frac{8x^4}{x+3}$
$=\frac{2x\cdot4x^3\cdot(x+3)(x-3)}{2x\cdot(x+3)}$
$=4x^3(x-3)$

61. 10 square feet $=\frac{10\text{ sq. ft}}{1}\cdot\frac{144\text{ sq. in.}}{1\text{ sq. ft}}$
$=1440$ square inches

63. 3,707,745 square feet
$=\frac{3,707,745\text{ sq. ft}}{1}\cdot\frac{1\text{ sq. yd}}{9\text{ sq. ft}}$
$\approx 411,972$ square yards

65. 50 miles per hour
$=\frac{50\text{ mi}}{1\text{ hr}}\cdot\frac{5280\text{ ft}}{1\text{ mi}}\cdot\frac{1\text{ hr}}{3600\text{ sec}}$
≈ 73 feet per second

67. 5023 feet per second
$=\frac{5023\text{ ft}}{1\text{ sec}}\cdot\frac{1\text{ mi}}{5280\text{ ft}}\cdot\frac{3600\text{ sec}}{1\text{ hr}}$
≈ 3424.8 miles per hour

69. $\frac{a^2+ac+ba+bc}{a-b}\div\frac{a+c}{a+b}$
$=\frac{a(a+c)+b(a+c)}{a-b}\cdot\frac{a+b}{a+c}$
$=\frac{(a+c)(a+b)}{a-b}\cdot\frac{a+b}{a+c}$
$=\frac{(a+c)\cdot(a+b)\cdot(a+b)}{(a-b)\cdot(a+c)}$
$=\frac{(a+b)^2}{a-b}$

71. $\frac{3x^2+8x+5}{x^2+8x+7}\cdot\frac{x+7}{x^2+4}$
$=\frac{(3x+5)(x+1)}{(x+7)(x+1)}\cdot\frac{x+7}{x^2+4}$
$=\frac{(3x+5)\cdot(x+1)\cdot(x+7)}{(x+7)\cdot(x+1)\cdot(x^2+4)}$
$=\frac{3x+5}{x^2+4}$

73. $\frac{x^3+8}{x^2-2x+4}\cdot\frac{4}{x^2-4}$
$=\frac{(x+2)(x^2-2x+4)}{x^2-2x+4}\cdot\frac{4}{(x+2)(x-2)}$
$=\frac{4\cdot(x+2)\cdot(x^2-2x+4)}{(x+2)(x-2)(x^2-2x+4)}$
$=\frac{4}{x-2}$

75. $\frac{a^2-ab}{6a^2+6ab} \div \frac{a^3-b^3}{a^2-b^2}$
$= \frac{a^2-ab}{6a^2+6ab} \cdot \frac{a^2-b^2}{a^3-b^3}$
$= \frac{a(a-b)}{6a(a+b)} \cdot \frac{(a-b)(a+b)}{(a-b)(a^2+ab+b^2)}$
$= \frac{a \cdot (a-b) \cdot (a-b) \cdot (a+b)}{6 \cdot a \cdot (a+b) \cdot (a-b) \cdot (a^2+ab+b^2)}$
$= \frac{a-b}{6(a^2+ab+b^2)}$

77. $\frac{1}{5}+\frac{4}{5}=\frac{5}{5}=1$

79. $\frac{9}{9}-\frac{19}{9}=-\frac{10}{9}$

81. $\frac{6}{5}+\left(\frac{1}{5}-\frac{8}{5}\right)=\frac{6}{5}+\left(-\frac{7}{5}\right)=-\frac{1}{5}$

83.

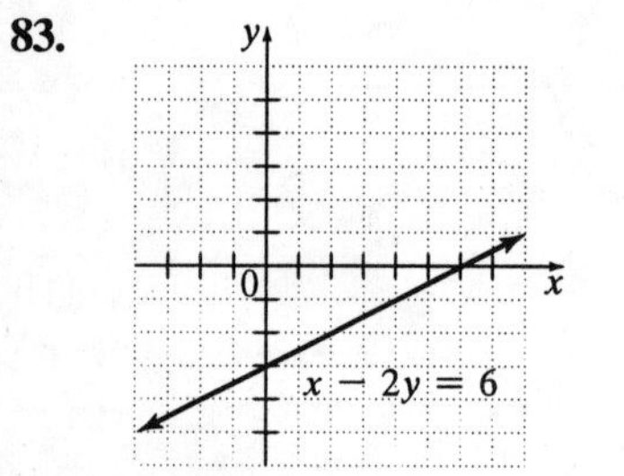

85. $\left(\frac{x^2-y^2}{x^2+y^2} \div \frac{x^2-y^2}{3x}\right) \cdot \frac{x^2+y^2}{6}$
$= \frac{x^2-y^2}{x^2+y^2} \cdot \frac{3x}{x^2-y^2} \cdot \frac{x^2+y^2}{6}$
$= \frac{(x+y)(x-y)}{x^2+y^2} \cdot \frac{3x}{(x+y)(x-y)} \cdot \frac{x^2+y^2}{6}$
$= \frac{3 \cdot x \cdot (x+y) \cdot (x-y) \cdot (x^2+y^2)}{2 \cdot 3 \cdot (x^2+y^2) \cdot (x+y) \cdot (x-y)}$
$= \frac{x}{2}$

87. $\left(\frac{2a+b}{b^2} \cdot \frac{3a^2-2ab}{ab+2b^2}\right) \div \frac{a^2-3ab+2b^2}{5ab-10b^2}$
$= \frac{2a+b}{b^2} \cdot \frac{3a^2-2ab}{ab+2b^2} \cdot \frac{5ab-10b^2}{a^2-3ab+2b^2}$
$= \frac{2a+b}{b^2} \cdot \frac{a(3a-2b)}{b(a+2b)} \cdot \frac{5b(a-2b)}{(a-2b)(a-b)}$
$= \frac{5 \cdot a \cdot b \cdot (2a+b) \cdot (3a-2b) \cdot (a-2b)}{b \cdot b^2 \cdot (a+2b) \cdot (a-2b) \cdot (a-b)}$
$= \frac{5a(2a+b)(3a-2b)}{b^2(a+2b)(a-b)}$

Section 6.3

Mental Math

1. $\frac{2}{3}+\frac{1}{3}=\frac{3}{3}=1$
2. $\frac{5}{11}+\frac{1}{11}=\frac{6}{11}$
3. $\frac{3x}{9}+\frac{4x}{9}=\frac{7x}{9}$
4. $\frac{3y}{8}+\frac{2y}{8}=\frac{5y}{8}$
5. $\frac{8}{9}-\frac{7}{9}=\frac{1}{9}$
6. $-\frac{4}{12}-\frac{3}{12}=-\frac{7}{12}$
7. $\frac{7}{5}+\frac{10y}{5}=\frac{7-10y}{5}$
8. $\frac{12x}{7}-\frac{4x}{7}=\frac{8x}{7}$

Exercise Set 6.3

1. $\frac{a}{13}+\frac{9}{13}=\frac{a+9}{13}$

3. $\frac{9}{3+y}+\frac{y+1}{3+y}=\frac{9+y+1}{3+y}=\frac{10+y}{3+y}$

5. $\frac{4m}{3n}+\frac{5m}{3n}=\frac{4m+5m}{3n}=\frac{9m}{3n}=\frac{3m}{n}$

7. $\frac{2x+1}{x-3}+\frac{3x+6}{x-3}=\frac{2x+1+3x+6}{x-3}=\frac{5x+7}{x-3}$

9. $\frac{7}{8}-\frac{3}{8}=\frac{4}{8}=\frac{1}{2}$

11. $\frac{4m}{m-6}-\frac{24}{m-6}=\frac{4m-24}{m-6}=\frac{4(m-6)}{m-6}=4$

13. $\frac{2x^2}{x-5}-\frac{25+x^2}{x-5}=\frac{2x^2-(25+x^2)}{x-5}$
$=\frac{2x^2-25-x^2}{x-5}$
$=\frac{x^2-25}{x-5}$
$=\frac{(x+5)(x-5)}{x-5}$
$=x+5$

15. $\frac{-3x^2-4}{x-4}-\frac{12-4x^2}{x-4}$
$=\frac{-3x^2-4-(12-4x^2)}{x-4}$
$=\frac{-3x^2-4-12+4x^2}{x-4}$
$=\frac{x^2-16}{x-4}$
$=\frac{(x+4)(x-4)}{x-4}$
$=x+4$

17. $\frac{2x+3}{x+1}-\frac{x+2}{x+1}=\frac{2x+3-(x+2)}{x+1}$
$=\frac{2x+3-x-2}{x+1}$
$=\frac{x+1}{x+1}$
$=1$

19. $\frac{3}{x^3}+\frac{9}{x^3}=\frac{3+9}{x^3}=\frac{12}{x^3}$

21. $\frac{5}{x+4}-\frac{10}{x+4}=\frac{5-10}{x+4}=-\frac{5}{x+4}$

23. $\frac{x}{x+y}-\frac{2}{x+y}=\frac{x-2}{x+y}$

25. $\frac{8x}{2x+5}+\frac{20}{2x+5}=\frac{8x+20}{2x+5}=\frac{4(2x+5)}{2x+5}=4$

27. $\frac{5x+4}{x-1}-\frac{2x+7}{x-1}=\frac{5x+4-(2x+7)}{x-1}$
$=\frac{5x+4-2x-7}{x-1}$
$=\frac{3x-3}{x-1}$
$=\frac{3(x-1)}{x-1}$
$=3$

29. $\frac{a}{a^2+2a-15}-\frac{3}{a^2+2a-15}=\frac{a-3}{a^2+2a-15}$
$=\frac{a-3}{(a+5)(a-3)}$
$=\frac{1}{a+5}$

31. $\frac{2x+3}{x^2-x-30}-\frac{x-2}{x^2-x-30}=\frac{2x+3-(x-2)}{x^2-x-30}$
$=\frac{2x+3-x+2}{x^2-x-30}$
$=\frac{x+5}{x^2-x-30}$
$=\frac{x+5}{(x-6)(x+5)}$
$=\frac{1}{x-6}$

33. $P=4s$
$P=4\left(\frac{5}{x-2}\right)=\frac{20}{x-2}$ meters

35. Answers may vary.

37. $3 = 3$
$33 = 3 \cdot 11$
$\text{LCD} = 3 \cdot 11 = 33$

39. $2x = 2 \cdot x$
$4x^3 = 2^2 \cdot x^3$
$\text{LCD} = 2^2 \cdot x^3 = 4x^3$

41. $8x = 2^3 \cdot x$
$2x + 4 = 2(x + 2)$
$\text{LCD} = 2^3 \cdot x \cdot (x + 2) = 8x(x + 2)$

43. $3x + 3 = 3(x + 1)$
$2x^2 + 4x + 2 = 2(x + 1)^2$
$\text{LCD} = 3 \cdot 2 \cdot (x + 1)^2 = 6(x + 1)^2$

45. $x - 8 = x - 8$
$8 - x = -1(x - 8)$
$\text{LCD} = x - 8$ or $8 - x$

47. $8x^2(x - 1)^2 = 2^3 \cdot x^2 \cdot (x - 1)^2$
$10x^3(x - 1) = 2 \cdot 5 \cdot x^3 \cdot (x - 1)$
$\text{LCD} = 2^3 \cdot 5 \cdot x^3 \cdot (x - 1)^2 = 40x^3(x - 1)^2$

49. $2x + 1 = (2x + 1)$
$2x - 1 = (2x - 1)$
$\text{LCD} = (2x + 1)(2x - 1)$

51. $2x^2 + 7x - 4 = (2x - 1)(x + 4)$
$2x^2 + 5x - 3 = (2x - 1)(x + 3)$
$\text{LCD} = (2x - 1)(x + 4)(x + 3)$

53. Answers may vary.

55. $\frac{3}{2x} \cdot \frac{2x}{2x} = \frac{6x}{4x^2}$

57. $\frac{6}{3a} \cdot \frac{4b^2}{4b^2} = \frac{24b^2}{12ab^2}$

59. $\frac{9}{x+3} \cdot \frac{2}{2} = \frac{18}{2(x+3)}$

61. $\frac{9a+2}{5a+10} \cdot \frac{b}{b} = \frac{9ab+2b}{5b(a+2)}$

63.
$$\frac{x}{x^2+6x+8} = \frac{x}{(x+4)(x+2)} = \frac{x(x+1)}{(x+4)(x+2)(x+1)} = \frac{x^2+x}{(x+4)(x+2)(x+1)}$$

65. $\frac{9y-1}{15x^2-30} = \frac{(9y-1)(2)}{(15x^2-30)(2)} = \frac{18y-2}{30x^2-60}$

67.
$$\frac{5}{2x^2-9x-5} = \frac{5}{(2x+1)(x-5)} \cdot \frac{3x(x-7)}{3x(x-7)} = \frac{15x(x-7)}{3x(2x+1)(x-7)(x-5)}$$

69. $\frac{5}{2-x} = \frac{5(-1)}{(2-x)(-1)} = -\frac{5}{x-2}$

71. $-\frac{7+x}{2-x} = \frac{7+x}{(-1)(2-x)} = \frac{7+x}{x-2}$

73. Since $88 = 2^3 \cdot 11$ and $4332 = 2^2 \cdot 3 \cdot 19^2$, the least common multiple is $2^3 \cdot 3 \cdot 11 \cdot 19^2 = 95{,}304$. It will take 95,304 Earth days for Jupiter and Mercury to align again.

75. Answers may vary.

77. $2x(x + 5) = 0$
$2x = 0$ or $x + 5 = 0$
$x = 0$ or $x = -5$

79. $x^2 - 6x + 5 = 0$
$(x - 5)(x - 1) = 0$
$x - 5 = 0$ or $x - 1 = 0$
$x = 5$ or $x = 1$

81. $\frac{9}{10} - \frac{3}{5} = \frac{9}{10} - \frac{3}{5} \cdot \frac{2}{2} = \frac{9}{10} - \frac{6}{10} = \frac{3}{10}$

83. $\frac{11}{15}+\frac{5}{9}=\frac{11}{15}\cdot\frac{3}{3}+\frac{5}{9}\cdot\frac{5}{5}=\frac{33}{45}+\frac{25}{45}=\frac{58}{45}$

Section 6.4

Mental Math

1. D
2. C
3. A
4. B

Exercise Set 6.4

1. $\frac{4}{2x}+\frac{9}{3x}$; LCD $=6x$

$\frac{4}{2x}\cdot\frac{3}{3}+\frac{9}{3x}\cdot\frac{2}{2}=\frac{12}{6x}+\frac{18}{6x}=\frac{30}{6x}=\frac{5}{x}$

3. $\frac{15a}{b}+\frac{6b}{5}$; LCD $=5b$

$\frac{15a}{b}\cdot\frac{5}{5}+\frac{6b}{5}\cdot\frac{b}{b}=\frac{75a}{5b}+\frac{6b^2}{5b}=\frac{75a+6b^2}{5b}$

5. $\frac{3}{x}+\frac{5}{2x^2}$; LCD $=2x^2$

$\frac{3}{x}\cdot\frac{2x}{2x}+\frac{5}{2x^2}=\frac{6x}{2x^2}+\frac{5}{2x^2}=\frac{6x+5}{2x^2}$

7. $\frac{6}{x+1}+\frac{9}{2x+2}=\frac{6}{x+1}+\frac{9}{2(x+1)}$;

LCD $=2(x+1)$

$\frac{6}{(x+1)}\cdot\frac{2}{2}+\frac{9}{2(x+1)}=\frac{12}{2(x+1)}+\frac{9}{2(x+1)}$

$=\frac{21}{2(x+1)}$

9. $\frac{15}{2x-4}+\frac{x}{x^2-4}=\frac{15}{2(x-2)}+\frac{x}{(x+2)(x-2)}$

LCD $=2(x-2)(x+2)$

$\frac{15}{2(x-2)}\cdot\frac{(x+2)}{(x+2)}+\frac{x}{(x+2)(x-2)}\cdot\frac{2}{2}$

$=\frac{15(x+2)}{2(x-2)(x+2)}+\frac{2x}{2(x-2)(x+2)}$

$=\frac{15x+30+2x}{2(x-2)(x+2)}$

$=\frac{17x+30}{2(x-2)(x+2)}$

11. $\frac{3}{4x}+\frac{8}{x-2}$; LCD $=4x(x-2)$

$\frac{3}{4x}\cdot\frac{(x-2)}{(x-2)}+\frac{8}{(x-2)}\cdot\frac{4x}{4x}$

$=\frac{3(x-2)}{4x(x-2)}+\frac{32x}{4x(x-2)}$

$=\frac{3x-6+32x}{4x(x-2)}$

$=\frac{35x-6}{4x(x-2)}$

13. $\frac{5}{y^2}-\frac{y}{2y+1}$; LCD $=y^2(2y+1)$

$\frac{5}{y^2}\cdot\frac{(2y+1)}{(2y+1)}-\frac{y}{(2y+1)}\cdot\frac{y^2}{y^2}$

$=\frac{5(2y+1)}{y^2(2y+1)}-\frac{y^3}{y^2(2y+1)}$

$=\frac{10y+5-y^3}{y^2(2y+1)}$

15. Answers may vary.

17. $\frac{6}{x-3}+\frac{8}{3-x}$

$=\frac{6}{x-3}-\frac{8}{x-3}$

$=\frac{6-8}{x-3}$

$=-\frac{2}{x-3}$

19. $\frac{-8}{x^2-1}-\frac{7}{1-x^2}=\frac{-8}{x^2-1}+\frac{7}{x^2-1}=-\frac{1}{x^2-1}$

21. $\frac{x}{x^2-4}-\frac{2}{4-x^2}=\frac{x}{x^2-4}+\frac{2}{x^2-4}$
$=\frac{x+2}{x^2-4}$
$=\frac{x+2}{(x+2)(x-2)}$
$=\frac{1}{x-2}$

23. $\frac{5}{x}+2;\qquad \text{LCD}=x$
$\frac{5}{x}+2\cdot\frac{x}{x}=\frac{5}{x}+\frac{2x}{x}=\frac{5+2x}{x}$

25. $\frac{5}{x-2}+6;\quad \text{LCD}=x-2$
$\frac{5}{x-2}+6\cdot\frac{(x-2)}{(x-2)}=\frac{5}{x-2}+\frac{6(x-2)}{x-2}$
$=\frac{5+6x-12}{x-2}$
$=\frac{6x-7}{x-2}$

27. $\frac{y+2}{y+3}-2;\quad \text{LCD}=y+3$
$\frac{y+2}{y+3}-2\cdot\frac{(y+3)}{(y+3)}=\frac{y+2}{y+3}-\frac{2(y+3)}{y+3}$
$=\frac{y+2-2y-6}{y+3}$
$=\frac{-y-4}{y+3}$
$=\frac{-1(y+4)}{y+3}$
$=-\frac{y+4}{y+3}$

29. $90°-\left(\frac{40}{x}\right)^{\circ}=\left(90-\frac{40}{x}\right)^{\circ}$
LCD $= x$
$\left(90\cdot\frac{x}{x}-\frac{40}{x}\right)^{\circ}=\left(\frac{90x}{x}-\frac{40}{x}\right)^{\circ}$
$=\left(\frac{90x-40}{x}\right)^{\circ}$

31. $\frac{5x}{x+2}-\frac{3x-4}{x+2}=\frac{5x-(3x-4)}{x+2}$
$=\frac{5x-3x+4}{x+2}$
$=\frac{2x+4}{x+2}$
$=\frac{2(x+2)}{x+2}$
$=2$

33. $\frac{3x^4}{x}-\frac{4x^2}{x^2}=3x^3-4$

35. $\frac{1}{x+3}-\frac{1}{(x+3)^2};\quad \text{LCD}=(x+3)^2$
$\frac{1}{x+3}\cdot\frac{(x+3)}{(x+3)}-\frac{1}{(x+3)^2}$
$=\frac{x+3}{(x+3)^2}-\frac{1}{(x+3)^2}$
$=\frac{x+3-1}{(x+3)^2}$
$=\frac{x+2}{(x+3)^2}$

37. $\frac{4}{5b}+\frac{1}{b-1};\quad \text{LCD}=5b(b-1)$
$\frac{4}{5b}\cdot\frac{(b-1)}{(b-1)}+\frac{1}{(b-1)}\cdot\frac{5b}{5b}$
$=\frac{4(b-1)}{5b(b-1)}+\frac{5b}{5b(b-1)}$
$=\frac{4b-4+5b}{5b(b-1)}$
$=\frac{9b-4}{5b(b-1)}$

39. $\frac{2}{m}+1;\qquad \text{LCD}=m$
$\frac{2}{m}+1\cdot\frac{m}{m}=\frac{2}{m}+\frac{m}{m}=\frac{2+m}{m}$

41. $\frac{6}{1-2x}-\frac{4}{2x-1}=\frac{6}{1-2x}+\frac{4}{1-2x}=\frac{10}{1-2x}$

43. $\frac{7}{(x+1)(x-1)}+\frac{8}{(x+1)^2};$

LCD $=(x+1)^2(x-1)$

$$\frac{7}{(x+1)(x-1)}\cdot\frac{(x+1)}{(x+1)}+\frac{8}{(x+1)^2}\cdot\frac{(x-1)}{(x-1)}$$
$$=\frac{7(x+1)}{(x+1)^2(x-1)}+\frac{8(x-1)}{(x+1)^2(x-1)}$$
$$=\frac{7x+7+8x-8}{(x+1)^2(x-1)}$$
$$=\frac{15x-1}{(x+1)^2(x-1)}$$

45. $\frac{x}{x^2-1}-\frac{2}{x^2-2x+1}$

$$=\frac{x}{(x+1)(x-1)}-\frac{2}{(x-1)^2}$$

LCD $=(x+1)(x-1)^2$

$$\frac{x}{(x+1)(x-1)}\cdot\frac{(x-1)}{(x-1)}-\frac{2}{(x-1)^2}\cdot\frac{(x+1)}{(x+1)}$$
$$=\frac{x(x-1)}{(x+1)(x-1)^2}-\frac{2(x+1)}{(x-1)^2(x+1)}$$
$$=\frac{x^2-x-2x-2}{(x+1)(x-1)^2}$$
$$=\frac{x^2-3x-2}{(x+1)(x-1)^2}$$

47. $\frac{3a}{2a+6}-\frac{a-1}{a+3}=\frac{3a}{2(a+3)}-\frac{a-1}{a+3}$

LCD $=2(a+3)$

$$\frac{3a}{2(a+3)}-\frac{(a-1)}{(a+3)}\cdot\frac{2}{2}=\frac{3a}{2(a+3)}-\frac{2(a-1)}{2(a+3)}$$
$$=\frac{3a-2a+2}{2(a+3)}$$
$$=\frac{a+2}{2(a+3)}$$

49. $\frac{5}{2-x}+\frac{x}{2x-4}=-\frac{5}{x-2}+\frac{x}{2(x-2)}$

LCD $=2(x-2)$

$$-\frac{5}{(x-2)}\cdot\frac{2}{2}+\frac{x}{2(x-2)}$$
$$=\frac{-10}{2(x-2)}+\frac{x}{2(x-2)}$$
$$=\frac{x-10}{2(x-2)}$$

51. $\frac{-7}{y^2-3y+2}-\frac{2}{y-1}=\frac{-7}{(y-2)(y-1)}-\frac{2}{y-1}$

LCD $=(y-2)(y-1)$

$$\frac{-7}{(y-2)(y-1)}-\frac{2}{(y-1)}\cdot\frac{(y-2)}{(y-2)}$$
$$=\frac{-7}{(y-2)(y-1)}-\frac{2(y-2)}{(y-1)(y-2)}$$
$$=\frac{-7-2y+4}{(y-2)(y-1)}$$
$$=\frac{-2y-3}{(y-2)(y-1)}$$

53. $\frac{13}{x^2-5x+6}-\frac{5}{x-3}=\frac{13}{(x-3)(x-2)}-\frac{5}{x-3}$

LCD $=(x-3)(x-2)$

$$\frac{13}{(x-3)(x-2)}-\frac{5}{(x-3)}\cdot\frac{(x-2)}{(x-2)}$$
$$=\frac{13}{(x-3)(x-2)}-\frac{5(x-2)}{(x-3)(x-2)}$$
$$=\frac{13-5x+10}{(x-3)(x-2)}$$
$$=\frac{-5x+23}{(x-3)(x-2)}$$

55. $\dfrac{8}{(x+2)(x-2)}+\dfrac{4}{(x+2)(x-3)}$

LCD $=(x+2)(x-2)(x-3)$

$\dfrac{8}{(x+2)(x-2)}\cdot\dfrac{(x-3)}{(x-3)}+\dfrac{4}{(x+2)(x-3)}\cdot\dfrac{(x-2)}{(x-2)}$

$=\dfrac{8(x-3)}{(x+2)(x-2)(x-3)}+\dfrac{4(x-2)}{(x+2)(x-3)(x-2)}$

$=\dfrac{8x-24+4x-8}{(x+2)(x-2)(x-3)}$

$=\dfrac{12x-32}{(x+2)(x-2)(x-3)}$

57. $\dfrac{5}{9x^2-4}+\dfrac{2}{3x-2}=\dfrac{5}{(3x+2)(3x-2)}+\dfrac{2}{3x-2}$

LCD $=(3x+2)(3x-2)$

$\dfrac{5}{(3x+2)(3x-2)}+\dfrac{2}{(3x-2)}\cdot\dfrac{(3x+2)}{(3x+2)}$

$=\dfrac{5}{(3x+2)(3x-2)}+\dfrac{2(3x+2)}{(3x-2)(3x+2)}$

$=\dfrac{5+6x+4}{(3x+2)(3x-2)}$

$=\dfrac{6x+9}{(3x+2)(3x-2)}$

59. $\dfrac{x+8}{x^2-5x-6}+\dfrac{x+1}{x^2-4x-5}$

$=\dfrac{x+8}{(x-6)(x+1)}+\dfrac{x+1}{(x-5)(x+1)}$

LCD $=(x-6)(x+1)(x-5)$

$\dfrac{(x+8)}{(x-6)(x+1)}\cdot\dfrac{(x-5)}{(x-5)}+\dfrac{(x+1)}{(x-5)(x+1)}\cdot\dfrac{(x-6)}{(x-6)}$

$=\dfrac{(x+8)(x-5)}{(x-6)(x+1)(x-5)}+\dfrac{(x+1)(x-6)}{(x-5)(x+1)(x-6)}$

$=\dfrac{x^2-5x+8x-40+x^2-6x+x-6}{(x-6)(x+1)(x-5)}$

$=\dfrac{2x^2-2x-46}{(x-6)(x+1)(x-5)}$

61. $\frac{3}{x+4}-\frac{1}{x-4}$
LCD $=(x+4)(x-4)$
$\frac{3}{(x+4)}\cdot\frac{(x-4)}{(x-4)}-\frac{1}{(x-4)}\cdot\frac{(x+4)}{(x+4)}$
$=\frac{3(x-4)}{(x+4)(x-4)}-\frac{1(x+4)}{(x-4)(x+4)}$
$=\frac{3x-12-x-4}{(x+4)(x-4)}$
$=\frac{2x-16}{(x+4)(x-4)}$ inches

63. C
$\frac{3}{x}+\frac{y}{x}=\frac{3+y}{x}$

65. B
$\frac{3}{x}\cdot\frac{y}{x}=\frac{3y}{x^2}$

67. $\frac{15x}{x+8}\cdot\frac{2x+16}{3x}=\frac{15x}{x+8}\cdot\frac{2(x+8)}{3x}$
$=\frac{2\cdot5\cdot3x\cdot(x+8)}{3x\cdot(x+8)}$
$=10$

69. $\frac{8x+7}{3x+5}-\frac{2x-3}{3x+5}=\frac{8x+7-(2x-3)}{3x+5}$
$=\frac{8x+7-2x+3}{3x+5}$
$=\frac{6x+10}{3x+5}$
$=\frac{2(3x+5)}{3x+5}$
$=2$

71. $\frac{5a+10}{18}\div\frac{a^2-4}{10a}=\frac{5(a+2)}{2\cdot9}\cdot\frac{2\cdot5a}{(a-2)(a+2)}$
$=\frac{25a}{9(a-2)}$

73. $\frac{5}{x^2-3x+2}+\frac{1}{x-2}=\frac{5}{(x-2)(x-1)}+\frac{1}{x-2}$
LCD $=(x-2)(x-1)$
$\frac{5}{(x-2)(x-1)}+\frac{1}{(x-2)}\cdot\frac{(x-1)}{(x-1)}$
$=\frac{5}{(x-2)(x-1)}+\frac{x-1}{(x-2)(x-1)}$
$=\frac{5+x-1}{(x-2)(x-1)}$
$=\frac{x+4}{(x-2)(x-1)}$

75. Answers may vary.

77. $\frac{\frac{3}{4}+\frac{1}{4}}{\frac{3}{8}+\frac{13}{8}}=\frac{\frac{4}{4}}{\frac{16}{8}}=\frac{4}{4}\cdot\frac{8}{16}=\frac{4\cdot8}{4\cdot8\cdot2}=\frac{1}{2}$

79. $\frac{\frac{2}{5}+\frac{1}{5}}{\frac{7}{10}+\frac{7}{10}}=\frac{\frac{3}{5}}{\frac{14}{10}}=\frac{3}{5}\cdot\frac{10}{14}=\frac{3\cdot2\cdot5}{5\cdot2\cdot7}=\frac{3}{7}$

81. (1, 2) and (–1, –2)
$m=\frac{-2-2}{-1-1}=\frac{-4}{-2}=2$

83. (0, 0) and (3, –1)
$m=\frac{-1-0}{3-0}=-\frac{1}{3}$

85. $\frac{5}{x^2-4}+\frac{2}{x^2-4x+4}-\frac{3}{x^2-x-6}=\frac{5}{(x+2)(x-2)}+\frac{2}{(x-2)^2}-\frac{3}{(x-3)(x+2)}$

$\text{LCD}=(x+2)(x-2)^2(x-3)$

$$\frac{5}{(x+2)(x-2)}\cdot\frac{(x-2)(x-3)}{(x-2)(x-3)}+\frac{2}{(x-2)^2}\cdot\frac{(x+2)(x-3)}{(x+2)(x-3)}-\frac{3}{(x-3)(x+2)}\cdot\frac{(x-2)^2}{(x-2)^2}$$

$$=\frac{5(x-2)(x-3)}{(x+2)(x-2)^2(x-3)}+\frac{2(x+2)(x-3)}{(x-2)^2(x+2)(x-3)}-\frac{3(x-2)^2}{(x-3)(x+2)(x-2)^2}$$

$$=\frac{5(x^2-5x+6)+2(x^2-x-6)-3(x^2-4x+4)}{(x+2)(x-2)^2(x-3)}$$

$$=\frac{5x^2-25x+30+2x^2-2x-12-3x^2+12x-12}{(x+2)(x-2)^2(x-3)}$$

$$=\frac{4x^2-15x+6}{(x+2)(x-2)^2(x-3)}$$

87. $\frac{5+x}{x^3-27}+\frac{x}{x^3+3x^2+9x}=\frac{5+x}{(x-3)(x^2+3x+9)}+\frac{x}{x(x^2+3x+9)}$

$\text{LCD}=x(x-3)(x^2+3x+9)$

$$\frac{(5+x)}{(x-3)(x^2+3x+9)}\cdot\frac{x}{x}+\frac{x}{x(x^2+3x+9)}\cdot\frac{(x-3)}{(x-3)}$$

$$=\frac{(5+x)(x)}{x(x-3)(x^2+3x+9)}+\frac{x(x-3)}{x(x-3)(x^2+3x+9)}$$

$$=\frac{5x+x^2+x^2-3x}{x(x-3)(x^2+3x+9)}$$

$$=\frac{2x^2+2x}{x(x-3)(x^2+3x+9)}$$

$$=\frac{2x(x+1)}{x(x-3)(x^2+3x+9)}$$

$$=\frac{2(x+1)}{(x-3)(x^2+3x+9)}$$

Section 6.5

Mental Math

1. $\frac{\frac{y}{2}}{\frac{5x}{2}}=\frac{2\left(\frac{y}{2}\right)}{2\left(\frac{5x}{2}\right)}=\frac{y}{5x}$

2. $\dfrac{\frac{10}{x}}{\frac{z}{x}}=\dfrac{x\left(\frac{10}{x}\right)}{x\left(\frac{z}{x}\right)}=\dfrac{10}{z}$

3. $\dfrac{\frac{3}{x}}{\frac{5}{x^2}}=\dfrac{x^2\left(\frac{3}{x}\right)}{x^2\left(\frac{5}{x^2}\right)}=\dfrac{3x}{5}$

4. $\dfrac{\frac{a}{10}}{\frac{b}{20}}=\dfrac{20\left(\frac{a}{10}\right)}{20\left(\frac{b}{20}\right)}=\dfrac{2a}{b}$

Exercise Set 6.5

1. $\dfrac{\frac{1}{2}}{\frac{3}{4}}=\dfrac{1}{2}\cdot\dfrac{4}{3}=\dfrac{2\cdot 2}{2\cdot 3}=\dfrac{2}{3}$

3. $\dfrac{-\frac{4x}{9}}{-\frac{2x}{3}}=-\dfrac{4x}{9}\cdot -\dfrac{3}{2x}=\dfrac{2\cdot 2\cdot x\cdot 3}{3\cdot 3\cdot 2\cdot x}=\dfrac{2}{3}$

5. $\dfrac{\frac{1+x}{6}}{\frac{1+x}{3}}=\dfrac{1+x}{6}\cdot\dfrac{3}{1+x}=\dfrac{3\cdot(1+x)}{2\cdot 3\cdot(1+x)}=\dfrac{1}{2}$

7. $$\begin{aligned}\frac{\frac{1}{2}+\frac{2}{3}}{\frac{5}{9}-\frac{5}{6}}&=\frac{\frac{1}{2}\cdot\frac{3}{3}+\frac{2}{3}\cdot\frac{2}{2}}{\frac{5}{9}\cdot\frac{2}{2}-\frac{5}{6}\cdot\frac{3}{3}}\\&=\frac{\frac{3}{6}+\frac{4}{6}}{\frac{10}{18}-\frac{15}{18}}\\&=\frac{\frac{7}{6}}{-\frac{5}{18}}\\&=\frac{7}{6}\cdot -\frac{18}{5}\\&=-\frac{7\cdot 3\cdot 6}{6\cdot 5}\\&=-\frac{21}{5}\end{aligned}$$

9. $$\begin{aligned}\frac{2+\frac{7}{10}}{1+\frac{3}{5}}&=\frac{10\left(2+\frac{7}{10}\right)}{10\left(1+\frac{3}{5}\right)}\\&=\frac{10(2)+10\left(\frac{7}{10}\right)}{10(1)+10\left(\frac{3}{5}\right)}\\&=\frac{20+7}{10+6}\\&=\frac{27}{16}\end{aligned}$$

11. $\dfrac{\frac{1}{3}}{\frac{1}{2}-\frac{1}{4}}=\dfrac{\frac{1}{3}}{\frac{1}{2}\cdot\frac{2}{2}-\frac{1}{4}}=\dfrac{\frac{1}{3}}{\frac{2}{4}-\frac{1}{4}}=\dfrac{\frac{1}{3}}{\frac{1}{4}}=\dfrac{1}{3}\cdot\dfrac{4}{1}=\dfrac{4}{3}$

13. $\dfrac{-\frac{2}{9}}{-\frac{14}{3}}=-\dfrac{2}{9}\cdot -\dfrac{3}{14}=\dfrac{2\cdot 3}{3\cdot 3\cdot 2\cdot 7}=\dfrac{1}{21}$

15. $$\begin{aligned}\frac{-\frac{5}{12x^2}}{\frac{25}{16x^3}}&=-\frac{5}{12x^2}\cdot\frac{16x^3}{25}\\&=-\frac{5\cdot 4\cdot 4\cdot x^2\cdot x}{4\cdot 3\cdot x^2\cdot 5\cdot 5}\\&=-\frac{4x}{15}\end{aligned}$$

17. $\dfrac{\frac{m}{n}-1}{\frac{m}{n}+1}=\dfrac{n\left(\frac{m}{n}-1\right)}{n\left(\frac{m}{n}+1\right)}=\dfrac{n\left(\frac{m}{n}\right)+n(-1)}{n\left(\frac{m}{n}\right)+n(1)}=\dfrac{m-n}{m+n}$

19. $$\begin{aligned}\frac{\frac{1}{5}-\frac{1}{x}}{\frac{7}{10}+\frac{1}{x^2}}&=\frac{10x^2\left(\frac{1}{5}-\frac{1}{x}\right)}{10x^2\left(\frac{7}{10}+\frac{1}{x^2}\right)}\\&=\frac{10x^2\left(\frac{1}{5}\right)+10x^2\left(-\frac{1}{x}\right)}{10x^2\left(\frac{7}{10}\right)+10x^2\left(\frac{1}{x^2}\right)}\\&=\frac{2x^2-10x}{7x^2+10}\\&=\frac{2x(x-5)}{7x^2+10}\end{aligned}$$

21. $\frac{1+\frac{1}{y-2}}{y+\frac{1}{y-2}} = \frac{(y-2)\left(1+\frac{1}{y-2}\right)}{(y-2)\left(y+\frac{1}{y-2}\right)}$

$= \frac{(y-2)(1)+(y-2)\cdot\frac{1}{y-2}}{(y-2)(y)+(y-2)\cdot\frac{1}{y-2}}$

$= \frac{y-2+1}{y^2-2y+1}$

$= \frac{y-1}{(y-1)(y-1)}$

$= \frac{1}{y-1}$

23. $\frac{\frac{4y-8}{16}}{\frac{6y-12}{4}} = \frac{4y-8}{16}\cdot\frac{4}{6y-12}$

$= \frac{4(y-2)}{16}\cdot\frac{4}{6(y-2)}$

$= \frac{16\cdot(y-2)}{16\cdot 6\cdot(y-2)}$

$= \frac{1}{6}$

25. $\frac{\frac{x}{y}+1}{\frac{x}{y}-1} = \frac{y\left(\frac{x}{y}+1\right)}{y\left(\frac{x}{y}-1\right)}$

$= \frac{y\left(\frac{x}{y}\right)+y(1)}{y\left(\frac{x}{y}\right)+y(-1)}$

$= \frac{x+y}{x-y}$

27. $\frac{1}{2+\frac{1}{3}} = \frac{1}{2\cdot\frac{3}{3}+\frac{1}{3}} = \frac{1}{\frac{6}{3}+\frac{1}{3}} = \frac{1}{\frac{7}{3}} = 1\cdot\frac{3}{7} = \frac{3}{7}$

29. $\frac{\frac{ax+ab}{x^2-b^2}}{\frac{x+b}{x-b}} = \frac{ax+ab}{x^2-b^2}\cdot\frac{x-b}{x+b}$

$= \frac{a(x+b)}{(x+b)(x-b)}\cdot\frac{x-b}{x+b}$

$= \frac{a\cdot(x+b)\cdot(x-b)}{(x+b)\cdot(x-b)\cdot(x+b)}$

$= \frac{a}{x+b}$

31. $\frac{\frac{-3+y}{4}}{\frac{8+y}{28}} = \frac{-3+y}{4}\cdot\frac{28}{8+y}$

$= \frac{4\cdot 7\cdot(-3+y)}{4\cdot(8+y)}$

$= \frac{7(y-3)}{8+y}$

33. $\frac{3+\frac{12}{x}}{1-\frac{16}{x^2}} = \frac{x^2\left(3+\frac{12}{x}\right)}{x^2\left(1-\frac{16}{x^2}\right)}$

$= \frac{x^2(3)+x^2\left(\frac{12}{x}\right)}{x^2(1)+x^2\left(-\frac{16}{x^2}\right)}$

$= \frac{3x^2+12x}{x^2-16}$

$= \frac{3x(x+4)}{(x-4)(x+4)}$

$= \frac{3x}{x-4}$

35. $\frac{\frac{8}{x+4}+2}{\frac{12}{x+4}-2} = \frac{(x+4)\left(\frac{8}{x+4}+2\right)}{(x+4)\left(\frac{12}{x+4}-2\right)}$

$= \frac{(x+4)\left(\frac{8}{x+4}\right)+(x+4)(2)}{(x+4)\left(\frac{12}{x+4}\right)+(x+4)(-2)}$

$= \frac{8+2x+8}{12-2x-8}$

$= \frac{2x+16}{-2x+4}$

$= \frac{2(x+8)}{-2(x-2)}$

$= -\frac{x+8}{x-2}$

37. $\frac{\frac{s}{r}+\frac{r}{s}}{\frac{s}{r}-\frac{r}{s}} = \frac{rs\left(\frac{s}{r}+\frac{r}{s}\right)}{rs\left(\frac{s}{r}-\frac{r}{s}\right)}$

$= \frac{rs\left(\frac{s}{r}\right)+rs\left(\frac{r}{s}\right)}{rs\left(\frac{s}{r}\right)+rs\left(-\frac{r}{s}\right)}$

$= \frac{s^2+r^2}{s^2-r^2}$

39. Answers may vary.

41. $\dfrac{\frac{1}{3}+\frac{3}{4}}{2}=\dfrac{\frac{1}{3}\cdot\frac{4}{4}+\frac{3}{4}\cdot\frac{3}{3}}{2}$
$=\dfrac{\frac{4}{12}+\frac{9}{12}}{2}$
$=\dfrac{\frac{13}{12}}{2}$
$=\dfrac{13}{12}\cdot\dfrac{1}{2}$
$=\dfrac{13}{24}$

43. $\dfrac{1}{\frac{1}{R_1}+\frac{1}{R_2}}=\dfrac{1}{\frac{R_2}{R_1R_2}+\frac{R_1}{R_1R_2}}=\dfrac{1}{\frac{R_2+R_1}{R_1R_2}}=\dfrac{R_1R_2}{R_2+R_1}$

45. $t=\dfrac{d}{r}$
$t=\dfrac{\frac{20x}{3}}{\frac{5x}{9}}=\dfrac{20x}{3}\cdot\dfrac{9}{5x}=\dfrac{4\cdot 5x\cdot 3\cdot 3}{3\cdot 5x}=12$ hours

47. $3x+5=7$
$3x=2$
$x=\dfrac{2}{3}$

49. $2x^2-x-1=0$
$(2x+1)(x-1)=0$
$2x+1=0$ or $x-1=0$
$2x=-1$ or $x=1$
$x=-\dfrac{1}{2}$

51. $\dfrac{2+x}{x+2}=\dfrac{2+x}{2+x}=1$

53. $\dfrac{2-x}{x-2}=-\dfrac{x-2}{x-2}=-1$

55. $\dfrac{x^{-1}+2^{-1}}{x^{-2}-4^{-1}}=\dfrac{\frac{1}{x}+\frac{1}{2}}{\frac{1}{x^2}-\frac{1}{4}}$
$=\dfrac{4x^2\left(\frac{1}{x}+\frac{1}{2}\right)}{4x^2\left(\frac{1}{x^2}-\frac{1}{4}\right)}$
$=\dfrac{4x+2x^2}{4-x^2}$
$=\dfrac{2x(2+x)}{(2-x)(2+x)}$
$=\dfrac{2x}{2-x}$

57. $\dfrac{x+y^{-1}}{\frac{x}{y}}=\dfrac{x+\frac{1}{y}}{\frac{x}{y}}=\dfrac{y\left(x+\frac{1}{y}\right)}{y\left(\frac{x}{y}\right)}=\dfrac{xy+1}{x}$

59. $\dfrac{y^{-2}}{1-y^{-2}}=\dfrac{\frac{1}{y^2}}{1-\frac{1}{y^2}}=\dfrac{y^2\left(\frac{1}{y^2}\right)}{y^2\left(1-\frac{1}{y^2}\right)}=\dfrac{1}{y^2-1}$

Section 6.6

Calculator Explorations

1. Graph $y_1=\dfrac{x-4}{2}-\dfrac{x-3}{9}$ and $y_2=\dfrac{5}{18}$.
Use INTERSECT to find the point of intersection.

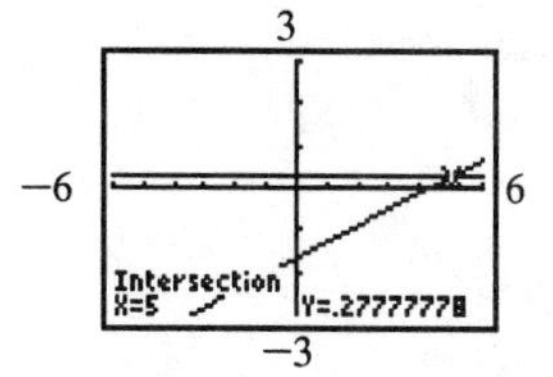

The point of intersection has an x-value of 5, so the solution of the equation is 5.

3. Graph $y_1 = 3 - \frac{6}{x}$ and $y_2 = x + 8$.

Use INTERSECT to find the point of intersection.

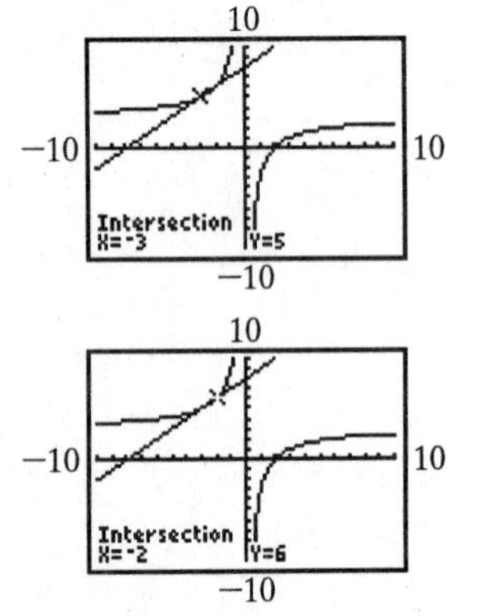

The first graph shows a point of intersection that has an x-value of -3. The second graph shows a point of intersection that has an x-value of -2. Thus, the equation has 2 solutions, $x = -3$ and $x = -2$.

5. Graph $y_1 = \frac{2x}{x-4}$ and $y_2 = \frac{8}{x-4} + 1$.

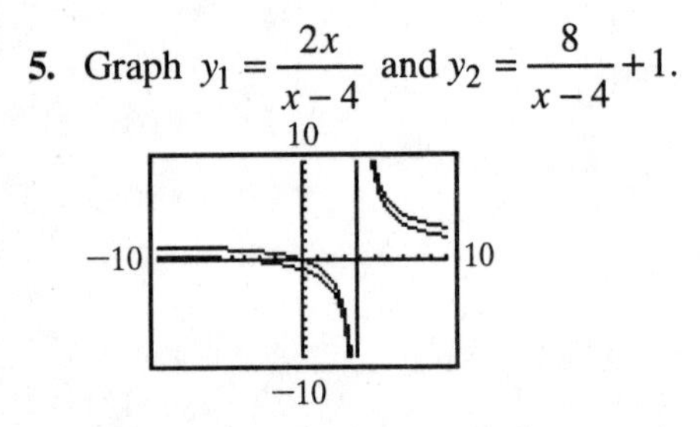

The graphs get closer and closer as they approach $x = 4$ but they never intersect.

Mental Math

1.
$$\frac{x}{5} = 2$$
$$5 \cdot \frac{x}{5} = 5 \cdot 2$$
$$x = 10$$

2.
$$\frac{x}{8} = 4$$
$$8 \cdot \frac{x}{8} = 8 \cdot 4$$
$$x = 32$$

3.
$$\frac{z}{6} = 6$$
$$6 \cdot \frac{z}{6} = 6 \cdot 6$$
$$z = 36$$

4.
$$\frac{y}{7} = 8$$
$$7 \cdot \frac{y}{7} = 7 \cdot 8$$
$$y = 56$$

Exercise Set 6.6

1.
$$\frac{x}{5} + 3 = 9$$
$$5\left(\frac{x}{5} + 3\right) = 5(9)$$
$$5\left(\frac{x}{5}\right) + 5(3) = 5(9)$$
$$x + 15 = 45$$
$$x = 45 - 15$$
$$x = 30$$

3.
$$\frac{x}{2} + \frac{5x}{4} = \frac{x}{12}$$
$$12\left(\frac{x}{2} + \frac{5x}{4}\right) = 12\left(\frac{x}{12}\right)$$
$$12\left(\frac{x}{2}\right) + 12\left(\frac{5x}{4}\right) = 12\left(\frac{x}{12}\right)$$
$$6x + 15x = x$$
$$21x = x$$
$$21x - x = 0$$
$$20x = 0$$
$$x = \frac{0}{20} = 0$$

5.
$$2 + \frac{10}{x} = x + 5$$
$$x\left(2 + \frac{10}{x}\right) = x(x+5)$$
$$2x + 10 = x^2 + 5x$$
$$0 = x^2 + 3x - 10$$
$$0 = (x+5)(x-2)$$
$$x + 5 = 0 \quad \text{or} \quad x - 2 = 0$$
$$x = -5 \quad \text{or} \quad x = 2$$

7.
$$\frac{a}{5}=\frac{a-3}{2}$$
$$10\left(\frac{a}{5}\right)=10\left(\frac{a-3}{2}\right)$$
$$2a=5(a-3)$$
$$2a=5a-15$$
$$2a-5a=-15$$
$$-3a=-15$$
$$a=\frac{-15}{-3}=5$$

9.
$$\frac{x-3}{5}+\frac{x-2}{2}=\frac{1}{2}$$
$$10\left(\frac{x-3}{5}+\frac{x-2}{2}\right)=10\left(\frac{1}{2}\right)$$
$$10\left(\frac{x-3}{5}\right)+10\left(\frac{x-2}{2}\right)=10\left(\frac{1}{2}\right)$$
$$2(x-3)+5(x-2)=5$$
$$2x-6+5x-10=5$$
$$7x-16=5$$
$$7x=5+16$$
$$7x=21$$
$$x=\frac{21}{7}=3$$

11.
$$\frac{20x}{3}+\frac{32x}{6}=180$$
$$6\left(\frac{20x}{3}+\frac{32x}{6}\right)=6\cdot 180$$
$$40x+32x=1080$$
$$72x=1080$$
$$x=15$$
$$\left(\frac{20x}{3}\right)^{\circ}=\left(\frac{20\cdot 15}{3}\right)^{\circ}=100^{\circ}$$
$$\left(\frac{32x}{6}\right)^{\circ}=\left(\frac{32\cdot 15}{6}\right)^{\circ}=80^{\circ}$$

13.
$$\frac{150}{x}+\frac{450}{x}=90$$
$$x\left(\frac{150}{x}+\frac{450}{x}\right)=x\cdot 90$$
$$150+450=90x$$
$$600=90x$$
$$\frac{600}{90}=x$$
$$\frac{20}{3}=x$$
$$\left(\frac{150}{x}\right)^{\circ}=\left(\frac{150}{\frac{20}{3}}\right)^{\circ}=\left(150\cdot\frac{3}{20}\right)^{\circ}=22.5^{\circ}$$
$$\left(\frac{450}{x}\right)^{\circ}=\left(\frac{450}{\frac{20}{3}}\right)^{\circ}=\left(450\cdot\frac{3}{20}\right)^{\circ}=67.5^{\circ}$$

15.
$$\frac{9}{2a-5}=-2$$
$$(2a-5)\left(\frac{9}{2a-5}\right)=(2a-5)(-2)$$
$$9=-4a+10$$
$$9-10=-4a$$
$$-1=-4a$$
$$\frac{-1}{-4}=a$$
$$\frac{1}{4}=a$$

17.
$$\frac{y}{y+4}+\frac{4}{y+4}=3$$
$$(y+4)\left(\frac{y}{y+4}+\frac{4}{y+4}\right)=(y+4)(3)$$
$$(y+4)\left(\frac{y}{y+4}\right)+(y+4)\left(\frac{4}{y+4}\right)=(y+4)(3)$$
$$y+4=3y+12$$
$$y-3y=12-4$$
$$-2y=8$$
$$y=\frac{8}{-2}=-4$$

-4 is an extraneous solution. If $y=-4$, the denominator would equal zero. The equation has no solution.

19.

$$\begin{aligned}
\frac{2x}{x+2}-2&=\frac{x-8}{x-2}\\
(x+2)(x-2)\left(\frac{2x}{x+2}-2\right)&=(x+2)(x-2)\left(\frac{x-8}{x-2}\right)\\
(x+2)(x-2)\left(\frac{2x}{x+2}\right)+(x+2)(x-2)(-2)&=(x+2)(x-8)\\
(x-2)(2x)+(x+2)(x-2)(-2)&=(x+2)(x-8)\\
2x^2-4x+(x^2-4)(-2)&=x^2-6x-16\\
2x^2-4x-2x^2+8&=x^2-6x-16\\
-4x+8&=x^2-6x-16\\
0&=x^2-6x+4x-16-8\\
0&=x^2-2x-24\\
0&=(x-6)(x+4)
\end{aligned}$$

$x-6=0$ or $x+4=0$

$x=6$ $\quad$ $x=-4$

21.

$$\begin{aligned}
\frac{4y}{y-4}+5&=\frac{5y}{y-4}\\
(y-4)\left(\frac{4y}{y-4}+5\right)&=(y-4)\left(\frac{5y}{y-4}\right)\\
(y-4)\left(\frac{4y}{y-4}\right)+(y-4)(5)&=(y-4)\left(\frac{5y}{y-4}\right)\\
4y+5y-20&=5y\\
4y+5y-5y&=20\\
4y&=20\\
y&=\frac{20}{4}=5
\end{aligned}$$

23.

$$\begin{aligned}
\frac{7}{x-2}+1&=\frac{x}{x+2}\\
(x-2)(x+2)\left(\frac{7}{x-2}+1\right)&=(x-2)(x+2)\left(\frac{x}{x+2}\right)\\
(x-2)(x+2)\left(\frac{7}{x-2}\right)+(x-2)(x+2)(1)&=(x-2)(x)\\
(x+2)(7)+(x-2)(x+2)(1)&=(x-2)(x)\\
7x+14+x^2-4&=x^2-2x\\
x^2+7x+10&=x^2-2x\\
x^2-x^2+7x+2x&=-10\\
9x&=-10\\
x&=-\frac{10}{9}
\end{aligned}$$

25.

$$\frac{x+1}{x+3}=\frac{2x^2-15x}{x^2+x-6}-\frac{x-3}{x-2}$$
$$\frac{x+1}{x+3}=\frac{2x^2-15x}{(x+3)(x-2)}-\frac{x-3}{x-2}$$
$$(x+3)(x-2)\left(\frac{x+1}{x+3}\right)=(x+3)(x-2)\left(\frac{2x^2-15x}{(x+3)(x-2)}-\frac{x-3}{x-2}\right)$$
$$(x-2)(x+1)=(x+3)(x-2)\left(\frac{2x^2-15x}{(x+3)(x-2)}\right)-(x+3)(x-2)\left(\frac{x-3}{x-2}\right)$$
$$(x-2)(x+1)=2x^2-15x-(x+3)(x-3)$$
$$x^2-x-2=2x^2-15x-(x^2-9)$$
$$x^2-x-2=2x^2-15x-x^2+9$$
$$x^2-x-2=x^2-15x+9$$
$$x^2-x^2-x+15x=9+2$$
$$14x=11$$
$$x=\frac{11}{14}$$

27.

$$\frac{y}{2y+2}+\frac{2y-16}{4y+4}=\frac{2y-3}{y+1}$$
$$\frac{y}{2(y+1)}+\frac{2y-16}{4(y+1)}=\frac{2y-3}{y+1}$$
$$4(y+1)\left(\frac{y}{2(y+1)}+\frac{2y-16}{4(y+1)}\right)=4(y+1)\left(\frac{2y-3}{y+1}\right)$$
$$4(y+1)\left(\frac{y}{2(y+1)}\right)+4(y+1)\left(\frac{2y-16}{4(y+1)}\right)=4(2y-3)$$
$$2y+2y-16=8y-12$$
$$4y-16=8y-12$$
$$4y-8y=-12+16$$
$$-4y=4$$
$$y=\frac{4}{-4}=-1$$

-1 is an extraneous solution. If $y=-1$, the denominator would equal zero. The equation has no solution.

29. Expression;

$$\frac{1}{x}+\frac{2}{3}=\frac{1}{x}\cdot\frac{3}{3}+\frac{2}{3}\cdot\frac{x}{x}=\frac{3}{3x}+\frac{2x}{3x}=\frac{3+2x}{3x}$$

31. Equation;

$$\frac{1}{x}+\frac{2}{3}=\frac{3}{x}$$
$$3x\left(\frac{1}{x}+\frac{2}{3}\right)=3x\left(\frac{3}{x}\right)$$
$$3x\left(\frac{1}{x}\right)+3x\left(\frac{2}{3}\right)=3x\left(\frac{3}{x}\right)$$
$$3+2x=9$$
$$2x=9-3$$
$$2x=6$$
$$x=3$$

33. Expression;

$$\frac{2}{x+1}-\frac{1}{x}=\frac{2}{x+1}\cdot\frac{x}{x}-\frac{1}{x}\cdot\frac{(x+1)}{(x+1)}$$
$$=\frac{2x}{x(x+1)}-\frac{x+1}{x(x+1)}$$
$$=\frac{2x-(x+1)}{x(x+1)}$$
$$=\frac{2x-x-1}{x(x+1)}$$
$$=\frac{x-1}{x(x+1)}$$

35. Equation;

$$\frac{2}{x+1}-\frac{1}{x}=1$$
$$x(x+1)\left(\frac{2}{x+1}-\frac{1}{x}\right)=x(x+1)\cdot 1$$
$$x(x+1)\left(\frac{2}{x+1}\right)+x(x+1)\left(\frac{-1}{x}\right)=x(x+1)$$
$$2x-(x+1)=x(x+1)$$
$$2x-x-1=x^2+x$$
$$x-1=x^2+x$$
$$-1=x^2$$

No solution

37. Answers may vary.

39.

$$\frac{2x}{7}-5x=9$$
$$7\left(\frac{2x}{7}-5x\right)=7(9)$$
$$7\left(\frac{2x}{7}\right)+7(-5x)=7(9)$$
$$2x-35x=63$$
$$-33x=63$$
$$x=-\frac{63}{33}=-\frac{21}{11}$$

41.

$$\frac{2}{y}+\frac{1}{2}=\frac{5}{2y}$$
$$2y\left(\frac{2}{y}+\frac{1}{2}\right)=2y\left(\frac{5}{2y}\right)$$
$$2y\left(\frac{2}{y}\right)+2y\left(\frac{1}{2}\right)=2y\left(\frac{5}{2y}\right)$$
$$4+y=5$$
$$y=5-4$$
$$y=1$$

43.

$$\frac{4x+10}{7}=\frac{8}{2}$$
$$14\left(\frac{4x+10}{7}\right)=14\left(\frac{8}{2}\right)$$
$$2(4x+10)=7(8)$$
$$8x+20=56$$
$$8x=56-20$$
$$8x=36$$
$$x=\frac{36}{8}=\frac{9}{2}$$

45.

$$2+\frac{3}{a-3}=\frac{a}{a-3}$$
$$(a-3)\left(2+\frac{3}{a-3}\right)=(a-3)\left(\frac{a}{a-3}\right)$$
$$(a-3)(2)+(a-3)\left(\frac{3}{a-3}\right)=a$$
$$2a-6+3=a$$
$$2a-3=a$$
$$-3=a-2a$$
$$-3=-a$$
$$\frac{-3}{-1}=a$$
$$3=a$$

3 is an extraneous solution. If $a = 3$, the denominator would equal zero. The equation has no solution.

47.

$$\frac{5}{x}+\frac{2}{3}=\frac{7}{2x}$$
$$6x\left(\frac{5}{x}+\frac{2}{3}\right)=6x\left(\frac{7}{2x}\right)$$
$$6x\left(\frac{5}{x}\right)+6x\left(\frac{2}{3}\right)=21$$
$$30+4x=21$$
$$4x=21-30$$
$$4x=-9$$
$$x=-\frac{9}{4}$$

49.

$$\frac{2a}{a+4}=\frac{3}{a-1}$$
$$(a+4)(a-1)\left(\frac{2a}{a+4}\right)=(a+4)(a-1)\left(\frac{3}{a-1}\right)$$
$$(a-1)(2a)=(a+4)(3)$$
$$2a^2-2a=3a+12$$
$$2a^2-2a-3a-12=0$$
$$2a^2-5a-12=0$$
$$(2a+3)(a-4)=0$$
$$2a+3=0 \quad \text{or} \quad a-4=0$$
$$2a=-3 \qquad\qquad a=4$$
$$a=-\frac{3}{2}$$

51.

$$\frac{x+1}{3}-\frac{x-1}{6}=\frac{1}{6}$$
$$6\left(\frac{x+1}{3}-\frac{x-1}{6}\right)=6\left(\frac{1}{6}\right)$$
$$6\left(\frac{x+1}{3}\right)-6\left(\frac{x-1}{6}\right)=1$$
$$2(x+1)-(x-1)=1$$
$$2x+2-x+1=1$$
$$x+3=1$$
$$x=1-3$$
$$x=-2$$

53.

$$\frac{4r-1}{r^2+5r-14}+\frac{2}{r+7}=\frac{1}{r-2}$$

$$(r+7)(r-2)\left(\frac{4r-1}{(r+7)(r-2)}+\frac{2}{r+7}\right)=(r+7)(r-2)\left(\frac{1}{r-2}\right)$$

$$(r+7)(r-2)\left(\frac{4r-1}{(r+7)(r-2)}\right)+(r+7)(r-2)\left(\frac{2}{r+7}\right)=r+7(1)$$

$$4r-1+(r-2)(2)=r+7$$

$$4r-1+2r-4=r+7$$

$$6r-5=r+7$$

$$6r-r=7+5$$

$$5r=12$$

$$r=\frac{12}{5}$$

55.

$$\frac{t}{t-4}=\frac{t+4}{6}$$

$$6(t-4)\left(\frac{t}{t-4}\right)=6(t-4)\left(\frac{t+4}{6}\right)$$

$$6t=(t-4)(t+4)$$

$$6t=t^2-16$$

$$0=t^2-6t-16$$

$$0=(t-8)(t+2)$$

$t-8=0$ or $t+2=0$

$t=8$ $\quad$ $t=-2$

57.

$$\frac{x}{2x+6}+\frac{x+1}{3x+9}=\frac{2}{4x+12}$$

$$\frac{x}{2(x+3)}+\frac{x+1}{3(x+3)}=\frac{2}{4(x+3)}$$

$$12(x+3)\left(\frac{x}{2(x+3)}+\frac{x+1}{3(x+3)}\right)=12(x+3)\left(\frac{2}{4(x+3)}\right)$$

$$12(x+3)\left(\frac{x}{2(x+3)}\right)+12(x+3)\left(\frac{x+1}{3(x+3)}\right)=3(2)$$

$$6x+4(x+1)=6$$

$$6x+4x+4=6$$

$$10x+4=6$$

$$10x=6-4$$

$$10x=2$$

$$x=\frac{2}{10}=\frac{1}{5}$$

59.
$$\frac{D}{R} = T$$
$$R\left(\frac{D}{R}\right) = R(T)$$
$$D = RT$$
$$\frac{D}{T} = R$$

61.
$$\frac{3}{x} = \frac{5y}{x+2}$$
$$x(x+2)\left(\frac{3}{x}\right) = x(x+2)\left(\frac{5y}{x+2}\right)$$
$$(x+2)(3) = x(5y)$$
$$3x+6 = 5xy$$
$$\frac{3x+6}{5x} = y$$

63.
$$\frac{3a+2}{3b-2} = -\frac{4}{2a}$$
$$2a(3b-2)\left(\frac{3a+2}{3b-2}\right) = 2a(3b-2)\left(-\frac{4}{2a}\right)$$
$$2a(3a+2) = (3b-2)(-4)$$
$$6a^2+4a = -12b+8$$
$$6a^2+4a-8 = -12b$$
$$-\frac{6a^2+4a-8}{2\cdot 6} = b$$
$$-\frac{2(3a^2+2a-4)}{2\cdot 6} = b$$
$$-\frac{3a^2+2a-4}{6} = b$$

65.
$$\frac{A}{BH} = \frac{1}{2}$$
$$2BH\left(\frac{A}{BH}\right) = 2BH\left(\frac{1}{2}\right)$$
$$2A = BH$$
$$\frac{2A}{H} = B$$

67.
$$\frac{C}{\pi r} = 2$$
$$\pi r\left(\frac{C}{\pi r}\right) = \pi r(2)$$
$$C = 2\pi r$$
$$\frac{C}{2\pi} = r$$

69.
$$\frac{1}{a} = \frac{1}{b} + \frac{1}{c}$$
$$abc\left(\frac{1}{a}\right) = abc\left(\frac{1}{b} + \frac{1}{c}\right)$$
$$bc = abc\left(\frac{1}{b}\right) + abc\left(\frac{1}{c}\right)$$
$$bc = ac + ab$$
$$bc = a(c+b)$$
$$\frac{bc}{c+b} = a$$

71.
$$\frac{m^2}{6} - \frac{n}{3} = \frac{p}{2}$$
$$6\left(\frac{m^2}{6} - \frac{n}{3}\right) = 6\left(\frac{p}{2}\right)$$
$$6\left(\frac{m^2}{6}\right) - 6\left(\frac{n}{3}\right) = 3p$$
$$m^2 - 2n = 3p$$
$$m^2 - 3p = 2n$$
$$\frac{m^2-3p}{2} = n$$

73.
$$\frac{5}{a^2+4a+3}+\frac{2}{a^2+a-6}-\frac{3}{a^2-a+2}=0$$
$$\frac{5}{(a+3)(a+1)}+\frac{2}{(a+3)(a-2)}-\frac{3}{(a-2)(a+1)}=0$$
$$(a+3)(a+1)(a-2)\left(\frac{5}{(a+3)(a+1)}+\frac{2}{(a+3)(a-2)}-\frac{3}{(a-2)(a+1)}\right)=(a+3)(a+1)(a-2)(0)$$
$$(a+3)(a+1)(a-2)\left(\frac{5}{(a+3)(a+1)}\right)+(a+3)(a+1)(a-2)\left(\frac{2}{(a+3)(a-2)}\right)$$
$$-(a+3)(a+1)(a-2)\left(\frac{3}{(a-2)(a+1)}\right)=0$$
$$5(a-2)+2(a+1)-3(a+3)=0$$
$$5a-10+2a+2-3a-9=0$$
$$4a-17=0$$
$$4a=17$$
$$a=\frac{17}{4}$$

75. The graph crosses the x-axis at $x=2$. It crosses the y-axis at $y=-2$. The x-intercept is (2, 0) and the y-intercept is (0, –2).

77. The graph crosses the x-axis at $x=-4$, $x=-2$, and $x=3$. It crosses the y-axis at $y=4$. The x-intercepts are (–4, 0), (–2, 0), and (3, 0) and the y-intercept is (0, 4).

Exercise Set 6.7

1. $\frac{2}{15}$

3. $\frac{10}{12}=\frac{5}{6}$

5. 3 gallons = 12 quarts
$\frac{5}{12}$

7. 2 dollars = 40 nickels
$\frac{4}{40}=\frac{1}{10}$

9. 5 meters = 500 centimeters
$\frac{175}{500}=\frac{7}{20}$

11. 3 hours = 180 minutes
$$\frac{190}{180} = \frac{19}{18}$$

13. Answers may vary.

15.
$$\frac{2}{3} = \frac{x}{6}$$
$$2 \cdot 6 = 3 \cdot x$$
$$12 = 3x$$
$$\frac{12}{3} = x$$
$$4 = x$$

17.
$$\frac{x}{10} = \frac{5}{9}$$
$$x \cdot 9 = 10 \cdot 5$$
$$9x = 50$$
$$x = \frac{50}{9}$$

19.
$$\frac{4x}{6} = \frac{7}{2}$$
$$4x \cdot 2 = 6 \cdot 7$$
$$8x = 42$$
$$x = \frac{42}{8} = \frac{21}{4}$$

21.
$$\frac{a}{25} = \frac{12}{10}$$
$$a \cdot 10 = 25 \cdot 12$$
$$10a = 300$$
$$a = \frac{300}{10} = 30$$

23.
$$\frac{x-3}{x} = \frac{4}{7}$$
$$7(x-3) = 4 \cdot x$$
$$7x - 21 = 4x$$
$$-21 = 4x - 7x$$
$$-21 = -3x$$
$$\frac{-21}{-3} = x$$
$$7 = x$$

25.
$$\frac{5x+1}{x} = \frac{6}{3}$$
$$3(5x+1) = 6 \cdot x$$
$$15x + 3 = 6x$$
$$3 = 6x - 15x$$
$$3 = -9x$$
$$\frac{3}{-9} = x$$
$$-\frac{1}{3} = x$$

27.
$$\frac{x+1}{2x+3} = \frac{2}{3}$$
$$3(x+1) = 2(2x+3)$$
$$3x + 3 = 4x + 6$$
$$3 - 6 = 4x - 3x$$
$$-3 = x$$

29.
$$\frac{9}{5} = \frac{12}{3x+2}$$
$$9(3x+2) = 5 \cdot 12$$
$$27x + 18 = 60$$
$$27x = 60 - 18$$
$$27x = 42$$
$$x = \frac{42}{27} = \frac{14}{9}$$

31.
$$\frac{3}{x+1} = \frac{5}{2x}$$
$$3 \cdot 2x = 5(x+1)$$
$$6x = 5x + 5$$
$$6x - 5x = 5$$
$$x = 5$$

33.
$$\frac{3}{100} = \frac{x}{4100}$$
$$3 \cdot 4100 = 100 \cdot x$$
$$12{,}300 = 100x$$
$$123 = x$$
The elephant's weight on Pluto is 123 pounds.

35. $\frac{110}{28.4} = \frac{x}{42.6}$

$110 \cdot 42.6 = 28.4 \cdot x$

$4686 = 28.4x$

$\frac{4686}{28.4} = x$

$165 = x$

42.6 grams of this cereal has 165 calories.

37. $\frac{1}{6} = \frac{x}{23{,}000}$

$1 \cdot 23{,}000 = 6 \cdot x$

$23{,}000 = 6x$

$\frac{23{,}000}{6} = x$

$3833 \approx x$

I would expect 3833 women to earn bigger paychecks.

39. $\frac{8}{2} = \frac{36}{x}$

$8 \cdot x = 2 \cdot 36$

$8x = 72$

$x = \frac{72}{8}$

$x = 9$

9 gallons of water are needed.

41. $\frac{39}{250} = \frac{x}{50{,}000}$

$39 \cdot 50{,}000 = 250 \cdot x$

$1{,}950{,}000 = 250x$

$\frac{1{,}950{,}000}{250} = x$

$7800 = x$

We would expect 7800 people to have no health insurance.

43. $\frac{1280}{14} = \frac{x}{2}$

$1280 \cdot 2 = 14 \cdot x$

$2560 = 14x$

$\frac{2560}{14} = x$

$\frac{1280}{7} = x$

$182\frac{6}{7} = x$

2 ounces of Eagle Brand Milk has $182\frac{6}{7}$ calories.

45. $\frac{\$5.79}{110} \approx \$0.0526$

$\frac{\$13.99}{240} \approx \$0.0583$

The best buy is 110 ounces for \$5.79.

47. $\frac{\$0.69}{6} = \$0.115$

$\frac{\$0.90}{8} = \$0.1125$

$\frac{\$1.89}{16} \approx \$0.1181$

The best buy is 8 ounces for \$0.90.

49. $\frac{\$8.99}{4} = \$2.2475$

$\frac{\$13.99}{6} \approx \$2.3317$

The best buy is the 4-pack for \$8.99.

51. $\frac{\$1.57}{1} = \$1.57$

$\frac{\$2.10}{2} = \$1.05$

$\frac{\$3.99}{4} = \$0.9975$

The best buy is 1 gallon for \$3.99.

53. The capacity in 1982 is approximately 70 megawatts. The capacity in 1984 is approximately 600 megawatts. The increase is approximately
$600 - 70 = 530$ megawatts.

55. The megawatt capacity in 2000 is approximately 2650 megawatts.

$$\frac{1000}{560{,}000} = \frac{2650}{x}$$
$$1000 \cdot x = 560{,}000 \cdot 2650$$
$$1000x = 1{,}484{,}000{,}000$$
$$x = 1{,}484{,}000$$

In 2000, the number of megawatts that can be generated from wind will serve the electricity needs of approximately 1,484,000 people.

57. Yes; answers may vary.

59. Notice that **a.** is a proportion and **b.** is not a proportion. We can immediately use cross products to solve for x in equation **a.**

61. (0, 4), (2, 10)

$$m = \frac{10-4}{2-0} = \frac{6}{2} = 3$$

Since the slope is positive, the line moves upward.

63. (–2, 7), (3, –2)

$$m = \frac{-2-7}{3-(-2)} = -\frac{9}{5}$$

Since the slope is negative, the line moves downward.

65. (0, –4), (2, –4)

$$m = \frac{-4-(-4)}{2-0} = \frac{0}{2} = 0$$

Since the slope is 0, the line is horizontal.

Exercise Set 6.8

1. Let x = the unknown number.

Its reciprocal $= \frac{1}{x}$.

$$3\left(\frac{1}{x}\right) = 9\left(\frac{1}{6}\right)$$
$$\frac{3}{x} = \frac{9}{6}$$
$$3 \cdot 6 = x \cdot 9$$
$$18 = 9x$$
$$\frac{18}{9} = x$$
$$2 = x$$

3. Let x = the unknown number.

$$\frac{2x+3}{x+1} = \frac{3}{2}$$
$$2(2x+3) = 3(x+1)$$
$$4x+6 = 3x+3$$
$$4x-3x = 3-6$$
$$x = -3$$

5.

	Time	In one hour
Experienced	4	$\frac{1}{4}$
Apprentice	5	$\frac{1}{5}$
Together	x	$\frac{1}{x}$

$$\frac{1}{4} + \frac{1}{5} = \frac{1}{x}$$
$$20x\left(\frac{1}{4} + \frac{1}{5}\right) = 20x\left(\frac{1}{x}\right)$$
$$20x\left(\frac{1}{4}\right) + 20x\left(\frac{1}{5}\right) = 20$$
$$5x + 4x = 20$$
$$9x = 20$$
$$x = \frac{20}{9} = 2\frac{2}{9}$$

Together it will take them $2\frac{2}{9}$ hours.

7.

	Time	In one minute
Belt	2	$\frac{1}{2}$
Smaller	6	$\frac{1}{6}$
Together	x	$\frac{1}{x}$

$$\frac{1}{2}+\frac{1}{6}=\frac{1}{x}$$
$$6x\left(\frac{1}{2}+\frac{1}{6}\right)=6x\left(\frac{1}{x}\right)$$
$$6x\left(\frac{1}{2}\right)+6x\left(\frac{1}{6}\right)=6$$
$$3x+x=6$$
$$4x=6$$
$$x=\frac{6}{4}=\frac{3}{2}=1\frac{1}{2}$$

If both are used, it takes $1\frac{1}{2}$ minutes.

9.

	distance	= rate	· time
Trip	12	$\frac{12}{x}$	x
Return Trip	18	$\frac{18}{x+1}$	$x+1$

$$\frac{12}{x}=\frac{18}{x+1}$$
$$x(x+1)\left(\frac{12}{x}\right)=x(x+1)\left(\frac{18}{x+1}\right)$$
$$12(x+1)=18x$$
$$12x+12=18x$$
$$12=18x-12x$$
$$12=6x$$
$$\frac{12}{6}=\frac{6x}{6}$$
$$2=x$$

Her jogging speed is

$\frac{12}{x}=\frac{12}{2}=6$ miles per hour.

11.

	distance	= rate	· time
First part	20	r	$\frac{20}{r}$
Cooldown	16	$r-2$	$\frac{16}{r-2}$

$$\frac{20}{r}=\frac{16}{r-2}$$
$$20(r-2)=r\cdot 16$$
$$20r-40=16r$$
$$20r-16r=40$$
$$4r=40$$
$$r=\frac{40}{4}=10$$

The first part is at 10 miles per hour, and the cooldown is at 8 miles per hour.

13. $\frac{4}{12}=\frac{x}{18}$
$$12\cdot x=4\cdot 18$$
$$12x=72$$
$$x=\frac{72}{12}=6$$

15. $\frac{x}{3.75}=\frac{12}{9}$
$$x\cdot 9=3.75\cdot 12$$
$$9x=45$$
$$x=\frac{45}{9}=5$$

17. Let x = the unknown number.
$$\frac{1}{4}=\frac{x}{8}$$
$$1\cdot 8=4\cdot x$$
$$8=4x$$
$$\frac{8}{4}=x$$
$$2=x$$

19.

	Time	In one hour
Marcus	6	$\frac{1}{6}$
Tony	4	$\frac{1}{4}$
Together	x	$\frac{1}{x}$

$$\frac{1}{6}+\frac{1}{4}=\frac{1}{x}$$
$$12x\left(\frac{1}{6}+\frac{1}{4}\right)=12x\left(\frac{1}{x}\right)$$
$$12x\left(\frac{1}{6}\right)+12x\left(\frac{1}{4}\right)=12$$
$$2x+3x=12$$
$$5x=12$$
$$x=\frac{12}{5}=2.4 \text{ hours}$$

2.4 hours · \$45/hour = \$108

21. Let x = speed of car in still air.

	distance = rate · time		
With the wind	11	$x+3$	$\frac{11}{x+3}$
Into wind	10	$x-3$	$\frac{10}{x-3}$

$$\frac{10}{x-3}=\frac{11}{x+3}$$
$$10(x+3)=11(x-3)$$
$$10x+30=11x-33$$
$$30+33=11x-10x$$
$$63=x$$

The speed of the car in still air is 63 miles per hour.

23.
$$\frac{10}{16}=\frac{y}{34}$$
$$16\cdot y=10\cdot 34$$
$$16y=340$$
$$y=\frac{340}{16}=21.25$$

25.
$$\frac{28\text{ ft}}{20\text{ ft}}=\frac{8\text{ ft}}{y}$$
$$28\text{ ft}\cdot y=20\text{ ft}\cdot 8\text{ ft}$$
$$28\text{ ft}\cdot y=160\text{ sq. ft}$$
$$y=\frac{160\text{ sq. ft}}{28\text{ ft}}$$
$$y=\frac{40}{7}\text{ ft}=5\frac{5}{7}\text{ ft}$$

27.
$$\frac{y}{25\text{ ft}}=\frac{3\text{ ft}}{2\text{ ft}}$$
$$y\cdot 2\text{ ft}=25\text{ ft}\cdot 3\text{ ft}$$
$$y\cdot 2\text{ ft}=75\text{ sq. ft}$$
$$y=\frac{75\text{ sq. ft}}{2\text{ ft}}$$
$$y=37\frac{1}{2}\text{ ft}$$

29. Let x = the unknown number.

$$\frac{2}{x-3}-\frac{4}{x+3}=8\left(\frac{1}{x^2-9}\right)$$
$$\frac{2}{x-3}-\frac{4}{x+3}=\frac{8}{x^2-9}$$
$$(x-3)(x+3)\left(\frac{2}{x-3}-\frac{4}{x+3}\right)=(x+3)(x-3)\left(\frac{8}{(x+3)(x-3)}\right)$$
$$(x-3)(x+3)\left(\frac{2}{x-3}\right)-(x-3)(x+3)\left(\frac{4}{x+3}\right)=8$$
$$2(x+3)-4(x-3)=8$$
$$2x+6-4x+12=8$$
$$-2x+18=8$$
$$-2x=8-18$$
$$-2x=-10$$
$$x=\frac{-10}{-2}=5$$

31. Let x = the speed of plane in still air.

	distance = rate · time		
With the wind	630	$x+35$	$\frac{630}{x+35}$
Against the wind	455	$x-35$	$\frac{455}{x-35}$

$$\frac{630}{x+35}=\frac{455}{x-35}$$
$$630(x-35)=455(x+35)$$
$$630x-22{,}050=455x+15{,}925$$
$$630x-455x=15{,}925+22{,}050$$
$$175x=37{,}975$$
$$x=\frac{37{,}975}{175}=217$$

The speed of the plane in still air is 217 miles per hour.

33. Let x = the speed of the wind.

	distance = rate · time		
With the wind	48	$16+x$	$\frac{48}{16+x}$
Against the wind	16	$16-x$	$\frac{16}{16-x}$

$$\frac{48}{16+x}=\frac{16}{16-x}$$
$$48(16-x)=16(16+x)$$
$$768-48x=256+16x$$
$$768-256=16x+48x$$
$$512=64x$$
$$\frac{512}{64}=x$$
$$8=x$$

The wind is 8 miles per hour.

35.

	Time	In one hour
1st custodian	3	$\frac{1}{3}$
2nd custodian	x	$\frac{1}{x}$
Together	$1\frac{1}{2}=\frac{3}{2}$	$\frac{1}{\frac{3}{2}}=\frac{2}{3}$

$$\frac{1}{3}+\frac{1}{x}=\frac{2}{3}$$
$$3x\left(\frac{1}{3}+\frac{1}{x}\right)=3x\left(\frac{2}{3}\right)$$
$$3x\left(\frac{1}{3}\right)+3x\left(\frac{1}{x}\right)=2x$$
$$x+3=2x$$
$$3=2x-x$$
$$3=x$$

It takes the 2nd custodian 3 hours to do the job alone.

37.

	Time	In one hour
First pipe	20	$\frac{1}{20}$
Second pipe	15	$\frac{1}{15}$
Third pipe	x	$\frac{1}{x}$
Together	6	$\frac{1}{6}$

$$\frac{1}{20}+\frac{1}{15}+\frac{1}{x}=\frac{1}{6}$$
$$60x\left(\frac{1}{20}+\frac{1}{15}+\frac{1}{x}\right)=60x\left(\frac{1}{6}\right)$$
$$60x\left(\frac{1}{20}\right)+60x\left(\frac{1}{15}\right)+60x\left(\frac{1}{x}\right)=60x\left(\frac{1}{6}\right)$$
$$3x+4x+60=10x$$
$$7x+60=10x$$
$$60=10x-7x$$
$$60=3x$$
$$20=x$$

The third pipe does the job in 20 hours.

39.

$$\frac{20\text{ feet}}{6\text{ inches}}=\frac{x}{8\text{ inches}}$$
$$20\text{ feet}\cdot 8\text{ inches}=6\text{ inches}\cdot x$$
$$160\text{ feet}\cdot\text{inches}=6\text{ inches}\cdot x$$
$$\frac{160\text{ feet}\cdot\text{inches}}{6\text{ inches}}=x$$
$$\frac{80}{3}\text{ feet}=x$$
$$26\frac{2}{3}\text{ feet}=x$$

41.

	Time	In one hour
Andrew	2	$\frac{1}{2}$
Timothy	3	$\frac{1}{3}$
Together	x	$\frac{1}{x}$

$$\frac{1}{2}+\frac{1}{3}=\frac{1}{x}$$
$$6x\left(\frac{1}{2}+\frac{1}{3}\right)=6x\left(\frac{1}{x}\right)$$
$$6x\left(\frac{1}{2}\right)+6x\left(\frac{1}{3}\right)=6$$
$$3x+2x=6$$
$$5x=6$$
$$\frac{5x}{5}=\frac{6}{5}$$
$$x=\frac{6}{5}=1\frac{1}{5}$$

Together it will take them $1\frac{1}{5}$ hours.

43.

	Time	In one hour
First cook	6	$\frac{1}{6}$
Second Cook	7	$\frac{1}{7}$
Third cook	x	$\frac{1}{x}$
Together	2	$\frac{1}{2}$

$$\frac{1}{6}+\frac{1}{7}+\frac{1}{x}=\frac{1}{2}$$
$$42x\left(\frac{1}{6}+\frac{1}{7}+\frac{1}{x}\right)=42x\left(\frac{1}{2}\right)$$
$$42x\left(\frac{1}{6}\right)+42x\left(\frac{1}{7}\right)+42x\left(\frac{1}{x}\right)=21x$$
$$7x+6x+42=21x$$
$$13x+42=21x$$
$$42=21x-13x$$
$$42=8x$$
$$\frac{42}{8}=x$$
$$\frac{21}{4}=x$$
$$5\frac{1}{4}=x$$

The third cook can prepare the pies in $5\frac{1}{4}$ hours.

45. Let x = the time for faster pump.
Then $3x$ = the time for slower pump.

	Time	In one minute
Faster pump	x	$\frac{1}{x}$
Slower pump	$3x$	$\frac{1}{3x}$
Together	21	$\frac{1}{21}$

$$\frac{1}{x}+\frac{1}{3x}=\frac{1}{21}$$
$$21x\left(\frac{1}{x}+\frac{1}{3x}\right)=21x\left(\frac{1}{21}\right)$$
$$21x\left(\frac{1}{x}\right)+21x\left(\frac{1}{3x}\right)=x$$
$$21+7=x$$
$$28=x$$

The faster pump takes 28 minutes and the slower pump takes 84 minutes.

47. From Exercise 46, we know that the age of his death is 84.
Age when son was born

$$= \frac{1}{6}x + \frac{1}{12}x + \frac{1}{7}x + 5$$
$$= \frac{1}{6}(84) + \frac{1}{12}(84) + \frac{1}{7}(84) + 5$$
$$= 14 + 7 + 12 + 5$$
$$= 38 \text{ years}$$

Age of son when he died $= \frac{1}{2}x$
$$= \frac{1}{2}(84)$$
$$= 42 \text{ years}$$

49. Answers may vary.

51. Let d = the distance the giraffe runs.

	distance =	rate ·	time
Hyena	$d + 0.5$	40	$\frac{d+0.5}{40}$
Giraffe	d	32	$\frac{d}{32}$

$$\frac{d+0.5}{40} = \frac{d}{32}$$
$$32(d + 0.5) = 40 \cdot d$$
$$32d + 16 = 40d$$
$$16 = 40d - 32d$$
$$16 = 8d$$
$$\frac{16}{8} = d$$
$$2 = d$$
$$\frac{d}{32} = \frac{2}{32} = \frac{1}{16}$$

It will take the hyena $\frac{1}{16}$ hour, or 3.75 minutes, to overtake the giraffe.

53. $-x + 3y = 6$

If $x = 0$, then
$$-0 + 3y = 6$$
$$3y = 6$$
$$y = 2$$

If $y = 0$, then
$$-x + 3(0) = 6$$
$$-x = 6$$
$$x = -6$$

If $x = -3$, then
$$-(-3) + 3y = 6$$
$$3 + 3y = 6$$
$$3y = 3$$
$$y = 1$$

55. $y = 2x$

If $x = 0$, then
$$y = 2(0)$$
$$y = 0$$

If $y = 0$, then
$$0 = 2x$$
$$0 = x$$

If $x = 1$, then
$$y = 2(1)$$
$$y = 2$$

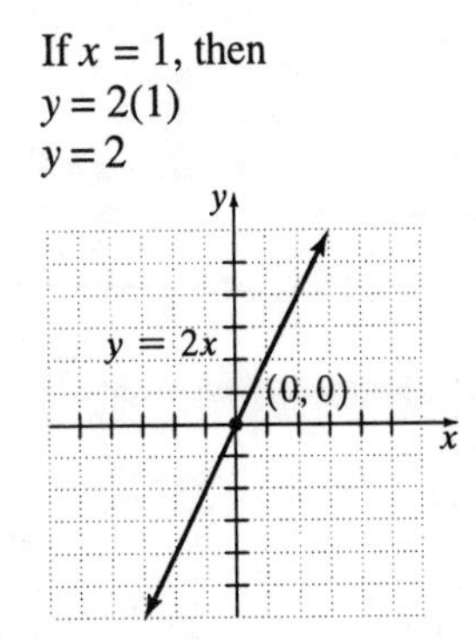

57. $y - x = -5$

If $x = 0$, then
$y - 0 = -5$
$y = -5$

If $y = 0$, then
$0 - x = -5$
$-x = -5$
$x = 5$
If $x = 1$, then
$y - 1 = -5$
$y = -4$

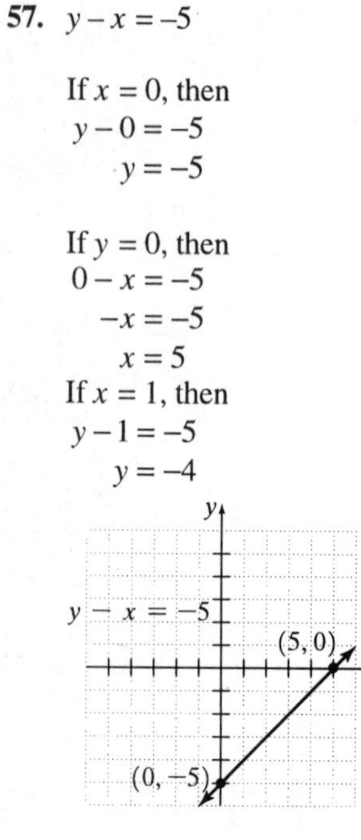

Chapter 6 Review Exercises

1. $\frac{x+5}{x^2-4}$

$x^2 - 4 = 0$
$(x+2)(x-2) = 0$
$x + 2 = 0$ or $x - 2 = 0$
$x = -2$ $\quad$ $x = 2$
It is undefined if $x = 2$ or $x = -2$.

2. $\frac{5x+9}{4x^2-4x-15}$

$4x^2 - 4x - 15 = 0$
$(2x+3)(2x-5) = 0$
$2x + 3 = 0$ or $2x - 5 = 0$
$\frac{2x}{2} = -\frac{3}{2}$ $\quad$ $\frac{2x}{2} = \frac{5}{2}$
$x = -\frac{3}{2}$ $\quad$ $x = \frac{5}{2}$

It is undefined if $x = -\frac{3}{2}$ or $x = \frac{5}{2}$.

3. If $x = 5$, $y = 7$, and $z = -2$:

$$\frac{z^2 - z}{z + xy} = \frac{(-2)^2 - (-2)}{-2 + (5)(7)} = \frac{4+2}{-2+35} = \frac{6}{33} = \frac{2}{11}$$

4. If $x = 5$, $y = 7$, and $z = -2$:

$$\frac{x^2 + xy - z^2}{x + y + z} = \frac{5^2 + (5)(7) - (-2)^2}{5 + 7 + (-2)}$$
$$= \frac{25 + 35 - 4}{10}$$
$$= \frac{56}{10}$$
$$= \frac{28}{5}$$

5. $\frac{x+2}{x^2-3x-10} = \frac{x+2}{(x-5)(x+2)} = \frac{1}{x-5}$

6. $\frac{x+4}{x^2+5x+4} = \frac{x+4}{(x+4)(x+1)} = \frac{1}{x+1}$

7.
$$\frac{x^3 - 4x}{x^2 + 3x + 2} = \frac{x(x^2-4)}{(x+2)(x+1)}$$
$$= \frac{x(x+2)(x-2)}{(x+2)(x+1)}$$
$$= \frac{x(x-2)}{x+1}$$

8.
$$\frac{5x^2 - 125}{x^2 + 2x - 15} = \frac{5(x^2 - 25)}{(x+5)(x-3)}$$
$$= \frac{5(x-5)(x+5)}{(x+5)(x-3)}$$
$$= \frac{5(x-5)}{(x-3)}$$

9. $\frac{x^2 - x - 6}{x^2 - 3x - 10} = \frac{(x-3)(x+2)}{(x-5)(x+2)} = \frac{x-3}{x-5}$

10. $\frac{x^2 - 2x}{x^2 + 2x - 8} = \frac{x(x-2)}{(x+4)(x-2)} = \frac{x}{x+4}$

11. $\frac{x^2 + 6x + 5}{2x^2 + 11x + 5} = \frac{(x+5)(x+1)}{(2x+1)(x+5)} = \frac{x+1}{2x+1}$

12. $\dfrac{x^2+xa+xb+ab}{x^2-xc+bx-bc}=\dfrac{x(x+a)+b(x+a)}{x(x-c)+b(x-c)}$
$=\dfrac{(x+a)(x+b)}{(x-c)(x+b)}$
$=\dfrac{x+a}{x-c}$

13. $\dfrac{x^2+5x-2x-10}{x^2-3x-2x+6}=\dfrac{x(x+5)-2(x+5)}{x(x-3)-2(x-3)}$
$=\dfrac{(x+5)(x-2)}{(x-3)(x-2)}$
$=\dfrac{x+5}{x-3}$

14. $\dfrac{x^2-9}{9-x^2}=\dfrac{(x-3)(x+3)}{(3-x)(3+x)}$
$=\dfrac{(x-3)(x+3)}{-(x-3)(3+x)}$
$=\dfrac{1}{-1}$
$=-1$

15. $\dfrac{4-x}{x^3-64}=-\dfrac{x-4}{x^3-64}$
$=-\dfrac{x-4}{(x-4)(x^2+4x+16)}$
$=-\dfrac{1}{x^2+4x+16}$

16. $\dfrac{15x^3\cdot y^2}{z}\cdot\dfrac{z}{5xy^3}=\dfrac{3\cdot 5\cdot x\cdot x^2\cdot y^2\cdot z}{z\cdot 5\cdot x\cdot y^2\cdot y}=\dfrac{3x^2}{y}$

17. $\dfrac{-y^3}{8}\cdot\dfrac{9x^2}{y^3}=-\dfrac{9x^2y^3}{8y^3}=-\dfrac{9x^2}{8}$

18. $\dfrac{x^2-9}{x^2-4}\cdot\dfrac{x-2}{x+3}=\dfrac{(x-3)(x+3)(x-2)}{(x-2)(x+2)(x+3)}$
$=\dfrac{x-3}{x+2}$

19. $\dfrac{2x+5}{x-6}\cdot\dfrac{2x}{-x+6}=\dfrac{(2x+5)\cdot 2\cdot x}{(x-6)\cdot -1(x-6)}$
$=-\dfrac{2x(2x+5)}{(x-6)^2}$

20. $\dfrac{x^2-5x-24}{x^2-x-12}\div\dfrac{x^2-10x+16}{x^2+x-6}$
$=\dfrac{(x-8)(x+3)}{(x-4)(x+3)}\cdot\dfrac{(x+3)(x-2)}{(x-8)(x-2)}$
$=\dfrac{(x-8)(x+3)(x+3)(x-2)}{(x-4)(x+3)(x-8)(x-2)}$
$=\dfrac{x+3}{x-4}$

21. $\dfrac{4x+4y}{xy^2}\div\dfrac{3x+3y}{x^2y}=\dfrac{4x+4y}{xy^2}\cdot\dfrac{x^2y}{3x+3y}$
$=\dfrac{4(x+y)}{xy^2}\cdot\dfrac{x^2y}{3(x+y)}$
$=\dfrac{4(x+y)\cdot x\cdot x\cdot y}{x\cdot y\cdot y\cdot 3(x+y)}$
$=\dfrac{4x}{3y}$

22. $\dfrac{x^2+x-42}{x-3}\cdot\dfrac{(x-3)^2}{x+7}$
$=\dfrac{(x+7)(x-6)(x-3)(x-3)}{(x-3)(x+7)}$
$=(x-6)(x-3)$

23. $\dfrac{2a+2b}{3}\cdot\dfrac{a-b}{a^2-b^2}=\dfrac{2(a+b)(a-b)}{3(a+b)(a-b)}=\dfrac{2}{3}$

24. $\dfrac{x^2-9x+14}{x^2-5x+6}\cdot\dfrac{x+2}{x^2-5x-14}$
$=\dfrac{(x-7)(x-2)(x+2)}{(x-3)(x-2)(x-7)(x+2)}$
$=\dfrac{1}{x-3}$

25. $(x-3)\cdot\frac{x}{x^2+3x-18}=\frac{(x-3)\cdot x}{(x+6)(x-3)}$
$=\frac{x}{x+6}$

26. $\frac{2x^2-9x+9}{8x-12}\div\frac{x^2-3x}{2x}$
$=\frac{(2x-3)(x-3)}{2\cdot 2(2x-3)}\cdot\frac{2x}{x(x-3)}$
$=\frac{(2x-3)(x-3)\cdot 2\cdot x}{2\cdot 2(2x-3)\cdot x(x-3)}$
$=\frac{1}{2}$

27. $\frac{x^2-y^2}{x^2+xy}\div\frac{3x^2-2xy-y^2}{3x^2+6x}$
$=\frac{x^2-y^2}{x^2+xy}\cdot\frac{3x^2+6x}{3x^2-2xy-y^2}$
$=\frac{(x+y)(x-y)}{x(x+y)}\cdot\frac{3x(x+2)}{(3x+y)(x-y)}$
$=\frac{(x+y)(x-y)\cdot 3\cdot x(x+2)}{x(x+y)(3x+y)(x-y)}$
$=\frac{3(x+2)}{3x+y}$

28. $\frac{x^2-y^2}{8x^2-16xy+8y^2}\div\frac{x+y}{4x-y}$
$=\frac{(x-y)(x+y)}{8(x-y)(x-y)}\cdot\frac{4x-y}{x+y}$
$=\frac{(x-y)(x+y)(4x-y)}{8(x-y)(x-y)(x+y)}$
$=\frac{4x-y}{8(x-y)}$

29. $\frac{x-y}{4}\div\frac{y^2-2y-xy+2x}{16x+24}$
$=\frac{x-y}{4}\cdot\frac{16x+24}{y^2-2y-xy+2x}$
$=\frac{x-y}{4}\cdot\frac{8(2x+3)}{y(y-2)-x(y-2)}$
$=\frac{x-y}{4}\cdot\frac{8(2x+3)}{(y-2)(y-x)}$
$=-\frac{y-x}{4}\cdot\frac{8(2x+3)}{(y-2)(y-x)}$
$=-\frac{2\cdot 4(y-x)(2x+3)}{4(y-2)(y-x)}$
$=-\frac{2(2x+3)}{y-2}$

30. $\frac{y-3}{4x+3}\div\frac{9-y^2}{4x^2-x-3}$
$=\frac{y-3}{4x+3}\cdot\frac{4x^2-x-3}{9-y^2}$
$=\frac{y-3}{4x+3}\cdot\frac{(4x+3)(x-1)}{-1(y-3)(y+3)}$
$=\frac{(y-3)(4x+3)(x-1)}{-(4x+3)(y-3)(y+3)}$
$=-\frac{x-1}{y+3}$

31. $\frac{5x-4}{3x-1}+\frac{6}{3x-1}=\frac{5x-4+6}{3x-1}=\frac{5x+2}{3x-1}$

32. $\frac{4x-5}{3x^2}-\frac{2x+5}{3x^2}=\frac{4x-5-(2x+5)}{3x^2}$
$=\frac{4x-5-2x-5}{3x^2}$
$=\frac{2x-10}{3x^2}$

33. $\frac{9x+7}{6x^2} - \frac{3x+4}{6x^2} = \frac{9x+7-(3x+4)}{6x^2}$
$= \frac{9x+7-3x-4}{6x^2}$
$= \frac{6x+3}{6x^2}$
$= \frac{3(2x+1)}{6x^2}$
$= \frac{2x+1}{2x^2}$

34. $2x = 2 \cdot x$
$7x = 7 \cdot x$
$\text{LCD} = 2 \cdot 7 \cdot x = 14x$

35. $x^2 - 5x - 24 = (x-8)(x+3)$
$x^2 + 11x + 24 = (x+8)(x+3)$
$\text{LCD} = (x-8)(x+8)(x+3)$

36. $\frac{x+2}{x^2+11x+18} = \frac{x+2}{(x+2)(x+9)} \cdot \frac{x-5}{x-5}$
$= \frac{(x+2)(x-5)}{(x+2)(x+9)(x-5)}$
$= \frac{x^2-3x-10}{(x+2)(x-5)(x+9)}$

37. $\frac{3x-5}{x^2+4x+4} = \frac{3x-5}{(x+2)^2} \cdot \frac{x+3}{x+3}$
$= \frac{(3x-5)(x+3)}{(x+2)^2(x+3)}$
$= \frac{3x^2+4x-15}{(x+2)^2(x+3)}$

38. $\frac{4}{5x^2} - \frac{6}{y} = \frac{4}{5x^2} \cdot \frac{y}{y} - \frac{6}{y} \cdot \frac{5x^2}{5x^2}$
$= \frac{4y}{5x^2y} - \frac{30x^2}{5x^2y}$
$= \frac{4y-30x^2}{5x^2y}$

39. $\frac{2}{x-3} - \frac{4}{x-1}$
$= \frac{2}{x-3} \cdot \frac{x-1}{x-1} - \frac{4}{x-1} \cdot \frac{x-3}{x-3}$
$= \frac{2(x-1)}{(x-3)(x-1)} - \frac{4(x-3)}{(x-1)(x-3)}$
$= \frac{2(x-1)-4(x-3)}{(x-3)(x-1)}$
$= \frac{2x-2-4x+12}{(x-3)(x-1)}$
$= \frac{-2x+10}{(x-3)(x-1)}$

40. $\frac{x+7}{x+3} - \frac{x-3}{x+7}$
$= \frac{x+7}{x+3} \cdot \frac{x+7}{x+7} - \frac{x-3}{x+7} \cdot \frac{x+3}{x+3}$
$= \frac{(x+7)^2}{(x+3)(x+7)} - \frac{(x-3)(x+3)}{(x+3)(x+7)}$
$= \frac{(x+7)^2-(x-3)(x+3)}{(x+3)(x+7)}$
$= \frac{x^2+14x+49-x^2+9}{(x+3)(x+7)}$
$= \frac{14x+58}{(x+3)(x+7)}$

41. $\frac{4}{x+3} - 2 = \frac{4}{x+3} - 2 \cdot \frac{(x+3)}{(x+3)}$
$= \frac{4}{x+3} - \frac{2(x+3)}{x+3}$
$= \frac{4-2(x+3)}{x+3}$
$= \frac{4-2x-6}{x+3}$
$= \frac{-2x-2}{x+3}$

42. $\frac{3}{x^2+2x-8}+\frac{2}{x^2-3x+2}$

$=\frac{3}{(x+4)(x-2)}+\frac{2}{(x-2)(x-1)}$

$=\frac{3}{(x+4)(x-2)}\cdot\frac{x-1}{x-1}+\frac{2}{(x-2)(x-1)}\cdot\frac{x+4}{x+4}$

$=\frac{3(x-1)}{(x+4)(x-2)(x-1)}+\frac{2(x+4)}{(x+4)(x-2)(x-1)}$

$=\frac{3x-3+2x+8}{(x+4)(x-2)(x-1)}$

$=\frac{5x+5}{(x+4)(x-2)(x-1)}$

43. $\frac{2x-5}{6x+9}-\frac{4}{2x^2+3x}$

$=\frac{2x-5}{3(2x+3)}-\frac{4}{x(2x+3)}$

$=\frac{2x-5}{3(2x+3)}\cdot\frac{x}{x}-\frac{4}{x(2x+3)}\cdot\frac{3}{3}$

$=\frac{x(2x-5)}{3x(2x+3)}-\frac{4(3)}{3x(2x+3)}$

$=\frac{2x^2-5x-12}{3x(2x+3)}$

$=\frac{(2x+3)(x-4)}{3x(2x+3)}$

$=\frac{x-4}{3x}$

44. $\frac{x-1}{x^2-2x+1}-\frac{x+1}{x-1}=\frac{x-1}{(x-1)(x-1)}-\frac{x+1}{x-1}$

$=\frac{1}{x-1}-\frac{x+1}{x-1}$

$=\frac{1-(x+1)}{x-1}$

$=\frac{1-x-1}{x-1}$

$=-\frac{x}{x-1}$

45. $\frac{x-1}{x^2+4x+4}+\frac{x-1}{x+2}$

$=\frac{x-1}{(x+2)^2}+\frac{x-1}{x+2}$

$=\frac{x-1}{(x+2)^2}+\frac{(x-1)}{(x+2)}\cdot\frac{(x+2)}{(x+2)}$

$=\frac{x-1}{(x+2)^2}+\frac{(x-1)(x+2)}{(x+2)^2}$

$=\frac{x-1+(x-1)(x+2)}{(x+2)^2}$

$=\frac{x-1+x^2+x-2}{(x+2)^2}$

$=\frac{x^2+2x-3}{(x+2)^2}$

46. $P=2l+2w$

$P=2\left(\frac{x}{8}\right)+2\left(\frac{x+2}{4x}\right)$

$P=\frac{x}{4}+\frac{x+2}{2x}$

$P=\frac{x}{4}\cdot\frac{x}{x}+\frac{x+2}{2x}\cdot\frac{2}{2}$

$P=\frac{x^2}{4x}+\frac{2(x+2)}{4x}$

$P=\frac{x^2+2x+4}{4x}$

$A=l\cdot w$

$A=\left(\frac{x}{8}\right)\left(\frac{x+2}{4x}\right)$

$A=\frac{x(x+2)}{8\cdot 4x}$

$A=\frac{x+2}{32}$

47. $P = \dfrac{3x}{4x-4} + \dfrac{2x}{3x-3} + \dfrac{x}{x-1}$

$P = \dfrac{3x}{4(x-1)} \cdot \dfrac{3}{3} + \dfrac{2x}{3(x-1)} \cdot \dfrac{4}{4} + \dfrac{x}{x-1} \cdot \dfrac{12}{12}$

$P = \dfrac{9x}{12(x-1)} + \dfrac{8x}{12(x-1)} + \dfrac{12x}{12(x-1)}$

$P = \dfrac{9x+8x+12x}{12(x-1)}$

$P = \dfrac{29x}{12(x-1)}$

$A = \dfrac{1}{2}bh$

$A = \dfrac{1}{2}\left(\dfrac{x}{x-1}\right)\left(\dfrac{6y}{5}\right)$

$A = \dfrac{6xy}{2 \cdot 5(x-1)}$

$A = \dfrac{3xy}{5(x-1)}$

48. $\dfrac{\frac{5x}{27}}{-\frac{10xy}{21}} = \dfrac{5x}{27} \cdot \dfrac{-21}{10xy} = \dfrac{5x(3)(-7)}{3 \cdot 9 \cdot 2 \cdot 5xy} = -\dfrac{7}{18y}$

49. $\dfrac{\frac{8x}{x^2-9}}{\frac{4}{x+3}} = \dfrac{8x}{x^2-9} \cdot \dfrac{x+3}{4}$

$= \dfrac{8x(x+3)}{(x+3)(x-3)4}$

$= \dfrac{2x}{x-3}$

50. $\dfrac{\frac{3}{5}+\frac{2}{7}}{\frac{1}{5}+\frac{5}{6}} = \dfrac{210\left(\frac{3}{5}+\frac{2}{7}\right)}{210\left(\frac{1}{5}+\frac{5}{6}\right)}$

$= \dfrac{210\left(\frac{3}{5}\right)+210\left(\frac{2}{7}\right)}{210\left(\frac{1}{5}\right)+210\left(\frac{5}{6}\right)}$

$= \dfrac{126+60}{42+175}$

$= \dfrac{186}{217}$

$= \dfrac{6 \cdot 31}{7 \cdot 31}$

$= \dfrac{6}{7}$

51. $\dfrac{\frac{2}{a}+\frac{1}{2a}}{a+\frac{a}{2}} = \dfrac{2a\left(\frac{2}{a}+\frac{1}{2a}\right)}{2a\left(a+\frac{a}{2}\right)} = \dfrac{4+1}{2a^2+a^2} = \dfrac{5}{3a^2}$

52. $\dfrac{3-\frac{1}{y}}{2-\frac{1}{y}} = \dfrac{y\left(3-\frac{1}{y}\right)}{y\left(2-\frac{1}{y}\right)} = \dfrac{y(3)-y\left(\frac{1}{y}\right)}{y(2)-y\left(\frac{1}{y}\right)} = \dfrac{3y-1}{2y-1}$

53. $\dfrac{2+\frac{1}{x^2}}{\frac{1}{x}+\frac{2}{x^2}} = \dfrac{x^2\left(2+\frac{1}{x^2}\right)}{x^2\left(\frac{1}{x}+\frac{2}{x^2}\right)}$

$= \dfrac{x^2(2)+x^2\left(\frac{1}{x^2}\right)}{x^2\left(\frac{1}{x}\right)+x^2\left(\frac{2}{x^2}\right)}$

$= \dfrac{2x^2+1}{x+2}$

54. $\dfrac{\frac{1}{a}+\frac{1}{b}}{\frac{1}{ab}} = \dfrac{ab\left(\frac{1}{a}+\frac{1}{b}\right)}{ab\left(\frac{1}{ab}\right)} = \dfrac{b+a}{1} = b+a$

55. $$\frac{\frac{6}{x+2}+4}{\frac{8}{x+2}-4} = \frac{\frac{6}{x+2}+\frac{4(x+2)}{x+2}}{\frac{8}{x+2}-\frac{4(x+2)}{x+2}}$$
$$= \frac{\frac{6+4(x+2)}{x+2}}{\frac{8-4(x+2)}{x+2}}$$
$$= \frac{6+4(x+2)}{x+2} \cdot \frac{x+2}{8-4(x+2)}$$
$$= \frac{6+4x+8}{8-4x-8}$$
$$= \frac{14+4x}{-4x}$$
$$= \frac{2(7+2x)}{2(-2x)}$$
$$= -\frac{7+2x}{2x}$$

56. $$\frac{x+4}{9} = \frac{5}{9}$$
$$9x+36 = 45$$
$$9x = 9$$
$$\frac{9x}{9} = \frac{9}{9}$$
$$x = 1$$

57. $$\frac{n}{10} = 9 - \frac{n}{5}$$
$$10\left(\frac{n}{10}\right) = 10\left(9 - \frac{n}{5}\right)$$
$$n = 10(9) - 10\left(\frac{n}{5}\right)$$
$$n = 90 - 2n$$
$$n + 2n = 90$$
$$3n = 90$$
$$\frac{3n}{3} = \frac{90}{3}$$
$$n = 30$$

58. $$\frac{5y-3}{7} = \frac{15y-2}{28}$$
$$28(5y-3) = 7(15y-2)$$
$$140y - 84 = 105y - 14$$
$$35y = 70$$
$$\frac{35y}{35} = \frac{70}{35}$$
$$y = 2$$

59.

$$\frac{2}{x+1}-\frac{1}{x-2}=-\frac{1}{2}$$
$$2(x+1)(x-2)\left(\frac{2}{x+1}-\frac{1}{x-2}\right)=2(x+1)(x-2)\left(-\frac{1}{2}\right)$$
$$2(x+1)(x-2)\left(\frac{2}{x+1}\right)-2(x+1)(x-2)\left(\frac{1}{x-2}\right)=-(x+1)(x-2)$$
$$4(x-2)-2(x+1)=-(x+1)(x-2)$$
$$4x-8-2x-2=-(x^2-x-2)$$
$$2x-10=-x^2+x+2$$
$$x^2+2x-x-10-2=0$$
$$x^2+x-12=0$$
$$(x+4)(x-3)=0$$

$x+4=0$ or $x-3=0$
$x=-4$ $\quad x=3$

60.

$$\frac{1}{a+3}+\frac{1}{a-3}=-\frac{5}{a^2-9}$$
$$\frac{1}{a+3}+\frac{1}{a-3}=-\frac{5}{(a-3)(a+3)}$$
$$(a-3)(a+3)\left(\frac{1}{a+3}+\frac{1}{a-3}\right)=(a-3)(a+3)\left(-\frac{5}{(a-3)(a+3)}\right)$$
$$a-3+a+3=-5$$
$$2a=-5$$
$$\frac{2a}{2}=-\frac{5}{2}$$
$$a=-\frac{5}{2}$$

61.

$$\frac{y}{2y+2}+\frac{2y-16}{4y+4}=\frac{y-3}{y+1}$$
$$\frac{y}{2(y+1)}+\frac{2(y-8)}{4(y+1)}=\frac{y-3}{y+1}$$
$$\frac{y}{2(y+1)}+\frac{y-8}{2(y+1)}=\frac{y-3}{y+1}$$
$$2(y+1)\left(\frac{y}{2(y+1)}+\frac{y-8}{2(y+1)}\right)=2(y+1)\left(\frac{y-3}{y+1}\right)$$
$$2(y+1)\left(\frac{y}{2(y+1)}\right)+2(y+1)\left(\frac{y-8}{2(y+1)}\right)=2(y-3)$$
$$y+y-8=2y-6$$
$$2y-8=2y-6$$
$$2y-2y=-6+8$$
$$0=2 \quad \text{False}$$

No solution

62.

$$\frac{4}{x+3}+\frac{8}{x^2-9}=0$$
$$\frac{4}{x+3}+\frac{8}{(x-3)(x+3)}=0$$
$$(x-3)(x+3)\left(\frac{4}{x+3}+\frac{8}{(x-3)(x+3)}\right)=(x-3)(x+3)(0)$$
$$(x-3)(x+3)\left(\frac{4}{x+3}\right)+(x-3)(x+3)\left(\frac{8}{(x-3)(x+3)}\right)=0$$
$$4(x-3)+8=0$$
$$4x-12+8=0$$
$$4x-4=0$$
$$4x=4$$
$$\frac{4x}{4}=\frac{4}{4}$$
$$x=1$$

63.

$$\frac{2}{x-3}-\frac{4}{x+3}=\frac{8}{x^2-9}$$
$$\frac{2}{x-3}-\frac{4}{x+3}=\frac{8}{(x+3)(x-3)}$$
$$(x+3)(x-3)\left(\frac{2}{x-3}-\frac{4}{x+3}\right)=(x+3)(x-3)\left(\frac{8}{(x+3)(x-3)}\right)$$
$$(x+3)(x-3)\left(\frac{2}{x-3}\right)-(x+3)(x-3)\left(\frac{4}{x+3}\right)=8$$
$$2(x+3)-4(x-3)=8$$
$$2x+6-4x+12=8$$
$$-2x+18=8$$
$$-2x=8-18$$
$$-2x=-10$$
$$\frac{-2x}{-2}=\frac{-10}{-2}$$
$$x=5$$

64.

$$\frac{x-3}{x+1}-\frac{x-6}{x+5}=0$$
$$(x+1)(x+5)\left(\frac{x-3}{x+1}-\frac{x-6}{x+5}\right)=(x+1)(x+5)0$$
$$(x+1)(x+5)\left(\frac{x-3}{x+1}\right)-(x+1)(x+5)\left(\frac{x-6}{x+5}\right)=0$$
$$(x-3)(x+5)-(x-6)(x+1)=0$$
$$x^2+2x-15-x^2+5x+6=0$$
$$7x-9=0$$
$$7x=9$$
$$\frac{7x}{7}=\frac{9}{7}$$
$$x=\frac{9}{7}$$

65.

$$x+5=\frac{6}{x}$$
$$x(x+5)=x\left(\frac{6}{x}\right)$$
$$x^2+5x=6$$
$$x^2+5x-6=0$$
$$(x+6)(x-1)=0$$
$$x+6=0 \quad \text{or} \quad x-1=0$$
$$x=-6 \qquad\qquad x=1$$

66.

$$\frac{4A}{5b}=x^2$$
$$5b\left(\frac{4A}{5b}\right)=5b\cdot x^2$$
$$4A=5bx^2$$
$$\frac{4A}{5x^2}=\frac{5bx^2}{5x^2}$$
$$\frac{4A}{5x^2}=b$$

67.
$$\frac{x}{7}+\frac{y}{8}=10$$
$$56\left(\frac{x}{7}+\frac{y}{8}\right)=56(10)$$
$$56\left(\frac{x}{7}\right)+56\left(\frac{y}{8}\right)=560$$
$$8x+7y=560$$
$$7y=560-8x$$
$$y=\frac{560-8x}{7}$$

68. 1 dollar = 100 cents
$$\frac{20}{100}=\frac{1}{5}$$

69. $\frac{4}{6}=\frac{2}{3}$

70.
$$\frac{x}{2}=\frac{12}{4}$$
$$4x=24$$
$$\frac{4x}{4}=\frac{24}{4}$$
$$x=6$$

71.
$$\frac{20}{1}=\frac{x}{25}$$
$$1x=20\cdot 25$$
$$x=500$$

72.
$$\frac{32}{100}=\frac{100}{x}$$
$$32x=10,000$$
$$\frac{32x}{32}=\frac{10,000}{32}$$
$$x=312.5$$

73.
$$\frac{20}{2}=\frac{c}{5}$$
$$2c=100$$
$$\frac{2c}{2}=\frac{100}{2}$$
$$c=50$$

74.
$$\frac{2}{x-1}=\frac{3}{x+3}$$
$$2(x+3)=3(x-1)$$
$$2x+6=3x-3$$
$$6+3=3x-2x$$
$$9=x$$

75.
$$\frac{4}{y-3}=\frac{2}{y-3}$$
$$4(y-3)=2(y-3)$$
$$4y-12=2y-6$$
$$4y-2y=-6+12$$
$$2y=6$$
$$\frac{2y}{2}=\frac{6}{2}$$
$$y=3$$
3 is an extraneous solution.
If y = 3, the denominator would be zero.
The equation has no solution.

76.
$$\frac{y+2}{y}=\frac{5}{3}$$
$$3(y+2)=5y$$
$$3y+6=5y$$
$$6=2y$$
$$\frac{6}{2}=\frac{2y}{2}$$
$$3=y$$

77.
$$\frac{x-3}{3x+2}=\frac{2}{6}$$
$$6(x-3)=2(3x+2)$$
$$6x-18=6x+4$$
$$6x-6x=4+18$$
$$0=22 \text{ False}$$
The equation has no solution.

78.
$$\frac{\$1.29}{10}=\$0.129$$
$$\frac{\$2.15}{16}\approx\$0.134$$
The best buy is 10 ounces for $1.29.

79. $\frac{\$0.89}{8} \approx \$0.111$

$\frac{\$1.63}{15} \approx \$0.109$

$\frac{\$2.36}{20} = \$0.118$

The best buy is 15 ounces for $1.63.

80. $\frac{300}{20} = \frac{x}{45}$

$20x = 300 \cdot 45$

$20x = 13,500$

$\frac{20x}{20} = \frac{13,500}{20}$

$x = 675$

675 parts can be processed in 45 minutes.

81. $\frac{90}{8} = \frac{x}{3}$

$8x = 90 \cdot 3$

$8x = 270$

$\frac{8x}{8} = \frac{270}{8}$

$x = 33.75$

He charges $33.75.

82. $\frac{100}{35} = \frac{x}{55}$

$35x = 5500$

$\frac{35x}{35} = \frac{5500}{35}$

$x = \frac{1100}{7} = 157\frac{1}{7}$

He can address 157 letters in 55 minutes.

83. Let x = the unknown number.

$5\left(\frac{1}{x}\right) = \frac{3}{2}\left(\frac{1}{x}\right) + \frac{7}{6}$

$\frac{5}{x} = \frac{3}{2x} + \frac{7}{6}$

$6x\left(\frac{5}{x}\right) = 6x\left(\frac{3}{2x} + \frac{7}{6}\right)$

$30 = 6x\left(\frac{3}{2x}\right) + 6x\left(\frac{7}{6}\right)$

$30 = 9 + 7x$

$30 - 9 = 7x$

$21 = 7x$

$\frac{21}{7} = \frac{7x}{7}$

$3 = x$

84. Let x = the unknown number.

$\frac{1}{x} = \frac{1}{4-x}$

$x = 4 - x$

$2x = 4$

$\frac{2x}{2} = \frac{4}{2}$

$x = 2$

85.

	distance	= rate	· time
Slower car	60	$x - 10$	$\frac{60}{x-10}$
Faster car	90	x	$\frac{90}{x}$

$\frac{60}{x-10} = \frac{90}{x}$

$60x = 90(x - 10)$

$60x = 90x - 900$

$60x - 90x = -900$

$-30x = -900$

$\frac{-30x}{-30} = \frac{-900}{-30}$

$x = 30$

The speed of the faster car is 30 mph and the speed of the slower car is 20 mph.

86.

	distance	= rate	· time
Upstream	48	$x-4$	$\frac{48}{x-4}$
Downstream	72	$x+4$	$\frac{72}{x+4}$

$$\frac{48}{x-4}=\frac{72}{x+4}$$
$$48(x+4)=72(x-4)$$
$$48x+192=72x-288$$
$$480=24x$$
$$\frac{480}{24}=\frac{24x}{24}$$
$$20=x$$

The speed of the boat is 20 miles per hour in still water.

87.

	Time	In one hour
Mark	7	$\frac{1}{7}$
Maria	x	$\frac{1}{x}$
Together	5	$\frac{1}{5}$

$$\frac{1}{7}+\frac{1}{x}=\frac{1}{5}$$
$$35x\left(\frac{1}{7}+\frac{1}{x}\right)=35x\left(\frac{1}{5}\right)$$
$$35x\left(\frac{1}{7}\right)+35x\left(\frac{1}{x}\right)=7x$$
$$5x+35=7x$$
$$35=7x-5x$$
$$35=2x$$
$$\frac{35}{2}=\frac{2x}{2}$$
$$17\frac{1}{2}=x$$

It takes Maria $17\frac{1}{2}$ hours to do it.

88.

	Time	In one day
Pipe A	20	$\frac{1}{20}$
Pipe B	15	$\frac{1}{15}$
Together	x	$\frac{1}{x}$

$$\frac{1}{20}+\frac{1}{15}=\frac{1}{x}$$
$$60x\left(\frac{1}{20}+\frac{1}{15}\right)=60x\left(\frac{1}{x}\right)$$
$$60x\left(\frac{1}{20}\right)+60x\left(\frac{1}{15}\right)=60$$
$$3x+4x=60$$
$$7x=60$$
$$\frac{7x}{7}=\frac{60}{7}$$
$$x=8\frac{4}{7}$$

It takes them $8\frac{4}{7}$ days to fill the pond.

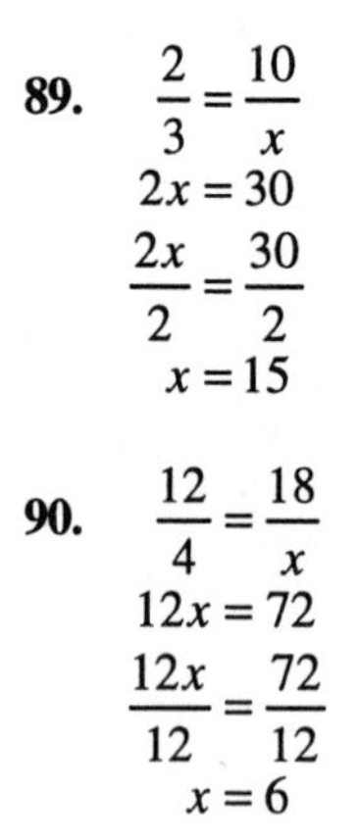

89.
$$\frac{2}{3}=\frac{10}{x}$$
$$2x=30$$
$$\frac{2x}{2}=\frac{30}{2}$$
$$x=15$$

90.
$$\frac{12}{4}=\frac{18}{x}$$
$$12x=72$$
$$\frac{12x}{12}=\frac{72}{12}$$
$$x=6$$

91. $\frac{9}{7\frac{1}{5}} = \frac{x}{12}$

$108 = 7\frac{1}{5}x$

$108 = \frac{36}{5}x$

$540 = 36x$

$\frac{540}{36} = \frac{36x}{36}$

$15 = x$

92. $\frac{x}{5} = \frac{30}{2.5}$

$2.5x = 150$

$\frac{2.5x}{2.5} = \frac{150}{2.5}$

$x = 60$

Chapter 6 Test

1. $\frac{x+5}{x^2+4x+3} = \frac{x+5}{(x+3)(x+1)}$

The expression is undefined if $x = -3$ or $x = -1$.

2. a. $C = \frac{100x+3000}{x}$

$C = \frac{100(200)+3000}{200} = \$115$

b. $C = \frac{100x+3000}{x}$

$C = \frac{100(1000)+3000}{1000} = \$103$

3. $\frac{3x-6}{5x-10} = \frac{3(x-2)}{5(x-2)} = \frac{3}{5}$

4. $\frac{x+10}{x^2-100} = \frac{x+10}{(x+10)(x-10)} = \frac{1}{x-10}$

5. $\frac{x+6}{x^2+12x+36} = \frac{x+6}{(x+6)(x+6)} = \frac{1}{x+6}$

6. $\frac{x+3}{x^3+27} = \frac{x+3}{(x+3)(x^2-3x+9)}$

$= \frac{1}{x^2-3x+9}$

7. $\frac{2m^3-2m^2-12m}{m^2-5m+6} = \frac{2m(m^2-m-6)}{(m-3)(m-2)}$

$= \frac{2m(m-3)(m+2)}{(m-3)(m-2)}$

$= \frac{2m(m+2)}{m-2}$

8. $\frac{ay+3a+2y+6}{ay+3a+5y+15} = \frac{a(y+3)+2(y+3)}{a(y+3)+5(y+3)}$

$= \frac{(y+3)(a+2)}{(y+3)(a+5)}$

$= \frac{a+2}{a+5}$

9. $\frac{y-x}{x^2-y^2} = -\frac{x-y}{x^2-y^2}$

$= -\frac{x-y}{(x+y)(x-y)}$

$= -\frac{1}{x+y}$

10. $\frac{x^2-13x+42}{x^2+10x+21} \div \frac{x^2-4}{x^2+x-6}$

$= \frac{x^2-13x+42}{x^2+10x+21} \cdot \frac{x^2+x-6}{x^2-4}$

$= \frac{(x-6)(x-7)}{(x+7)(x+3)} \cdot \frac{(x+3)(x-2)}{(x-2)(x+2)}$

$= \frac{(x-6)(x-7)(x+3)(x-2)}{(x+7)(x+3)(x-2)(x+2)}$

$= \frac{(x-6)(x-7)}{(x+7)(x+2)}$

11. $\frac{3}{x-1} \cdot (5x-5) = \frac{3}{x-1} \cdot \frac{5(x-1)}{1}$

$= \frac{15(x-1)}{x-1}$

$= 15$

12. $\frac{y^2-5y+6}{2y+4}\cdot\frac{y+2}{2y-6}$
$=\frac{(y-3)(y-2)}{2(y+2)}\cdot\frac{y+2}{2(y-3)}$
$=\frac{(y-3)(y-2)(y+2)}{4(y+2)(y-3)}$
$=\frac{y-2}{4}$

13. $\frac{5}{2x+5}-\frac{6}{2x+5}=\frac{5-6}{2x+5}$
$=\frac{-1}{2x+5}$
$=-\frac{1}{2x+5}$

14. $\frac{5a}{a^2-a-6}-\frac{2}{a-3}$
$=\frac{5a}{(a-3)(a+2)}-\frac{2}{a-3}$
$=\frac{5a}{(a-3)(a+2)}-\frac{2}{a-3}\cdot\frac{a+2}{a+2}$
$=\frac{5a}{(a-3)(a+2)}-\frac{2(a+2)}{(a-3)(a+2)}$
$=\frac{5a-2(a+2)}{(a-3)(a+2)}$
$=\frac{5a-2a-4}{(a-3)(a+2)}$
$=\frac{3a-4}{(a-3)(a+2)}$

15. $\frac{6}{x^2-1}+\frac{3}{x+1}$
$=\frac{6}{(x+1)(x-1)}+\frac{3}{x+1}$
$=\frac{6}{(x+1)(x-1)}+\frac{3}{x+1}\cdot\frac{x-1}{x-1}$
$=\frac{6}{(x+1)(x-1)}+\frac{3(x-1)}{(x+1)(x-1)}$
$=\frac{6+3(x-1)}{(x+1)(x-1)}$
$=\frac{6+3x-3}{(x+1)(x-1)}$
$=\frac{3x+3}{(x+1)(x-1)}$
$=\frac{3(x+1)}{(x+1)(x-1)}$
$=\frac{3}{x-1}$

16. $\frac{x^2-9}{x^2-3x}\div\frac{xy+5x+3y+15}{2x+10}$
$=\frac{x^2-9}{x^2-3x}\cdot\frac{2x+10}{xy+5x+3y+15}$
$=\frac{(x+3)(x-3)}{x(x-3)}\cdot\frac{2(x+5)}{x(y+5)+3(y+5)}$
$=\frac{(x+3)(x-3)}{x(x-3)}\cdot\frac{2(x+5)}{(y+5)(x+3)}$
$=\frac{2(x+3)(x-3)(x+5)}{x(x-3)(y+5)(x+3)}$
$=\frac{2(x+5)}{x(y+5)}$

17. $\frac{x+2}{x^2+11x+18}+\frac{5}{x^2-3x-10}$

$=\frac{x+2}{(x+9)(x+2)}+\frac{5}{(x-5)(x+2)}$

$=\frac{(x+2)}{(x+9)(x+2)}\cdot\frac{x-5}{x-5}+\frac{5}{(x-5)(x+2)}\cdot\frac{x+9}{x+9}$

$=\frac{(x+2)(x-5)}{(x+9)(x+2)(x-5)}+\frac{5(x+9)}{(x-5)(x+2)(x+9)}$

$=\frac{x^2-3x-10}{(x+9)(x+2)(x-5)}+\frac{5x+45}{(x+9)(x+2)(x-5)}$

$=\frac{x^2-3x-10+5x+45}{(x+9)(x+2)(x-5)}$

$=\frac{x^2+2x+35}{(x+9)(x+2)(x-5)}$

18. $\frac{4y}{y^2+6y+5}-\frac{3}{y^2+5y+4}$

$=\frac{4y}{(y+5)(y+1)}-\frac{3}{(y+4)(y+1)}$

$=\frac{4y}{(y+5)(y+1)}\cdot\frac{(y+4)}{(y+4)}-\frac{3}{(y+4)(y+1)}\cdot\frac{(y+5)}{(y+5)}$

$=\frac{4y(y+4)}{(y+5)(y+1)(y+4)}-\frac{3(y+5)}{(y+4)(y+1)(y+5)}$

$=\frac{4y(y+4)-3(y+5)}{(y+5)(y+1)(y+4)}$

$=\frac{4y^2+16y-3y-15}{(y+5)(y+1)(y+4)}$

$=\frac{4y^2+13y-15}{(y+5)(y+1)(y+4)}$

19. $\frac{4}{y}-\frac{5}{3}=\frac{-1}{5}$

$15y\left(\frac{4}{y}-\frac{5}{3}\right)=15y\left(-\frac{1}{5}\right)$

$15y\left(\frac{4}{y}\right)+15y\left(-\frac{5}{3}\right)=-3y$

$60-25y=-3y$

$60=-3y+25y$

$60=22y$

$\frac{60}{22}=\frac{22y}{22}$

$\frac{30}{11}=y$

20. $\frac{5}{y+1}=\frac{4}{y+2}$

$5(y+2)=4(y+1)$

$5y+10=4y+4$

$5y-4y=4-10$

$y=-6$

21.
$$\frac{a}{a-3}=\frac{3}{a-3}-\frac{3}{2}$$
$$2(a-3)\left(\frac{a}{a-3}\right)=2(a-3)\left(\frac{3}{a-3}-\frac{3}{2}\right)$$
$$2(a-3)\left(\frac{a}{a-3}\right)=2(a-3)\left(\frac{3}{a-3}\right)+2(a-3)\left(-\frac{3}{2}\right)$$
$$2a=6-3(a-3)$$
$$2a=6-3a+9$$
$$2a=15-3a$$
$$2a+3a=15$$
$$5a=15$$
$$\frac{5a}{5}=\frac{15}{5}$$
$$a=3$$

3 is an extraneous solution. If $a=3$, the denominator would be zero. The equation has no solution.

22.
$$\frac{10}{x^2-25}=\frac{3}{x+5}+\frac{1}{x-5}$$
$$\frac{10}{(x+5)(x-5)}=\frac{3}{x+5}+\frac{1}{x-5}$$
$$(x+5)(x-5)\left(\frac{10}{(x+5)(x-5)}\right)=(x+5)(x-5)\left(\frac{3}{x+5}+\frac{1}{x-5}\right)$$
$$10=(x+5)(x-5)\left(\frac{3}{x+5}\right)+(x+5)(x-5)\left(\frac{1}{x-5}\right)$$
$$10=3(x-5)+1(x+5)$$
$$10=3x-15+x+5$$
$$10=4x-10$$
$$10+10=4x$$
$$20=4x$$
$$\frac{20}{4}=\frac{4x}{4}$$
$$5=x$$

5 is an extraneous solution. If $x=5$, the denominator would be zero. The equation has no solution.

23. $\dfrac{\frac{5x^2}{yz^2}}{\frac{10x}{z^3}}=\dfrac{5x^2}{yz^2}\cdot\dfrac{z^3}{10x}=\dfrac{5\cdot x\cdot x\cdot z\cdot z^2}{y\cdot z^2\cdot 2\cdot 5\cdot x}=\dfrac{xz}{2y}$

24. $$\frac{\frac{b}{a}-\frac{a}{b}}{\frac{b}{a}+\frac{b}{a}}=\frac{ab\left(\frac{b}{a}-\frac{a}{b}\right)}{ab\left(\frac{b}{a}+\frac{b}{a}\right)}$$
$$=\frac{ab\left(\frac{b}{a}\right)-ab\left(\frac{a}{b}\right)}{ab\left(\frac{b}{a}\right)+ab\left(\frac{b}{a}\right)}$$
$$=\frac{b^2-a^2}{b^2+b^2}$$
$$=\frac{b^2-a^2}{2b^2}$$

25. $$\frac{5-\frac{1}{y^2}}{\frac{1}{y}+\frac{2}{y^2}}=\frac{\frac{5y^2}{y^2}-\frac{1}{y^2}}{\frac{y}{y^2}+\frac{2}{y^2}}$$
$$=\frac{\frac{5y^2-1}{y^2}}{\frac{y+2}{y^2}}$$
$$=\frac{5y^2-1}{y^2}\cdot\frac{y^2}{y+2}$$
$$=\frac{5y^2-1}{y+2}$$

26. $$\frac{3}{85}=\frac{x}{510}$$
$$3\cdot 510=85x$$
$$1530=85x$$
$$\frac{1530}{85}=\frac{85x}{85}$$
$$18=x$$

27. Let x = the unknown number.
$$x+5\left(\frac{1}{x}\right)=6$$
$$x+\frac{5}{x}=6$$
$$x\left(x+\frac{5}{x}\right)=x(6)$$
$$x(x)+x\left(\frac{5}{x}\right)=6x$$
$$x^2+5=6x$$
$$x^2-6x+5=0$$
$$(x-1)(x-5)=0$$
$$x-1=0 \quad \text{or} \quad x-5=0$$
$$x=1 \qquad\qquad x=5$$

28.

	distance	rate	time
downstream	16	$x+2$	$\frac{16}{x+2}$
upstream	14	$x-2$	$\frac{14}{x-2}$

(distance = rate · time)

$$\frac{16}{x+2}=\frac{14}{x-2}$$
$$16(x-2)=14(x+2)$$
$$16x-32=14x+28$$
$$16x-14x=28+32$$
$$2x=60$$
$$\frac{2x}{2}=\frac{60}{2}$$
$$x=30$$
The speed of the boat is 30 miles per hour in still water.

29.

	Time	In one hour
First pipe	12	$\frac{1}{12}$
Second pipe	15	$\frac{1}{15}$
Together	x	$\frac{1}{x}$

$$\frac{1}{12}+\frac{1}{15}=\frac{1}{x}$$
$$60x\left(\frac{1}{12}+\frac{1}{15}\right)=60x\left(\frac{1}{x}\right)$$
$$60x\left(\frac{1}{12}\right)+60x\left(\frac{1}{15}\right)=60x\left(\frac{1}{x}\right)$$
$$5x+4x=60$$
$$9x=60$$
$$x=\frac{60}{9}=\frac{20}{3}=6\frac{2}{3}$$

It takes them $6\frac{2}{3}$ hours to fill the tank.

30. $\frac{\$1.19}{6} \approx \$0.198$

$\frac{\$2.15}{10} = \$0.215$

$\frac{\$3.25}{16} \approx \$0.203$

The best buy is 6 ounces for $1.19.

31. $\frac{8}{x} = \frac{10}{15}$

$8 \cdot 15 = 10x$

$120 = 10x$

$\frac{120}{10} = \frac{10x}{10}$

$12 = x$

Chapter 7

Section 7.1

Calculator Explorations

1. $y = x; y = 6x; y = -6x$

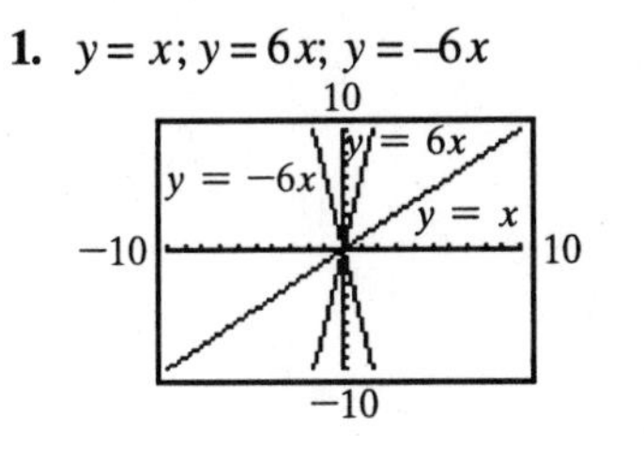

3. $y = \frac{1}{2}x + 2; \; y = \frac{3}{4}x + 2; \; y = x + 2$

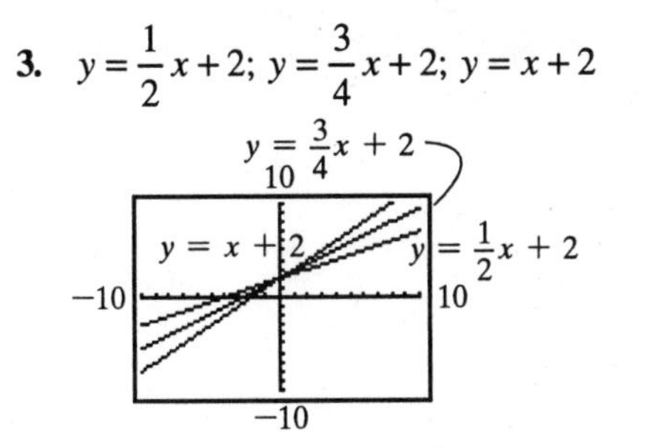

5. $y = -7x + 5; y = 7x + 5$

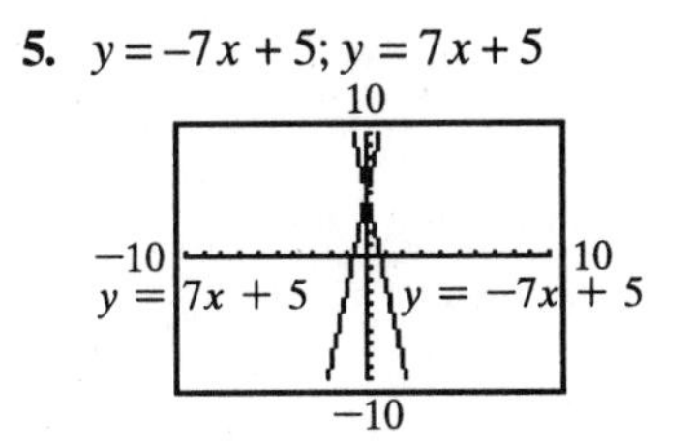

Mental Math

1. $y = 2x - 1; m = 2; (0, -1)$

2. $y = -7x + 3; m = -7; (0, 3)$

3. $y = x + \frac{1}{3}; \; m = 1; \; \left(0, \; \frac{1}{3}\right)$

4. $y = -x - \frac{2}{9}; \; m = -1; \; \left(0, \; -\frac{2}{9}\right)$

5. $y = \frac{5}{7}x - 4; \; m = \frac{5}{7}; \; (0, -4)$

6. $y = -\frac{1}{4}x + \frac{3}{5}; \; m = -\frac{1}{4}; \; \left(0, \; \frac{3}{5}\right)$

Exercise Set 7.1

1. $2x + y = 4$
$y = -2x + 4$
$m = -2; (0, 4)$

3. $x + 9y = 1$
$9y = -x + 1$
$y = -\frac{1}{9}x + \frac{1}{9}$
$m = -\frac{1}{9}; \; \left(0, \; \frac{1}{9}\right)$

5. $4x - 3y = 12$
$-3y = -4x + 12$
$y = \frac{-4x}{-3} + \frac{12}{-3}$
$y = \frac{4}{3}x - 4$
$m = \frac{4}{3}; \; (0, -4)$

7. $x + y = 0$
$y = -x$
$m = -1; (0, 0)$

9. $y = -3$
$m = 0; (0, -3)$

11. $-x + 5y = 20$
$5y = x + 20$
$y = \frac{x}{5} + \frac{20}{5}$
$y = \frac{1}{5}x + 4$
$m = \frac{1}{5}; \; (0, 4)$

13. $m = 2$; y-intercept = (0, 1); B

15. $m = -3$; y-intercept = (0, −2); D

17. $x - 3y = -6$
$-3y = -x - 6$
$y = \frac{1}{3}x + 2$
$m = \frac{1}{3}$
$3x - y = 0$
$-y = -3x + 0$
$y = 3x$
$m = 3$
Because the slopes are not the same and their product is not -1, the lines are neither parallel nor perpendicular.

19. $2x - 7y = 1$
$-7y = -2x + 1$
$y = \frac{2}{7}x - \frac{1}{7}$
$m = \frac{2}{7}$
$2y = 7x - 2$
$y = \frac{7}{2}x - 1$
$m = \frac{7}{2}$
Because the slopes are not the same and their product is not -1, the lines are neither parallel nor perpendicular.

21. $10 + 3x = 5y$
$y = \frac{3}{5}x + 2$
$m = \frac{3}{5}$
$5x + 3y = 1$
$3y = -5x + 1$
$y = -\frac{5}{3}x + \frac{1}{3}$
$m = -\frac{5}{3}$
Because the product of the two slopes is -1, the lines are perpendicular.

23. $6x = 5y + 1$
$-5y = -6x + 1$
$y = \frac{6}{5}x - \frac{1}{5}$
$m = \frac{6}{5}$; y-intercept: $\left(0, -\frac{1}{5}\right)$
$-12x + 10y = 1$
$10y = 12x + 1$
$y = \frac{6}{5}x + \frac{1}{10}$
$m = \frac{6}{5}$; y-intercept: $\left(0, \frac{1}{10}\right)$
Because the slopes are the same and their y-intercepts are different, the lines are parallel.

25. Answers may vary.

27. $y = -x + 1$

29. $y = 2x + \frac{3}{4}$

31. $y = \frac{2}{7}x$

33. $y = \frac{2}{3}x + 5$

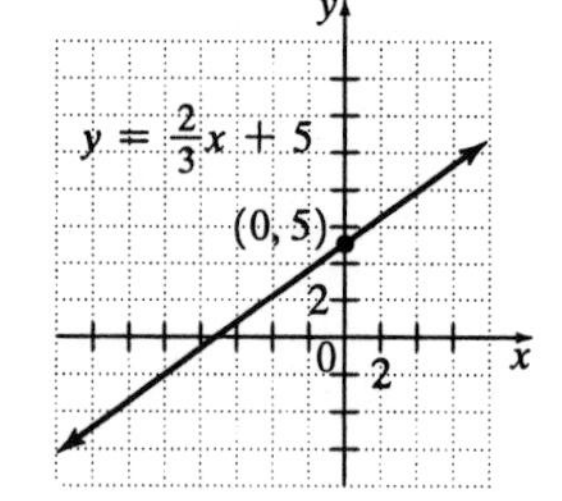

35. $y = -\frac{3}{5}x - 2$

37. $y = 2x + 1$

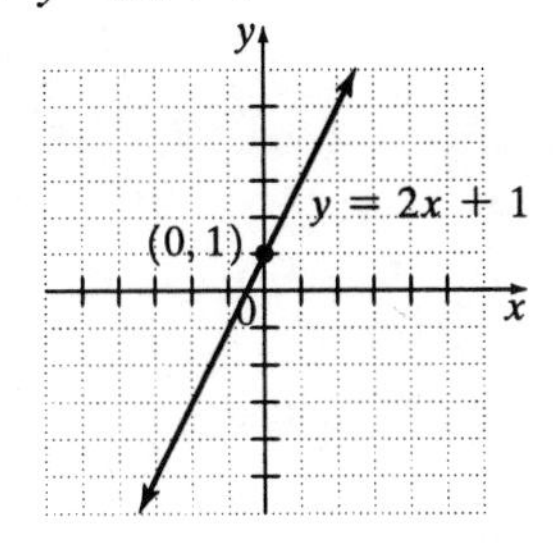

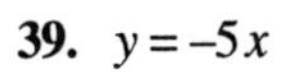

39. $y = -5x$

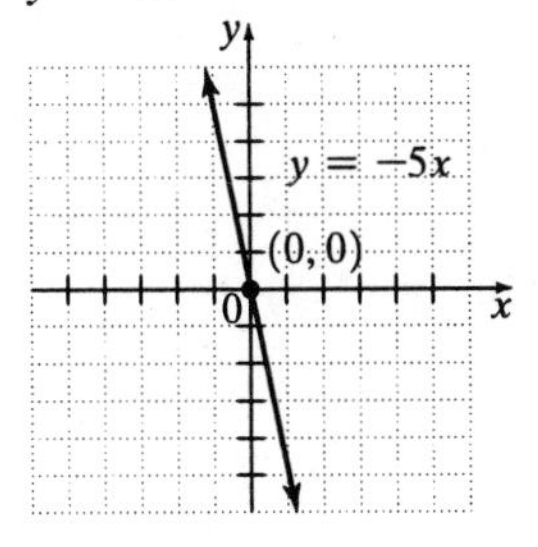

41. $4x + y = 6$

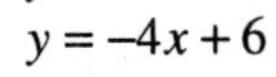

$y = -4x + 6$

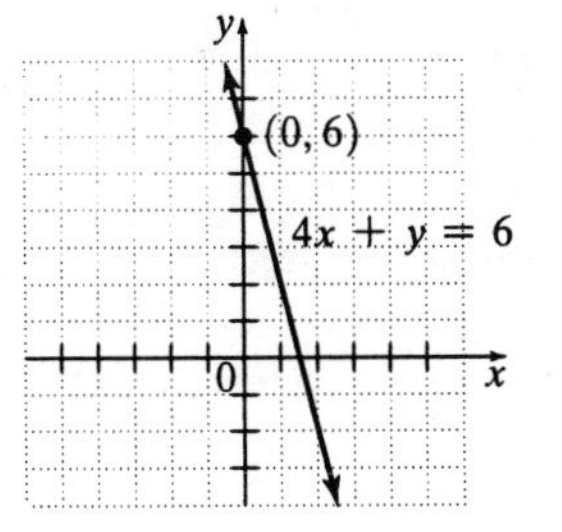

43. $x - y = -2$

$-y = -x - 2$

$y = x + 2$

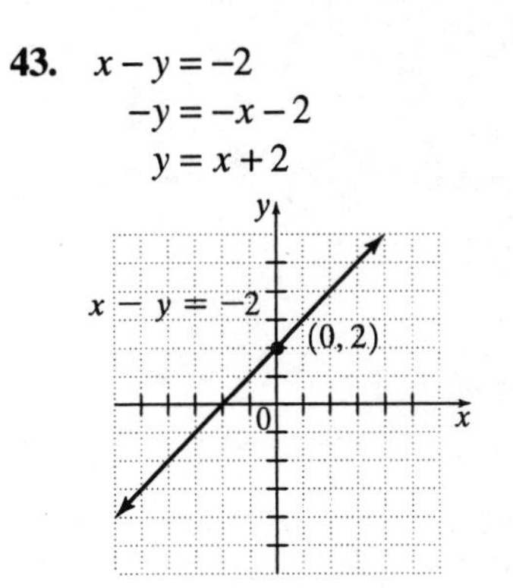

45. $3x + 5y = 10$

$5y = -3x + 10$

$y = -\frac{3}{5}x + 2$

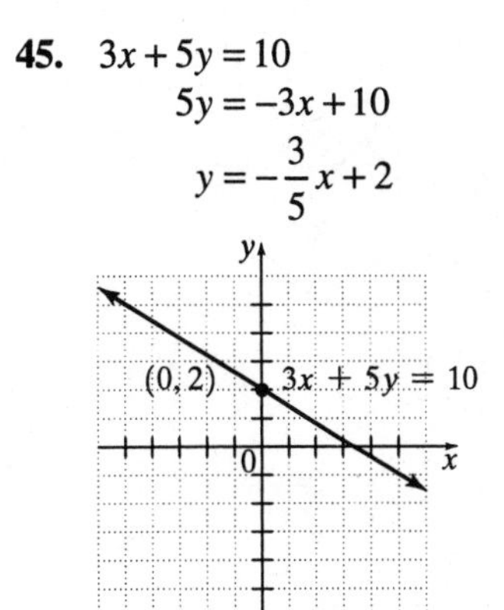

47. $4x - 7y = -14$

$-7y = -4x - 14$

$y = \frac{4}{7}x + 2$

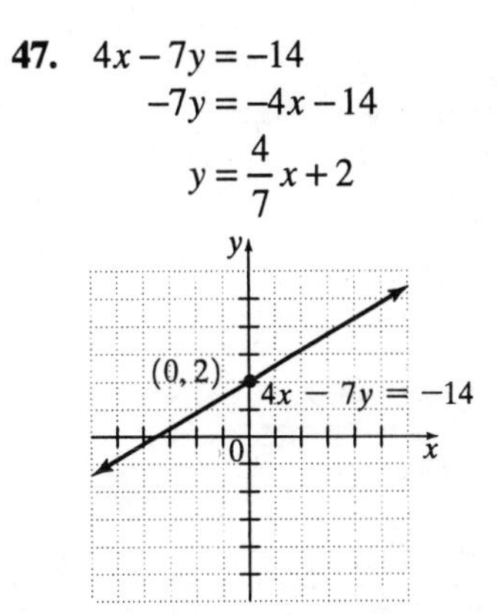

49. a. (0, 28); (5, 22)

b. $m = \frac{22-28}{5-0} = \frac{-6}{5} = -\frac{6}{5} = -1.2$
$y = -1.2x + 28$

c. In 2001, $x = 9$:
$y = -1.2(9) + 28$
$y = 17.2$ heads per square foot

51. a. The temperature 100° Celsius is equivalent to 212° Fahrenheit.

b. 68°F

c. 27°C

d. $m = \frac{212-32}{100-0} = \frac{180}{100} = \frac{9}{5}$
$F = \frac{9}{5}C + 32$

e. $F = \frac{9}{5}(20) + 32$
$= 68$
$20°C = 68°F$
$80 = \frac{9}{5}C + 32$
$48 = \frac{9}{5}C$
$\frac{240}{9} = C$
$\frac{80}{3} = C$
$27 \approx C$
$80°F \approx 27°C$

53. Answers may vary.

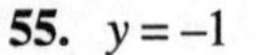

55. $y = -1$

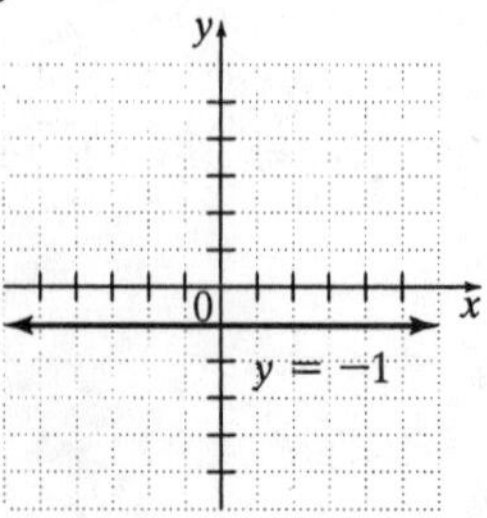

57. $x = 2$

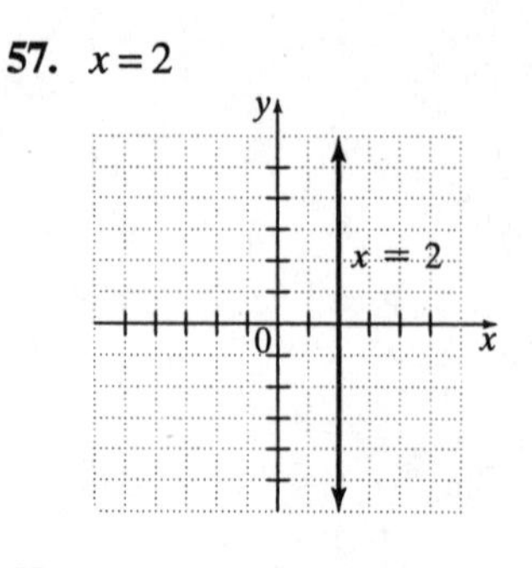

59.
$$\begin{aligned} y-2 &= 3(x-6) \\ y-2 &= 3x-18 \\ -3x+y-2 &= -18 \\ -3x+y &= -16 \\ 3x-y &= 16 \end{aligned}$$

61.
$$\begin{aligned} y+4 &= -6(x+1) \\ y+4 &= -6x-6 \\ 6x+y+4 &= -6 \\ 6x+y &= -10 \end{aligned}$$

Section 7.2

Mental Math

1. $y - 8 = 3(x - 4)$
$m = 3$
A point of the line is (4, 8).

2. $y - 1 = 5(x - 2)$
$m = 5$
A point of the line is (2, 1).

3. $y + 3 = -2(x - 10)$
$m = -2$
A point of the line is (10, –3).

4. $y + 6 = -7(x - 2)$
$m = -7$
A point of the line is (2, –6).

5. $y = \frac{2}{5}(x + 1)$
$m = \frac{2}{5}$
A point of the line is (–1, 0).

6. $y = \frac{3}{7}(x+4)$
$m = \frac{3}{7}$
A point of the line is (–4, 0).

Exercise Set 7.2

1. Slope 6; through (2, 2)
$$\begin{aligned} y - y_1 &= m(x - x_1) \\ y - 2 &= 6(x-2) \\ y - 2 &= 6x - 12 \\ -2 &= 6x - y - 12 \\ -2 + 12 &= 6x - y \\ 10 &= 6x - y \\ 6x - y &= 10 \end{aligned}$$

3. Slope –8; through (–1, –5)
$$\begin{aligned} y - y_1 &= m(x - x_1) \\ y - (-5) &= -8[x - (-1)] \\ y + 5 &= -8(x+1) \\ y + 5 &= -8x - 8 \\ 8x + y + 5 &= -8 \\ 8x + y &= -8 - 5 \\ 8x + y &= -13 \end{aligned}$$

5. Slope $\frac{1}{2}$; through (5, –6)
$$\begin{aligned} y - y_1 &= m(x - x_1) \\ y - (-6) &= \frac{1}{2}(x-5) \\ y + 6 &= \frac{1}{2}(x-5) \\ 2(y+6) &= 2\left[\frac{1}{2}(x-5)\right] \\ 2y + 12 &= x - 5 \\ 12 &= x - 2y - 5 \\ 12 + 5 &= x - 2y \\ 17 &= x - 2y \\ x - 2y &= 17 \end{aligned}$$

7. Through (3, 2) and (5, 6)
$$\begin{aligned} m &= \frac{6-2}{5-3} = \frac{4}{2} = 2 \\ y - y_1 &= m(x - x_1) \\ y - 2 &= 2(x-3) \\ y - 2 &= 2x - 6 \\ -2 &= 2x - y - 6 \\ -2 + 6 &= 2x - y \\ 4 &= 2x - y \\ 2x - y &= 4 \end{aligned}$$

9. Through (–1, 3) and (–2, –5)
$$\begin{aligned} m &= \frac{-5-3}{-2-(-1)} = \frac{-8}{-2+1} = \frac{-8}{-1} = 8 \\ y - y_1 &= m(x - x_1) \\ y - 3 &= 8[x - (-1)] \\ y - 3 &= 8(x+1) \\ y - 3 &= 8x + 8 \\ -3 &= 8x - y + 8 \\ -3 - 8 &= 8x - y \\ -11 &= 8x - y \\ 8x - y &= -11 \end{aligned}$$

11. Through (2, 3) and (–1, –1)
$$\begin{aligned} m &= \frac{-1-3}{-1-2} = \frac{-4}{-3} = \frac{4}{3} \\ y - y_1 &= m(x - x_1) \\ y - 3 &= \frac{4}{3}(x-2) \\ 3(y-3) &= 3\left[\frac{4}{3}(x-2)\right] \\ 3(y-3) &= 4(x-2) \\ 3y - 9 &= 4x - 8 \\ -9 &= 4x - 3y - 8 \\ -9 + 8 &= 4x - 3y \\ -1 &= 4x - 3y \\ 4x - 3y &= -1 \end{aligned}$$

13. Vertical line through (0, 2)
On a vertical line, the x-coordinate stays the same.
$x = 0$

15. Horizontal line through (–1, 3)
On a horizontal line, the y-coordinate stays the same.
$y = 3$

17. Vertical line through $\left(\frac{-7}{3}, \frac{-2}{5}\right)$
On a vertical line, the x-coordinate stays the same.
$x = -\frac{7}{3}$

19. Parallel to $y = 5$, through (1, 2)
Since the graph of $y = 5$ is a horizontal line, any line parallel to it is also horizontal. On a horizontal line, the y-coordinate stays the same.
$y = 2$

21. Perpendicular to $x = -3$, through (–2, 5)
Since the graph of $x = -3$ is a vertical line, any line perpendicular to it is horizontal. On a horizontal line, the y-coordinate stays the same.
$y = 5$

23. Parallel to $x = 0$, through (6, –8)
Since the graph of $x = 0$ is a vertical line, any line parallel to it is also vertical. On a vertical line, the x-coordinate stays the same.
$x = 6$

25. Slope $-\frac{1}{2}$, through $\left(0, \frac{5}{3}\right)$

$$\begin{aligned} y - y_1 &= m(x - x_1) \\ y - \frac{5}{3} &= -\frac{1}{2}(x - 0) \\ y - \frac{5}{3} &= -\frac{1}{2}x \\ 6\left(y - \frac{5}{3}\right) &= 6\left(-\frac{1}{2}x\right) \\ 6y - 10 &= -3x \\ 3x + 6y - 10 &= 0 \\ 3x + 6y &= 10 \end{aligned}$$

27. Slope 1, through (–7, 9)

$$\begin{aligned} y - y_1 &= m(x - x_1) \\ y - 9 &= 1[x - (-7)] \\ y - 9 &= 1(x + 7) \\ y - 9 &= x + 7 \\ -9 &= x - y + 7 \\ -9 - 7 &= x - y \\ -16 &= x - y \\ x - y &= -16 \end{aligned}$$

29. Through (10, 7) and (7, 10)

$$m = \frac{10 - 7}{7 - 10} = \frac{3}{-3} = -1$$

$$\begin{aligned} y - y_1 &= m(x - x_1) \\ y - 7 &= -1(x - 10) \\ y - 7 &= -x + 10 \\ x + y - 7 &= 10 \\ x + y &= 10 + 7 \\ x + y &= 17 \end{aligned}$$

31. Through (6, 7), parallel to x-axis
The x-axis is a horizontal line, so the parallel line is horizontal. On a horizontal line, the y-coordinate stays the same.
$y = 7$

33. Slope $-\frac{4}{7}$, through (–1, –2)

$$\begin{aligned} y - y_1 &= m(x - x_1) \\ y - (-2) &= -\frac{4}{7}[x - (-1)] \\ y + 2 &= -\frac{4}{7}(x + 1) \\ 7(y + 2) &= 7\left[-\frac{4}{7}(x + 1)\right] \\ 7(y + 2) &= -4(x + 1) \\ 7y + 14 &= -4x - 4 \\ 4x + 7y + 14 &= -4 \\ 4x + 7y &= -4 - 14 \\ 4x + 7y &= -18 \end{aligned}$$

35. Through (–8, 1) and (0, 0)

$$m = \frac{0-1}{0-(-8)} = \frac{-1}{8} = -\frac{1}{8}$$
$$y - y_1 = m(x - x_1)$$
$$y - 0 = -\frac{1}{8}(x - 0)$$
$$y = -\frac{1}{8}x$$
$$8(y) = 8\left(-\frac{1}{8}x\right)$$
$$8y = -x$$
$$x + 8y = 0$$

37. Through (0, 0) with slope 3

$$y - y_1 = m(x - x_1)$$
$$y - 0 = 3(x - 0)$$
$$y = 3x$$
$$0 = 3x - y$$
$$3x - y = 0$$

39. Through (–6, –6) and (0, 0)

$$m = \frac{0-(-6)}{0-(-6)} = \frac{6}{6} = 1$$
$$y - y_1 = m(x - x_1)$$
$$y - 0 = 1(x - 0)$$
$$y = x$$
$$0 = x - y$$
$$x - y = 0$$

41. Slope –5, y-intercept 7

$$y = mx + b$$
$$y = -5x + 7$$
$$5x + y = 7$$

43. Through (–1, 5) and (0, –6)

$$m = \frac{-6-5}{0-(-1)} = \frac{-11}{1} = -11$$
$$y - y_1 = m(x - x_1)$$
$$y - (-6) = -11(x - 0)$$
$$y + 6 = -11x$$
$$11x + y + 6 = 0$$
$$11x + y = -6$$

45. With undefined slope, through $\left(-\frac{3}{4}, 1\right)$

When the slope is undefined, the line is vertical. On a vertical line, the x-coordinate stays the same.

$$x = -\frac{3}{4}$$

47. Through (–2, –3), perpendicular to the y-axis.
Since the y-axis is a vertical line, any line perpendicular to it is horizontal. On a horizontal line, the y-coordinate stays the same.

$$y = -3$$

49. Slope 7, through (1, 3)

$$y - y_1 = m(x - x_1)$$
$$y - 3 = 7(x - 1)$$
$$y - 3 = 7x - 7$$
$$-3 = 7x - y - 7$$
$$-3 + 7 = 7x - y$$
$$4 = 7x - y$$
$$7x - y = 4$$

51. a. (0, 3280) and (2, 4760)

$$m = \frac{4760-3280}{2-0} = \frac{1480}{2} = 740$$
$$y = 740x + 3280$$

b. In 2005, $x = 9$:

$$y = 740(9) + 3280$$
$$y = 9940 \text{ vehicles}$$

53. a. (1, 32) and (3, 96)

$$m = \frac{96-32}{3-1} = \frac{64}{2} = 32$$
$$s - s_1 = m(t - t_1)$$
$$s - 32 = 32(t - 1)$$
$$s - 32 = 32t - 32$$
$$s = 32t$$

b. $s = 32(4) = 128$
128 ft/sec

55. a. (0, 150); (6, 135)

$$m = \frac{135-150}{6-0} = \frac{-15}{6} = -2.5$$

$$y = -2.5x + 150$$

b. In 2008, $x = 18$:

$$y = -2.5(18) + 150$$
$$y = 105$$

105 thousand apparel and accessory stores

57. (10, 63) and (15, 94)

Let x = radius and y = circumference.

$$m = \frac{94-63}{15-10} = \frac{31}{5}$$

$$\begin{aligned} y - y_1 &= m(x - x_1) \\ y - 63 &= \frac{31}{5}(x-10) \\ 5(y-63) &= 5\left[\frac{31}{5}(x-10)\right] \\ 5(y-63) &= 31(x-10) \\ 5y - 315 &= 31x - 310 \\ -315 &= 31x - 5y - 310 \\ -315 + 310 &= 31x - 5y \\ -5 &= 31x - 5y \\ 31x - 5y &= -5 \end{aligned}$$

59. a. (2, 2600) and (5, 2000)

$$m = \frac{2000-2600}{5-2} = \frac{-600}{3} = -200$$

$$\begin{aligned} V - V_1 &= m(t - t_1) \\ V - 2600 &= -200(t-2) \\ V - 2600 &= -200t + 400 \\ V &= -200t + 400 + 2600 \\ V &= -200t + 3000 \end{aligned}$$

b. In 2005, $t = 10$:

$$V = -200(10) + 3000$$
$$V = 1000$$

\$1000

61. Answers may vary.

63. a. Since the slope of $y = 3x - 1$ is 3, the slope of any line parallel to it is 3.

Slope = 3, point (–1, 2)

$$\begin{aligned} y - y_1 &= m(x - x_1) \\ y - 2 &= 3(x+1) \\ y - 2 &= 3x + 3 \\ -2 &= 3x - y + 3 \\ -5 &= 3x - y \\ 3x - y &= -5 \end{aligned}$$

b. Since the slope of $y = 3x - 1$ is 3, the slope of any line perpendicular to it is m where:

$$3 \cdot m = -1$$
$$m = -\frac{1}{3}$$

Slope = $-\frac{1}{3}$, point (–1, 2)

$$\begin{aligned} y - y_1 &= m(x - x_1) \\ y - 2 &= -\frac{1}{3}(x+1) \\ -3(y-2) &= -3\left[-\frac{1}{3}(x+1)\right] \\ -3y + 6 &= x + 1 \\ 6 &= x + 3y + 1 \\ 5 &= x + 3y \\ x + 3y &= 5 \end{aligned}$$

65. $3x+2y=7$

$$2y=-3x+7$$

$$y=-\frac{3}{2}x+\frac{7}{2}$$

a. Since the slope of $3x+2y=7$ is $-\frac{3}{2}$, the slope of any line parallel to it is $-\frac{3}{2}$.

Slope $= -\frac{3}{2}$, point $(3, -5)$

$$y-y_1=m(x-x_1)$$
$$y-(-5)=-\frac{3}{2}(x-3)$$
$$y+5=-\frac{3}{2}(x-3)$$
$$2(y+5)=2\left[-\frac{3}{2}(x-3)\right]$$
$$2y+10=-3(x-3)$$
$$2y+10=-3x+9$$
$$3x+2y+10=9$$
$$3x+2y=-1$$

b. Since the slope of $3x+2y=7$ is $-\frac{3}{2}$, the slope of any line perpendicular to it is m where:

$$-\frac{3}{2}m=-1$$
$$m=\frac{2}{3}$$

Slope $= \frac{2}{3}$, point $(3, -5)$

$$y-y_1=m(x-x_1)$$
$$y-(-5)=\frac{2}{3}(x-3)$$
$$y+5=\frac{2}{3}(x-3)$$
$$3(y+5)=3\left[\frac{2}{3}(x-3)\right]$$
$$3y+15=2(x-3)$$
$$3y+15=2x-6$$
$$15=2x-3y-6$$
$$21=2x-3y$$
$$2x-3y=21$$

67. $y=2x-6$

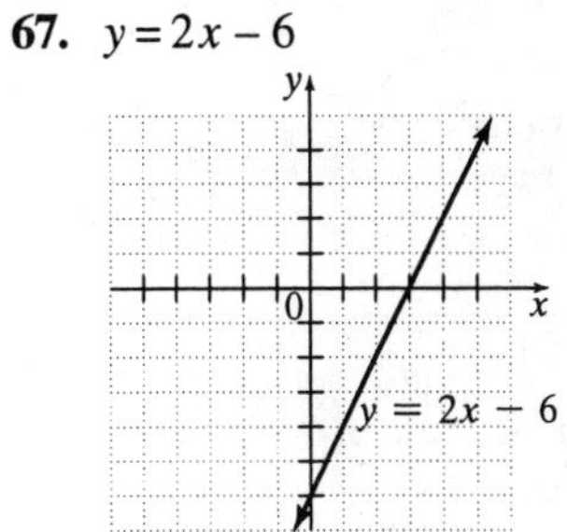

69. $x+3y=5$

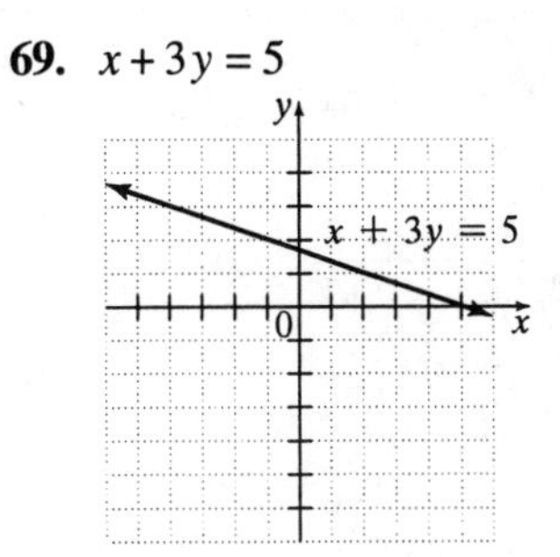

71. $y=-2$

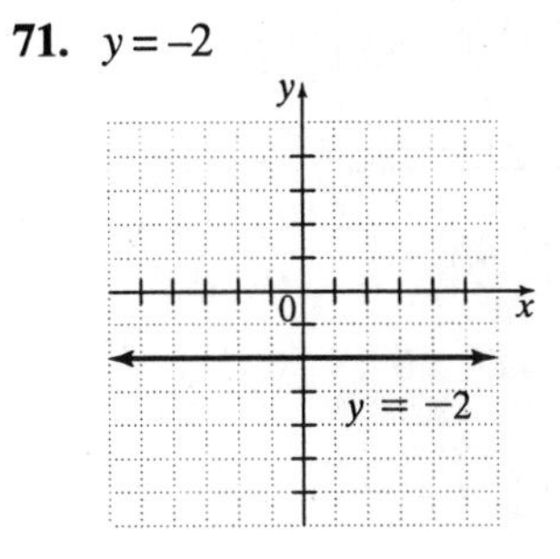

Section 7.3

Calculator Explorations

1. $y = x^2 + 3x - 2$

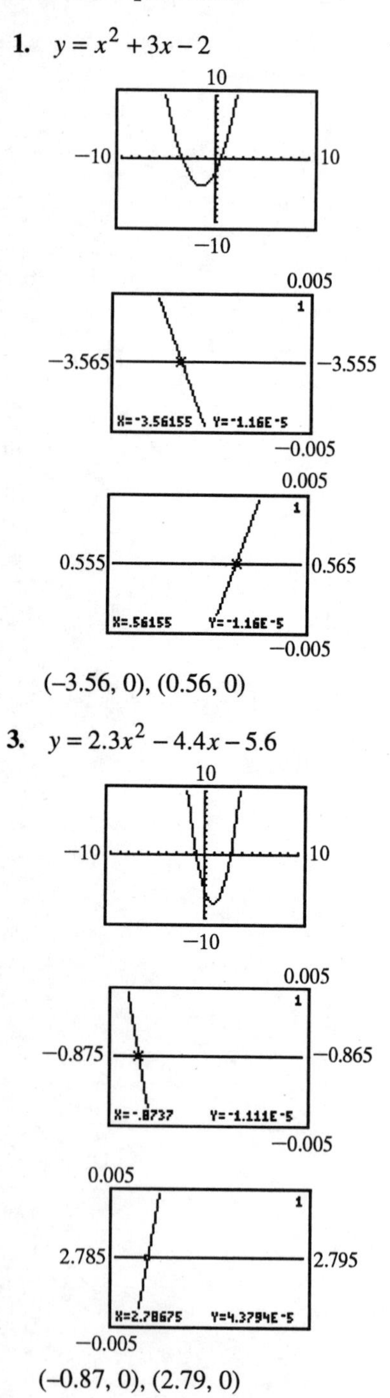

(−3.56, 0), (0.56, 0)

3. $y = 2.3x^2 - 4.4x - 5.6$

(−0.87, 0), (2.79, 0)

5. $y = 2|x| - 1.3$

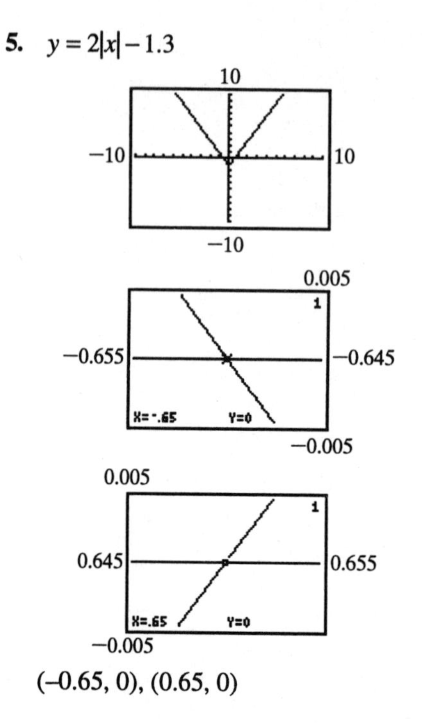

(−0.65, 0), (0.65, 0)

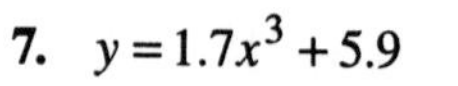

7. $y = 1.7x^3 + 5.9$

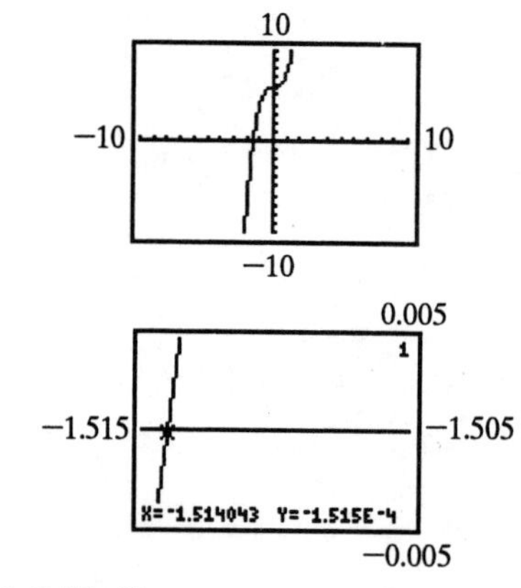

(−1.51, 0)

Exercise Set 7.3

For Exercises 1 through 7, plot the ordered pair solutions and connect with a smooth curve.

1. $y = x^2 + 2$

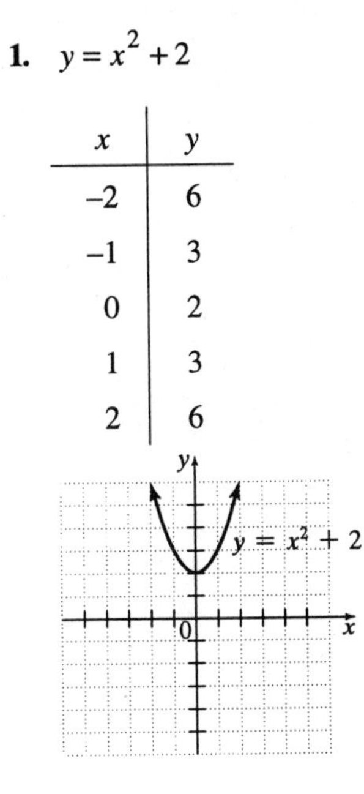

x	y
–2	6
–1	3
0	2
1	3
2	6

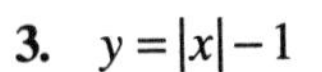

3. $y = |x| - 1$

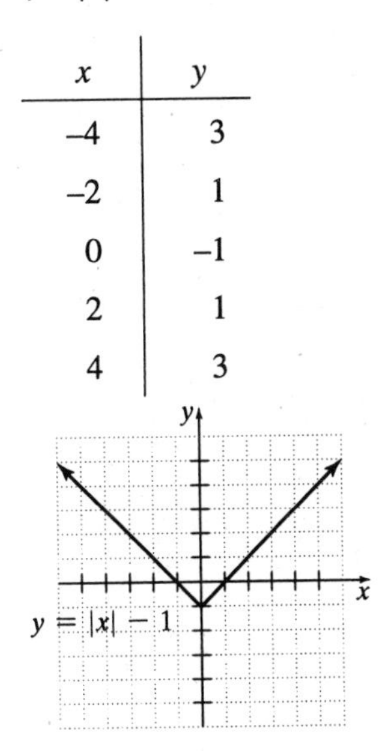

x	y
–4	3
–2	1
0	–1
2	1
4	3

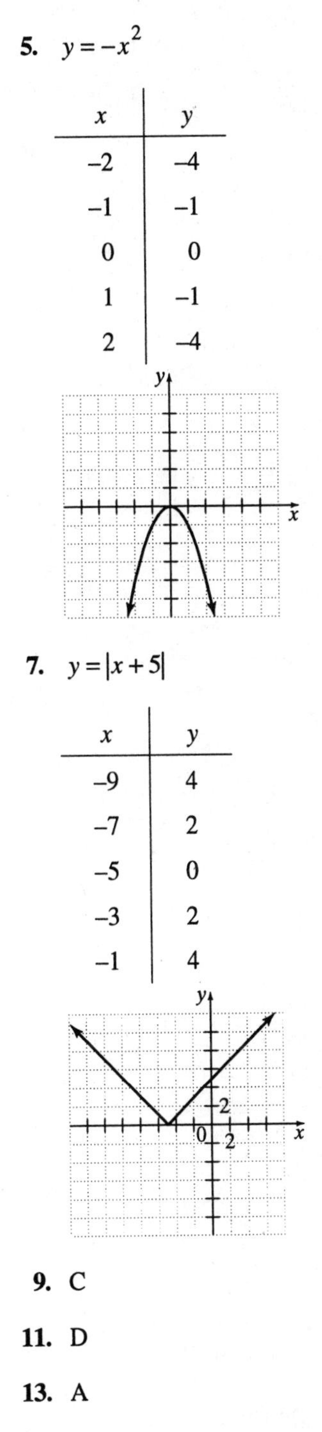

5. $y = -x^2$

x	y
–2	–4
–1	–1
0	0
1	–1
2	–4

7. $y = |x + 5|$

x	y
–9	4
–7	2
–5	0
–3	2
–1	4

9. C

11. D

13. A

15. (0, 1), (0, –1); (–2, 0), (2, 0)

17. $(2, 0); \left(\frac{2}{3}, -2\right)$

19. (2, any real number)

21. There is no such point.

23. $(2, -1)$

25. Linear

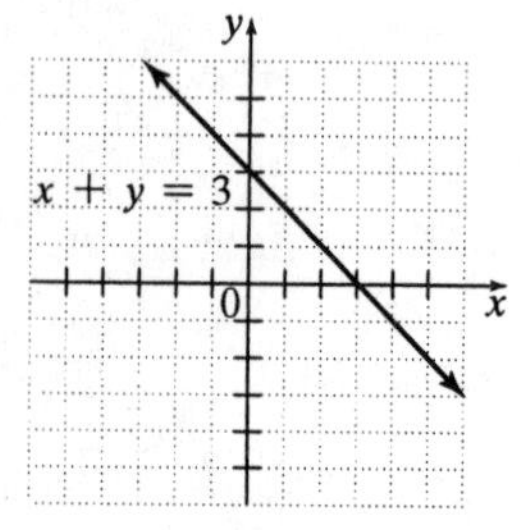

27. Linear

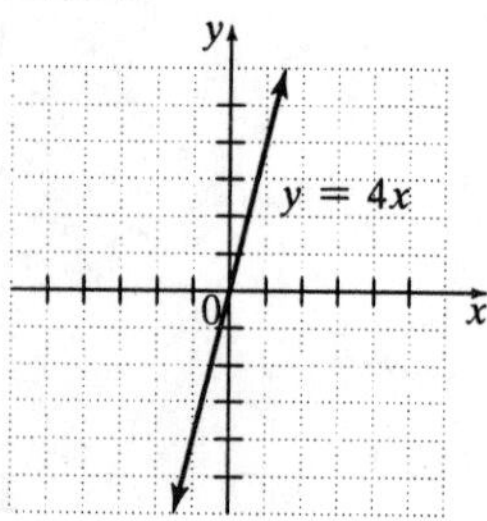

29. Linear

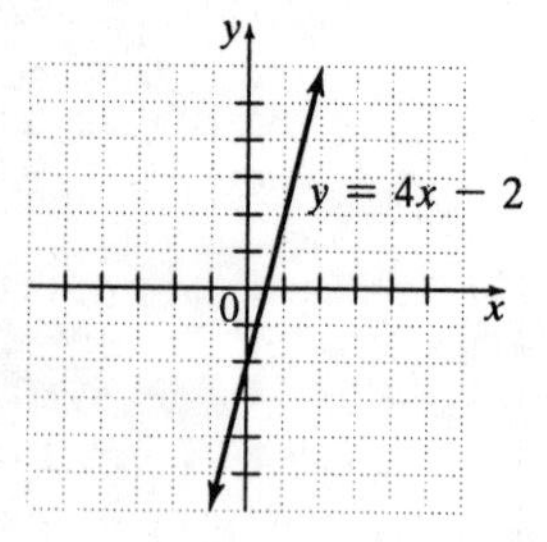

31. Not linear

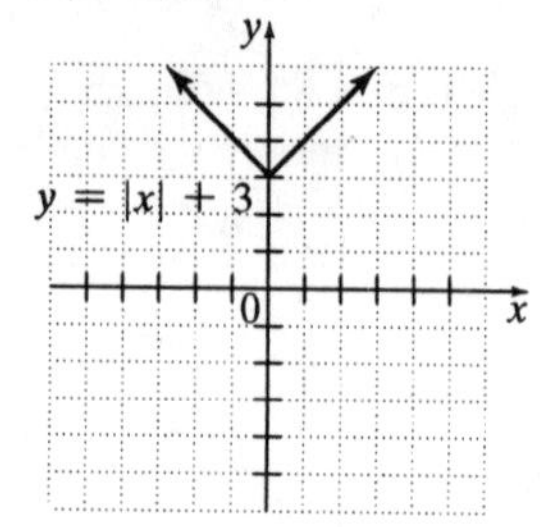

33. Linear

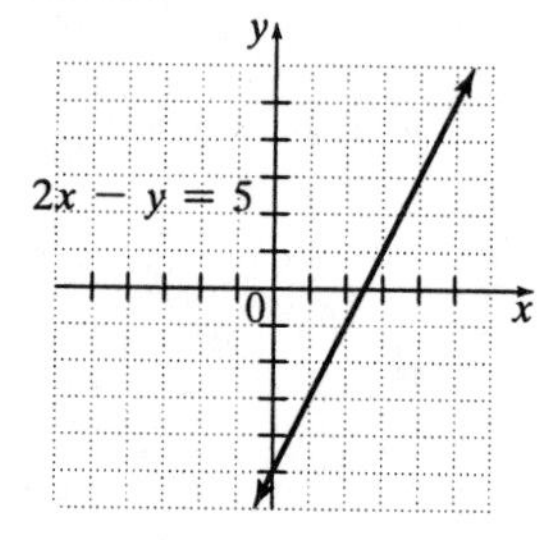

35. Not linear

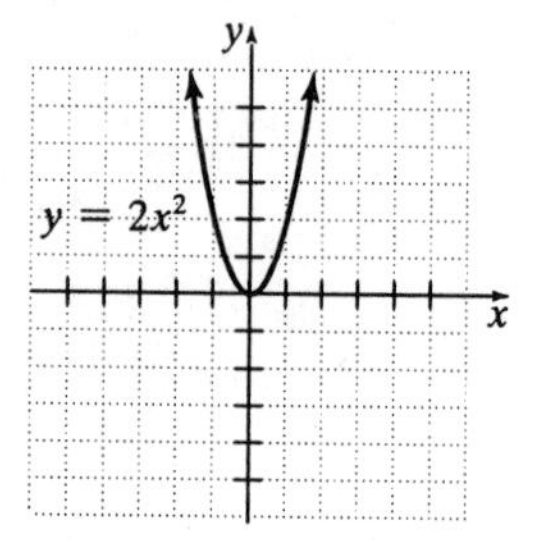

37. Not linear

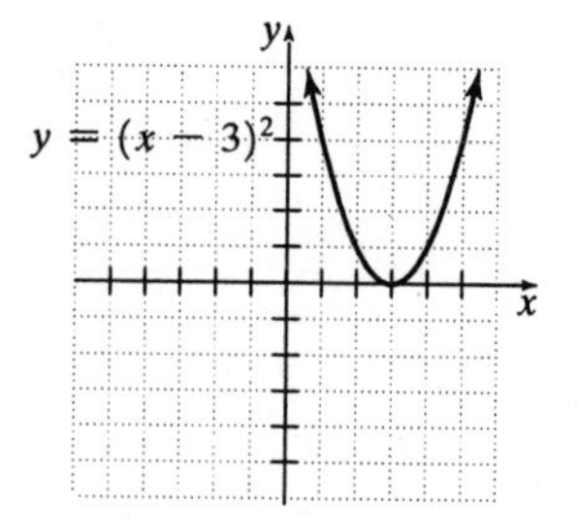

39. Linear

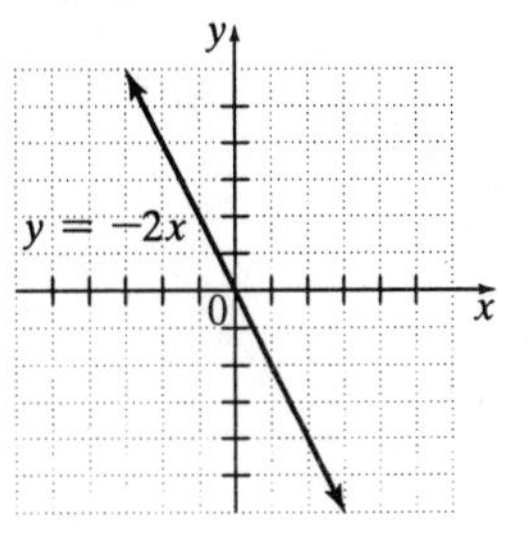

41. Linear

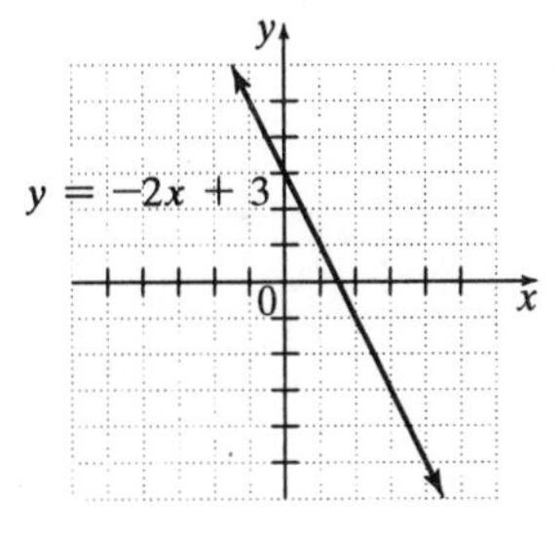

43. Not Linear

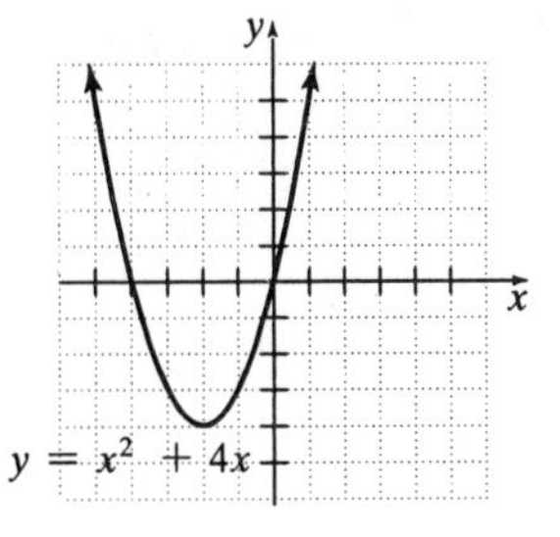

45. 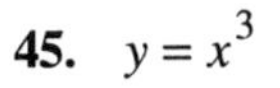 $y = x^3$

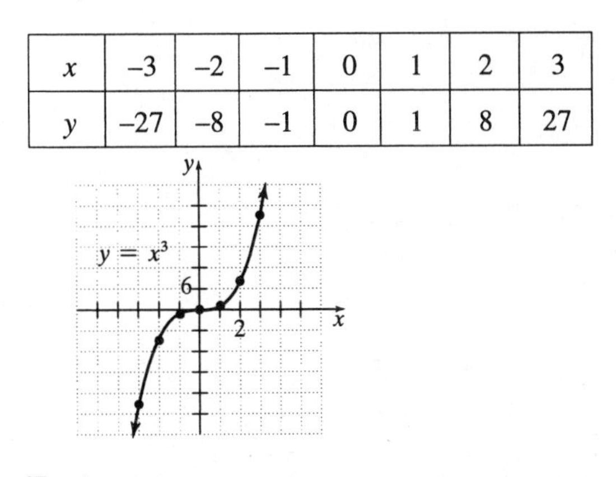

x	−3	−2	−1	0	1	2	3
y	−27	−8	−1	0	1	8	27

47. Answers may vary.

49. Answers may vary.

51.
$$\begin{aligned} x^2 - 3x + 1 &= (5)^2 - 3(5) + 1 \\ &= 25 - 15 + 1 \\ &= 11 \end{aligned}$$

53.
$$\begin{aligned} x^2 - 3x + 1 &= (-3)^2 - 3(-3) + 1 \\ &= 9 + 9 + 1 \\ &= 19 \end{aligned}$$

55. No

57. Yes

Exercise Set 7.4

1. {(2, 4), (0, 0), (−7, 10), (10, −7)}
Domain: (−7, 0, 2, 10}
Range: {−7, 0, 4, 10}

3. {(0, −2), (1, −2), (5, −2)}
Domain: {0, 1, 5}
Range: {−2}

5. Yes, because each x-value is assigned to only one y-value.

7. No, because the x-value −1 is paired with more than one y-value.

9. No, because the vertical line $x = 1$ would intersect more than one point.

11. Yes, because there is no vertical line that would intersect more than one point.

13. Yes, because there is no vertical line that would intersect more than one point.

15. No, because there is a vertical line that would intersect more than one point.

17. No, because there is a vertical line that would intersect more than one point.

19. Yes, because there is no vertical line that would intersect more than one point.

21. $y = x + 1$
Yes, it is a function. Each x-value will produce exactly one y-value.

23. $y - x = 7$
Yes, it is a function. Each x-value will produce exactly one y-value.

25. $y = 6$
Yes, it is a function. Each x-value will produce exactly one y-value.

27. $x = -2$
No, it is not a function.
The ordered pairs (–2, 0) and (–2, 1) make the equation true. Therefore, an x-value has more than one y-value, so it is not a function.

29. $y < 2x + 1$
No, it is not a function. A vertical line would pass through more than one point in the shaded portion of the graph.

31. 5:20 A.M.

33. Answers may vary.

35. $4.75 per hour

37. 2002

39. Yes; answers may vary.

41. $f(x) = 2x - 5$

a. $f(-2) = 2(-2) - 5 = -4 - 5 = -9$

b. $f(0) = 2(0) - 5 = 0 - 5 = -5$

c. $f(3) = 2(3) - 5 = 6 - 5 = 1$

43. $f(x) = x^2 + 2$

a. $f(-2) = (-2)^2 + 2 = 4 + 2 = 6$

b. $f(0) = (0)^2 + 2 = 0 + 2 = 2$

c. $f(3) = (3)^2 + 2 = 9 + 2 = 11$

45. $f(x) = x^3$

a. $f(-2) = (-2)^3 = -8$

b. $f(0) = (0)^3 = 0$

c. $f(3) = (3)^3 = 27$

47. $f(x) = |x|$

a. $f(-2) = |-2| = 2$

b. $f(0) = |0| = 0$

c. $f(3) = |3| = 3$

49. $h(x) = 5x$

a. $h(-1) = 5(-1) = -5$

b. $h(0) = 5(0) = 0$

c. $h(4) = 5(4) = 20$

51. $h(x) = 2x^2 + 3$

a.
$$\begin{aligned} h(-1) &= 2(-1)^2 + 3 \\ &= 2(1) + 3 \\ &= 2 + 3 \\ &= 5 \end{aligned}$$

b.
$$\begin{aligned} h(0) &= 2(0)^2 + 3 \\ &= 2(0) + 3 \\ &= 0 + 3 \\ &= 3 \end{aligned}$$

c.
$$\begin{aligned} h(4) &= 2(4)^2 + 3 \\ &= 2(16) + 3 \\ &= 32 + 3 \\ &= 35 \end{aligned}$$

53. $h(x) = -x^2 - 2x + 3$

a.
$$\begin{aligned} h(-1) &= -(-1)^2 - 2(-1) + 3 \\ &= -1 + 2 + 3 \\ &= 4 \end{aligned}$$

b. $h(0) = -0^2 - 2(0) + 3 = 0 - 0 + 3 = 3$

c. $h(4) = -4^2 - 2(4) + 3$
$= -16 - 8 + 3$
$= -21$

55. $h(x) = 6$

a. $h(-1) = 6$

b. $h(0) = 6$

c. $h(4) = 6$

57. $f(x) = 3x - 7$
The domain is all real numbers.

59. $h(x) = \dfrac{1}{x+5}$
The domain is all real numbers except –5.

61. $g(x) = |x + 1|$
The domain is all real numbers.

63. Domain: all real numbers
Range: $y \geq -4$

65. Domain: all real numbers
Range: all real numbers

67. Domain: all real numbers
Range: $y = 2$

69. $H(x) = 2.59x + 47.24$

a. $H(46) = 2.59(46) + 47.24 = 166.38$ cm

b. $H(39) = 2.59(39) + 47.24 = 148.25$ cm

71. Answers may vary.

73. $f(x) = x + 7$

75. $(3, 0)$

77. $(-3, -3)$

79. $g(x) = -3x + 12$

a. $g(s) = -3(s) + 12 = -3s + 12$

b. $g(r) = -3(r) + 12 = -3r + 12$

81. $f(x) = x^2 - 12$

a. $f(12) = (12)^2 - 12 = 144 - 12 = 132$

b. $f(a) = (a)^2 - 12 = a^2 - 12$

Chapter 7 Review Exercises

1. $3x + y = 7$
$y = -3x + 7$
$m = -3$; $(0, 7)$

2. $x - 6y = -1$
$-6y = -x - 1$
$y = \frac{1}{6}x + \frac{1}{6}$
$m = \frac{1}{6}$; $\left(0, \frac{1}{6}\right)$

3. $y = 2$
$m = 0$; $(0, 2)$

4. $x = -5$
undefined slope; no y-intercept

5. $x - y = -6$
$-y = -x - 6$
$y = x + 6$
$m = 1$
$x + y = 3$
$y = -x + 3$
$m = -1$
Since the product of the slopes is –1, the lines are perpendicular.

6. $3x + y = 7$
$y = -3x + 7$
$m = -3$; y-intercept = $(0, 7)$
$-3x - y = 10$
$y = -3x - 10$
$m = -3$; y-intercept = $(0, -10)$
Since the slopes are the same and the y-intercepts are different, the lines are parallel.

7. $y = 4x + \frac{1}{2}$
$m = 4$
$4x + 2y = 1$
$2y = -4x + 1$
$y = -2x + \frac{1}{2}$
$m = -2$
Since the slopes are not the same and their product is not -1, the lines are neither parallel nor perpendicular.

8. $y = -5x + \frac{1}{2}$

9. $y = \frac{2}{3}x + 6$

10. $y = -3x$
Slope = -3
y-intercept = (0, 0)

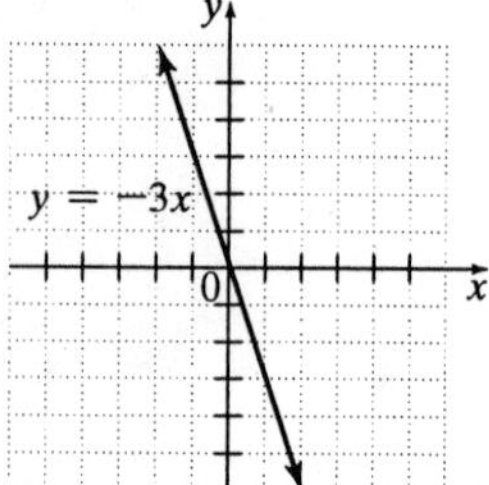

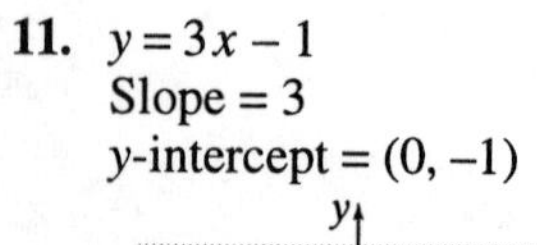

11. $y = 3x - 1$
Slope = 3
y-intercept = (0, −1)

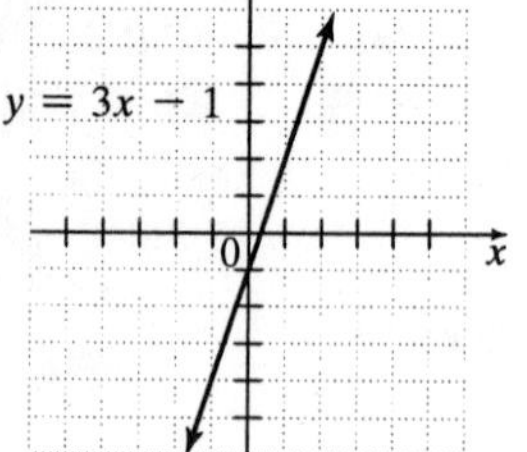

12. $-x + 2y = 8$
$2y = x + 8$
$y = \frac{1}{2}x + 4$
Slope = $\frac{1}{2}$
y-intercept = (0, 4)

13. $5x - 3y = 15$
$-3y = -5x + 15$
$y = \frac{5}{3}x - 5$
Slope = $\frac{5}{3}$
y-intercept = (0, −5)

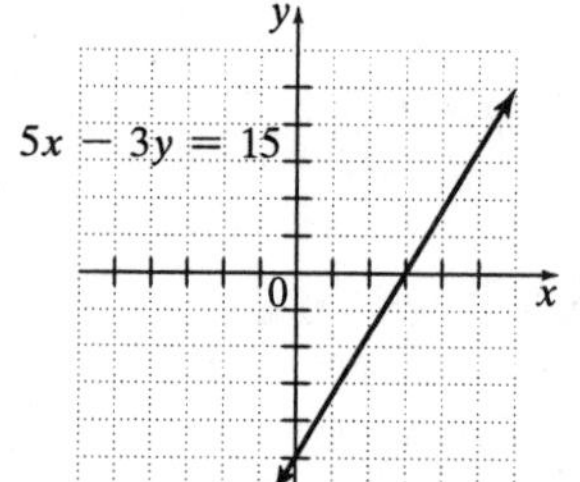

14. D

15. C

16. A

17. B

18. $m = 4$, (2, 0)
$y - y_1 = m(x - x_1)$
$y - 0 = 4(x - 2)$
$y = 4x - 8$
$0 = 4x - y - 8$
$8 = 4x - y$
$4x - y = 8$

19. $m = -3$, $(0, -5)$
$$y - y_1 = m(x - x_1)$$
$$y - (-5) = -3(x - 0)$$
$$y + 5 = -3(x - 0)$$
$$y + 5 = -3x$$
$$3x + y + 5 = 0$$
$$3x + y = -5$$

20. $m = \frac{1}{2}$, $\left(0, -\frac{7}{2}\right)$
$$y - y_1 = m(x - x_1)$$
$$y - \left(-\frac{7}{2}\right) = \frac{1}{2}(x - 0)$$
$$y + \frac{7}{2} = \frac{1}{2}x$$
$$2\left(y + \frac{7}{2}\right) = 2\left(\frac{1}{2}x\right)$$
$$2y + 7 = x$$
$$7 = x - 2y$$
$$x - 2y = 7$$

21. $m = 0$, $(-2, -3)$
$$y - y_1 = m(x - x_1)$$
$$y - (-3) = 0[x - (-2)]$$
$$y + 3 = 0(x + 2)$$
$$y + 3 = 0$$
$$y = -3$$

22. $m = 0$, $(0, 0)$
Since the slope is 0, the line is a horizontal line. On a horizontal line, the y-coordinate stays the same.
$y = 0$

23. $m = -6$, $(2, -1)$
$$y - y_1 = m(x - x_1)$$
$$y - (-1) = -6(x - 2)$$
$$y + 1 = -6(x - 2)$$
$$y + 1 = -6x + 12$$
$$6x + y + 1 = 12$$
$$6x + y = 11$$

24. $m = 12$, $\left(\frac{1}{2}, 5\right)$
$$y - y_1 = m(x - x_1)$$
$$y - 5 = 12\left(x - \frac{1}{2}\right)$$
$$y - 5 = 12x - 6$$
$$-5 = 12x - y - 6$$
$$-5 + 6 = 12x - y$$
$$1 = 12x - y$$
$$12x - y = 1$$

25. $(0, 6)$ and $(6, 0)$
$$m = \frac{0 - 6}{6 - 0} = \frac{-6}{6} = -1$$
$$y - y_1 = m(x - x_1)$$
$$y - 6 = -1(x - 0)$$
$$y - 6 = -x$$
$$x + y - 6 = 0$$
$$x + y = 6$$

26. $(0, -4)$ and $(-8, 0)$
$$m = \frac{0 - (-4)}{-8 - 0} = \frac{4}{-8} = -\frac{1}{2}$$
$$y - y_1 = m(x - x_1)$$
$$y - (-4) = -\frac{1}{2}(x - 0)$$
$$y + 4 = -\frac{1}{2}x$$
$$2(y + 4) = 2\left(-\frac{1}{2}x\right)$$
$$2y + 8 = -x$$
$$x + 2y + 8 = 0$$
$$x + 2y = -8$$

27. Vertical line, through $(5, 7)$
On a vertical line, the x-coordinate stays the same.
$x = 5$

28. Horizontal line, through $(-6, 8)$
On a horizontal line, the y-coordinate stays the same.
$y = 8$

29. Through (6, 0), perpendicular to $y = 8$
Since $y = 8$ is a horizontal line, any line perpendicular to it is vertical. On a vertical line, the x-coordinate stays the same.
$x = 6$

30. Through (10, 12), perpendicular to $x = -2$
Since $x = -2$ is a vertical line, any line perpendicular to it is horizontal. On a horizontal line, the y-coordinate stays the same.
$y = 12$

31. a. $m = -3$; point (5, 0)

$$y - 0 = -3(x - 5)$$
$$y = -3x + 15$$
$$3x + y = 15$$

b. $m = \frac{1}{3}$; point (5, 0)

$$y - 0 = \frac{1}{3}(x - 5)$$
$$y = \frac{1}{3}x - \frac{5}{3}$$
$$3y = x - 5$$
$$x - 3y = 5$$

32.

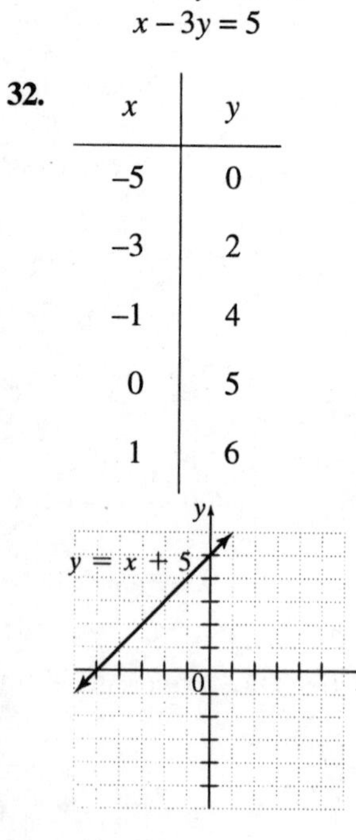

x	y
−5	0
−3	2
−1	4
0	5
1	6

33.

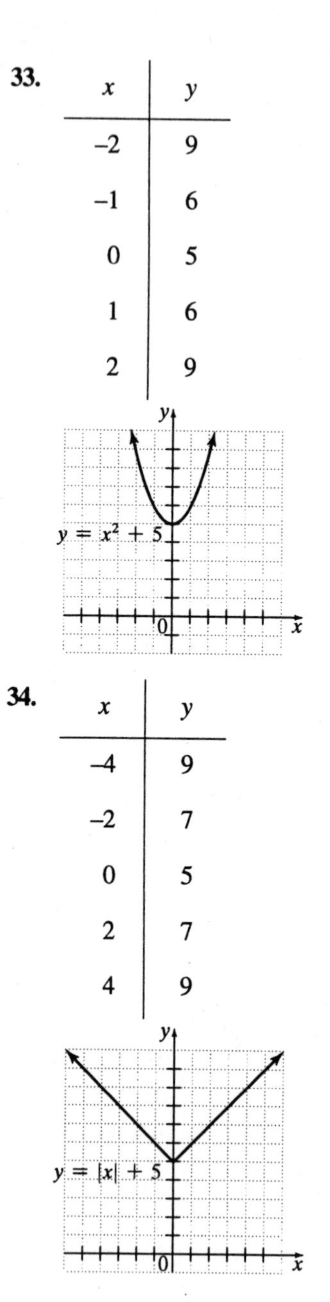

x	y
−2	9
−1	6
0	5
1	6
2	9

34.

x	y
−4	9
−2	7
0	5
2	7
4	9

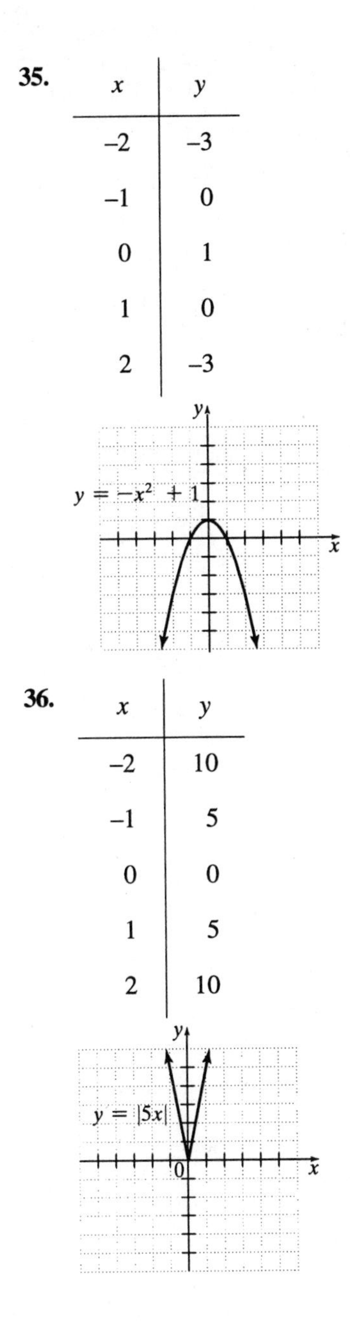

35.

x	y
–2	–3
–1	0
0	1
1	0
2	–3

36.

x	y
–2	10
–1	5
0	0
1	5
2	10

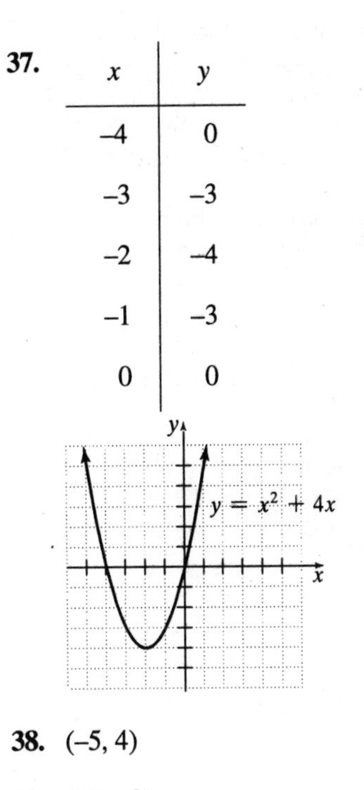

37.

x	y
–4	0
–3	–3
–2	–4
–1	–3
0	0

38. (–5, 4)

39. (–1, –3)

40. (–5, 4)

41. (6, –1)

42. No, because $x = 7$ is paired with more than one y-value.

43. Yes, because every x-value is paired with exactly one value.

44. Yes, because each x-value will produce exactly one y-value.

45. Yes, because each x-value will produce exactly one y-value.

46. No, because $x = 2$ is paired with more than one y-value.

47. Yes, because each x-value will produce exactly one y-value.

48. No, because a vertical line will intersect more than one point in the shaded region.

49. No, because there is a vertical line that will intersect the graph in more than one point.

50. Yes, because there is no vertical line that would intersect the graph in more than one point.

51. $f(x) = -2x + 6$

a. $f(0) = -2(0) + 6 = 0 + 6 = 6$

b. $f(-2) = -2(-2) + 6 = 4 + 6 = 10$

c. $f\left(\frac{1}{2}\right) = -2\left(\frac{1}{2}\right) + 6 = -1 + 6 = 5$

52. $h(x) = -5 - 3x$

a. $h(2) = -5 - 3(2) = -5 - 6 = -11$

b. $h(-3) = -5 - 3(-3) = -5 + 9 = 4$

c. $h(0) = -5 - 3(0) = -5 - 0 = -5$

53. $g(x) = x^2 + 12x$

a. $g(3) = 3^2 + 12(3) = 9 + 36 = 45$

b. $g(-5) = (-5)^2 + 12(-5) = 25 - 60 = -35$

c. $g(0) = 0^2 + 12(0) = 0$

54. $h(x) = 6 - |x|$

a. $h(-1) = 6 - |-1| = 6 - 1 = 5$

b. $h(1) = 6 - |1| = 6 - 1 = 5$

c. $h(-4) = 6 - |-4| = 6 - 4 = 2$

55. All real numbers

56. All real numbers except 2

57. Domain: $-3 \le x \le 5$
Range: $-4 \le y \le 2$

58. Domain: all real numbers
Range: $y \ge 0$

59. Domain: $x = 3$
Range: all real numbers

60. Domain: all real numbers
Range: $y \le 2$

Chapter 7 Test

1. $7x - 3y = 2$

$$-3y = -7x + 2$$

$$y = \frac{7}{3}x - \frac{2}{3}$$

$$m = \frac{7}{3};\ \left(0,\ -\frac{2}{3}\right)$$

2. $y = 2x - 6$

$$m = 2$$

$$-4x = 2y$$

$$y = -2x$$

$$m = -2$$

neither

3. Slope $-\frac{1}{4}$, through (2, 2)

$$y - y_1 = m(x - x_1)$$

$$y - 2 = -\frac{1}{4}(x - 2)$$

$$-4(y - 2) = -4\left(-\frac{1}{4}(x - 2)\right)$$

$$-4y + 8 = x - 2$$

$$10 = x + 4y$$

$$x + 4y = 10$$

4. Through the origin and (6, –7);
(0, 0) and (6, –7)

$$m = \frac{-7-0}{6-0} = -\frac{7}{6}$$
$$y - y_1 = m(x - x_1)$$
$$y - 0 = -\frac{7}{6}(x - 0)$$
$$y = -\frac{7}{6}x$$
$$6(y) = 6\left(-\frac{7}{6}x\right)$$
$$6y = -7x$$
$$7x + 6y = 0$$

5. Through (2, –5) and (1, 3)

$$m = \frac{3-(-5)}{1-2} = \frac{3+5}{-1} = \frac{8}{-1} = -8$$
$$y - y_1 = m(x - x_1)$$
$$y - (-5) = -8(x - 2)$$
$$y + 5 = -8x + 16$$
$$8x + y + 5 = 16$$
$$8x + y = 16 - 5$$
$$8x + y = 11$$

6. Through (–5, –1), parallel to $x = 7$;
Since $x = 7$ is a vertical line, any line parallel to it would be vertical. On a vertical line, the x-coordinate stays the same.
$x = -5$

7. Slope $\frac{1}{8}$, y-intercept 12

$$y - y_1 = m(x - x_1)$$
$$y - 12 = \frac{1}{8}(x - 0)$$
$$y - 12 = \frac{1}{8}x$$
$$8(y - 12) = 8\left(\frac{1}{8}x\right)$$
$$8y - 96 = x$$
$$-96 = x - 8y$$
$$x - 8y = -96$$

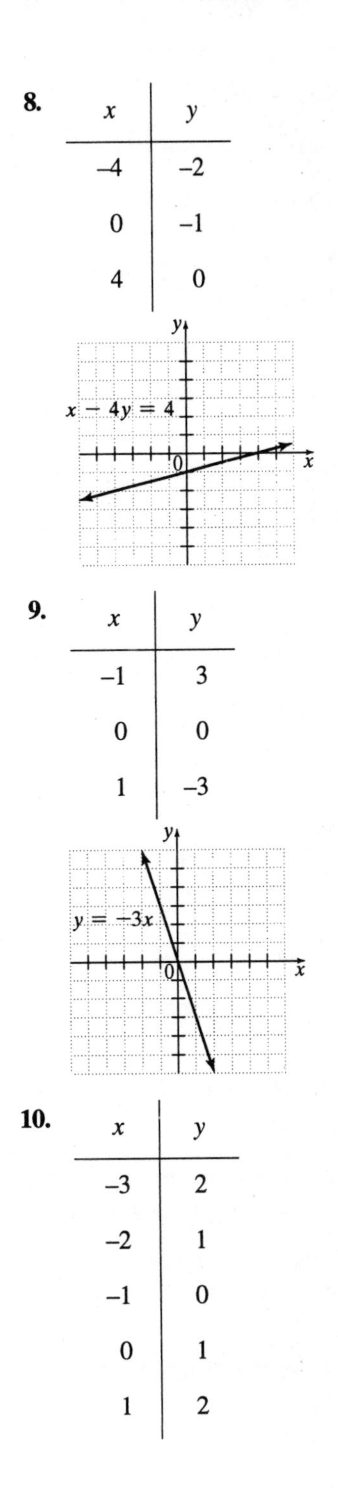

8.

x	y
–4	–2
0	–1
4	0

9.

x	y
–1	3
0	0
1	–3

10.

x	y
–3	2
–2	1
–1	0
0	1
1	2

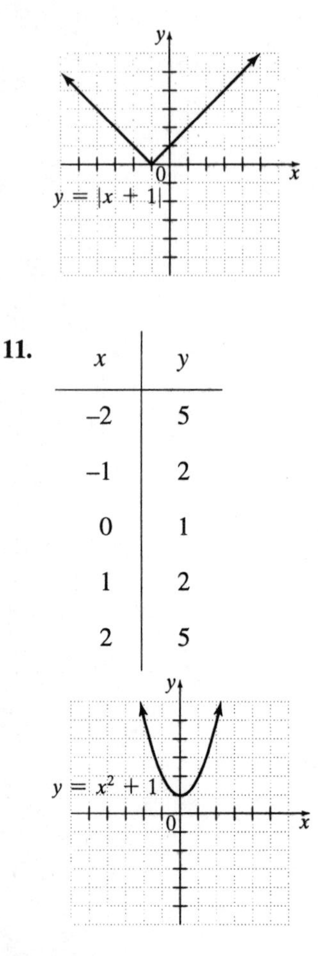

11.

x	y
−2	5
−1	2
0	1
1	2
2	5

12. Yes, because each x-value is paired with exactly one y-value.

13. Yes, because each x-value is paired with exactly one y-value.

14. Yes, because no vertical line would intersect the graph in more than one point.

15. No, because there is a vertical line that will intersect the graph in more than one point.

16. No, because there is a vertical line that will intersect the graph in more than one point.

17. $f(x) = 2x - 4$

a. $f(-2) = 2(-2) - 4 = -4 - 4 = -8$

b. $f(0.2) = 2(0.2) - 4 = 0.4 - 4 = -3.6$

c. $f(0) = 2(0) - 4 = 0 - 4 = -4$

18. $h(x) = x^3 - x$

a. $h(-1) = (-1)^3 - (-1) = -1 + 1 = 0$

b. $h(0) = 0^3 - 0 = 0 - 0 = 0$

c. $h(4) = 4^3 - 4 = 64 - 4 = 60$

19. $g(x) = 6$

a. $g(0) = 6$

b. $g(a) = 6$

c. $g(242) = 6$

20. All real numbers except −1

21. Domain: all real numbers
Range: $y \leq 4$

22. Domain: all real numbers
Range: all real numbers

Chapter 8

Section 8.1

Calculator Explorations

1. $\begin{cases} y = -2.68x + 1.21 \\ y = 5.22x - 1.68 \end{cases}$

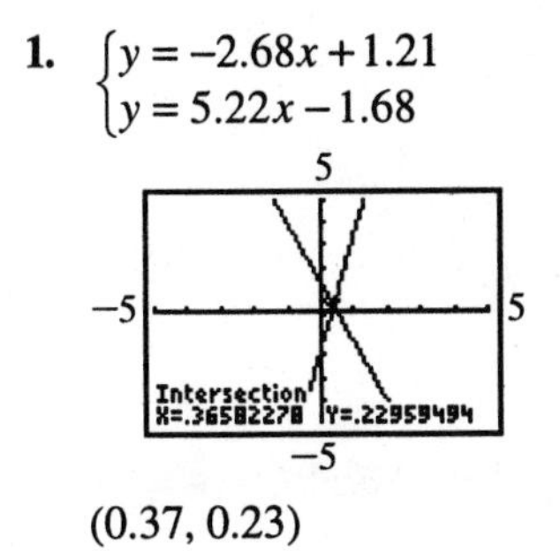

(0.37, 0.23)

3. $\begin{cases} 4.3x - 2.9y = 5.6 \\ 8.1x + 7.6y = -14.1 \end{cases}$

First, solve each equation for *y*.

$$\begin{cases} y = \dfrac{4.3x - 5.6}{2.9} \\ y = \dfrac{-8.1x - 14.1}{7.6} \end{cases}$$

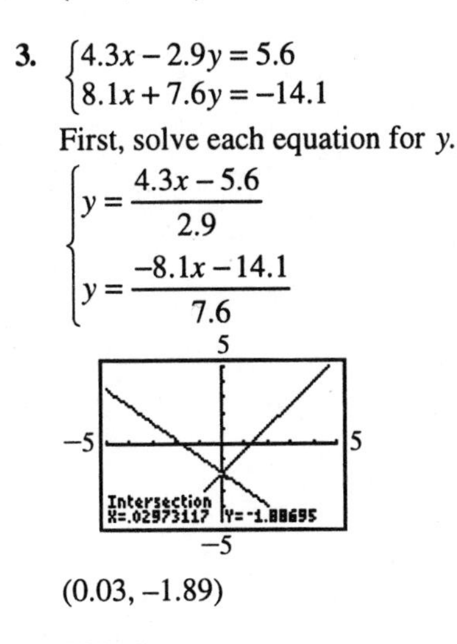

(0.03, −1.89)

Mental Math

1. 1 solution, (−1, 3)

2. no solution

3. Infinite number of solutions

4. 1 solution, (3, 4)

5. no solution

6. Infinite number of solutions

7. 1 solution, (3, 2)

8. 1 solution, (0 −3)

Exercise Set 8.1

1. $\begin{cases} x + y = 8 \\ 3x + 2y = 21 \end{cases}$

a. (2, 4)

$x + y = 8$
$2 + 4 \stackrel{?}{=} 8$
$6 = 8$ False

$3x + 2y = 21$
$3(2) + 2(4) \stackrel{?}{=} 21$
$6 + 8 \stackrel{?}{=} 21$
$14 = 21$ False

(2, 4) is not a solution.

b. (5, 3)

$x + y = 8$
$5 + 3 \stackrel{?}{=} 8$
$8 = 8$ True

$3x + 2y = 21$
$3(5) + 2(3) \stackrel{?}{=} 21$
$15 + 6 \stackrel{?}{=} 21$
$21 = 21$ True

(5, 3) is a solution.

c. (1, 9)

$x + y = 8$
$1 + 9 \stackrel{?}{=} 8$
$10 = 8$ False

$3x + 2y = 21$
$3(1) + 2(9) \stackrel{?}{=} 21$
$3 + 18 \stackrel{?}{=} 21$
$21 = 21$ True

(1, 9) is not a solution.

3. $\begin{cases} 3x - y = 5 \\ x + 2y = 11 \end{cases}$

a. (2, –1)

$$\begin{aligned} 3x - y &= 5 \\ 3(2) - (-1) &\stackrel{?}{=} 5 \\ 6 + 1 &\stackrel{?}{=} 5 \\ 7 &= 5 \text{ False} \end{aligned}$$

$$\begin{aligned} x + 2y &= 11 \\ 2 + 2(-1) &\stackrel{?}{=} 11 \\ 2 - 2 &\stackrel{?}{=} 11 \\ 0 &= 11 \text{ False} \end{aligned}$$

(2, –1) is not a solution.

b. (3, 4)

$$\begin{aligned} 3x - y &= 5 \\ 3(3) - 4 &\stackrel{?}{=} 5 \\ 9 - 4 &\stackrel{?}{=} 5 \\ 5 &= 5 \text{ True} \end{aligned}$$

$$\begin{aligned} x + 2y &= 11 \\ 3 + 2(4) &\stackrel{?}{=} 11 \\ 3 + 8 &\stackrel{?}{=} 11 \\ 11 &= 11 \text{ True} \end{aligned}$$

(3, 4) is a solution.

c. (0, –5)

$$\begin{aligned} 3x - y &= 5 \\ 3(0) - (-5) &\stackrel{?}{=} 5 \\ 0 + 5 &\stackrel{?}{=} 5 \\ 5 &= 5 \text{ True} \end{aligned}$$

$$\begin{aligned} x + 2y &= 11 \\ 0 + 2(-5) &\stackrel{?}{=} 11 \\ -10 &\stackrel{?}{=} 11 \\ -10 &= 11 \text{ False} \end{aligned}$$

(0, –5) is not a solution.

5. $\begin{cases} 2y = 4x \\ 2x - y = 0 \end{cases}$

a. (–3, –6)

$$\begin{aligned} 2y &= 4x \\ 2(-6) &\stackrel{?}{=} 4(-3) \\ -12 &= -12 \text{ True} \end{aligned}$$

$$\begin{aligned} 2x - y &= 0 \\ 2(-3) - (-6) &\stackrel{?}{=} 0 \\ -6 + 6 &\stackrel{?}{=} 0 \\ 0 &= 0 \text{ True} \end{aligned}$$

(–3, –6) is a solution.

b. (0, 0)

$$\begin{aligned} 2y &= 4x \\ 2(0) &\stackrel{?}{=} 4(0) \\ 0 &= 0 \text{ True} \end{aligned}$$

$$\begin{aligned} 2x - y &= 0 \\ 2(0) - 0 &\stackrel{?}{=} 0 \\ 0 &= 0 \text{ True} \end{aligned}$$

(0, 0) is a solution.

c. (1, 2)

$$\begin{aligned} 2y &= 4x \\ 2(2) &\stackrel{?}{=} 4(1) \\ 4 &= 4 \text{ True} \end{aligned}$$

$$\begin{aligned} 2x - y &= 0 \\ 2(1) - 2 &\stackrel{?}{=} 0 \\ 2 - 2 &\stackrel{?}{=} 0 \\ 0 &= 0 \text{ True} \end{aligned}$$

(1, 2) is a solution.

7. Answers may vary.

9. $\begin{cases} y = x + 1 \\ y = 2x - 1 \end{cases}$

Graph each linear equation on a single set of axes.

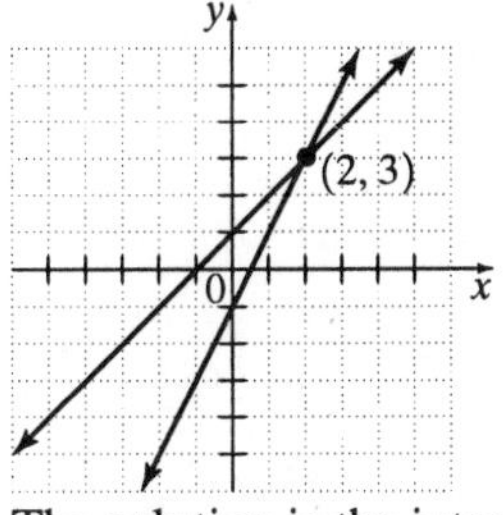

The solution is the intersection point of the two lines, (2, 3). Since this system has only one solution, it is consistent and independent.

11. $\begin{cases} 2x + y = 0 \\ 3x + y = 1 \end{cases}$

Graph each linear equation on a single set of axes.

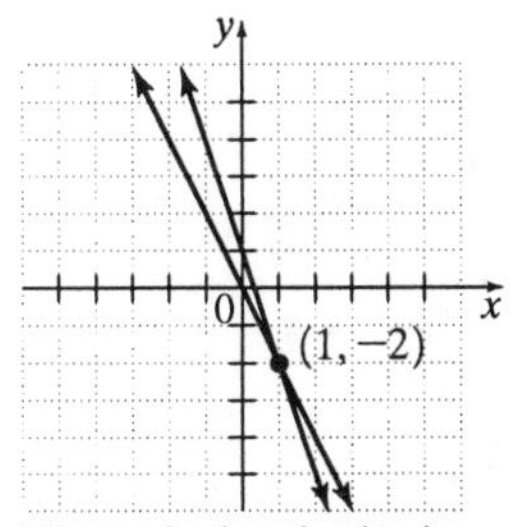

The solution is the intersection point of the two lines, (1, –2). Since this system has only one solution, it is consistent and independent.

13. $\begin{cases} y = -x - 1 \\ y = 2x + 5 \end{cases}$

Graph each linear equation on a single set of axes.

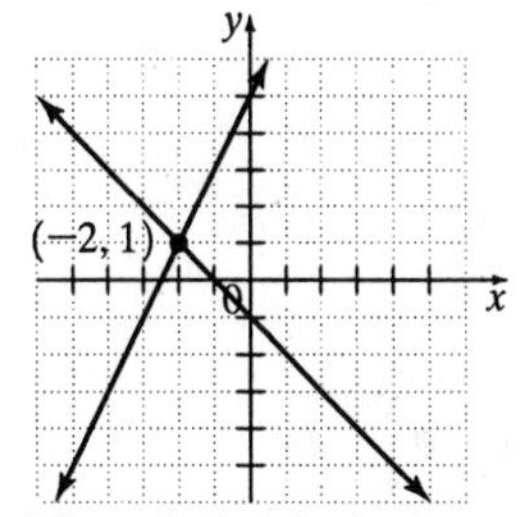

The solution is the intersection point of the two lines, (–2, 1). Since this system has only one solution, it is consistent and independent.

15. $\begin{cases} 2x - y = 6 \\ y = 2 \end{cases}$

Graph each linear equation on a single set of axes.

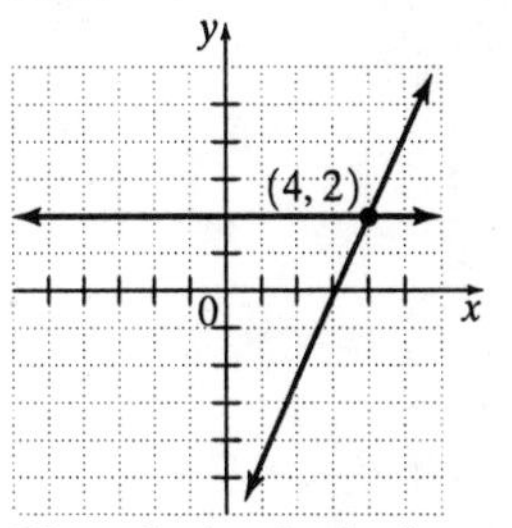

The solution is the intersection point of the two lines, (4, 2). Since this system has only one solution, it is consistent and independent.

17. $\begin{cases} x+y=5 \\ x+y=6 \end{cases}$

Graph each linear equation on a single set of axes.

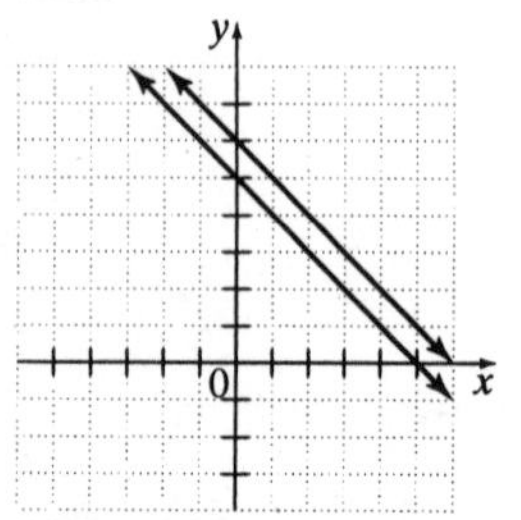

Since the lines are parallel, the system has no solution. The system is inconsistent and independent.

19. $\begin{cases} y-3x=-2 \\ 6x-2y=4 \end{cases}$

Graph each linear equation on a single set of axes.

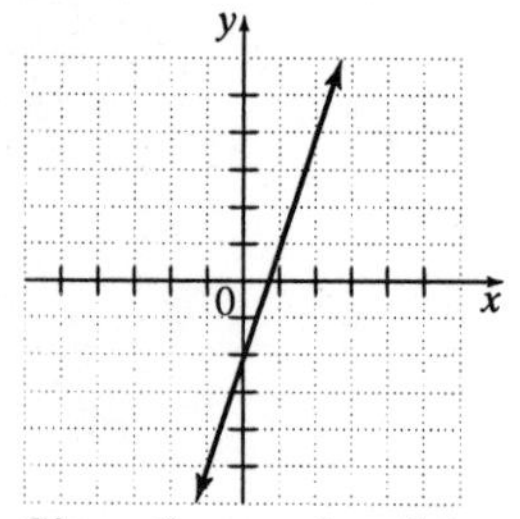

Since the graphs of the equations are the same line, there is an infinite number of solutions. This system is consistent and dependent.

21. $\begin{cases} x-2y=2 \\ 3x+2y=-2 \end{cases}$

Graph each linear equation on a single set of axes.

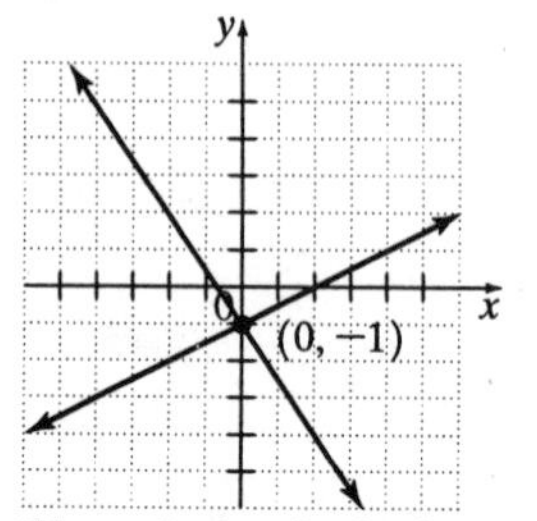

The solution is the intersection point of the two lines, (0, –1). Since this system has only one solution, it is consistent and independent.

23. $\begin{cases} \frac{1}{2}x+y=-1 \\ x=4 \end{cases}$

Graph each linear equation on a single set of axes.

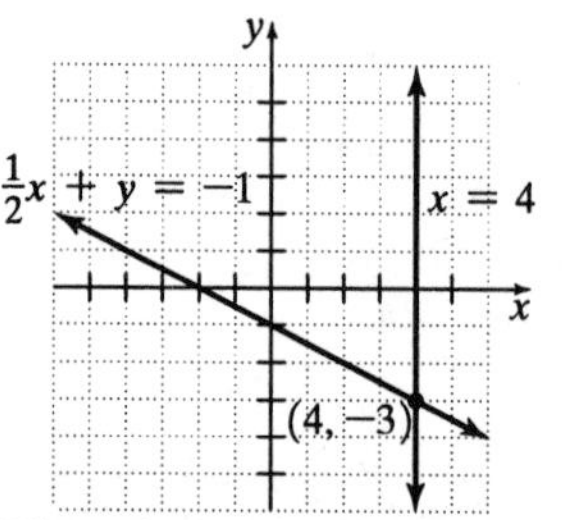

The solution is the intersection point of the two lines, (4, –3). Since this system has only one solution, it is inconsistent and independent.

25. $\begin{cases} y = x - 2 \\ y = 2x + 3 \end{cases}$

Graph each linear equation on a single set of axes.

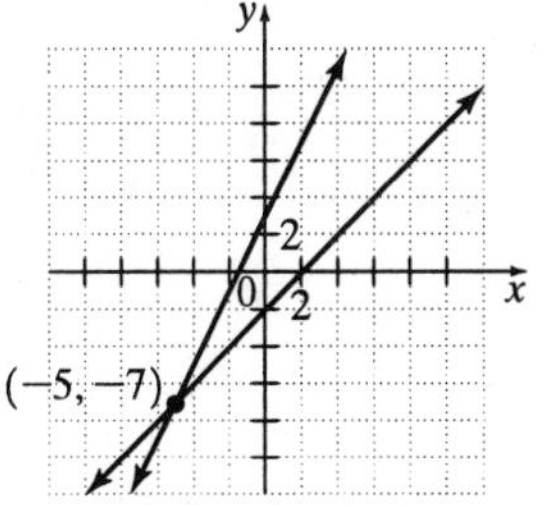

The solution is the intersection point of the two lines, (–5, –7). Since this system has only one solution, it is consistent and independent.

27. $\begin{cases} x + y = 7 \\ x - y = 3 \end{cases}$

Graph each linear equation on a single set of axes.

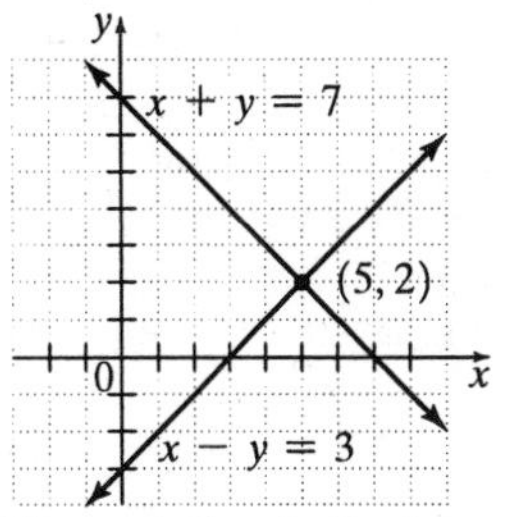

The solution is the intersection point of the two lines, (5, 2). Since this system has only one solution, it is consistent and independent.

29. Answers may vary.

31. $\begin{cases} 4x + y = 24 \\ x + 2y = 2 \end{cases}$

$4x + y = 24$
$y = -4x + 24$
$m = -4$

$x + 2y = 2$
$2y = -x + 2$
$\frac{2y}{2} = \frac{-x}{2} + \frac{2}{2}$
$y = -\frac{1}{2}x + 1$
$m = -\frac{1}{2}$

Slopes are different.

a. Lines intersect at a single point.

b. One solution

33. $\begin{cases} 2x + y = 0 \\ 2y = 6 - 4x \end{cases}$

$2x + y = 0$
$y = -2x$
$m = -2,\ b = 0$

$2y = 6 - 4x$
$\frac{2y}{2} = \frac{6}{2} - \frac{4x}{2}$
$y = 3 - 2x$
$y = -2x + 3$
$m = -2,\ b = 3$

Slopes are the same.
y-intercepts are different.

a. The lines are parallel.

b. No solution

35. $\begin{cases} 6x - y = 4 \\ \frac{1}{2}y = -2 + 3x \end{cases}$

$6x - y = 4$
$-y = -6x + 4$
$\frac{-y}{-1} = \frac{-6x}{-1} + \frac{4}{-1}$
$y = 6x - 4$
$m = 6,\ b = -4$

$\frac{1}{2}y = -2 + 3x$
$2\left(\frac{1}{2}y\right) = 2(-2 + 3x)$
$y = -4 + 6x$
$y = 6x - 4$
$m = 6,\ b = -4$

Slopes are the same.
y-intercepts are the same.

a. Identical lines

b. Infinite number of solutions

37. $\begin{cases} x=5 \\ y=-2 \end{cases}$

$x=5$ | $y=-2$
m is undefined. | $m=0$
b = none | $b=-2$

Slopes are different.

a. Lines intersect at a single point.

b. One solution

39. $\begin{cases} 3y-2x=3 \\ x+2y=9 \end{cases}$

$$3y-2x=3 \qquad x+2y=9$$
$$3y=2x+3 \qquad 2y=-x+9$$
$$\frac{3y}{3}=\frac{2x}{3}+\frac{3}{3} \qquad \frac{2y}{2}=\frac{-y}{2}+\frac{9}{2}$$
$$y=\frac{2}{3}x+1 \qquad y=-\frac{1}{2}x+\frac{9}{2}$$
$$m=\frac{2}{3},\ b=1 \qquad m=-\frac{1}{2},\ b=\frac{9}{2}$$

Slopes are different.

a. The lines intersect at a single point.

b. One solution

41. $\begin{cases} 6y+4x=6 \\ 3y-3=-2x \end{cases}$

$$6y+4x=6 \qquad 3y-3=-2x$$
$$6y=-4x+6 \qquad 3y=-2x+3$$
$$\frac{6y}{6}=-\frac{4}{6}x+\frac{6}{6} \qquad \frac{3y}{3}=-\frac{2}{3}x+\frac{3}{3}$$
$$y=-\frac{2}{3}x+1 \qquad y=-\frac{2}{3}x+1$$
$$m=-\frac{2}{3},\ b=1 \qquad m=-\frac{2}{3},\ b=1$$

Slopes are the same.
y-intercepts are the same.

a. Identical lines

b. Infinite number of solutions

43. $\begin{cases} x+y=4 \\ x+y=3 \end{cases}$

$$x+y=4 \qquad x+y=3$$
$$y=-x+4 \qquad y=-x+3$$
$$m=-1,\ b=4 \qquad m=-1,\ b=3$$

Slopes are the same.
y-intercepts are different.

a. The lines are parallel.

b. No solution

45. Answers may vary.

47. 1984, 1988; the lines intersect at the approximate points (1984, 6.2) and (1988, 7.3).

49. a. (4, 9); each of the tables has the point (4, 9).

b. Yes

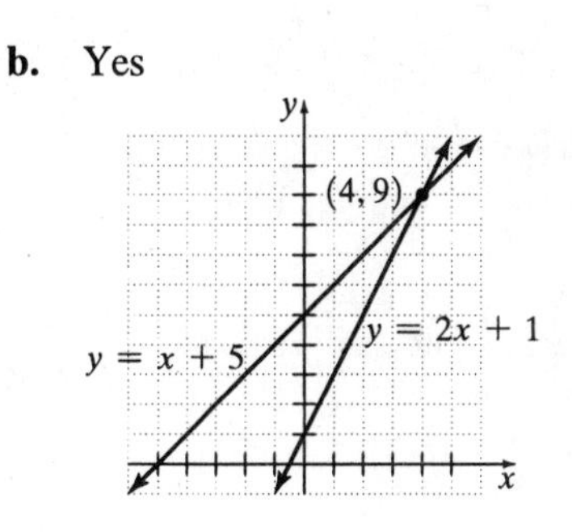

51. $-2x+3(x+6)=17$
$-2x+3x+18=17$
$x+18=17$
$x=-1$

53. $-y+12\left(\frac{y-1}{4}\right)=3$
$-y+3(y-1)=3$
$-y+3y-3=3$
$2y-3=3$
$2y=6$
$y=3$

55. $3z-(4z-2)=9$
$3z-4z+2=9$
$-z+2=9$
$-z=7$
$z=-7$

Exercise Set 8.2

1. $\begin{cases} x+y=3 \\ x=2y \end{cases}$
Replace x with $2y$ in the first equation.
$2y+y=3$
$3y=3$
$y=1$
To find x, use $y = 1$ in the equation
$x=2y$
$x=2(1)$
$x=2$
The solution is (2, 1).

3. $\begin{cases} x+y=6 \\ y=-3x \end{cases}$
Replace y with $-3x$ in the first equation.
$x+(-3x)=6$
$-2x=6$
$x=\frac{6}{-2}=-3$
To find y, use $x = -3$ in the equation
$y=-3x$
$y=-3(-3)$
$y=9$
The solution is (–3, 9).

5. $\begin{cases} 3x+2y=16 \\ x=3y-2 \end{cases}$
Replace x with $3y-2$ in the first equation.
$3(3y-2)+2y=16$
$9y-6+2y=16$
$11y-6=16$
$11y=16+6$
$11y=22$
$y=\frac{22}{11}=2$
To find x, use $y = 2$ in the equation
$x=3y-2$
$x=3(2)-2$
$x=6-2$
$x=4$
The solution is (4, 2).

7. $\begin{cases} 3x-4y=10 \\ x=2y \end{cases}$
Replace x with $2y$ in the first equation.
$3(2y)-4y=10$
$6y-4y=10$
$2y=10$
$y=\frac{10}{2}=5$
To find x, use $y = 5$ in the equation
$x=2y$
$x=2(5)$
$x=10$
The solution is (10, 5).

9. $\begin{cases} y = 3x+1 \\ 4y - 8x = 12 \end{cases}$

Replace y with $3x + 1$ in the second equation.

$$4(3x+1) - 8x = 12$$
$$12x + 4 - 8x = 12$$
$$4x + 4 = 12$$
$$4x = 12 - 4$$
$$4x = 8$$
$$x = \frac{8}{4} = 2$$

To find y, use $x = 2$ in the equation

$y = 3x + 1$
$y = 3(2) + 1$
$y = 6 + 1$
$y = 7$

The solution is (2, 7).

11. $\begin{cases} x + 2y = 6 \\ 2x + 3y = 8 \end{cases}$

Solve the first equation for x.

$x + 2y = 6$
$x = -2y + 6$

Replace x with $-2y + 6$ in the second equation.

$$2(-2y+6) + 3y = 8$$
$$-4y + 12 + 3y = 8$$
$$-y + 12 = 8$$
$$-y = +8 - 12$$
$$-y = -4$$
$$y = 4$$

To find x, use $y = 4$ in the equation

$x = -2y + 6$
$x = -2(4) + 6$
$x = -8 + 6$
$x = -2$

The solution is (–2, 4).

13. $\begin{cases} 2x - 5y = 1 \\ 3x + y = -7 \end{cases}$

Solve the second equation for y.

$3x + y = -7$
$y = -3x - 7$

Replace y with $-3x - 7$ in the first equation.

$$2x - 5(-3x - 7) = 1$$
$$2x + 15x + 35 = 1$$
$$17x + 35 = 1$$
$$17x = 1 - 35$$
$$17x = -34$$
$$x = \frac{-34}{17} = -2$$

To find y, use $x = -2$ in the equation

$y = -3x - 7$
$y = -3(-2) - 7$
$y = 6 - 7$
$y = -1$

The solution is (–2, –1).

15. $\begin{cases} 2y = x + 2 \\ 6x - 12y = 0 \end{cases}$

Solve the first equation for x.

$2y = x + 2$
$2y - 2 = x$

Replace x with $2y - 2$ in the second equation.

$$6(2y - 2) - 12y = 0$$
$$12y - 12 - 12y = 0$$
$$-12 = 0$$

This is a contradiction. Therefore, there is no solution.

17. $\begin{cases} \frac{1}{3}x - y = 2 \\ x - 3y = 6 \end{cases}$

Solve the first equation for *y*.

$$\frac{1}{3}x - y = 2$$
$$\frac{1}{3}x = 2 + y$$
$$\frac{1}{3}x - 2 = y$$

Replace *y* with $\frac{1}{3}x - 2$ in the second equation.

$$x - 3\left(\frac{1}{3}x - 2\right) = 6$$
$$x - x + 6 = 6$$
$$6 = 6$$

This is an identity.
The equations are dependent and there is an infinite number of solutions.

19. $\begin{cases} 4x + y = 11 \\ 2x + 5y = 1 \end{cases}$

Solve the first equation for *y*.

$$4x + y = 11$$
$$y = -4x + 11$$

Replace *y* with $-4x + 11$ in the second equation.

$$2x + 5(-4x + 11) = 1$$
$$2x - 20x + 55 = 1$$
$$-18x + 55 = 1$$
$$-18x = 1 - 55$$
$$-18x = -54$$
$$x = \frac{-54}{-18} = 3$$

To find *y*, use $x = 3$ in the equation

$$4x + y = 11$$
$$4(3) + y = 11$$
$$12 + y = 11$$
$$y = 11 - 12$$
$$y = -1$$

The solution is (3, –1).

21. $\begin{cases} 2x - 3y = -9 \\ 3x = y + 4 \end{cases}$

Solve the second equation for *y*.

$$3x = y + 4$$
$$3x - 4 = y$$

Replace *y* with $3x - 4$ in the first equation.

$$2x - 3(3x - 4) = -9$$
$$2x - 9x + 12 = -9$$
$$-7x + 12 = -9$$
$$-7x = -9 - 12$$
$$-7x = -21$$
$$x = \frac{-21}{-7} = 3$$

To find *y*, use $x = 3$ in the equation,

$$3x - 4 = y$$
$$3(3) - 4 = y$$
$$9 - 4 = y$$
$$5 = y$$

The solution is (3, 5).

23. $\begin{cases} 6x - 3y = 5 \\ x + 2y = 0 \end{cases}$

Solve the second equation for *x*.

$$x + 2y = 0$$
$$x = -2y$$

Replace *x* with $-2y$ in the first equation.

$$6(-2y) - 3y = 5$$
$$-12y - 3y = 5$$
$$-15y = 5$$
$$y = \frac{5}{-15} = -\frac{1}{3}$$

To find *x*, use $y = -\frac{1}{3}$ in the equation

$$x = -2y$$
$$x = -2\left(-\frac{1}{3}\right)$$
$$x = \frac{2}{3}$$

The solution is $\left(\frac{2}{3}, -\frac{1}{3}\right)$.

25. $\begin{cases} 3x - y = 1 \\ 2x - 3y = 10 \end{cases}$

Solve the first equation for y.

$3x - y = 1$
$-y = -3x + 1$
$y = \frac{-3}{-1}x + \frac{1}{-1}$
$y = 3x - 1$

Replace y with $3x - 1$ in the second equation.

$2x - 3(3x - 1) = 10$
$2x - 9x + 3 = 10$
$-7x + 3 = 10$
$-7x = 10 - 3$
$-7x = 7$
$x = \frac{7}{-7} = -1$

To find y, use $x = -1$ in the equation

$y = 3x - 1$
$y = 3(-1) - 1$
$y = -3 - 1$
$y = -4$

The solution is $(-1, -4)$.

27. $\begin{cases} -x + 2y = 10 \\ -2x + 3y = 18 \end{cases}$

Solve the first equation for x.

$-x + 2y = 10$
$2y = 10 + x$
$2y - 10 = x$

Replace x with $2y - 10$ in the second equation.

$-2(2y - 10) + 3y = 18$
$-4y + 20 + 3y = 18$
$-y + 20 = 18$
$-y = 18 - 20$
$-y = -2$
$y = 2$

To find x, use $y = 2$ in the equation

$2y - 10 = x$
$2(2) - 10 = x$
$4 - 10 = x$
$-6 = x$

The solution is $(-6, 2)$.

29. $\begin{cases} 5x + 10y = 20 \\ 2x + 6y = 10 \end{cases}$

Solve the second equation for x.

$2x + 6y = 10$
$2x = 10 - 6y$
$x = \frac{10}{2} - \frac{6}{2}y$
$x = 5 - 3y$

Replace x with $5 - 3y$ in the first equation.

$5(5 - 3y) + 10y = 20$
$25 - 15y + 10y = 20$
$25 - 5y = 20$
$-5y = 20 - 25$
$-5y = -5$
$y = \frac{-5}{-5} = 1$

To find x, use $y = 1$ in the equation

$x = 5 - 3y$
$x = 5 - 3(1)$
$x = 5 - 3$
$x = 2$

The solution is $(2, 1)$.

31. $\begin{cases} 3x + 6y = 9 \\ 4x + 8y = 16 \end{cases}$

Solve the first equation for x.

$3x + 6y = 9$
$3x = -6y + 9$
$x = \frac{-6y}{3} + \frac{9}{3}$
$x = -2y + 3$

Replace x with $-2y + 3$ in the second equation.

$4(-2y + 3) + 8y = 16$
$-8y + 12 + 8y = 16$
$12 = 16$

There is a contradiction. There is no solution.

33. $\begin{cases} y = 2x + 9 \\ y = 7x + 10 \end{cases}$

Replace y with $2x + 9$ in the second equation.

$$2x + 9 = 7x + 10$$
$$9 = 7x - 2x + 10$$
$$9 = 5x + 10$$
$$9 - 10 = 5x$$
$$-1 = 5x$$
$$-\frac{1}{5} = x$$

To find y, use $x = -\frac{1}{5}$ in the equation

$$y = 2x + 9$$
$$y = 2\left(-\frac{1}{5}\right) + 9$$
$$y = -\frac{2}{5} + 9$$
$$y = -\frac{2}{5} + \frac{45}{5}$$
$$y = \frac{43}{5}$$

The solution is $\left(-\frac{1}{5}, \frac{43}{5}\right)$

35. Answers may vary.

37. $-5y + 6y = 3x + 2(x - 5) - 3x + 5$

$$-5y + 6y = 3x + 2x - 10 - 3x + 5$$
$$y = 2x - 5$$

$$4(x + y) - x + y = -12$$
$$4x + 4y - x + y = -12$$
$$3x + 5y = -12$$

$$3x + 5(2x - 5) = -12$$
$$3x + 10x - 25 = -12$$
$$13x - 25 = -12$$
$$13x = 13$$
$$x = 1$$

$$y = 2x - 5$$
$$y = 2(1) - 5$$
$$y = 2 - 5$$
$$y = -3$$

The solution is (1, –3).

39. a. $\begin{cases} y = -0.65x + 32.02 \\ y = 0.78x + 1.32 \end{cases}$

Substitute $-0.65x + 32.02$ for y in the second equation. Then solve for x.

$$-0.65x + 32.02 = 0.78x + 1.32$$
$$-1.43x = -30.7$$
$$x \approx 21.47$$

Substitute 21.47 for x in the first equation. Then solve for y.

$$y \approx -0.65(21.47) + 32.02$$
$$y \approx 18.06$$

The solution is approximately (21, 18).

b. Answers may vary.

c.

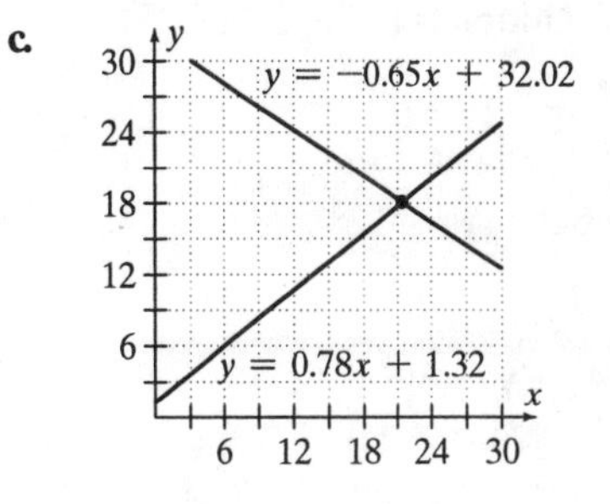

Answers may vary.

41. $\begin{cases} y = 5.1x + 14.56 \\ y = -2x - 3.9 \end{cases}$

$$\begin{aligned} 5.1x + 14.56 &= -2x - 3.9 \\ 7.1x &= -18.46 \\ x &= -2.6 \end{aligned}$$

$$\begin{aligned} y &= -2x - 3.9 \\ y &= -2(-2.6) - 3.9 \\ y &= 5.2 - 3.9 \\ y &= 1.3 \end{aligned}$$

The solution is (–2.6, 1.3).

43. $3x + 2y = 14.05$
$5x + y = 18.5$
Solve the second equation for x.

$$\begin{aligned} 5x + y &= 18.5 \\ 5x &= 18.5 - y \\ x &= \frac{18.5}{5} - \frac{y}{5} \\ x &= 3.7 - 0.2y \end{aligned}$$

$$\begin{aligned} 3x + 2y &= 14.05 \\ 3(3.7 - 0.2y) + 2y &= 14.05 \\ 11.1 - 0.6y + 2y &= 14.05 \\ 1.4y &= 2.95 \\ y &= 2.11 \end{aligned}$$

$$\begin{aligned} 3x + 2y &= 14.05 \\ 3x + 2(2.11) &= 14.05 \\ 3x + 4.22 &= 14.05 \\ 3x &= 9.83 \\ x &= 3.28 \end{aligned}$$

The solution is (3.28, 2.11).

45.
$$\begin{aligned} 3x + 2y &= 6 \\ -2(3x + 2y) &= -2(6) \\ -6x - 4y &= -12 \end{aligned}$$

47.
$$\begin{aligned} -4x + y &= 3 \\ 3(-4x + y) &= 3(3) \\ -12x + 3y &= 9 \end{aligned}$$

49.
$$\begin{array}{r} 3n + 6m \\ \underline{+\,2n - 6m} \\ 5n \end{array}$$

51.
$$\begin{array}{r} -5a - 7b \\ \underline{+\,5a - 8b} \\ -15b \end{array}$$

Exercise Set 8.3

1. $\begin{cases} 3x + y = 5 \\ 6x - y = 4 \end{cases}$

$$\begin{array}{l} 3x + y = 5 \\ \underline{6x - y = 4} \\ 9x \quad\; = 9 \\ x \quad\;\; = 1 \end{array}$$

To find y, use $x = 1$ in the equation

$$\begin{aligned} 3x + y &= 5 \\ 3(1) + y &= 5 \\ 3 + y &= 5 \\ y &= 5 - 3 \\ y &= 2 \end{aligned}$$

The solution is (1, 2).

3. $\begin{cases} x - 2y = 8 \\ -x + 5y = -17 \end{cases}$

$$\begin{array}{l} x - 2y = 8 \\ \underline{-x + 5y = -17} \\ 3y = -9 \\ y = \frac{-9}{3} = -3 \end{array}$$

To find x, use $y = -3$ in the equation

$$\begin{aligned} x - 2y &= 8 \\ x - 2(-3) &= 8 \\ x + 6 &= 8 \\ x &= 8 - 6 \\ x &= 2 \end{aligned}$$

The solution is (2, –3).

5. $\begin{cases} x+y=6 \\ x-y=6 \end{cases}$

$$\begin{array}{r} x+y = \ \ 6 \\ x-y = \ \ 6 \\ \hline 2x \qquad = 12 \\ x \qquad = \ \ 6 \end{array}$$

To find y, use $x = 6$ in the equation

$x+y=6$
$6+y=6$
$y=6-6$
$y=0$

The solution is (6, 0).

7. $\begin{cases} 3x+y=4 \\ 9x+3y=6 \end{cases}$

Multiply 1st equation by –3.

$-3(3x+y)=-3(4)$
$-9x-3y=-12$

Add the equations.

$$\begin{array}{r} -9x-3y = -12 \\ 9x+3y = \ \ \ 6 \\ \hline 0 = \ -6 \end{array}$$

This is a contradiction. There is no solution.

9. $\begin{cases} 3x-2y=7 \\ 5x+4y=8 \end{cases}$

Multiply 1st equation by 2.

$2(3x-2y)=2(7)$
$6x-4y=14$

Add the equations.

$$\begin{array}{r} 6x-4y = 14 \\ 5x+4y = \ \ 8 \\ \hline 11x \qquad = 22 \\ x \qquad = \dfrac{22}{11} = 2 \end{array}$$

To find y, use $x = 2$ in the equation

$3x-2y=7$
$3(2)-2y=7$
$6-2y=7$
$-2y=7-6$
$-2y=1$
$y=-\dfrac{1}{2}$

The solution is $\left(2, -\dfrac{1}{2}\right)$.

11. $\begin{cases} \dfrac{2}{3}x+4y=-4 \\ 5x+6y=18 \end{cases}$

Multiply 1st equation by 3.

$3\left(\dfrac{2}{3}x+4y\right)=3(-4)$
$2x+12y=-12$

Since addition now would not eliminate a variable, multiply the second equation by –2.

$-2(5x+6y)=-2(18)$
$-10x-12y=-36$

Add the equations.

$$\begin{array}{r} 2x+12y = -12 \\ -10x-12y = -36 \\ \hline -8x \qquad = -48 \\ x \qquad = \dfrac{-48}{-8} = 6 \end{array}$$

To find y, use $x = 6$ in the equation

$5x+6y=18$
$5(6)+6y=18$
$30+6y=18$
$6y=18-30$
$6y=-12$
$y=-\dfrac{12}{6}=-2$

The solution is (6, –2).

13. $\begin{cases} 4x-6y=8 \\ 6x-9y=12 \end{cases}$

Multiply 1st equation by 3.
Multiply 2nd equation by –2.

$3(4x-6y)=3(8)$
$-2(6x-9x)=-2(12)$

Add the resulting equations.

$$\begin{aligned} 12x-18y &= 24 \\ -12x+18y &= -24 \\ \hline 0 &= 0 \end{aligned}$$

This is an identity.
The equations are dependent.
There is an infinite number of solutions.

15. $\begin{cases} 3x+y=-11 \\ 6x-2y=-2 \end{cases}$

Multiply 1st equation by 2.

$2(3x+y)=2(-11)$
$6x+2y=-22$

Add the two equations.

$$\begin{aligned} 6x+2y &= -22 \\ 6x-2y &= -2 \\ \hline 12x \quad &= -24 \\ x \quad &= \frac{-24}{12}=-2 \end{aligned}$$

To find y, use $x=-2$ in the equation

$$\begin{aligned} 3x+y &= -11 \\ 3(-2)+y &= -11 \\ -6+y &= -11 \\ y &= -11+6 \\ y &= -5 \end{aligned}$$

The solution is (–2, –5).

17. $\begin{cases} 3x+2y=11 \\ 5x-2y=29 \end{cases}$

$$\begin{aligned} 3x+2y &= 11 \\ 5x-2y &= 29 \\ \hline 8x \quad &= 40 \\ x \quad &= \frac{40}{8}=5 \end{aligned}$$

To find y, use $x=5$ in the equation

$$\begin{aligned} 3x+2y &= 11 \\ 3(5)+2y &= 11 \\ 15+2y &= 11 \\ 2y &= 11-15 \\ 2y &= -4 \\ y &= \frac{-4}{2}=-2 \end{aligned}$$

The solution is (5, –2).

19. $\begin{cases} x+5y=18 \\ 3x+2y=-11 \end{cases}$

Multiply 1st equation by –3.

$-3(x+5y)=-3(18)$
$-3x-15y=-54$

Add the two equations.

$$\begin{aligned} -3x-15y &= -54 \\ 3x+2y &= -11 \\ \hline -13y &= -65 \\ y &= \frac{-65}{-13}=5 \end{aligned}$$

To find x, use $y=5$ in the equation

$$\begin{aligned} x+5y &= 18 \\ x+5(5) &= 18 \\ x+25 &= 18 \\ x &= 18-25 \\ x &= -7 \end{aligned}$$

The solution is (–7, 5).

21. $\begin{cases} 2x-5y=4 \\ 3x-2y=4 \end{cases}$

Multiply the 1st equation by –3.
Multiply 2nd equation by 2.

$-3(2x-5y)=-3(4)$
$2(3x-2y)=2(4)$

$$\begin{aligned} -6x+15y &= -12 \\ 6x-4y &= 8 \\ \hline 11y &= -4 \\ y &= -\frac{4}{11} \end{aligned}$$

To find x, use $y=-\frac{4}{11}$ in the equation

$$2x - 5y = 4$$
$$2x - 5\left(-\frac{4}{11}\right) = 4$$
$$2x + \frac{20}{11} = 4$$
$$2x = 4 - \frac{20}{11}$$
$$2x = \frac{44}{11} - \frac{20}{11}$$
$$2x = \frac{24}{11}$$
$$\frac{1}{2}(2x) = \frac{1}{2}\left(\frac{24}{11}\right)$$
$$x = \frac{12}{11}$$

The solution is $\left(\frac{12}{11}, -\frac{4}{11}\right)$.

23. $\begin{cases} 2x + 3y = 0 \\ 4x + 6y = 3 \end{cases}$

Multiply 1st equation by –2.

$$-2(2x + 3y) = -2(0)$$
$$-4x - 6y = 0$$

Add the equations.

$$\begin{array}{r} -4x - 6y = 0 \\ 4x + 6y = 3 \\ \hline 0 = 3 \end{array}$$

This is a contradiction. There is no solution.

25. $\begin{cases} \frac{x}{3} + \frac{y}{6} = 1 \\ \frac{x}{2} - \frac{y}{4} = 0 \end{cases}$

Multiply 1st equation by 6.
Multiply 2nd equation by 4.

$$6\left(\frac{x}{3} + \frac{y}{6}\right) = 6(1)$$
$$4\left(\frac{x}{2} - \frac{y}{4}\right) = 4(0)$$

Add the equations.

$$\begin{array}{r} 2x + y = 6 \\ 2x - y = 0 \\ \hline 4x \quad = 6 \end{array}$$
$$x = \frac{6}{4} = \frac{3}{2}$$

To find y, use $x = \frac{3}{2}$ in the equation

$$2x + y = 6$$
$$2\left(\frac{3}{2}\right) + y = 6$$
$$3 + y = 6$$
$$y = 6 - 3$$
$$y = 3$$

The solution is $\left(\frac{3}{2}, 3\right)$.

27. $\begin{cases} x - \frac{y}{3} = -1 \\ -\frac{x}{2} + \frac{y}{8} = \frac{1}{4} \end{cases}$

Multiply 1st equation by 3.
Multiply 2nd equation by 8.

$$3\left(x - \frac{y}{3}\right) = 3(-1)$$
$$8\left(-\frac{x}{2} + \frac{y}{8}\right) = 8\left(\frac{1}{4}\right)$$

Add the resulting equations.

$$\begin{array}{r} 3x - y = -3 \\ -4x + y = 2 \\ \hline -x \quad = -1 \end{array}$$
$$x = \frac{-1}{-1} = 1$$

To find y, use $x = 1$ in the equation

$$-4x + y = 2$$
$$-4(1) + y = 2$$
$$-4 + y = 2$$
$$y = 2 + 4$$
$$y = 6$$

The solution is (1, 6).

29. $\begin{cases} \dfrac{x}{3} - y = 2 \\ -\dfrac{x}{2} + \dfrac{3y}{2} = -3 \end{cases}$

Multiply 1st equation by 3.
Multiply 2nd equation by 2.

$$3\left(\frac{x}{3} - y\right) = 3(2)$$

$$2\left(-\frac{x}{2} + \frac{3y}{2}\right) = 2(-3)$$

Add the equations.

$$\begin{aligned} x - 3y &= 6 \\ -x + 3y &= -6 \\ \hline 0 &= 0 \end{aligned}$$

This is an identity.
The equations are dependent.
There is an infinite number of solutions.

31. $\begin{cases} 8x = -11y - 16 \\ 2x + 3y = -4 \end{cases}$

Multiply the 2nd equation by –4.

$$-4(2x + 3y) = -4(-4)$$

$$-8x - 12y = 16$$

Rearrange the first equation.

$$8x = -11y - 16$$

$$8x + 11y = -16$$

Add the equations.

$$\begin{aligned} -8x - 12y &= 16 \\ 8x + 11y &= -16 \\ \hline -y &= 0 \\ y &= 0 \end{aligned}$$

To find x, use $y = 0$ in the equation

$$2x + 3y = -4$$

$$2x + 3(0) = -4$$

$$2x = -4$$

$$x = \frac{-4}{2} = -2$$

The solution is (–2, 0).

33. Answers may vary.

35. $\begin{cases} 2x - 3y = -11 \\ y = 4x - 3 \end{cases}$

Replace y with $4x - 3$ in the 1st equation.

$$2x - 3(4x - 3) = -11$$

$$2x - 12x + 9 = -11$$

$$-10x + 9 = -11$$

$$-10x = -11 - 9$$

$$-10x = -20$$

$$x = \frac{-20}{-10} = 2$$

To find y, use $x = 2$ in the equation

$$y = 4x - 3$$

$$y = 4(2) - 3$$

$$y = 8 - 3$$

$$y = 5$$

The solution is (2, 5).

37. $\begin{cases} x + 2y = 1 \\ 3x + 4y = -1 \end{cases}$

Multiply the 1st equation by –3.

$$-3(x + 2y) = -3(1)$$

$$-3x - 6y = -3$$

Add the equations.

$$\begin{aligned} -3x - 6y &= -3 \\ 3x + 4y &= -1 \\ \hline -2y &= -4 \end{aligned}$$

$$y = \frac{-4}{-2} = 2$$

To find x, use $y = 2$ in the equation

$$x + 2y = 1$$

$$x + 2(2) = 1$$

$$x + 4 = 1$$

$$x = 1 - 4$$

$$x = -3$$

The solution is (–3, 2).

39. $\begin{cases} 2y = x+6 \\ 3x-2y=-6 \end{cases}$

Solve the 1st equation for x.

$2y = x + 6$

$2y - 6 = x$

Replace x with $2y - 6$ in the second equation.

$3(2y-6)-2y=-6$

$6y-18-2y=-6$

$4y-18=-6$

$4y=-6+18$

$4y=12$

$y=\frac{12}{4}=3$

To find x, use $y = 3$ in the equation

$2y-6=x$

$2(3)-6=x$

$6-6=x$

$0=x$

The solution is (0, 3).

41. $\begin{cases} y=2x-3 \\ y=5x-18 \end{cases}$

Replace y with $2x-3$ in the second equation.

$2x-3=5x-18$

$2x-5x-3=-18$

$-3x-3=-18$

$-3x=-18+3$

$-3x=-15$

$x=\frac{-15}{-3}=5$

To find y, use $x = 5$ in the equation

$y=2x-3$

$y=2(5)-3$

$y=10-3$

$y=7$

The solution is (5, 7).

43. $\begin{cases} x+\frac{1}{6}y=\frac{1}{2} \\ 3x+2y=3 \end{cases}$

Multiply 1st equation by 6.

$6\left(x+\frac{1}{6}y\right)=6\left(\frac{1}{2}\right)$

$6x+y=3$

Since addition now would not eliminate a variable, multiply this equation by −2.

$-2(6x+y)=-2(3)$

$-12x-2y=-6$

Add the equations.

$$\begin{array}{r} -12x-2y=-6 \\ 3x+2y=\ \ 3 \\ \hline -9x \qquad =-3 \end{array}$$

$x=\frac{-3}{-9}=\frac{1}{3}$

To find y, use $x=\frac{1}{3}$ in the equation

$3x+2y=3$

$3\left(\frac{1}{3}\right)+2y=3$

$1+2y=3$

$2y=3-1$

$2y=2$

$y=\frac{2}{2}=1$

The solution is $\left(\frac{1}{3}, 1\right)$.

45. $\begin{cases} \frac{x+2}{2}=\frac{y+11}{3} \\ \frac{x}{2}=\frac{2y+16}{6} \end{cases}$

Multiply 1st equation by 6.

$6\left(\frac{x+2}{2}\right)=6\left(\frac{y+11}{3}\right)$

$3(x+2)=2(y+11)$

$3x+6=2y+22$

$3x-2y=22-6$

$3x-2y=16$

Multiply 2nd equation by 6.

$$6\left(\frac{x}{2}\right)=6\left(\frac{2y+16}{6}\right)$$
$$3x=2y+16$$
$$3x-2y=16$$
$$-1(3x-2y)=-1(16)$$
$$-3x+2y=-16$$
Add the equations.
$$\begin{array}{r} 3x-2y=\ \ 16 \\ -3x+2y=-16 \\ \hline 0=\ \ \ 0 \end{array}$$
This is an identity.
The equations are dependent.
There is an infinite number of solutions.

47. $\begin{cases} 2x+3y=14 \\ 3x-4y=69.1 \end{cases}$

Multiply the 1st equation by 3 and the 2nd equation by –2.
$$3(2x+3y)=3(14)$$
$$-2(3x-4y)=-2(-69.1)$$
Add the resulting equations.
$$\begin{array}{r} 6x+9y=\ \ 42 \\ -6x+8y=138.2 \\ \hline 17y=180.2 \\ y=\ \ 10.6 \end{array}$$
To find x, use y = 10.6 in the equation
$$2x+3y=14$$
$$2x+3(10.6)=14$$
$$2x+31.8=14$$
$$2x=-17.8$$
$$x=-8.9$$

The solution is (–8.9, 10.6).

49. a. $\begin{cases} 10x-2y=-986 \\ -21x+y=295 \end{cases}$

Multiply the 1st equation by $\frac{1}{2}$.
$$\frac{1}{2}(10x-2y)=\frac{1}{2}(-986)$$
$$5x-y=-493$$
Add the equations
$$\begin{array}{r} 5x-y=\ -493 \\ -21x+y=\ \ \ \ 295 \\ \hline -16x\ \ \ \ \ \ =\ -198 \end{array}$$
$$x=12.375$$
To find y, use x = 12.375 in the equation
$$-21x+y=295$$
$$-21(12.375)+y=295$$
$$-259.875+y=295$$
$$y=554.875$$
The solution is approximately (12, 555).

b. Answers may vary.

c. Since they were equal 12 years after 1980, then from 1980 + 13 = 1993 to 1997, there were more UHF stations than VHF stations.

51. a.
$$x+y=5$$
$$3(x+y)=3(5)$$
$$3x+3y=15$$
$$b=15$$

b. Any real number except 15

53. Answers may vary.

55. Let x = number
$2x+6=x-3$

57. Let x = number
$20-3x=2$

59. Let x = number
$4(x+6)=2x$

Exercise Set 8.4

1. c; length = 9 ft, width = 6 ft; the length is 3 ft longer than the width and the perimeter is 2(9) + 2(6) = 18 + 12 = 30 ft.

3. b; notebook = \$3, computer disk = \$4;
2 computer disks and 3 notebooks
= 2(4) + 3(3)
= 8 + 9
= \$17
5 computer disks and 4 notebooks
= 5(4) + 4(3)
= 20 + 12
= \$32.

5. a; 80 dimes and 20 quarters;
80 + 20 = 100 coins;
80(0.10) + 20(0.25) = 8 + 5 = \$13

7. Let $x =$ one number
$y =$ another number

$$\begin{cases} x+y=15 \\ x-y=7 \end{cases}$$

9. Let $x =$ amount invested in larger account
$y =$ amount invested in smaller account

$$\begin{cases} x+y=6500 \\ x=y+800 \end{cases}$$

11. Let $x =$ one number
$y =$ another number

$$\begin{cases} x+y=83 \\ x-y=17 \end{cases}$$
$$2x = 100$$
$$x = 50$$

Let $x = 50$ in the first equation.
$$50 + y = 83$$
$$y = 33$$
The two numbers are 33 and 50.

13. Let $x =$ first number
$y =$ second number

$$\begin{cases} x+2y=8 \\ 2x+y=25 \end{cases}$$

$$\begin{cases} -2(x+2y)=-2(8) \\ 2x+y=25 \end{cases}$$

$$\begin{cases} -2x-4y=-16 \\ 2x+y=25 \end{cases}$$
$$-3y=9$$
$$y=-3$$

Let $y = -3$ in the first equation.
$$x+2(-3)=8$$
$$x-6=8$$
$$x=14$$
The numbers are 14 and −3.

15. Let $x =$ number of points Cooper scored
$y =$ number of points Swoops scored

$$\begin{cases} x=101+y \\ x+y=1271 \end{cases}$$

Substitute $101 + y$ for x in the second equation.
$$101+y+y=1271$$
$$2y=1170$$
$$y=585$$
Let $y = 585$ in the first equation.
$$x = 101 + 585$$
$$x = 686$$
Cooper scored 686 points and Swoops scores 585 points.

17. Let $x =$ price of adult' s ticket
$y =$ price of child' s ticket

$$\begin{cases} 3x+4y=159 \\ 2x+3y=112 \end{cases}$$

$$\begin{cases} -2(3x+4y)=-2(159) \\ 3(2x+3y)=3(112) \end{cases}$$

$$\begin{cases} -6x-8y=-318 \\ 6x+9y=336 \end{cases}$$
$$y=18$$

Let $y = 18$ in the first equation.
$$3x+4(18)=159$$
$$3x+72=159$$
$$3x=87$$
$$x=29$$
An adult's ticket is \$29 and a child's ticket is \$18.

19. Let $x =$ number of quarters
$y =$ number of nickels

$$\begin{cases} x + y = 80 \\ 0.25x + 0.05y = 14.6 \end{cases}$$

Substitute $80 - x$ for y in the second equation.

$$0.25x + 0.05(80 - x) = 14.6$$
$$0.25x + 4 - 0.05x = 14.6$$
$$0.2x = 10.6$$
$$x = 53$$

Let $x = 53$ in the first equation.

$$53 + y = 80$$
$$y = 27$$

There are 53 quarters and 27 nickels.

21. Let $x =$ Price of IBM stock
$y =$ price of GA Financial stock

$$\begin{cases} 50x + 40y = 6485.90 \\ y = x + 64.25 \end{cases}$$

Substitute $x + 64.25$ for y in the first equation.

$$50x + 40(x + 64.25) = 6485.90$$
$$50x + 40x + 2570 = 6485.90$$
$$90x = 3915.90$$
$$x = 43.51$$

Let $x = 43.51$ in the second equation.

$$y = 43.51 + 64.25$$
$$y = 107.76$$

The stock of IBM was $43.51 and the stock of GA Financial was $107.76.

23. Let $x =$ Pratap's rate in still water, in miles per hour
$y =$ rate of current in miles per hour

$$\begin{cases} 2(x + y) = 18 \\ 4.5(x - y) = 18 \end{cases}$$

$$\begin{cases} 2x + 2y = 18 \\ 4.5x - 4.5y = 18 \end{cases}$$

$$\begin{cases} 2.25(2x + 2y) = 2.25(18) \\ 4.5x - 4.5y = 18 \end{cases}$$

$$\begin{cases} 4.5x + 4.5y = 40.5 \\ 4.5x - 4.5y = 18 \end{cases}$$
$$9x = 58.5$$
$$x = 6.5$$

Let $x = 6.5$ in the first equation.

$$2(6.5) + 2y = 18$$
$$2y = 5$$
$$y = 2.5$$

Pratap's rate in still water was 6.5 mph and the current's rate was 2.5 mph.

25. Let $x =$ speed of plane in still air, in miles per hour
$y =$ speed of wind, in miles per hour

$$\begin{cases} 780 = 2(x - y) \\ 780 = 1.5(x + y) \end{cases}$$

$$\begin{cases} 390 = x - y \\ 520 = x + y \end{cases}$$
$$910 = 2x$$
$$455 = x$$

Let $x = 455$ in the equation $520 = x + y$.

$$520 = 455 + y$$
$$65 = y$$

The plane's speed is 455 mph in still air and the wind's speed is 65 mph.

27. Let $x =$ amount of 12% solution
$y =$ amount of 4% solution

$$\begin{cases} x + y = 12 \\ 0.12x + 0.04y = 0.09(12) \end{cases}$$

Substitute $12 - x$ for y in the second equation.

$$0.12x + 0.04(12 - x) = 0.09(12)$$
$$0.12x + 0.48 - 0.04x = 1.08$$
$$0.08x = 0.6$$
$$x = 7.5$$

Let $x = 7.5$ in the first equation.

$$7.5 + y = 12$$
$$y = 4.5$$

She needs $7\frac{1}{2}$ oz of 12% solution and $4\frac{1}{2}$ oz of 4% solution.

29. Let $x =$ number of pounds of \$4.95 per pound beans
$y =$ number of pounds of \$2.65 per pound beans

$$\begin{cases} x + y = 200 \\ 4.95x + 2.65y = 200(3.95) \end{cases}$$

Substitute $200 - x$ for y in the second equation.

$$4.95x + 2.65(200 - x) = 200(3.95)$$
$$4.95x + 530 - 2.65x = 790$$
$$2.3x = 260$$
$$x \approx 113.04$$

Substitute 113.04 for x in the first equation.

$$113 + y \approx 200$$
$$y \approx 86.96$$

To the nearest pound, he needs 113 pounds of the \$4.95 per pound beans and 87 pounds of the
\$2.65 per pound beans.

31. Let $x =$ first angle
$y =$ second angle

$$\begin{cases} x + y = 90 \\ x = 2y \end{cases}$$

Let $x = 2y$ in the first equation.

$$2y + y = 90$$
$$3y = 90$$
$$y = 30$$

Let $y = 30$ in the second equation.

$$x = 2(30)$$
$$x = 60$$

The angles measure 60° and 30°.

33. Let $x =$ first angle
$y =$ second angle

$$\begin{cases} x + y = 90 \\ y = 3x + 10 \end{cases}$$

Let $y = 3x + 10$ in the first equation.

$$x + 3x + 10 = 90$$
$$4x = 80$$
$$x = 20$$

Let $x = 20$ in the second equation.

$$y = 3(20) + 10$$
$$y = 70$$

The angles measure 20° and 70°.

35. $x =$ liters of 20% solution
$y =$ liters of 70% solution

$$\begin{cases} x + y = 50 \\ 0.20x + 0.70y = 0.60(50) \end{cases}$$

Multiply 1st equation by –0.20 and add the equations.

$$-0.20x - 0.20y = -10$$
$$0.20x + 0.70y = 30$$
$$0.50y = 20$$
$$y = 40$$
$$x + 40 = 50$$
$$x = 10$$

She needs 10 liters of 20% solution and 40 liters of 70% solution.

37. Let $x =$ number sold at \$9.50
$y =$ number sold at \$7.50

$$\begin{cases} x + y = 90 \\ 9.5x + 7.5y = 721 \end{cases}$$

Substitute $90 - y$ for x in the second equation.

$$9.5(90 - y) + 7.5y = 721$$
$$855 - 9.5y + 7.5y = 721$$
$$-2y = -134$$
$$y = 67$$

Let $y = 67$ in the first equation.

$$x + 67 = 90$$
$$x = 23$$

They sold 23 at \$9.50 each and 67 at \$7.50 each.

39. Let $x =$ width
$y =$ length

$$\begin{cases} 2x + y = 33 \\ y = 2x - 3 \end{cases}$$

Substitute $2x - 3$ for y in the first equation.

$$2x + 2x - 3 = 33$$
$$4x = 36$$
$$x = 9$$

Let $x = 9$ in the second equation.

$$y = 2(9) - 3$$
$$y = 15$$

The width is 9 feet and the length is 15 feet.

41. Let x = time bicycling
y = time walking

$$\begin{cases} x+y=6 \\ 40x+4y=186 \end{cases}$$

Solve the 1st equation for x.
$x=6-y$
Replace x with $6-y$ in the second equation.

$$40(6-y)+4y=186$$
$$240-40y+4y=186$$
$$240-36y=186$$
$$-36y=186-240$$
$$-36y=-54$$
$$y=\frac{-54}{-36}=1.5$$

To find x, use $y = 1.5$ in the equation
$x=6-y$
$x=6-1.5$
$x=4.5$
The time bicycling is 4.5 hours.

43. Let y = eastbound train's speed
x = westbound train's speed

$$\begin{cases} \frac{5}{4}(x+y)=150 \end{cases}$$

Let $x=2y$ in the 1st equation.

$$\frac{5}{4}(2y+y)=150$$
$$\frac{15y}{15}=\frac{600}{15}$$
$$y=40$$

Let $y = 40$ in the 2nd equation.
$x=2y$
$x=2(40)$
$x=80$
The eastbound train is traveling at 40 mph and the westbound train is traveling at 80 mph.

45. B
The resulting mixture must have an acid strength that is between the strengths of the two solutions.

47. $y \ge 4-2x$
Find two points.

Let $x=0$	$x=2$
$y=4-2(0)$	$y=4-2(2)$
$y=4-0$	$y=4-4$
$y=4$	$y=0$
(0, 4)	(2, 0)

The boundary line is solid.
Choose (0, 0) as a test point.
$0 \; ? \; 4-2(0)$
$0 \; ? \; 4-0$
$0 \ge 4$ False
The side containing (0, 0) is not shaded.

49. $3x+5y<15$
Find two points.

Let $x=5$	$y=3$
$3(5)+5y=15$	$3x+5(3)=15$
$15+5y=15$	$3x+15=15$
$5y=0$	$3x=0$
$y=0$	$x=0$
(5, 0)	(0, 3)

The boundary line is dashed.
Choose (0, 0) as a test point.
$3(0)+5(0) \; ? \; 15$
$0+0 \; ? \; 15$
$0<15$ True

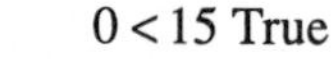

The side containing (0, 0) is shaded.

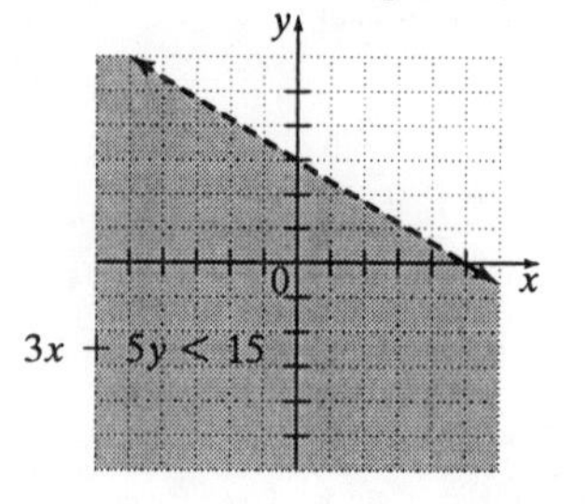

Exercise Set 8.5

1. $\begin{cases} y \geq x+1 \\ y \geq 3-x \end{cases}$

Graph $y = x + 1$.
The boundary line is solid.
Choose (0, 0) as a test point.
$y \geq x+1$
$0 \stackrel{?}{\geq} 0+1$
$0 \stackrel{?}{\geq} 1$
$0 \not\geq 1$, so shade the side *not* containing (0, 0).
Graph $y = 3 - x$.
The boundary line is solid. Choose (0, 0) as a test point.
$y \geq 3-x$
$0 \stackrel{?}{\geq} 3-0$
$0 \stackrel{?}{\geq} 3$
$0 \not\geq 3$, so shade the side *not* containing (0, 0).

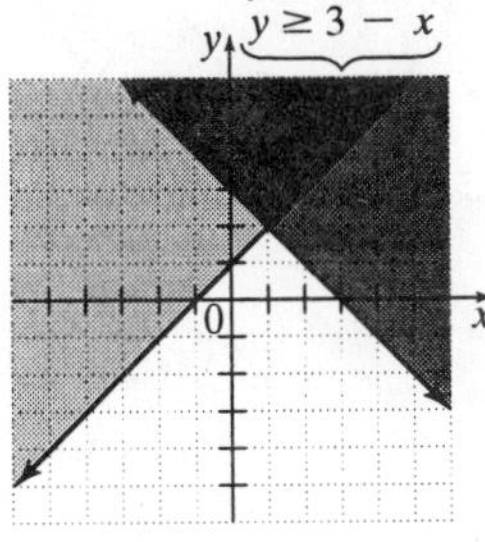

3. $\begin{cases} y < 3x-4 \\ y \leq x+2 \end{cases}$

Graph $y = 3x - 4$.
The boundary line is dashed.
Choose (0, 0) as a test point.
$y < 3x-4$
$0 \stackrel{?}{<} 3(0)-4$
$0 \stackrel{?}{<} -4$
$0 \not< -4$, so shade the side *not* containing (0, 0).
Graph $y = x + 2$.
The boundary line is solid.
Choose (0, 0) as a test point.
$y \leq x+2$
$0 \stackrel{?}{\leq} 0+2$
$0 \stackrel{?}{\leq} 2$
$0 \leq 2$, so shade the side containing (0, 0).

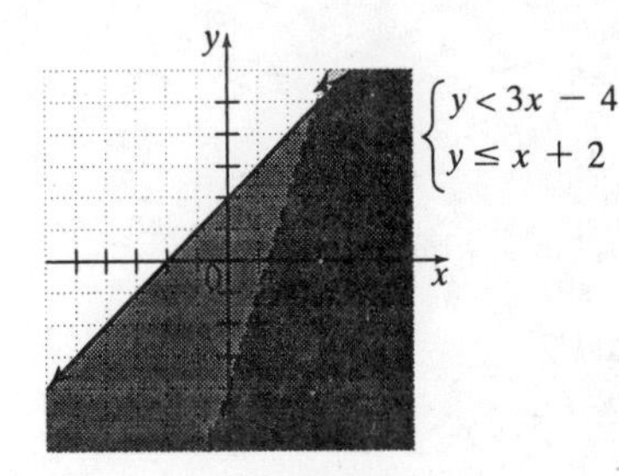

5. 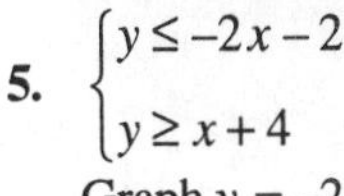

$\begin{cases} y \leq -2x-2 \\ y \geq x+4 \end{cases}$

Graph $y = -2x - 2$.
The boundary line is solid.
Choose (0, 0) as a test point.
$y \leq -2x-2$
$0 \stackrel{?}{\leq} -2(0)-2$
$0 \stackrel{?}{\leq} -2$
$0 \not\leq -2$, so shade the side *not* containing (0, 0).

Graph $y = x + 4$.
The boundary line is solid.
Choose (0, 0) as a test point.
$y \geq x+4$
$0 \stackrel{?}{\geq} 0+4$
$0 \stackrel{?}{\geq} 4$
$0 \not\geq 4$, so shade the side *not* containing (0, 0).

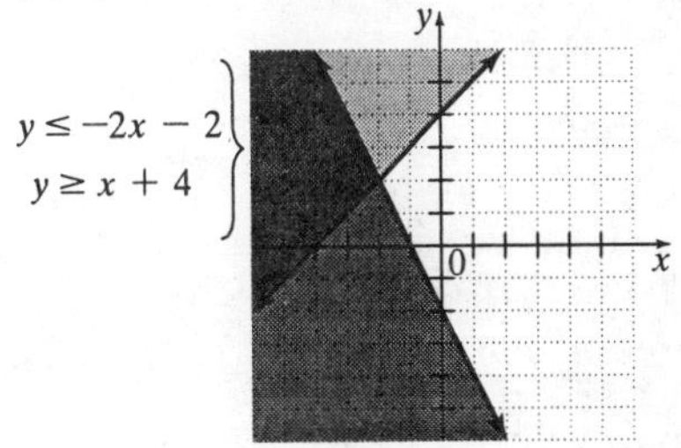

7. $\begin{cases} y \geq -x+2 \\ y \leq 2x+5 \end{cases}$

Graph $y = -x + 2$.
The boundary line is solid.
Choose (0, 0) as a test point.
$y \geq -x+2$
$0 \stackrel{?}{\geq} -0 + 2$
$0 \stackrel{?}{\geq} 2$
$0 \not\geq 2$, so shade the side *not* containing (0, 0).

Graph $y = 2x + 5$.
The boundary line is solid.
Choose (0, 0) as a test point.
$y \leq 2x+5$
$0 \stackrel{?}{\leq} 2(0) + 5$
$0 \stackrel{?}{\leq} 5$
$0 \leq 5$, so shade the side containing (0, 0).

$y \leq -x + 2$
$y \geq 2x + 5$

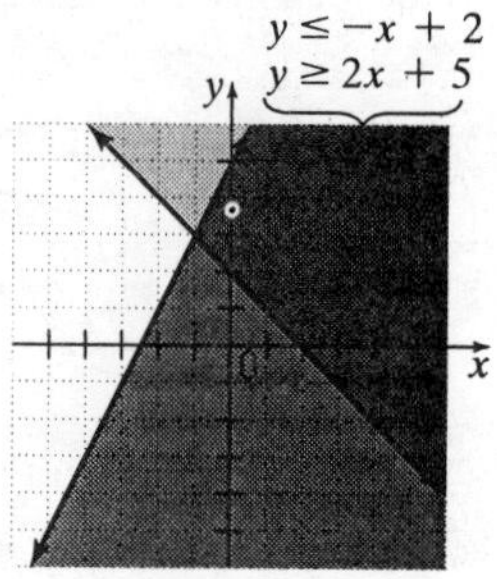

9. $\begin{cases} x \geq 3y \\ x+3y \leq 6 \end{cases}$

Graph $x = 3y$.
The boundary line is solid.
Choose (4, 0) as a test point.
$x \geq 3y$
$4 \stackrel{?}{\geq} 3(0)$
$4 \stackrel{?}{\geq} 0$
$4 \geq 0$, so shade the side containing (4, 0).
Graph $x + 3y = 6$
The boundary line is solid.
Choose (0, 0) as a test point.
$x+3y \leq 6$
$0 + 3(0) \stackrel{?}{\leq} 6$
$0 \stackrel{?}{\leq} 6$
$0 \leq 6$, so shade the side containing (0, 0).

$x \geq 3y$
$x + 3y \leq 6$

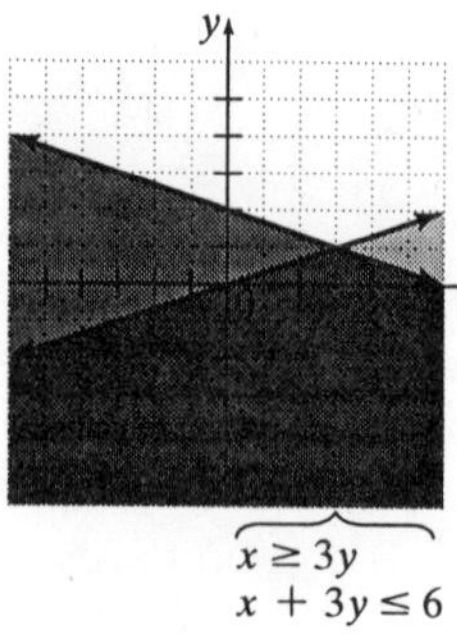

11. $\begin{cases} y+2x \geq 0 \\ 5x-3y \leq 12 \end{cases}$

Graph $y + 2x = 0$.
The boundary line is solid.
Choose (4, 0) as a test point.
$y+2x \geq 0$
$0 + 2(4) \stackrel{?}{\geq} 0$
$8 \stackrel{?}{\geq} 0$
$8 \geq 0$, so shade the side containing (4, 0).

Graph $5x - 3y = 12$.
The boundary line is solid.
Choose (0, 0) as a test point.
$5x-3y \leq 12$
$5(0) - 3(0) \stackrel{?}{\leq} 12$
$0 \stackrel{?}{\leq} 12$
$0 \leq 12$, so shade the side containing (0, 0).

$y + 2x \geq 0$
$5x - 3y \leq 12$

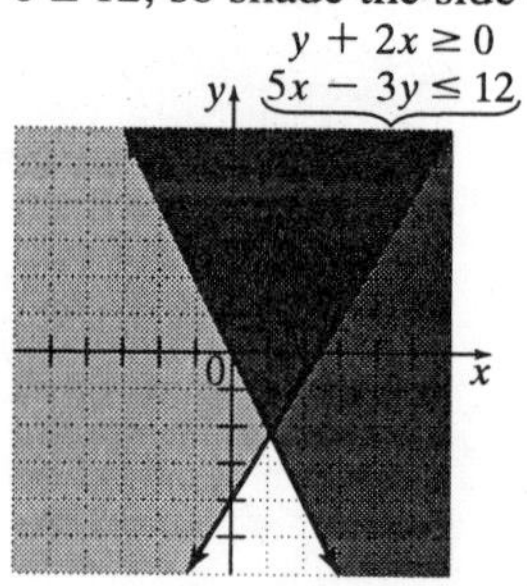

13. $\begin{cases} 3x - 4y \geq -6 \\ 2x + y \leq 7 \end{cases}$

Graph $3x - 4y = -6$.
The boundary line is solid.
Choose (0, 0) for a test point.

$3x - 4y \geq -6$
$3(0) - 4(0) \stackrel{?}{\geq} -6$
$0 \stackrel{?}{\geq} -6$

$0 \geq -6$, so shade the side containing (0, 0).

Graph $2x + y = 7$.
The boundary line is solid.
Choose (0, 0) for a test point.

$2x + y \leq 7$
$2(0) + 0 \stackrel{?}{\leq} 7$
$0 \stackrel{?}{\leq} 7$

$0 \leq 7$, so shade the side containing (0, 0).

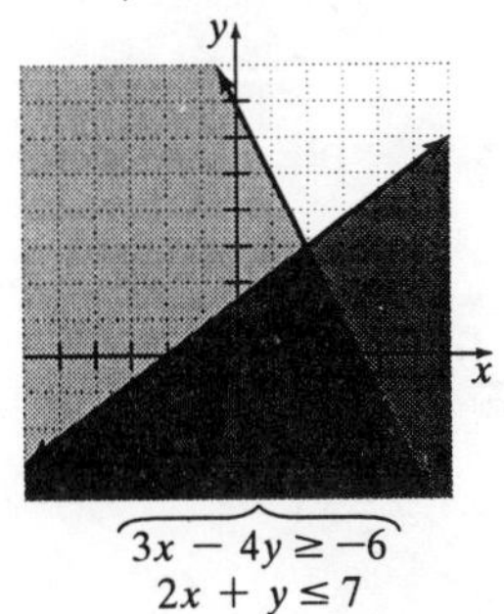

15. $\begin{cases} x \leq 2 \\ y \geq -3 \end{cases}$

Graph $x = 2$.
The boundary line is solid.
Since (0, 0) satisfies $x \leq 2$, shade the side containing (0, 0).

Graph $y = -3$.
The boundary line is solid.
Since (0, 0) satisfies $y \geq -3$, shade the side containing (0, 0).

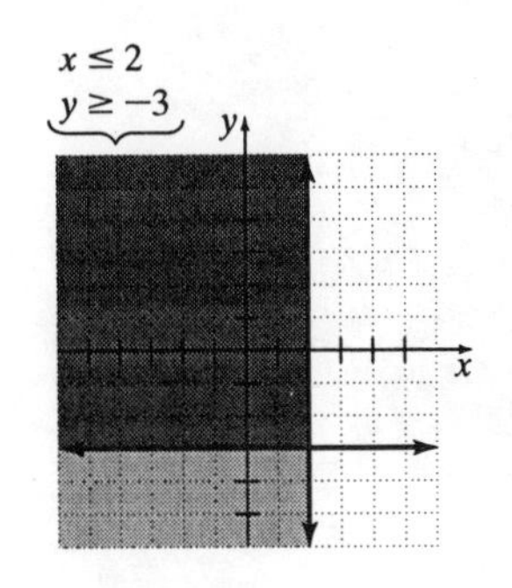

17. $\begin{cases} y \geq 1 \\ x < -3 \end{cases}$

Graph $y = 1$.
The boundary line is solid.
Since (0, 0) does *not* satisfy $y \geq 1$, shade the side *not* containing (0, 0).

Graph $x = -3$
The boundary line is dashed.
Since (0, 0) does *not* satisfy $x < -3$, shade the side *not* containing (0, 0).

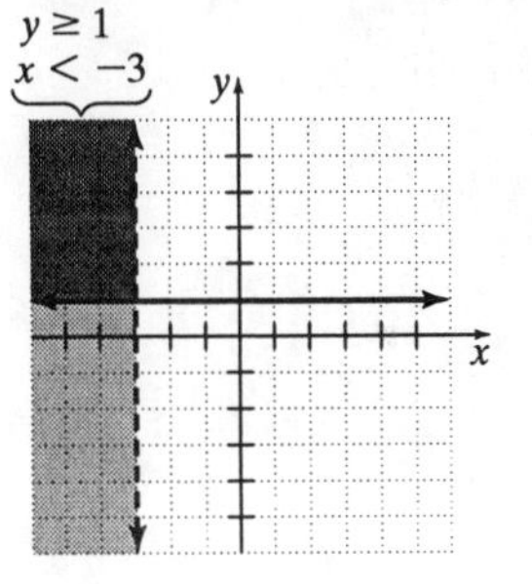

19. $\begin{cases} 2x + 3y < -8 \\ x \geq -4 \end{cases}$

Graph $2x + 3y = -8$.
The boundary line is dashed.
Choose (0, 0) for a test point.

$2x + 3y < -8$
$2(0) + 3(0) \stackrel{?}{<} -8$
$0 \stackrel{?}{<} -8$

$0 \not< -8$, so the side *not* containing (0, 0) is shaded.

Graph $x = -4$.
The boundary line is solid.
Since (0, 0) does satisfy $x \geq -4$, shade the side containing (0, 0).

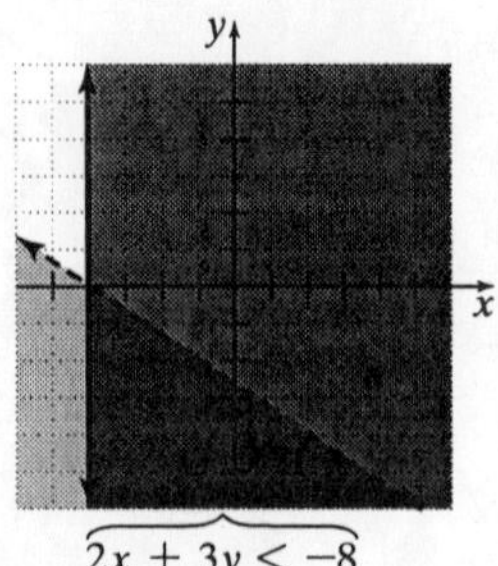

21. $\begin{cases} 2x-5y \le 9 \\ y \le -3 \end{cases}$

Graph $2x - 5y = 9$.
The boundary line is solid.
Choose (0, 0) for a test point.

$2x-5y \le 9$
$2(0)-5(0) \overset{?}{\le} 9$
$0 \overset{?}{\le} 9$

$0 \le 9$, so the side containing (0, 0) is shaded.

Graph $y = -3$.
The boundary line is solid.
Since (0, 0) does *not* satisfy $y \le -3$, shade the side not containing (0, 0).

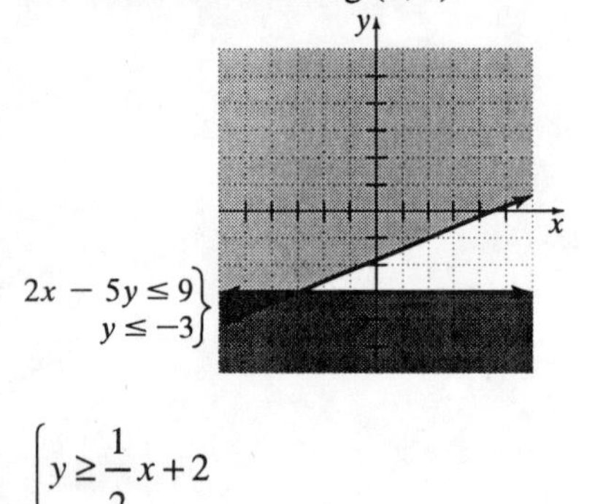

23. $\begin{cases} y \ge \frac{1}{2}x+2 \\ y \le \frac{1}{2}x-3 \end{cases}$

Graph $y = \frac{1}{2}x + 2$.
The boundary line is solid.
Choose (0, 0) for a test point.

$y \ge \frac{1}{2}x+2$
$0 \ ? \ \frac{1}{2}(0)+2$
$0 \overset{?}{\ge} 2$

$0 \not\ge 2$, so the side *not* containing (0, 0) is shaded.

Graph $y = \frac{1}{2}x - 3$.
The boundary line is solid.
Choose (0, 0) for a test point.

$y \le \frac{1}{2}x-3$
$0 \ ? \ \frac{1}{2}(0)-3$
$0 \overset{?}{\le} -3$

$0 \not\le -3$, so shade the side *not* containing (0, 0).

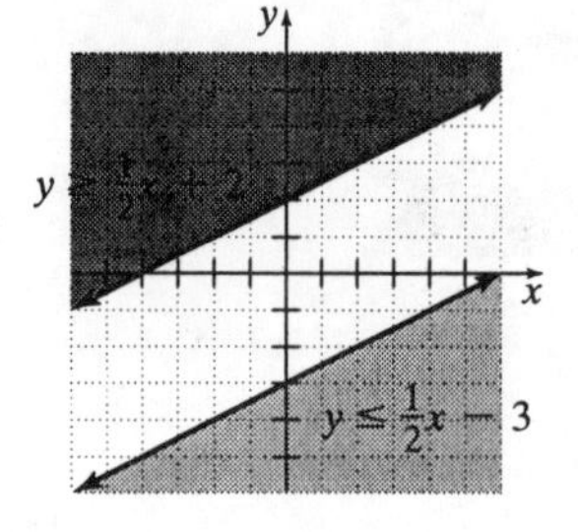

25. C

27. D

29. a. Let x = hours for writing bills
y = hours for writing purchase orders

$\begin{cases} x+y \le 8 \\ x < 3 \end{cases}$

b. Graph $x + y = 8$.
The boundary line is solid.
Choose (0, 0) for a test point.
$x + y \le 8$
$0 + 0 \stackrel{?}{\le} 8$
$0 \stackrel{?}{\le} 8$
$0 \le 8$, so shade the side containing (0, 0).

Graph $x = 3$.
Since (0, 0) does satisfy $x < 3$, shade the side containing (0, 0).

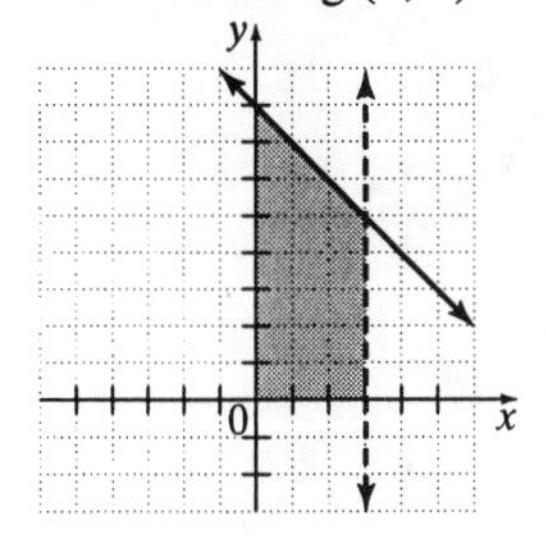

31. Answers may vary.

33. $4^2 = 16$

35. $(6x)^2 = 6^2 \cdot x^2 = 36x^2$

37. $(10y^3)^2 = (10)^2 \cdot (y^3)^2$
$= (10)^2 \cdot y^{3\cdot 2}$
$= 100y^6$

Chapter 8 Review Exercises

1. $\begin{cases} 2x - 3y = 12 \\ 3x + 4y = 1 \end{cases}$

a. (12, 4)
$2x - 3y = 12$
$2(12) - 3(4) \stackrel{?}{=} 12$
$24 - 12 \stackrel{?}{=} 12$
$12 = 12$ True

$3x + 4y = 1$
$3(12) + 4(4) \stackrel{?}{=} 1$
$36 + 16 \stackrel{?}{=} 1$
$52 = 1$ False
(12, 4) is not a solution.

b. (3, −2)
$2x - 3y = 12$
$2(3) - 3(-2) \stackrel{?}{=} 12$
$6 + 6 \stackrel{?}{=} 12$
$12 = 12$ True

$3x + 4y = 1$
$3(3) + 4(-2) \stackrel{?}{=} 1$
$9 - 8 \stackrel{?}{=} 1$
$1 = 1$ True
(3, −2) is a solution.

c. (−3, 6)

$2x - 3y = 12$
$2(-3) - 3(6) \stackrel{?}{=} 12$
$-6 - 18 \stackrel{?}{=} 12$
$-24 = 12$ False

$3x + 4y = 1$
$3(-3) + 4(6) \stackrel{?}{=} 1$
$-9 + 24 \stackrel{?}{=} 1$
$15 = 1$ False
(−3, 6) is not a solution.

2. $\begin{cases} 4x + y = 0 \\ -8x - 5y = 9 \end{cases}$

a. $\left(\frac{3}{4}, -3\right)$
$4x + y = 0$
$4\left(\frac{3}{4}\right) + (-3) \stackrel{?}{=} 0$
$3 + (-3) \stackrel{?}{=} 0$
$0 = 0$ True
$-8x - 5y = 9$
$-8\left(\frac{3}{4}\right) - 5(-3) \stackrel{?}{=} 9$
$-6 + 15 \stackrel{?}{=} 9$
$9 = 9$ True

$\left(\frac{3}{4}, -3\right)$ is a solution.

b. (–2, 8)

$$4x + y = 0$$
$$4(-2) + 8 \stackrel{?}{=} 0$$
$$-8 + 8 \stackrel{?}{=} 0$$
$$0 = 0 \text{ True}$$

$$-8x - 5y = 9$$
$$-8(-2) - 5(8) \stackrel{?}{=} 9$$
$$16 - 40 \stackrel{?}{=} 9$$
$$-24 = 9 \text{ False}$$

(–2, 8) is not a solution.

c. $\left(\frac{1}{2}, -2\right)$

$$4x + y = 0$$
$$4\left(\frac{1}{2}\right) + (-2) \stackrel{?}{=} 0$$
$$2 + (-2) \stackrel{?}{=} 0$$
$$0 = 0 \text{ True}$$

$$-8x - 5y = 9$$
$$-8\left(\frac{1}{2}\right) - 5(-2) \stackrel{?}{=} 9$$
$$-4 + 10 \stackrel{?}{=} 9$$
$$6 = 9 \text{ False}$$

$\left(\frac{1}{2}, -2\right)$ is not a solution.

3. $\begin{cases} 5x - 6y = 18 \\ 2y - x = -4 \end{cases}$

a. (–6, –8)

$$5x - 6y = 18$$
$$5(-6) - 6(-8) \stackrel{?}{=} 18$$
$$-30 + 48 \stackrel{?}{=} 18$$
$$18 = 18 \text{ True}$$

$$2y - x = -4$$
$$2(-8) - (-6) \stackrel{?}{=} -4$$
$$-16 + 6 \stackrel{?}{=} -4$$
$$-10 = -4 \text{ False}$$

(–6, –8) is not a solution.

b. $\left(3, \frac{5}{2}\right)$

$$5x - 6y = 18$$
$$5(3) - 6\left(\frac{5}{2}\right) \stackrel{?}{=} 18$$
$$15 - 15 \stackrel{?}{=} 18$$
$$0 = 18 \text{ False}$$

$$2y - x = -4$$
$$2\left(\frac{5}{2}\right) - 3 \stackrel{?}{=} -4$$
$$5 - 3 \stackrel{?}{=} -4$$
$$2 = -4 \text{ False}$$

$\left(3, \frac{5}{2}\right)$ is not a solution.

c. $\left(3, -\frac{1}{2}\right)$

$$5x - 6y = 18$$
$$5(3) - 6\left(-\frac{1}{2}\right) \stackrel{?}{=} 18$$
$$15 + 3 \stackrel{?}{=} 18$$
$$18 = 18 \text{ True}$$

$$2y - x = -4$$
$$2\left(-\frac{1}{2}\right) - 3 \stackrel{?}{=} -4$$
$$-1 - 3 \stackrel{?}{=} -4$$
$$-4 = -4 \text{ True}$$

$\left(3, -\frac{1}{2}\right)$ is a solution.

4. $\begin{cases} 2x+3y=1 \\ 3y-x=4 \end{cases}$

a. (2, 2)

$$2x+3y=1$$
$$2(2)+3(2)\stackrel{?}{=}1$$
$$4+6\stackrel{?}{=}1$$
$$10=1 \text{ False}$$

(2, 2) is not a solution.

b. (–1, 1)

$$2x+3y=1$$
$$2(-1)+3(1)\stackrel{?}{=}1$$
$$-2+3\stackrel{?}{=}1$$
$$1=1 \text{ True}$$

$$3y-x=4$$
$$3(1)-(-1)\stackrel{?}{=}4$$
$$3+1\stackrel{?}{=}4$$
$$4=4 \text{ True}$$

(–1, 1) is a solution.

c. (2, –1)

$$2x+3y=1$$
$$2(2)+3(-1)\stackrel{?}{=}1$$
$$4-3\stackrel{?}{=}1$$
$$1=1 \text{ True}$$

$$3y-x=4$$
$$3(-1)-2\stackrel{?}{=}4$$
$$-3-2\stackrel{?}{=}4$$
$$-5=4 \text{ False}$$

(2, –1) is not a solution.

5. $\begin{cases} 2x+y=5 \\ 3y=-x \end{cases}$

Graph each linear equation on a single set of axes.

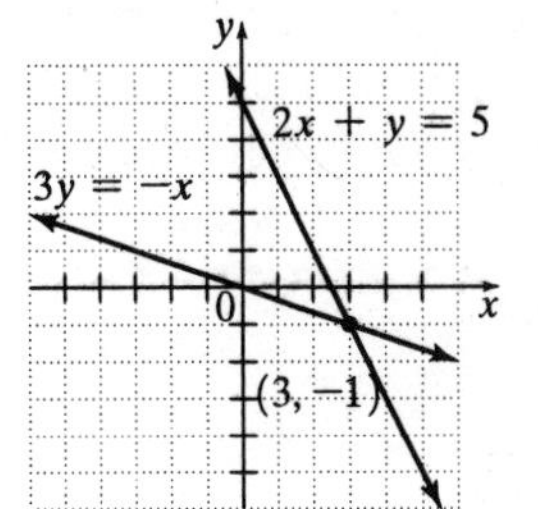

The solution is the intersection point of the two lines, (3, –1).

6. $\begin{cases} 3x+y=-2 \\ 2x-y=-3 \end{cases}$

Graph each linear equation on a single set of axes.

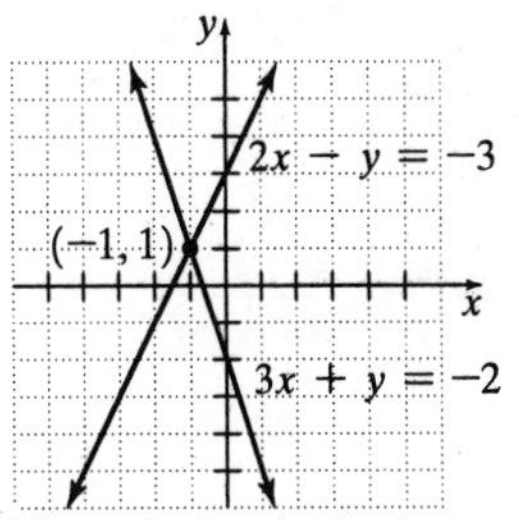

The solution is the intersection point of the two lines, (–1, 1).

7. 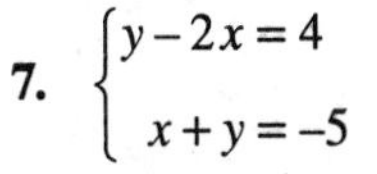

$\begin{cases} y-2x=4 \\ x+y=-5 \end{cases}$

Graph each linear equation on a single set of axes.

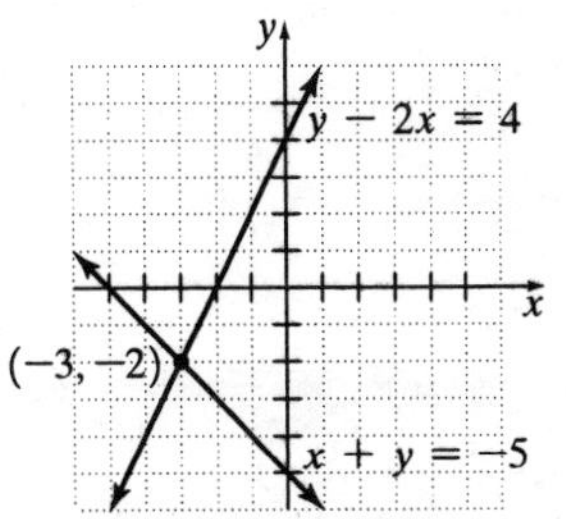

The solution is the intersection point of the two lines (–3, –2).

8. $\begin{cases} y-3x=0 \\ 2y-3=6x \end{cases}$

Graph each linear equation on a single set of axes.

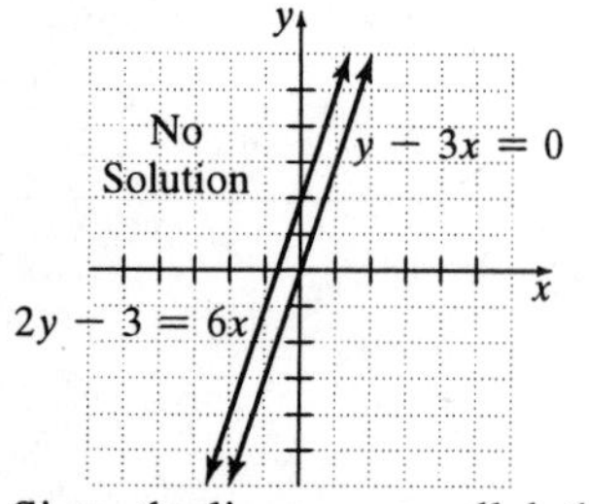

Since the lines are parallel, the system has no solution.

9. $\begin{cases} 3x+y=2 \\ 3x-6=-9y \end{cases}$

Graph each linear equation on a single set of axes.

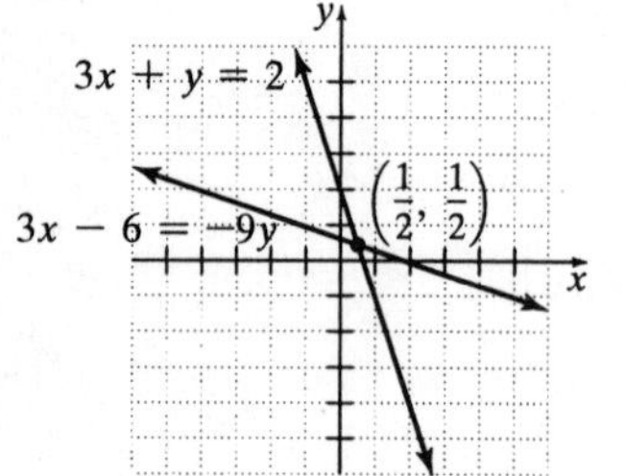

The solution is the intersection point of the two lines, $\left(\frac{1}{2}, \frac{1}{2}\right)$.

10. $\begin{cases} 2y+x=2 \\ x-y=5 \end{cases}$

Graph each linear equation on a single set of axes.

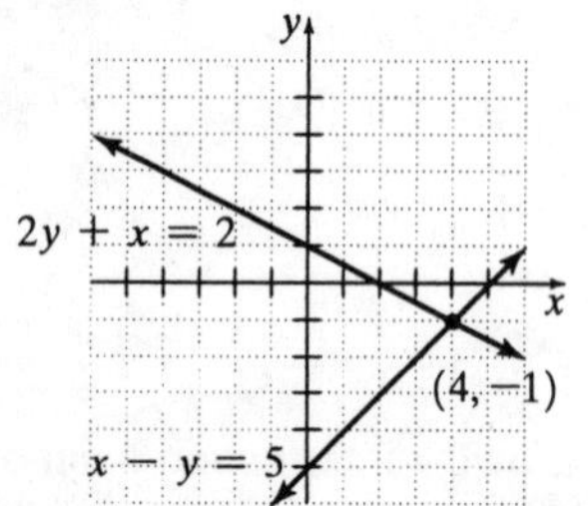

The solution is the intersection point of the two lines (4, –1).

11. $\begin{cases} 2x-y=3 \\ y=3x+1 \end{cases}$

$2x-y=3$
$-y=-2x+3$
$\frac{-y}{-1}=\frac{-2}{-1}x+\frac{3}{-1}$
$y=2x-3$
$m=2,\ b=-3$

$y=3x+1$
$m=3,\ b=1$

Since the slopes are different, the lines intersect at a single point; one solution.

12. $\begin{cases} 3x+y=4 \\ y=-3x+1 \end{cases}$

$3x+y=4$
$y=-3x+4$

Since the lines have the same slope but different
y-intercepts, the lines are parallel; no solution.

13. $\begin{cases} \frac{2}{3}x+\frac{1}{6}y=0 \\ y=-4x \end{cases}$

$\frac{2}{3}x+\frac{1}{6}y=0$
$\frac{1}{6}y=-\frac{2}{3}x$
$6\left(\frac{1}{6}y\right)=6\left(-\frac{2}{3}x\right)$
$y=-4x$

$y=-4x$

Since the equations are identical, there are an infinite number of solutions.

14. $\begin{cases} \frac{1}{4}x+\frac{1}{8}y=0 \\ y=-6x \end{cases}$

$\frac{1}{4}x+\frac{1}{8}y=0$
$2x+y=0$
$y=-2x$

Since the lines have different slopes, they intersect at a single point; one solution.

15. $\begin{cases} y = 2x + 6 \\ 3x - 2y = -11 \end{cases}$

Replace y with $2x + 6$ in the second equation.

$$3x - 2(2x + 6) = -11$$
$$3x - 4x - 12 = -11$$
$$-x - 12 = -11$$
$$-x = -11 + 12$$
$$-x = 1$$
$$\frac{-x}{-1} = \frac{1}{-1}$$
$$x = -1$$

To find y, use $x = -1$ in the equation

$y = 2x + 6$
$y = 2(-1) + 6$
$y = -2 + 6$
$y = 4$

The solution is (–1, 4).

16. $\begin{cases} y = 3x - 7 \\ 2x - 3y = 7 \end{cases}$

Replace y with $3x - 7$ in the second equation.

$$2x - 3(3x - 7) = 7$$
$$2x - 9x + 21 = 7$$
$$-7x = -14$$
$$\frac{-7x}{-7} = \frac{-14}{-7}$$
$$x = 2$$

To find y, use $x = 2$ in the equation

$y = 3x - 7$
$y = 3(2) - 7$
$y = 6 - 7$
$y = -1$

The solution is (2, –1).

17. $\begin{cases} x + 3y = -3 \\ 2x + y = 4 \end{cases}$

Solve the 1st equation for x.

$x = -3y - 3$

Replace x with $-3y - 3$ in the second equation.

$$2(-3y - 3) + y = 4$$
$$-6y - 6 + y = 4$$
$$-5y - 6 = 4$$
$$-5y = 4 + 6$$
$$-5y = 10$$
$$y = \frac{10}{-5} = -2$$

To find x, use $y = -2$ in the equation.

$x = -3y - 3$
$x = -3(-2) - 3$
$x = 6 - 3$
$x = 3$

The solution is (3, –2).

18. $\begin{cases} 3x + y = 11 \\ x + 2y = 12 \end{cases}$

Solve the 1st equation for y.

$y = -3x + 11$

Replace y with $-3x + 11$ in the second equation.

$$x + 2(-3x + 11) = 12$$
$$x - 6x + 22 = 12$$
$$-5x = 10$$
$$\frac{-5x}{-5} = \frac{-10}{-5}$$
$$x = 2$$

To find y, let $x = 2$ in the equation $y = -3x + 11$

$y = -3(2) + 11$
$y = -6 + 11$
$y = 5$

The solution is (2, 5).

19. $\begin{cases} 4y = 2x - 3 \\ x - 2y = 4 \end{cases}$

Solve the 2nd equation for x.

$x = 2y + 4$

Replace x with $2y + 4$ in the 1st equation.

$$4y = 2(2y+4) - 3$$
$$4y = 4y + 8 - 3$$
$$4y = 4y + 5$$
$$4y - 4y = 5$$
$$0 = 5$$

This is a contradiction.
There is no solution.
The system is inconsistent.

20. $\begin{cases} 2x = 3y - 18 \\ x + 4y = 2 \end{cases}$

Solve the 2nd equation for x.

$x = 2 - 4y$

Replace x with $2 - 4y$ in the 1st equation.

$$2(2 - 4y) = 3y - 18$$
$$4 - 8y = 3y - 18$$
$$22 = 11y$$
$$\frac{22}{11} = \frac{11y}{11}$$
$$2 = y$$

To find x, use $y = 2$ in the equation

$x = 2 - 4y$
$x = 2 - 4(2)$
$x = 2 - 8$
$x = -6$

The solution is $(-6, 2)$.

21. $\begin{cases} 2(3x - y) = 7x - 5 \\ 3(x - y) = 4x - 6 \end{cases}$

Simplify the equations.

$$2(3x - y) = 7x - 5$$
$$6x - 2y = 7x - 5$$
$$6x - 7x - 2y = -5$$
$$-x - 2y = -5$$

$$3(x - y) = 4x - 6$$
$$3x - 3y = 4x - 6$$
$$3x - 4x - 3y = -6$$
$$-x - 3y = -6$$

Solve the 1st equation for x.

$$-x - 2y = -5$$
$$-x = 2y - 5$$
$$\frac{-x}{-1} = \frac{2y}{-1} - \frac{5}{-1}$$
$$x = -2y + 5$$

Replace x with $-2y + 5$ in the 2nd equation.

$$-(-2y+5) - 3y = -6$$
$$2y - 5 - 3y = -6$$
$$-y - 5 = -6$$
$$-y = -6 + 5$$
$$-y = -1$$
$$\frac{-y}{-1} = \frac{-1}{-1}$$
$$y = 1$$

To find x, use $y = 1$ in the equation

$x = -2y + 5$
$x = -2(1) + 5$
$x = -2 + 5$
$x = 3$

The solution is $(3, 1)$.

22. $\begin{cases} 4(x - 3y) = 3x - 1 \\ 3(4y - 3x) = 1 - 8x \end{cases}$

Simplify the 1st equation and solve for x.

$$4x - 12y = 3x - 1$$
$$x = 12y - 1$$

Replace x with $12y - 1$ in the 2nd equation.

$$3[4y - 3(12y - 1)] = 1 - 8(12y - 1)$$
$$3[4y - 36y + 3] = 1 - 96y + 8$$
$$12y - 108y + 9 = 1 - 96y + 8$$
$$-96y + 9 = -96y + 9$$
$$9 = 9$$

There is an infinite number of solutions. The system is dependent.

23. $\begin{cases} \frac{3}{4}x + \frac{2}{3}y = 2 \\ 3x + y = 18 \end{cases}$

Solve the 2nd equation for y.

$y = -3x + 18$

Replace y with $-3x + 18$ in the 1st equation.

$$\frac{3}{4}x + \frac{2}{3}(-3x + 18) = 2$$
$$\frac{3}{4}x - 2x + 12 = 2$$
$$\frac{3}{4}x - \frac{8}{4}x + 12 = 2$$
$$-\frac{5}{4}x + 12 = 2$$
$$-\frac{5}{4}x = 2 - 12$$
$$-\frac{5}{4}x = -10$$
$$-\frac{4}{5}\left(-\frac{5}{4}x\right) = -\frac{4}{5}(-10)$$
$$x = 8$$

To find y, use $x = 8$ in the equation

$y = -3x + 18$

$y = -3(8) + 18$

$y = -24 + 18$

$y = -6$

The solution is (8, –6).

24. $\begin{cases} \frac{2}{5}x + \frac{3}{4}y = 1 \\ x + 3y = -2 \end{cases}$

Solve the 2nd equation for x.

$x = -3y - 2$

Replace x with $-3y - 2$ in the 1st equation

$$\frac{2}{5}(-3y - 2) + \frac{3}{4}y = 1$$
$$20\left[\frac{2}{5}(-3y - 2) + \frac{3}{4}y = 1\right]$$
$$8(-3y - 2) + 15y = 20$$
$$-24y - 16 + 15y = 20$$
$$-9y = 36$$
$$\frac{-9y}{-9} = \frac{36}{-9}$$
$$y = -4$$

To find x, use $y = -4$ in the equation

$x = -3y - 2$

$x = -3(-4) - 2$

$x = 12 - 2$

$x = 10$

The solution is (10, –4).

25. $\begin{cases} 2x + 3y = -6 \\ x - 3y = -12 \end{cases}$

Add the equations.

$$\begin{array}{r} 2x + 3y = -6 \\ x - 3y = -12 \\ \hline 3x \quad = -18 \end{array}$$
$$x = \frac{-18}{3} = -6$$

To find y, use $x = -6$ in the equation

$$x - 3y = -12$$
$$-6 - 3y = -12$$
$$-3y = -12 + 6$$
$$-3y = -6$$
$$y = \frac{-6}{-3} = 2$$

The solution is (–6, 2).

26. $\begin{cases} 4x + y = 15 \\ -4x + 3y = -19 \end{cases}$

Add the equations.

$$4x + y = 15$$
$$-4x + 3y = -19$$
$$4y = -4$$
$$y = -1$$

To find x, use $y = -1$ in the equation

$$4x + y = 15$$
$$4x - 1 = 15$$
$$4x = 16$$
$$x = 4$$

The solution is (4, –1).

27. $\begin{cases} 2x-3y=-15 \\ x+4y=31 \end{cases}$

Multiply the 2nd equation by –2.

$-2(x+4y)=-2(31)$

$-2x-8y=-62$

Add the equations.

$$\begin{array}{r} -2x-8y=-62 \\ 2x-3y=-15 \\ \hline -11y=-77 \end{array}$$

$y=\dfrac{-77}{-11}=7$

To find x, use $y = 7$ in the equation

$x+4y=31$

$x+4(7)=31$

$x+28=31$

$x=31-28$

$x=3$

The solution is (3, 7).

28. $\begin{cases} x-5y=-22 \\ 4x+3y=4 \end{cases}$

Multiply the 1st equation by –4 and add to the 2nd equation.

$$\begin{array}{r} -4x+20y=88 \\ 4x\ +3y=\ 4 \\ \hline 23y=92 \end{array}$$

$y=4$

To find x, use $y = 4$ in the equation

$x-5y=-22$

$x-5(4)=-22$

$x-20=-22$

$x=-2$

The solution is (–2, 4).

29. $\begin{cases} 2x=6y-1 \\ \dfrac{1}{3}x-y=-\dfrac{1}{6} \end{cases}$

Multiply the 2nd equation by 6.

$6\left(\dfrac{1}{3}x-y\right)=6\left(-\dfrac{1}{6}\right)$

$2x-6y=-1$

Multiply the 1st equation by –1.

$-1(2x)=-(6y-1)$

$-2x=-6y+1$

$-2x+6y=1$

Add the equations.

$$\begin{array}{r} 2x-6y=-1 \\ -2x+6y=\ 1 \\ \hline 0=\ 0 \end{array}$$

This is an identity.

The system is dependent.

There is an infinite number of solutions.

30. $\begin{cases} 8x=3y-2 \\ \dfrac{4}{7}x-y=-\dfrac{5}{2} \end{cases}$

Multiply the 2nd equation by –14 and add to the 1st equation.

$$\begin{array}{r} 8x\ -3y=-2 \\ -8x+14y=35 \\ \hline 11y=33 \end{array}$$

$y=3$

To find x, use $y = 3$ in the equation

$8x=3y-2$

$8x=3(3)-2$

$8x=9-2$

$8x=7$

$\dfrac{8x}{8}=\dfrac{7}{8}$

$x=\dfrac{7}{8}$

The solution is $\left(\dfrac{7}{8},\ 3\right)$.

31. $\begin{cases} 5x=6y+25 \\ -2y=7x-9 \end{cases}$

Rearrange the equations.

$5x-6y=25$

$-7x-2y=-9$

Multiply the 2nd equation by –3.

$-3(-7x-2y)=-3(-9)$

$21x+6y=27$

Add the equations.

$$\begin{array}{rl} 21x+6y &= 27 \\ 5x-6y &= 25 \\ \hline 26x &= 52 \end{array}$$

$$x = \frac{52}{26} = 2$$

To find y, use $x = 2$ in the equation

$$5x-6y=25$$
$$5(2)-6y=25$$
$$10-7y=25$$
$$-6y=25-10$$
$$-6y=15$$
$$y=\frac{15}{-6}=-\frac{5}{2}$$

The solution is $\left(2, -\frac{5}{2}\right)$.

32. $\begin{cases} -4x = 8+6y \\ -3y = 2x-3 \end{cases}$

Rearrange the equations.

$$-4x-6y=8$$
$$-2x-3y=-3$$

Multiply the 2nd equation by -2.

$$-2(-2x-3y)=-2(-3)$$
$$4x+6y=6$$

Add the equations.

$$\begin{array}{rl} -4x-6y &= 8 \\ 4x+6y &= 6 \\ \hline 0 &= 14 \end{array}$$

This is a contradiction.
There is no solution.
The system is inconsistent.

33. $\begin{cases} 3(x-4) = -2y \\ 2x = 3(y-19) \end{cases}$

Simplify each equation.

$$3(x-4)=-2y$$
$$3x-12=-2y$$
$$3x+2y-12=0$$
$$3x+2y=12$$

$$2x=3(y-19)$$
$$2x=3y-57$$
$$2x-3y=-57$$

Multiply the 1st equation by -2.

$$-2(3x+2y)=-2(12)$$
$$-6x-4y=-24$$

Multiply the 2nd equation by 3.

$$3(2x-3y)=3(-57)$$
$$6x-9y=-171$$

Add the equations.

$$\begin{array}{rl} -6x-4y &= -24 \\ 6x-9y &= -171 \\ \hline -13y &= -195 \end{array}$$

$$y=\frac{-195}{-13}=15$$

To find x, use $y = 15$ in the equation

$$2x-3y=-57$$
$$2x-3(15)=-57$$
$$2x-45=-57$$
$$2x=-57+45$$
$$2x=-12$$
$$x=\frac{-12}{2}=-6$$

The solution is $(-6, 15)$.

34. $\begin{cases} 4(x+5) = -3y \\ 3x-2(y+18) = 0 \end{cases}$

Simplify each equation.

$$4(x+5)=-3y$$
$$4x+20=-3y$$
$$4x+3y=-20$$

$$3x-2(y+18)=0$$
$$3x-2y-36=0$$
$$3x-2y=36$$

Multiply the 1st equation by 2.

$$2(4x+3y)=2(-20)$$
$$8x+6y=-40$$

Multiply the 2nd equation by 3.

$$3(3x-2y)=3(36)$$
$$9x-6y=108$$

Add the equations.

$$\begin{array}{rl} 8x+6y &= -40 \\ 9x-6y &= 108 \\ \hline 17x &= 68 \end{array}$$

$$x=4$$

To find y, use $x = 4$ in the equation

$$4x+3y=-20$$
$$4(4)+3y=-20$$
$$16+3y=-20$$
$$3y=-36$$
$$y=-12$$

The solution is (4, –12).

35. $\begin{cases} \frac{2x+9}{3}=\frac{y+1}{2} \\ \frac{x}{3}=\frac{y-7}{6} \end{cases}$

Simplify the equations.

$$6\left(\frac{2x+9}{3}\right)=6\left(\frac{y+1}{2}\right)$$
$$2(2x+9)=3(y+1)$$
$$4x+18=3y+3$$
$$4x-3y+18=3$$
$$4x-3y=3-18$$
$$4x-3y=-15$$
$$6\left(\frac{x}{3}\right)=6\left(\frac{y-7}{6}\right)$$
$$2x=y-7$$
$$2x-y=-7$$

Multiply the 2nd equation by –3.

$$-3(2x-y)=-3(-7)$$
$$-6x+3y=21$$

Add the equations.

$$\begin{aligned} -6x+3y &= 21 \\ 4x-3y &= -15 \\ \hline -2x &= 6 \end{aligned}$$
$$x=\frac{6}{-2}=-3$$

To find y, use $x = -3$ in the equation

$$2x-y=-7$$
$$2(-3)-y=-7$$
$$-6-y=-7$$
$$-y=-7+6$$
$$-y=-1$$
$$y=\frac{-1}{-1}=1$$

The solution is (–3, 1).

36. $\begin{cases} \frac{2-5x}{4}=\frac{2y-4}{2} \\ \frac{x+5}{3}=\frac{y}{5} \end{cases}$

Simplify each equation.

$$4\left(\frac{2-5x}{4}\right)=4\left(\frac{2y-4}{2}\right)$$
$$2-5x=4y-8$$
$$5x+4y=10$$
$$15\left(\frac{x+5}{3}\right)=15\left(\frac{y}{5}\right)$$
$$5x+25=3y$$
$$-5x+3y=25$$

Add the equations.

$$\begin{aligned} 5x+4y &= 10 \\ -5x+3y &= 25 \\ \hline 7y &= 35 \end{aligned}$$
$$y=5$$

To find x, use $y = 5$ in the equation

$$5x+4y=10$$
$$5x+4(5)=10$$
$$5x+20=10$$
$$5x=-10$$
$$x=-2$$

The solution is (–2, 5).

37. Let x = smaller number

y = larger number

$$\begin{cases} x+y=16 \\ 3y-x=72 \end{cases}$$

Solve the 1st equation for x.

$x = 16 - y$

Replace x with $16 - y$ in the 2nd equation.

$$3y-(16-y)=72$$
$$3y-16+y=72$$
$$4y-16=72$$
$$4y=72+16$$
$$4y=88$$
$$y=\frac{88}{4}=22$$

To find x, use $y = 22$ in the equation

$x = 16 - y$

$x = 16 - 22$

$x = -6$

The numbers are 22 and –6.

38. Let x = number of orchestra seats
y = number of balcony seats

$$\begin{cases} x+y=360 \\ 45x+35y=15{,}150 \end{cases}$$

Multiply the 1st equation by –45.

$-45(x+y)=-45(360)$

$-45x-45y=-16,200$

Add the equations.

$$\begin{aligned} -45x-45y&=-16,200 \\ 45x+35y&=15,150 \\ \hline -10y&=-1050 \\ y&=105 \end{aligned}$$

To find x, let y = 105 in the equation

$x+y=360$

$x+105=360$

$x=255$

255 people can be seated in the orchestra section.

39. Let x = speed of boat in still water
y = speed of current

$$\begin{cases} 19(x-y)=340 \\ 14(x+y)=340 \end{cases}$$

Simplify the equations.

$$\frac{19(x-y)}{19}=\frac{340}{19}$$

$x-y=17.9$

$$\frac{14(x+y)}{14}=\frac{340}{14}$$

$x+y=24.3$

Add the equations.

$$\begin{aligned} x-y&=17.9 \\ x+y&=24.3 \\ \hline 2x&=42.2 \\ x&=\frac{42.2}{2}=21.1 \end{aligned}$$

To find y, use x = 21.1 in the equation

$x+y=24.3$

$21.1+y=24.3$

$y=24.3-21.1$

$y=3.2$

Boat's speed = 21.1 mph
Current's speed = 3.2 mph

40. Let x = amount invested at 6%
y = amount invested at 10%

$$\begin{cases} x+y=9000 \\ 0.06x+0.10y=652.80 \end{cases}$$

Multiply the first equation by –6 and the second equation by 100.

$-6(x+y)=-6(9000)$

$100(0.06x+0.10y)=100(652.80)$

Add the resulting equations.

$$\begin{aligned} -6x-6y&=-54,000 \\ 6x+10y&=65,280 \\ \hline 4y&=11,280 \\ y&=2820 \end{aligned}$$

To find x, let y = 2820 in the equation

$x+y=9000$

$x+2820=9000$

$x=6180$

\$6180 was invested at 6% and \$2820 was invested at 10%.

41. Let x = width
y = length

$$\begin{cases} 2x+2y=6 \\ 1.6x=y \end{cases}$$

Replace $y=1.6x$ in the 1st equation.

$2x+2(1.6x)=6$

$2x+3.2x=6$

$5.2x=6$

$$x=\frac{6}{5.2}=1.15$$

To find y, use x = 1.15 in the equation

$y=1.6x$

$y=1.6(1.15)$

$y=1.84$

width ≈ 1.15 ft.
length ≈ 1.84 ft.

42. Let x = amount of 6% solution

y = amount of 14% solution

$$\begin{cases} x + y = 50 \\ 0.06x + 0.14y = 0.12(50) \end{cases}$$

Multiply the first equation by –6 and the second equation by 100.

$-6(x + y) = -6(50)$

$100(0.06x + 0.14y) = 100(0.12)(50)$

Add the resulting equations.

$$\begin{array}{r} -6x - 6y = -300 \\ 6x + 14y = 600 \\ \hline 8y = 300 \\ y = 37.5 \end{array}$$

To find x, use $y = 37.5$ in the equation

$x + y = 50$

$x + 37.5 = 50$

$x = 12.5$

12.5 cc of 6% solution;

37.5 cc of 14% solution

43. Let x = cost of an egg

y = cost of a strip of bacon

$$\begin{cases} 3x + 4y = 3.80 \\ 2x + 3y = 2.75 \end{cases}$$

Multiply the 1st equation by –2.

$-2(3x + 4y) = -2(3.80)$

$-6x - 8y = -7.60$

Multiply the 2nd equation by 3.

$3(2x + 3y) = 3(2.75)$

$6x + 9y = 8.25$

Add the equations.

$$\begin{array}{r} -6x - 8y = -7.60 \\ 6x + 9y = 8.25 \\ \hline y = 0.65 \end{array}$$

To find x, use $y = 0.65$ in the equation

$2x + 3y = 2.75$

$2x + 3(0.65) = 2.75$

$2x + 1.95 = 2.75$

$2x = 2.75 - 1.95$

$2x = 0.80$

$x = \frac{0.80}{2} = 0.40$

One egg is \$0.40 and a strip of bacon is \$0.65.

44. Let x = time spent jogging

y = time spent walking

$$\begin{cases} 7.5x + 4y = 15 \\ x + y = 3 \end{cases}$$

Multiply the second equation by –4.

$-4(x + y) = -4(3)$

$-4x - 4y = -12$

Add the equations.

$$\begin{array}{r} \frac{15}{2}x + 4y = 15 \\ -4x - 4y = -12 \\ \hline \frac{7}{2}x = 3 \\ 7x = 6 \\ x = \frac{6}{7} \end{array}$$

$x = \frac{6}{7} = 0.86$

He spend about 0.86 hours jogging.

45. $\begin{cases} y \ge 2x - 3 \\ y \le -2x + 1 \end{cases}$

Graph $y = 2x + 3$.

The boundary line is solid.

Choose (0, 0) as a test point.

$y \ge 2x - 3$

$0 \ ? \ 2(0) - 3$

$0 \ ? -3$

$0 \ge -3$, so shade the side containing (0, 0).

Graph $y = -2x + 1$.

The boundary line is solid.

Choose (0, 0) for a test point.

$y \le -2x + 1$

$0 \ ? -2(0) + 1$

$0 \ ? \ 1$

$0 \le 1$, so shade the side containing (0, 0).

$y \ge 2x - 3$

$y \le -2x + 1$

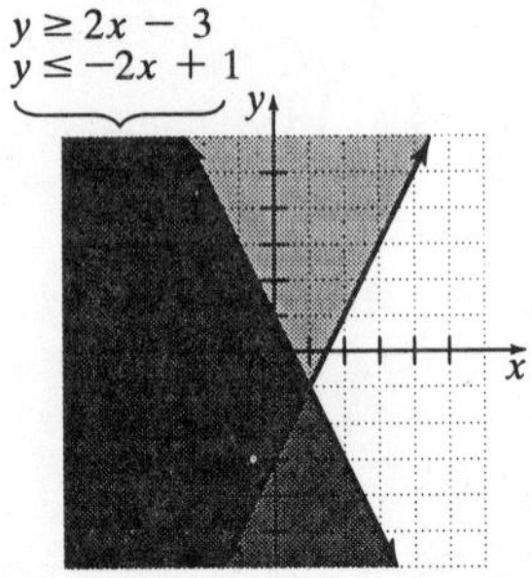

46. $\begin{cases} y \le -3x - 3 \\ y \le 2x + 7 \end{cases}$

Graph $y = -3x - 3$.
The boundary line is solid.
Choose (0, 0) as a test point.

$y \le -3x - 3$
$0 \,?\, -3(0) - 3$
$0 \,?\, 0 - 3$
$0 \,?\, -3$

$0 \not\le -3$, so shade the side that does *not* contain (0, 0).
Graph $y = 2x + 7$.
The boundary line is solid.
Choose (0, 0) as a test point.

$y \le 2x + 7$
$0 \,?\, 2(0) + 7$
$0 \,?\, 0 + 7$
$0 \,?\, 7$

$0 \le 7$, so shade the side containing (0, 0).

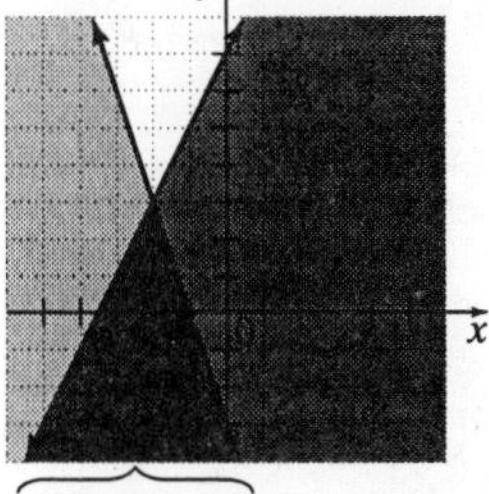

47. $\begin{cases} x + 2y > 0 \\ x - y \le 6 \end{cases}$

Graph $x + 2y = 0$.
The boundary line is dashed.
Choose (4, 0) as a test point.

$x + 2y > 0$
$4 + 2(0) \,?\, 0$
$4 \,?\, 0$

$4 > 0$, so shade the side containing (4, 0).

Graph $x - y \le 6$.
The boundary line is solid.
Choose (0, 0) as a test point.

$x - y \le 6$
$0 - 0 \,?\, 6$
$0 \,?\, 6$

$0 \le 6$, so shade the side containing (0, 0).

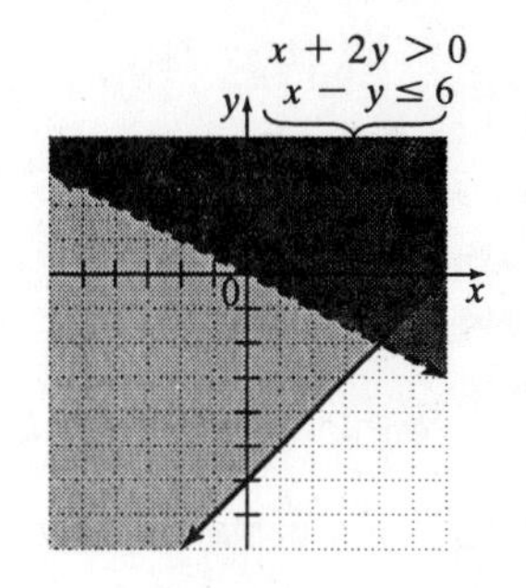

48. $\begin{cases} x - 2y \ge 7 \\ x + y \le -5 \end{cases}$

Graph $x - 2y = 7$.
The boundary line is solid.
Choose (0, 0) as a test point.

$x - 2y \ge 7$
$0 - 2(0) \,?\, 7$
$0 - 0 \,?\, 7$
$0 \,?\, 7$

$0 \not\ge 7$, so shade the side that does *not* contain
(0, 0).
Graph $x + y = -5$.
The boundary line is solid.
Choose (0, 0) as a test point.

$x + y \le -5$
$0 + 0 \,?\, -5$
$0 \,?\, -5$

$0 \not\le -5$, so shade the side that does *not* contain (0, 0).

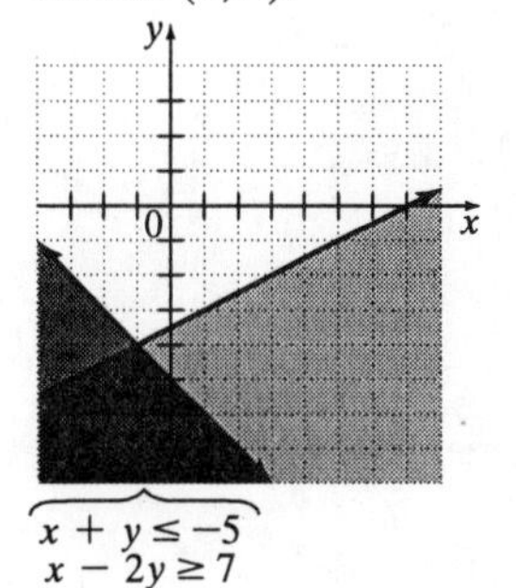

49. $\begin{cases} 3x-2y \le 4 \\ 2x+y \ge 5 \end{cases}$

Graph $3x - 2y = 4$.
The boundary line is solid.
Choose (0, 0) as a test point.

$3x-2y \le 4$
$3(0)-2(0) \ ?\ 4$
$0 \ ?\ 4$

$0 \le 4$, so shade the side containing (0, 0).

Graph $2x + y = 5$
The boundary line is solid.
Choose (0, 0) as a test point.

$2x+y \ge 5$
$2(0)+0 \ ?\ 5$
$0 \ ?\ 5$

$0 \not\ge 5$, so shade the side *not* containing (0, 0).

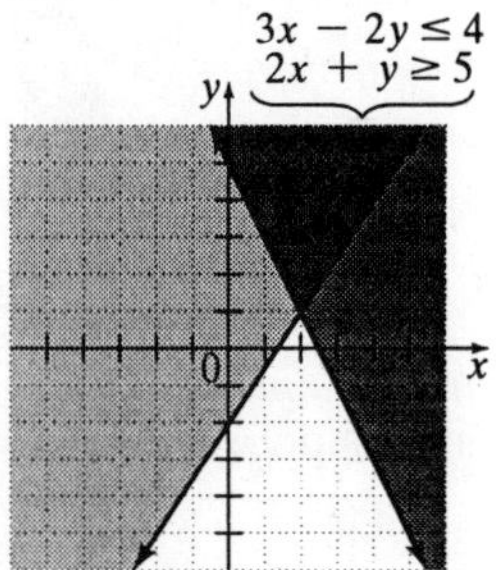

50. $\begin{cases} 4x-y \le 0 \\ 3x-2y \ge -5 \end{cases}$

Graph $4x - y = 0$.
The boundary line is solid.
Choose (0, 1) as a test point.

$4x-y \le 0$
$4(0)-1 \ ?\ 0$
$0-1 \ ?\ 0$
$-1 \ ?\ 0$

$-1 \le 0$, so shade the side containing (0, 1).
Graph $3x - 2y = -5$.
The boundary line is solid.
Choose (0, 0) as a test point.

$3x-2y \ge -5$
$3(0)-2(0) \ ?\ -5$
$0 \ ?\ -5$

$0 \ge -5$, so shade the side containing (0, 0).

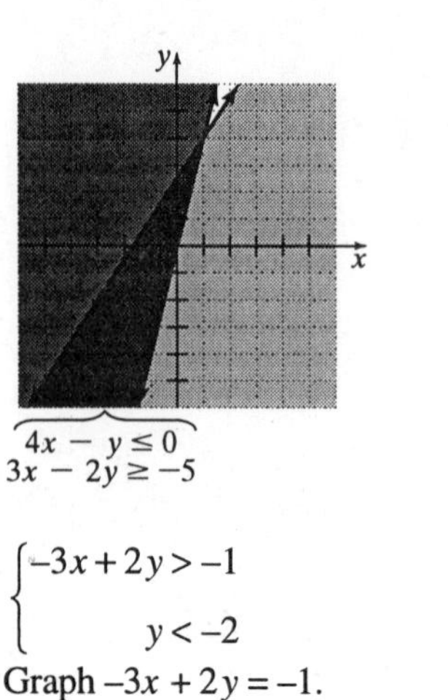

51. $\begin{cases} -3x+2y > -1 \\ y < -2 \end{cases}$

Graph $-3x + 2y = -1$.
The boundary line is dashed.
Choose (0, 0) as a test point.

$-3x+2y > -1$
$-3(0)+2(0) \ ?\ -1$
$0 \ ?\ -1$

$0 > -1$, so shade the side containing (0, 0).
Graph $y = -2$.
The boundary line is dashed.
Since (0, 0) does not satisfy $y > -2$, shade the side that does *not* contain (0, 0).

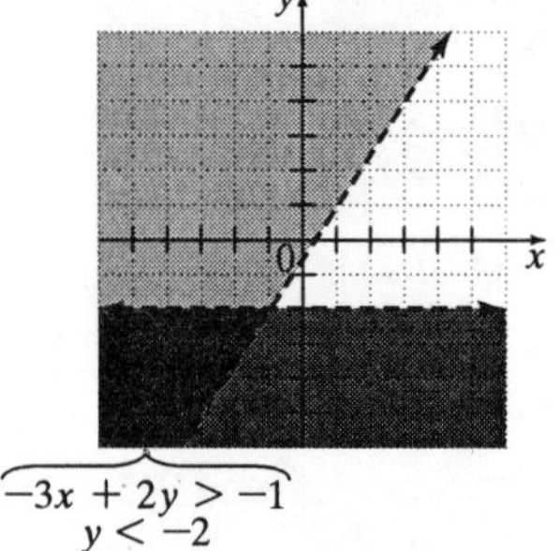

52. $\begin{cases} -2x+3y>-7 \\ x \geq -2 \end{cases}$

Graph $-2x+3y=-7$
The boundary line is dashed.
Choose (0, 0) as a test point.

$$-2x+3y>-7$$
$$-2(0)+3(0) \ ? -7$$
$$0 \ ? -7$$

$0>-7$, so shade the side containing (0, 0).
Graph $x=-2$.
The boundary line is solid.
Since (0, 0) satisfies $x \geq -2$, shade the side containing (0, 0).

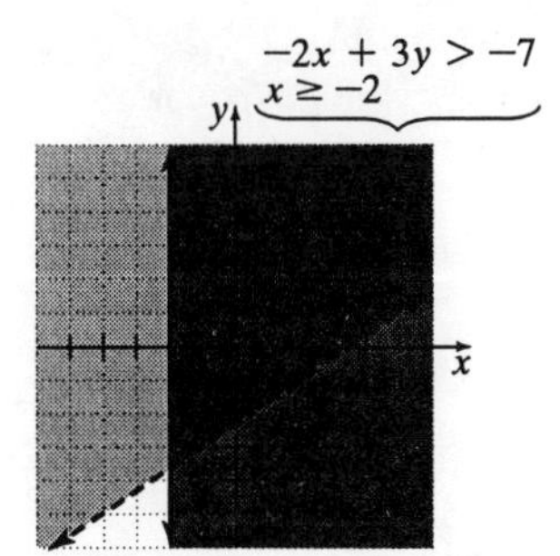

Chapter 8 Test

1. False; the system can have one solution, infinitely many solutions, or no solution.

2. False; if the ordered pair is not a solution of one of the equations, it is not a solution of the system.

3. True; the system is inconsistent.

4. False; if $3x=0$, then $\frac{3x}{3}=\frac{0}{3}$ or $x=0$.

5. $\begin{cases} 2x-3y=5 \\ 6x+y=1 \end{cases}$

(1, −1)

$$2x-3y=5$$
$$2(1)-3(-1) \stackrel{?}{=} 5$$
$$2+3 \stackrel{?}{=} 5$$
$$5=5 \text{ True}$$

$$6x+y=1$$
$$6(1)-1 \stackrel{?}{=} 1$$
$$6-1 \stackrel{?}{=} 1$$
$$5=1 \text{ False}$$

(1, −1) is not a solution.

6. $\begin{cases} 4x-3y=24 \\ 4x+5y=-8 \end{cases}$

(3, −4)

$$4x-3y=24$$
$$4(3)-3(-4) \stackrel{?}{=} 24$$
$$12+12 \stackrel{?}{=} 24$$
$$24=24 \text{ True}$$

$$4x+5y=-8$$
$$4(3)+5(-4) \stackrel{?}{=} -8$$
$$12-20 \stackrel{?}{=} -8$$
$$-8=-8 \text{ True}$$

(3, −4) is a solution.

7. $\begin{cases} y-x=6 \\ y-2x=-6 \end{cases}$

Graph each equation on a single set of axes.

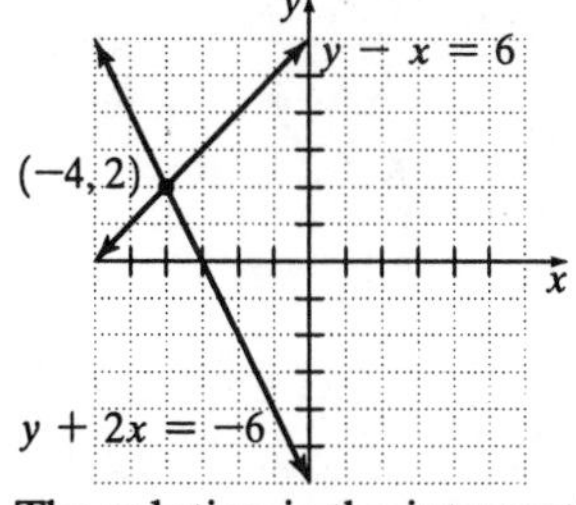

The solution is the intersection point of the two lines, (−4, 2).

8. $\begin{cases} 3x-2y=-14 \\ x+3y=-1 \end{cases}$

Solve the 2nd equation for x.

$x=-3y-1$

Replace x with $-3y-1$ in the 1st equation.

$$3(-3y-1)-2y=-14$$
$$-9y-3-2y=-14$$
$$-11y-3=-14$$
$$-11y=-14+3$$
$$-11y=-11$$
$$y=\frac{-11}{-11}=1$$

To find x, use $y = 1$ in the equation

$x=-3y-1$

$x=-3(1)-1$

$x=-3-1$

$x=-4$

The solution is $(-4, 1)$.

9. $\begin{cases} \frac{1}{2}x+2y=-\frac{15}{4} \\ 4x=-y \end{cases}$

Solve the 2nd equation for y.

$$4x=-y$$
$$\frac{4x}{-1}=y$$
$$-4x=y$$

Replace y with $-4x$ in the 1st equation.

$$\frac{1}{2}x+2(-4x)=-\frac{15}{4}$$
$$\frac{1}{2}x-8x=-\frac{15}{4}$$
$$-\frac{15}{2}x=-\frac{15}{4}$$
$$-\frac{2}{15}\left(-\frac{15}{2}x\right)=-\frac{2}{15}\left(-\frac{15}{4}\right)$$
$$x=\frac{2}{4}=\frac{1}{2}$$

To find y, use $x=\frac{1}{2}$ in the equation

$$y=-4x$$
$$y=-4\left(\frac{1}{2}\right)$$
$$y=-2$$

The solution is $\left(\frac{1}{2}, -2\right)$.

10. $\begin{cases} 3x+5y=2 \\ 2x-3y=14 \end{cases}$

Multiply the 1st equation by 3.

$3(3x + 5y) = 3(2)$

$9x+15y=6$

Multiply the 2nd equation by 5.

$5(2x - 3y) = 5(14)$

$10x - 15y = 70$

Add the equations.

$$\begin{array}{rl} 9x+15y= & 6 \\ 10x+15y= & 70 \\ \hline 19x \quad = & 76 \end{array}$$
$$x=\frac{76}{19}=4$$

To find y, use $x = 4$ in the equation

$$2x-3y=14$$
$$2(4)-3y=14$$
$$8-3y=14$$
$$-3y=14-8$$
$$-3y=6$$
$$y=\frac{6}{-3}=-2$$

The solution is $(4, -2)$.

11. $\begin{cases} 5x-6y=7 \\ 7x-4y=12 \end{cases}$

Multiply the 1st equation by -7.

$-7(5x - 6y) = -7(7)$

$-35x+42y=-49$

Multiply the 2nd equation by 5.

$5(7x - 4y) = 5(12)$

$35x - 20y = 60$

Add the equations.

$$\begin{array}{rl} -35x+42y= & -49 \\ 35x-20y= & 60 \\ \hline 22y= & 11 \end{array}$$
$$y=\frac{11}{22}=\frac{1}{2}$$

To find x, use $y = \frac{1}{2}$ in the equation

$$5x - 6y = 7$$
$$5x - 6\left(\frac{1}{2}\right) = 7$$
$$5x - 3 = 7$$
$$5x = 7 + 3$$
$$5x = 10$$
$$x = \frac{10}{5} = 2$$

The solution is $\left(2, \frac{1}{2}\right)$.

12. $\begin{cases} 3x + y = 7 \\ 4x + 3y = 1 \end{cases}$

Multiply the 1st equation by –3.

$$-3(3x + y) = -3(7)$$
$$-9x - 3y = -21$$

Add the equations.

$$\begin{array}{rl} -9x - 3y &= -21 \\ 4x + 3y &= 1 \\ \hline -5x &= -20 \end{array}$$
$$x = \frac{-20}{-5} = 4$$

To find y, use $x = 4$ in the equation

$$3x + y = 7$$
$$3(4) + y = 7$$
$$12 + y = 7$$
$$y = 7 - 12$$
$$y = -5$$

The solution is (4, –5).

13. $\begin{cases} 3(2x + y) = 4x + 20 \\ x - 2y = 3 \end{cases}$

Simplify the 1st equation.

$$6x + 3y = 4x + 20$$
$$6x - 4x + 3y = 20$$
$$2x + 3y = 20$$

Multiply the 2nd equation by –2.

$$-2(x - 2y) = -2(3)$$
$$-2x + 4y = -6$$

Add the equations.

$$\begin{array}{rl} 2x + 3y &= 20 \\ -2x + 4y &= -6 \\ \hline 7y &= 14 \end{array}$$
$$y = \frac{14}{7} = 2$$

To find x, use $y = 2$ in the equation

$$x - 2y = 3$$
$$x - 2(2) = 3$$
$$x - 4 = 3$$
$$x = 3 + 4$$
$$x = 7$$

The solution is (7, 2).

14. $\begin{cases} \frac{x-3}{2} = \frac{2-y}{4} \\ \frac{7-2x}{3} = \frac{y}{2} \end{cases}$

Simplify each equation.

$$4\left(\frac{x-3}{2}\right) = 4\left(\frac{2-y}{4}\right)$$
$$2(x - 3) = 2 - y$$
$$2x - 6 = 2 - y$$
$$2x + y - 6 = 2$$
$$2x + y = 8$$
$$6\left(\frac{7-2x}{3}\right) = 6\left(\frac{y}{2}\right)$$
$$2(7 - 2x) = 3y$$
$$14 - 4x = 3y$$
$$14 - 4x - 3y = 0$$
$$-4x - 3y = -14$$

Multiply the 1st equation by 3.

$$3(2x + y) = 3(8)$$
$$6x + 3y = 24$$

Add the equations.

$$\begin{array}{rl} -4x - 3y &= -14 \\ 6x + 3y &= 24 \\ \hline 2x &= 10 \end{array}$$
$$x = \frac{10}{2} = 5$$

To find y, use $x = 5$ in the equation

$$2x + y = 8$$
$$2(5) + y = 8$$
$$10 + y = 8$$
$$y = 8 - 10$$
$$y = -2$$

The solution is (5, –2).

15. Let x = number of \$1 bills
y = number of \$5 bills

$$\begin{cases} x + y = 62 \\ 1x + 5y = 230 \end{cases}$$

Multiply the 1st equation by –1.

$$-1(x + y) = -1(62)$$
$$-x - y = -62$$

Add the equations.

$$\begin{array}{r} x + 5y = 230 \\ -x - y = -62 \\ \hline 4y = 168 \end{array}$$

$$y = \frac{168}{4} = 42$$

To find x, use $y = 42$ in the equation

$$x + y = 62$$
$$x + 42 = 62$$
$$x = 62 - 42$$
$$x = 20$$

20 → \$1 bills
42 → \$5 bills

16. Let x = money at 5%
y = money at 9%

$$\begin{cases} x + y = 4000 \\ 0.05x + 0.09y = 311 \end{cases}$$

Solve the 1st equation for x.
$x = 4000 - y$
Replace x with $4000 - y$ in the second equation.

$$0.05(4000 - y) + 0.09y = 311$$
$$200 - 0.05y + 0.09y = 311$$
$$200 + 0.04y = 311$$
$$0.04y = 311 - 200$$
$$0.04y = 111$$
$$y = \frac{111}{0.04} = 2775$$

To find x, use $y = 2775$ in the equation
$x = 4000 - y$
$x = 4000 - 2775$
$x = 1225$
\$1225 at 5%
\$2775 at 9%

17. Let
x = number of farms in Missouri (in thousands)
y = number of farms in Texas (in thousands)

$$\begin{cases} x + y = 336 \\ y = 116 + x \end{cases}$$

Substitute $116 + x$ for y in the 1st equation.

$$x + 116 + x = 336$$
$$2x = 220$$
$$x = 110$$

To find y, let $x = 110$ in the equation

$$y = 116 + x$$
$$y = 116 + 110$$
$$y = 226$$

Missouri has 226 thousand farms and Texas has 110 thousand farms.

18. $\begin{cases} y + 2x \le 4 \\ y \ge 2 \end{cases}$

Graph $y + 2x = 4$.
The boundary line is solid.
Choose (0, 0) as a test point.

$$y + 2x \le 4$$
$$0 + 2(0) \ ?\ 4$$
$$0 \ ?\ 4$$

$0 \le 4$, so shade the side containing (0, 0).
Graph $y = 2$.
The boundary line is solid.
Since (0, 0), does *not* satisfy $y \ge 2$, shade the side that does *not* contain (0, 0).

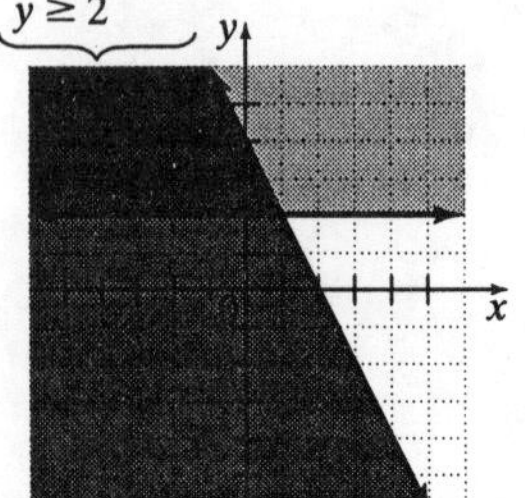

19. $\begin{cases} 2y - x \geq 1 \\ x + y \geq -4 \end{cases}$

Graph $2y - x = 1$.
The boundary line is solid.
Choose (0, 0) as a test point.

$2y - x \geq 1$
$2(0) - 0 \; ? \; 1$
$0 \; ? \; 1$

$0 \not\geq 1$, so shade the side that does *not* contain
(0, 0).

Graph $x + y = -4$.
The boundary line is solid.
Choose (0, 0) as a test point.

$x + y \geq -4$
$0 + 0 \; ? \; -4$
$0 \; ? \; -4$

$0 \geq -4$, so shade the side containing (0, 0).

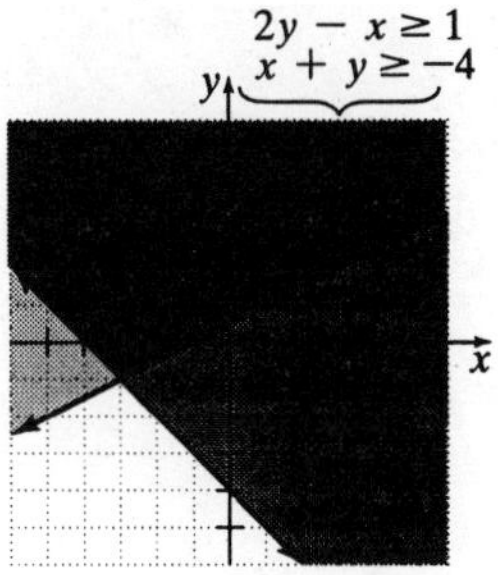

$2y - x \geq 1$
$x + y \geq -4$

Chapter 9

Section 9.1

Calculator Explorations

1. $\sqrt{7} \approx 2.646$; yes

3. $\sqrt{11} \approx 3.317$; yes

5. $\sqrt{82} \approx 9.055$; yes

7. $\sqrt[3]{40} \approx 3.420$; yes

9. $\sqrt[4]{20} \approx 2.115$; yes

11. $\sqrt[5]{18} \approx 1.783$; yes

Mental Math

1. False; the index is even and the radicand is negative.

2. True; $8^2 = 64$ and $4^3 = 64$.

3. True; $(-3)^2 = 9$ and $3^2 = 9$.

4. True; $0^2 = 0$ and $1^2 = 1$.

5. True; $(x^5)^2 = x^{10}$.

6. False; $(x^4)^2 = x^8$, not x^{16}.

Exercise Set 9.1

1. $\sqrt{16} = 4$ because $4^2 = 16$ and 4 is positive.

3. $\sqrt{81} = 9$ because $9^2 = 81$ and 9 is positive.

5. $\sqrt{\frac{1}{25}} = \frac{1}{5}$ because $\left(\frac{1}{5}\right)^2 = \frac{1}{25}$ and $\frac{1}{5}$ is positive.

7. $-\sqrt{100} = -10$ because the negative sign in front of the radical indicates the negative square root of 100.

9. $\sqrt{-4}$ is not a real number because the index is even and the radicand is negative.

11. $-\sqrt{121} = -11$ because the negative sign in front of the radical indicates the negative square root of 121.

13. $\sqrt{\frac{9}{25}} = \frac{3}{5}$ because $\left(\frac{3}{5}\right)^2 = \frac{9}{25}$ and $\frac{3}{5}$ is positive.

15. $\sqrt{144} = 12$ because $12^2 = 144$ and 12 is positive.

17. $\sqrt{\frac{49}{36}} = \frac{7}{6}$ because $\left(\frac{7}{6}\right)^2 = \frac{49}{36}$ and $\frac{7}{6}$ is positive.

19. $-\sqrt{1} = -1$ because the negative sign in front of the radical indicates the negative square root of 1.

21. $\sqrt{37} \approx 6.083$

23. $\sqrt{136} \approx 11.662$

25. $\sqrt{2} \approx 1.41$
$90 \cdot \sqrt{2} \approx 90(1.41) = 126.90$ feet

27. $\sqrt{z^2} = z$ because $(z)^2 = z^2$.

29. $\sqrt{x^4} = x^2$ because $\left(x^2\right)^2 = x^4$.

31. $\sqrt{9x^8} = 3x^4$ because $\left(3x^4\right)^2 = 9x^8$.

33. $\sqrt{81x^2} = 9x$ because $(9x)^2 = 81x^2$.

35. $\sqrt{\frac{x^6}{36}} = \frac{x^3}{6}$ because $\left(\frac{x^3}{6}\right)^2 = \frac{x^6}{36}$.

37. $\sqrt{\frac{25y^2}{9}} = \frac{5y}{3}$ because $\left(\frac{5y}{3}\right)^2 = \frac{25y^2}{9}$.

39. $\sqrt[3]{125} = 5$ because $5^3 = 125$.

41. $\sqrt[3]{-64} = -4$ because $(-4)^3 = -64$

43. $-\sqrt[3]{8} = -2$. because $\sqrt[3]{8} = 2$.

45. $\sqrt[3]{\frac{1}{8}} = \frac{1}{2}$ because $\left(\frac{1}{2}\right)^3 = \frac{1}{8}$.

47. $\sqrt[3]{-125} = -5$ because $(-5)^3 = -125$.

49. $\sqrt[3]{-1000} = -10$ because $(-10)^3 = -1000$.

51. Answers may vary.

53. $\sqrt[5]{32} = 2$ because $2^5 = 32$.

55. $\sqrt[4]{-16}$ is not a real number.

57. $-\sqrt[4]{625} = -5$ because $\sqrt[4]{625} = 5$.

59. $\sqrt[6]{1} = 1$ because $1^6 = 1$.

61. $\sqrt[5]{-32} = -2$ because $(-2)^5 = -32$.

63. $\sqrt[4]{256} = 4$ because $4^4 = 256$.

65. $\sqrt[3]{195,112} = 58$
because $(58)^3 = 195,112$. Each side would be 58 feet.

67.

x	$y = \sqrt[3]{x}$
–8	–2
–2	–1.3 (approx.)
–1	–1
0	0
1	1
2	1.3 (approx.)
8	2

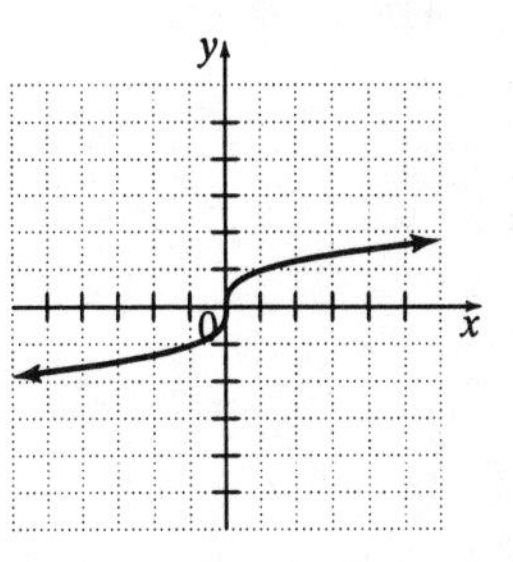

69. $\sqrt[3]{x^{21}} = x^7$ because $(x^7)^3 = x^{21}$.

71. $\sqrt[4]{x^{20}} = x^5$ because $(x^5)^4 = x^{20}$.

73. $y = \sqrt{x+3}$
The beginning of the graph is at (–3, 0).

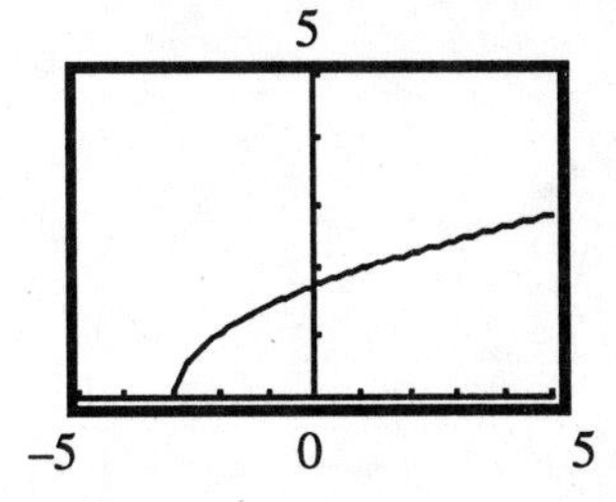

75. $y = \sqrt{x-5}$

The beginning of the graph is at (5, 0).
$x - 5$ must be ≥ 0, so $x \geq 5$. At $x = 5$, $y = 0$.

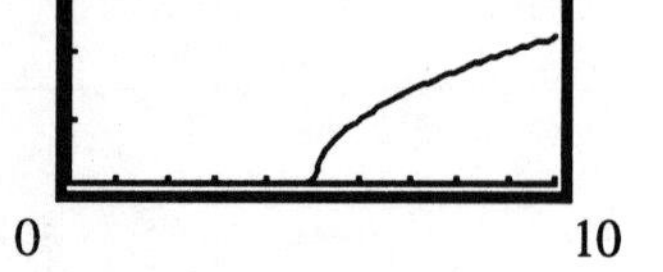

77. $8 = 4 \cdot 2$, 4 is a perfect square.

79. $75 = 25 \cdot 3$, 25 is a perfect square.

81. $44 = 4 \cdot 11$, 4 is a perfect square.

83. $90 = 9 \cdot 10$, 9 is a perfect square.

Section 9.2

Mental Math

1. $\sqrt{4 \cdot 9} = 2 \cdot 3 = 6$

2. $\sqrt{9 \cdot 36} = 3 \cdot 6 = 18$

3. $\sqrt{x^2} = x$

4. $\sqrt{y^4} = y^2$

5. $\sqrt{0} = 0$

6. $\sqrt{1} = 1$

7. $\sqrt{25x^4} = 5x^2$

8. $\sqrt{49x^2} = 7x$

Exercise Set 9.2

1. $\sqrt{20} = \sqrt{4 \cdot 5} = \sqrt{4} \cdot \sqrt{5} = 2\sqrt{5}$

3. $\sqrt{18} = \sqrt{9 \cdot 2} = \sqrt{9} \cdot \sqrt{2} = 3\sqrt{2}$

5. $\sqrt{50} = \sqrt{25 \cdot 2} = \sqrt{25} \cdot \sqrt{2} = 5\sqrt{2}$

7. $\sqrt{33}$ cannot be simplified further.

9. $\sqrt{60} = \sqrt{4 \cdot 15} = \sqrt{4} \cdot \sqrt{15} = 2\sqrt{15}$

11. $\sqrt{180} = \sqrt{36 \cdot 5} = \sqrt{36} \cdot \sqrt{5} = 6\sqrt{5}$

13. $\sqrt{52} = \sqrt{4 \cdot 13} = \sqrt{4} \cdot \sqrt{13} = 2\sqrt{13}$

15. $\sqrt{\frac{8}{25}} = \frac{\sqrt{8}}{\sqrt{25}} = \frac{\sqrt{4} \cdot \sqrt{2}}{5} = \frac{2\sqrt{2}}{5}$

17. $\sqrt{\frac{27}{121}} = \frac{\sqrt{27}}{\sqrt{121}} = \frac{\sqrt{9} \cdot \sqrt{3}}{11} = \frac{3\sqrt{3}}{11}$

19. $\sqrt{\frac{9}{4}} = \frac{\sqrt{9}}{\sqrt{4}} = \frac{3}{2}$

21. $\sqrt{\frac{125}{9}} = \frac{\sqrt{125}}{\sqrt{9}} = \frac{\sqrt{25} \cdot \sqrt{5}}{3} = \frac{5\sqrt{5}}{3}$

23. $\sqrt{\frac{11}{36}} = \frac{\sqrt{11}}{\sqrt{36}} = \frac{\sqrt{11}}{6}$

25. $$\begin{aligned} -\sqrt{\frac{27}{144}} &= -\frac{\sqrt{27}}{\sqrt{144}} \\ &= -\frac{\sqrt{9} \cdot \sqrt{3}}{12} \\ &= -\frac{3\sqrt{3}}{12} \\ &= -\frac{\sqrt{3}}{4} \end{aligned}$$

27. $\sqrt{x^7} = \sqrt{x^6 \cdot x} = \sqrt{x^6} \cdot \sqrt{x} = x^3\sqrt{x}$

29. $\sqrt{x^{13}} = \sqrt{x^{12} \cdot x} = \sqrt{x^{12}} \cdot \sqrt{x} = x^6\sqrt{x}$

31. $\sqrt{75x^2} = \sqrt{25x^2 \cdot 3} = \sqrt{25x^2} \cdot \sqrt{3} = 5x\sqrt{3}$

33. $\sqrt{96x^4} = \sqrt{16x^4 \cdot 6} = \sqrt{16x^4} \cdot \sqrt{6} = 4x^2\sqrt{6}$

35. $\sqrt{\frac{12}{y^2}} = \frac{\sqrt{12}}{\sqrt{y^2}} = \frac{\sqrt{4}\cdot\sqrt{3}}{y} = \frac{2\sqrt{3}}{y}$

37. $\sqrt{\frac{9x}{y^2}} = \frac{\sqrt{9x}}{\sqrt{y^2}} = \frac{\sqrt{9}\cdot\sqrt{x}}{y} = \frac{3\sqrt{x}}{y}$

39. $\sqrt{\frac{88}{x^4}} = \frac{\sqrt{88}}{\sqrt{x^4}} = \frac{\sqrt{4}\cdot\sqrt{22}}{x^2} = \frac{2\sqrt{22}}{x^2}$

41. $\sqrt[3]{24} = \sqrt[3]{8\cdot 3} = \sqrt[3]{8}\cdot\sqrt[3]{3} = 2\sqrt[3]{3}$

43. $\sqrt[3]{250} = \sqrt[3]{125\cdot 2} = \sqrt[3]{125}\cdot\sqrt[3]{2} = 5\sqrt[3]{2}$

45. $\sqrt[3]{\frac{5}{64}} = \frac{\sqrt[3]{5}}{\sqrt[3]{64}} = \frac{\sqrt[3]{5}}{4}$

47. $\sqrt[3]{\frac{7}{8}} = \frac{\sqrt[3]{7}}{\sqrt[3]{8}} = \frac{\sqrt[3]{7}}{2}$

49. $\sqrt[3]{\frac{15}{64}} = \frac{\sqrt[3]{15}}{\sqrt[3]{64}} = \frac{\sqrt[3]{15}}{4}$

51. $\sqrt[3]{80} = \sqrt[3]{8\cdot 10} = \sqrt[3]{8}\cdot\sqrt[3]{10} = 2\sqrt[3]{10}$

53. $\sqrt[4]{48} = \sqrt[4]{16\cdot 3} = \sqrt[4]{16}\cdot\sqrt[4]{3} = 2\sqrt[4]{3}$

55. $\sqrt[4]{\frac{8}{81}} = \frac{\sqrt[4]{8}}{\sqrt[4]{81}} = \frac{\sqrt[4]{8}}{3}$

57. $\sqrt[5]{96} = \sqrt[5]{32\cdot 3} = \sqrt[5]{32}\cdot\sqrt[5]{3} = 2\sqrt[5]{3}$

59. $\sqrt[5]{\frac{5}{32}} = \frac{\sqrt[5]{5}}{\sqrt[5]{32}} = \frac{\sqrt[5]{5}}{2}$

61. $\sqrt[3]{80} = \sqrt[3]{8\cdot 10} = \sqrt[3]{8}\cdot\sqrt[3]{10} = 2\sqrt[3]{10}$
Each side has length $2\sqrt[3]{10}$ in.

63. Answers may vary.

65. $C = 100\sqrt[3]{n} + 700$
$= 100\sqrt[3]{1000} + 700$
$= 100\cdot 10 + 700$
$= 1000 + 700$
$= \$1700$

67. $\sqrt[3]{-8x^6} = -2x^2$

69. $\sqrt[3]{\frac{2}{x^9}} = \frac{\sqrt[3]{2}}{\sqrt[3]{x^9}} = \frac{\sqrt[3]{2}}{x^3}$

71. $6x + 8x = 14x$

73. $(2x+3)(x-5) = 2x^2 - 10x + 3x - 15$
$= 2x^2 - 7x - 15$

75. $9y^2 - 9y^2 = 0$

77. $\frac{x}{12} = \frac{6}{9}$
$9x = 12\cdot 6$
$\frac{9x}{9} = \frac{72}{9}$
$x = 8$ cm

Section 9.3

Mental Math

1. $3\sqrt{2} + 5\sqrt{2} = 8\sqrt{2}$
2. $2\sqrt{3} + 7\sqrt{3} = 9\sqrt{3}$
3. $5\sqrt{x} + 2\sqrt{x} = 7\sqrt{x}$
4. $8\sqrt{x} + 3\sqrt{x} = 11\sqrt{x}$
5. $5\sqrt{7} - 2\sqrt{7} = 3\sqrt{7}$
6. $8\sqrt{6} - 5\sqrt{6} = 3\sqrt{6}$

Exercise Set 9.3

1. $4\sqrt{3} - 8\sqrt{3} = (4-8)\sqrt{3} = -4\sqrt{3}$

3. $3\sqrt{6}+8\sqrt{6}-2\sqrt{6}-5=(3+8-2)\sqrt{6}-5$
$=9\sqrt{6}-5$

5. $6\sqrt{5}-5\sqrt{5}+\sqrt{2}=(6-5)\sqrt{5}+\sqrt{2}$
$=\sqrt{5}+\sqrt{2}$

7. $2\sqrt[3]{3}+5\sqrt[3]{3}-\sqrt{3}=(2+5)\sqrt[3]{3}-\sqrt{3}$
$=7\sqrt[3]{3}-\sqrt{3}$

9. $2\sqrt[3]{2}-7\sqrt[3]{2}-6=(2-7)\sqrt[3]{2}-6=-5\sqrt[3]{2}-6$

11. $3\sqrt{5}+3\sqrt{5}+\sqrt{5}+\sqrt{5}=(3+3+1+1)\sqrt{5}$
$=8\sqrt{5}$ inches

13. Answers may vary.

15. $\sqrt{12}+\sqrt{27}=\sqrt{4\cdot 3}+\sqrt{9\cdot 3}$
$=2\sqrt{3}+3\sqrt{3}$
$=5\sqrt{3}$

17. $\sqrt{45}+3\sqrt{20}=\sqrt{9\cdot 5}+3\sqrt{4\cdot 5}$
$=3\sqrt{5}+3(2)\sqrt{5}$
$=3\sqrt{5}+6\sqrt{5}$
$=9\sqrt{5}$

19. $2\sqrt{54}-\sqrt{20}+\sqrt{45}-\sqrt{24}$
$=2\sqrt{9}\sqrt{6}-\sqrt{4}\sqrt{5}+\sqrt{9}\sqrt{5}-\sqrt{4}\sqrt{6}$
$=2(3)\sqrt{6}-2\sqrt{5}+3\sqrt{5}-2\sqrt{6}$
$=6\sqrt{6}-2\sqrt{5}+3\sqrt{5}-2\sqrt{6}$
$=4\sqrt{6}+\sqrt{5}$

21. $4x-3\sqrt{x^2}+\sqrt{x}=4x-3x+\sqrt{x}=x+\sqrt{x}$

23. $\sqrt{25x}+\sqrt{36x}-11\sqrt{x}$
$=5\sqrt{x}+6\sqrt{x}-11\sqrt{x}$
$=11\sqrt{x}-11\sqrt{x}$
$=0$

25. $\sqrt{16x}-\sqrt{x^3}=4\sqrt{x}-\sqrt{x^2\cdot x}$
$=4\sqrt{x}-x\sqrt{x}$

27. $12\sqrt{5}-\sqrt{5}-4\sqrt{5}=11\sqrt{5}-4\sqrt{5}=7\sqrt{5}$

29. $\sqrt{5}+\sqrt[3]{5}$ cannot be simplified.

31. $4+8\sqrt{2}-9=-5+8\sqrt{2}$

33. $8-\sqrt{2}-5\sqrt{2}=8-6\sqrt{2}$

35. $5\sqrt{32}-\sqrt{72}=5\sqrt{16}\sqrt{2}-\sqrt{36}\sqrt{2}$
$=5(4)\sqrt{2}-6\sqrt{2}$
$=20\sqrt{2}-6\sqrt{2}$
$=14\sqrt{2}$

37. $\sqrt{8}+\sqrt{9}+\sqrt{18}+\sqrt{81}$
$=\sqrt{4}\sqrt{2}+3+\sqrt{9}\sqrt{2}+9$
$=2\sqrt{2}+3+3\sqrt{2}+9$
$=5\sqrt{2}+12$

39. $\sqrt{\frac{5}{9}}+\sqrt{\frac{5}{81}}=\frac{\sqrt{5}}{\sqrt{9}}+\frac{\sqrt{5}}{\sqrt{81}}$
$=\frac{\sqrt{5}}{3}+\frac{\sqrt{5}}{9}$
$=\frac{\sqrt{5}}{3}\cdot\frac{3}{3}+\frac{\sqrt{5}}{9}$
$=\frac{3\sqrt{5}}{9}+\frac{\sqrt{5}}{9}$
$=\frac{4\sqrt{5}}{9}$

41. $\sqrt{\frac{3}{4}}-\sqrt{\frac{3}{64}}=\frac{\sqrt{3}}{\sqrt{4}}-\frac{\sqrt{3}}{\sqrt{64}}$
$=\frac{\sqrt{3}}{2}-\frac{\sqrt{3}}{8}$
$=\frac{\sqrt{3}}{2}\cdot\frac{4}{4}-\frac{\sqrt{3}}{8}$
$=\frac{4\sqrt{3}}{8}-\frac{\sqrt{3}}{8}$
$=\frac{3\sqrt{3}}{8}$

43. $2\sqrt{45}-2\sqrt{20}=2\sqrt{9}\sqrt{5}-2\sqrt{4}\sqrt{5}$
$=2(3)\sqrt{5}-2(2)\sqrt{5}$
$=6\sqrt{5}-4\sqrt{5}$
$=2\sqrt{5}$

45. $\sqrt{35}-\sqrt{140}=\sqrt{35}-\sqrt{4}\sqrt{35}$
$=\sqrt{35}-2\sqrt{35}$
$=-\sqrt{35}$

47. $5\sqrt{2x}+\sqrt{98x}=5\sqrt{2x}+\sqrt{49\cdot 2x}$
$=5\sqrt{2x}+\sqrt{49}\cdot\sqrt{2x}$
$=5\sqrt{2x}+7\sqrt{2x}$
$=12\sqrt{2x}$

49. $5\sqrt{x}+4\sqrt{4x}-13\sqrt{x}=5\sqrt{x}+8\sqrt{x}-13\sqrt{x}$
$=0$

51. $\sqrt{3x^3}+3x\sqrt{x}=\sqrt{3x\cdot x^2}+3x\sqrt{x}$
$=x\sqrt{3x}+3x\sqrt{x}$

53. $\sqrt[3]{81}+\sqrt[3]{24}=\sqrt[3]{27}\sqrt[3]{3}+\sqrt[3]{8}\sqrt[3]{3}$
$=3\sqrt[3]{3}+2\sqrt[3]{3}$
$=5\sqrt[3]{3}$

55. $4\sqrt[3]{9}-\sqrt[3]{243}=4\sqrt[3]{9}-\sqrt[3]{27}\sqrt[3]{9}$
$=4\sqrt[3]{9}-3\sqrt[3]{9}$
$=\sqrt[3]{9}$

57. $2\sqrt[3]{8}+2\sqrt[3]{16}=2(2)+2\sqrt[3]{8\cdot 2}=4+4\sqrt[3]{2}$

59. $\sqrt[3]{8}+\sqrt[3]{54}-5=2+\sqrt[3]{27\cdot 2}-5=-3+3\sqrt[3]{2}$

61. $\sqrt{32x^2}+\sqrt[3]{32}+\sqrt{4x^2}$
$=\sqrt{16\cdot 2x^2}+\sqrt[3]{8\cdot 4}+\sqrt{4x^2}$
$=4x\sqrt{2}+2\sqrt[3]{4}+2x$

63. $\sqrt{40x}+\sqrt[3]{40}-2\sqrt{10x}-\sqrt[3]{5}$
$=\sqrt{4\cdot 10x}+\sqrt[3]{8\cdot 5}-2\sqrt{10x}-\sqrt[3]{5}$
$=2\sqrt{10x}+2\sqrt[3]{5}-2\sqrt{10x}-\sqrt[3]{5}$
$=\sqrt[3]{5}$

65. $2(3\cdot 8)+2\left(\frac{3\sqrt{27}}{4}\right)=2(24)+\frac{3\sqrt{27}}{2}$
$=48+3\frac{\sqrt{9\cdot 3}}{2}$
$=48+\frac{9\sqrt{3}}{2}$
$=\left(48+\frac{9\sqrt{3}}{2}\right)$ sq ft

67. $(x+6)^2=(x)^2+2(x)(6)+(6)^2$
$=x^2+12x+36$

69. $(2x-1)^2=(2x)^2+2(2x)(-1)+(1)^2$
$=4x^2-4x+1$

71. $\begin{cases}x=2y\\ x+5y=14\end{cases}$

Replace x with $2y$ in the 2nd equation.
$2y+5y=14$
$7y=14$
$y=\frac{14}{7}=2$
To find x, use $y=2$ in the equation
$x=2y$
$x=2(2)$
$x=4$
The solution is (4, 2).

Section 9.4

Mental Math

1. $\sqrt{2}\cdot\sqrt{3}=\sqrt{6}$
2. $\sqrt{5}\cdot\sqrt{7}=\sqrt{35}$
3. $\sqrt{1}\cdot\sqrt{6}=\sqrt{6}$
4. $\sqrt{7}\cdot\sqrt{x}=\sqrt{7x}$
5. $\sqrt{10}\cdot\sqrt{y}=\sqrt{10y}$
6. $\sqrt{x}\cdot\sqrt{y}=\sqrt{xy}$

Exercise Set 9.4

1. $\sqrt{8}\sqrt{2} = \sqrt{16} = 4$

3. $\sqrt{10}\sqrt{5} = \sqrt{50} = \sqrt{25}\sqrt{2} = 5\sqrt{2}$

5. $\sqrt{10}(\sqrt{2}+\sqrt{5}) = \sqrt{20}+\sqrt{50}$
$= \sqrt{4}\sqrt{5}+\sqrt{25}\sqrt{2}$
$= 2\sqrt{5}+5\sqrt{2}$

7. $(3\sqrt{5}-\sqrt{10})(\sqrt{5}-4\sqrt{3})$
$= 3\sqrt{25}-12\sqrt{15}-\sqrt{50}+4\sqrt{30}$
$= 3(5)-12\sqrt{15}-\sqrt{25}\sqrt{2}+4\sqrt{30}$
$= 15-12\sqrt{15}-5\sqrt{2}+4\sqrt{30}$

9. $(\sqrt{x}+6)(\sqrt{x}-6) = (\sqrt{x})^2-(6)^2 = x-36$

11. $(\sqrt{3}+8)^2 = (\sqrt{3})^2+2(\sqrt{3})(8)+(8)^2$
$= 3+16\sqrt{3}+64$
$= 67+16\sqrt{3}$

13. $A = lw$
$A = (13\sqrt{2})(5\sqrt{6})$
$A = 65\sqrt{12}$
$A = 65\sqrt{4}\sqrt{3}$
$A = 65(2)\sqrt{3}$
$A = 130\sqrt{3}$ sq. meters

15. $\dfrac{\sqrt{32}}{\sqrt{2}} = \sqrt{\dfrac{32}{2}} = \sqrt{16} = 4$

17. $\dfrac{\sqrt{90}}{\sqrt{5}} = \sqrt{\dfrac{90}{5}} = \sqrt{18} = \sqrt{9}\sqrt{2} = 3\sqrt{2}$

19. $\dfrac{\sqrt{75y^5}}{\sqrt{3y}} = \sqrt{\dfrac{75y^5}{3y}} = \sqrt{25y^4} = 5y^2$

21. $\sqrt{\dfrac{3}{5}} = \dfrac{\sqrt{3}}{\sqrt{5}}\cdot\dfrac{\sqrt{5}}{\sqrt{5}} = \dfrac{\sqrt{15}}{5}$

23. $\dfrac{1}{\sqrt{6y}} = \dfrac{1}{\sqrt{6y}}\cdot\dfrac{\sqrt{6y}}{\sqrt{6y}} = \dfrac{\sqrt{6y}}{6y}$

25. $\sqrt{\dfrac{5}{18}} = \dfrac{\sqrt{5}}{\sqrt{18}}$
$= \dfrac{\sqrt{5}}{\sqrt{9}\sqrt{2}}$
$= \dfrac{\sqrt{5}}{3\sqrt{2}}$
$= \dfrac{\sqrt{5}}{3\sqrt{2}}\cdot\dfrac{\sqrt{2}}{\sqrt{2}}$
$= \dfrac{\sqrt{10}}{3(2)}$
$= \dfrac{\sqrt{10}}{6}$

27. $r = \sqrt{\dfrac{A}{\pi}} = \dfrac{\sqrt{A}}{\sqrt{\pi}}\cdot\dfrac{\sqrt{\pi}}{\sqrt{\pi}} = \dfrac{\sqrt{A\pi}}{\sqrt{\pi^2}} = \dfrac{\sqrt{A\pi}}{\pi}$

29. Answers may vary.

31. $\dfrac{3}{\sqrt{2}+1} = \dfrac{3(\sqrt{2}-1)}{(\sqrt{2}+1)(\sqrt{2}-1)}$
$= \dfrac{3(\sqrt{2}-1)}{2-1}$
$= \dfrac{3\sqrt{2}-3}{1}$
$= 3\sqrt{2}-3$

33. $\dfrac{2}{\sqrt{10}-3} = \dfrac{2(\sqrt{10}+3)}{(\sqrt{10}-3)(\sqrt{10}+3)}$
$= \dfrac{2(\sqrt{10}+3)}{10-9}$
$= \dfrac{2\sqrt{10}+6}{1}$
$= 2\sqrt{10}+6$

35. $\dfrac{\sqrt{5}+1}{\sqrt{6}-\sqrt{5}} = \dfrac{(\sqrt{5}+1)(\sqrt{6}+\sqrt{5})}{(\sqrt{6}-\sqrt{5})(\sqrt{6}+\sqrt{5})}$
$= \dfrac{\sqrt{30}+\sqrt{25}+\sqrt{6}+\sqrt{5}}{6-5}$
$= \dfrac{\sqrt{30}+5+\sqrt{6}+\sqrt{5}}{1}$
$= \sqrt{30}+5+\sqrt{6}+\sqrt{5}$

37. $\dfrac{6+2\sqrt{3}}{2} = \dfrac{2(3+\sqrt{3})}{2} = 3+\sqrt{3}$

39. $\dfrac{18-12\sqrt{5}}{6} = \dfrac{6(3-2\sqrt{5})}{6} = 3-2\sqrt{5}$

41. $\dfrac{15\sqrt{3}+5}{5} = \dfrac{5(3\sqrt{3}+1)}{5} = 3\sqrt{3}+1$

43. $2\sqrt{3}\cdot 4\sqrt{15} = 8\sqrt{45}$
$= 8\sqrt{9}\sqrt{5}$
$= 8(3)\sqrt{5}$
$= 24\sqrt{5}$

45. $(2\sqrt{5})^2 = 4(5) = 20$

47. $\left(6\sqrt{x}\right)^2 = 6^2\left(\sqrt{x}\right)^2 = 36x$

49. $\sqrt{6}(\sqrt{5}+\sqrt{7}) = \sqrt{30}+\sqrt{42}$

51. $4\sqrt{5x}(\sqrt{x}-3\sqrt{5}) = 4\sqrt{5x^2}-12\sqrt{25x}$
$= 4\sqrt{x^2}\sqrt{5}-12\sqrt{25}\sqrt{x}$
$= 4x\sqrt{5}-12(5)\sqrt{x}$
$= 4x\sqrt{5}-60\sqrt{x}$

53. $(\sqrt{3}+\sqrt{5})(\sqrt{2}-\sqrt{5})$
$= \sqrt{6}-\sqrt{15}+\sqrt{10}-\sqrt{25}$
$= \sqrt{6}-\sqrt{15}+\sqrt{10}-5$

55. $(\sqrt{7}-2\sqrt{3})(\sqrt{7}+2\sqrt{3}) = (\sqrt{7})^2-(2\sqrt{3})^2$
$= 7-4(3)$
$= 7-12$
$= -5$

57. $(\sqrt{x}-3)(\sqrt{x}+3) = (\sqrt{x})^2-(3)^2 = x-9$

59. $(\sqrt{6}+3)^2 = (\sqrt{6})^2+2(\sqrt{6})(3)+(3)^2$
$= 6+6\sqrt{6}+9$
$= 15+6\sqrt{6}$

61. $(3\sqrt{x}-5)^2 = (3\sqrt{x})^2+2(3\sqrt{x})(-5)+(5)^2$
$= 9x-30\sqrt{x}+25$

63. $\dfrac{\sqrt{150}}{\sqrt{2}} = \sqrt{\dfrac{150}{2}} = \sqrt{75} = \sqrt{25}\sqrt{3} = 5\sqrt{3}$

65. $\dfrac{\sqrt{72y^5}}{\sqrt{3y^3}} = \sqrt{\dfrac{72y^5}{3y^3}}$
$= \sqrt{24y^2}$
$= \sqrt{4y^2}\sqrt{6}$
$= 2y\sqrt{6}$

67. $\dfrac{\sqrt{24x^3y^4}}{\sqrt{2xy}} = \sqrt{\dfrac{24x^3y^4}{2xy}}$
$= \sqrt{12x^2y^3}$
$= \sqrt{4x^2y^2}\sqrt{3y}$
$= 2xy\sqrt{3y}$

69. $\sqrt{\dfrac{2}{15}} = \dfrac{\sqrt{2}}{\sqrt{15}}\cdot\dfrac{\sqrt{15}}{\sqrt{15}} = \dfrac{\sqrt{30}}{15}$

71. $\sqrt{\frac{3}{20}} = \frac{\sqrt{3}}{\sqrt{20}}$
$= \frac{\sqrt{3}}{\sqrt{4}\sqrt{5}}$
$= \frac{\sqrt{3}}{2\sqrt{5}}$
$= \frac{\sqrt{3}}{2\sqrt{5}} \cdot \frac{\sqrt{5}}{\sqrt{5}}$
$= \frac{\sqrt{15}}{2(5)}$
$= \frac{\sqrt{15}}{10}$

73. $\frac{3x}{\sqrt{2x}} = \frac{3x}{\sqrt{2x}} \cdot \frac{\sqrt{2x}}{\sqrt{2x}} = \frac{3x\sqrt{2x}}{2x} = \frac{3\sqrt{2x}}{2}$

75. $\frac{4}{2-\sqrt{5}} = \frac{4(2+\sqrt{5})}{(2-\sqrt{5})(2+\sqrt{5})}$
$= \frac{4(2+\sqrt{5})}{4-5}$
$= \frac{8+4\sqrt{5}}{-1}$
$= \frac{-1(-8-4\sqrt{5})}{-1}$
$= -8-4\sqrt{5}$

77. $\frac{5}{3+\sqrt{10}} = \frac{5(3-\sqrt{10})}{(3+\sqrt{10})(3-\sqrt{10})}$
$= \frac{5(3-\sqrt{10})}{9-10}$
$= \frac{15-5\sqrt{10}}{-1}$
$= \frac{-1(-15+5\sqrt{10})}{-1}$
$= -15+5\sqrt{10}$

79. $\frac{2\sqrt{3}}{\sqrt{15}+2} = \frac{2\sqrt{3}(\sqrt{15}-2)}{(\sqrt{15}+2)(\sqrt{15}-2)}$
$= \frac{2\sqrt{3}(\sqrt{15}-2)}{15-4}$
$= \frac{2\sqrt{45}-4\sqrt{3}}{11}$
$= \frac{2\sqrt{9}\sqrt{5}-4\sqrt{3}}{11}$
$= \frac{2(3)\sqrt{5}-4\sqrt{3}}{11}$
$= \frac{6\sqrt{5}-4\sqrt{3}}{11}$

81. $\frac{\sqrt{3}+1}{\sqrt{2}-1} = \frac{(\sqrt{3}+1)(\sqrt{2}+1)}{(\sqrt{2}-1)(\sqrt{2}+1)}$
$= \frac{(\sqrt{3}+1)(\sqrt{2}+1)}{2-1}$
$= \frac{\sqrt{6}+\sqrt{3}+\sqrt{2}+1}{1}$
$= \sqrt{6}+\sqrt{3}+\sqrt{2}+1$

83. $\sqrt[3]{12} \cdot \sqrt[3]{4} = \sqrt[3]{12 \cdot 4}$
$= \sqrt[3]{48}$
$= \sqrt[3]{8 \cdot 6}$
$= \sqrt[3]{8} \cdot \sqrt[3]{6}$
$= 2\sqrt[3]{6}$

85. $2\sqrt[3]{5} \cdot 6\sqrt[3]{2} = 12\sqrt[3]{10}$

87. $\sqrt[3]{15} \cdot \sqrt[3]{25} = \sqrt[3]{375} = \sqrt[3]{125} \cdot \sqrt[3]{3} = 5\sqrt[3]{3}$

89. $\frac{\sqrt[3]{54}}{\sqrt[3]{2}} = \sqrt[3]{\frac{54}{2}} = \sqrt[3]{27} = 3$

91. $\frac{\sqrt[3]{120}}{\sqrt[3]{5}} = \sqrt[3]{\frac{120}{5}}$
$= \sqrt[3]{24}$
$= \sqrt[3]{8 \cdot 3}$
$= \sqrt[3]{8} \cdot \sqrt[3]{3}$
$= 2\sqrt[3]{3}$

93. $\sqrt[3]{\frac{5}{4}} = \frac{\sqrt[3]{5}}{\sqrt[3]{4}} \cdot \frac{\sqrt[3]{2}}{\sqrt[3]{2}} = \frac{\sqrt[3]{10}}{\sqrt[3]{8}} = \frac{\sqrt[3]{10}}{2}$

95. $\frac{6}{\sqrt[3]{2}} = \frac{6}{\sqrt[3]{2}} \cdot \frac{\sqrt[3]{4}}{\sqrt[3]{4}} = \frac{6\sqrt[3]{4}}{\sqrt[3]{8}} = \frac{6\sqrt[3]{4}}{2} = 3\sqrt[3]{4}$

97. $\sqrt[3]{\frac{1}{9}} = \frac{\sqrt[3]{1}}{\sqrt[3]{9}} = \frac{1}{\sqrt[3]{9}} \cdot \frac{\sqrt[3]{3}}{\sqrt[3]{3}} = \frac{\sqrt[3]{3}}{\sqrt[3]{27}} = \frac{\sqrt[3]{3}}{3}$

99. $\sqrt[3]{\frac{2}{9}} = \frac{\sqrt[3]{2}}{\sqrt[3]{9}} = \frac{\sqrt[3]{2}}{\sqrt[3]{9}} \cdot \frac{\sqrt[3]{3}}{\sqrt[3]{3}} = \frac{\sqrt[3]{6}}{3}$

101. Answers may vary.

103.
$$\begin{aligned} \frac{\sqrt{2}-2}{2-\sqrt{3}} &= \frac{(\sqrt{2}-2)}{(2-\sqrt{3})} \cdot \frac{(\sqrt{2}+2)}{(\sqrt{2}+2)} \\ &= \frac{2-4}{(2-\sqrt{3})(\sqrt{2}+2)} \\ &= \frac{-2}{2\sqrt{2}+4-\sqrt{6}-2\sqrt{3}} \end{aligned}$$

105. $\frac{12x+8}{4} = \frac{4(3x+2)}{4} = 3x+2$

107. $\frac{8y^2-2y}{2y} = \frac{2y(4y-1)}{2y} = 4y-1$

109.
$$\begin{aligned} 2y-1 &= 3^2 \\ 2y-1 &= 9 \\ 2y &= 10 \\ y &= 5 \end{aligned}$$

111.
$$\begin{aligned} 9x^2+5x+4 &= (3x+1)^2 \\ 9x^2+5x+4 &= 9x^2+6x+1 \\ 5x+4 &= 6x+1 \\ 4 &= x+1 \\ 3 &= x \end{aligned}$$

Exercise Set 9.5

1.
$$\begin{aligned} \sqrt{x} &= 9 \\ \left(\sqrt{x}\right)^2 &= 9^2 \\ x &= 81 \end{aligned}$$

3.
$$\begin{aligned} \sqrt{x+5} &= 2 \\ \left(\sqrt{x+5}\right)^2 &= 2^2 \\ x+5 &= 4 \\ x &= -1 \end{aligned}$$

5.
$$\begin{aligned} \sqrt{2x+6} &= 4 \\ \left(\sqrt{2x+6}\right)^2 &= 4^2 \\ 2x+6 &= 16 \\ 2x &= 10 \\ x &= 5 \end{aligned}$$

7.
$$\begin{aligned} \sqrt{x}-2 &= 5 \\ \sqrt{x} &= 7 \\ \left(\sqrt{x}\right)^2 &= 7^2 \\ x &= 49 \end{aligned}$$

9.
$$\begin{aligned} 3\sqrt{x}+5 &= 2 \\ 3\sqrt{x} &= -3 \\ \sqrt{x} &= -1 \end{aligned}$$

There is no solution since $\sqrt{x}$ cannot equal a negative number.

11.
$$\begin{aligned} \sqrt{x+6}+1 &= 3 \\ \sqrt{x+6} &= 2 \\ \left(\sqrt{x+6}\right)^2 &= 2^2 \\ x+6 &= 4 \\ x &= -2 \end{aligned}$$

13.
$$\begin{aligned} \sqrt{2x+1}+3 &= 5 \\ \sqrt{2x+1} &= 2 \\ \left(\sqrt{2x+1}\right)^2 &= 2^2 \\ 2x+1 &= 4 \\ 2x &= 3 \\ x &= \frac{3}{2} \end{aligned}$$

15.
$$\begin{aligned} \sqrt{x}+3 &= 7 \\ \sqrt{x} &= 4 \\ \left(\sqrt{x}\right)^2 &= 4^2 \\ x &= 16 \end{aligned}$$

17. $\sqrt{x+6}+5=3$
$\sqrt{x+6}=-2$
There is no solution since the result of a square root cannot be negative.

19. $\sqrt{4x-3}=\sqrt{x+3}$
$\left(\sqrt{4x-3}\right)^2=\left(\sqrt{x+3}\right)^2$
$4x-3=x+3$
$3x=6$
$x=2$

21. $\sqrt{x}=\sqrt{3x-8}$
$\left(\sqrt{x}\right)^2=\left(\sqrt{3x-8}\right)^2$
$x=3x-8$
$-2x=-8$
$x=4$

23. $\sqrt{4x}=\sqrt{2x+6}$
$\left(\sqrt{4x}\right)^2=\left(\sqrt{2x+6}\right)^2$
$4x=2x+6$
$2x=6$
$x=3$

25. $\sqrt{9x^2+2x-4}=3x$
$\left(\sqrt{9x^2+2x-4}\right)^2=(3x)^2$
$9x^2+2x-4=9x^2$
$2x=4$
$x=2$

27. $\sqrt{16x^2-3x+6}=4x$
$\left(\sqrt{16x^2-3x+6}\right)^2=(4x)^2$
$16x^2-3x+6=16x^2$
$3x=6$
$x=2$

29. $\sqrt{16x^2+2x+2}=4x$
$\left(\sqrt{16x^2+2x+2}\right)^2=(4x)^2$
$16x^2+2x+2=16x^2$
$2x=-2$
$x=-1$
A check shows that $x=-1$ is an extraneous solution. Therefore, there is no solution.

31. $\sqrt{2x^2+6x+9}=3$
$\left(\sqrt{2x^2+6x+9}\right)^2=3^2$
$2x^2+6x+9=9$
$2x(x+3)=0$
$2x=0$ or $x+3=0$
$x=0$ or $x=-3$

33. $\sqrt{x+7}=x+5$
$\left(\sqrt{x+7}\right)^2=(x+5)^2$
$x+7=x^2+10x+25$
$x^2+9x+18=0$
$(x+6)(x+3)=0$
$x+6=0$ or $x+3=0$
$x=-6$ (extraneous) $x=-3$

35. $\sqrt{x}=x-6$
$\left(\sqrt{x}\right)^2=(x-6)^2$
$x=x^2-12x+36$
$0=x^2-13x+36$
$0=(x-9)(x-4)$
$x-9=0$ or $x-4=0$
$x=9$ $x=4$ (extraneous)

37. $\sqrt{2x+1}=x-7$
$\left(\sqrt{2x+1}\right)^2=(x-7)^2$
$2x+1=x^2-14x+49$
$0=x^2-16x+48$
$0=(x-12)(x-4)$
$x-12=0$ or $x-4=0$
$x=12$ $x=4$ (extraneous)

39.
$$x = \sqrt{2x-2}+1$$
$$x-1 = \sqrt{2x-2}$$
$$(x-1)^2 = \left(\sqrt{2x-2}\right)^2$$
$$x^2-2x+1 = 2x-2$$
$$x^2-4x+3=0$$
$$(x-3)(x-1)=0$$
$$x-3=0 \text{ or } x-1=0$$
$$x=3 \text{ or } x=1$$

41.
$$\sqrt{1-8x}-x=4$$
$$\sqrt{1-8x}=x+4$$
$$\left(\sqrt{1-8x}\right)^2=(x+4)^2$$
$$1-8x=x^2+8x+16$$
$$0=x^2+16x+15$$
$$0=(x+15)(x+1)$$
$$x+15=0 \text{ or } x+1=0$$
$$x=-15 \text{ (extraneous)} \quad x=-1$$

43.
$$\sqrt{2x+5}-1=x$$
$$\sqrt{2x+5}=1+x$$
$$\left(\sqrt{2x+5}\right)^2=(1+x)^2$$
$$2x+5=1+2x+x^2$$
$$x^2=4$$
$$x=2 \text{ or } x=-2 \text{ (extraneous)}$$

45.
$$\sqrt{x-7}=\sqrt{x}-1$$
$$\left(\sqrt{x-7}\right)^2=\left(\sqrt{x}-1\right)^2$$
$$x-7=x-2\sqrt{x}+1$$
$$2\sqrt{x}=8$$
$$\sqrt{x}=4$$
$$\left(\sqrt{x}\right)^2=4^2$$
$$x=16$$

47.
$$\sqrt{x}+3=\sqrt{x+15}$$
$$\left(\sqrt{x}+3\right)^2=\left(\sqrt{x+15}\right)^2$$
$$x+6\sqrt{x}+9=x+15$$
$$6\sqrt{x}=6$$
$$\sqrt{x}=1$$
$$\left(\sqrt{x}\right)^2=1^2$$
$$x=1$$

49.
$$\sqrt{x+8}=\sqrt{x}+2$$
$$\left(\sqrt{x+8}\right)^2=\left(\sqrt{x}+2\right)^2$$
$$x+8=x+4\sqrt{x}+4$$
$$4=4\sqrt{x}$$
$$1=\sqrt{x}$$
$$1^2=\left(\sqrt{x}\right)^2$$
$$1=x$$
$$x=1$$

51. Let x = number
$$x=6+\sqrt{x}$$
$$x-6=\sqrt{x}$$
$$(x-6)^2=\left(\sqrt{x}\right)^2$$
$$(x)^2+2(x)(-6)+(-6)^2=x$$
$$x^2-12x+36=x$$
$$x^2-12x-x+36=0$$
$$x^2-13x+36=0$$
$$(x-9)(x-4)=0$$
$$x-9=0 \text{ or } x-4=0$$
$$x=9 \text{ or } x=4$$

Check $x=9$

$9=6+\sqrt{9}$

$9=6+3$

$9=9$ True

Check $x=4$

$4=6+\sqrt{4}$

$4=6+2$

$4=8$ False

The solution is 9.

53. a. $b = \sqrt{\frac{V}{2}}$

$b = \sqrt{\frac{20}{2}} \approx 3.2$

$b = \sqrt{\frac{200}{2}} = 10$

$b = \sqrt{\frac{2000}{2}} \approx 31.6$

V	20	200	2000
b	3.2	10	31.6

b. No; it increases by a factor of $\sqrt{10}$.

55. Answers may vary.

57. $\sqrt{x+1} = 2x - 3$

$y_1 = \sqrt{x+1}$

$y_2 = 2x - 3$

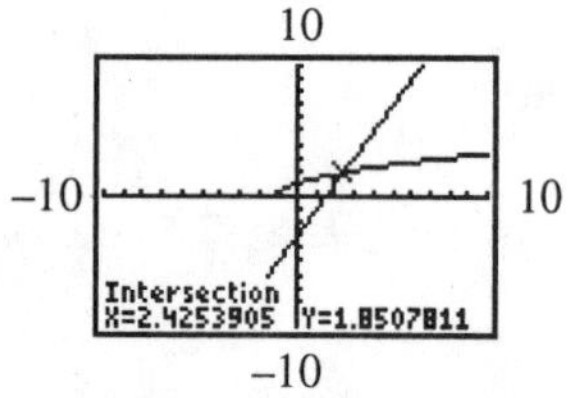

The solution is the x-value of the intersection, 2.43.

59. $-\sqrt{x+5} = -7x + 1$

$y_1 = -\sqrt{x+5}$

$y_2 = -7x + 1$

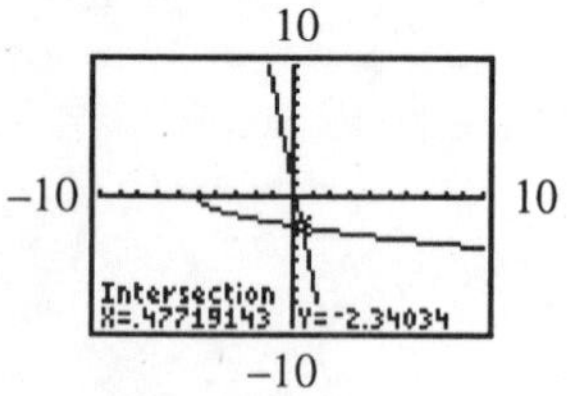

The solution is the x-value of the intersection, 0.48.

61.
$$
\begin{aligned}
2x - (x+3) &= 11 \\
2x - x - 3 &= 11 \\
x - 3 &= 11 \\
x - 3 + 3 &= 11 + 3 \\
x &= 14
\end{aligned}
$$

63. Let x = width

$x + 2$ = length

$$
\begin{aligned}
2x + 2(x+2) &= 24 \\
2x + 2x + 4 &= 24 \\
4x + 4 &= 24 \\
4x + 4 - 4 &= 24 - 4 \\
4x &= 20 \\
\frac{4x}{4} &= \frac{20}{4} \\
x &= 5
\end{aligned}
$$

$x + 2 = 7$

The length is 7 in.

Exercise Set 9.6

1.
$$
\begin{aligned}
a^2 + b^2 &= c^2 \\
2^2 + 3^2 &= c^2 \\
4 + 9 &= c^2 \\
13 &= c^2 \\
\sqrt{13} &= c
\end{aligned}
$$

The hypotenuse has a length of $\sqrt{13} \approx 3.61$.

3.
$$
\begin{aligned}
a^2 + b^2 &= c^2 \\
3^2 + b^2 &= 6^2 \\
9 + b^2 &= 36 \\
b^2 &= 27 \\
b &= \sqrt{27} \\
b &= 3\sqrt{3}
\end{aligned}
$$

The unknown side has a length of $3\sqrt{3} \approx 5.20$.

5.
$$
\begin{aligned}
a^2 + b^2 &= c^2 \\
7^2 + 24^2 &= c^2 \\
49 + 576 &= c^2 \\
625 &= c^2 \\
\sqrt{625} &= c \\
25 &= c
\end{aligned}
$$

The hypotenuse has a length of 25.

7. $a^2+b^2=c^2$

$$a^2+\left(\sqrt{3}\right)^2=5^2$$
$$a^2+3=25$$
$$a^2=22$$
$$a=\sqrt{22}$$

The unknown side has a length of $\sqrt{22}\approx 4.69$.

9. $a^2+b^2=c^2$

$$4^2+b^2=13^2$$
$$16+b^2=169$$
$$b^2=153$$
$$b=\sqrt{153}$$
$$b=3\sqrt{17}$$

The unknown side has a length of $3\sqrt{17}\approx 12.37$.

11. $a^2+b^2=c^2$

$$4^2+5^2=c^2$$
$$16+25=c^2$$
$$41=c^2$$
$$\sqrt{41}=c$$
$$c=\sqrt{41}\approx 6.40$$

13. $a^2+b^2=c^2$

$$a^2+2^2=6^2$$
$$a^2+4=36$$
$$a^2=32$$
$$a=\sqrt{32}$$
$$a=4\sqrt{2}\approx 5.66$$

15. $a^2+b^2=c^2$

$$\left(\sqrt{10}\right)^2+b^2=10^2$$
$$10+b^2=100$$
$$b^2=90$$
$$b=\sqrt{90}$$
$$b=3\sqrt{10}\approx 9.49$$

17.

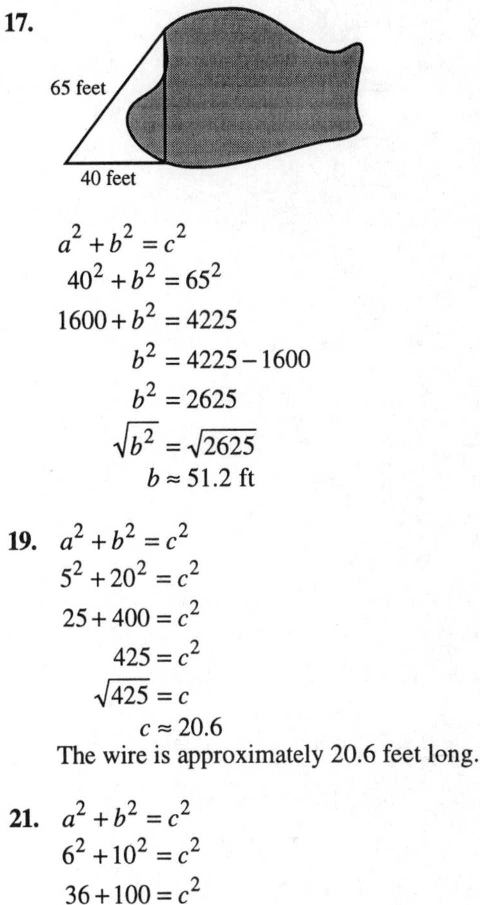

$$a^2+b^2=c^2$$
$$40^2+b^2=65^2$$
$$1600+b^2=4225$$
$$b^2=4225-1600$$
$$b^2=2625$$
$$\sqrt{b^2}=\sqrt{2625}$$
$$b\approx 51.2 \text{ ft}$$

19. $a^2+b^2=c^2$

$$5^2+20^2=c^2$$
$$25+400=c^2$$
$$425=c^2$$
$$\sqrt{425}=c$$
$$c\approx 20.6$$

The wire is approximately 20.6 feet long.

21. $a^2+b^2=c^2$

$$6^2+10^2=c^2$$
$$36+100=c^2$$
$$136=c^2$$
$$\sqrt{136}=c$$
$$c\approx 11.7$$

The brace is approximately 11.7 feet long.

23. (3, 6) and (5, 11)

$$d=\sqrt{(x_2-x_1)^2+(y_2-y_1)^2}$$
$$=\sqrt{(5-3)^2+(11-6)^2}$$
$$=\sqrt{2^2+5^2}$$
$$=\sqrt{4+25}$$
$$=\sqrt{29}$$

25. (–3, 1) and (5, –2)
$$d = \sqrt{(x_2 - x_1)^2 + (y_2 - y_1)^2}$$
$$= \sqrt{[5-(-3)]^2 + (-2-1)^2}$$
$$= \sqrt{(8)^2 + (-3)^2}$$
$$= \sqrt{64+9}$$
$$= \sqrt{73}$$

27. (3, –2) and (1, –8)
$$d = \sqrt{(x_2 - x_1)^2 + (y_2 - y_1)^2}$$
$$= \sqrt{(1-3)^2 + [-8-(-2)]^2}$$
$$= \sqrt{(-2)^2 + (-6)^2}$$
$$= \sqrt{4+36}$$
$$= \sqrt{40}$$
$$= \sqrt{4 \cdot 10}$$
$$= 2\sqrt{10}$$

29. $\left(\frac{1}{2}, 2\right)$ and (2, –1)
$$d = \sqrt{(x_2 - x_1)^2 + (y_2 - y_1)^2}$$
$$= \sqrt{\left(2-\frac{1}{2}\right)^2 + (-1-2)^2}$$
$$= \sqrt{\left(\frac{3}{2}\right)^2 + (-3)^2}$$
$$= \sqrt{\frac{9}{4}+9}$$
$$= \sqrt{\frac{45}{4}}$$
$$= \frac{\sqrt{45}}{\sqrt{4}}$$
$$= \frac{3\sqrt{5}}{2}$$

31. (3, –2) and (5, 7)
$$d = \sqrt{(x_2 - x_1)^2 + (y_2 - y_1)^2}$$
$$= \sqrt{(5-3)^2 + [7-(-2)]^2}$$
$$= \sqrt{2^2 + 9^2}$$
$$= \sqrt{4+81}$$
$$= \sqrt{85}$$

33. $b = \sqrt{\frac{3V}{h}}$
$$6 = \sqrt{\frac{3V}{2}}$$
$$6^2 = \frac{3V}{2}$$
$$2(36) = 3V$$
$$\frac{2(36)}{3} = V$$
$$V = 24$$
The volume is 24 cubic feet.

35. $s = \sqrt{30fd}$
$$s = \sqrt{30(0.35)(280)}$$
$$s = \sqrt{2940}$$
$$s \approx 54$$
It was traveling approximately 54 mph.

37. $r = \sqrt{2.5r}$
$$r = \sqrt{2.5(300)}$$
$$r = \sqrt{750}$$
$$r \approx 27$$
The car can travel at approximately 27 mph.

39. $d = 3.5\sqrt{h}$
$$d = 3.5\sqrt{305.4}$$
$$d \approx 61.2$$
You can see approximately 61.2 km.

41. First find the length of the whole base, and label it *y*.

$y^2 + 3^2 = 7^2$
$y^2 + 9 = 49$
$y^2 = 40$
$y = \sqrt{40}$
$y = 2\sqrt{10}$

Then find the length of the short unknown side, label it z.

$z^2 + 3^2 = 5^2$
$z^2 + 9 = 25$
$z^2 = 16$
$z = 4$

Then find *x*.

$x = y - z$
$x = 2\sqrt{10} - 4$

43. $a^2 + b^2 = c^2$
$[60(3)]^2 + [30(3)]^2 = c^2$
$(180)^2 + (90)^2 = c^2$
$32,400 + 8100 = c^2$
$40,500 = c^2$
$201 \approx c$

They are approximately 201 miles apart.

45. Answers may vary.

47. $(-3)^3 = (-3)(-3)(-3) = -27$

49. $\left(\frac{2}{7}\right)^3 = \left(\frac{2}{7}\right)\left(\frac{2}{7}\right)\left(\frac{2}{7}\right) = \frac{8}{343}$

51. $x^4 \cdot x^2 = x^{4+2} = x^6$

53. $x \cdot x^7 = x^{1+7} = x^8$

Exercise Set 9.7

1. $8^{1/3} = \sqrt[3]{8} = 2$

3. $9^{1/2} = \sqrt{9} = 3$

5. $16^{3/4} = (\sqrt[4]{16})^3 = 2^3 = 8$

7. $32^{2/5} = \left(\sqrt[5]{32}\right)^2 = 2^2 = 4$

9. $-16^{-1/4} = -\frac{1}{16^{1/4}} = -\frac{1}{\sqrt[4]{16}} = -\frac{1}{2}$

11. $16^{-3/2} = \frac{1}{16^{3/2}} = \frac{1}{(\sqrt{16})^3} = \frac{1}{4^3} = \frac{1}{64}$

13. $81^{-3/2} = \frac{1}{81^{3/2}} = \frac{1}{(\sqrt{81})^3} = \frac{1}{9^3} = \frac{1}{729}$

15. $\left(\frac{4}{25}\right)^{-1/2} = \frac{1}{\left(\frac{4}{25}\right)^{1/2}} = \frac{1}{\sqrt{\frac{4}{25}}} = \frac{1}{\frac{2}{5}} = \frac{5}{2}$

17. Answers may vary.

19. $2^{1/3} \cdot 2^{2/3} = 2^{3/3} = 2^1 = 2$

21. $\frac{4^{3/4}}{4^{1/4}} = 4^{3/4-1/4} = 4^{2/4} = 4^{1/2} = \sqrt{4} = 2$

23. $\frac{x^{1/6}}{x^{5/6}} = x^{\frac{1}{6}-\frac{5}{6}} = x^{-4/6} = x^{-2/3} = \frac{1}{x^{2/3}}$

25. $(x^{1/2})^6 = x^{6/2} = x^3$

27. Answers may vary.

29. $81^{1/2} = \sqrt{81} = 9$

31. $(-8)^{1/3} = \sqrt[3]{-8} = -2$

33. $-81^{1/4} = -(81^{1/4}) = -(\sqrt[4]{81}) = -(3) = -3$

35. $\left(\frac{1}{81}\right)^{1/2} = \frac{1^{1/2}}{81^{1/2}} = \frac{\sqrt{1}}{\sqrt{81}} = \frac{1}{9}$

37. $\left(\frac{27}{64}\right)^{1/3} = \frac{27^{1/3}}{64^{1/3}} = \frac{\sqrt[3]{27}}{\sqrt[3]{64}} = \frac{3}{4}$

39. $9^{3/2} = (\sqrt{9})^3 = (3)^3 = 27$

41. $64^{3/2} = (\sqrt{64})^3 = (8)^3 = 512$

43. $-8^{2/3} = -(8^{2/3})$
$= -(\sqrt[3]{8})^2$
$= -(2)^2$
$= -(4)$
$= -4$

45. $4^{5/2} = (\sqrt{4})^5 = (2)^5 = 32$

47. $\left(\frac{4}{9}\right)^{3/2} = \frac{4^{3/2}}{9^{3/2}} = \frac{(\sqrt{4})^3}{(\sqrt{9})^3} = \frac{2^3}{3^3} = \frac{8}{27}$

49. $\left(\frac{1}{81}\right)^{3/4} = \frac{1^{3/4}}{81^{3/4}} = \frac{(\sqrt[4]{1})^3}{(\sqrt[4]{81})^3} = \frac{1^3}{3^3} = \frac{1}{27}$

51. $4^{-1/2} = \frac{1}{4^{1/2}} = \frac{1}{\sqrt{4}} = \frac{1}{2}$

53. $125^{-1/3} = \frac{1}{125^{1/3}} = \frac{1}{\sqrt[3]{125}} = \frac{1}{5}$

55. $625^{-3/4} = \frac{1}{625^{3/4}} = \frac{1}{(\sqrt[4]{625})^3} = \frac{1}{5^3} = \frac{1}{125}$

57. $3^{4/3} \cdot 3^{2/3} = 3^{4/3+2/3} = 3^{6/3} = 3^2 = 9$

59. $\frac{6^{2/3}}{6^{1/3}} = 6^{2/3-1/3} = 6^{1/3}$

61. $\left(x^{2/3}\right)^9 = x^{\frac{2}{3}\cdot 9} = x^6$

63. $\frac{6^{1/3}}{6^{-5/3}} = 6^{1/3-(-5/3)}$
$= 6^{\frac{1}{3}+\frac{5}{3}}$
$= 6^{6/3}$
$= 6^2$
$= 36$

65. $\frac{3^{-3/5}}{3^{2/5}} = 3^{-3/5-2/5} = 3^{-5/5} = 3^{-1} = \frac{1}{3}$

67. $\left(\frac{x^{1/3}}{y^{3/4}}\right)^2 = \frac{x^{\frac{1}{3}\cdot 2}}{x^{\frac{3}{4}\cdot 2}} = \frac{x^{2/3}}{y^{3/2}}.$

69. $\left(\frac{x^{2/5}}{y^{3/4}}\right)^8 = \frac{x^{\frac{2}{5}\cdot 8}}{x^{\frac{3}{4}\cdot 8}} = \frac{x^{16/5}}{y^6}$

71. $P = P_0(1.08)^N$
$P = 10,000(1.08)^{3/2}$
$P = 10,000(\sqrt{1.08})^3$
$P = 10,000(1.0392)^3$
$P = 10,000(1.1224)$
$P = 11,224$ people

73. $5^{3/4} = 3.344$

75. $18^{3/5} = 5.665$

77. $\begin{cases} x + y < 6 \\ y \geq 2x \end{cases}$
Graph $x + y = 6$.
The boundary line is dashed. Choose (0, 0) as a test point.
$x + y < 6$
$0 + 0 \ ? \ 6$
$0 \ ? \ 6$
Since $0 < 6$, shade the side containing (0, 0).
Graph $y = 2x$.
The boundary line is solid.
Choose (–2, 0) as a test point.
$y \geq 2x$
$0 \ ? \ 2(-2)$
$0 \ ? \ -4$
Since $0 \geq -4$, shade the side containing (–2, 0).

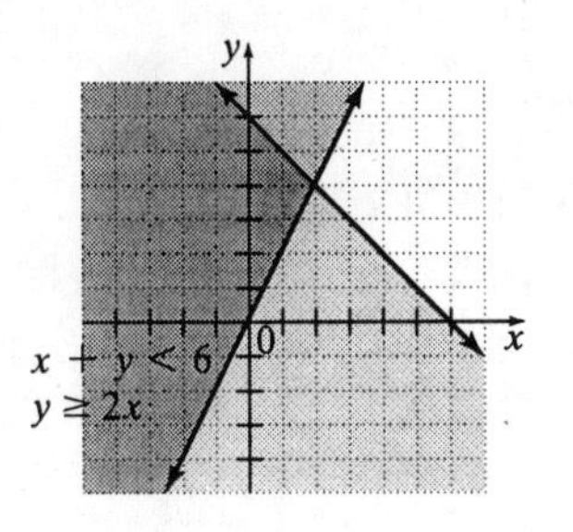

79. $x^2 - 4 = 3x$

$x^2 - 3x - 4 = 0$

$(x-4)(x+1) = 0$

$x - 4 = 0$ or $x + 1 = 0$

$x = 4$ or $x = -1$

$x = -1, 4$

81. $2x^2 - 5x - 3 = 0$

$(2x+1)(x-3) = 0$

$2x + 1 = 0$ or $x - 3 = 0$

$2x = -1$ or $x = 3$

$x = -\frac{1}{2}$

Chapter 9 Review Exercises

1. $\sqrt{81} = 9$ because $9^2 = 81$.

2. $-\sqrt{49} = -7$ because $7^2 = 49$.

3. $\sqrt[3]{27} = 3$ because $3^3 = 27$.

4. $\sqrt[4]{16} = 2$ because $2^4 = 16$.

5. $-\sqrt{\frac{9}{64}} = -\frac{3}{8}$ because $\left(\frac{3}{8}\right)^2 = \frac{9}{64}$.

6. $\sqrt{\frac{36}{81}} = \frac{6}{9} = \frac{2}{3}$ because $\left(\frac{6}{9}\right)^2 = \frac{36}{81}$.

7. $\sqrt[4]{-\frac{16}{81}}$; not a real number

8. $\sqrt[3]{-\frac{27}{64}} = -\frac{3}{4}$ because $\left(-\frac{3}{4}\right)^3 = -\frac{27}{64}$.

9. $\sqrt{76}$; irrational, 8.718

10. $\sqrt{576}$; rational, 24

11. $\sqrt{x^{12}} = x^6$ because $(x^6)^2 = x^{12}$.

12. $\sqrt{x^8} = x^4$ because $(x^4)^2 = x^8$.

13. $\sqrt{9x^6} = 3x^3$ because $(3x^3)^2 = 9x^6$.

14. $\sqrt{25x^4} = 5x^2$ because $(5x^2)^2 = 25x^4$.

15. $\sqrt{\frac{16}{y^{10}}} = \frac{4}{y^5}$ because $\left(\frac{4}{y^5}\right)^2 = \frac{16}{y^{10}}$.

16. $\sqrt{\frac{y^{12}}{49}} = \frac{y^6}{7}$ because $\left(\frac{y^6}{7}\right)^2 = \frac{y^{12}}{49}$.

17. $\sqrt{54} = \sqrt{9}\sqrt{6} = 3\sqrt{6}$

18. $\sqrt{88} = \sqrt{4 \cdot 22} = 2\sqrt{22}$

19. $\sqrt{150x^3} = \sqrt{25x^2}\sqrt{6x} = 5x\sqrt{6x}$

20. $\sqrt{92y^5} = \sqrt{4 \cdot 23 \cdot y^4 \cdot y} = 2y^2\sqrt{23y}$

21. $\sqrt[3]{54} = \sqrt[3]{27}\sqrt[3]{2} = 3\sqrt[3]{2}$

22. $\sqrt[3]{88} = \sqrt[3]{8 \cdot 11} = 2\sqrt[3]{11}$

23. $\sqrt[4]{48} = \sqrt[4]{16}\sqrt[4]{3} = 2\sqrt[4]{3}$

24. $\sqrt[4]{162} = \sqrt[4]{81 \cdot 2} = 3\sqrt[4]{2}$

25. $\sqrt{\frac{18}{25}} = \frac{\sqrt{18}}{\sqrt{25}} = \frac{\sqrt{9}\sqrt{2}}{5} = \frac{3\sqrt{2}}{5}$

26. $\sqrt{\frac{75}{64}} = \frac{\sqrt{75}}{\sqrt{64}} = \frac{\sqrt{25 \cdot 3}}{8} = \frac{5\sqrt{3}}{8}$

27. $\sqrt{\frac{45y^2}{4x^4}} = \frac{\sqrt{45y^2}}{\sqrt{4x^4}} = \frac{\sqrt{9y^2}\sqrt{5}}{2x^2} = \frac{3y\sqrt{5}}{2x^2}$

28. $\sqrt{\frac{20x^5}{9x^2}} = \sqrt{\frac{20x^3}{9}} = \frac{\sqrt{4\cdot 5\cdot x^2\cdot x}}{\sqrt{9}} = \frac{2x\sqrt{5x}}{3}$

29. $\sqrt[4]{\frac{9}{16}} = \frac{\sqrt[4]{9}}{\sqrt[4]{16}} = \frac{\sqrt[4]{9}}{2}$

30. $\sqrt[3]{\frac{40}{27}} = \frac{\sqrt[3]{8\cdot 5}}{\sqrt[3]{27}} = \frac{2\sqrt[3]{5}}{3}$

31. $\sqrt[3]{\frac{3}{8}} = \frac{\sqrt[3]{3}}{\sqrt[3]{8}} = \frac{\sqrt[3]{3}}{2}$

32. $\sqrt[4]{\frac{5}{81}} = \frac{\sqrt[4]{5}}{\sqrt[4]{81}} = \frac{\sqrt[4]{5}}{3}$

33. $3\sqrt[3]{2} + 2\sqrt[3]{3} - 4\sqrt[3]{2} = (3-4)\sqrt[3]{2} + 2\sqrt[3]{3} = -\sqrt[3]{2} + 2\sqrt[3]{3}$

34. $5\sqrt{2} + 2\sqrt[3]{2} - 8\sqrt{2} = (5-8)\sqrt{2} + 2\sqrt[3]{2} = -3\sqrt{2} + 2\sqrt[3]{2}$

35. $\sqrt{6} + 2\sqrt[3]{6} - 4\sqrt[3]{6} + 5\sqrt{6}$
$= (1+5)\sqrt{6} + (2-4)\sqrt[3]{6}$
$= 6\sqrt{6} - 2\sqrt[3]{6}$

36. $3\sqrt{5} - \sqrt[3]{5} - 2\sqrt{5} + 3\sqrt[3]{5}$
$= (3-2)\sqrt{5} + (-1+3)\sqrt[3]{5}$
$= \sqrt{5} + 2\sqrt[3]{5}$

37. $\sqrt{28x} + \sqrt{63x} + \sqrt[3]{56}$
$= \sqrt{4}\sqrt{7x} + \sqrt{9}\sqrt{7x} + \sqrt[3]{8}\sqrt[3]{7}$
$= 2\sqrt{7x} + 3\sqrt{7x} + 2\sqrt[3]{7}$
$= 5\sqrt{7x} + 2\sqrt[3]{7}$

38. $\sqrt{75y} + \sqrt{48y} - \sqrt[4]{16}$
$= \sqrt{25\cdot 3y} + \sqrt{16\cdot 3y} - 2$
$= 5\sqrt{3y} + 4\sqrt{3y} - 2$
$= 9\sqrt{3y} - 2$

39. $\sqrt{\frac{5}{9}} - \sqrt{\frac{5}{36}} = \frac{\sqrt{5}}{\sqrt{9}} - \frac{\sqrt{5}}{\sqrt{36}} = \frac{\sqrt{5}}{3} - \frac{\sqrt{5}}{6} = \frac{\sqrt{5}}{3}\cdot\frac{2}{2} - \frac{\sqrt{5}}{6} = \frac{2\sqrt{5}}{6} - \frac{\sqrt{5}}{6} = \frac{\sqrt{5}}{6}$

40. $\sqrt{\frac{11}{25}} + \sqrt{\frac{11}{16}} = \frac{\sqrt{11}}{5} + \frac{\sqrt{11}}{4} = \frac{4\sqrt{11} + 5\sqrt{11}}{20} = \frac{9\sqrt{11}}{20}$

41. $2\sqrt[3]{125} - 5\sqrt[3]{8} = 2(5) - 5(2) = 10 - 10 = 0$

42. $3\sqrt[3]{16} - 2\sqrt[3]{2} = 3\sqrt[3]{8\cdot 2} - 2\sqrt[3]{2} = 6\sqrt[3]{2} - 2\sqrt[3]{2} = 4\sqrt[3]{2}$

43. $3\sqrt{10}\cdot 2\sqrt{5} = 6\sqrt{50} = 6\sqrt{25}\sqrt{2} = 6(5)\sqrt{2} = 30\sqrt{2}$

44. $2\sqrt[3]{4}\cdot 5\sqrt[3]{6}=10\sqrt[3]{24}=10\sqrt[3]{8\cdot 3}=20\sqrt[3]{3}$

45. $$\begin{aligned}\sqrt{3}(2\sqrt{6}-3\sqrt{12}) &= 2\sqrt{18}-3\sqrt{36}\\ &= 2\sqrt{9}\sqrt{2}-3(6)\\ &= 2(3)\sqrt{2}-18\\ &= 6\sqrt{2}-18\end{aligned}$$

46. $$\begin{aligned}4\sqrt{5}(2\sqrt{10}-5\sqrt{5}) &= 8\sqrt{50}-20\sqrt{25}\\ &= 8\sqrt{25\cdot 2}-20(5)\\ &= 40\sqrt{2}-100\end{aligned}$$

47. $$\begin{aligned}(\sqrt{3}+2)(\sqrt{6}-5) &= \sqrt{18}-5\sqrt{3}+2\sqrt{6}-10\\ &= \sqrt{9}\sqrt{2}-5\sqrt{3}+2\sqrt{6}-10\\ &= 3\sqrt{2}-5\sqrt{3}+2\sqrt{6}-10\end{aligned}$$

48. $$\begin{aligned}(2\sqrt{5}+1)(4\sqrt{5}-3) &= 8\sqrt{25}-6\sqrt{5}+4\sqrt{5}-3\\ &= 40-3-2\sqrt{5}\\ &= 37-2\sqrt{5}\end{aligned}$$

49. $\dfrac{\sqrt{96}}{\sqrt{3}}=\sqrt{\dfrac{96}{3}}=\sqrt{32}=\sqrt{16}\sqrt{2}=4\sqrt{2}$

50. $\dfrac{\sqrt{160}}{\sqrt{8}}=\sqrt{\dfrac{160}{8}}=\sqrt{20}=\sqrt{4\cdot 5}=2\sqrt{5}$

51. $$\begin{aligned}\frac{\sqrt{15x^6}}{\sqrt{12x^3}} &= \sqrt{\frac{15x^6}{12x^3}}\\ &= \sqrt{\frac{5x^3}{4}}\\ &= \frac{\sqrt{5x^3}}{\sqrt{4}}\\ &= \frac{\sqrt{x^2}\sqrt{5x}}{2}\\ &= \frac{x\sqrt{5x}}{2}\end{aligned}$$

52. $$\begin{aligned}\frac{\sqrt{50y^8}}{\sqrt{72y^3}} &= \frac{\sqrt{25\cdot 2y^8}}{\sqrt{36\cdot 2\cdot y^2\cdot y}}\\ &= \frac{5y^4\sqrt{2}}{6y\sqrt{2y}}\\ &= \frac{5y^3}{6}\sqrt{\frac{2}{2y}}\\ &= \frac{5y^3}{6\sqrt{y}}\\ &= \frac{5y^3\sqrt{y}}{6y}\\ &= \frac{5y^2\sqrt{y}}{6}\end{aligned}$$

53. $\sqrt{\dfrac{5}{6}}=\dfrac{\sqrt{5}}{\sqrt{6}}\cdot\dfrac{\sqrt{6}}{\sqrt{6}}=\dfrac{\sqrt{30}}{6}$

54. $\sqrt{\dfrac{7}{10}}=\dfrac{\sqrt{7}}{\sqrt{10}}\cdot\dfrac{\sqrt{10}}{\sqrt{10}}=\dfrac{\sqrt{70}}{\sqrt{100}}=\dfrac{\sqrt{70}}{10}$

55. $\sqrt{\dfrac{3}{2x}}=\dfrac{\sqrt{3}}{\sqrt{2x}}\cdot\dfrac{\sqrt{2x}}{\sqrt{2x}}=\dfrac{\sqrt{6x}}{2x}$

56. $\sqrt{\dfrac{6}{5y}}=\dfrac{\sqrt{6}}{\sqrt{5y}}\cdot\dfrac{\sqrt{5y}}{\sqrt{5y}}=\dfrac{\sqrt{30y}}{\sqrt{25y^2}}=\dfrac{\sqrt{30y}}{5y}$

57. $$\begin{aligned}\sqrt{\frac{7}{20y^2}} &= \frac{\sqrt{7}}{\sqrt{20y^2}}\\ &= \frac{\sqrt{7}}{\sqrt{4y^2}\sqrt{5}}\\ &= \frac{\sqrt{7}}{2y\sqrt{5}}\cdot\frac{\sqrt{5}}{\sqrt{5}}\\ &= \frac{\sqrt{35}}{2y(5)}\\ &= \frac{\sqrt{35}}{10y}\end{aligned}$$

58. $\sqrt{\dfrac{5z}{12x^2}} = \dfrac{\sqrt{5z}}{\sqrt{12x^2}} \cdot \dfrac{\sqrt{3}}{\sqrt{3}} = \dfrac{\sqrt{15z}}{\sqrt{36x^2}} = \dfrac{\sqrt{15z}}{6x}$

59. $\sqrt[3]{\dfrac{7}{9}} = \dfrac{\sqrt[3]{7}}{\sqrt[3]{9}} \cdot \dfrac{\sqrt[3]{3}}{\sqrt[3]{3}} = \dfrac{\sqrt[3]{21}}{\sqrt[3]{27}} = \dfrac{\sqrt[3]{21}}{3}$

60. $\sqrt[3]{\dfrac{3}{4}} = \dfrac{\sqrt[3]{3}}{\sqrt[3]{4}} \cdot \dfrac{\sqrt[3]{2}}{\sqrt[3]{2}} = \dfrac{\sqrt[3]{6}}{\sqrt[3]{8}} = \dfrac{\sqrt[3]{6}}{2}$

61. $\sqrt[3]{\dfrac{3}{2}} = \dfrac{\sqrt[3]{3}}{\sqrt[3]{2}} \cdot \dfrac{\sqrt[3]{4}}{\sqrt[3]{4}} = \dfrac{\sqrt[3]{12}}{\sqrt[3]{8}} = \dfrac{\sqrt[3]{12}}{2}$

62. $\sqrt[3]{\dfrac{5}{4}} = \dfrac{\sqrt[3]{5}}{\sqrt[3]{4}} \cdot \dfrac{\sqrt[3]{2}}{\sqrt[3]{2}} = \dfrac{\sqrt[3]{10}}{\sqrt[3]{8}} = \dfrac{\sqrt[3]{10}}{2}$

63.
$$\begin{aligned}\frac{3}{\sqrt{5}-2} &= \frac{3(\sqrt{5}+2)}{(\sqrt{5}-2)(\sqrt{5}+2)}\\ &= \frac{3(\sqrt{5}+2)}{5-4}\\ &= \frac{3\sqrt{5}+6}{1}\\ &= 3\sqrt{5}+6\end{aligned}$$

64.
$$\begin{aligned}\frac{8}{\sqrt{10}-3} &= \frac{8}{\sqrt{10}-3} \cdot \frac{\sqrt{10}+3}{\sqrt{10}+3}\\ &= \frac{8(\sqrt{10}+3)}{10-9}\\ &= \frac{8\sqrt{10}+24}{1}\\ &= 8\sqrt{10}+24\end{aligned}$$

65.
$$\begin{aligned}\frac{8}{\sqrt{6}+2} &= \frac{8(\sqrt{6}-2)}{(\sqrt{6}+2)(\sqrt{6}-2)}\\ &= \frac{8(\sqrt{6}-2)}{6-4}\\ &= \frac{8\left(\sqrt{6}-2\right)}{2}\\ &= 4\left(\sqrt{6}-2\right)\\ &= 4\sqrt{6}-8\end{aligned}$$

66.
$$\begin{aligned}\frac{12}{\sqrt{15}-3} &= \frac{12}{\sqrt{15}-3} \cdot \frac{\sqrt{15}+3}{\sqrt{15}+3}\\ &= \frac{12(\sqrt{15}+3)}{\sqrt{225}-9}\\ &= \frac{12\sqrt{15}+36}{15-9}\\ &= \frac{12\sqrt{15}+36}{6}\\ &= 2\sqrt{15}+6\end{aligned}$$

67.
$$\begin{aligned}\frac{\sqrt{2}}{4+\sqrt{2}} &= \frac{\sqrt{2}(4-\sqrt{2})}{(4+\sqrt{2})(4-\sqrt{2})}\\ &= \frac{\sqrt{2}(4-\sqrt{2})}{16-2}\\ &= \frac{4\sqrt{2}-2}{14}\\ &= \frac{2\left(2\sqrt{2}-1\right)}{14}\\ &= \frac{2\sqrt{2}-1}{7}\end{aligned}$$

68.
$$\begin{aligned}\frac{\sqrt{3}}{5+\sqrt{3}} &= \frac{\sqrt{3}}{5+\sqrt{3}} \cdot \frac{5-\sqrt{3}}{5-\sqrt{3}}\\ &= \frac{\sqrt{3}(5-\sqrt{3})}{25-\sqrt{9}}\\ &= \frac{5\sqrt{3}-\sqrt{9}}{25-3}\\ &= \frac{5\sqrt{3}-3}{22}\end{aligned}$$

69.
$$\frac{2\sqrt{3}}{\sqrt{3}-5} = \frac{2\sqrt{3}(\sqrt{3}+5)}{(\sqrt{3}-5)(\sqrt{3}+5)}$$
$$= \frac{2\sqrt{3}(\sqrt{3}+5)}{3-25}$$
$$= \frac{2(3)+10\sqrt{3}}{-22}$$
$$= \frac{6+10\sqrt{3}}{-22}$$
$$= \frac{2\left(3+5\sqrt{3}\right)}{-22}$$
$$= -\frac{3+5\sqrt{3}}{11}$$

70.
$$\frac{7\sqrt{2}}{\sqrt{2}-4} = \frac{7\sqrt{2}}{\sqrt{2}-4} \cdot \frac{\sqrt{2}+4}{\sqrt{2}+4}$$
$$= \frac{7\sqrt{2}(\sqrt{2}+4)}{\sqrt{4}-16}$$
$$= \frac{7\sqrt{4}+28\sqrt{2}}{2-16}$$
$$= \frac{14+28\sqrt{2}}{-14}$$
$$= -1-2\sqrt{2}$$

71.
$$\sqrt{2x} = 6$$
$$\left(\sqrt{2x}\right)^2 = 6^2$$
$$2x = 36$$
$$x = \frac{36}{2} = 18$$

72.
$$\sqrt{x+3} = 4$$
$$\left(\sqrt{x+3}\right)^2 = (4)^2$$
$$x+3 = 16$$
$$x = 13$$

73.
$$\sqrt{x}+3 = 8$$
$$\sqrt{x} = 8-3$$
$$\sqrt{x} = 5$$
$$\left(\sqrt{x}\right)^2 = 5^2$$
$$x = 25$$

74.
$$\sqrt{x}+8 = 3$$
$$\sqrt{x} = -5$$
No solution because the positive square root of a number cannot equal a negative number.

75.
$$\sqrt{2x+1} = x-7$$
$$\left(\sqrt{2x+1}\right)^2 = (x-7)^2$$
$$2x+1 = (x)^2+2(x)(-7)+(7)^2$$
$$2x+1 = x^2-14x+49$$
$$0 = x^2-14x-2x+49-1$$
$$0 = x^2-16x+48$$
$$0 = (x-12)(x-4)$$
$x-12=0$ or $x-4=0$
$x=12$ or $x=4$
(extraneous)

76.
$$\sqrt{3x+1} = x-1$$
$$\left(\sqrt{3x+1}\right)^2 = (x-1)^2$$
$$3x+1 = x^2-2x+1$$
$$0 = x^2-5x$$
$$0 = x(x-5)$$
$x=0$ or $x-5=0$
extraneous $x=5$

77.
$$\sqrt{x+3}+x = 9$$
$$\sqrt{x+3} = 9-x$$
$$\left(\sqrt{x+3}\right)^2 = (9-x)^2$$
$$x+3 = (9)^2+2(9)(-x)+(x)^2$$
$$x+3 = 81-18x+x^2$$
$$0 = 81-3-18x-x+x^2$$
$$0 = 78-19x+x^2$$
$$0 = x^2-19x+78$$
$$0 = (x-6)(x-13)$$
$x-6=0$ or $x-13=0$
$x=6$ or $x=13$ (extraneous)

78. $\sqrt{2x} + x = 4$

$\left(\sqrt{2x}\right)^2 = (4-x)^2$

$2x = 16 - 8x + x^2$

$0 = x^2 - 10x + 16$

$0 = (x-8)(x-2)$

$x - 8 = 0$ or $x - 2 = 0$

$x = 8$ or $x = 2$

$x = 2$; 8 is extraneous.

79. $a^2 + b^2 = c^2$

$5^2 + b^2 = 9^2$

$25 + b^2 = 81$

$b^2 = 81 - 25$

$b^2 = 56$

$\sqrt{b^2} = \sqrt{56}$

$b = \sqrt{4}\sqrt{14}$

$b = 2\sqrt{14}$

80. $a^2 + b^2 = c^2$

$9^2 + 6^2 = c^2$

$81 + 36 = c^2$

$\sqrt{117} = \sqrt{c^2}$

$\sqrt{117} = c$

81. $a^2 + b^2 = c^2$

$12^2 + 20^2 = c^2$

$144 + 400 = c^2$

$544 = c^2$

$\sqrt{544} = \sqrt{c^2}$

$\sqrt{16}\sqrt{34} = c$

$4\sqrt{34}$ ft $= c$

82. $a^2 + b^2 = c^2$

$5^2 + b^2 = 10^2$

$25 + b^2 = 100$

$b^2 = 75$

$\sqrt{b^2} = \sqrt{75}$

$b = \sqrt{25 \cdot 3}$

$b = 5\sqrt{3}$ inches

83. (6, –2) and (–3, 5)

$d = \sqrt{(x_2 - x_1)^2 + (y_2 - y_1)^2}$

$d = \sqrt{(-3-6)^2 + [5-(-2)]^2}$

$d = \sqrt{(-9)^2 + (5+2)^2}$

$d = \sqrt{81 + (7)^2}$

$d = \sqrt{81 + 49}$

$d = \sqrt{130}$

84. (2, 8) and (–6, 10)

$\sqrt{(-6-2)^2 + (10-8)^2} = \sqrt{(-8)^2 + 2^2}$

$= \sqrt{64 + 4}$

$= \sqrt{68}$

$= \sqrt{4 \cdot 17}$

$= 2\sqrt{17}$

85. $r = \sqrt{\dfrac{A}{4\pi}}$

$r = \sqrt{\dfrac{72}{4(3.14)}}$

$r = \sqrt{\dfrac{72}{12.56}}$

$r = \sqrt{5.732}$

$r \approx 2.4$ in.

86. $r = \sqrt{\frac{A}{4\pi}}$
$6 = \sqrt{\frac{A}{4\pi}}$
$36 = \frac{A}{4\pi}$
$36(4\pi) = A \Rightarrow A = 144\pi$
144π sq. in.

87. $\sqrt{a^5} = a^{5/2}$

88. $\sqrt[5]{a^3} = a^{3/5}$

89. $\sqrt[6]{x^{15}} = x^{15/6} = x^{5/2}$

90. $\sqrt[4]{x^{12}} = x^{12/4} = x^3$

91. $16^{1/2} = \sqrt{16} = 4$

92. $36^{1/2} = \sqrt{36} = 6$

93. $(-8)^{1/3} = \sqrt[3]{-8} = -2$

94. $(-32)^{1/5} = \sqrt[5]{-32} = -2$

95. $-64^{3/2} = -(64^{3/2})$
$= -(\sqrt{64})^3$
$= -(8)^3$
$= -512$

96. $-8^{2/3} = -\sqrt[3]{8^2} = -\sqrt[3]{64} = -4$

97. $\left(\frac{16}{81}\right)^{3/4} = \frac{16^{3/4}}{81^{3/4}} = \frac{(\sqrt[4]{16})^3}{(\sqrt[4]{81})^3} = \frac{2^3}{3^3} = \frac{8}{27}$

98. $\left(\frac{9}{25}\right)^{3/2} = \left(\sqrt{\frac{9}{25}}\right)^3 = \left(\frac{3}{5}\right)^3 = \frac{27}{125}$

99. $25^{-1/2} = \frac{1}{25^{1/2}} = \frac{1}{\sqrt{25}} = \frac{1}{5}$

100. $64^{-2/3} = \frac{1}{64^{2/3}} = \frac{1}{\left(\sqrt[3]{64}\right)^2} = \frac{1}{(4)^2} = \frac{1}{16}$

101. $8^{1/3} \cdot 8^{4/3} = 8^{5/3} = (\sqrt[3]{8})^5 = 2^5 = 32$

102. $4^{3/2} \cdot 4^{1/2} = 4^{\frac{3}{2}+\frac{1}{2}} = 4^{4/2} = 4^2 = 16$

103. $\frac{3^{1/6}}{3^{5/6}} = 3^{\frac{1}{6}-\frac{5}{6}} = 3^{-4/6} = 3^{-2/3} = \frac{1}{3^{2/3}}$

104. $\frac{2^{1/4}}{2^{-3/5}} = 2^{\frac{1}{4}-\left(-\frac{3}{5}\right)} = 2^{\frac{1}{4}+\frac{3}{5}} = 2^{\frac{5+12}{20}} = 2^{17/20}$

105. $\left(x^{-1/3}\right)^6 = x^{-\frac{1}{3}\cdot 6} = x^{-2} = \frac{1}{x^2}$

106. $\left(\frac{x^{1/2}}{y^{1/3}}\right)^2 = \frac{x^{2/2}}{y^{2/3}} = \frac{x}{y^{2/3}}$

Chapter 9 Test

1. $\sqrt{16} = 4$ because $4^2 = 16$.

2. $\sqrt[3]{125} = 5$ because $5^3 = 125$.

3. $16^{3/4} = (\sqrt[4]{16})^3 = 2^3 = 8$

4. $\left(\frac{9}{16}\right)^{1/2} = \frac{9^{1/2}}{16^{1/2}} = \frac{\sqrt{9}}{\sqrt{16}} = \frac{3}{4}$

5. $\sqrt[4]{-81}$; not a real number

6. $27^{-2/3} = \frac{1}{27^{2/3}} = \frac{1}{(\sqrt[3]{27})^2} = \frac{1}{3^2} = \frac{1}{9}$

7. $\sqrt{54} = \sqrt{9}\sqrt{6} = 3\sqrt{6}$

8. $\sqrt{92} = \sqrt{4}\sqrt{23} = 2\sqrt{23}$

9. $\sqrt{3x^6} = \sqrt{x^6}\sqrt{3} = x^3\sqrt{3}$

10. $\sqrt{8x^4y^7} = \sqrt{4x^4y^6}\sqrt{2y} = 2x^2y^3\sqrt{2y}$

11. $\sqrt{9x^9} = \sqrt{9x^8}\sqrt{x} = 3x^4\sqrt{x}$

12. $\sqrt[3]{40} = \sqrt[3]{8}\sqrt[3]{5} = 2\sqrt[3]{5}$

13. $\sqrt[3]{8} = 2$

14. $\sqrt{12} - 2\sqrt{75} = \sqrt{4}\sqrt{3} - 2\sqrt{25}\sqrt{3}$
$= 2\sqrt{3} - 2(5)\sqrt{3}$
$= 2\sqrt{3} - 10\sqrt{3}$
$= -8\sqrt{3}$

15. $\sqrt{2x^2} + \sqrt[3]{54} - x\sqrt{18}$
$= \sqrt{x^2}\sqrt{2} + \sqrt[3]{27}\sqrt[3]{2} - x\sqrt{9}\sqrt{2}$
$= x\sqrt{2} + 3\sqrt[3]{2} - x(3)\sqrt{2}$
$= x\sqrt{2} + 3\sqrt[3]{2} - 3x\sqrt{2}$
$= -2x\sqrt{2} + 3\sqrt[3]{2}$

16. $\sqrt{\frac{5}{16}} = \frac{\sqrt{5}}{\sqrt{16}} = \frac{\sqrt{5}}{4}$

17. $\sqrt[3]{\frac{2}{27}} = \frac{\sqrt[3]{2}}{\sqrt[3]{27}} = \frac{\sqrt[3]{2}}{3}$

18. $3\sqrt{8x} = 3\sqrt{4}\sqrt{2x} = 3(2)\sqrt{2x} = 6\sqrt{2x}$

19. $\sqrt{\frac{2}{3}} = \frac{\sqrt{2}}{\sqrt{3}} = \frac{\sqrt{2}}{\sqrt{3}} \cdot \frac{\sqrt{3}}{\sqrt{3}} = \frac{\sqrt{6}}{3}$

20. $\sqrt[3]{\frac{5}{9}} = \frac{\sqrt[3]{5}}{\sqrt[3]{9}} = \frac{\sqrt[3]{5}}{\sqrt[3]{9}} \cdot \frac{\sqrt[3]{3}}{\sqrt[3]{3}} = \frac{\sqrt[3]{15}}{\sqrt[3]{27}} = \frac{\sqrt[3]{15}}{3}$

21. $\sqrt{\frac{5}{12x^2}} = \frac{\sqrt{5}}{\sqrt{12x^2}}$
$= \frac{\sqrt{5}}{\sqrt{4x^2 \cdot 3}}$
$= \frac{\sqrt{5}}{2x\sqrt{3}}$
$= \frac{\sqrt{5}}{2x\sqrt{3}} \cdot \frac{\sqrt{3}}{\sqrt{3}}$
$= \frac{\sqrt{15}}{2x(3)}$
$= \frac{\sqrt{15}}{6x}$

22. $\frac{8}{\sqrt{6}+2} = \frac{8(\sqrt{6}-2)}{(\sqrt{6}+2)(\sqrt{6}-2)}$
$= \frac{8(\sqrt{6}-2)}{6-4}$
$= \frac{8(\sqrt{6}-2)}{2}$
$= 4(\sqrt{6}-2)$
$= 4\sqrt{6} - 8$

23. $\frac{2\sqrt{3}}{\sqrt{3}-3} = \frac{2\sqrt{3}(\sqrt{3}+3)}{(\sqrt{3}-3)(\sqrt{3}+3)}$
$= \frac{2\sqrt{3}(\sqrt{3}+3)}{3-9}$
$= \frac{2(3)+6\sqrt{3}}{-6}$
$= \frac{6+6\sqrt{3}}{-6}$
$= \frac{6(1+\sqrt{3})}{-6}$
$= -1(1+\sqrt{3})$
$= -1-\sqrt{3}$

24. $\sqrt{x}+8=11$

$\sqrt{x}=11-8$

$\sqrt{x}=3$

$\left(\sqrt{x}\right)^2=(3)^2$

$x=9$

Check

$\sqrt{9}+8=11$

$3+8=11$

$11=11$ True

The solution is 9.

25. $\sqrt{3x-6}=\sqrt{x+4}$

$\left(\sqrt{3x-6}\right)^2=\left(\sqrt{x+4}\right)^2$

$3x-6=x+4$

$3x-x-6=4$

$2x-6=4$

$2x=4+6$

$2x=10$

$x=\frac{10}{2}=5$

Check

$\sqrt{3(5)-6}=\sqrt{5+4}$

$\sqrt{15-6}=\sqrt{9}$

$\sqrt{9}=\sqrt{9}$ True

The solution is 5.

26. $\sqrt{2x-2}=x-5$

$\left(\sqrt{2x-2}\right)^2=(x-5)^2$

$2x-2=(x)^2+2(x)(-5)+(5)^2$

$2x-2=x^2-10x+25$

$0=x^2-10x-2x+25+2$

$0=x^2-12x+27$

$0=(x-9)(x-3)$

$x-9=0$ or $x-3=0$

$x=9$ or $x=3$

Check $x=9$

$\sqrt{2(9)-2}=9-5$

$\sqrt{18-2}=4$

$\sqrt{16}=4$

$4=4$ True

Check $x=3$

$\sqrt{2(3)-2}=3-5$

$\sqrt{6-2}=-2$

$\sqrt{4}=-2$

$2=-2$ False

The solution is 9.

27.

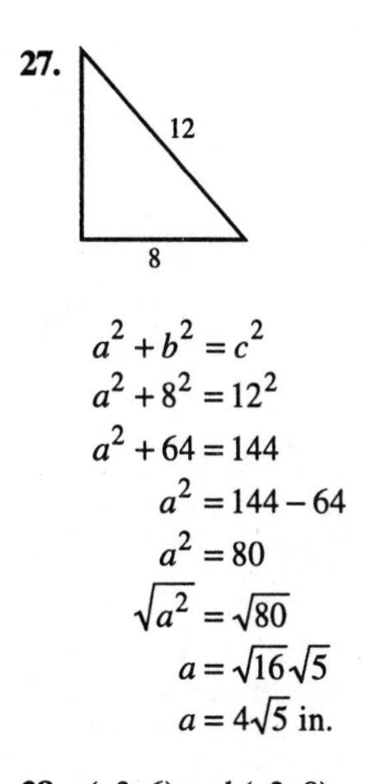

$a^2+b^2=c^2$

$a^2+8^2=12^2$

$a^2+64=144$

$a^2=144-64$

$a^2=80$

$\sqrt{a^2}=\sqrt{80}$

$a=\sqrt{16}\sqrt{5}$

$a=4\sqrt{5}$ in.

28. $(-3, 6)$ and $(-2, 8)$

$d=\sqrt{(x_2-x_1)^2+(y_2-y_1)^2}$

$d=\sqrt{[-2-(-3)]^2+(8-6)^2}$

$d=\sqrt{(-2+3)^2+(2)^2}$

$d=\sqrt{1^2+4}$

$d=\sqrt{1+4}$

$d=\sqrt{5}$

29. $16^{-3/4}\cdot 16^{-1/4}=16^{-4/4}=16^{-1}=\frac{1}{16}$

30. $\left(x^{2/3}\right)^5=x^{10/3}$

Chapter 10

Exercise Set 10.1

1. $x^2 = 64$
$x = \pm\sqrt{64}$
$x = \pm 8$
The solutions are ± 8.

3. $x^2 = 21$
$x = \pm\sqrt{21}$
The solutions are $\pm\sqrt{21}$.

5. $x^2 = \frac{1}{25}$
$x = \pm\sqrt{\frac{1}{25}}$
$x = \pm\frac{\sqrt{1}}{\sqrt{25}}$
$x = \pm\frac{1}{5}$
The solutions are $\pm\frac{1}{5}$.

7. $x^2 = -4$
This equation has no real solution because the square root of –4 is not a real number.

9. $3x^2 = 13$
$x^2 = \frac{13}{3}$
$x = \pm\sqrt{\frac{13}{3}}$
$x = \pm\frac{\sqrt{13}}{\sqrt{3}}$
$x = \pm\frac{\sqrt{13}\cdot\sqrt{3}}{\sqrt{3}\cdot\sqrt{3}}$
$x = \pm\frac{\sqrt{39}}{3}$
The solutions are $\pm\frac{\sqrt{39}}{3}$.

11. $7x^2 = 4$
$x^2 = \frac{4}{7}$
$x = \pm\sqrt{\frac{4}{7}}$
$x = \pm\frac{\sqrt{4}}{\sqrt{7}}$
$x = \pm\frac{2\cdot\sqrt{7}}{\sqrt{7}\cdot\sqrt{7}}$
$x = \pm\frac{2\sqrt{7}}{7}$
The solutions are $\pm\frac{2\sqrt{7}}{7}$.

13. $x^2 - 2 = 0$
$x^2 = 2$
$x = \pm\sqrt{2}$
The solutions are $\pm\sqrt{2}$.

15. $2x^2 - 10 = 0$
$2x^2 = 10$
$x^2 = 5$
$x = \pm\sqrt{5}$
The solutions are $\pm\sqrt{5}$.

17. Answers may vary.

19. $(x-5)^2 = 49$
$x - 5 = \pm\sqrt{49}$
$x - 5 = \pm 7$
$x = 5 \pm 7$
$x = 5 - 7$ or $x = 5 + 7$
$x = -2$ or $x = 12$
The solutions are –2 and 12.

21. $(x+2)^2 = 7$
$x + 2 = \pm\sqrt{7}$
$x = -2 \pm \sqrt{7}$
The solutions are $-2 \pm \sqrt{7}$.

23. $\left(m-\frac{1}{2}\right)^2=\frac{1}{4}$

$$m-\frac{1}{2}=\pm\sqrt{\frac{1}{4}}$$
$$m-\frac{1}{2}=\pm\frac{1}{2}$$
$$m=\frac{1}{2}\pm\frac{1}{2}$$
$$m=\frac{1}{2}-\frac{1}{2} \quad \text{or} \quad m=\frac{1}{2}+\frac{1}{2}$$
$$m=0 \quad \text{or} \quad m=1$$

The solutions are 0 and 1.

25. $(p+2)^2=10$

$$p+2=\pm\sqrt{10}$$
$$p=-2\pm\sqrt{10}$$

The solutions are $-2\pm\sqrt{10}$.

27. $(3y+2)^2=100$

$$3y+2=\pm\sqrt{100}$$
$$3y+2=\pm 10$$
$$3y=-2\pm 10$$
$$y=\frac{-2\pm 10}{3}$$
$$y=\frac{-2-10}{3} \quad \text{or} \quad y=\frac{-2+10}{3}$$
$$y=-4 \quad \text{or} \quad y=\frac{8}{3}$$

The solutions are –4 and $\frac{8}{3}$.

29. $(z-4)^2=-9$

This equation has no real solution because the square root of –9 is not a real number.

31. $(2x-11)^2=50$

$$2x-11=\pm\sqrt{50}$$
$$2x-11=\pm 5\sqrt{2}$$
$$2x=11\pm 5\sqrt{2}$$
$$x=\frac{11\pm 5\sqrt{2}}{2}$$

The solutions are $\frac{11\pm 5\sqrt{2}}{2}$.

33. $(3x-7)^2=32$

$$3x-7=\pm\sqrt{32}$$
$$3x-7=\pm 4\sqrt{2}$$
$$3x=7\pm 4\sqrt{2}$$
$$x=\frac{7\pm 4\sqrt{2}}{3}$$

The solutions are $x=\frac{7\pm 4\sqrt{2}}{3}$.

35. $(2p-5)^2=121$

$$2p-5=\pm\sqrt{121}$$
$$2p-5=11 \quad \text{or} \quad 2p-5=-11$$
$$2p=16 \quad \text{or} \quad 2p=-6$$
$$p=8 \quad \text{or} \quad p=-3$$

The solutions are 8 and –3.

37. $x^2+4x+4=16$

$$(x+2)^2=16$$
$$x+2=\pm\sqrt{16}$$
$$x+2=\pm 4$$
$$x=-2\pm 4$$
$$x=-2-4 \quad \text{or} \quad x=-2+4$$
$$x=-6 \quad \text{or} \quad x=2$$

The solutions are –6 and 2.

39. $y^2-10y+25=11$

$$(y-5)^2=11$$
$$y-5=\pm\sqrt{11}$$
$$y=5\pm\sqrt{11}$$

The solutions are $5\pm\sqrt{11}$.

41. $A=\pi r^2$

$$36\pi=\pi r^2$$
$$36=r^2$$
$$\sqrt{36}=r$$
$$6=r$$

The radius is 6 in.

43.
$$\begin{aligned} d &= 16t^2 \\ 400 &= 16t^2 \\ \frac{400}{16} &= t^2 \\ \sqrt{\frac{400}{16}} &= t \\ \frac{\sqrt{400}}{\sqrt{16}} &= t \\ \frac{20}{4} &= t \\ 5 &= t \end{aligned}$$
It will take 5 seconds.

45.
$$\begin{aligned} y &= 3x^2 + 41 \\ 116 &= 3x^2 + 41 \\ 75 &= 3x^2 \\ 25 &= x^2 \\ 5 &= x \end{aligned}$$
$1997 + 5 = 2002$
The year will be 2002.

47.
$$\begin{aligned} y^2 &= 9.86 \\ y &= \pm\sqrt{9.86} \\ y &= \pm 3.14 \end{aligned}$$
The solutions are ± 3.14.

49.
$$\begin{aligned} (z + 10.68)^2 &= 16.61 \\ z + 10.68 &= \pm\sqrt{16.61} \\ z &= -10.68 \pm \sqrt{16.61} \\ z &= -10.68 \pm 4.08 \\ z &= -14.76, -6.60 \end{aligned}$$
The solutions are -14.76 and -6.60.

51.
$$\begin{aligned} (5z - 5.95)^2 &= 14.19 \\ 5z - 5.95 &= \pm\sqrt{14.19} \\ 5z &= 5.95 \pm \sqrt{14.19} \\ z &= \frac{5.95 \pm 3.77}{5} \\ z &= 0.44, 1.94 \end{aligned}$$
The solutions are 0.44 and 1.94.

53. $y^2 + 10y + 25 = (y + 5)(y + 5) = (y + 5)^2$

55.
$$\begin{aligned} x^2 - 20x + 100 &= (x - 10)(x - 10) \\ &= (x - 10)^2 \end{aligned}$$

57.
$$\begin{aligned} m &= \frac{43 - 36.6}{3 - 0} = \frac{6.4}{3} = 2.1 \\ y - 36.6 &= 2.1(x - 0) \\ y - 36.6 &= 2.1x \\ y &= 2.1x + 36.6 \end{aligned}$$

Section 10.2

Mental Math

1. $p^2 + 8p \Rightarrow \left(\frac{8}{2}\right)^2 = 4^2 = 16$

2. $p^2 + 6p \Rightarrow \left(\frac{6}{2}\right)^2 = 3^2 = 9$

3. $x^2 + 20x \Rightarrow \left(\frac{20}{2}\right)^2 = 10^2 = 100$

4. $x^2 + 18x \Rightarrow \left(\frac{18}{2}\right)^2 = 9^2 = 81$

5. $y^2 + 14y \Rightarrow \left(\frac{14}{2}\right)^2 = 7^2 = 49$

6. $y^2 + 2y \Rightarrow \left(\frac{2}{2}\right)^2 = 1^2 = 1$

Exercise Set 10.2

1. $x^2 + 4x \Rightarrow \left(\frac{4}{2}\right)^2 = 2^2 = 4$
$x^2 + 4x + 4 = (x + 2)^2$

3. $k^2 - 12k \Rightarrow \left(\frac{-12}{2}\right)^2 = 6^2 = 36$
$k^2 - 12k + 36 = (k - 6)^2$

5. $x^2 - 3x \Rightarrow \left(\frac{-3}{2}\right)^2 = \frac{9}{4}$

$x^2 - 3x + \frac{9}{4} = \left(x - \frac{3}{2}\right)^2$

7. $m^2 - m \Rightarrow \left(\frac{-1}{2}\right)^2 = \frac{1}{4}$

$m^2 - m + \frac{1}{4} = \left(m - \frac{1}{2}\right)^2$

9.
$$x^2 - 6x = 0$$
$$x^2 - 6x + 9 = 0 + 9$$
$$(x-3)^2 = 9$$
$$x - 3 = \pm\sqrt{9}$$
$$x - 3 = \pm 3$$
$$x = 3 \pm 3$$

$x = 3 + 3$ or $x = 3 - 3$

$x = 6$ or $x = 0$

The solutions are 6 and 0.

11.
$$x^2 + 8x = -12$$
$$x^2 + 8x + 16 = -12 + 16$$
$$(x+4)^2 = 4$$
$$x + 4 = \pm\sqrt{4}$$
$$x + 4 = \pm 2$$
$$x = -4 \pm 2$$

$x = -4 + 2$ or $x = -4 - 2$

$x = -2$ or $x = -6$

The solutions are –2 and –6.

13.
$$x^2 + 2x - 5 = 0$$
$$x^2 + 2x = 5$$
$$x^2 + 2x + 1 = 5 + 1$$
$$(x+1)^2 = 6$$
$$x + 1 = \pm\sqrt{6}$$
$$x = -1 \pm \sqrt{6}$$

The solutions are $-1 \pm \sqrt{6}$.

15.
$$x^2 + 6x - 25 = 0$$
$$x^2 + 6x = 25$$
$$x^2 + 6x + 9 = 25 + 9$$
$$(x+3)^2 = 34$$
$$x + 3 = \pm\sqrt{34}$$
$$x = -3 \pm \sqrt{34}$$

The solutions are $-3 \pm \sqrt{34}$.

17.
$$z^2 + 5z = 7$$
$$z^2 + 5z + \frac{25}{4} = 7 + \frac{25}{4}$$
$$\left(z + \frac{5}{2}\right)^2 = \frac{28}{4} + \frac{25}{4}$$
$$\left(z + \frac{5}{2}\right)^2 = \frac{53}{4}$$
$$z + \frac{5}{2} = \pm\sqrt{\frac{53}{4}}$$
$$z + \frac{5}{2} = \pm\frac{\sqrt{53}}{2}$$
$$z = -\frac{5}{2} \pm \frac{\sqrt{53}}{2}$$
$$z = \frac{-5 \pm \sqrt{53}}{2}$$

The solutions are $\frac{-5 \pm \sqrt{53}}{2}$.

19.
$$x^2 - 2x - 1 = 0$$
$$x^2 - 2x = 1$$
$$x^2 - 2x + 1 = 1 + 1$$
$$(x-1)^2 = 2$$
$$x - 1 = \pm\sqrt{2}$$
$$x = 1 \pm \sqrt{2}$$

The solutions are $1 \pm \sqrt{2}$.

21.
$$y^2+5y+4=0$$
$$y^2+5y=-4$$
$$y^2+5y+\frac{25}{4}=-4+\frac{25}{4}$$
$$\left(y+\frac{5}{2}\right)^2=-\frac{16}{4}+\frac{25}{4}$$
$$\left(y+\frac{5}{2}\right)^2=\frac{9}{4}$$
$$y+\frac{5}{2}=\pm\sqrt{\frac{9}{4}}$$
$$y+\frac{5}{2}=\pm\frac{3}{2}$$
$$y=-\frac{5}{2}\pm\frac{3}{2}$$
$$y=-\frac{5}{2}+\frac{3}{2} \quad \text{or} \quad y=-\frac{5}{2}-\frac{3}{2}$$
$$y=-\frac{2}{2}=-1 \quad \text{or} \quad y=-\frac{8}{2}=-4$$
The solutions are −1 and −4.

23.
$$x(x+3)=18$$
$$x^2+3x=18$$
$$x^2+3x+\frac{9}{4}=18+\frac{9}{4}$$
$$\left(x+\frac{3}{2}\right)^2=\frac{72}{4}+\frac{9}{4}$$
$$\left(x+\frac{3}{2}\right)^2=\frac{81}{4}$$
$$x+\frac{3}{2}=\pm\sqrt{\frac{81}{4}}$$
$$x+\frac{3}{2}=\pm\frac{9}{2}$$
$$x=-\frac{3}{2}\pm\frac{9}{2}$$
$$x=-\frac{3}{2}+\frac{9}{2} \quad \text{or} \quad x=-\frac{3}{2}-\frac{9}{2}$$
$$x=\frac{6}{2}=3 \quad \text{or} \quad x=\frac{-12}{2}=-6$$
The solutions are 3 and −6.

25.
$$4x^2-24x=13$$
$$\frac{4x^2}{4}-\frac{24x}{4}=\frac{13}{4}$$
$$x^2-6x=\frac{13}{4}$$
$$x^2-6x+9=\frac{13}{4}+9$$
$$(x-3)^2=\frac{13}{4}+\frac{36}{4}$$
$$(x-3)^2=\frac{49}{4}$$
$$x-3=\pm\sqrt{\frac{49}{4}}$$
$$x-3=\pm\frac{7}{2}$$
$$x=3\pm\frac{7}{2}$$
$$x=3+\frac{7}{2} \quad \text{or} \quad x=3-\frac{7}{2}$$
$$x=\frac{6}{2}+\frac{7}{2} \quad \text{or} \quad x=\frac{6}{2}-\frac{7}{2}$$
$$x=\frac{13}{2} \quad \text{or} \quad x=-\frac{1}{2}$$
The solutions are $\frac{13}{2}$ and $-\frac{1}{2}$.

27.
$$5x^2+10x+6=0$$
$$5x^2+10x=-6$$
$$\frac{5x^2}{5}+\frac{10x}{5}=\frac{-6}{5}$$
$$x^2+2x=-\frac{6}{5}$$
$$x^2+2x+1=-\frac{6}{5}+1$$
$$(x+1)^2=-\frac{6}{5}+\frac{5}{5}$$
$$x+1=\pm\sqrt{-\frac{1}{5}}$$
$\sqrt{-\frac{1}{5}}$ is not a real number. No real solutions.

29.
$$2x^2 = 6x + 5$$
$$2x^2 - 6x = 5$$
$$\frac{2x^2}{2} - \frac{6x}{2} = \frac{5}{2}$$
$$x^2 - 3x = \frac{5}{2}$$
$$x^2 - 3x + \frac{9}{4} = \frac{5}{2} + \frac{9}{4}$$
$$\left(x - \frac{3}{2}\right)^2 = \frac{10}{4} + \frac{9}{4}$$
$$\left(x - \frac{3}{2}\right)^2 = \frac{19}{4}$$
$$x - \frac{3}{2} = \pm\sqrt{\frac{19}{4}}$$
$$x - \frac{3}{2} = \pm\frac{\sqrt{19}}{2}$$
$$x = \frac{3}{2} \pm \frac{\sqrt{19}}{2}$$
$$x = \frac{3 \pm \sqrt{19}}{2}$$

The solutions are $\frac{3 \pm \sqrt{19}}{2}$.

31.
$$3x^2 - 6x = 24$$
$$\frac{3x^2}{3} - \frac{6x}{3} = \frac{24}{3}$$
$$x^2 - 2x = 8$$
$$x^2 - 2x + 1 = 8 + 1$$
$$(x-1)^2 = 9$$
$$x - 1 = \pm\sqrt{9}$$
$$x - 1 = \pm 3$$
$$x = 1 \pm 3$$

$x = 1 + 3$ or $x = 1 - 3$

$x = 4$ or $x = -2$

The solutions are 4 and -2.

33.
$$2y^2 + 8y + 5 = 0$$
$$2y^2 + 8y = -5$$
$$\frac{2y^2}{2} + \frac{8y}{2} = \frac{-5}{2}$$
$$y^2 + 4y = -\frac{5}{2}$$
$$y^2 + 4y + 4 = -\frac{5}{2} + 4$$
$$(y+2)^2 = -\frac{5}{2} + \frac{8}{2}$$
$$(y+2)^2 = \frac{3}{2}$$
$$y + 2 = \pm\sqrt{\frac{3}{2}}$$
$$y + 2 = \pm\frac{\sqrt{3}}{\sqrt{2}}$$
$$y + 2 = \pm\frac{\sqrt{3}}{\sqrt{2}} \cdot \frac{\sqrt{2}}{\sqrt{2}}$$
$$y + 2 = \pm\frac{\sqrt{6}}{2}$$
$$y = -2 \pm \frac{\sqrt{6}}{2}$$
$$y = -\frac{4}{2} \pm \frac{\sqrt{6}}{2}$$
$$y = \frac{-4 \pm \sqrt{6}}{2}$$

The solutions are $\frac{-4 \pm \sqrt{6}}{2}$.

35.
$$2y^2 - 3y + 1 = 0$$
$$2y^2 - 3y = -1$$
$$\frac{2y^2}{2} - \frac{3y}{2} = \frac{-1}{2}$$
$$y^2 - \frac{3}{2}y = -\frac{1}{2}$$
$$y^2 - \frac{3}{2}y + \frac{9}{16} = -\frac{1}{2} + \frac{9}{16}$$
$$\left(y - \frac{3}{4}\right)^2 = -\frac{8}{16} + \frac{9}{16}$$
$$\left(y - \frac{3}{4}\right)^2 = \frac{1}{16}$$
$$y - \frac{3}{4} = \pm\sqrt{\frac{1}{16}}$$
$$y - \frac{3}{4} = \pm\frac{1}{4}$$
$$y = \frac{3}{4} \pm \frac{1}{4}$$
$$y = \frac{3}{4} + \frac{1}{4} \quad \text{or} \quad y = \frac{3}{4} - \frac{1}{4}$$
$$y = \frac{4}{4} = 1 \quad \text{or} \quad y = \frac{2}{4} = \frac{1}{2}$$
The solutions are 1 and $\frac{1}{2}$.

37.
$$3y^2 - 2y - 4 = 0$$
$$3y^2 - 2y = 4$$
$$\frac{3y^2}{3} - \frac{2y}{3} = \frac{4}{3}$$
$$y^2 - \frac{2}{3}y = \frac{4}{3}$$
$$y^2 - \frac{2}{3}y + \frac{1}{9} = \frac{4}{3} + \frac{1}{9}$$
$$\left(y - \frac{1}{3}\right)^2 = \frac{12}{9} + \frac{1}{9}$$
$$\left(y - \frac{1}{3}\right)^2 = \frac{13}{9}$$
$$y - \frac{1}{3} = \pm\sqrt{\frac{13}{9}}$$
$$y - \frac{1}{3} = \pm\frac{\sqrt{13}}{3}$$
$$y = \frac{1}{3} \pm \frac{\sqrt{13}}{3}$$
$$y = \frac{1 \pm \sqrt{13}}{3}$$
The solutions are $\frac{1 \pm \sqrt{13}}{3}$.

39. Answers may vary.

41.
$$x^2 + kx + 16$$
$$\left(\frac{k}{2}\right)^2 = 16$$
$$\frac{k}{2} = \pm\sqrt{16}$$
$$\frac{k}{2} = \pm 4$$
$$k = \pm 8$$

43. $x^2 + 8x = -12$
$x = -6, -2$

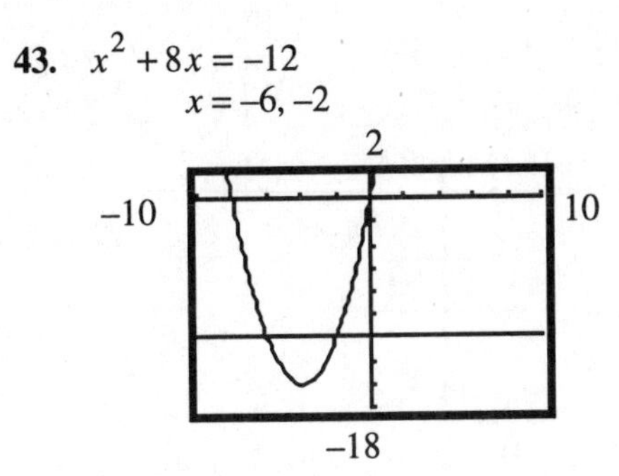

45. $2x^2 = 6x + 5$
$x \approx -0.68, 3.68$

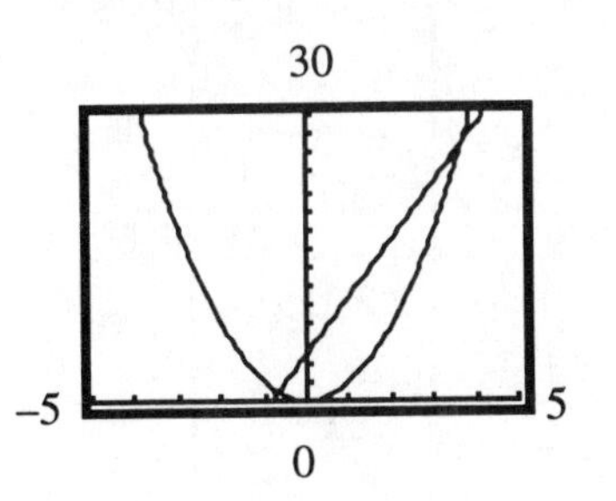

47. $\frac{3}{4} - \sqrt{\frac{25}{16}} = \frac{3}{4} - \frac{\sqrt{25}}{\sqrt{16}} = \frac{3}{4} - \frac{5}{4} = -\frac{2}{4} = -\frac{1}{2}$

49. $\frac{1}{2} - \sqrt{\frac{9}{4}} = \frac{1}{2} - \frac{\sqrt{9}}{\sqrt{4}} = \frac{1}{2} - \frac{3}{2} = \frac{-2}{2} = -1$

51. $\frac{6 + 4\sqrt{5}}{2} = \frac{2(3 + 2\sqrt{5})}{2} = 3 + 2\sqrt{5}$

53. $\frac{3 - 9\sqrt{2}}{6} = \frac{3(1 - 3\sqrt{2})}{3 \cdot 2} = \frac{1 - 3\sqrt{2}}{2}$

Section 10.3

Mental Math

1. $2x^2 + 5x + 3 = 0$
$a = 2,\ b = 5,\ c = 3$

2. $5x^2 - 7x + 1 = 0$
$a = 5,\ b = -7,\ c = 1$

3. $10x^2 - 13x - 2 = 0$
$a = 10,\ b = -13,\ c = -2$

4. $x^2 + 3x - 7 = 0$
$a = 1,\ b = 3,\ c = -7$

5. $x^2 - 6 = 0$
$a = 1,\ b = 0,\ c = -6$

6. $9x^2 - 4 = 0$
$a = 9,\ b = 0,\ c = -4$

Exercise Set 10.3

1.
$$\frac{-1 \pm \sqrt{1^2 - 4(1)(-2)}}{2(1)} = \frac{-1 \pm \sqrt{1+8}}{2} = \frac{-1 \pm \sqrt{9}}{2} = \frac{-1 \pm 3}{2} = 1, -2$$

3.
$$\frac{-5 \pm \sqrt{5^2 - 4(1)(2)}}{2(1)} = \frac{-5 \pm \sqrt{25-8}}{2} = \frac{-5 \pm \sqrt{17}}{2}$$

5.
$$\frac{-(-4) \pm \sqrt{(-4)^2 - 4(2)(1)}}{2(2)} = \frac{4 \pm \sqrt{16-8}}{4} = \frac{4 \pm \sqrt{8}}{4} = \frac{4 \pm \sqrt{4}\sqrt{2}}{4} = \frac{4 \pm 2\sqrt{2}}{4} = \frac{2(2 \pm \sqrt{2})}{4} = \frac{2 \pm \sqrt{2}}{2}$$

7. $x^2 - 3x + 2 = 0$
$a = 1,\ b = -3,\ c = 2$

$$x = \frac{-(-3) \pm \sqrt{(-3)^2 - 4(1)(2)}}{2(1)}$$

$$x = \frac{3 \pm \sqrt{9-8}}{2}$$

$$x = \frac{3 \pm \sqrt{1}}{2}$$

$$x = \frac{3 \pm 1}{2}$$

$$x = \frac{3+1}{2} \quad \text{or} \quad x = \frac{3-1}{2}$$

$$x = \frac{4}{2} = 2 \quad \text{or} \quad x = \frac{2}{2} = 1$$

The solutions are 2 and 1.

9. $3k^2 + 7k + 1 = 0$
$a = 3,\ b = 7,\ c = 1$

$$k = \frac{-7 \pm \sqrt{7^2 - 4(3)(1)}}{2(3)}$$

$$k = \frac{-7 \pm \sqrt{49-12}}{6}$$

$$k = \frac{-7 \pm \sqrt{37}}{6}$$

The solutions are $\frac{-7 \pm \sqrt{37}}{6}$.

11. $49x^2 - 4 = 0$
$a = 49,\ b = 0,\ c = -4$

$$x = \frac{-0 \pm \sqrt{0^2 - 4(49)(-4)}}{2(49)}$$

$$x = \frac{\pm\sqrt{784}}{98}$$

$$x = \pm\frac{28}{98} = \pm\frac{2}{7}$$

The solutions are $\pm\frac{2}{7}$.

13. $5z^2 - 4z + 3 = 0$
$a = 5,\ b = -4,\ c = 3$

$$z = \frac{-(-4) \pm \sqrt{(-4)^2 - 4(5)(3)}}{2(5)}$$

$$z = \frac{4 \pm \sqrt{16-60}}{10}$$

$$z = \frac{4 \pm \sqrt{-44}}{10}$$

$\sqrt{-44}$ is not a real number. No real solutions.

15. $y^2 = 7y + 30$
$y^2 - 7y - 30 = 0$
$a = 1,\ b = -7,\ c = -30$

$$y = \frac{-(-7) \pm \sqrt{(-7)^2 - 4(1)(-30)}}{2(1)}$$

$$y = \frac{7 \pm \sqrt{49+120}}{2}$$

$$y = \frac{7 \pm \sqrt{169}}{2}$$

$$y = \frac{7 \pm 13}{2}$$

$$y = \frac{7+13}{2} \quad \text{or} \quad y = \frac{7-13}{2}$$

$$y = \frac{20}{2} = 10 \quad \text{or} \quad y = \frac{-6}{2} = -3$$

The solutions are 10 and –3.

17. $2x^2 = 10$

$2x^2 - 10 = 0$

$a = 2, b = 0, c = -10$

$$x = \frac{-0 \pm \sqrt{0^2 - 4(2)(-10)}}{2(2)}$$

$$x = \frac{\pm\sqrt{80}}{4}$$

$$x = \frac{\pm\sqrt{16}\sqrt{5}}{4}$$

$$x = \pm\frac{4\sqrt{5}}{4}$$

$$x = \pm\sqrt{5}$$

The solutions are $\pm\sqrt{5}$.

19. $m^2 - 12 = m$

$m^2 - m - 12 = 0$

$a = 1, b = -1, c = -12$

$$m = \frac{-(-1) \pm \sqrt{(-1)^2 - 4(1)(-12)}}{2(1)}$$

$$m = \frac{1 \pm \sqrt{1+48}}{2}$$

$$m = \frac{1 \pm \sqrt{49}}{2}$$

$$m = \frac{1 \pm 7}{2}$$

$$m = \frac{1+7}{2} \quad \text{or} \quad m = \frac{1-7}{2}$$

$$m = \frac{8}{2} = 4 \quad \text{or} \quad m = \frac{-6}{2} = -3$$

The solutions are 4 and −3.

21. $3 - x^2 = 4x$

$-x^2 - 4x + 3 = 0$

$a = -1, b = -4, c = 3$

$$x = \frac{-(-4) \pm \sqrt{(-4)^2 - 4(-1)(3)}}{2(-1)}$$

$$x = \frac{4 \pm \sqrt{16+12}}{-2}$$

$$x = \frac{4 \pm \sqrt{28}}{-2}$$

$$x = \frac{4 \pm \sqrt{4}\sqrt{7}}{-2}$$

$$x = \frac{4 \pm 2\sqrt{7}}{-2}$$

$$x = \frac{2(2 \pm \sqrt{7})}{-2}$$

$$x = -1(2 \pm \sqrt{7})$$

$$x = -2 \pm \sqrt{7}$$

The solutions are $-2 \pm \sqrt{7}$.

23. $2a^2 - 7a + 3 = 0$

$a = 2, b = -7, c = 3$

$$a = \frac{-(-7) \pm \sqrt{(-7)^2 - 4(2)(3)}}{2(2)}$$

$$a = \frac{7 \pm \sqrt{49-24}}{4}$$

$$a = \frac{7 \pm \sqrt{25}}{4}$$

$$a = \frac{7 \pm 5}{4}$$

$$a = \frac{7+5}{4} \quad \text{or} \quad a = \frac{7-5}{4}$$

$$a = \frac{12}{4} = 3 \quad \text{or} \quad a = \frac{2}{4} = \frac{1}{2}$$

The solutions are 3 and $\frac{1}{2}$.

25. $x^2 - 5x - 2 = 0$
$a = 1,\ b = -5,\ c = -2$

$$x = \frac{-(-5) \pm \sqrt{(-5)^2 - 4(1)(-2)}}{2(1)}$$

$$x = \frac{5 \pm \sqrt{25+8}}{2}$$

$$x = \frac{5 \pm \sqrt{33}}{2}$$

The solutions are $\frac{5 \pm \sqrt{33}}{2}$.

27. $3x^2 - x - 14 = 0$
$a = 3,\ b = -1,\ c = -14$

$$x = \frac{-(-1) \pm \sqrt{(-1)^2 - 4(3)(-14)}}{2(3)}$$

$$x = \frac{1 \pm \sqrt{1+168}}{6}$$

$$x = \frac{1 \pm \sqrt{169}}{6}$$

$$x = \frac{1 \pm 13}{6}$$

$$x = \frac{1+13}{6} \quad \text{or} \quad x = \frac{1-13}{6}$$

$$x = \frac{14}{6} = \frac{7}{3} \quad \text{or} \quad x = \frac{-12}{6} = -2$$

The solutions are $\frac{7}{3}$ and -2.

29. $6x^2 + 9x = 2$
$6x^2 + 9x - 2 = 0$
$a = 6,\ b = 9,\ c = -2$

$$x = \frac{-9 \pm \sqrt{9^2 - 4(6)(-2)}}{2(6)}$$

$$x = \frac{-9 \pm \sqrt{81+48}}{12}$$

$$x = \frac{-9 \pm \sqrt{129}}{12}$$

The solutions are $\frac{-9 \pm \sqrt{129}}{12}$.

31. $7p^2 + 2 = 8p$
$7p^2 - 8p + 2 = 0$
$a = 7,\ b = -8,\ c = 2$

$$p = \frac{-(-8) \pm \sqrt{(-8)^2 - 4(7)(2)}}{2(7)}$$

$$p = \frac{8 \pm \sqrt{64-56}}{14}$$

$$p = \frac{8 \pm \sqrt{8}}{14}$$

$$p = \frac{8 \pm \sqrt{4}\sqrt{2}}{14}$$

$$p = \frac{8 \pm 2\sqrt{2}}{14}$$

$$p = \frac{2(4 \pm \sqrt{2})}{14}$$

$$p = \frac{4 \pm \sqrt{2}}{7}$$

The solutions are $\frac{4 \pm \sqrt{2}}{7}$.

33. $a^2 - 6a + 2 = 0$
$a = 1,\ b = -6,\ c = 2$

$$a = \frac{-(-6) \pm \sqrt{(-6)^2 - 4(1)(2)}}{2(1)}$$

$$a = \frac{6 \pm \sqrt{36-8}}{2}$$

$$a = \frac{6 \pm \sqrt{28}}{2}$$

$$a = \frac{6 \pm \sqrt{4}\sqrt{7}}{2}$$

$$a = \frac{6 \pm 2\sqrt{7}}{2}$$

$$a = \frac{2(3 \pm \sqrt{7})}{2}$$

$$a = 3 \pm \sqrt{7}$$

The solutions are $3 \pm \sqrt{7}$.

35. $2x^2 - 6x + 3 = 0$
$a = 2, b = -6, c = 3$

$$x = \frac{-(-6) \pm \sqrt{(-6)^2 - 4(2)(3)}}{2(2)}$$
$$x = \frac{6 \pm \sqrt{36 - 24}}{4}$$
$$x = \frac{6 \pm \sqrt{12}}{4}$$
$$x = \frac{6 \pm \sqrt{4}\sqrt{3}}{4}$$
$$x = \frac{6 \pm 2\sqrt{3}}{4}$$
$$x = \frac{2(3 \pm \sqrt{3})}{4}$$
$$x = \frac{3 \pm \sqrt{3}}{2}$$

The solutions are $\frac{3 \pm \sqrt{3}}{2}$.

37. $3x^2 = 1 - 2x$
$3x^2 + 2x - 1 = 0$
$a = 3, b = 2, c = -1$

$$x = \frac{-2 \pm \sqrt{2^2 - 4(3)(-1)}}{2(3)}$$
$$x = \frac{-2 \pm \sqrt{4 + 12}}{6}$$
$$x = \frac{-2 \pm \sqrt{16}}{6}$$
$$x = \frac{-2 \pm 4}{6}$$
$$x = \frac{-2 + 4}{6} \quad \text{or} \quad x = \frac{-2 - 4}{6}$$
$$x = \frac{2}{6} = \frac{1}{3} \quad \text{or} \quad x = \frac{-6}{6} = -1$$

The solutions are $\frac{1}{3}$ and -1.

39. $20y^2 = 3 - 11y$
$20y^2 + 11y - 3 = 0$
$a = 20, b = 11, c = -3$

$$y = \frac{-11 \pm \sqrt{11^2 - 4(20)(-3)}}{2(20)}$$
$$y = \frac{-11 \pm \sqrt{121 + 240}}{40}$$
$$y = \frac{-11 \pm \sqrt{361}}{40}$$
$$y = \frac{-11 \pm 19}{40}$$
$$y = \frac{-11 + 19}{40} \quad \text{or} \quad y = \frac{-11 - 19}{40}$$
$$y = \frac{8}{40} = \frac{1}{5} \quad \text{or} \quad y = \frac{-30}{40} = -\frac{3}{4}$$

The solutions are $\frac{1}{5}$ and $-\frac{3}{4}$.

41. $x^2 + x + 1 = 0$
$a = 1, b = 1, c = 1$

$$x = \frac{-1 \pm \sqrt{1^2 - 4(1)(1)}}{2(1)}$$
$$x = \frac{-1 \pm \sqrt{1 - 4}}{2}$$
$$x = \frac{-1 \pm \sqrt{-3}}{2}$$

$\sqrt{-3}$ is not a real number. No real solutions.

43. $4y^2 = 6y + 1$

$4y^2 - 6y - 1 = 0$

$a = 4,\ b = -6,\ c = -1$

$$y = \frac{-(-6) \pm \sqrt{(-6)^2 - 4(4)(-1)}}{2(4)}$$

$$y = \frac{6 \pm \sqrt{36 + 16}}{8}$$

$$y = \frac{6 \pm \sqrt{52}}{8}$$

$$y = \frac{6 \pm \sqrt{4}\sqrt{13}}{8}$$

$$y = \frac{6 \pm 2\sqrt{13}}{8}$$

$$y = \frac{2(3 \pm \sqrt{13})}{8}$$

$$y = \frac{3 \pm \sqrt{13}}{4}$$

The solutions are $\frac{3 \pm \sqrt{13}}{4}$.

45. $3p^2 - \frac{2}{3}p + 1 = 0$

$$3\left(3p^2 - \frac{2}{3}p + 1\right) = 3(0)$$

$9p^2 - 2p + 3 = 0$

$a = 9,\ b = -2,\ c = 3$

$$p = \frac{-(-2) \pm \sqrt{(-2)^2 - 4(9)(3)}}{2(9)}$$

$$p = \frac{2 \pm \sqrt{4 - 108}}{18}$$

$$p = \frac{2 \pm \sqrt{-104}}{18}$$

$\sqrt{-104}$ is not a real number. No real solutions.

47. $\frac{m^2}{2} = m + \frac{1}{2}$

$$2\left(\frac{m^2}{2}\right) = 2\left(m + \frac{1}{2}\right)$$

$m^2 = 2m + 1$

$m^2 - 2m - 1 = 0$

$a = 1,\ b = -2,\ c = -1$

$$m = \frac{-(-2) \pm \sqrt{(-2)^2 - 4(1)(-1)}}{2(1)}$$

$$m = \frac{2 \pm \sqrt{4 + 4}}{2}$$

$$m = \frac{2 \pm \sqrt{8}}{2}$$

$$m = \frac{2 \pm \sqrt{4}\sqrt{2}}{2}$$

$$m = \frac{2 \pm 2\sqrt{2}}{2}$$

$$m = \frac{2(1 \pm \sqrt{2})}{2}$$

$m = 1 \pm \sqrt{2}$

The solutions are $1 \pm \sqrt{2}$.

49. $4p^2 + \frac{3}{2} = -5p$

$$2\left(4p^2 + \frac{3}{2}\right) = 2(-5p)$$

$8p^2 + 3 = -10p$

$8p^2 + 10p + 3 = 0$

$a = 8,\ b = 10,\ c = 3$

$$p = \frac{-10 \pm \sqrt{10^2 - 4(8)(3)}}{2(8)}$$

$$p = \frac{-10 \pm \sqrt{100 - 96}}{16}$$

$$p = \frac{-10 \pm \sqrt{4}}{16}$$

$$p = \frac{-10 \pm 2}{16}$$

$p = \frac{-10+2}{16}$ or $p = \frac{-10-2}{16}$

$p = \frac{-8}{16} = -\frac{1}{2}$ or $p = \frac{-12}{16} = -\frac{3}{4}$

The solutions are $-\frac{1}{2}$ and $-\frac{3}{4}$.

51. $5x^2 = \frac{7}{2}x + 1$

$2(5x^2) = 2\left(\frac{7}{2}x + 1\right)$

$10x^2 = 7x + 2$

$10x^2 - 7x - 2 = 0$

$a = 10,\ b = -7,\ c = -2$

$x = \frac{-(-7) \pm \sqrt{(-7)^2 - 4(10)(-2)}}{2(10)}$

$x = \frac{7 \pm \sqrt{49+80}}{20}$

$x = \frac{7 \pm \sqrt{129}}{20}$

The solutions are $\frac{7 \pm \sqrt{129}}{20}$.

53. $28x^2 + 5x + \frac{11}{4} = 0$

$4\left(28x^2 + 5x + \frac{11}{4}\right) = 4(0)$

$112x^2 + 20x + 11 = 0$

$a = 112,\ b = 20,\ c = 11$

$x = \frac{-20 \pm \sqrt{20^2 - 4(112)(11)}}{2(112)}$

$x = \frac{-20 \pm \sqrt{400 - 4928}}{224}$

$x = \frac{-20 \pm \sqrt{-4528}}{224}$

$\sqrt{-4528}$ is not a real number. No real solutions.

55. $5z^2 - 2z = \frac{1}{5}$

$5(5z^2 - 2z) = 5\left(\frac{1}{5}\right)$

$25z^2 - 10z = 1$

$25z^2 - 10z - 1 = 0$

$a = 25,\ b = -10,\ c = -1$

$z = \frac{-(-10) \pm \sqrt{(-10)^2 - 4(25)(-1)}}{2(25)}$

$z = \frac{10 \pm \sqrt{100+100}}{50}$

$z = \frac{10 \pm \sqrt{200}}{50}$

$z = \frac{10 \pm \sqrt{100}\sqrt{2}}{50}$

$z = \frac{10 \pm 10\sqrt{2}}{50}$

$z = \frac{10(1 \pm \sqrt{2})}{50}$

$z = \frac{1 \pm \sqrt{2}}{5}$

The solutions are $\frac{1 \pm \sqrt{2}}{5}$.

57. $x^2 + 3\sqrt{2}x - 5 = 0$

$a = 1,\ b = 3\sqrt{2},\ c = -5$

$x = \frac{-3\sqrt{2} \pm \sqrt{(3\sqrt{2})^2 - 4(1)(-5)}}{2(1)}$

$x = \frac{-3\sqrt{2} \pm \sqrt{18+20}}{2}$

$x = \frac{-3\sqrt{2} \pm \sqrt{38}}{2}$

The solutions are $\frac{-3\sqrt{2} \pm \sqrt{38}}{2}$.

59. $x^2+3x-1=0$
$a=1,\ b=3,\ c=-1$
$$\begin{aligned} b^2-4ac &= 3^2-4(1)(-1) \\ &= 9+4 \\ &= 13 \end{aligned}$$
Since the discriminant is a positive number, this equation has two distinct real solutions.

61. $3x^2+x+5=0$
$a=3,\ b=1,\ c=5$
$$\begin{aligned} b^2-4ac &= 1^2-4(3)(5) \\ &= 1-60 \\ &= -59 \end{aligned}$$
Since the discriminant is a negative number, this equation has no real solution.

63. $4x^2+4x=-1$
$4x^2+4x+1=0$
$a=4,\ b=4,\ c=1$
$$\begin{aligned} b^2-4ac &= 4^2-4(4)(1) \\ &= 16-16 \\ &= 0 \end{aligned}$$
Since the discriminant is 0, this equation has one real solution.

65. $9x^2+2x=0$
$a=9,\ b=2,\ c=0$
$$\begin{aligned} b^2-4ac &= 2^2-4(9)(0) \\ &= 4-0 \\ &= 4 \end{aligned}$$
Since the discriminant is a positive number, this equation has two distinct real solutions.

67. $5x^2+1=0$
$a=5,\ b=0,\ c=1$
$$\begin{aligned} b^2-4ac &= 0^2-4(5)(1) \\ &= 0-20 \\ &= -20 \end{aligned}$$
Since the discriminant is a negative number, this equation has no real solution.

69. $x^2+36=-12x$
$x^2+12x+36=0$
$a=1,\ b=12,\ c=36$
$$\begin{aligned} b^2-4ac &= 12^2-4(1)(36) \\ &= 144-144 \\ &= 0 \end{aligned}$$
Since the discriminant is 0, this equation has one real solution.

71. $2x^2-5=7x$
$2x^2-7x-5=0$
$b=-7$
The answer is d.

73. $x^2+x=15$
$x^2+x-15=0$
$a=1,\ b=1,\ c=-15$
$$x=\frac{-1\pm\sqrt{1^2-4(1)(-15)}}{2(1)}$$
$$x=\frac{-1\pm\sqrt{61}}{2}$$
$x\approx-4.4,\ 3.4$
The solutions are –4.4 and 3.4.

75. $1.2x^2-5.2x-3.9=0$
$a=1.2,\ b=-5.2,\ c=-3.9$
$$x=\frac{-(-5.2)\pm\sqrt{(-5.2)^2-4(1.2)(-3.9)}}{2(1.2)}$$
$$x=\frac{5.2\pm\sqrt{45.76}}{2.4}$$
$x\approx-0.7,\ 5.0$
The solutions are –0.7 and 5.0.

77. $h = -16t^2 + 120t + 80$
$30 = -16t^2 + 120t + 80$
$0 = -16t^2 + 120t + 50$
$0 = -8t^2 + 60t + 25$
$a = -8,\ b = 60,\ c = 25$
$$t = \frac{-60 \pm \sqrt{(60)^2 - 4(-8)(25)}}{2(-8)}$$
$$t = \frac{-60 \pm \sqrt{4400}}{-16}$$
$t \approx 7.9, -0.4$
Disregard the negative.
In 7.9 seconds it will be 30 feet from the ground.

79. $\frac{7x}{2} = 3$
$7x = 6$
$\frac{7x}{7} = \frac{6}{7}$
$x = \frac{6}{7}$

81. $\frac{5}{7}x - \frac{2}{3} = 0$
$21\left(\frac{5}{7}x - \frac{2}{3}\right) = 21(0)$
$15x - 14 = 0$
$15x = 14$
$\frac{15x}{15} = \frac{14}{15}$
$x = \frac{14}{15}$

83. $\frac{3}{4}z + 3 = 0$
$4\left(\frac{3}{4}z + 3\right) = 4(0)$
$3z + 12 = 0$
$3z = -12$
$\frac{3z}{3} = -\frac{12}{3}$
$z = -4$

Exercise Set 10.4

1. $5x^2 - 11x + 2 = 0$
$(5x - 1)(x - 2) = 0$
$5x - 1 = 0$ or $x - 2 = 0$
$5x = 1$ or $x = 2$
$x = \frac{1}{5}$
The solutions are $\frac{1}{5}$ and 2.

3. $x^2 - 1 = 2x$
$x^2 - 2x - 1 = 0$
$a = 1,\ b = -2,\ c = -1$
$$x = \frac{-(-2) \pm \sqrt{(-2)^2 - 4(1)(-1)}}{2(1)}$$
$$x = \frac{2 \pm \sqrt{4+4}}{2}$$
$$x = \frac{2 \pm \sqrt{8}}{2}$$
$$x = \frac{2 \pm \sqrt{4}\sqrt{2}}{2}$$
$$x = \frac{2 \pm 2\sqrt{2}}{2}$$
$$x = \frac{2(1 \pm \sqrt{2})}{2}$$
$x = 1 \pm \sqrt{2}$
The solutions are $1 \pm \sqrt{2}$.

5. $a^2 = 20$
$a = \pm\sqrt{20}$
$a = \pm\sqrt{4}\sqrt{5}$
$a = \pm 2\sqrt{5}$
The solutions are $\pm 2\sqrt{5}$.

7. $x^2 - x + 4 = 0$
$a = 1,\ b = -1,\ c = 4$

$$x = \frac{-(-1) \pm \sqrt{(-1)^2 - 4(1)(4)}}{2(1)}$$

$$x = \frac{1 \pm \sqrt{1-16}}{2}$$

$$x = \frac{1 \pm \sqrt{-15}}{2}$$

$\sqrt{-15}$ is not a real number. No real solutions.

9.
$$3x^2 - 12x + 12 = 0$$
$$3(x^2 - 4x + 4) = 0$$
$$3(x-2)^2 = 0$$
$$(x-2)^2 = 0$$
$$x - 2 = \pm\sqrt{0}$$
$$x - 2 = 0$$
$$x = 2$$

The solution is 2.

11.
$$9 - 6p + p^2 = 0$$
$$(3-p)^2 = 0$$
$$3 - p = \pm\sqrt{0}$$
$$3 - p = 0$$
$$3 = p$$

The solution is 3.

13.
$$4y^2 - 16 = 0$$
$$4(y^2 - 4) = 0$$
$$4(y+2)(y-2) = 0$$

$y + 2 = 0$ or $y - 2 = 0$
$y = -2$ or $y = 2$

The solutions are –2 and 2.

15.
$$x^4 - 3x^3 + 2x^2 = 0$$
$$x^2(x^2 - 3x + 2) = 0$$
$$x^2(x-2)(x-1) = 0$$

$x^2 = 0$ or $x - 2 = 0$ or $x - 1 = 0$
$x = 0$ or $x = 2$ or $x = 1$

The solutions are 0, 2, and 1.

17.
$$(2z+5)^2 = 25$$
$$(2z)^2 + 2(2z)(5) + (5)^2 = 25$$
$$4z^2 + 20z + 25 = 25$$
$$4z^2 + 20z + 25 - 25 = 0$$
$$4z^2 + 20z = 0$$
$$4z(z+5) = 0$$

$4z = 0$ or $z + 5 = 0$
$z = \frac{0}{4} = 0$ or $z = -5$

The solutions are 0 and –5.

19.
$$30x = 25x^2 + 2$$
$$0 = 25x^2 - 30x + 2$$

$a = 25,\ b = -30,\ c = 2$

$$x = \frac{-(-30) \pm \sqrt{(-30)^2 - 4(25)(2)}}{2(25)}$$

$$x = \frac{30 \pm \sqrt{900-200}}{50}$$

$$x = \frac{30 \pm \sqrt{700}}{50}$$

$$x = \frac{30 \pm \sqrt{100}\sqrt{7}}{50}$$

$$x = \frac{30 \pm 10\sqrt{7}}{50}$$

$$x = \frac{10(3 \pm \sqrt{7})}{50}$$

$$x = \frac{3 \pm \sqrt{7}}{5}$$

The solutions are $\frac{3 \pm \sqrt{7}}{5}$.

21.
$$\frac{2}{3}m^2 - \frac{1}{3}m - 1 = 0$$
$$3\left(\frac{2}{3}m^2 - \frac{1}{3}m - 1\right) = 3(0)$$
$$2m^2 - m - 3 = 0$$
$$(2m - 3)(m + 1) = 0$$
$$2m - 3 = 0 \quad \text{or} \quad m + 1 = 0$$
$$2m = 3 \quad \text{or} \quad m = -1$$
$$m = \frac{3}{2}$$
The solutions are $\frac{3}{2}$ and -1.

23.
$$x^2 - \frac{1}{2}x - \frac{1}{5} = 0$$
$$10\left(x^2 - \frac{1}{2}x - \frac{1}{5}\right) = 10(0)$$
$$10x^2 - 5x - 2 = 0$$
$a = 10$, $b = -5$, $c = -2$
$$x = \frac{-(-5) \pm \sqrt{(-5)^2 - 4(10)(-2)}}{2(10)}$$
$$x = \frac{5 \pm \sqrt{25 + 80}}{20}$$
$$x = \frac{5 \pm \sqrt{105}}{20}$$
The solutions are $\frac{5 \pm \sqrt{105}}{20}$.

25.
$$4x^2 - 27x + 35 = 0$$
$$(4x - 7)(x - 5) = 0$$
$$4x - 7 = 0 \quad \text{or} \quad x - 5 = 0$$
$$4x = 7 \quad \text{or} \quad x = 5$$
$$x = \frac{7}{4}$$
The solutions are $\frac{7}{4}$ and 5.

27.
$$(7 - 5x)^2 = 18$$
$$(7)^2 + 2(7)(-5x) + (5x)^2 = 18$$
$$49 - 70x + 25x^2 = 18$$
$$25x^2 - 70x + 49 - 18 = 0$$
$$25x^2 - 70x + 31 = 0$$
$a = 25$, $b = -70$, $c = 31$
$$x = \frac{-(-70) \pm \sqrt{(-70)^2 - 4(25)(31)}}{2(25)}$$
$$x = \frac{70 \pm \sqrt{4900 - 3100}}{50}$$
$$x = \frac{70 \pm \sqrt{1800}}{50}$$
$$x = \frac{70 \pm \sqrt{900}\sqrt{2}}{50}$$
$$x = \frac{70 \pm 30\sqrt{2}}{50}$$
$$x = \frac{10(7 \pm 3\sqrt{2})}{50}$$
$$x = \frac{7 \pm 3\sqrt{2}}{5}$$
The solutions are $\frac{7 \pm 3\sqrt{2}}{5}$.

29.
$$3z^2 - 7z = 12$$
$$3z^2 - 7z - 12 = 0$$
$a = 3$, $b = -7$, $c = -12$
$$z = \frac{-(-7) \pm \sqrt{(-7)^2 - 4(3)(-12)}}{2(3)}$$
$$z = \frac{7 \pm \sqrt{49 + 144}}{6}$$
$$z = \frac{7 \pm \sqrt{193}}{6}$$
The solutions are $\frac{7 \pm \sqrt{193}}{6}$.

31. $x = x^2 - 110$
$0 = x^2 - x - 110$
$0 = (x-11)(x+10)$
$x - 11 = 0$ or $x + 10 = 0$
$x = 11$ or $x = -10$
The solutions are 11 and −10.

33. $\frac{3}{4}x^2 - \frac{5}{2}x - 2 = 0$
$4\left(\frac{3}{4}x^2 - \frac{5}{2}x - 2\right) = 4(0)$
$3x^2 - 10x - 8 = 0$
$(3x+2)(x-4) = 0$
$3x + 2 = 0$ or $x - 4 = 0$
$3x = -2$ or $x = 4$
$x = -\frac{2}{3}$
The solutions are $-\frac{2}{3}$ and 4.

35. $x^2 - 0.6x + 0.05 = 0$
$(x - 0.1)(x - 0.5) = 0$
$x - 0.1 = 0$ or $x - 0.5 = 0$
$x = 0.1$ or $x = 0.5$
The solutions are 0.1 and 0.5.

37. $10x^2 - 11x + 2 = 0$
$a = 10,\ b = -11,\ c = 2$
$$x = \frac{-(-11) \pm \sqrt{(-11)^2 - 4(10)(2)}}{2(10)}$$
$$x = \frac{11 \pm \sqrt{121 - 80}}{20}$$
$$x = \frac{11 \pm \sqrt{41}}{20}$$
The solutions are $\frac{11 \pm \sqrt{41}}{20}$.

39. $\frac{1}{2}z^2 - 2z + \frac{3}{4} = 0$
$4\left(\frac{1}{2}z^2 - 2z + \frac{3}{4}\right) = 4(0)$
$2z^2 - 8z + 3 = 0$
$a = 2,\ b = -8,\ c = 3$
$$z = \frac{-(-8) \pm \sqrt{(-8)^2 - 4(2)(3)}}{2(2)}$$
$$z = \frac{8 \pm \sqrt{64 - 24}}{4}$$
$$z = \frac{8 \pm \sqrt{40}}{4}$$
$$z = \frac{8 \pm \sqrt{4}\sqrt{10}}{4}$$
$$z = \frac{8 \pm 2\sqrt{10}}{4}$$
$$z = \frac{2(4 \pm \sqrt{10})}{4}$$
$$z = \frac{4 \pm \sqrt{10}}{2}$$
The solutions are $\frac{4 \pm \sqrt{10}}{2}$.

41. $h = 16t^2$
$87.6 = 16t^2$
$5.475 = t^2$
$\sqrt{5.475} = t$
$2.3 \approx t$
The time of the dive is approximately 2.3 seconds.

43. $16 \text{ miles} \cdot \frac{5280 \text{ feet}}{1 \text{ mile}} = 84,480 \text{ feet}$
$h = 16t^2$
$84,480 = 16t^2$
$5280 = t^2$
$\sqrt{5280} = t$
$72.7 \approx t$
His free-fall lasted approximately 72.7 seconds.

45.
$$y = 3x^2 + 80x + 340$$
$$1172 = 3x^2 + 80x + 340$$
$$0 = 3x^2 + 80x - 832$$
$a = 3$, $b = 80$, $c = -832$
$$x = \frac{-80 \pm \sqrt{80^2 - 4(3)(-832)}}{2(3)}$$
$$x = \frac{-80 \pm \sqrt{64,000 + 9984}}{6}$$
$$x = \frac{-80 \pm \sqrt{16,384}}{6}$$
$$x = \frac{-80 \pm 128}{3}$$
$$x = \frac{-80+128}{6} \quad \text{or} \quad x = \frac{-80-128}{6}$$
$$x = 8 \quad \text{or} \quad x = -\frac{208}{6}$$
Disregard a negative time.
1994 + 8 = 2002
In 2002, there will be 1172 Home Depot stores.

47.
$$y = 10x^2 + 34x + 567$$
$$1295 = 10x^2 + 34x + 567$$
$$0 = 10x^2 + 34x - 728$$
$$0 = (10x + 104)(x - 7)$$
$$10x + 104 = 0 \quad \text{or} \quad x - 7 = 0$$
$$10x = -104 \quad \text{or} \quad x = 7$$
$$x = -\frac{104}{10}$$
Disregard a negative time.
1994 + 7 = 2001
Goodyear's net income will be $1295 in 2001.

49.
$$\frac{AB}{AC} = \frac{AC}{CB}$$
$$\frac{x}{1} = \frac{1}{x-1}$$
$$x(x-1) = 1(1)$$
$$x^2 - x = 1$$
$$x^2 - x - 1 = 0$$
$a = 1$, $b = -1$, $c = -1$
$$x = \frac{-(-1) \pm \sqrt{(-1)^2 - 4(1)(-1)}}{2(1)}$$
$$x = \frac{1 \pm \sqrt{5}}{2}$$
$$AB = \frac{1 \pm \sqrt{5}}{2}$$
Since length cannot be negative,
$$AB = \frac{1+\sqrt{5}}{2}.$$

51. Answers may vary.

53. $\sqrt{104} = \sqrt{4 \cdot 26} = \sqrt{4} \cdot \sqrt{26} = 2\sqrt{26}$

55. $\sqrt{80} = \sqrt{16 \cdot 5} = \sqrt{16} \cdot \sqrt{5} = 4\sqrt{5}$

57. width $= x$ length $= x + 6$
$$A = lw$$
$$391 = (x+6)(x)$$
$$391 = x^2 + 6x$$
$$0 = x^2 + 6x - 391$$
$$0 = (x+23)(x-17)$$
$$x + 23 = 0 \quad \text{or} \quad x - 17 = 0$$
$$x = -23 \quad \text{or} \quad x = 17$$
Disregard a negative length.
width = 17 in., length = 23 in.

Exercise Set 10.5

1. $\sqrt{-9} = \sqrt{-1 \cdot 9} = \sqrt{-1}\sqrt{9} = i \cdot 3 = 3i$

3. $\sqrt{-100} = \sqrt{-1 \cdot 100} = \sqrt{-1}\sqrt{100} = i \cdot 10 = 10i$

5.
$$\sqrt{-50} = \sqrt{-1 \cdot 25 \cdot 2}$$
$$= \sqrt{-1}\sqrt{25}\sqrt{2}$$
$$= i \cdot 5\sqrt{2}$$
$$= 5i\sqrt{2}$$

7.
$$\sqrt{-63} = \sqrt{-1 \cdot 9 \cdot 7}$$
$$= \sqrt{-1}\sqrt{9}\sqrt{7}$$
$$= i \cdot 3\sqrt{7}$$
$$= 3i\sqrt{7}$$

9. $(2-i)+(-5+10i)=2-5+(-i+10i)$
$=-3+9i$

11. $(3-4i)-(2-i)=3-4i-2+i$
$=3-2+(-4i+i)$
$=1-3i$

13. $4i(3-2i)=12i-8i^2$
$=12i-8(-1)$
$=12i+8$
$=8+12i$

15. $(6-2i)(4+i)=6(4)+6i-2i(4)-2i(i)$
$=24+6i-8i-2i^2$
$=24-2i-2(-1)$
$=24-2i+2$
$=26-2i$

17. Answers may vary.

19. $\frac{8-12i}{4}=\frac{4(2-3i)}{4}=2-3i$

21. $\frac{7-i}{4-3i}=\frac{(7-i)}{(4-3i)}\cdot\frac{(4+3i)}{(4+3i)}$
$=\frac{7(4)+7(3i)-i(4)-i(3i)}{(4)^2-(3i)^2}$
$=\frac{28+21i-4i-3i^2}{16-9i^2}$
$=\frac{28+17i-3(-1)}{16-9(-1)}$
$=\frac{28+17i+3}{16+9}$
$=\frac{31+17i}{25}$
$=\frac{31}{25}+\frac{17}{25}i$

23. $(x+1)^2=-9$
$x+1=\pm\sqrt{-9}$
$x+1=\pm\sqrt{-1}\sqrt{9}$
$x+1=\pm 3i$
$x=-1\pm 3i$
The solutions are $-1\pm 3i$.

25. $(2z-3)^2=-12$
$2z-3=\pm\sqrt{-12}$
$2z-3=\pm\sqrt{-1}\sqrt{4}\sqrt{3}$
$2z-3=\pm 2i\sqrt{3}$
$2z=3\pm 2i\sqrt{3}$
$z=\frac{3\pm 2i\sqrt{3}}{2}$
The solutions are $\frac{3\pm 2i\sqrt{3}}{2}$.

27. $y^2+6y+13=0$
$a=1,\ b=6,\ c=13$
$y=\frac{-6\pm\sqrt{6^2-4(1)(13)}}{2(1)}$
$y=\frac{-6\pm\sqrt{36-52}}{2}$
$y=\frac{-6\pm\sqrt{-16}}{2}$
$y=\frac{-6\pm 4i}{2}$
$y=\frac{2(-3\pm 2i)}{2}$
$y=-3\pm 2i$
The solutions are $-3\pm 2i$.

29. $4x^2+7x+4=0$
$a=4,\ b=7,\ c=4$
$x=\frac{-7\pm\sqrt{7^2-4(4)(4)}}{2(4)}$
$x=\frac{-7\pm\sqrt{49-64}}{8}$
$x=\frac{-7\pm\sqrt{-15}}{8}$
$x=\frac{-7\pm i\sqrt{15}}{8}$
The solutions are $\frac{-7\pm i\sqrt{15}}{8}$.

31. $2m^2 - 4m + 5 = 0$
$a = 2, b = -4, c = 5$

$$m = \frac{-(-4) \pm \sqrt{(-4)^2 - 4(2)(5)}}{2(2)}$$
$$m = \frac{4 \pm \sqrt{16-40}}{4}$$
$$m = \frac{4 \pm \sqrt{-24}}{4}$$
$$m = \frac{4 \pm \sqrt{-4}\sqrt{6}}{4}$$
$$m = \frac{4 \pm 2i\sqrt{6}}{4}$$
$$m = \frac{2(2 \pm i\sqrt{6})}{4}$$
$$m = \frac{2 \pm i\sqrt{6}}{2}$$

The solutions are $\frac{2 \pm i\sqrt{6}}{2}$.

33. $3 + (12 - 7i) = 3 + 12 - 7i = 15 - 7i$

35. $-9i(5i - 7) = -45i^2 + 63i$
$= -45(-1) + 63i$
$= 45 + 63i$

37. $(2 - i) - (3 - 4i) = 2 - i - 3 + 4i$
$= 2 - 3 + (-i + 4i)$
$= -1 + 3i$

39.
$$\frac{15+10i}{5i} = \frac{(15+10i)}{5i} \cdot \frac{(-i)}{(-i)}$$
$$= \frac{-15i - 10i^2}{-5i^2}$$
$$= \frac{-15i - 10(-1)}{-5(-1)}$$
$$= \frac{-15i + 10}{5}$$
$$= \frac{5(-3i + 2)}{5}$$
$$= -3i + 2$$
$$= 2 - 3i$$

41. $-5 + i - (2 + 3i) = -5 + i - 2 - 3i$
$= -5 - 2 + (i - 3i)$
$= -7 - 2i$

43. $(4 - 3i)(4 + 3i) = (4)^2 - (3i)^2$
$= 16 - 9i^2$
$= 16 - 9(-1)$
$= 16 + 9$
$= 25$

45.
$$\frac{4-i}{1+2i} = \frac{(4-i)(1-2i)}{(1+2i)(1-2i)}$$
$$= \frac{4(1) + 4(-2i) - i(1) - i(-2i)}{(1)^2 - (2i)^2}$$
$$= \frac{4 - 8i - i + 2i^2}{1 - 4i^2}$$
$$= \frac{4 - 9i + 2(-1)}{1 - 4(-1)}$$
$$= \frac{4 - 9i - 2}{1 + 4}$$
$$= \frac{2 - 9i}{5}$$
$$= \frac{2}{5} - \frac{9}{5}i$$

47. $(5 + 2i)^2 = (5)^2 + 2(5)(2i) + (2i)^2$
$= 25 + 20i + 4i^2$
$= 25 + 20i + 4(-1)$
$= 25 + 20i - 4$
$= 21 + 20i$

49. $(y - 4)^2 = -64$
$y - 4 = \pm\sqrt{-64}$
$y - 4 = \pm 8i$
$y = 4 \pm 8i$
The solutions are $4 \pm 8i$.

51. $4x^2 = -100$
$x^2 = -25$
$x = \pm\sqrt{-25}$
$x = \pm 5i$
The solutions are $\pm 5i$.

53. $z^2 + 6z + 10 = 0$
$a = 1,\ b = 6,\ c = 10$
$z = \frac{-6 \pm \sqrt{6^2 - 4(1)(10)}}{2(1)}$
$z = \frac{-6 \pm \sqrt{36 - 40}}{2}$
$z = \frac{-6 \pm \sqrt{-4}}{2}$
$z = \frac{-6 \pm 2i}{2}$
$z = \frac{2(-3 \pm i)}{2}$
$z = -3 \pm i$
The solutions are $-3 \pm i$.

55. $2a^2 - 5a + 9 = 0$
$a = 2,\ b = -5,\ c = 9$
$a = \frac{-(-5) \pm \sqrt{(-5)^2 - 4(2)(9)}}{2(2)}$
$a = \frac{5 \pm \sqrt{25 - 72}}{4}$
$a = \frac{5 \pm \sqrt{-47}}{4}$
$a = \frac{5 \pm i\sqrt{47}}{4}$
The solutions are $\frac{5 \pm i\sqrt{47}}{4}$.

57. $(2x + 8)^2 = -20$
$2x + 8 = \pm\sqrt{-20}$
$2x + 8 = \pm\sqrt{-1}\sqrt{4}\sqrt{5}$
$2x + 8 = \pm 2i\sqrt{5}$
$2x = -8 \pm 2i\sqrt{5}$
$x = \frac{-8 \pm 2i\sqrt{5}}{2}$
$x = \frac{2\left(-4 \pm i\sqrt{5}\right)}{2}$
$x = -4 \pm i\sqrt{5}$
The solutions are $-4 \pm i\sqrt{5}$.

59. $3m^2 + 108 = 0$
$3m^2 = -108$
$m^2 = -\frac{108}{3}$
$m^2 = -36$
$m = \pm\sqrt{-36}$
$m = \pm 6i$
The solutions are $\pm 6i$.

61. $x^2 + 14x + 50 = 0$
$a = 1,\ b = 14,\ c = 50$
$x = \frac{-14 \pm \sqrt{14^2 - 4(1)(50)}}{2(1)}$
$x = \frac{-14 \pm \sqrt{196 - 200}}{2}$
$x = \frac{-14 \pm \sqrt{-4}}{2}$
$x = \frac{-14 \pm 2i}{2}$
$x = \frac{2(-7 \pm i)}{2}$
$x = -7 \pm i$
The solutions are $-7 \pm i$.

63. True

65. True

67. $y = -3$

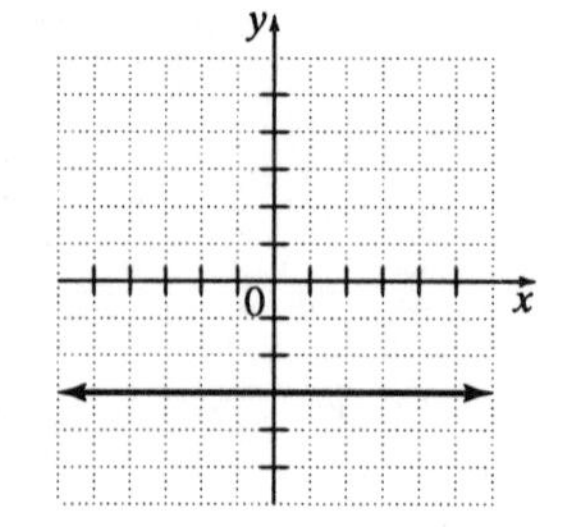

69. $y = 3x - 2$

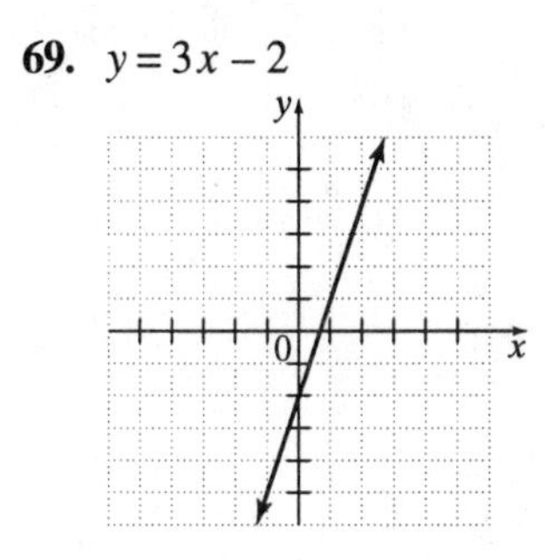

71. $x^2 + 7^2 = 10^2$

$x^2 + 49 = 100$

$\sqrt{x^2} = \pm\sqrt{51}$

$x = \sqrt{51}$ meters or 7.14 meters

Disregard the negative.

Section 10.6

Calculator Explorations

1. $x^2 - 7x - 3 = 0$

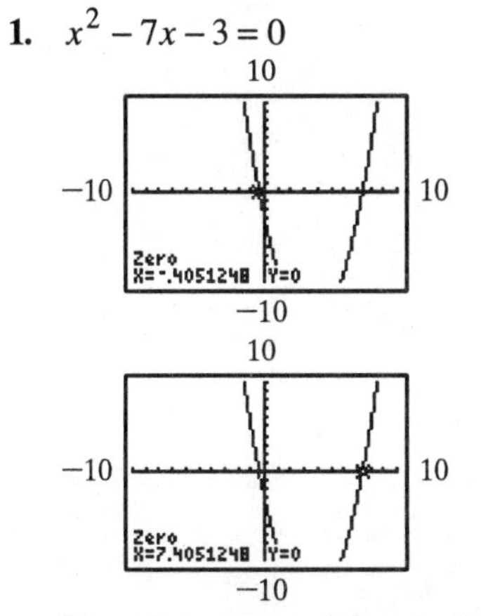

The x-intercepts of the graph are the solutions of the equation.

$x = -0.41, 7.41$

3. $-1.7x^2 + 5.6x - 3.7 = 0$

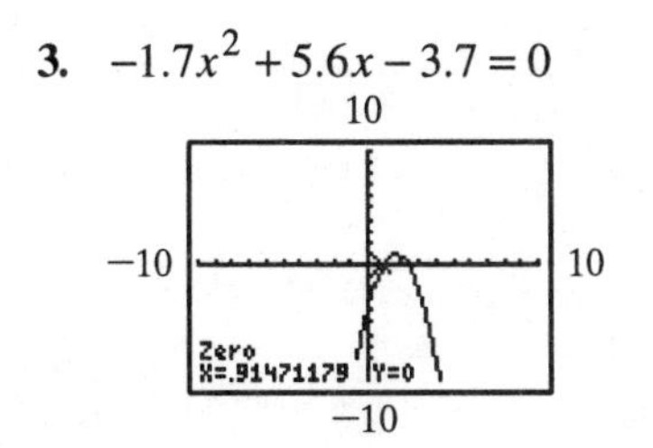

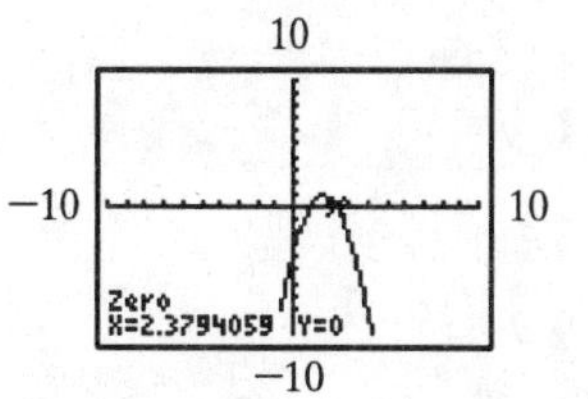

The x-intercepts of the graph are the solutions of the equation.

$x = 0.91, 2.38$

5. $5.8x^2 - 2.6x - 1.9 = 0$

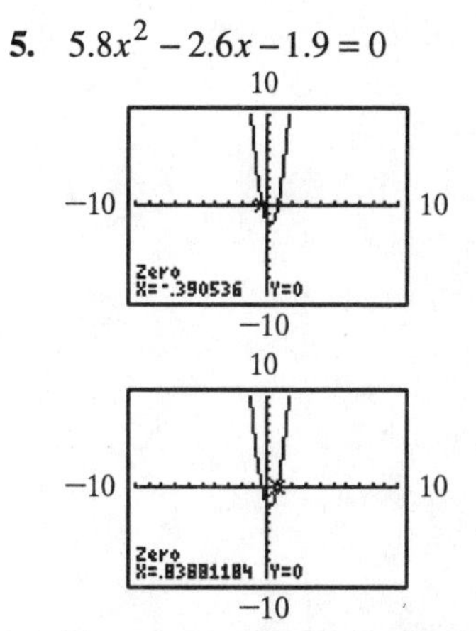

The x-intercepts of the graph are the solutions of the equation.

$x = -0.39, 0.84$

Exercise Set 10.6

1. $y = 2x^2$

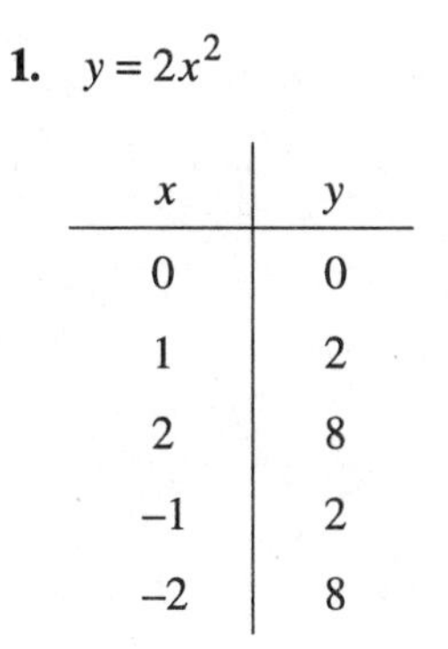

x	y
0	0
1	2
2	8
–1	2
–2	8

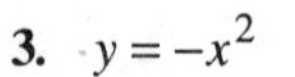

3. $y = -x^2$

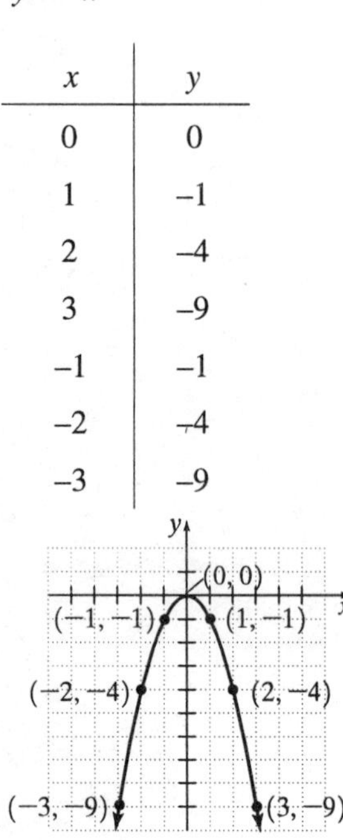

x	y
0	0
1	−1
2	−4
3	−9
−1	−1
−2	−4
−3	−9

5. $y = \frac{1}{3}x^2$

x	y
0	0
3	3
5	$\frac{25}{3}$
−3	3
−5	$\frac{25}{3}$

7. $y = x^2 - 1$

Find vertex.

$x = \frac{-b}{2a} = \frac{-0}{2(1)} = 0$

$y = 0^2 - 1 = -1$

vertex = (0, −1)

y-intercept = (0, −1)

Find x-intercepts. Let $y = 0$.

$0 = x^2 - 1$

$1 = x^2$

$\pm 1 = x$

x-intercepts = (−1, 0), (1, 0)

9. $y = x^2 + 4$

Find vertex.

$x = \frac{-b}{2a} = \frac{-0}{2(1)} = 0$

$y = 0^2 + 4 = 4$

vertex = (0, 4)

y-intercept = (0, 4)

Find x-intercepts. Let $y = 0$.

$0 = x^2 + 4$

$x^2 = -4$

There are no x-intercepts because there is no solution to this equation.

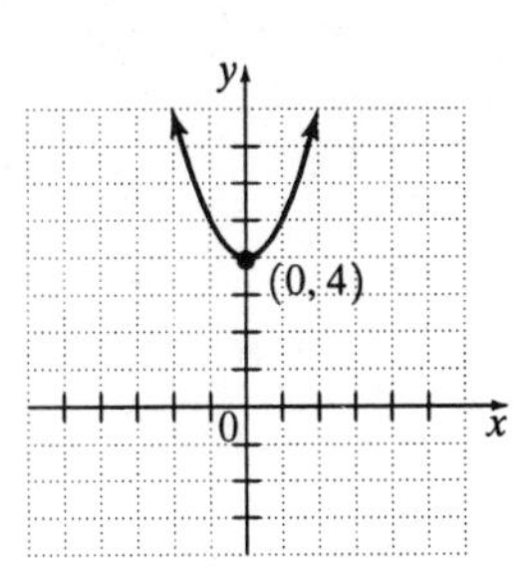

11. $y = x^2 + 6x$

Find vertex.

$$x = \frac{-b}{2a} = \frac{-6}{2(1)} = -3$$

$y = (-3)^2 + 6(-3) = -9$

vertex = $(-3, -9)$

Find x-intercepts. Let $y = 0$.

$0 = x^2 + 6x$

$0 = x(x+6)$

$x = 0$ or $x = -6$

x-intercepts = $(0, 0)$, $(-6, 0)$

y-intercept = $(0, 0)$

13. $y = x^2 + 2x - 8$

Find vertex.

$$x = \frac{-b}{2a} = \frac{-2}{2(1)} = -1$$

$y = (-1)^2 + 2(-1) - 8 = -9$

vertex = $(-1, -9)$

Find x-intercepts. Let $y = 0$.

$0 = x^2 + 2x - 8$

$0 = (x+4)(x-2)$

$x = -4$ or $x = 2$

x-intercepts = $(-4, 0)$, $(2, 0)$

Find y-intercept. Let $x = 0$.

$y = 0^2 + 2(0) - 8 = -8$

y-intercept = $(0, -8)$

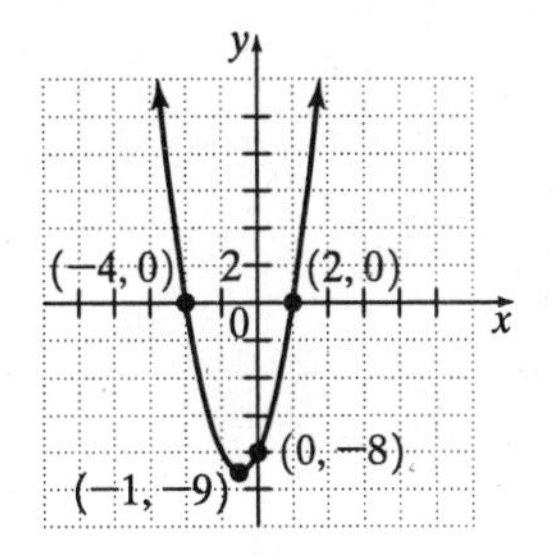

15. $y = -x^2 + x + 2$

Find vertex.

$$x = \frac{-b}{2a} = \frac{-1}{2(-1)} = \frac{1}{2}$$

$$y = -\left(\frac{1}{2}\right)^2 + \frac{1}{2} + 2 = \frac{9}{4}$$

vertex = $\left(\frac{1}{2}, \frac{9}{4}\right)$

Find x-intercepts. Let $y = 0$.

$0 = -x^2 + x + 2$

$0 = -1(x-2)(x+1)$

$x = 2$ or $x = -1$

x-intercepts = $(2, 0)$, $(-1, 0)$

Find y-intercept. Let $x = 0$.

$y = -0^2 + 0 + 2 = 2$

y-intercept = $(0, 2)$.

17. $y = x^2 + 5x + 4$

Find vertex.

$x = \frac{-b}{2a} = \frac{-5}{2(1)} = -\frac{5}{2}$

$y = \left(-\frac{5}{2}\right)^2 + 5\left(\frac{5}{2}\right) + 4 = -\frac{9}{4}$

vertex $= \left(-\frac{5}{2}, -\frac{9}{4}\right)$

Find x-intercepts. Let $y = 0$.

$0 = x^2 + 5x + 4$

$0 = (x+4)(x+1)$

$x = -4$ or $x = -1$

x-intercepts = (–4, 0), (–1, 0)

Find y-intercept. Let $x = 0$.

$y = 0^2 + 5(0) + 4 = 4$

y-intercept = (0, 4)

19. $y = -x^2 + 4x - 3$

Find vertex.

$x = \frac{-b}{2a} = \frac{-4}{2(-1)} = 2$

$y = -2^2 + 4(2) - 3 = 1$

vertex = (2, 1)

Find x-intercepts. Let $y = 0$.

$0 = -x^2 + 4x - 3$

$0 = -1(x-3)(x-1)$

$x = 3$ or $x = 1$

x-intercepts = (1, 0), (3, 0)

Find y-intercept. Let $x = 0$.

$y = -0^2 + 4(0) - 3 = -3$

y-intercept = (0, –3)

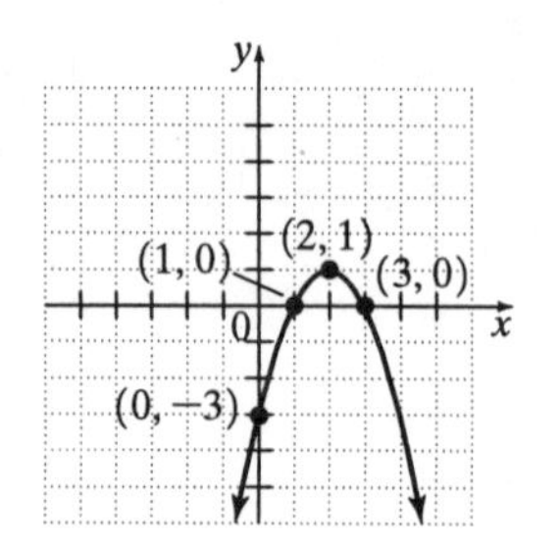

21. $y = x^2 + 2x - 2$

Find vertex.

$x = \frac{-b}{2a} = \frac{-2}{2(1)} = -1$

$y = (-1)^2 + 2(-1) - 2$
$= 1 - 2 - 2$
$= -3$

vertex = (–1, –3)

Find y-intercept.
Let $x = 0$.

$y = 0^2 + 2(0) - 2$

$y = -2$

y-intercept = (0, –2)

Find x-intercepts.
Let $y = 0$.

$0 = x^2 + 2x - 2$

$x = \frac{-2 \pm \sqrt{2^2 - 4(1)(-2)}}{2(1)}$
$= \frac{-2 \pm \sqrt{12}}{2}$
$= \frac{-2 \pm 2\sqrt{3}}{2}$

$x = -1 \pm \sqrt{3}$

x-intercepts $= \left(-1-\sqrt{3}, 0\right), \left(-1+\sqrt{3}, 0\right)$

23. $y = x^2 - 3x + 1$
Find vertex.
$x = \frac{-b}{2a} = \frac{-(-3)}{2(1)} = \frac{3}{2} = 1\frac{1}{2}$
$y = \left(\frac{3}{2}\right)^2 - 3\left(\frac{3}{2}\right) + 1$
$= \frac{9}{4} - \frac{9}{2} + 1$
$= \frac{9}{4} - \frac{18}{4} + \frac{4}{4}$
$= -\frac{5}{4}$
$= -1\frac{1}{4}$
vertex = $\left(1\frac{1}{2}, -1\frac{1}{4}\right)$
Find y-intercept. Let $x = 0$.
$y = 0^2 - 3(0) + 1$
$y = 1$
y-intercept = (0, 1)
Find x-intercepts. Let $y = 0$.
$0 = x^2 - 3x + 1$
$x = \frac{3 \pm \sqrt{(-3)^2 - 4(1)(1)}}{2(1)}$
$= \frac{3 \pm \sqrt{5}}{2}$
x-intercepts = $\left(\frac{3-\sqrt{5}}{2}, 0\right), \left(\frac{3+\sqrt{5}}{2}, 0\right)$

y
$\left(\frac{3-\sqrt{5}}{2}, 0\right)$ (0, 1) $\left(\frac{3+\sqrt{5}}{2}, 0\right)$
x
$\left(1\frac{1}{2}, -1\frac{1}{4}\right)$

25. Domain: all real numbers
Range: $y \le 3$

27. Domain: all real numbers
Range: $y \le 1$

29. a. The maximum height is at 4 seconds.
Let $t = 4$.
$h = -16(4)^2 + 128(4) = 256$ feet

b. 4 seconds

c. 8 seconds

31. B

33. D

35. $\frac{\frac{3}{8}}{\frac{1}{7}} = \frac{3}{8} \cdot \frac{7}{1} = \frac{21}{8}$

37. $\frac{\frac{x}{5}}{\frac{2}{x}} = \frac{\left(\frac{x}{5}\right)5x}{\left(\frac{2}{x}\right)5x} = \frac{x^2}{10}$

39. $\frac{x}{x - \frac{1}{x}} = \frac{(x)x}{\left(x - \frac{1}{x}\right)x} = \frac{x^2}{x^2 - 1}$

41. $\frac{\frac{2a^2}{a-3}}{\frac{a}{3-a}} = \frac{\frac{2a^2}{a-3}}{\frac{a}{-1(a-3)}}$
$= \frac{\left(\frac{2a^2}{a-3}\right)(-1)(a-3)}{\frac{a}{-1(a-3)}(-1)(a-3)}$
$= \frac{-2a^2}{a}$
$= -2a$

Chapter 10 Review Exercises

1. $(x - 4)(5x + 3) = 0$
$x - 4 = 0$ or $5x + 3 = 0$
$x = 4$ or $5x = -3$
$x = -\frac{3}{5}$

The solutions are 4, $-\frac{3}{5}$.

2. $(x+7)(3x+4)=0$

$x+7=0$ or $3x+4=0$

$x=-7$ or $3x=-4$

$x=-\frac{4}{3}$

The solutions are –7 and $-\frac{4}{3}$.

3. $3m^2-5m=2$

$3m^2-5m-2=0$

$(3m+1)(m-2)=0$

$3m+1=0$ or $m-2=0$

$3m=-1$ or $m=2$

$m=-\frac{1}{3}$

The solutions are $-\frac{1}{3}$ and 2.

4. $7m^2+2m=5$

$7m^2+2m-5=0$

$(7m-5)(m+1)=0$

$7m-5=0$ or $m+1=0$

$7m=5$ or $m=-1$

$m=\frac{5}{7}$

The solutions are $\frac{5}{7}$ and –1.

5. $k^2=50$

$k=\pm\sqrt{50}$

$k=\pm\sqrt{25}\sqrt{2}$

$k=\pm5\sqrt{2}$

The solutions are $\pm5\sqrt{2}$.

6. $k^2=45$

$k=\pm\sqrt{45}$

$k=\pm\sqrt{9\cdot5}$

$k=\pm3\sqrt{5}$

The solutions are $\pm3\sqrt{5}$.

7. $(x-5)(x-1)=12$

$x(x)+x(-1)-5(x)-5(-1)=12$

$x^2-x-5x+5=12$

$x^2-6x+5-12=0$

$x^2-6x-7=0$

$(x-7)(x+1)=0$

$x-7=0$ or $x+1=0$

$x=7$ or $x=-1$

The solutions are 7 and –1.

8. $(x-3)(x+2)=6$

$x^2-x-6=6$

$x^2-x-12=0$

$(x-4)(x+3)=0$

$x-4=0$ or $x+3=0$

$x=4$ or $x=-3$

The solutions are 4 and –3.

9. $(x-11)^2=49$

$x-11=\pm\sqrt{49}$

$x-11=\pm7$

$x=11\pm7$

$x=11+7$ or $x=11-7$

$x=18$ or $x=4$

The solutions are 18 and 4.

10. $(x+3)^2=100$

$x+3=\pm\sqrt{100}$

$x+3=\pm10$

$x=-3\pm10$

$x=-3+10$ or $x=-3-10$

$x=7$ or $x=-13$

The solutions are 7 and –13.

11. $6x^3-54x=0$

$6x(x^2-9)=0$

$6x(x+3)(x-3)=0$

$6x=0$ or $x+3=0$ or $x-3=0$

$x=0$ or $x=-3$ or $x=3$

The solutions are 0, –3, and 3.

12. $2x^2 - 8 = 0$
$$2x^2 = 8$$
$$x^2 = 4$$
$$x = \pm\sqrt{4}$$
The solutions are ±2.

13. $(4p+2)^2 = 100$
$$4p+2 = \pm\sqrt{100}$$
$$4p+2 = \pm 10$$
$$4p = -2 \pm 10$$
$$p = \frac{-2 \pm 10}{4}$$
$$p = \frac{-2+10}{4} \quad \text{or} \quad p = \frac{-2-10}{4}$$
$$p = \frac{8}{4} = 2 \quad \text{or} \quad p = \frac{-12}{4} = -3$$
The solutions are 2 and –3.

14. $(3p+6)^2 = 81$
$$3p+6 = \pm\sqrt{81}$$
$$3p+6 = \pm 9$$
$$3p = -6 \pm 9$$
$$p = \frac{-6 \pm 9}{3}$$
$$p = \frac{-6-9}{3} \quad \text{or} \quad p = \frac{-6+9}{3}$$
$$p = -5 \quad \text{or} \quad p = 1$$
The solutions are –5 and 1.

15. $x^2 - 10x \Rightarrow \left(\frac{-10}{2}\right)^2 = -5^2 = 25$
$$x^2 - 10x + 25 = (x-5)^2$$

16. $x^2 + 16x \Rightarrow \left(\frac{16}{2}\right)^2 = 8^2 = 64$
$$x^2 + 16x + 64 = (x+8)^2$$

17. $a^2 + 4a \Rightarrow \left(\frac{4}{2}\right)^2 = 2^2 = 4$
$$a^2 + 4a + 4 = (a+2)^2$$

18. $a^2 - 12a \Rightarrow \left(\frac{-12}{2}\right)^2 = 36$
$$a^2 - 12a + 36 = (a-6)^2$$

19. $m^2 - 3m \Rightarrow \left(\frac{-3}{2}\right)^2 = \frac{9}{4}$
$$m^2 - 3m + \frac{9}{4} = \left(m - \frac{3}{2}\right)^2$$

20. $m^2 + 5m \Rightarrow \left(\frac{5}{2}\right)^2 = \frac{25}{4}$
$$m^2 + 5m + \frac{25}{4} = \left(m + \frac{5}{2}\right)^2$$

21. $x^2 - 6x + 7 = 0$
$$x^2 - 6x = -7$$
$$x^2 - 6x + 9 = -7 + 9$$
$$(x-3)^2 = 2$$
$$x - 3 = \pm\sqrt{2}$$
$$x = 3 \pm \sqrt{2}$$
The solutions are $3 \pm \sqrt{2}$.

22. $x^2 + 6x + 7 = 0$
$$x^2 + 6x = -7$$
$$x^2 + 6x + 9 = 9 - 7$$
$$(x+3)^2 = 2$$
$$x + 3 = \pm\sqrt{2}$$
$$x = -3 \pm \sqrt{2}$$
The solutions are $-3 \pm \sqrt{2}$.

23.
$$2y^2 + y - 1 = 0$$
$$2y^2 + y = 1$$
$$\frac{2y^2}{2} + \frac{1y}{2} = \frac{1}{2}$$
$$y^2 + \frac{1}{2}y + \frac{1}{16} = \frac{1}{2} + \frac{1}{16}$$
$$\left(y^2 + \frac{1}{4}\right)^2 = \frac{8}{16} + \frac{1}{16}$$
$$\left(y^2 + \frac{1}{4}\right)^2 = \frac{9}{16}$$
$$y + \frac{1}{4} = \pm\sqrt{\frac{9}{16}}$$
$$y + \frac{1}{4} = \pm\frac{3}{4}$$
$$y = -\frac{1}{4} \pm \frac{3}{4}$$
$$y = -\frac{1}{4} + \frac{3}{4} \quad \text{or} \quad y = -\frac{1}{4} - \frac{3}{4}$$
$$y = \frac{2}{4} = \frac{1}{2} \quad \text{or} \quad y = -\frac{4}{4} = -1$$
The solutions are $\frac{1}{2}$ and -1.

24.
$$y^2 + 3y - 1 = 0$$
$$y^2 + 3y = 1$$
$$y^2 + 3y + \frac{9}{4} = \frac{9}{4} + 1$$
$$\left(y + \frac{3}{2}\right)^2 = \frac{13}{4}$$
$$y + \frac{3}{2} = \pm\sqrt{\frac{13}{4}}$$
$$y + \frac{3}{2} = \pm\frac{\sqrt{13}}{2}$$
$$y = -\frac{3}{2} \pm \frac{\sqrt{13}}{2}$$
$$y = \frac{-3 \pm \sqrt{13}}{2}$$
The solutions are $\frac{-3 \pm \sqrt{13}}{2}$.

25. $x^2 - 10x + 7 = 0$

$a = 1$, $b = -10$, $c = 7$
$$x = \frac{-(-10) \pm \sqrt{(-10)^2 - 4(1)(7)}}{2(1)}$$
$$x = \frac{10 \pm \sqrt{100 - 28}}{2}$$
$$x = \frac{10 \pm \sqrt{72}}{2}$$
$$x = \frac{10 \pm \sqrt{36}\sqrt{2}}{2}$$
$$x = \frac{10 \pm 6\sqrt{2}}{2}$$
$$x = \frac{2(5 \pm 3\sqrt{2})}{2}$$
$$x = 5 \pm 3\sqrt{2}$$
The solutions are $5 \pm 3\sqrt{2}$.

26. $x^2 + 4x - 7 = 0$

$a = 1$, $b = 4$, $c = -7$
$$x = \frac{-4 \pm \sqrt{4^2 - 4(1)(-7)}}{2(1)}$$
$$x = \frac{-4 \pm \sqrt{16 + 28}}{2}$$
$$x = \frac{-4 \pm \sqrt{44}}{2}$$
$$x = \frac{-4 \pm \sqrt{4 \cdot 11}}{2}$$
$$x = \frac{-4 \pm 2\sqrt{11}}{2}$$
$$x = -2 \pm \sqrt{11}$$
The solutions are $-2 \pm \sqrt{11}$.

27. $2x^2+x-1=0$

$a=2,\ b=1,\ c=-1$

$$x=\frac{-1\pm\sqrt{1^2-4(2)(-1)}}{2(2)}$$

$$x=\frac{-1\pm\sqrt{1+8}}{4}$$

$$x=\frac{-1\pm\sqrt{9}}{4}$$

$$x=\frac{-1\pm3}{4}$$

$$x=\frac{-1+3}{4} \quad\text{or}\quad x=\frac{-1-3}{4}$$

$$x=\frac{2}{4}=\frac{1}{2} \quad\text{or}\quad x=\frac{-4}{4}=-1$$

The solutions are -1 and $\frac{1}{2}$.

28. $x^2+3x-1=0$

$a=1,\ b=3,\ c=-1$

$$x=\frac{-3\pm\sqrt{3^2-4(1)(-1)}}{2(1)}$$

$$x=\frac{-3\pm\sqrt{9+4}}{2}$$

$$x=\frac{-3\pm\sqrt{13}}{2}$$

The solutions are $\frac{-3\pm\sqrt{13}}{2}$.

29. $9x^2+30x+25=0$

$a=9,\ b=30,\ c=25$

$$x=\frac{-30\pm\sqrt{30^2-4(9)(25)}}{2(9)}$$

$$x=\frac{-30\pm\sqrt{900-900}}{18}$$

$$x=\frac{-30\pm\sqrt{0}}{18}$$

$$x=\frac{-30}{18}=-\frac{5}{3}$$

The solutions is $-\frac{5}{3}$.

30. $16x^2-72x+81=0$

$a=16,\ b=-72,\ c=81$

$$x=\frac{-(-72)\pm\sqrt{(-72)^2-4(16)(81)}}{2(16)}$$

$$x=\frac{72\pm\sqrt{5184-5184}}{32}$$

$$x=\frac{72\pm\sqrt{0}}{32}$$

$$x=\frac{72\pm0}{32}$$

$$x=\frac{9}{4}$$

The solution is $\frac{9}{4}$.

31. $15x^2+2=11x$

$15x^2-11x+2=0$

$a=15,\ b=-11,\ c=2$

$$x=\frac{-(-11)\pm\sqrt{(-11)^2-4(15)(2)}}{2(15)}$$

$$x=\frac{11\pm\sqrt{121-120}}{30}$$

$$x=\frac{11\pm\sqrt{1}}{30}$$

$$x=\frac{11\pm1}{30}$$

$$x=\frac{11+1}{30} \quad\text{or}\quad x=\frac{11-1}{30}$$

$$x=\frac{12}{30}=\frac{2}{5} \quad\text{or}\quad x=\frac{10}{30}=\frac{1}{3}$$

The solution is $\frac{2}{5}$ and $\frac{1}{3}$.

32. $15x^2 + 2 = 13x$

$15x^2 - 13x + 2 = 0$

$a = 15,\ b = -13,\ c = 2$

$$x = \frac{-(-13) \pm \sqrt{(-13)^2 - 4(15)(2)}}{2(15)}$$

$$x = \frac{13 \pm \sqrt{169 - 120}}{30}$$

$$x = \frac{13 \pm \sqrt{49}}{30}$$

$$x = \frac{13 \pm 7}{30}$$

$$x = \frac{13+7}{30} \quad \text{or} \quad x = \frac{13-7}{30}$$

$$x = \frac{20}{30} = \frac{2}{3} \quad \text{or} \quad x = \frac{6}{30} = \frac{1}{5}$$

The solutions are $\frac{2}{3}$ and $\frac{1}{5}$.

33. $2x^2 + x + 5 = 0$

$a = 2,\ b = 1,\ c = 5$

$$x = \frac{-1 \pm \sqrt{1^2 - 4(2)(5)}}{2(2)}$$

$$x = \frac{-1 \pm \sqrt{1 - 40}}{4}$$

$$x = \frac{-1 \pm \sqrt{-39}}{4}$$

$$x = \frac{-1 \pm i\sqrt{39}}{4}$$

$\sqrt{-39}$ is not a real number. No real solutions.

34. $7x^2 - 3x + 1 = 0$

$a = 7,\ b = -3,\ c = 1$

$$x = \frac{-(-3) \pm \sqrt{(-3)^2 - 4(7)(1)}}{2(7)}$$

$$x = \frac{3 \pm \sqrt{9 - 28}}{14}$$

$$x = \frac{3 \pm \sqrt{-19}}{14}$$

$\sqrt{-19}$ is not a real number. No real solutions.

35. $x^2 - 7x - 1 = 0$

$a = 1,\ b = -7,\ c = -1$

$$\begin{aligned} b^2 - 4ac &= (-7)^2 - 4(1)(-1) \\ &= 49 + 4 \\ &= 53 \end{aligned}$$

Since the discriminant is a positive number, this equation has two distinct real solutions.

36. $x^2 + x + 5 = 0$

$a = 1,\ b = 1,\ c = 5$

$$\begin{aligned} b^2 - 4ac &= 1^2 - 4(1)(5) \\ &= 1 - 20 \\ &= -19 \end{aligned}$$

Since the discriminant is a negative number, this equation has no real solutions.

37. $9x^2 + 1 = 6x$

$9x^2 - 6x + 1 = 0$

$a = 9,\ b = -6,\ c = 1$

$$\begin{aligned} b^2 - 4ac &= (-6)^2 - 4(9)(1) \\ &= 36 - 36 \\ &= 0 \end{aligned}$$

Since the discriminant is 0, this equation has one real solution.

38. $x^2 + 6x = 5$

$x^2 + 6x - 5 = 0$

$a = 1,\ b = 6,\ c = -5$

$$\begin{aligned} b^2 - 4ac &= 6^2 - 4(1)(-5) \\ &= 36 + 20 \\ &= 56 \end{aligned}$$

Since the discriminant is a positive number, this equation has two distinct real solutions.

39. $5x^2 + 4 = 0$
$a = 5,\ b = 0,\ c = 4$
$$b^2 - 4ac = 0^2 - 4(5)(4) = 0 - 80 = -80$$
Since the discriminant is a negative number, this equation has no real solutions.

40. $x^2 + 25 = 10x$
$x^2 - 10x + 25 = 0$
$a = 1,\ b = -10,\ c = 25$
$$b^2 - 4ac = (-10)^2 - 4(1)(25) = 100 - 100 = 0$$
Since the discriminant is 0, this equation has one real solution.

41. $5z^2 + z - 1 = 0$
$a = 5,\ b = 1,\ c = -1$
$$z = \frac{-1 \pm \sqrt{1^2 - 4(5)(-1)}}{2(5)}$$
$$z = \frac{-1 \pm \sqrt{1 + 20}}{10}$$
$$z = \frac{-1 \pm \sqrt{21}}{10}$$
The solutions are $\frac{-1 \pm \sqrt{21}}{10}$.

42. $4z^2 + 7z - 1 = 0$
$a = 4,\ b = 7,\ c = -1$
$$x = \frac{-7 \pm \sqrt{7^2 - 4(4)(-1)}}{2(4)}$$
$$x = \frac{-7 \pm \sqrt{49 + 16}}{8}$$
$$x = \frac{-7 \pm \sqrt{65}}{8}$$
The solutions are $\frac{-7 \pm \sqrt{65}}{8}$.

43. $4x^4 = x^2$
$4x^4 - x^2 = 0$
$x^2(4x^2 - 1) = 0$
$x^2(2x + 1)(2x - 1) = 0$
$x^2 = 0$ or $2x + 1 = 0$ or $2x - 1 = 0$
$x = 0$ or $2x = -1$ or $2x = 1$
$x = -\frac{1}{2}$ or $x = \frac{1}{2}$
The solutions are 0, $-\frac{1}{2}$, and $\frac{1}{2}$.

44. $9x^3 = x$
$9x^3 - x = 0$
$x(9x^2 - 1) = 0$
$x(3x - 1)(3x + 1) = 0$
$x = 0$ or $3x - 1 = 0$ or $3x + 1 = 0$
$3x = 1$ or $3x = -1$
$x = \frac{1}{3}$ or $x = -\frac{1}{3}$
The solutions are 0, $\frac{1}{3}$, and $-\frac{1}{3}$.

45. $2x^2 - 15x + 7 = 0$
$(2x - 1)(x - 7) = 0$
$2x - 1 = 0$ or $x - 7 = 0$
$2x = 1$ or $x = 7$
$x = \frac{1}{2}$
The solutions are $\frac{1}{2}$ and 7.

46. $x^2 - 6x - 7 = 0$
$(x - 7)(x + 1) = 0$
$x - 7 = 0$ or $x + 1 = 0$
$x = 7$ or $x = -1$

47. $(3x - 1)^2 = 0$
$3x - 1 = \pm\sqrt{0}$
$3x - 1 = 0$
$3x = 1$
$x = \frac{1}{3}$
The solution is $\frac{1}{3}$.

48. $(2x-3)^2 = 0$

$2x-3 = \pm\sqrt{0}$

$2x-3 = 0$

$2x = 3$

$x = \frac{3}{2}$

The solution is $\frac{3}{2}$.

49. $x^2 = 6x-9$

$x^2-6x+9 = 0$

$(x-3)(x-3) = 0$

$(x-3)^2 = 0$

$x-3 = \pm\sqrt{0}$

$x-3 = 0$

$x = 3$

The solution is 3.

50. $x^2 = 10x-25$

$x^2-10x+25 = 0$

$(x-5)(x-5) = 0$

$(x-5)^2 = 0$

$x-5 = \pm\sqrt{0}$

$x-5 = 0$

$x = 5$

The solution is 5.

51. $\left(\frac{1}{2}x-3\right)^2 = 64$

$\frac{1}{2}x-3 = \pm\sqrt{64}$

$\frac{1}{2}x-3 = \pm 8$

$\frac{1}{2}x = 3\pm 8$

$x = 2(3\pm 8)$

$x = 2(3+8)$ or $x = 2(3-8)$

$x = 2(11)$ or $x = 2(-5)$

$x = 22$ or $x = -10$

The solutions are 22 and –10.

52. $\left(\frac{1}{3}x+1\right)^2 = 49$

$\frac{1}{3}x+1 = \pm\sqrt{49}$

$\frac{1}{3}x+1 = \pm 7$

$\frac{1}{3}x = -1\pm 7$

$\frac{1}{3}x = -8$ or $\frac{1}{3}x = 6$

$x = -24$ or $x = 18$

The solutions are –24 and 18.

53. $x^2-0.3x+0.01 = 0$

$100(x^2-0.3x+0.01) = 100(0)$

$100x^2-30x+1 = 0$

$a = 100,\ b = -30,\ c = 1$

$x = \frac{-(-30)\pm\sqrt{(-30)^2-4(100)(1)}}{2(100)}$

$x = \frac{30\pm\sqrt{900-400}}{200}$

$x = \frac{30\pm\sqrt{500}}{200}$

$x = \frac{30\pm\sqrt{100}\sqrt{5}}{200}$

$x = \frac{30\pm 10\sqrt{5}}{200}$

$x = \frac{10(3\pm\sqrt{5})}{200}$

$x = \frac{3\pm\sqrt{5}}{20}$

The solutions are $\frac{3\pm\sqrt{5}}{20}$.

54. $x^2 + 0.6x - 0.16 = 0$

$100x^2 + 60x - 16 = 0$

$a = 100,\ b = 60,\ c = -16$

$$x = \frac{-60 \pm \sqrt{60^2 - 4(100)(-16)}}{2(100)}$$

$$x = \frac{-60 \pm \sqrt{3600 + 6400}}{200}$$

$$x = \frac{-60 \pm \sqrt{10000}}{200}$$

$$x = \frac{-60 \pm 100}{200}$$

$$x = \frac{-60 + 100}{200} \quad \text{or} \quad x = \frac{-60 - 100}{200}$$

$$x = \frac{40}{200} = \frac{1}{5} \quad \text{or} \quad x = \frac{-160}{200} = -\frac{4}{5}$$

The solutions are $\frac{1}{5}$ and $-\frac{4}{5}$.

55. $\frac{1}{10}x^2 + x - \frac{1}{2} = 0$

$10\left(\frac{1}{10}x^2 + x - \frac{1}{2}\right) = 0$

$x^2 + 10x - 5 = 0$

$a = 1,\ b = 10,\ c = -5$

$$x = \frac{-10 \pm \sqrt{10^2 - 4(1)(-5)}}{2(1)}$$

$$x = \frac{-10 \pm \sqrt{100 + 20}}{2}$$

$$x = \frac{-10 \pm \sqrt{120}}{2}$$

$$x = \frac{-10 \pm \sqrt{4}\sqrt{30}}{2}$$

$$x = \frac{-10 \pm 2\sqrt{30}}{2}$$

$$x = \frac{2(-5 \pm \sqrt{30})}{2}$$

$x = -5 \pm \sqrt{30}$

The solutions are $-5 \pm \sqrt{30}$.

56. $\frac{1}{12}x^2 - \frac{1}{2}x + \frac{1}{3} = 0$

$x^2 - 6x + 4 = 0$

$a = 1,\ b = -6,\ c = 4$

$$x = \frac{-(-6) \pm \sqrt{(-6)^2 - 4(1)(4)}}{2(1)}$$

$$x = \frac{6 \pm \sqrt{36 - 16}}{2}$$

$$x = \frac{6 \pm \sqrt{20}}{2}$$

$$x = \frac{6 \pm \sqrt{4 \cdot 5}}{2}$$

$$x = \frac{6 \pm 2\sqrt{5}}{2}$$

$x = 3 \pm \sqrt{5}$

The solutions are $3 \pm \sqrt{5}$.

57. $h = 16t^2$

$100 = 16t^2$

$\frac{100}{16} = t^2$

$\pm\sqrt{\frac{100}{16}} = t$

$t = \pm\frac{10}{4} = \pm\frac{5}{2}$

Disregard a negative time. It took her 2.5 seconds before she hit the water.

58. $5 \text{ miles} \cdot \frac{5280 \text{ feet}}{1 \text{ mile}} = 26,400 \text{ feet}$

$h = 16t^2$

$26,400 = 16t^2$

$\frac{26,400}{16} = t^2$

$\pm\sqrt{\frac{26,400}{16}} = t$

$t = \pm 40.6$

Disregard a negative time. A 5-mile free-fall will take approximately 40.6 seconds.

59.
$$y = 25x^2 - 54x + 519$$
$$1687 = 25x^2 - 54x + 519$$
$$25x^2 - 54x - 1168 = 0$$
$a = 25,\ b = -54,\ c = -1168$
$$x = \frac{-(-54) \pm \sqrt{(-54)^2 - 4(25)(-1168)}}{2(25)}$$
$$x = \frac{54 \pm \sqrt{119{,}716}}{50}$$
$$x = \frac{54 \pm 346}{50}$$
$$x = \frac{54 - 346}{50} \quad \text{or} \quad x = \frac{54 + 346}{50}$$
$$x = -5.84 \quad \text{or} \quad x = 8$$
Disregard a negative time.
1996 + 8 = 2004
The price of silver will be 1687 cents per ounce in 2004.

60.
$$y = 5x^2 - 6x + 398$$
$$670 = 5x^2 - 6x + 398$$
$$5x^2 - 6x - 272 = 0$$
$a = 5,\ b = -6,\ c = -272$
$$x = \frac{-(-6) \pm \sqrt{(-6)^2 - 4(5)(-272)}}{2(5)}$$
$$x = \frac{6 \pm \sqrt{5476}}{10}$$
$$x = \frac{6 \pm 74}{10}$$
$$x = \frac{6 - 74}{10} \quad \text{or} \quad x = \frac{6 + 74}{10}$$
$$x = -6.8 \quad \text{or} \quad x = 8$$
Disregard a negative time.
1996 + 8 = 2004
The price of platinum will be 670 dollars per ounce in 2004.

61.
$$\sqrt{-144} = \sqrt{-1 \cdot 144} = \sqrt{-1} \cdot \sqrt{144} = i \cdot 12 = 12i$$

62. $\sqrt{-36} = \sqrt{36 \cdot -1} = \sqrt{36} \cdot \sqrt{-1} = 6i$

63.
$$\sqrt{-108} = \sqrt{-1 \cdot 36 \cdot 3} = \sqrt{-1} \cdot \sqrt{36} \cdot \sqrt{3} = i \cdot 6\sqrt{3} = 6i\sqrt{3}$$

64.
$$\sqrt{-500} = \sqrt{100 \cdot 5 \cdot -1} = \sqrt{100} \cdot \sqrt{-1} \cdot \sqrt{5} = 10i\sqrt{5}$$

65.
$$(7 - i) + (14 - 9i) = 7 - i + 14 - 9i = 7 + 14 + (-i - 9i) = 21 - 10i$$

66.
$$(10 - 4i) + (9 - 21i) = 10 - 4i + 9 - 21i = 19 - 25i$$

67. $3 - (11 + 2i) = 3 - 11 - 2i = -8 - 2i$

68. $(-4 - 3i) + 5i = -4 - 3i + 5i = -4 + 2i$

69.
$$(2 - 3i)(3 - 2i)$$
$$= 2(3) + 2(-2i) - 3i(3) - 3i(-2i)$$
$$= 6 - 4i - 9i + 6i^2$$
$$= 6 - 13i + 6(-1)$$
$$= 6 - 13i - 6$$
$$= -13i$$

70.
$$(2 + 5i)(5 - i) = 10 - 2i + 25i - 5i^2 = 10 - 2i + 25i - 5(-1) = 10 + 5 - 2i + 25i = 15 + 23i$$

71.
$$(3 - 4i)(3 + 4i) = (3)^2 - (4i)^2 = 9 - 16i^2 = 9 - 16(-1) = 9 + 16 = 25$$

72.
$$(7 - 2i)(7 - 2i) = 49 - 14i - 14i + 4i^2 = 49 - 4 - 28i = 45 - 28i$$

73. $\frac{2-6i}{4i} = \frac{(2-6i)(-i)}{4i(-i)}$

$= \frac{-2i+6i^2}{-4i^2}$

$= \frac{-2i+6(-1)}{-4(-1)}$

$= \frac{-2i-6}{4}$

$= \frac{2(-i-3)}{4}$

$= -\frac{i}{2} - \frac{3}{2}$

$= -\frac{3}{2} - \frac{1}{2}i$

74. $\frac{5-i}{2i} = \frac{5-i}{2i} \cdot \frac{2i}{2i}$

$= \frac{2i(5-i)}{4i^2}$

$= \frac{10i-21i^2}{-4}$

$= \frac{2+10i}{-4}$

$= \frac{1+5i}{-2}$

$= -\frac{1}{2} - \frac{5}{2}i$

75. $\frac{4-i}{1+2i} = \frac{(4-i)(1-2i)}{(1+2i)(1-2i)}$

$= \frac{4(1)+4(-2i)-i(1)-i(-2i)}{(1)^2-(2i)^2}$

$= \frac{4-8i-i+2i^2}{1-4i^2}$

$= \frac{4-9i+2(-1)}{1-4(-1)}$

$= \frac{4-9i-2}{1+4}$

$= \frac{2-9i}{5}$

$= \frac{2}{5} - \frac{9}{5}i$

76. $\frac{1+3i}{2-7i} = \frac{1+3i}{2-7i} \cdot \frac{2+7i}{2+7i}$

$= \frac{2+7i+6i+21i^2}{4-49i^2}$

$= \frac{2-21+13i}{4+49}$

$= \frac{-19+13i}{53}$

$= -\frac{19}{53} + \frac{13}{53}i$

77. $3x^2 = -48$

$x^2 = -16$

$x = \pm\sqrt{-16}$

$x = \pm 4i$

The solutions are $\pm 4i$.

78. $5x^2 = -125$

$\frac{5x^2}{5} = \frac{-125}{5}$

$x^2 = -25$

$x = \pm\sqrt{-25}$

$x = \pm\sqrt{25 \cdot -1}$

$x = \pm 5i$

The solutions are $\pm 5i$.

79. $x^2 - 4x + 13 = 0$

$a = 1,\ b = -4,\ c = 13$

$x = \frac{-(-4) \pm \sqrt{(-4)^2 - 4(1)(13)}}{2(1)}$

$x = \frac{4 \pm \sqrt{16-52}}{2}$

$x = \frac{4 \pm \sqrt{-36}}{2}$

$x = \frac{4 \pm 6i}{2}$

$x = \frac{2(2 \pm 3i)}{2}$

$x = 2 \pm 3i$

The solutions are $2 \pm 3i$.

80. $x^2 + 4x + 11 = 0$
$a = 1$, $b = 4$, $c = 11$

$$x = \frac{-4 \pm \sqrt{4^2 - 4(1)(11)}}{2(1)}$$

$$x = \frac{-4 \pm \sqrt{16 - 44}}{2}$$

$$x = \frac{-4 \pm \sqrt{-28}}{2}$$

$$x = \frac{-4 \pm \sqrt{4 \cdot 7 \cdot -1}}{2}$$

$$x = \frac{-4 \pm 2i\sqrt{7}}{2}$$

$$x = -2 \pm i\sqrt{7}$$

The solutions are $-2 \pm i\sqrt{7}$.

81. $y = -3x^2$

$$x = \frac{-b}{2a} = \frac{-0}{2(-3)} = 0$$

$y = -3(0)^2 = 0$
vertex (0, 0)
axis of symmetry $x = 0$
Parabola opens downward because $a < 0$.

82. $y = -\frac{1}{2}x^2$

$$x = \frac{-b}{2a} = \frac{-0}{2\left(-\frac{1}{2}\right)} = 0$$

$y = -\frac{1}{2}(0)^2 = 0$
vertex (0, 0)
axis of symmetry $x = 0$
Parabola opens downward because $a < 0$.

83. $y = (x - 3)^2$
$y = x^2 - 6x + 9$

$$x = \frac{-b}{2a} = \frac{-(-6)}{2(1)} = 3$$

$y = 3^2 - 6(3) + 9 = 0$
vertex (3, 0)
axis of symmetry $x = 3$
Parabola opens upward because $a > 0$.

84. $y = (x - 5)^2$
$y = x^2 - 10x + 25$

$$x = \frac{-b}{2a} = \frac{-(-10)}{2(1)} = 5$$

$y = 5^2 - 10(5) + 25 = 0$
vertex (5, 0)
axis of symmetry $x = 5$
Parabola opens upward because $a > 0$.

85. $y = 3x^2 - 7$

$$x = \frac{-b}{2a} = \frac{-0}{2(-3)} = 0$$

$y = 3(0)^2 - 7 = -7$
vertex (0, –7)
axis of symmetry $x = 0$
Parabola opens upward because $a > 0$.

86. $y = -2x^2 + 25$

$$x = \frac{-b}{2a} = \frac{-0}{2(-2)} = 0$$

$y = -2(0)^2 + 25 = 25$
vertex (0, 25)
axis of symmetry $x = 0$
Parabola opens downward because $a < 0$.

87. $y = -5(x - 72)^2 + 14$
vertex (72, 14)
axis of symmetry $x = 72$
Parabola opens downward.

88. $y = 2(x - 35)^2 - 21$
vertex (35, –21)
axis of symmetry $x = 35$
Parabola opens upward.

89. $y = -x^2$
Find vertex.

$$x = \frac{-b}{2a} = \frac{-0}{2(-1)} = 0$$

$y = -0^2 = 0$
vertex = (0, 0)
y-intercept = (0, 0)
x-intercept = (0, 0)

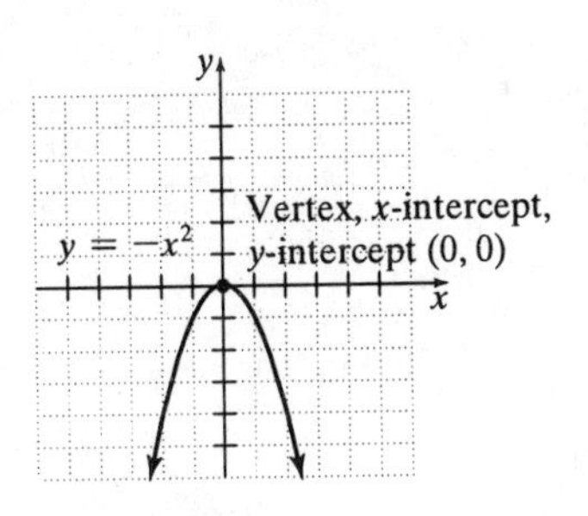

90. $y = 4x^2$
Find vertex.
$$x = \frac{-b}{2a} = \frac{-0}{2(4)} = 0$$
$$y = 4(0)^2 = 0$$
vertex = (0, 0)
y-intercept = (0, 0)
x-intercept = (0, 0)

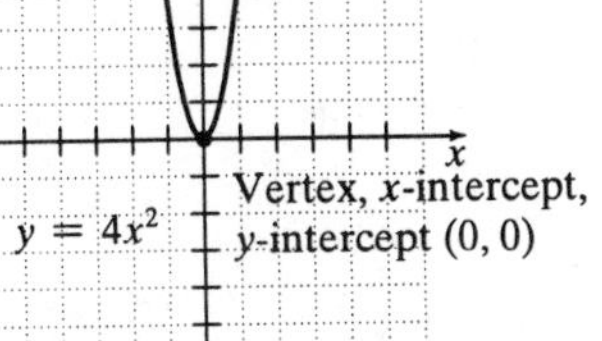

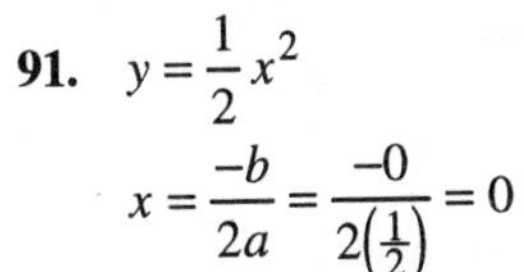

91. $y = \frac{1}{2}x^2$
$$x = \frac{-b}{2a} = \frac{-0}{2\left(\frac{1}{2}\right)} = 0$$
$$y = \frac{1}{2}(0)^2 = 0$$
vertex = (0, 0)
y-intercept = (0, 0)
x-intercept = (0, 0)

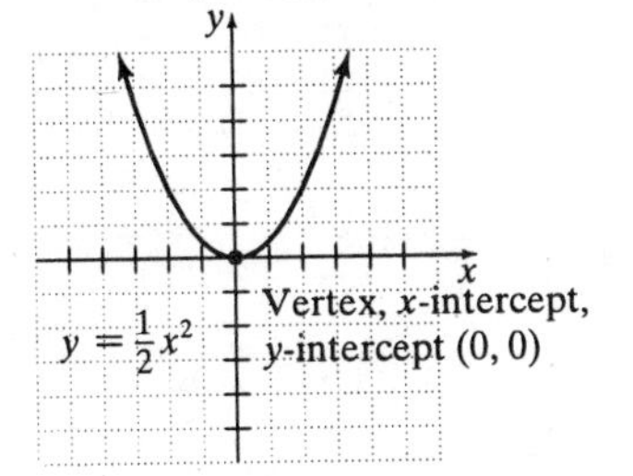

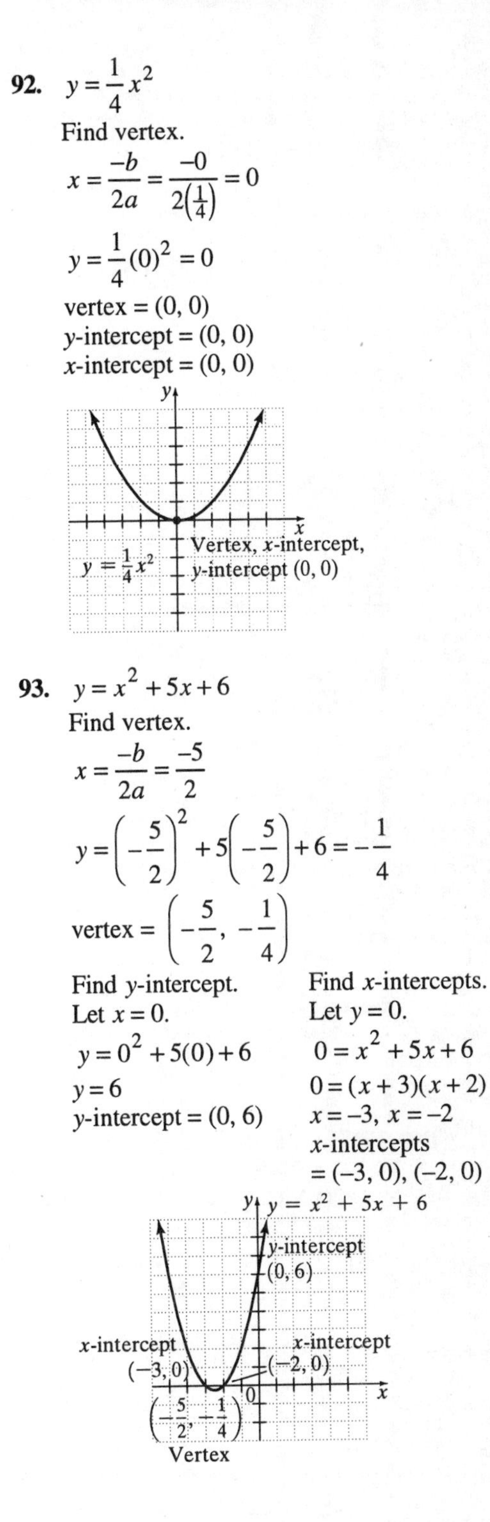

92. $y = \frac{1}{4}x^2$
Find vertex.
$$x = \frac{-b}{2a} = \frac{-0}{2\left(\frac{1}{4}\right)} = 0$$
$$y = \frac{1}{4}(0)^2 = 0$$
vertex = (0, 0)
y-intercept = (0, 0)
x-intercept = (0, 0)

93. $y = x^2 + 5x + 6$
Find vertex.
$$x = \frac{-b}{2a} = \frac{-5}{2}$$
$$y = \left(-\frac{5}{2}\right)^2 + 5\left(-\frac{5}{2}\right) + 6 = -\frac{1}{4}$$
$$\text{vertex} = \left(-\frac{5}{2}, -\frac{1}{4}\right)$$

Find y-intercept.
Let $x = 0$.
$y = 0^2 + 5(0) + 6$
$y = 6$
y-intercept = (0, 6)

Find x-intercepts.
Let $y = 0$.
$0 = x^2 + 5x + 6$
$0 = (x + 3)(x + 2)$
$x = -3$, $x = -2$
x-intercepts
= (−3, 0), (−2, 0)

94. $y = x^2 - 4x - 8$

Find vertex.

$x = \frac{-b}{2a} = \frac{-(-4)}{2 \cdot 1} = \frac{4}{2} = 2$

$y = 2^2 - 4(2) - 8 = -12$

vertex = (2, −12)

Find y-intercept.

Let $x = 0$

$y = 0^2 - 4(0) - 8$

$y = -8$

y-intercept = (0, −8)

Find x-intercepts.

Let $y = 0$

$0 = x^2 - 4x - 8$

$x = \frac{-(-4) \pm \sqrt{(-4)^2 - 4(1)(-8)}}{2(1)}$

$x = \frac{4 \pm \sqrt{48}}{2}$

$x = \frac{4 \pm 4\sqrt{3}}{2}$

$x = 2 \pm 2\sqrt{3}$

x-intercepts = $(2 - 2\sqrt{3},\ 0),\ (2 + 2\sqrt{3},\ 0)$

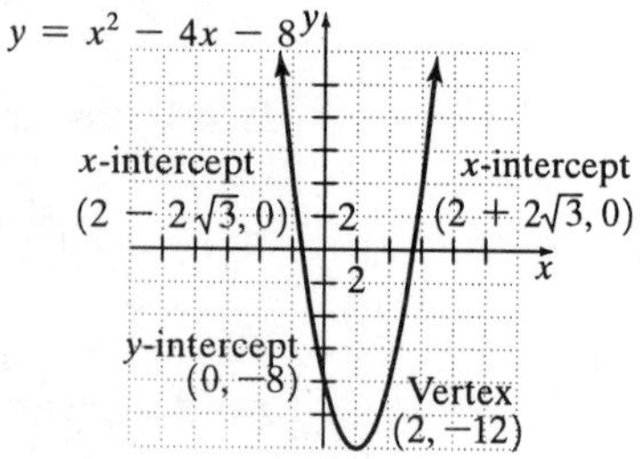

95. $y = 2x^2 - 11x - 6$

Find vertex.

$x = \frac{-b}{2a} = \frac{-(-11)}{2 \cdot 2} = \frac{11}{4}$

$y = 2\left(\frac{11}{4}\right)^2 - 11\left(\frac{11}{4}\right) - 6$

$y = -\frac{169}{8}$

vertex = $\left(\frac{11}{4},\ -\frac{169}{8}\right)$

Find y-intercept.

Let $x = 0$.

$y = 2(0)^2 - 11(0) - 6$

$y = -6$

y-intercept = (0, −6)

Find x-intercepts.

Let $y = 0$.

$0 = 2x^2 - 11x - 6$

$0 = (2x + 1)(x - 6)$

$x = -\frac{1}{2},\ x = 6$

x-intercepts = $\left(-\frac{1}{2},\ 0\right),\ (6,\ 0)$

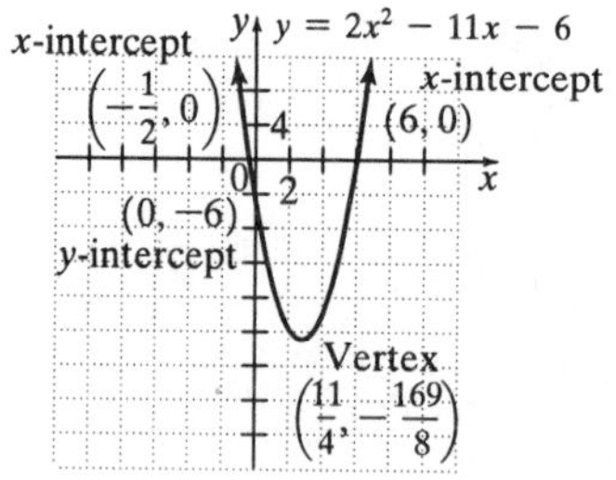

96. $y = 3x^2 - x - 2$

Find vertex.

$x = \frac{-b}{2a} = \frac{-(-1)}{2 \cdot 3} = \frac{1}{6}$

$y = 3\left(\frac{1}{6}\right)^2 - \frac{1}{6} - 2$

$y = -\frac{25}{12}$

vertex $= \left(\frac{1}{6}, -\frac{25}{12}\right)$

Find y-intercept.
Let $x = 0$.

$y = 3(0)^2 - 0 - 2$

$y = -2$

y-intercept $= (0, -2)$

Find x-intercepts.
Let $y = 0$.

$0 = 3x^2 - x - 2$

$0 = (3x + 2)(x - 1)$

$x = -\frac{2}{3}$, $x = 1$

x-intercepts $= \left(-\frac{2}{3}, 0\right), (1, 0)$

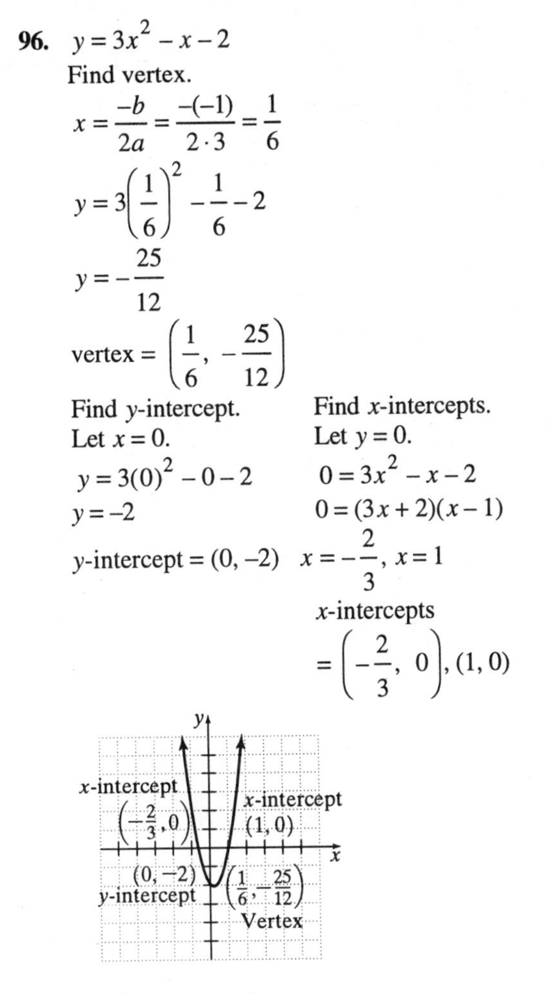

97. 1 solution; $x = -2$

98. 2 solutions; $x = 3$, $x = -1.5$

99. No real solutions

100. 2 solutions; $x = \pm 2$

Chapter 10 Test

1. $2x^2 - x = 21$

$2x^2 - 11x - 21 = 0$

$(2x + 3)(x - 7) = 0$

$2x + 3 = 0$ or $x - 7 = 0$

$2x = -3$ or $x = 7$

$x = -\frac{3}{2}$

The solutions are $-\frac{3}{2}$ and 7.

2. $x^4 + x^3 - 2x^2 = 0$

$x^2(x^2 + x - 2) = 0$

$x^2(x + 2)(x - 1) = 0$

$x^2 = 0$ or $x + 2 = 0$ or $x - 1 = 0$

$x = 0$ or $x = -2$ or $x = 1$

The solutions are 0, –2, and 1.

3. $5k^2 = 80$

$k^2 = 16$

$k = \pm\sqrt{16}$

$k = \pm 4$

The solutions are ± 4.

4. $(3m - 5)^2 = 8$

$3m - 5 = \pm\sqrt{8}$

$3m - 5 = \pm\sqrt{4}\sqrt{2}$

$3m - 5 = \pm 2\sqrt{2}$

$3m = 5 \pm 2\sqrt{2}$

$m = \frac{5 \pm 2\sqrt{2}}{3}$

The solutions are $\frac{5 \pm 2\sqrt{2}}{3}$.

5. $x^2 - 26x + 160 = 0$

$$x^2 - 26x = -160$$
$$x^2 - 26x + 169 = -160 + 169$$
$$(x-13)^2 = 9$$
$$x - 13 = \pm\sqrt{9}$$
$$x - 13 = \pm 3$$
$$x = 13 \pm 3$$

$x = 13 + 3$ or $x = 13 - 3$

$x = 16$ or $x = 10$

The solutions are 16 and 10.

6. $5x^2 + 9x = 2$

$$\frac{5x^2}{5} + \frac{9}{5}x = \frac{2}{5}$$
$$x^2 + \frac{9}{5}x = \frac{2}{5}$$
$$x^2 + \frac{9}{5}x + \frac{81}{100} = \frac{2}{5} + \frac{81}{100}$$
$$\left(x + \frac{9}{10}\right)^2 = \frac{40}{100} + \frac{81}{100}$$
$$\left(x + \frac{9}{10}\right)^2 = \frac{121}{100}$$
$$x + \frac{9}{10} = \pm\sqrt{\frac{121}{100}}$$
$$x + \frac{9}{10} = \pm\frac{11}{10}$$
$$x = -\frac{9}{10} \pm \frac{11}{10}$$

$x = -\frac{9}{10} + \frac{11}{10}$ or $x = -\frac{9}{10} - \frac{11}{10}$

$x = \frac{2}{10} = \frac{1}{5}$ or $x = \frac{-20}{10} = -2$

The solutions are $\frac{1}{5}$ and -2.

7. $x^2 - 3x - 10 = 0$

$a = 1, b = -3, c = -10$

$$x = \frac{-(-3) \pm \sqrt{(-3)^2 - 4(1)(-10)}}{2(1)}$$
$$x = \frac{3 \pm \sqrt{9 + 40}}{2}$$
$$x = \frac{3 \pm \sqrt{49}}{2}$$
$$x = \frac{3 \pm 7}{2}$$

$x = \frac{3+7}{2}$ or $x = \frac{3-7}{2}$

$x = \frac{10}{2} = 5$ or $x = \frac{-4}{2} = -2$

The solutions are 5 and -2.

8. $p^2 - \frac{5}{3}p - \frac{1}{3} = 0$

$$3\left(p^2 - \frac{5}{3}p - \frac{1}{3}\right) = 3(0)$$
$$3p^2 - 5p - 1 = 0$$

$a = 3, b = -5, c = -1$

$$p = \frac{-(-5) \pm \sqrt{(-5)^2 - 4(3)(-1)}}{2(3)}$$
$$p = \frac{5 \pm \sqrt{25 + 12}}{6}$$
$$p = \frac{5 \pm \sqrt{37}}{6}$$

The solutions are $\frac{5 \pm \sqrt{37}}{6}$.

9.
$$(3x-5)(x+2)=-6$$
$$3x(x)+3x(2)-5(x)-5(2)=-6$$
$$3x^2+6x-5x-10=-6$$
$$3x^2+x-10+6=0$$
$$3x^2+x-4=0$$
$$(3x+4)(x-1)=0$$
$3x+4=0$ or $x-1=0$

$3x=-4$ or $x=1$

$x=-\frac{4}{3}$

The solutions are $-\frac{4}{3}$ and 1.

10. $(3x-1)^2=16$
$$3x-1=\pm\sqrt{16}$$
$$3x-1=\pm 4$$
$$3x=1\pm 4$$
$$x=\frac{1\pm 4}{3}$$
$x=\frac{1+4}{3}$ or $x=\frac{1-4}{3}$

$x=\frac{5}{3}$ or $x=-\frac{3}{3}=-1$

The solutions are $\frac{5}{3}$ and -1.

11. $3x^2-7x-2=0$

$a=3,\ b=-7,\ c=-2$
$$x=\frac{-(-7)\pm\sqrt{(-7)^2-4(3)(-2)}}{2(3)}$$
$$x=\frac{7\pm\sqrt{49+24}}{6}$$
$$x=\frac{7\pm\sqrt{73}}{6}$$
The solutions are $\frac{7\pm\sqrt{73}}{6}$.

12. $x^2-4x+5=0$

$a=1,\ b=-4,\ c=5$
$$x=\frac{-(-4)\pm\sqrt{(-4)^2-4(1)(5)}}{2(1)}$$
$$x=\frac{4\pm\sqrt{16-20}}{2}$$
$$x=\frac{4\pm\sqrt{-4}}{2}$$
$$x=\frac{4\pm 2i}{2}$$
$$x=\frac{2(2\pm i)}{2}$$
$$x=2\pm i$$
The solutions are $2\pm i$.

13. $3x^2-7x+2=0$
$$(3x-1)(x-2)=0$$
$3x-1=0$ or $x-2=0$

$3x=1$ or $x=2$

$x=\frac{1}{3}$

The solutions are $\frac{1}{3}$ and 2.

14. $2x^2 - 6x + 1 = 0$
$a = 2,\ b = -6,\ c = 1$

$$x = \frac{-(-6) \pm \sqrt{(-6)^2 - 4(2)(1)}}{2(2)}$$
$$x = \frac{6 \pm \sqrt{36 - 8}}{4}$$
$$x = \frac{6 \pm \sqrt{28}}{4}$$
$$x = \frac{6 \pm \sqrt{4}\sqrt{7}}{4}$$
$$x = \frac{6 \pm 2\sqrt{7}}{4}$$
$$x = \frac{2(3 \pm \sqrt{7})}{4}$$
$$x = \frac{3 \pm \sqrt{7}}{2}$$

The solutions are $\frac{3 \pm \sqrt{7}}{2}$.

15. $2x^5 + 5x^4 - 3x^3 = 0$
$x^3(2x^2 + 5x - 3) = 0$
$x^3(2x - 1)(x + 3) = 0$
$x^3 = 0$ or $2x - 1 = 0$ or $x + 3 = 0$
$x = 0$ or $2x = 1$ or $x = -3$
$x = \frac{1}{2}$

The solutions are 0, $\frac{1}{2}$, and –3.

16. $9x^3 = x$
$9x^3 - x = 0$
$x(9x^2 - 1) = 0$
$x(3x - 1)(3x + 1) = 0$
$x = 0$ or $3x - 1 = 0$ or $3x + 1 = 0$
$3x = 1$ or $3x = -1$
$x = \frac{1}{3}$ or $x = -\frac{1}{3}$

The solutions are 0, $\frac{1}{3}$, and $-\frac{1}{3}$.

17. $\sqrt{-25} = \sqrt{-1 \cdot 25} = \sqrt{-1} \cdot \sqrt{25} = i \cdot 5 = 5i$

18.
$$\begin{aligned}\sqrt{-200} &= \sqrt{-1 \cdot 100 \cdot 2}\\ &= \sqrt{-1} \cdot \sqrt{100} \cdot \sqrt{2}\\ &= i \cdot 10\sqrt{2}\\ &= 10i\sqrt{2}\end{aligned}$$

19.
$$\begin{aligned}(3 + 2i) + (5 - i) &= 3 + 2i + 5 - i\\ &= 3 + 5 + (2i - i)\\ &= 8 + i\end{aligned}$$

20.
$$\begin{aligned}(4 - i) - (-3 + 5i) &= 4 - i + 3 - 5i\\ &= 4 + 3 + (-i - 5i)\\ &= 7 - 6i\end{aligned}$$

21.
$$\begin{aligned}(3 + 2i) - (3 - 2i) &= 3 + 2i - 3 + 2i\\ &= 3 - 3 + (2i + 2i)\\ &= 4i\end{aligned}$$

22.
$$\begin{aligned}(3 + 2i) + (3 - 2i) &= 3 + 2i + 3 - 2i\\ &= 3 + 3 + (2i - 2i)\\ &= 6\end{aligned}$$

23.
$$\begin{aligned}(3 + 2i)(3 - 2i) &= (3)^2 - (2i)^2\\ &= 9 - 4i^2\\ &= 9 - 4(-1)\\ &= 9 + 4\\ &= 13\end{aligned}$$

24.
$$\begin{aligned}\frac{3 - i}{1 + 2i} &= \frac{(3 - i)(1 - 2i)}{(1 + 2i)(1 - 2i)}\\ &= \frac{3(1) + 3(-2i) - i(1) - i(-2i)}{(1)^2 - (2i)^2}\\ &= \frac{3 - 6i - i + 2i^2}{1 - 4i^2}\\ &= \frac{3 - 7i + 2(-1)}{1 - 4(-1)}\\ &= \frac{3 - 7i - 2}{1 + 4}\\ &= \frac{1 - 7i}{5}\\ &= \frac{1}{5} - \frac{7}{5}i\end{aligned}$$

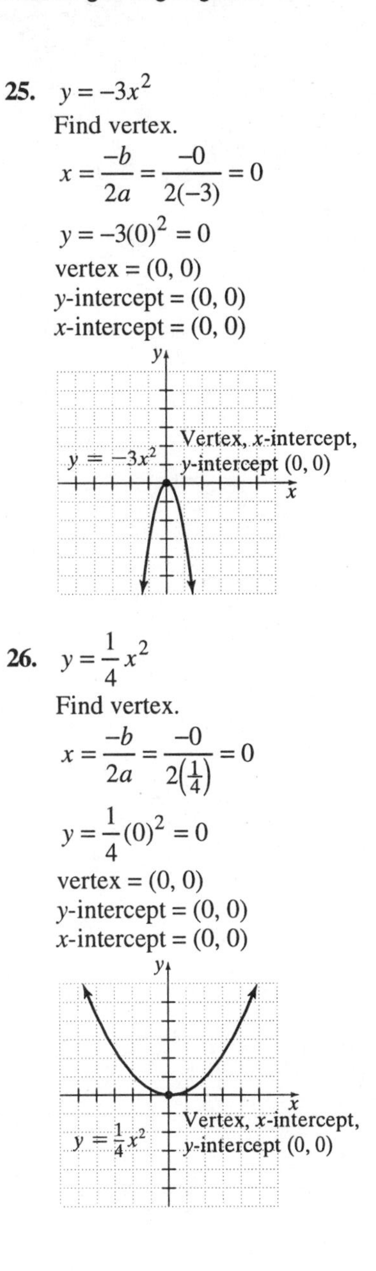

25. $y = -3x^2$

Find vertex.

$$x = \frac{-b}{2a} = \frac{-0}{2(-3)} = 0$$

$$y = -3(0)^2 = 0$$

vertex = (0, 0)

y-intercept = (0, 0)

x-intercept = (0, 0)

26. $y = \frac{1}{4}x^2$

Find vertex.

$$x = \frac{-b}{2a} = \frac{-0}{2\left(\frac{1}{4}\right)} = 0$$

$$y = \frac{1}{4}(0)^2 = 0$$

vertex = (0, 0)

y-intercept = (0, 0)

x-intercept = (0, 0)

27. $y = x^2 - 7x + 10$

Find vertex.

$$x = \frac{-b}{2a} = \frac{-(-7)}{2(1)} = \frac{7}{2}$$

$$y = \left(\frac{7}{2}\right)^2 - 7\left(\frac{7}{2}\right) + 10$$

$$y = -\frac{9}{4}$$

$$\text{vertex} = \left(\frac{7}{2}, -\frac{9}{4}\right)$$

Find y-intercept.

Let $x = 0$.

$y = 0^2 - 7(0) + 10$

$y = 10$

y-intercept = (0, 10)

Find x-intercepts.

Let $y = 0$.

$0 = x^2 - 7x + 10$

$0 = (x-2)(x-5)$

$x = 2$, $x = 5$

x-intercepts = (2, 0), (5, 0)

y, $y = x^2 - 7x + 10$; (0, 10) y-intercept; (2, 0) x-intercept (5, 0); 2; 0; x; $\left(\frac{7}{2}, -\frac{9}{4}\right)$ Vertex

28.

$$h = 16t^2$$

$$120.75 = 16t^2$$

$$\frac{120.75}{16} = t^2$$

$$\pm\sqrt{\frac{120.75}{16}} = t$$

$t = -2.7$ or $t = 2.7$

Disregard a negative time. It took her approximately 2.7 seconds for the dive.

29.

$$y = 28x^2 + 555$$
$$1003 = 28x^2 + 555$$
$$28x^2 - 448 = 0$$
$$28(x^2 - 16) = 0$$
$$28(x + 4)(x - 4) = 0$$
$$x + 4 = 0 \quad \text{or} \quad x - 4 = 0$$
$$x = -4 \quad \text{or} \quad x = 4$$

Disregard a negative time.
1996 + 4 = 2000
The value of mineral production is $1003 million in 2000.

Appendix A

1.
```
   9.076
 + 8.004
  17.080
```

3.
```
   6 10
  27.004
 − 14.2
  12.804
```

5.
```
 107.92
 + 3.04
 110.96
```

7.
```
 0 9 10
  10.0
 − 7.6
   2.4
```

9.
```
 011151212
  126.32
 − 97.89
   28.43
```

11.
```
   3.25
 ×   70
 227.50
```

13.
```
     2.7
 3)  8.1
    −6
     21
    −21
```

15.
```
 415 310410
  55.4050
 − 6.1711
  49.2339
```

17.
```
          80
 75.)  6000.
       −600
         00
         −0
```

19.
```
       0.07612
 100)  7.61200
      −700
        612
       −600
         120
        −100
          200
         −200
```

21.
```
        4.56
 27.)  123.12
      −108
        151
       −135
         162
        −162
```

23.
```
 569.2
  71.25
 + 8.01
 648.46
```

25.
```
    7 910
  768.00
  − 0.17
  767.83
```

27.
```
  12
 + 0.062
 12.062
```

29.
```
   5 910
   76.00
 − 14.52
   61.48
```

31.
```
        7.7
 43.)  331.1
      −301
        30 1
       −30 1
```

33.
$$\begin{array}{r} 762.12 \\ 89.7 \\ +\ 11.55 \\ \hline 863.37 \end{array}$$

35.
$$\begin{array}{r} {\scriptstyle 2\ 13\ 9\ 10} \\ 23.400 \\ -\ 0.821 \\ \hline 22.579 \end{array}$$

37.
$$\begin{array}{r} {\scriptstyle 5\ 10\ 12} \\ 476.12 \\ -\ 112.97 \\ \hline 363.15 \end{array}$$

39.
$$\begin{array}{r} 0.007 \\ +\ 7 \\ \hline 7.007 \end{array}$$

40.
$$\begin{array}{r} 51.77 \\ +\ 3.6 \\ \hline 55.37 \end{array}$$

Appendix B

1. $90° - 19° = 71°$

3. $90° - 70.8° = 19.2°$

5. $90° - 11\frac{1}{4}° = 78\frac{3}{4}°$

7. $180° - 150° = 30°$

9. $180° - 30.2° = 149.8°$

11. $180° - 79\frac{1}{2}° = 100\frac{1}{2}°$

13.
$$\begin{aligned} m\angle 1 &= 110° \\ m\angle 2 &= 180° - 110° = 70° \\ m\angle 3 &= m\angle 2 = 70° \\ m\angle 4 &= m\angle 2 = 70° \\ m\angle 5 &= m\angle 1 = 110° \\ m\angle 6 &= m\angle 4 = 70° \\ m\angle 7 &= m\angle 5 = 110° \end{aligned}$$

15. $180° - 11° - 79° = 90°$

17. $180° - 25° - 65° = 90°$

19. $180° - 30° - 60° = 90°$

21. $90° - 45° = 45°$
$45°, 90°$

23. $90° - 17° = 73°$
$73°, 90°$

25. $90° - 39\frac{3}{4}° = 50\frac{1}{4}°$
$50\frac{1}{4}°, 90°$

27.
$$\begin{aligned} \frac{12}{4} &= \frac{18}{x} \\ 4x\left(\frac{12}{4}\right) &= 4x\left(\frac{18}{x}\right) \\ 12x &= 72 \\ x &= 6 \end{aligned}$$

29.
$$\begin{aligned} \frac{6}{9} &= \frac{3}{x} \\ 9x\left(\frac{6}{9}\right) &= 9x\left(\frac{3}{x}\right) \\ 6x &= 27 \\ x &= 4.5 \end{aligned}$$

31.
$$\begin{aligned} a^2 + b^2 &= c^2 \\ 6^2 + 8^2 &= c^2 \\ 36 + 64 &= c^2 \\ 100 &= c^2 \\ 10 &= c \end{aligned}$$

33.
$$\begin{aligned} a^2 + b^2 &= c^2 \\ 5^2 + b^2 &= 13^2 \\ 25 + b^2 &= 169 \\ b^2 &= 144 \\ b &= 12 \end{aligned}$$

Appendix D

1. 21, 28, 16, 42, 38

$$\bar{x} = \frac{21+28+16+42+38}{5} = \frac{145}{5} = 29$$

16, 21, *28*, 38, 42

median = 28

no mode

3. 7.6, 8.2, 8.2, 9.6, 5.7, 9.1

$$\bar{x} = \frac{7.6+8.2+8.2+9.6+5.7+9.1}{6} = \frac{48.4}{6} = 8.1$$

5.7, 7.6, *8.2*, *8.2*, 9.1, 9.6

$$\text{median} = \frac{8.2+8.2}{2} = 8.2$$

mode = 8.2

5. 0.2, 0.3, 0.5, 0.6, 0.6, 0.9, 0.2, 0.7, 1.1

$$\bar{x} = \frac{0.2+0.3+0.5+0.6+0.6+0.9+0.2+0.7+1.1}{9}$$

$$= \frac{5.1}{9}$$

$$= 0.6$$

0.2, 0.2, 0.3, 0.5, *0.6*, 0.6, 0.7, 0.9, 1.1

median = 0.6

mode = 0.2 and 0.6

7. 231, 543, 601, 293, 588, 109, 334, 268

$$\bar{x} = \frac{231+543+601+293+588+109+334+268}{8}$$

$$= \frac{2967}{8}$$

$$= 370.9$$

109, 231, 268, *293*, *334*, 543, 588, 601

$$\text{median} = \frac{293+334}{2} = 313.5$$

no mode

9. $$\bar{x} = \frac{1454+1368+1362+1250+1136}{5}$$

$$= \frac{5670}{5}$$

$$= 1314 \text{ feet}$$

11. 1454, 1368, 1362, 1250, *1136*, *1127*, 1107, 1046, 1023, 1002

$$\text{median} = \frac{1136+1127}{2} = 1131.5 \text{ feet}$$

13. $\bar{x} = \dfrac{7.8+6.9+7.5+4.7+6.9+7.0}{6}$
$= \dfrac{40.8}{6}$
$= 6.8$ seconds

15. 4.7, 6.9, 6.9, 7.0, 7.5, 7.8
mode = 6.9

17. 74, 77, *85*, *86*, 91, 95
$\text{median} = \dfrac{85+86}{2} = 85.5$

19. $\bar{x} = \dfrac{78+80+66+68+71+64+82+71+70+65+70+75+77+86+72}{15}$
$= \dfrac{1095}{15}$
$= 73$

21. 64, 65, 66, 68, 70, 70, 71, 71, 72, 75, 77, 78, 80, 82, 86
mode = 70 and 71

23. 64, 65, 66, 68, 70, 70, 71, 71, 72, ↑ 75, 77, 78, 80, 82, 86
mean = 73
9 rates were lower than the mean.

25. _, _, 16, 18, _;
Since the mode is 21, at least two of the missing numbers must be 21. The mean is 20. Let the one unknown number be x.

$$\bar{x} = \frac{21+21+16+18+x}{6} = 20$$
$$\frac{96+x}{6} = 20$$
$$96+x = 120$$
$$x = 24$$

The missing numbers are 21, 21, 24.

Appendix F

1. Volume $= lwh = 6(4)(3) = 72$ cu in.
   Surface area $= 2lh + 2wh + 2lw$
   $= 2(6)(3) + 2(4)(3) + 2(6)(4)$
   $= 36 + 24 + 48$
   $= 108$ sq in.

3. Volume $= s^3 = 8^3 = 512$ cu cm
   Surface area $= 6s^2 = 6(8)^2 = 384$ sq cm

5. Volume $= \frac{1}{3}\pi r^2 h$
   $= \frac{1}{3}\pi(2)^2(3)$
   $= 4\pi$ cu yd
   $\approx 4\left(\frac{22}{7}\right)$
   $= 12\frac{4}{7}$ cu yd

   Surface area $= \pi r\sqrt{r^2 + h^2} + \pi r^2$
   $= \pi(2)\sqrt{2^2 + 3^2} + \pi(2)^2$
   $= 2\sqrt{13}\pi + 4\pi$ sq yd
   $\approx 2\sqrt{13}(3.14) + 4(3.14)$
   $= 35.20$ sq yd

7. Volume $= \frac{4}{3}\pi r^3$
   $= \frac{4}{3}\pi(5)^3$
   $= \frac{500}{3}\pi$ cu in.
   $\approx \frac{500}{3}\left(\frac{22}{7}\right)$
   $= 523\frac{17}{21}$ cu in.

   Surface area $= 4\pi r^2$
   $= 4\pi(5)^2$
   $= 100\pi$ sq in.
   $\approx 100\left(\frac{22}{7}\right)$
   $= 314\frac{2}{7}$ sq in.

9. Volume $= \frac{1}{3}s^2h = \frac{1}{3}(5)^2(9) = 75$ cu cm

   Surface area $= B + \frac{1}{2}pl$
   $= 25 + \frac{1}{2}(20)(9.34)$
   $= 118.4$ sq cm

11. Volume $= s^3 = \left(1\frac{1}{3}\right)^3 = 2\frac{10}{27}$ cu in.

13. Surface area $= 2lh + 2wh + 2lw$
    $= 2(2)(1.4) + 2(3)(1.4) + 2(2)(3)$
    $= 5.6 + 8.4 + 12$
    $= 26$ sq ft

15. Volume $= \frac{1}{3}s^2h = \frac{1}{3}(5)^2(1.3) = 10\frac{5}{6}$ cu in.

17. Volume $= \frac{1}{3}s^2h = \frac{1}{3}(12)^2(20) = 960$ cu cm

19. Surface area $= 4\pi r^2 = 4\pi(7)^2 = 196\pi$ sq in.

21. Volume $= lwh = 2\left(2\frac{1}{2}\right)\left(1\frac{1}{2}\right) = 7\frac{1}{2}$ cu ft

23. Volume $= \frac{1}{3}\pi r^2 h$
    $\approx \frac{1}{3}\left(\frac{22}{7}\right)(2)^2(3)$
    $= 12\frac{4}{7}$ cu cm